Complete
20th Century History
for Cambridge IGCSE® & O Level

Second Edition

John Cantrell
Neil Smith
Peter Smith

Oxford excellence for Cambridge IGCSE® & O Level

OXFORD
UNIVERSITY PRESS

OXFORD
UNIVERSITY PRESS

Great Clarendon Street, Oxford, OX2 6DP, United Kingdom

Oxford University Press is a department of the University of Oxford.
It furthers the University's objective of excellence in research,
scholarship, and education by publishing worldwide. Oxford is a
registered trade mark of Oxford University Press in the UK and in
certain other countries

British Library Cataloguing in Publication Data
Data available

ISBN: 978-0-19-842492-5

5 7 9 10 8 6

Paper used in the production of this book is a natural, recyclable
product made from wood grown in sustainable forests.
The manufacturing process conforms to the environmental
regulations of the country of origin.

Printed in the UK by Bell & Bain Ltd.

Acknowledgements

The publisher and authors would like to thank the following for permission to use
photographs and other copyright material:

Cover: solar22/Shutterstock; **Photos: p2:** Pictorial Press Ltd/Alamy Stock Photo;
p3: The Print Collector/Alamy Stock Photo; **p10:** Sueddeutsche Zeitung Photo/
Alamy Stock Photo; **p11:** Chronicle/Alamy Stock Photo; **p12:** Robert Cicchetti /
Alamy Stock Photo; **p13:** Photo 12/Alamy Stock Photo; **p14:** John Frost Newspapers
/ Alamy Stock Photo; **p16:** Chronicle/Alamy Stock Photo; **p19:** Punch Limited/
Punch Cartoons; **p20:** John Frost Newspapers/Alamy Stock Photo; **p23:** Hulton
Archive/Getty Images; **p25 (l):** Punch Magazine/The League Of Nations. London:
The Historical Association; **p25 (r):** Library of Congress/Corbis Historical/Getty
Images; **p31:** Hulton-Deutsch Collection/CORBIS/Getty Images; **p33:** Bettmann/
Getty Images; **p34:** Bettmann/Getty Images; **p35:** Hulton-Deutsch Collection/
Corbis/Getty Images; **p36 (t):** Bettmann/Getty Images; **p36 (b):** Photo 12/Alamy
Stock Photo; **p37:** Art Media/Print Collector/Getty Images; **p38:** Bettmann/Getty
Images; **p39:** Universal History Archive/Getty Images; **p43:** Hulton-Deutsch
Collection/CORBIS/Corbis/Getty Images; **p45:** Image Source/Getty Images; **p47:**
Popperfoto/Getty Images; **p49 (l):** Bettmann/Getty Images; **p49 (r):** Hulton-
Deutsch/Hulton-Deutsch Collection/Corbis/Getty Images; **p50 (t):** imageBROKER/
Alamy Stock Photo; **p50 (b):** Ernest Howard/Punch Cartoons; **p51:** Bettmann/
Getty Images; **p52:** Partridge Bernard/Punch Cartoons; **p53 (t):** Partridge Bernard/
Punch Cartoons; **p53 (l):** The Print Collector/Alamy Stock Photo; **p53 (r):** Pictorial
Press Ltd/Alamy Stock Photo; **p55:** ZUMA Press, Inc./Alamy Stock Photo; **p56:**
CTK/Alamy Stock Photo; **p60:** Associated Newspapers Ltd./Solo Syndication/British
Cartoon Archive; **p65:** Science History Images/Alamy Stock Photo; **p73:** Associated
Newspaper Photos/Archive Photos/Getty Images; **p79:** PhotoQuest/
Archive Photos/Getty Images; **p82:** Ernest Howard Shepard/Punch Cartoon Library;
p83: INTERFOTO/Alamy Stock Photo; **p85:** Granger Historical Picture Archive/
Alamy Stock Photo; **p88:** Granger Historical Picture Archive / Alamy Stock Photo;
p92 (l): Bettmann/Getty Images; **p92 (r):** Chronicle/Alamy Stock Photo; **p94:**
Bettmann/Getty Images; **p96:** Bettmann/Getty Images; **p99:** Gib Crockett./Library
of Congress; **p100:** Matt Trommer/Shutterstock; **p101:** ClassicStock/Alamy Stock
Photo; **p104 (l):** Rolls Press/Popperfoto/Getty Images; **p104 (r):** Herbert L. Block/
Library Of Congress; **p104 (b):** © 2018 Anthony Nardo, Jr.; **p105:** Bettmann/
Getty Images; **p106:** ASSOCIATED PRESS; **p108 (t):** Everett Collection Inc/Alamy
Stock Photo; **p108 (b):** Agence France Presse/Agence France Presse/Getty Images;
p110 (t): Topfoto; **p110 (b):** Bettmann/Getty Images; **p111:** Jack Novak/DOD/G.
Schoolfield/Mary Evans; **p117:** Popperfoto/Getty Images; **p118:** Sovfoto/UIG/Getty
Images; **p119:** HIP/Topfoto; **p121 (t):** Josef Koudelka/Magnum Photos; **p121 (b):**

GERARD LEROUX/AFP/Getty Images; **p124:** Bettmann/Getty Images; **p125:** Jean-
Louis Atlan/Sygma/Getty Images; **p126:** Telegraph Media Group Ltd/British Cartoon
Archive; **p127:** Mpworks/Alamy Stock Photo; **p130 (t):** Ullsteinbild/Topfoto; **p130
(b):** Marx Memorial Library/Mary Evans Picture Library; **p136:** Bettmann/Getty
Images; **p137:** Jacques Pavlovsky/Sygma/Getty Images; **p138:** Shepard Sherbell/
CORBIS SABA/Corbis/Getty Images; **p140 (t):** Shepard Sherbell/CORBIS SABA/Corbis/
Getty Images; **p140 (b):** Shepard Sherbell/CORBIS SABA/Corbis/Getty Images;
p145: Bettmann/Getty Images; **p146:** Bettmann/Getty Images; **p149:** Kazuyoshi
Nomachi/Corbis Documentary/Getty Images; **p150:** Stocktrek Images, Inc./Alamy
Stock Photo; **p157:** Punch Limited; **p159:** Hulton-Deutsch Collection/Corbis/Getty
Images; **p160 (t):** Illustrated London News Ltd/Mary Evans; **p160 (b):** Mary Evans/
Robert Hunt Collection; **p163 (t):** Universal History Archive/UIG/Getty Images;
p163 (b): Robert Hunt Collection/Mary Evans; **p172:** Albert Harlingue/Roger
Viollet/Getty Images; p173: Topical Press Agency/Getty Images; **p175:** Tofoto.
co.uk; p176: Tofoto.co.uk; **p177:** Print Collector/Hip/Topfoto; **p179:** Chronicle/
Alamy Stock Photo; **p182:** © IWM (Q 56278); **p183:** Amoret Tanner/Alamy Stock
Photo; **p184:** Granger Historical Picture Archive/Alamy Stock Photo; **p185:** Mary
Evans/Sueddeutsche Zeitung Photo; **p191:** INTERFOTO/Alamy Stock Photo; **p194
(l):** Bettmann/Getty Images; **p194 (r):** Bettmann/Getty Images; **p197:** AF archive/
Alamy Stock Photo; **p202:** Joe Vogan/Alamy Stock Photo; **p203:** Bernard Partridge/
Punch Cartoon Library; **p205:** Hulton-Deutsch Collection/CORBIS/Corbis/Getty
Images; **p210 (t):** Robert Hunt Library/Mary Evans; **p210 (b):** LAPI/Roger Viollet/
Getty Images; **p211:** Peter Langer/ Perspectives/Getty Images; **p213:** World
History Archive/Alamy Stock Photo; **p217:** Mary Evans Picture Library/WEIMAR
ARCHIVE; **p218:** INTERFOTO/Alamy Stock Photo; **p219 (l):** The Print Collector/
Alamy Stock Photo; **p219 (r):** INTERFOTO/Alamy Stock Photo; **p225:** John Massey
Stewart Russian Collection/Mary Evans Picture Library; **p226:** Pictorial Press Ltd/
Alamy Stock Photo; **p227:** Hulton Archive/Getty Images; **p228 (l):** Mirrorpix/
British Cartoon Archive; **p228 (r):** Mirrorpix/British Cartoon Archive; **p232:** Mary
Evans Picture Library; **p237:** Science History Images/Alamy Stock Photo; **p241
(t):** Heritage Image Partnership Ltd/Alamy Stock Photo; **p241 (b):** Mary Evans
Picture Library; **p243:** Associated Newspapers Ltd./Solo Syndication/British Cartoon
Archive; **p244 (t):** Mary Evans Picture Library; **p244 (b):** Sz Photo/Scherl/Mary
Evans Picture Library; **p245:** Sueddeutsche Zeitung Photo/Mary Evans Picture
Library; **p251:** Library of Congress; **p252:** Glasshouse Images/Alamy Stock Photo;
p253 (l): After Guerassimov, Serguei; **p253 (r):** After Guerassimov, Serguei; **p258:**
Arthur Gerlach/Time Life Pictures/Getty Images; **p259 (t):** Bettmann/Getty Images;
p259 (b): INTERFOTO/Alamy Stock Photo; **p262:** Pictorial Press Ltd/Alamy Stock
Photo; **p265:** ZUMA Press, Inc./Alamy Stock Photo; **p266:** FPG/Hulton Archive/
Getty Images; **p268:** George Rinhart/Corbis/Getty Images; **p271 (t):** INTERFOTO/
Alamy Stock Photo; **p271 (b):** Universal History Archive/Getty Images; **p272:** Niday
Picture Library/Alamy Stock Photo; **p274:** MPI/Getty Images; **p277:** GRANGER/
GRANGER, NYC; **p279 (l):** Fotosearch/Getty Images; **p279 (r):** Fotosearch/Getty
Images; **p285 (r):** Mary Evans Picture Library; **p285 (l):** Iberfoto/Mary Evans
Picture Library; **p287:** Robert Hunt Library/Mary Evans Picture Library; **p291:**
Sz Photo/Scherl/Mary Evans Picture Library; **p293:** Mary Evans Picture Library;
p294: Mary Evans Picture Library; **p296:** Shanghai Renmin Chubanshe/Chinese
Poster; **p297:** Henri Cartier-Bresson/Magnum Photos; **p298:** Interfoto/Mary Evan
Picture Library; **p299 (t):** Mary Evans Picture Library; **p299 (b):** Ivy Close Images/
Alamy Stock Photo; **p304:** INTERFOTO/Alamy Stock Photo; **p305:** INTERFOTO/
Alamy Stock Photo; **p307:** Mark Avery/AP Images; **p308:** Swim ink 2/Corbis via
Getty Images; **p309 (l):** Keystone/HIP/Topfoto; **p309 (r):** INTERFOTO/Alamy Stock
Photo; **p311 (t):** Mary Evans Picture Library; **p311 (bl):** INTERFOTO/Alamy Stock
Photo; **p311 (br):** Ryan Warkentin/Shutterstock; **p312:** AFP/Getty Images; **p323:**
Everett Historical/Shutterstock; **p326:** Juda Ngwenya/Reuters; **p328:** Diriye Amey/
Alamy Stock Photo; **p330:** Associated Newspapers Ltd./Solo Syndication/British
Cartoon Archive; **p333:** Keystone/Getty Images; **p335:** Associated Newspapers Ltd./
Solo Syndication/British Cartoon Archive; **p339:** Bettmann/Getty Images; **p349:**
David Turnley/Corbis/VCG/Getty Images; **p353:** Telegraph Media Group Ltd/British
Cartoon Archive; **p367:** Micha Perry/National Photographic Collection; **p370:**
TopFoto; **p373:** TopFoto; **p380:** Nsf/Alamy Stock Photo; **p382:** ZUMA Press, Inc./
Alamy Stock Photo; **p383:** ASSOCIATED PRESS/AP Images; **p388:** Associated
Newspapers Ltd./Solo Syndication/British Cartoon Archive; **Artworks:** QBS Learning

Every effort has been made to contact copyright holders of material reproduced in
this book. Any omissions will be rectified in subsequent printings if notice is given
to the publisher.

IGCSE® is the registered trademark of Cambridge Assessment International
Education. All examination-style questions and answers within this publication
have been written by the authors. In examination, the way marks are awarded may
be different.

Acknowledgements continue on the last page.

Contents

 Additional exam practice and study tips can be found on your free support website. Access the support website here:
www.oxfordsecondary.com/9780198424925

Introduction

History is an exciting subject, driven by a strong narrative and populated by dynamic characters. Equally important, however, is the process of analysis—looking at how and why this narrative was created. History is constructed from a series of questions which help us to explore how, why, when, and with what results, events in the past took place.

20th Century History for Cambridge IGCSE® and O Level focuses on the major international issues of the twentieth century and provides a detailed study of the regions which dominated the period. This book aims to provide an in-depth account of major events, and help students to develop the skills required to be successful at Cambridge IGCSE® (0470 and 0977 syllabuses) and Cambridge O Level (2147 syllabus).

The chapters follow the curriculum content for each of the Core and Depth Studies for the twentieth century topics offered by the Cambridge IGCSE® and O Level History courses. Each chapter contains Key Questions and Focus Points, reflecting the structure of the different options in the syllabus. Throughout each chapter you will find descriptions of key terms, mini-biographies of the major historical figures, short structured tasks, as well as exam-style questions. Starting on page v, you will find a series of syllabus matching grids indicating where each Key Question and Focus Point is covered in the book.

Cambridge IGCSE® and O Level overviews

For Cambridge IGCSE® and O Level candidates:
Paper 1: two questions on the Core Content and one question on a Depth Study
and
Paper 2: six questions on one prescribed topic taken from the Core Content

For Cambridge IGCSE® candidates only:
either Component 3 (coursework): a 2000-word extended piece of writing based on a Depth Study from the syllabus or a Depth Study devised by the Centre
or
Paper 4 (written paper): one question on a Depth Study

While the book provides students with a detailed coverage of each topic, it also contains a wide range of accessible and stimulating visual materials designed to provoke questions about the period and to help with the development of skills in analysing historical sources. The Cambridge IGCSE® and O Level syllabuses require students to demonstrate proficiency in the use of sources in a variety of ways, whether it be cross-referencing, testing them for utility, assessing reliability, or using them to test hypotheses. One of the strengths of **20th Century History for Cambridge IGCSE® and O Level** is that it provides a solid source of factual content, while providing an array of useful tips for tackling source questions, and many opportunities to practise source skills.

The support website supplements the material in the book by including a range of revision resources, such as timelines and revision tips. Furthermore, it features even more exam-style questions for students to assess their understanding of each topic and provides suggested exemplar responses. A list of useful links is also included on the support website.

We hope that **20th Century History for Cambridge IGCSE® and O Level** will be an invaluable tool for all students studying Cambridge IGCSE® and O Level History.

CAIE syllabus matching grids

Matching grids for Cambridge IGCSE® syllabuses 0470 and 0977, and Cambridge O Level syllabus 2147, for examination from 2020.

Core Content Option B: The twentieth century: international relations since 1919

The seven Key Questions in Core Content Option B are covered in Chapters 1 to 7 of this book.

Depth Studies

The seven Depth Studies are covered in Chapters 8 to 14 of this book.

4 Why has it proved impossible to resolve the Arab–Israeli issue?	
Focus Points	

What's on the support website?

Everything in the book and support website has been designed to help you prepare for your examination and achieve your best.

Glossary
A comprehensive revision tool that unpacks the vocabulary of the subject.

Exam-style questions
Additional questions for exam practice.

Revision checklists and timelines
Check your understanding and print out timelines for revision.

Exam-style questions with sample answers
Exam-style questions with sample answers to review and consolidate exam technique.

General study skills
Extra support material to help students with their reading and writing skills.

Interactive multiple choice tests
Test your knowledge on every chapter of the book with interactive multiple choice tests that encourage reflection and revision.

Weblinks
A list of useful links to provide additional background information on each topic.

1 | Were the peace treaties of 1919–23 fair?

Introduction

The First World War was described by British Prime Minister David Lloyd George as "the cruellest and most terrible war that has ever scourged mankind". In its simplest form it was a bid by the Central Powers—Germany assisted by Austria-Hungary, Turkey, and Bulgaria—to achieve supremacy or domination in Europe. When this bid failed in the autumn of 1918, the initiative lay with Germany's opponents, the Allies—principally Britain, France, and the United States—to bring about a new peace in Europe.

This aims of this chapter are to:

- Consider the roles of individuals such as Wilson, Clemenceau, and Lloyd George in the peacemaking process.

- Examine the impact of the treaties on the defeated countries.

- Look at contemporary opinions about the treaties.

As soon as the First World War came to an end in November 1918, plans were immediately made for a peace conference to take place in Paris during 1919. This conference produced a number of peace treaties that are referred to collectively as the **Versailles Settlement**.

The Versailles Settlement		
Treaty	**Date**	**Country affected**
Versailles	June 1919	Germany
Saint Germain	September 1919	Austria
Neuilly	November 1919	Bulgaria
Trianon	June 1920	Hungary
Sèvres	August 1920	Turkey
Lausanne	June 1923	Turkey

▲ **Table 1.1**

The Versailles Settlement was the result of discussions held between the victorious countries. Every country concerned wanted a peace settlement that would last and prevent a repeat of the slaughter of the First World War. The problem was that this could be achieved in a variety of ways. This led to strong disagreement among the peacemakers on a number of key issues, such as the extent to which the defeated countries should be punished or the victorious countries rewarded. Disagreement led to compromise with the result that the Versailles Settlement, and especially the Treaty of Versailles, soon became the focus of fierce criticism and debate.

▲ **Fig. 1.1** *San Francisco Examiner*, 1918

Versailles Settlement

A term used to describe the entire peace settlement of 1919–23. The phrase does not mean the same as Treaty of Versailles which is just one part of the Versailles Settlement.

What were the motives and aims of the Big Three at Versailles?

The Paris Peace Conference was attended by 32 states representing more than two-thirds of the world's population. Soviet Russia was not invited following the Bolshevik Revolution of October 1917 and the defeated powers were also excluded from the negotiations. The main peacemakers were the countries primarily responsible for the defeat of Germany and its allies: France, Italy, the United States, Britain, and Japan. But within this group the major players were France, the United States, and Britain. These countries were represented by Prime Minister Clemenceau, President Wilson, and Prime Minister Lloyd George respectively. The aims and motives of these three statesmen, the "Big Three", were to determine the nature of the peace settlement.

France

SOURCE 1

Extract from a speech by Georges Clemenceau to the Paris Peace Conference, 16 June 1919.

The conduct of Germany is almost unexampled in human history ... not less than seven million dead lie buried in Europe, while more than twenty million others carry upon them the evidence of wounds and sufferings, because Germany saw fit to gratify her lust for tyranny by resort to war. ... Justice, therefore, is the only possible basis for the settlement of the accounts of this terrible war.

George Clemenceau (1841–1929)

Nicknamed "The Tiger".

Pre-political career

Medical doctor, journalist, schoolteacher, newspaper proprietor.

Political positions

Minister of the Interior (1906); Prime Minister of France (1906–9 and 1917–20); President of the Paris Peace Conference (1919–20).

Character and outlook

A hard-headed, tough, and uncompromising politician. His unforgiving attitude towards Germany developed following the German invasions of France in 1870 and 1914. Wanted a harsh peace to be imposed on Germany.

▲ **Fig. 1.2** Aerial view of the war damage to the French town of Albert, 1914–18

QUICK QUESTION 1

How would photographs such as that in Figure 1.2 have affected Clemenceau's approach to the peace settlement with Germany?

French Prime Minister George Clemenceau's primary concern at Paris was to achieve a peace that would ensure the future security of France. He thought that if Germany was sufficiently weakened it would be unable to threaten the peace of Europe again. There were a number of reasons why Clemenceau thought that his country was open to future attack across its eastern frontier.

- France shared a common border with Germany.

- This border was not defined by a natural frontier such as a major river.

- The invasion of France in August 1914 was the second time in 50 years that France had been invaded by Germany. On the first occasion in 1870, during the Franco–Prussian War, France had lost the province of Alsace-Lorraine.

In addition to this France had made a much greater sacrifice during the course of the war than either Britain or the United States and there was a national desire for revenge against Germany. This was bolstered by the behaviour of the German army as it retreated across north-eastern France during the final stages of the war, causing deliberate damage by flooding mines and destroying bridges, railways, small towns, and villages.

As a result of his desire to increase the security of his country, Clemenceau went into the conference chamber with a series of demands designed to weaken Germany. These demands included:

- permanent disarmament involving disbanding most of Germany's army, navy, and air force

- a very high level of **reparations** with a definite figure to be named in the treaty

- the return of Alsace-Lorraine to France

- a significant portion of Germany's colonies to be handed over to France

- the Rhineland area to be formed into an independent state so that France no longer shared a common border with Germany

- the Saar Basin to be transferred to France.

In total, these demands represented an extremely stern form of justice, though not as extreme as recommended by the French President Poincaré. He wanted Germany to be broken up into a collection of smaller states. If Germany had been dismembered and crippled absolutely by the peace terms as many of the French insisted, then it would not have been in a position to challenge the peace of Europe 20 years later.

	Military deaths	Civilian deaths	Wounded
France	1.4	0.3	4.3
Britain	0.9	0.1	1.7
United States	0.1	0.001	0.2
Italy	0.6	0.6	0.9

▲ **Table 1.2** First World War casualties (in millions)

Reparations

The name given to the compensation that the defeated powers had to pay the Allies for damage caused and for war pensions. Reparations could be paid in cash or in goods such as coal or timber.

DISCUSSION

How far does Source 1 (page 3) agree with Source 2 (page 5) about the motives behind the peace settlement?

The United States

Thomas Woodrow Wilson (1856–1924)

Pre-political career
Lawyer, academic (political science), President of Princeton University.

Political career
Governor of New Jersey (1911–13); President of the United States (1913–21).

Character and outlook
Idealist who took America into the First World War to make the world "safe for democracy". Devised the Fourteen Points in early 1918 which he hoped would form the basis for a peace settlement. Was the main inspiration behind the League of Nations.

SOURCE 2

Extract from a speech by President Woodrow Wilson to a joint session of Congress, 2 April 1917.

The world must be made safe for democracy. Its peace must be planted upon the tested foundations of political liberty. We have no selfish ends to serve. We desire no conquest, no dominion. We seek no indemnities for ourselves, no material compensation for the sacrifices we shall freely make. We are but one of the champions of the rights of mankind.

President Woodrow Wilson's hopes and expectations from the peace settlement were very different from the French. But America's experience of the war was also very different.

- America had not declared war on Germany until April 1917 and was not fully involved in the war until more than a year later.

- At no point was American territory invaded and relatively few American lives were lost with civilian fatalities of less than 800.

- The war had provided profitable trading and business opportunities for American manufacturers, merchants, and financiers.

Lack of a national grievance meant that Wilson could stand back and take a more detached view of the peace proceedings. He was determined to earn his place in history as the guiding spirit behind what he hoped would be a "fair and lasting peace". This objective could be achieved, so Wilson believed, by making his Fourteen Points the basis of the peace settlement.

The Fourteen Points had been drawn up during the later stages of the war. They resulted from Wilson trying to identify the general causes of the conflict and then devising remedies for each cause. Here are three examples.

- Wilson believed that secret treaties had led to misunderstandings and suspicion between the most important countries before the war. He therefore recommended that there should be open diplomacy and no secret treaties (see Point 1).

- He decided that one of the causes of the war had been the build-up of armaments—naval ships, aircraft, and weaponry for the army such as artillery and rifles. Wilson therefore recommended that all states should disarm, maintaining just what was needed for basic defence (see Point 4).

- Wilson hoped to promote the long-term stability of Europe by recognising the principle of **self-determination**. In practice this meant allowing national groups such as Slovaks, Czechs, and Poles to form independent national states (see Points 9, 10, 12, and 13).

Wilson's approach to the peace was based on ideals and high principles and he inevitably clashed with the self-interested ambitions of Britain and France, especially with regard to acquiring Germany's colonies. Nevertheless, several aspects of his Fourteen Points were incorporated into the peace settlement.

Wilson's Fourteen Points	
1	No more secret treaties.
2	Free navigation of the seas in peacetime and wartime.
3	Removal of economic trade barriers.
4	Reduction of armaments for all countries.
5	Impartial settlement of colonial disputes taking into account the interests of both the colonial populations and the governing countries.
6	German troops to leave Russia.
7	Independence for Belgium.
8	Return of Alsace-Lorraine to France.
9	Readjustment of Italian frontiers in line with nationality.
10	Self-determination for peoples of Austria-Hungary.
11	Evacuation and restoration of invaded Balkan countries.
12	Self-determination for peoples in the Turkish Empire.
13	Establishment of an independent Poland with access to the sea.
14	Establishment of a general association of nations.

▲ **Table 1.3**

DISCUSSION

To what extent were Points 1, 4, 8, and 14 of Wilson's Fourteen Points reflected in the Treaty of Versailles?

Self-determination

Allowing an area to decide its own political future, usually by means of a vote.

Britain

David Lloyd George (1863–1945)

Pre-political career

Lawyer.

Political career

Entered national politics as a Liberal in 1890. Held various Cabinet positions (1906–16) including Chancellor of the Exchequer and Minister for Munitions; Prime Minister (1916–22).

Character and outlook

A dynamic, persuasive, and unconventional politician. Acclaimed as the man who won the war. More of a realist than an idealist. Wanted a peace which would punish Germany but not too harshly.

Lloyd George's views in November/December 1918

Before the Paris Peace Conference began, it looked as if Britain shared the French desire for a harsh peace settlement to be imposed on Germany. This was quite understandable given Britain's experience of the war.

- Unlike the United States, Britain had suffered direct attacks on her mainland both in 1914, when German naval ships bombarded a number of Yorkshire coastal towns, and during the Zeppelin raids of 1915–18 when London, Edinburgh, and other towns were attacked.

- Britain had sustained heavy casualties during the war.

- Britain's economy had been severely disrupted, especially the export sectors.

- Britain was concerned about the security of France's eastern frontier because if that were to be crossed by hostile troops it would only be a matter of time before Britain was directly threatened also. France's eastern frontier was effectively Britain's outer defence.

Britain was as concerned as France that Germany's war-making potential be reduced. Furthermore, the British public demanded vengeance against Germany immediately after the war. In the general election of November 1918, Prime Minister Lloyd George knew that if he was to be re-elected then he would have to reflect these views. Accordingly he insisted that Germany should pay for the full cost of the war. Lloyd George also wanted a sizeable share of Germany's colonies.

Lloyd George's views from January 1919

Yet, despite every indication that Lloyd George would unite with the French against the high principles of President Wilson, he soon changed his outlook. By the time that he had arrived in Paris in January 1919, Lloyd George had decided that a more moderate peace settlement was in British interests. What had caused Lloyd George to change his mind?

- Lloyd George came to realise that the future economic well-being of Britain depended largely upon the economic revival of Europe. This, in turn, depended upon the revival of the German economy. Germany was Britain's most important European customer prior to 1914.

SOURCE 3

Extract from an election speech by Lloyd George given in Bristol, 11 December 1918.

We propose to demand the whole cost of the war from Germany. Germany must pay to the last penny.

SOURCE 4

Extract from a speech by Lloyd George to the House of Commons, 16 April 1919.

We want a peace which will be just, but not vindictive. We want a stern peace because the occasion demands it. The crime demands it. But its severity must be designed, not to gratify vengeance, but to vindicate justice. ... Above all, we want to protect the future against a repetition of the horrors of this War.

DISCUSSION

How far do Sources 3 and 4 suggest that Lloyd George wanted a harsh peace to be imposed on Germany?

- If Germany was deprived of the Rhineland, where much of its industry was located, it would not be wealthy enough to buy British goods on the same scale as before the war.

- A very high reparations figure would also check Germany's economic recovery since it would take away money that could otherwise be used for investment.

- A weak Germany would provide an inadequate barrier against the spread of communism from the east. Communism was regarded by many as a much greater threat to Europe than the revival of German military power.

- Lloyd George was also anxious that the treaty should not be regarded as excessively harsh by the Germans as he was convinced that this would give rise to a sense of intense grievance. This might lead to attempts to overturn the treaty.

Lloyd George's impact on Clemenceau

Because of these factors Lloyd George managed to persuade Clemenceau to make a number of key concessions:

- to abandon the idea of an independent Rhineland state

- to abandon the idea of naming a definite and very high figure for reparations in the treaty

- to abandon the idea that the Saar Basin on the border shared by Germany and France be transferred to France

- to abandon the idea that Danzig be handed over to Poland.

These concessions by the French had the added advantage for Britain that German domination in Europe would not be replaced by French domination. It was in Britain's interest to maintain a balance of power in Europe for this would help preserve Britain's position as a world power.

What were the main terms of the Treaty of Versailles?

There were a number of key points in the treaty.

1. War Guilt Clause (Article 231)—Germany and her allies had to accept total responsibility for starting the war.

2. Reparations—Germany had to accept liability for reparations, the amount of which would be decided by a Reparations Commission.

3. Disarmament—this restricted Germany's ability to wage war in the future.

   - The German army was to be restricted to 100 000 with no conscription.

   - No tanks, armoured vehicles or heavy artillery were permitted.

   - No military or naval air force was permitted.

   - The navy was to be restricted to 6 battleships, 12 destroyers, 6 light cruisers, 12 torpedo boats, and no submarines.

   - The Rhineland was to become a **demilitarised** zone with no German troops or fortifications allowed in the area. In addition there was to be an Allied army of occupation on the west bank of the Rhine for 15 years.

Demilitarised

Without troops, armaments or fortifications.

4. Territory—German territory was taken away.

- Germany was to lose all her colonies in Africa and the Far East (see Table 1.5).

- Alsace-Lorraine was to be returned to France.

- Eupen, Malmédy, and Moresnet were to be transferred to Belgium.

- North Schleswig was to be transferred to Denmark.

- West Prussia, Posen, and parts of Upper Silesia were to be transferred to Poland.

- Hultschin was to be transferred to Czechoslovakia.

- The Saar Basin was to be administered by the League of Nations for 15 years when a **plebiscite** would decide whether it should belong to France, to Germany or remain under League control. During the period of League administration the profits of the coal mines were to go to France.

- Memel was to be transferred to Lithuania.

- Danzig was to become a Free City administered by the League of Nations. Poland could use the port for its external trade.

- The Treaty of Brest-Litovsk was to be cancelled, with Estonia, Latvia, and Lithuania taken away from Germany and set up as independent states.

- Union between Germany and Austria was forbidden.

5. The Covenant of the League of Nations—Germany had to accept the Covenant or constitution of the League of Nations even though it was excluded from the original membership.

TASKS

Copy and complete the table below in your workbook. You will not be able to complete the final column until later in the chapter.

	Leader	Main aims	Reason for these aims	Were these aims achieved?
France				
United States				
Britain				

▲ Table 1.4

Plebiscite

A vote on a single issue in the manner of a referendum. Plebiscites were held after 1918 in areas of uncertain nationality to establish which country the populations wished to be governed by.

Why was Danzig important?

- There were heated discussions about the status of Danzig during the peace negotiations.

- Before the war Danzig was a flourishing German sea port. With the recreation of Poland, Germany was set to lose West Prussia and Danzig to the new state.

- The population of Danzig was overwhelmingly German and transfer to Poland might have created an unstable situation. Yet Poland needed a sea port from which to trade with the outside world.

- A compromise was reached whereby Danzig was made a Free City and placed under League of Nations control.

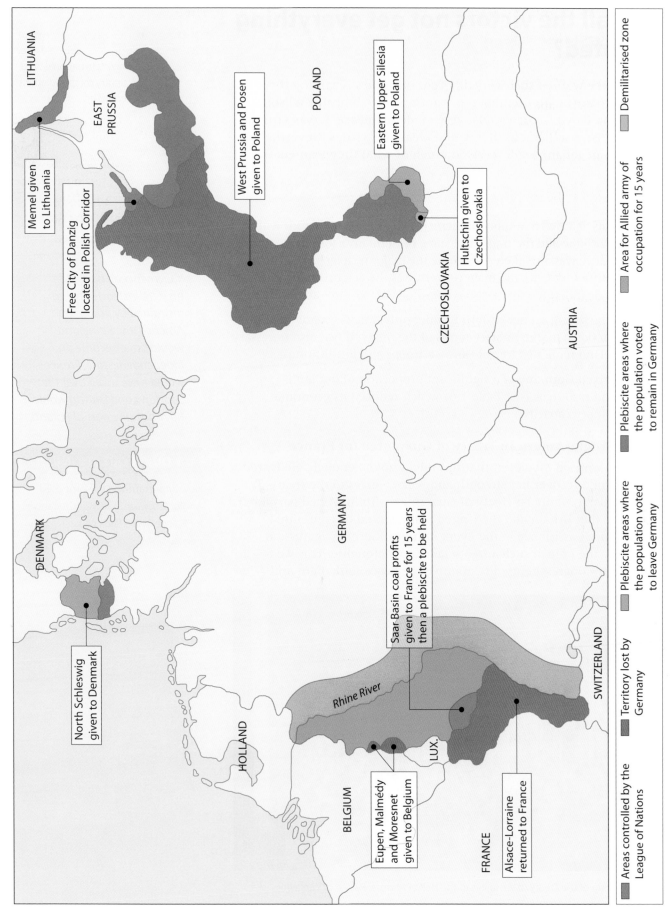

▲ **Fig. 1.3** The Treaty of Versailles: territorial changes

Memel given to Lithuania

Free City of Danzig located in Polish Corridor

West Prussia and Posen given to Poland

Eastern Upper Silesia given to Poland

Hultschin given to Czechoslovakia

North Schleswig given to Denmark

Saar Basin coal profits given to France for 15 years then a plebiscite to be held

Eupen, Malmédy and Moresnet given to Belgium

Alsace-Lorraine returned to France

LITHUANIA

EAST PRUSSIA

POLAND

CZECHOSLOVAKIA

AUSTRIA

DENMARK

GERMANY

HOLLAND

Rhine River

BELGIUM

LUX.

FRANCE

SWITZERLAND

Areas controlled by the League of Nations

Territory lost by Germany

Plebiscite areas where the population voted to leave Germany

Plebiscite areas where the population voted to remain in Germany

Area for Allied army of occupation for 15 years

Demilitarised zone

Why did all the victors not get everything they wanted?

Since the Big Three wanted such very different outcomes regarding the treatment of Germany, with Clemenceau wanting a harsh peace, Wilson a lenient peace, and Lloyd George a relatively moderate peace, it was virtually impossible to devise a settlement that would please all parties. Nevertheless, each of the main negotiators still received much of what they wanted.

France

The Versailles Treaty satisfied a number of Clemenceau's specific demands with regard to Alsace-Lorraine and the transfer of some of Germany's former colonies (see Table 1.5). France was also likely to become the major recipient of German reparations. Of course Clemenceau's main concern was the defence and security of France and it was clear that the treaty also went some way towards achieving this.

- France would be secure on her eastern frontier providing Germany kept to, or was forced to keep to, the military terms of the treaty. It was also necessary that the Rhineland remained free of German troops and fortifications.

- Versailles deprived Germany of a significant proportion of her land, population, and resources (see Table 1.6) which reduced its economic power and military capacity.

The proposed Anglo/American Treaty of Guarantee for France

Clemenceau was worried, however, that this might not be enough. He feared that Germany would recover her strength and seek changes to the treaty. To protect against this he wanted a Treaty of Guarantee with his Allied partners. This would mean that Britain and the United States would be committed to coming to France's assistance in the event of future German aggression. Unfortunately for the French such a treaty failed to materialise. This was because American Congress refused to approve the peace settlement and

SOURCE 5

Extract from *A History of Germany, 1815–1945* by William Carr, published in 1972.

If Clemenceau had had his way, instead of being restrained by Britain and America, the Rhineland would have become an independent state, France would have taken over the Saarland and Danzig would have become part of Poland.

QUICK QUESTION 2

How important was the proposed Anglo/American Treaty of Guarantee for France in the Paris peace negotiations?

▲ **Fig. 1.4** The signing of the Treaty of Versailles in the Hall of Mirrors, Palace of Versailles, 28 June 1919

America withdrew into diplomatic isolation. Britain was unwilling to provide any guarantees to France on its own.

This meant that despite all the positive features of the Versailles Treaty France still felt dangerously exposed on her eastern frontier. Clemenceau's relative failure led to his defeat in the presidential elections of January 1920 and resignation from the office of Prime Minister shortly afterwards.

Versailles Settlement: distribution of major German and Turkish colonies			
German colonies	**Britain**	**France**	**Japan**
Togoland	•	•	
Cameroons	•	•	
German south-west Africa	•		
German east Africa	•		
Mariana Islands			•
Caroline Islands			•
Marshall Islands			•
German New Guinea	•		
Turkish colonies			
Iraq	•		
Transjordan	•		
Palestine	•		
Syria		•	
Lebanon		•	

▲ **Table 1.5**

The United States

President Wilson had mixed feelings about the peace settlement. The positive features were as follows.

- He was pleased that he had successfully persuaded his partners to accept that the Covenant or constitution of the League of Nations should be included in all the peace treaties; this would help to make the new peacekeeping organisation become a reality.

- Wilson was also partly satisfied by the requirement in all the peace treaties that the defeated powers should disarm. This represented at least some movement towards his objective of disarmament for all countries.

- Wilson was relieved that the Rhineland was not going to be made into a separate state and was going to remain part of Germany. Not only did this reduce the potential harshness of the peace, it made it much more likely that Germany would remain a major economic power able to do business with the United States.

- For very similar reasons he was pleased that Germany was not going to be burdened with a very high reparations figure in the treaty.

Colonies	100%
European land	13%
Population	10%
Coal resources	26%
Iron ore deposits	75%

▲ **Table 1.6** Versailles Settlement: Germany's loss of resources

▲ **Fig. 1.5** A Parisian newspaper claims that the Treaty of Versailles has avenged France for her defeat in the Franco–Prussian War

SOURCE 6

Extract from *The Kings Depart: The German Revolution and the Treaty of Versailles* by Richard M. Watt, published in 1969.

Woodrow Wilson had first come to Paris with great hopes – the conference represented the opportunity he had always dreamed of – to completely remake the world according to the liberal and democratic ideas to which he had dedicated his life. But he had found the task so dominated with conflicting claims, hatreds, fears and greeds, that he was forced to settle for a compromise that satisfied no one.

- With regard to the Versailles Settlement as a whole, Wilson was delighted by the recreation of an independent Poland together with the two entirely new **"successor states"**, Czechoslovakia and Yugoslavia.

But overall Wilson thought that the Versailles Treaty was too harsh on Germany and there were also particular elements of the Versailles Settlement with which Wilson was less than happy.

- At the insistence of Britain the principle of free navigation of the seas was abandoned.

- There was little disguising the fact that Britain, France, and Japan had rewarded themselves with Germany's former colonies even though, officially, these colonies were to be governed as **mandated territories** on behalf of the League of Nations (see Table 1.5).

- While national self-determination for the peoples of the former Austro-Hungarian Empire was broadly implemented there were some noticeable exceptions.

  - Austria was not allowed to unite with Germany.

  - The Sudeten Germans were not consulted about their future.

The most upsetting circumstance concerning the peace settlement for Wilson, however, came when he failed to persuade the necessary two-thirds of American Congress to approve the treaties together with the League of Nations.

Why American Congress rejected the peace settlement

- Wilson's political opponents, the Republicans, had gained a small majority in the Senate in November 1918.

- Wilson's health and persuasive powers were clearly in decline after his stroke in October 1919.

- Many Americans did not want to be further involved in European affairs. There were fears that if America signed up to the peace settlement and became a leading member of the League of Nations, then it would be in danger of being drawn into another European war.

Britain

SOURCE 7

Extract from a speech by Lloyd George to the House of Commons, 21 July 1919.

We have restored where restoration was just, we have organised reparations where damage and injury have been inflicted, and we have established guarantees and securities ... against the repetition of these crimes and horrors from which the world is just emerging. We have disarmed; we have punished. We have demonstrated ... that you cannot trample on national rights and liberties, that you cannot break solemn covenants with impunity.

Lloyd George was probably the most satisfied of the major peacemakers. He had wanted a moderate peace which would allow the European economy to revive, and that is largely what he achieved. There were some features of the peace settlement that he did not like, such as the placing of German-speaking peoples under French or Polish rule, but on the whole he got his way. Lloyd George's main achievements at Paris were twofold.

Successor states

The successor states from the Versailles Peace Settlement were Poland, Czechoslovakia, and Yugoslavia. Poland had been eliminated from the map of Europe at the end of the eighteenth century but the peacemakers wanted to recreate the country. In contrast, Czechoslovakia was a completely new state forged out of provinces of the former Austro-Hungarian Empire such as Bohemia and Moravia. Similarly, Yugoslavia was a new state formed by merging Serbia with south-western provinces of the former empire such as Dalmatia, Croatia, and Bosnia.

Mandated territories

Mandates were former German or Turkish colonies handed over to the Allies to be governed by them on behalf of the League of Nations.

▲ **Fig. 1.6** US Congress

- He successfully persuaded Clemenceau to adopt a more moderate approach towards Germany by offering him an Anglo/American guarantee against future German aggression.

- He directly promoted British interests by extending her colonies, adding an additional 1.8 million square miles and 13 million new subjects (see Table 1.5). The British Empire was at its peak in 1919. Fortune also favoured Lloyd George when the Germans decided to scuttle their fleet at Scapa Flow. This meant that any German naval threat was removed for the foreseeable future.

Lloyd George felt that the Versailles Treaty punished Germany without destroying its economy or ability to contribute to the future prosperity of Europe. This was good for British business and reassuring for those who feared the westward spread of communism. In contrast to Clemenceau, Lloyd George returned from Paris in triumph and the House of Commons voted to approve the treaty with an overwhelming majority.

DISCUSSION

1. Study Sources 5, 6, and 7. Who was the more satisfied with the Versailles Treaty, Wilson, Clemenceau or Lloyd George? Use the sources and your own knowledge to explain your answer.

TASKS

Copy and complete the table below in your workbook.

	Positive features	Negative features
France		
United States		
Britain		

▲ **Table 1.7** The Versailles Settlement: positive and negative features

What was the impact of the peace treaty on Germany up to 1923?

Germany had numerous criticisms of the Versailles Treaty.

Too harsh

Germany's general objection to the treaty was that it was too harsh. Many Germans felt that their country was being punished twice over.

- They had to pay reparations.

- They were deprived of the very resources (coal, iron ore) that were needed to pay these reparations.

Germany had, however, imposed an equally harsh treaty on Soviet Russia at Brest-Litovsk in March 1918. The Russians had been expected to pay reparations and suffer drastic losses of territory and resources. So it could be argued that Germany was now getting a taste of its own medicine.

▲ **Fig. 1.7** Berlin protests against the Treaty of Versailles

Diktat

Germany objected that the treaty was a **"diktat"** or a dictated peace. German statesmen and officials were excluded from the negotiations leading up to the treaty. They were simply handed a draft copy and invited to express comments and criticisms in writing. This led to some minor changes including the holding of a plebiscite in Upper Silesia. The Germans had little choice but to sign the treaty. If they had refused then the Allied naval blockade would have continued and the Allies would have restarted the war.

War Guilt Clause

Article 231 or the War Guilt Clause was included in the treaty at the insistence of the Allied lawyers. They wanted to establish a legal basis for reparations: if you cause damage, and it is entirely your fault, then you must pay compensation. The Germans felt that this clause rubbed salt into their wounds. They were also not convinced that they, together with their allies, were totally responsible for starting the war. After all, it could be argued that the first military action in the immediate lead-up to the conflict was the Russian mobilisation of July 1914.

The political and economic impact of the Treaty of Versailles

Political impact

When on 28 June 1919 two representatives of the new German Government, the Weimar Government, signed the Treaty of Versailles this was an action made under duress. The Allies had made it clear that they would restart the war if Germany refused to sign and, in the opinion of leading German generals, this would have led to military defeat. But though the Weimar Government had little option but to sign the Treaty, it became instantly unpopular for having done so. The Treaty was the symbol of Germany's dishonour and humiliation and now the Weimar Government had agreed to it. The authority of the new republic was seriously undermined.

- Right-wing politicians and activists expressed their disapproval by supporting attempts to overthrow the government, such as the Munich Putsch of November 1923.

- Right-wing extremists carried out a number of assassinations of high-ranking government ministers, such as Walter Rathenau (foreign minister) and Matthias Erzberger (finance minister).

- Left-wing extremist groups exploited the unpopularity of the Weimar Government by promoting rebellions, such as that in the Ruhr of March 1920.

- Many members of the army, furious with the government for agreeing to the disarmament clauses of the Treaty, joined the Freikorps, an unofficial, anti-communist vigilante group. When the government tried to disband this group in March 1923 following pressure from the Allies, Freikorps units under the command of Wolfgang Kapp staged a coup in Berlin and declared a new national government. The army refused to intervene and the Weimar Government was on the point of collapse. It survived thanks to a general workers' strike which brought public services to a standstill.

Diktat

Something that is imposed or dictated without discussion.

▲ **Fig. 1.8** Headline in the London *Evening Standard* newspaper, 8 May 1919

> **QUICK QUESTION 3**
>
> Why was Germany angry about the terms of the Treaty of Versailles?

> **QUICK QUESTION 4**
>
> How far was the 1923 hyperinflation caused by the Treaty of Versailles?

The signing of the Treaty of Versailles, therefore, meant that the new democratic Weimar Republic was operating under a major disadvantage from the very beginning of its existence and was deprived of much needed support during its early years.

Economic impact

The Germans claimed that in signing the treaty they were also signing a blank cheque since although they had to agree to the principle of paying reparations, no figure was actually stated in the treaty. When the figure of £6.6 billion was announced by the Reparations Commission in 1921, Germany claimed that this amount was more than it could afford to pay. Whether this was true or not is difficult to assess, but there is no doubt that Germany did not want to pay such an amount.

The Versailles Treaty undoubtedly caused major economic problems for Germany and the Weimar Republic. Germany lost valuable economic resources, yet had to repay war debts together with reparations. The immediate post-war period was characterised by inflation, rising unemployment and the attendant problems of poverty and homelessness. Crisis came in 1923 and was triggered by the reparations issue.

- Germany had paid its first instalment of reparations in 1921 but then claimed that it was unable to make the 1922 payment.

- The French felt that Germany was simply trying to escape from its Treaty obligations and together with Belgium decided to take direct action. In January 1923 French and Belgian troops occupied the Ruhr, Germany's most valuable industrial area. The intention was to seize coal and other resources to the value of the missed payments.

- The German Government was not in a position to order armed resistance and so instead ordered the German population of the Ruhr to offer passive resistance or peaceful strike action.

- The French responded to this by expelling more than 100 000 Germans from the region and killing over 130.

- The German Government now faced a situation in which its expenditure had increased, due to the need to re-house and feed the displaced Ruhr population, yet its income had declined due to the ending of Ruhr taxation receipts.

- To make up for the lost revenue the German Government began to print money. This stoked up the existing high inflation into hyperinflation. The German mark became worthless and middle class savings lost their value. Bartering became increasingly popular as the best means to protect the value of a payment. Hence eggs, cigarettes or bags of sugar were used as a form of currency.

Clearly such a state of affairs had to be resolved quickly. In August 1923 Gustav Stresemann became Chancellor and the following month took the unpopular decision of ending the passive resistance in the Ruhr. In October he introduced a temporary new currency, the Rentenmark, with a strictly controlled circulation and soon after this he agreed to resume reparation payments. Germany's finances had been stabilised. The reparations problem was partly solved by the Dawes Plan of April 1924 which introduced a more flexible repayments schedule (see page 14). Five years later the

Young Plan reduced the outstanding amount to £2 billion. The whole issue of reparations caused enormous bitterness and achieved very little since Germany received more in American loans during the 1920s than it ever paid back to the Allies.

QUICK QUESTION 5

How far was the 1923 hyperinflation caused by the Treaty of Versailles?

Disarmament

Germany's dislike of the disarmament clauses was partly to do with status and prestige but there were also practical objections.

- Germany claimed that 100 000 men was insufficient for border defence.

- It would also be difficult to deal with revolts and uprisings.

Wilson's Fourteen Points

Germany always maintained that the armistice was signed on the understanding that the peace settlement would be based upon Wilson's Fourteen Points. However, the Treaty of Versailles was seen by the German people as a betrayal of this promise in a number of ways.

- There is no mention in the Fourteen Points of war guilt or reparations.

▲ **Fig. 1.9** The wreckage of German warplanes in a Munich scrap yard following the disarmament clauses of the Treaty of Versailles which disallowed a German military or naval air force

- The Fourteen Points proposed disarmament for all and a general assembly of nations. In the Treaty, Germany was required to disarm but there was no equivalent requirement for the victorious countries. Similarly, Germany was not allowed to join the League of Nations, at least not for the time being.

- The Fourteen Points stressed the idea of self-determination yet in the treaty it was clear that this was not to apply to Austria, Alsace-Lorraine or, until 15 years had passed, the Saar Basin.

In fact, the Allies never made a promise to follow Wilson's principles to the letter though they did indicate that they would use them as guiding principles for the peace settlement. The principle of self-determination was used in many areas including parts of East Prussia, Upper Silesia, and Schleswig.

Area	Year	Result
Schleswig	1920	Partitioned between Germany and Denmark
East Prussia: Allenstein and Marienwerder	1920	Remained part of Germany
Upper Silesia	1921	Partitioned between Germany and Poland
Saar Basin	1935	Returned to Germany

▲ **Table 1.8** Plebiscite areas

DISCUSSION

Imagine that in June 1919 a debate takes place in a town hall in central Germany. The motion is: "The German Government has no alternative but to sign and accept the Treaty of Versailles". The following guest speakers have been invited.

1. An armaments manufacturer

2. A shopkeeper from Danzig

3. A coal miner from the Saar Basin

4. A farmer with land on the west bank of the Rhine

What do you think each of these speakers would say? Would they be for or against the motion? How would their personal circumstances be likely to affect their views?

What were the terms of the other peace treaties?

The treaties affecting Germany's allies had a number of features in common with the Treaty of Versailles.

- A war guilt clause
- An obligation to pay reparations
- Reduction in armaments
- Acceptance of the Covenant of the League of Nations

It was principally in the territorial provisions that the various treaties differed from one another.

The Treaty of Saint Germain with Austria, 10 September 1919

The main points of this treaty were the following.

- The new Republic of Austria had to accept the break-up of the Austro-Hungarian Empire.

- Austria had to recognise the independence of Hungary, Czechoslovakia, Yugoslavia, and Poland.

- Territory from the former Empire was transferred to Czechoslovakia, Poland, Yugoslavia, Italy, and Romania.

- Union between Austria and Germany was forbidden.

Instead of being at the heart of a grand empire, one of the great powers of Europe, Austria was now a small landlocked nation surrounded by hostile states. Austria particularly resented the fact that union with Germany was forbidden and that three million Sudeten Germans were placed under Czech rule. This was seen as a violation of the principle of self-determination.

▲ **Fig. 1.10** The Treaties of Saint Germain and Trianon: territorial changes

The Treaty of Trianon with Hungary, 4 June 1920

The main points of this treaty were the following.

- Hungary had to accept the break-up of the Austro-Hungarian Empire.

- Hungary had to recognise the independence of Yugoslavia and Czechoslovakia.

- Territory from the former Empire was transferred to Czechoslovakia, Yugoslavia, and Romania.

Hungary was dismayed by these terms as more than 70 per cent of its territory and one third of its population had been lost. Since the treaty also deprived Hungary of its seaports it was now, like Austria, a landlocked nation.

The Treaty of Neuilly with Bulgaria, 27 November 1919

The main points of this treaty were the following.

- Bulgaria had to recognise the independence of Yugoslavia.

- Bulgaria lost territory to Greece, Yugoslavia, and Romania.

Bulgarians regarded the treaty as a national catastrophe. It brought to an end the 40-year struggle for the unification of the Bulgarian-populated territories. With the loss of land and the blow to its national pride Bulgaria faced an uncertain future.

The Treaty of Sèvres with Turkey, 10 August 1920

The main points of this treaty were the following.

- Turkey had to recognise the independence of the Kingdom of Hejaz (later to form part of Saudi Arabia) and Armenia.

- Turkey lost its provinces in the Middle East to Britain and France.

- Turkey lost territory to Greece and Italy.

- The Dardanelles Strait was to become an international waterway.

Bulgarian territory lost to Greece and Yugoslavia
Turkish territory lost to Italy
Turkish territory lost to Greece (returned by the Treaty of Lausanne, 1923)

▲ **Fig. 1.11** The Treaties of Neuilly and Sèvres: territorial changes

The plight of Turkey after the First World War sparked off a nationalist movement led by Mustapha Kemal. He strongly objected to the terms of Sèvres and challenged the peace treaty by force, driving the Greeks out of Smyrna. This led to a renegotiated treaty.

The Treaty of Lausanne with Turkey, 24 July 1923

The main points of this treaty were the following.

- Turkey confirmed the loss of its provinces in the Middle East.
- Turkey received back most of its European territory.
- The Dardanelles Strait was to return to Turkish sovereignty.
- Restrictions on armed forces were removed.
- Turkey was no longer to pay reparations.

DISCUSSION

1. Which of Germany's former allies suffered most from the peace settlement?
2. How do you think each of the following would have reacted to the peace settlement?
    - An export agent living in Budapest, the capital city of Hungary
    - A Czech writer and poet living in Prague, once one of the main cities of the Austro-Hungarian Empire and now the capital city of Czechoslovakia
    - A senior civil servant living in Vienna, once the capital city of the Austro-Hungarian Empire and now the capital city of Austria
    - A Bulgarian army officer living in the port of Dedeagach in western Thrace given to Greece by the Treaty of Neuilly

TASKS

1. Which of Wilson's Fourteen Points (see Table 1.3, page 5) can be identified in the treaties dealing with Germany's former allies?

▲ **Fig. 1.12** The Reckoning, British cartoon published in 1919

QUICK QUESTION 6

Do you think Clemenceau would have agreed with the point of view expressed in Figure 1.12?

Could the treaties be justified at the time?

The Versailles Settlement soon became the subject of fierce debate though it was the Versailles Treaty that attracted the most attention. Opinions on the treaty can be divided three ways.

Those who thought the treaty was too harsh

Most Germans would have taken this view although it was shared by many others from other countries.

SOURCE 8

Extract from a speech made by a German member of the Reichstag in 1919.

The criminal madness of this peace will drain Germany's national life-blood. It is a shameless blow in the face of common sense. It is inflicting the deepest wounds on us Germans as our world lies in wreckage about us.

SOURCE 9

Extract from an article written by a British journalist in 1922 quoted in *International Relations* by K. Shephard published in 1992.

It was a peace of revenge. It was full of injustice. It was incapable of fulfilment. It sowed a thousand seeds from which new wars might spring. The wild impossibility of extracting those vast reparations from the defeated enemy ought to have been obvious to the most ignorant schoolboy.

Those who thought the Versailles Treaty was not harsh enough

Many French supported this view.

SOURCE 10

Comment by Marshal Foch at the signing of the Treaty of Versailles, 1919.

This is not a peace treaty, it is an armistice for twenty years.

SOURCE 11

Extract from a memorandum given by President Raymond Poincaré of France to the Paris Peace Conference, 1919.

Germany is supposedly going to undertake to have neither troops nor fortresses on the left bank and within a zone extending 50 kilometres east of the Rhine. But the Treaty does not provide for any permanent supervision of troops and armaments on the left bank any more than elsewhere in Germany. ... We can thus have no guarantee that after ... fifteen years and the evacuation of the left bank, the Germans will not filter troops by degrees into this district.

PEACE AND FUTURE CANNON FODDER

The Tiger: "Curious! I seem to hear a child weeping!"

▲ **Fig. 1.13** Peace And Future Cannon Fodder, *Daily Herald*, 13 May 1919. The caption reads, The Tiger: "Curious, I seem to hear a child weeping!"

Those who thought that the Versailles Treaty was fair

There were some that believed the treaty to be fair or that it represented the best that could have been achieved in the circumstances.

SOURCE 12

Extract from the diary of Edward M. House, an American diplomat, June 1919.

To those who are saying that the Treaty is bad ... I feel like admitting it. But I would also say in reply that empires cannot be shattered and new states raised upon their ruins without disturbance. To create new boundaries is always to create new troubles. The one follows the other. While I should have preferred a different peace, I doubt whether it could have been made.

SOURCE 13

Extract from a speech by President Wilson delivered to the League of Nations, September 1919.

Do not think of this treaty of peace as merely a settlement with Germany. It is that. It is a very severe settlement with Germany, but there is not anything in it that she did not earn. Indeed, she earned more than she can ever be able to pay for, and the punishment exacted of her is not a punishment greater than she can bear, and it is absolutely necessary in order that no other nation may ever plot such a thing against humanity and civilization.

KEY POINTS

▶ The aims and motives of Clemenceau, Lloyd George and Wilson between November 1918 and the signing of the peace treaties.

▶ The terms of the Treaty of Versailles.

▶ The reactions of the "Big Three" to the Treaty.

▶ How the Treaty affected Germany up to 1923.

▶ The main terms of the treaties that dealt with Austria, Hungary, Bulgaria and Turkey.

▶ The range of contemporary opinions on the peace settlement.

Revision tips

- Make sure you know why the "Big Three" held the positions they did with regard to Germany. You will find that the differences between the "Big Three" reflected their different wartime experiences and defensive positions. You will need to be familiar with Wilson's Fourteen Points and the reasons Lloyd George's views changed after November 1918.

- The terms of the Treaty of Versailles have to be learnt. You will also need to be able to identify which terms pleased or displeased each of the "Big Three".

- You will need to be able to explain the various reasons why Germany objected to the Versailles Treaty.

- You should also cover the terms that each of the minor treaties had in common, together with an understanding of how Czechoslovakia and Yugoslavia were formed out of the territory of the former Austro-Hungarian Empire.

DISCUSSION

1. How useful is Source 8 as evidence of German objections to the Treaty of Versailles?

2. Does Source 9 surprise you? Explain your answer using the source and your own knowledge.

3. Does Figure 1.12 show that Sources 8 and 9 were wrong? Explain your answer using the sources and your own knowledge.

4. What message is the cartoonist trying to give in Figure 1.13?

5. How far do Sources 8 to 10 and Figures 1.12 and 1.13 support the view that the Treaty of Versailles was a compromise that satisfied no-one?

Review questions

1. What were the aims of each of the "Big Three" at the Paris Peace Conference?

2. To what extent were the aims of the "Big Three" achieved at the Paris Peace Conference?

3. Describe the military restrictions imposed on Germany by the Treaty of Versailles.

4. Describe Germany's territorial losses under the Treaty of Versailles.

5. What problems did the Treaty of Versailles cause for Germany?

6. Explain why there was so much bitterness over the Treaty of Versailles in Germany.

7. Which was more important in causing Germany's dissatisfaction with the Treaty: the imposing of reparations or the War Guilt Clause?

8. To what extent was the Treaty of Versailles justifiable at the time?

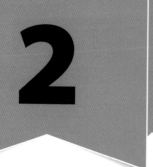

2

To what extent was the League of Nations a success?

Introduction

During the First World War a number of statesmen began discussing ways to avoid another international conflict. These statesmen included Jan Smuts of South Africa, Lloyd George of Britain, and Woodrow Wilson of the United States. A variety of possible schemes were considered. These included:

- a narrowly-focused organisation that would meet to sort out disputes and crises

- an organisation backed by an army that would exist to enforce the peace settlement

- a broad-based organisation that would address a wide range of international problems as well as meet to sort out disputes and crises.

▲ **Fig. 2.1** First session of the Assembly of the League of Nations, Geneva, Switzerland, 1920

The third option favoured by Smuts and Wilson formed the basis for the League of Nations which came into existence in January 1920.

The aims of this chapter are to:

- Examine the strengths and weaknesses of the structure and organisation of the League of Nations, as well as its successes and failures in peacekeeping during the 1920s.

- Estimate the impact of the World Depression on the work of the League after 1929.

- Consider the failures of the League in the 1930s including the Manchurian and Abyssinian crises.

According to the **Covenant of the League of Nations** its primary aim was to preserve world peace, but it also attempted to promote international cooperation over a wide range of economic and social problems including disarmament. Everyone accepts that the League of Nations failed in its main purpose as war broke out again in September 1939, but this does not mean that the League was a total failure. As will be seen, it did resolve a number of disputes and performed some very useful work in tackling a host of international problems.

Covenant of the League of Nations

The Covenant was the name chosen by President Wilson to describe the constitution or charter of the League of Nations. It comprised 26 articles which laid out the structure, rules, procedures, and functions of the League.

How was the League organised?

The key organs of the League were the Secretariat, Assembly, and Council.

Secretariat	• The civil service of the League. • Performed all the administrative and financial work: organising conferences, distributing agendas, monitoring budgets, publishing reports, etc.
Assembly	• Met once a year. • Every member of the League had one vote. • Considered matters of general policy. • Controlled the League's budget. • Admitted new members. • Elected non-permanent members of the Council.
Council	• The executive body of the League. • Met four or five times a year and in times of crisis. • Had permanent and non-permanent members. • In 1920, permanent members were Britain, France, Italy, and Japan. • In 1926 Germany became a permanent member. • Number of non-permanent members increased from 4 in 1920 to 11 in 1936.

▲ **Table 2.1**

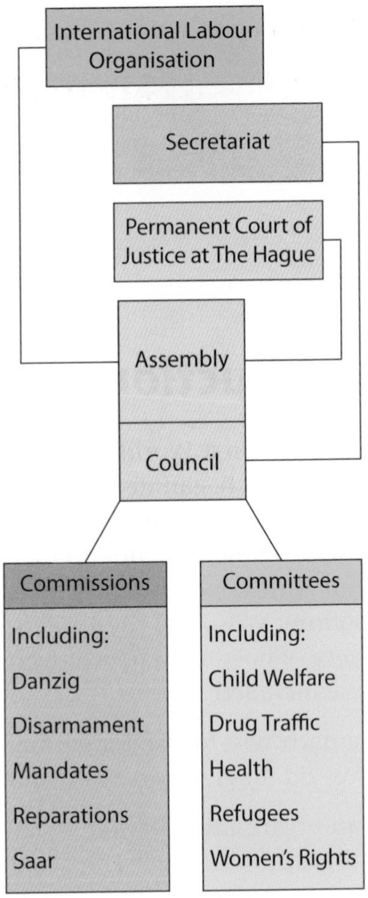

Two largely independent organisations that were also closely associated with the League were the Permanent Court of International Justice and the International Labour Organisation.

Permanent Court of International Justice	• Based in The Hague. • Offered an arbitration service to countries in dispute. • Provided legal advice to the Council. • Staffed by 11 judges and 4 deputy judges elected for 9 years by the Council and Assembly.
International Labour Organisation	• Based in Geneva. • Included representatives of government, employers, and workers among its various committees. • Central purpose was to promote good working practices with regard to issues such as working hours, women's rights, child labour, employers' liability, etc.

▲ **Table 2.2**

▲ **Fig. 2.2** Diagram of the structure of the League

During the early years of its existence the League established a number of agencies, committees, and commissions to deal with matters arising from the peace settlement and to address various social and economic problems. Here are a few examples.

Mandates Commission	• Supervised the administration of Germany's and Turkey's former colonies by the victorious countries, especially Britain and France.
Danzig Commission	• Exercised direct League control over the former German city.
Minorities Commission	• Attempted to bring about a general improvement in the way that some racial minorities were ill-treated.
Intellectual Cooperation Organisation	• Promoted cultural exchanges and intellectual contact between academics, artists, and writers.
Special Committee for Drug Traffic	• Campaigned to reduce drug misuse and drug smuggling.

▲ **Table 2.3**

How far did weaknesses in the League's organisation make failure inevitable?

Membership

The Assembly and the Council would have been far more effective in their operations and influence if they had represented all the major countries of the world. This had been President Wilson's intention when he called for a general assembly of nations, but the League of Nations was never in this position.

The United States

Despite the fact that President Wilson was one of the main inspirations behind the League, America refused to join. This was because a majority in the American Senate thought that the League would drag America into future wars and disputes. America's absence was a body blow to the prospects of the League as the new organisation was deprived of the world's most powerful, influential, and wealthy country. This meant that the ability of the League to take action against aggressive countries would be much reduced and the general prestige of the League would be significantly affected.

▲ **Fig. 2.3** German magazine cartoon, May 1919. Germany is represented by the figure on the ground with, from left to right, Lloyd George, Clemenceau and President Wilson standing above

QUICK QUESTION 1

What is Figure 2.3 suggesting about the League of Nations?

THE GAP IN THE BRIDGE.

▲ **Fig. 2.4** British magazine cartoon, 10 December 1919

QUICK QUESTION 2

What point is the cartoonist making about the United States in Figure 2.4?

Germany

Germany was not allowed to join the League until it had demonstrated its peaceful intentions. This had the unfortunate effect of making the League look like a club for the victorious powers closely associated with the Treaty of Versailles. Germany was allowed to join in 1926 and became a permanent member of the Council, but its membership was short-lived and one of Adolf Hitler's first significant foreign policy actions was to take Germany out of the League in 1933.

Soviet Russia

Soviet Russia was not invited to join the League, mainly for ideological reasons—it was communist and committed to the overthrow of capitalism. Neither was there any desire in Soviet Russia itself to join the new organisation as a number of its members, such as Britain, France, and Japan, had been actively assisting the counter-revolution during the Russian Civil War (1918–21). By the late 1920s, however, there was more tolerance on both sides and Soviet Russia joined the League in 1934. It was expelled in December 1939 following the invasion of Finland.

Japan

Japan was one of the original members of the League but left in 1933 when it received criticism for invading Manchuria.

Italy

Italy was also one of the original members of the League but left in 1937 following its invasion of Abyssinia and the imposition of sanctions.

Britain and France

Britain and France were the only major countries that were members of the League throughout its existence. These two countries, both weakened by the First World War, had to shoulder the responsibility of trying to make the League work. Yet Britain was also concerned with trying to maintain its empire while France was primarily concerned with increasing security against Germany. The League often took second place in the minds of British and French politicians.

Collective security

Collective security was the intended means by which the League was to maintain peace. There were three stages that could be followed to stop an aggressive power.

Moral disapproval	• Following an act of aggression the Council would meet and vote to condemn the action.
	• The aggressive country, knowing that it had the weight of world opinion directed against it, might drop its aggressive action.
Economic sanctions	• If moral disapproval failed then the Council could impose economic sanctions on the aggressor.
	• This meant arranging a trade boycott and refusing credit.
Military sanctions	• If economic sanctions failed then, as a last resort, the Council could impose military sanctions.
	• This might involve sending an army to assist the victim of the aggression.

▲ Table 2.4

In theory at least the system of collective security looked like a promising new way to preserve the peace of the world, but the absence of the United States would reduce the effectiveness of both moral disapproval and sanctions. Unfortunately there were other problems.

SOURCE 1

Article 16 of the Covenant of the League of Nations

Should any Member of the League resort to war in disregard of its covenants ... it shall be deemed to have committed an act of war against all other Members of the League, which hereby undertake immediately to subject it to the severance of all trade or financial relations. ... It shall be the duty of the Council in such case to recommend ... what effective military, naval or air force the Members of the League shall severally contribute to the armed forces to be used to protect the covenants of the League.

QUICK QUESTION 3

Does Source 1 prove that the League of Nations was likely to be a powerful and effective organisation for preserving world peace?

Unanimous decisions

All decisions taken by the Assembly or Council had to be unanimous. This meant that if the Assembly or Council was meeting to vote on aggressive action by a country, it would take just one negative vote, not including the negative vote of the aggressor, for the motion to fail. A majority or even an overwhelming majority was not enough. This could obviously make it very difficult to take decisive action against a country that decided to disturb the peace.

Lack of an army

Surprisingly, the League did not have an army of its own. The lack of an army meant that the League did not have standing forces to call upon if it wished to impose military sanctions. If such sanctions were to be imposed, then member states would be asked to contribute towards a military force. This would take time and there was no guarantee that an appropriate army could be assembled. The uncertainty created by this serious oversight meant that military sanctions could never be contemplated seriously where a major country was threatening world peace.

How successful was the League of Nations in the 1920s?

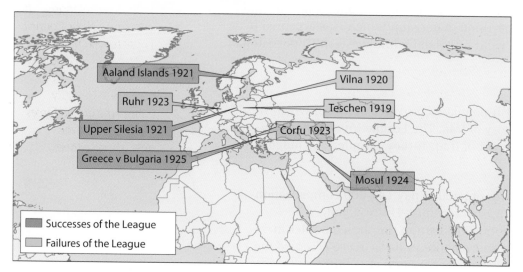

▲ **Fig. 2.5** Map showing successes and failures of the League of Nations during the 1920s

At first glance it would appear that the League was very successful during the 1920s. There was no major conflict or threat to world peace during this decade and many of the League's agencies and commissions performed useful work. Germany and all the parts of the former Austro-Hungarian Empire were League members by the end of 1926 and by the late 1920s the defeated powers appeared peaceful in their intentions.

Yet these surface features were perhaps misleading. During the 1920s most of the great powers, with the exception of the United States, were exhausted after the exertions of the First World War. The emphasis was on domestic and economic reconstruction, with little spare capacity or energy to pursue international disputes.

The European powers were recharging their batteries. It is with this in mind that the achievements of the League of Nations should be judged.

League successes

Most of the League's successes during the 1920s related to relatively minor disputes. This should not take away from their importance, however, as minor disputes have the potential to grow into much more serious affairs. This was demonstrated during the Balkan crises in the lead-up to the First World War.

Aaland Islands, 1921

The first dispute to be satisfactorily resolved by the League concerned the rival claims of Sweden and Finland to the Aaland Islands situated in the Baltic Sea. Most of the islanders wanted to be ruled by Sweden. The League investigated the matter and awarded the islands to Finland but with safeguards for the islanders including demilitarisation. Sweden accepted the judgment.

Upper Silesia, 1921

Upper Silesia, which contained a valuable industrial area, was located on the border between Germany and Poland. Originally granted to Poland by the draft Treaty of Versailles, the Germans protested and it was agreed to hold a plebiscite in the region. The overall results of the vote suggested it should be awarded to Germany but in some rural parts of the Silesian territory there was a clear majority in favour of Poland. Following riots and protests the League suggested a partition, a decision which was accepted by both sides. Eastern Upper Silesia went to Poland while western Upper Silesia went to Germany.

Mosul, 1924

In 1924 Turkey claimed the Kurdish-populated province of Mosul which was part of the British-mandated territory of Iraq. The League investigated the problem and made an award in favour of Iraq. Turkey accepted the judgment.

Bulgaria, 1925

In south-eastern Europe, Greece was ordered to pay £45 000 compensation to Bulgaria after its invasion of Bulgarian territory. This was judged a disproportionate response to a shooting incident on the shared border in which a Greek sentry was killed in an exchange of fire. Greece accepted the ruling but felt it was unfair that Italy had been treated very differently and more generously in similar circumstances (see the Corfu Incident).

SOURCE 2

Extract from *Essential Modern History* by Steven Waugh published in 1990.

In the 1920s everything seemed to run smoothly. The League's agencies were working extremely well and the world's statesmen were actually getting together and talking with each other. They met at the League's headquarters in Geneva. They were able to sort out international problems over brandy and a cigar in front of a fire.

How successful was the work of the League agencies?

The League was not simply concerned with the resolution of disputes. It also attempted to identify those social, economic and military issues that directly or indirectly affected the peace and wellbeing of the world—disease, poverty, exploitation, militarism, etc. It was the task of the agencies, commissions and committees to address these problems and try to bring about improvements. Some of the most important of these agencies are considered below.

Refugee Organisation

The Refugee Organisation faced the problem of former First World War prisoners-of-war stranded principally in Soviet Russia, Poland, France, Germany and Turkey. There was an estimated 250 000 Russians in German or French camps and 300 000 Germans and former Austro-Hungarians in Soviet Russia. In addition more than a million Greeks were made homeless during the Turkish War of Independence (1919–23). The Norwegian explorer and scientist, Fridtjof Nansen, was given the responsibility of devising a solution to this challenge. Despite the daunting scale of the problem, and with little more than a shoestring budget, Nansen and his staff worked alongside the Red Cross and helped 425 000 displaced persons either return to their homes or find new homes between 1920 and 1922. Nansen's methods involved a series of sometimes ingenuous improvisations—finding suitable transport, setting up camps, creating new settlements, teaching new trades and skills, issuing identity documents, etc. It was an imaginative and logistical triumph that brought nothing but praise and thanks for the work of the League.

Health Organisation

Under the inspirational leadership of its Director, Ludwig Rajchman, this is regarded as one of the most successful of the League agencies. It established links with non-member countries such as Germany, Soviet Russia and the United States to provide an information service, technical assistance and advice on public health matters. In particular, it helped Soviet Russia prevent a typhus epidemic in Siberia in part by organising a public education campaign on health and sanitation. It also helped reduce the incidence of leprosy and began an international campaign to exterminate mosquitoes, so reducing the spread of malaria and yellow fever. The Health Organisation was instrumental in setting up a number of research institutions based in London, Copenhagen and Singapore which developed internationally accepted vaccines for diseases such as diphtheria, tetanus and tuberculosis. The success of the Health Organisation was later demonstrated when, after the demise of the League, it became the World Health Organisation affiliated to the **United Nations (UN)**.

Economic and Financial Organisation

Following the end of the First World War, a number of countries faced economic crisis. Austria, for example, was in danger of financial collapse as it tried to adjust to its new status as a small landlocked country now dependent upon agriculture for its wealth. Expenditure had to be brought in line with the inevitably reduced revenues and in 1922 the League devised a rescue plan to achieve this. Action was taken to stabilise the currency by controlling the level of interest rates, the circulation of banknotes, and the issuing of credit. Austria was also given a substantial loan. As a result of this trade soon revived, unemployment fell, and the budget was balanced. Similarly successful rescue programmes were devised for other ailing countries including Hungary, Greece and Bulgaria.

United Nations (UN)

The international organisation founded in 1945 to promote peace, security, and economic development.

DISCUSSION

How could each of the following affect world peace?

- Disease
- Poverty
- Labour exploitation
- Production of armaments

International Labour Organisation

During the 1920s the ILO, under the direction of the French socialist Albert Thomas, achieved some success in pursuit of its main objective which was to bring about a general improvement in working conditions. It collected data on employment practices throughout the world, published the results and tried to persuade governments to take action by issuing recommendations. These included the eight-hour working day and forty-eight-hour working week, annual holidays with pay, the right to join trade unions, and a minimum employment age. The ILO also published information on health and safety in the workplace, demonstrating that the use of white lead in print manufacturing was dangerous to health. Inevitably the readiness of different countries to implement the recommendations was somewhat patchy. For example, the recommended minimum age for employment was 15, yet even in Britain the school leaving age was not raised to that level until after the Second World War. In the United States some employers were denying their employees the right to join trade unions until well into the 1930s. Yet the ILO established and popularised a new series of benchmarks with regard to work and employment. It became increasingly difficult for member states to ignore the existence of enlightened work practices with regard to working hours, minimum wages, sickness and unemployment insurance and pensions.

TASKS

Which of the following people made the greatest and most lasting contribution to the work of the League of Nations?

a. Fridtjof Nansen

b. Ludwik Rajchman

c. Albert Thomas

Slavery Commission

The principal objective of the Slavery Commission was to stamp out slavery and slave dealing together with other exploitative practices such as forcing young women and children into prostitution—the 'white slave' traffic. Its methods were those of persistent enquiry, publication of reports, and the constant coaxing of governments that appeared slow or evasive in taking effective action. Successes included the freeing of 200 000 slaves in Sierra Leone and the reduction of the death rate for African workers engaged on the Tanganyikan railway from 50 per cent to 4 per cent. A number of countries abolished slavery altogether such as Iraq, Jordan, and Nepal. Yet the success was far from universal and the continued existence of slave trading was acknowledged in the Commission's report for 1937 while the 'white slave' traffic remains a serious social problem, even in advanced countries, in the twenty-first century.

Disarmament Commission

It is probably true to say that the Disarmament Commission made the most disappointing progress of the all League's various agencies and commissions. Article 8 of the League Covenant had called on all nations to disarm "to the lowest point consistent with national safety" yet by the end of the 1920s only the defeated powers had disarmed and that is because they had been forced to by the terms of the peace treaties imposed on them. There was a minor success for the Commission in organising the Washington Naval Conference of 1921, which led to agreement on naval limitation by the United States, Britain, France, and Japan but this represented the high water mark of voluntary disarmament during the 1920s. It even proved impossible for the Commission to convene a World Disarmament Conference before 1932 largely due to a failure to agree on a series of technicalities such as definitions, classifications, and methods of armaments counting. It was easy for Germany to think that there was no real desire among the former Allies to bring about a state of general disarmament and this suspicion forms part of the background to the failure of the World Disarmament Conference of 1932–1934.

In fact, all the League agencies achieved some positive results or were engaged in ongoing research, publicity, and persuasion. This often took the form of bombarding member states with questionnaires or requests for reports. Through such persistent methods the incidence of illegal drugs trading, black slavery, and white slave traffic was much reduced.

League failures

There were a number of occasions during the 1920s, however, when the League seemed to accept the role of passive bystander. On other occasions its authority was ignored or undermined. A number of agreements made outside the League seemed to suggest that many countries had less than complete confidence in the ability of the League to maintain peace.

Vilna, 1920

Following the Versailles Settlement, Vilna, with a largely Polish population, was made the capital of the newly created state of Lithuania. A Polish army seized the city in 1920 as a result of which Lithuania made an appeal to the League. The League asked the Polish troops to withdraw while a plebiscite was arranged but Poland refused. The matter was then passed on to the **Conference of Ambassadors** who awarded Vilna to Poland.

Occupation of the Ruhr, 1923

When Germany defaulted on its reparations payment in 1922 the matter should have been referred to the League. Instead France, supported by Belgium, decided to take swift and unilateral action by ordering their troops to occupy the Ruhr in January 1923. This action only served to confirm the impression of many that the League was little more than a victors club for the pursuit of victors' interests.

Corfu Incident, 1923

Conference of Ambassadors

Established in 1920, this was a group of senior diplomats representing the Allied powers who oversaw matters arising from the peace settlement. As such it duplicated some of the functions of the League. It played a major role in the resolution of the Vilna dispute and the Corfu Incident. After 1925 it became increasingly inactive until it was dissolved in 1931.

▲ **Fig. 2.6** Italian troops landing in Corfu, 1923

The Corfu Incident of 1923 was probably the most important dispute with which the League was involved during the 1920s. This was because it exposed the weakness and ineffectiveness of the League when dealing with a relatively major power.

In August 1923 Mussolini, the Italian Prime Minister, ordered the naval bombardment and occupation of the Greek island of Corfu. This action was in response to the murder of an Italian general and some of his staff, who had been patrolling part of the border frontier between Greece and Albania. The murders had taken place on Greek soil and Mussolini had immediately demanded 50 million lira in compensation as well as the execution of the assassins. When Greece was unable to locate the culprits Mussolini resorted to direct action.

Greece appealed to the League whose initial response was to condemn the invasion but Mussolini insisted that final arbitration should be passed on to the Conference of Ambassadors. This body ordered Greece to pay the compensation and Italy to withdraw its troops from Corfu.

The impression created was that Italy's bullying tactics had paid off and that Greece had had to pay an excessive amount of compensation. It appeared that the Conference of Ambassadors had taken the line of least resistance without regard for the principles of international justice. Partly as a result of the weaknesses in the League exposed by the Corfu Incident, the British and French devised the **Geneva Protocol**. This attempt to strengthen the League failed, however, following a change of government in Britain.

Agreements made outside the League

It is probably true to say that the leading European powers had little faith in the League's ability to deal with a major challenge during the 1920s. Its committees and commissions performed useful work and it could resolve disputes between minor states, but there the matter ended.

France was the country most concerned about its security during this period and far from relying upon the new collective security system it set about establishing mutual assistance pacts with various eastern European states such as Poland and Czechoslovakia. These pacts were designed to give France added protection in the event of German aggression.

At **Locarno** in 1925 the mutual frontiers of France, Belgium, and Germany were guaranteed by the three countries concerned, backed up by Britain and Italy. In 1928 the French became one of the original signatories in what became known as the **Kellogg-Briand Pact**. Alliances and pacts were not abandoned now that the League of Nations existed; instead they were run in parallel with collective security. The approach was one of hope that the League would work, but in case it did not, having a safety net to fall back on.

Geneva Protocol

This was drafted in 1924 on the initiative of MacDonald, the British Prime Minister, together with Herriot, his counterpart in France. League members were required to agree to the compulsory arbitration of disputes by the Permanent Court of International Justice failing agreement between the parties concerned. The decision would be backed up by the economic and military power of all members. If the protocol had been adopted the League would have been significantly strengthened. Macdonald lost a general election later in 1924 and the incoming government refused to approve the scheme.

Locarno

The Locarno Treaties signed in 1925 were thought at the time to mark the beginning of a new era of international harmony. For the first time since 1918 Germany was treated on a par with the other European powers. The treaties provided guarantees for the frontiers of north-eastern Europe and confirmed the demilitarised status of the Rhineland. They said nothing, however, about the frontiers of eastern Europe.

Kellogg-Briand Pact

In 1927 Briand, the French Foreign Minister, suggested to the American Secretary of State Kellogg that the two countries should sign a pact renouncing war. Kellogg suggested that the pact be extended to include more countries and by 1928 it had 65 signatories including Germany, Italy, and Japan. The pact amounted to little more than an international statement of good intentions.

DISCUSSION

1. Does Source 2 give a fair and accurate summary of the League's activities during the 1920s? Explain your answer.

2. What part did the following play in the League's failure to settle the Corfu Incident?
   i. The fact that Italy was a major power
   ii. The Conference of Ambassadors

3. Why did France make a number of agreements outside the League of Nations during the 1920s?

How far did the Depression make the work of the League more difficult?

In October 1929 the **Wall Street Crash** marked the beginning of a worldwide economic recession. There was a dramatic contraction in production and trade over the next three years and a steep rise in unemployment. Every country in the capitalist world was affected, especially the United States of America, although the unemployment levels were at their highest in Germany, peaking at approximately one third of the workforce, or six million, in 1932.

Wall Street Crash

In October 1929 shares on the New York stock exchange on Wall Street plummeted. This happened because investors thought a recession was just around the corner and wanted to sell their stocks and shares before they fell in value. The "crash" did not cause the depression, rather it was an indication that an economic slump was on its way.

Reduced inclination of League members to impose economic sanctions. World markets were shrinking and all countries wanted to maintain their existing trade contacts.

Brought extremists to power in Germany who were committed to destroying Versailles Settlement. Before the Wall Street Crash the Nazis were a fringe party polling less than 3% of the vote. As the recession deepened so the Nazis picked up support.

World Depression

Put pressure on governments to cut expenditure to balance the books. Serious rearmament had to be delayed. As a result League members lacked the military means to deal with aggressors.

Put pressure on countries to find new markets and sources of raw materials. One way this could be done was through colonisation or the annexation of new territories. But this was likely to involve war.

Encouraged militarism in Japan. The Japanese army appreciated how Japan's survival depended upon its overseas trade and, in 1931, decided to take the law into its own hands.

▲ **Fig. 2.7** Consequences of the Wall Street Crash

So the World Depression brought extremist parties to power in both Europe and the Far East, created an additional need for expansionist foreign policies, and undermined the ability of League members to devise effective ways of preventing or containing such action. In short, the World Depression made the work of the League very much more difficult.

▲ **Fig. 2.8** Panic at New York Stock Exchange, 24 October 1929

How successful was the League in the 1930s?

Those seeking to make a case for the positive achievements of the League during the 1930s would point to the following.

- The continuing good work of the agencies, committees and commissions. The Saar Commission, for example, successfully organised the plebiscite which led to the return of the region to Germany in January 1935.

- The contribution made towards the resolution of border disputes in South America between Bolivia and Paraguay over the Chaco and between Peru and Columbia over Leticia.

But overall there is no disguising the fact that the 1930s was a disastrous decade for the League of Nations. Three of the permanent members of the Council—Japan, Germany, and Italy—left the League and Soviet Russia was expelled for invading Finland in November 1939. The events of the early autumn of 1939 undermined the purpose of the League. It had come into existence with the primary intention of preventing another world war and failed.

Following the German invasion of Poland in September 1939, there were no further meetings of the League until April 1946, when it was wound up and its assets transferred to the newly formed United Nations.

There were three main events that collectively demonstrated the complete inadequacy of the League in the face of determined action to pursue national rather than international interests during the 1930s.

1. The Japanese invasion of Manchuria

2. The failure of the Disarmament Conference

3. The Italian invasion of Abyssinia

By 1936 the League had become an irrelevancy and was thereafter largely ignored by European statesmen.

Why did Japan invade Manchuria?

Background

Manchuria was a province of north-east China with part of its southern frontier bordering Korea. It was a sparsely populated province, rich in mineral wealth, agricultural land, and forestry.

Since 1905 the Japanese had been in control of Korea with additional trading rights extending northwards into the Manchurian interior. In connection with these rights Japanese guards were permitted along the route of the South Manchurian Railway. The purpose of these guards was to maintain order in a lawless, chaotic area so as to protect Japanese business interests.

Japan's economic position

As an island trading nation Japan was very badly affected by the Depression. Japan was not self-sufficient in food and depended upon imports to feed its rapidly rising population. These imports had to be paid for with exports but Japan's main export commodity was silk, a luxury item. As exports declined due to falling overseas demand Japan faced a growing economic crisis.

▲ **Fig. 2.9** Japanese patrol behind sandbags in North Manchuria

Manchuria seemed to offer the answer to Japan's problems: it could provide a source of food and raw materials, a market for Japanese exports, as well as land for the surplus Japanese population.

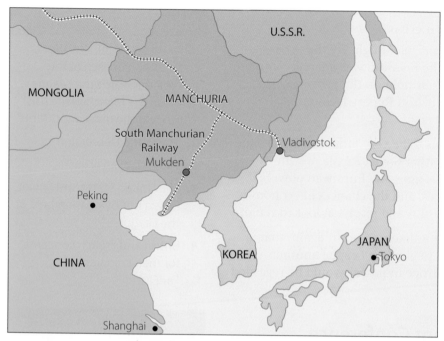

▲ **Fig. 2.10** Manchuria

▲ **Fig. 2.11** Japanese troops enter Manchuria, 1931

The Mukden Railway Incident

Japanese soldiers staged an incident along the railway line in September 1931, using the excuse of Chinese banditry to launch an invasion of the local area. China appealed to the League following the initial attacks and the Japanese government promised to withdraw. It soon became clear, however, that the civilian government was no longer in control of events and the Japanese army proceeded to occupy the whole province. In March 1932 Manchuria was renamed Manchukuo.

What was the response of the League?

At this stage the League could have called for sanctions but it failed to do so. There were several reasons for this.

- None of the European powers wanted to reduce their trade with the Far East, especially since American firms could have taken over the lost business.

- The alternative of military sanctions was even less appealing. This would have involved European states sending a naval task force to the other side of the world with very uncertain prospects of success.

- Both Britain and France possessed colonies in the Far East, including Hong Kong and Singapore, and feared sanctions might provoke a Japanese attack.

The Lytton Commission

But the League did not feel it could do absolutely nothing and appointed Lord Lytton to lead a commission of enquiry to Manchuria. Together with a four-man team, including a representative from the United States, Lytton spent six weeks in the province and came to the conclusion that although the Japanese were provoked in various ways by the Chinese, the invasion was not justified. The Lytton Report was considered by the Assembly in February 1933 where the findings were accepted by a vote of 42 to 1. Japan's response was to terminate its membership of the League.

What were the lessons of the Manchurian crisis?

The League can be criticised for not acting quickly enough. By the time that Lytton arrived in the Far East in April 1932 the invasion was a fait accompli and the Japanese were busy strengthening their hold on the province. The Assembly of the League finally voted on the Lytton Report 18 months after the original Japanese action.

Even with the benefit of hindsight there seems to be very little that the League could have done to resolve the crisis. With neither Soviet Russia nor the United States as members of the League at this time, the European powers were unable to call upon nearby military forces, and the chances of economic sanctions achieving a positive result at a time of world recession looked remote.

It was because of these factors, thought to be unlikely to occur again, that politicians and world opinion were prepared to give the League another chance. A successful challenge by a major European power would be regarded very differently.

Why did the World Disarmament Conference of 1932–4 fail?

Background

Before the First World War there had been an arms race, one element of which had been the naval arms race between Germany and Britain. It was thought that this arms race had made war more likely. After 1918 disarmament was considered to be a central issue in promoting world peace. It was one of Wilson's Fourteen Points and a prominent feature of the Versailles Settlement, although only the defeated powers were required to disarm.

The Disarmament Commission arranged a Disarmament Conference to meet in Geneva between 1932 and 1934 so that the issues surrounding disarmament could be debated and resolutions adopted.

Why did the members of the conference fail to agree?

In view of the ongoing economic recession it might have been thought that disarmament would have been an attractive idea for the 54 states attending the conference and so it was in theory. The problems lay with the fears and anxieties of individual states and their reluctance to trust one another.

- France, Poland, and Czechoslovakia were all worried about their future defensive security in the event of an attack by Germany and were reluctant to place their faith in a system of collective security that had already shown flaws.

▲ **Fig. 2.12** Official opening of the World Disarmament Conference, Geneva, Switzerland, 1932

UNDER THE SPREADING ARMAMENT TREE
THE DISARMAMENT CONFERENCE SITS

(Yesterday Was Chestnut Sunday)

▲ **Fig. 2.13** British newspaper cartoon of the World Disarmament Conference, 1934

- France was willing to disarm, but only if additional guarantees were provided by Britain and the United States. This is something that the latter countries were not prepared to give.

- Hitler, who had no intention of disarming, was able to exploit these fears and claimed that France was not serious about disarmament, using this as an excuse to withdraw from the conference altogether. Shortly afterwards Germany left the League.

- With the exit of Japan over the League's attitude to its conquest of Manchuria, it soon became apparent that general disarmament was going to remain a pipe dream.

If disarmament was going to work all the major countries had to participate and by 1934 it was clear that this was not going to happen. The following year Hitler announced his violations of the disarmament clauses of the Treaty of Versailles and this point marked the beginning of the German military build-up. Italian and Japanese rearmament soon followed.

▲ **Fig. 2.14** French journal cartoon, March 1935

QUICK QUESTION 4

What point is the cartoonist making about the World Disarmament Conference in Figure 2.13?

QUICK QUESTION 5

What threats to the League of Nations can you identify in Figure 2.14?

Did Italy's invasion of Abyssinia destroy the League?

Background

Abyssinia was the last remaining independent state in Africa. It was ruled by Emperor Haile Selassie. Unlike Manchuria, Abyssinia was of relatively minor economic value. While it possessed some mineral resources, much of the country was little more than rocky wasteland.

Abyssinia was located between Italy's other territories in east Africa: Eritrea and Somaliland. In 1896 an Italian army had been humiliatingly defeated at Adowa in northern Abyssinia in a failed attempt to conquer the country and turn it into a colony. Ever since then Italians had been set upon revenge.

Mussolini, Italy's leader, was looking for ways to boost his popularity following the economic problems of recession such as unemployment. War with Abyssinia looked like a low-risk way of achieving this. Conquest of Abyssinia would also help to resolve the disappointments of 1919 when Italy had failed to get a significant share of Germany's and Turkey's colonies. The Abyssinian army, equipped with outdated rifles supplemented by spears and arrows, was unlikely to be a match for the Italian tanks, planes and poison gas.

Benito Mussolini (1883–1945)

Pre-political career

Teacher, labourer, trade unionist, journalist and newspaper editor.

Political career

Socialist until 1915 then Nationalist. Formed Fascist Party in 1919. Appointed Prime Minister of Italy in 1922. Had become dictator, *Il Duce*, by 1925. Deposed 1943.

Character and outlook

Confident, self-centred, and sometimes aggressive. Keen nationalist. Wanted to create new Roman Empire and make Italy "great, respected and feared".

▲ Fig. 2.15 Map of Abyssinia

The invasion

Following a border incident at Wal Wal in December 1934, Mussolini began a build-up of Italian forces in Eritrea and Somaliland. The two-pronged Italian attack, involving a quarter of a million men, was launched in October 1935 without any formal declaration of war. The world was soon shocked at the ruthlessness of the Italian action as primitive villages and small towns under the rule of local chieftains were destroyed by the invaders' modern military equipment.

How friendly were Britain, France, and Italy before the Abyssinian crisis? ⓘ

- Britain, France, and Italy had been allies during the First World War.

- The three countries had also collaborated at the Paris Peace Conference, although Italy had not got everything it wanted in terms of territory.

- Britain, France, and Italy had formed the Stresa Front in April 1935. This was a united stand against German rearmament.

- Until the Italian invasion of October 1935 the three countries could be considered to be close associates.

▲ Fig. 2.16 A large canvas portrait of Mussolini on display in northern Abyssinia, where the Italians camped out during November 1935

What was the response of the League?

The Italian invasion was a clear example of unprovoked aggression and the League promptly condemned the action and imposed economic sanctions. It appeared as if the League was determined not to repeat the mistakes made over the Japanese invasion of Manchuria and for a while it appeared strong and resolute. But it soon became apparent that economic sanctions were having little impact on the progress of the war. There were several reasons for this.

- Essential war materials such as oil and coal had been excluded from the list of prohibited items.
- The Suez Canal, the main artery for the supply of the Italian army, was kept open for fear of possible Italian naval attacks on the British colonial possessions of Gibraltar and Malta.

To avoid embarrassment, in December 1935 the British and French governments concocted a secret deal, the infamous Hoare-Laval Pact. Italy would receive approximately two-thirds of Abyssinia in return for stopping the war. The remaining mountainous rump and ancient kingdom would be compensated for this loss by being given a narrow strip of territory to provide access to the sea through Italian Eritrea.

Mussolini indicated that he would accept this deal but news of it was leaked to the French press. The consequent storm of public protest in both France and Britain meant that the plan had to be abandoned, with immediate blame heaped on the shoulders of the two hapless foreign ministers. The war continued with Addis Ababa, the Abyssinian capital, being captured in May 1936. Sanctions were lifted in July.

▲ **Fig. 2.17** Italian propaganda postcard

Why did the League fail to give effective help to Abyssinia?

During the Abyssinian crisis Britain and France had been trying to pursue two contradictory objectives. On the one hand, these two countries felt that they were duty-bound to support the League of Nations and the idea of collective security. Hence, they nominally applied economic sanctions against Italy. On the other hand, they were fearful of offending Italy to the extent that it would decide to become an ally of Germany. The second objective was regarded as more important than the first, and during the Abyssinian crisis the main, but unstated, policy of Britain and France was to retain Italy as a potential ally against Germany.

By pursuing two contradictory policies simultaneously, Britain and France ended up with nothing. The League of Nations was dealt a death blow from which it never recovered, while Italy was so offended by the imposition of economic sanctions that it decided to make common cause with Germany and left the League in 1937.

DISCUSSION

How did each of the following contribute to the failure of the League over Abyssinia?

1. Continuing economic recession
2. Lack of faith in the League
3. Determination to keep Germany isolated, without friends and allies
4. Fear of war against Italy

How did the Abyssinian crisis affect the work of the League after 1936?

While the committees and commissions of the League continued to perform useful, if largely unpublicised, work during the late 1930s, the League was ignored on most of the major issues of foreign policy.

The League played little or no part in the diplomacy leading up to the Anschluss or union between Germany and Austria in March 1938. It was not consulted over the Sudetenland Crisis and the Munich Conference in September of the same year. Britain and France realised that the only way to check an increasingly aggressive Germany was to rearm and seek military allies. There were no meetings of the Council or Assembly during the Second World War and when the League met again in April 1946 it was for the last time.

Yet, important elements of the League, such as the Permanent Court of International Justice and the International Labour Organisation, were built into the United Nations which used a similar structure in the form of an assembly and council. The League of Nations was the world's first experiment in the practice of collective security. Although it failed, the central idea of collective security and the more general idea of working together to solve the world's social and economic problems continued to attract the support of leading politicians and statesmen.

Why did the League of Nations fail to preserve world peace?

1. How useful is Source 4 as evidence of Japanese aggression against China in the early 1930s?

2. How far do Sources 3 and 5 support the view that the Japanese invasion of Manchuria was the prime cause of the failure of the League of Nations?

3. How far do Sources 6 to 8 support the view that it was an absence of willpower, especially on the part of Britain and France, that led to the failure of the League of Nations?

SOURCE 3

Extract from *20th Century World History* by Martin Cannon et al published in 2009.

The Great Depression exposed the weakness of the post-Versailles settlements and is regarded by some as the greatest cause of the Second World War. It encouraged Japanese aggression and the rise of Hitler and exposed the inability of the League to maintain peace.

SOURCE 4

Extract from the Lytton Report published in 1932.

It is a fact that, without declaration of war, a large area of what was indisputably the Chinese territory has been forcibly seized and occupied by the armed forces of Japan ...

SOURCE 5

Extract from *Modern World History* by Ben Walsh published in 1996.

The significance of the Manchurian crisis was obvious. As many of its critics had predicted, the League was powerless if a strong nation decided to pursue an aggressive policy and invade its neighbours. Japan had committed blatant aggression and got away with it. Back in Europe both Hitler and Mussolini observed with interest. Within three years they would follow Japan's example.

SOURCE 6

Extract from a speech by Emperor Haile Selassie to the League in 1936.

I thought it to be impossible that fifty-two nations, including the most powerful in the world, should be successfully opposed by a single aggressor. ...This is not a case of the impossibility of stopping an aggressor but of the refusal to stop an aggressor.

SOURCE 7

Extract from the introduction of *The United Nations and Its Agencies* by R.J. and J. Owen published in 1985.

In the 1930s the League failed to stop Italian aggression in Abyssinia and German aggression in Europe because the members would not agree to combine their armed forces against Italy and Germany.

SOURCE 8

Extract from *Success in Twentieth Century World Affairs* by Jack Watson published in 1974.

The Ethiopian [Abyssinian] war was a disaster for collective security through the League of Nations. The League had failed miserably, undermined by the feebleness of Britain and France, although the absence from the League of important states such as Germany and the USA was a contributory factor.

KEY POINTS

▶ The organisation and structure of the League; especially the Assembly, Council and Permanent Court of Justice.

▶ Problems with membership, the unanimous decisions requirement, and the lack of an army.

▶ The record of the League during the 1920s with regard to various crises such as the Corfu Incident of 1923, together with the work of the agencies and commissions.

▶ The negative impact of the Great Depression on the work of the League.

▶ The record of the League during the 1930s with special reference to the Japanese invasion of Manchuria, the World Disarmament Conference, and the Italian invasion of Abyssinia.

▶ Reasons for the failure of the League.

Revision tips

- It is important to understand the roles of the different organisations of the League and to understand how the main bodies operated. Remember to revise the weaknesses in the League's structure and organisation. Make sure you know why the membership of the League was incomplete and how the absence of the United States affected the League's work.

- Make sure you can make a case for the successful work of the League with regard to its agencies and commissions.

- Make sure you can give examples of the peacekeeping successes and failures of the League during the 1920s and be able to explain the reasons for the various outcomes. Why were a number of agreements, such as Locarno, made outside the League?

- To understand the failure of the League during the 1930s you must first understand how the Great Depression affected the work of the League. You must be able to give plenty of reasons as to how the Great Depression made the League's work more difficult.

- The general circumstances surrounding the Japanese invasion of Manchuria, the World Disarmament Conference, and the Italian invasion of Abyssinia must be thoroughly understood. You may be asked to consider the relative contribution of any two of these episodes to the failure of the League.

- Finally, you must have a clear idea of why the League failed. Was it doomed from the outset or was it later events that undermined its ability to preserve world peace?

Review questions

1. What were the roles of the Council and the Permanent Court of Justice in the organisation of the League of Nations?

2. How was the League of Nations weakened by its structure and membership?

3. What did the League of Nations hope to achieve when it was set up in 1920?

4. What work was carried out by the agencies of the League of Nations?

5. Describe the impact of the Depression on the work of the League.

6. Describe how the lack of an army affected the work of the League.

7. What were the main successes of the League of Nations?

8. "The refusal of the United States to become a member was the main reason for the failure of the league of Nations." How far do you agree with this view. Explain your answer.

3

Why had international peace collapsed by 1939?

Introduction

The 1930s was a decade of increasing tension and conflict in Europe and the Far East. Few were surprised when war broke out again in September 1939. The first major act of aggression had come with Japan's invasion of Manchuria in 1931. This set the tone for what was to follow. Over the course of the next eight years Abyssinia, China, Austria, Czechoslovakia, Memel, Albania, and finally Poland fell victim to the ambitions of Italy, Germany, and Japan. Yet in the mid to late 1920s everything had looked so very different. The League of Nations seemed to be finding its feet and a series of international agreements such as Locarno and the Kellogg-Briand Pact appeared to suggest the dawn of a new age of peace and tranquillity. Something had gone very wrong.

The aims of this chapter are to:

- Look at the collapse of international order in the 1930s.

- Examine the increasing militarism of Germany, Italy, and Japan.

- Consider Hitler's foreign policy up to 1939 including actions with regards to the Saar, remilitarisation of the Rhineland, involvement in the Spanish Civil War, Anschluss with Austria, appeasement, crises with Czechoslovakia and Poland, and the outbreak of war.

▲ **Fig. 3.1** Newspaper headlines September 1939

What were the long-term consequences of the peace treaties of 1919–23?

Dissatisfied powers

One of the most important consequences of the peace settlement was that it left a number of countries feeling dissatisfied.

- Japan was disappointed because its idea for a racial equality clause had been rejected at the Paris Peace Conference and it had expected to receive a greater share of Germany's former trading rights in China.

- Italy had hoped to receive the Adriatic port of Fiume and a greater share of the former colonies of Germany and Turkey.

- Germany objected to just about every aspect of the Treaty of Versailles—the territorial provisions, the disarmament clauses, war guilt, and reparations.

The dissatisfied powers were likely to seek peace settlement changes when the circumstances were favourable. Germany's dissatisfaction was sharpened by the conviction among many that it had been "stabbed in the back" in 1918.

SOURCE 1

Extract from a right-wing German newspaper published in June 1919.

Today in the Hall of Mirrors in Versailles the disgraceful Treaty is being signed. Do not forget it! The German people will with unceasing labour press forward to reconquer the place amongst nations to which it is entitled. Then will come vengeance for the shame of 1919.

Germany's potential

Not only did the Versailles Treaty leave Germany extremely dissatisfied, it also failed to disable her and prevent her from growing into a powerful European state. Even though Germany had lost a significant amount of territory, including all her colonies, she was still left with considerable resources.

It was the combination of Germany's extreme dissatisfaction with Versailles together with its ability to bring about a revision of the settlement that proved to be so dangerous.

Hitler's foreign policy

Destruction of the Versailles Settlement provided Hitler with a foreign policy agenda. Virtually every foreign policy action and demand that Hitler made between 1933 and September 1939 involved the violation of the Treaty of Versailles or the Treaty of Saint Germain. These actions included:

- German rearmament and the remilitarisation of the Rhineland

- the Anschluss or union with Austria

- the transfer of the **Sudetenland** from Czechoslovakia

- the occupation of Prague

- the seizure of Memel

- claims made over Danzig and the Polish Corridor.

What was the "stab in the back" myth?

- After the First World War the myth developed that Germany had not really lost the war at all but was betrayed by group of weak, unpatriotic, and socialist-inclined politicians. These were the "November Criminals", who hoped to profit from Germany's surrender.

- There was no truth in this myth as Germany had only surrendered in 1918 because she was on the brink of military defeat. Surrender was certainly preferable to the destruction of the German army.

- Nevertheless, the "stab in the back" myth gained popularity in right-wing, extremist circles in Germany and gave rise to the thinking that if the war had not really been lost, then the peace settlement was unnecessary and deserved to be overturned at the earliest opportunity.

- Many of those who joined or supported the Nazi Party thought this way.

Sudetenland

Territory located along the extended border areas of western Czechoslovakia mostly populated by Germans. The area contained many of Czechoslovakia's military defences, together with valuable raw materials and centres of engineering and textile manufacture. The famous Skoda engineering factory was located here.

Extract from Hitler's *Mein Kampf* written in 1924.

What a use could be made of the Treaty of Versailles! ... How each one of the points of that Treaty could be branded in the minds and hearts of the German people until 60 million men and women find their souls aflame with a feeling of rage and shame.

The Treaty of Versailles, in particular, was detested by the German people and Hitler could ensure his short-term popularity by dismantling the treaty clause by clause.

Impact on British and French opinion

The Treaty of Versailles clearly made a major impact on Germany. It also made an impact on British and French opinion.

To begin with, the British were fully satisfied by the harsh, punitive aspect of the treaty. But it did not take long for many to question whether the treaty was fair. By the early 1930s a common view in British government circles was that the treatment of Germany had been too harsh. The emergence of Hitler and the Nazis was seen as an understandable response to the excessive punishment meted out to Germany in 1919. It followed from this line of thought that if many aspects of Versailles were unfair, then it was the duty of British politicians to assist Germany in achieving the peaceful revision of the treaty. After all, the British were partly responsible for the nature of the settlement.

The French reaction to the treaty was that it was not harsh enough. The French had wanted a treaty that would permanently disable Germany in order to guarantee their security. By the mid-1930s, however, it was clear that Hitler was seeking to overturn the peace settlement. The French did not feel confident or strong enough to stand up to Hitler on their own so they acted in partnership with the British.

A settlement of inconsistencies

The Versailles Settlement had created a whole series of inconsistencies or anomalies:

- the separation of East Prussia from the main bulk of German territory by the Polish Corridor

- the placing of Danzig, overwhelmingly populated by Germans, under League of Nations control

- the placing of three and a half million Germans under Czech rule in the Sudetenland.

All of these inconsistencies could be justified in one way or another, yet to many German people they represented a series of grievances that had to be dealt with. The British were sympathetic over many of these issues but they believed that they should be addressed in a peaceful and orderly manner. Unfortunately, Hitler had very different ideas.

QUICK QUESTION 1

How useful are Sources 1 and 2 as evidence that the German people wanted to overturn the Treaty of Versailles?

QUICK QUESTION 2

Select one of the inconsistencies or anomalies created by the Versailles Settlement. Explain how it would have been justified by the peacemakers in 1919. You may need to refer back to Chapter 1 for information to help you with your answer.

▲ **Fig. 3.2** Today, Danzig is known as Gdańsk; it is one of Poland's largest metropolitan areas

What were the consequences of the failures of the League in the 1930s?

After the First World War collective security, administered by the League of Nations, was meant to be the main way of preserving world peace. By 1929, the halfway point between the two world wars, there were some grounds for optimism regarding the new organisation. While the League had experienced some early teething problems, it had survived and grown in membership and influence. Yet within six years the League had shown that it was not fit for purpose. The Great Depression, followed by the Japanese invasion of Manchuria, and the Italian invasion of Abyssinia, essentially finished off the League (see Chapter 2). The League's failure had a major impact on the actions of Japan, Italy, and Germany.

Manchuria

When Japan invaded Manchuria in 1931 the eyes of the world were focused upon the League. This was the first time it had faced a serious challenge from a great power. If the League was firm and decisive then this would act as a warning to those powers seeking to expand their territory.

When the League failed to take any effective action the very opposite effect was achieved. Japan must have realised that without the membership of either the United States or Soviet Russia there was little the League could do to prevent her from further expansion at the expense of China.

While Soviet Russia was admitted to the League in 1934, it was clear that Stalin's immediate concerns lay with agricultural and industrial reform. This meant that there were no obstacles to prevent Japan from doing whatever it wanted and the invasion of China continued in 1937.

For both Italy and Germany, the lessons of Manchuria were certainly encouraging, making them think that their territorial ambitions were feasible. But it would take a successful European challenge to the League to give Mussolini and Hitler sufficient confidence to take action.

Abyssinia

At first the Italian invasion of Abyssinia in October 1935 appeared to jolt the League into taking firm action as it imposed economic sanctions on Italy. When it became clear, however, that these sanctions excluded certain key commodities such as coal and oil, the League was exposed as guilty of double dealing. The Hoare-Laval Pact of December 1935 confirmed this impression.

Both Mussolini and Hitler were delighted with the outcome; the League appeared to be incapable of effective action and it was proving impossible to put internationalism ahead of national interests. This meant that further aggressive behaviour from Italy was extremely likely and that Hitler would soon be furthering his policy of destroying the Treaty of Versailles.

SOURCE 3

Mussolini speaking in 1935.

The League is very well when sparrows shout, but no good at all when eagles fall out.

QUICK QUESTION 3

What point do you think Mussolini is making in Source 3? Give an example of which countries and disputes he might be referring to in the source.

The failure of the League and rearmament

The failure of the League also affected the thoughts and actions of Britain and France. Although they had never placed much confidence in the League, it was now obvious to both that collective security was dead and that alternative means had to be found to preserve world peace.

This meant both countries needed to rearm to deter Germany and Italy from taking further action. Rearmament had not happened before for a number of reasons.

- Following the world recession, money had been scarce and neither Britain nor France had spent what they should have on their defences.

- Both countries had used collective security as an excuse for underspending on arms.

- Public opinion was firmly against any major arms spending, partly because the public placed more faith in the League than politicians did.

The failure of the League and appeasement

By the summer of 1936 it was clear that rearmament was a top priority, but it was unlikely to preserve world peace on its own. This was partly because it would take several years for Britain and France to get rearmament programmes fully underway. Therefore while defences were being repaired and reconstructed, a policy of appeasement was adopted towards the dictators. Both rearmament and appeasement were, to a large extent, the result of the failures of the League of Nations.

▲ **Fig. 3.3** Neville Chamberlain with Munich Agreement

What was appeasement?

- Appeasement was the name given to the foreign policy adopted towards Hitler and Mussolini by Britain and France during the mid to late 1930s.

- It involved making pacts and deals with the dictators in order to satisfy their demands without going to war.

- Although opposed by a small number of high profile figures such as Churchill, appeasement was supported by the majority of British and French politicians between 1935 and 1939.

- The most famous example of appeasement was the Munich Agreement of September 1938.

> **❝** *I believe it is peace for our time.* **❞**
>
> Chamberlain on his return from Munich

How far was Hitler's foreign policy to blame for the outbreak of war in 1939?

What were Hitler's foreign policy aims?

When Hitler became Chancellor of Germany in January 1933 he had one overriding foreign policy objective: he wanted to make Germany great again. This could be achieved by pursuing a number of secondary objectives.

Policy	Implications of policy
Destroy the Treaty of Versailles	• The disarmament clauses would be broken by introducing conscription and by building up the army, navy, and air force. • Germany's western frontier would be secured by remilitarising and refortifying the Rhineland. • Lost territory would be regained.
Create a Greater Germany	• All German-speaking peoples would be brought into the **Reich**. • The frontiers of Germany would be extended to cover those areas where the population was predominantly German. This might include Austria and parts of Czechoslovakia and Poland.
Destroy communism	• Germany would be drawn into conflict with Soviet Russia.
Acquire lebensraum or "living space"	• Hitler thought that it was the entitlement of all Germans to have "living space". • This meant more land for their recreation and cultivation. • Lebensraum implied expansion eastwards at the expense of Poland and Soviet Russia.
Build up a central European empire	• Once Hitler had achieved all this he would be master of a new central European empire, the most powerful state in Europe, if not the world.

▲ **Table 3.1**

Whether Hitler's ambition would have been satisfied once he had achieved these objectives is open to debate. Possibly he would have wanted to have France as a **client state** and so extend the range of German domination from the Urals to the Atlantic. Hitler was a man with a grand vision for Germany.

Reich

Empire or realm.

Client state

A state that is effectively controlled or under the influence of another. The form of control or influence might be political, economic or military.

How far was Hitler's early foreign policy 1933–5 directed towards war?

The early stages of Hitler's foreign policy were quite tame compared with what followed. It was not clear to begin with that Hitler was heading towards war in Europe. Much of what he did in this period could be interpreted as trying to achieve equality with the western powers such as Britain and France.

Date	Event or action	Comment
1933	Germany refused to pay any more reparations, walked out of the World Disarmament Conference, and left the League of Nations.	• These were Hitler's first strikes against the Versailles Settlement. • Germany also began to rearm in secret.
January 1934	Ten-year non-aggression pact with Poland agreed.	• This would remove the prospect of war with Poland if Hitler decided to make a move against Austria or Czechoslovakia

July 1934	Attempted union or Anschluss with Austria.	• This followed the murder of the Austrian Chancellor Dollfuss by Austrian Nazis.
		• In the resulting confusion Hitler was poised to strike but Mussolini signalled his disapproval by moving Italian troops to the Brenner Pass.
		• Hitler backed down and denied any responsibility for the murder of Dollfuss.
January 1935	**Saar** plebiscite.	• This took place in accordance with the Treaty of Versailles.
		• The results showed that over 90 per cent were in favour of a return to Germany.
		• Germany had now regained its first piece of lost territory by legal and peaceful means.
March 1935	Reintroduction of conscription.	• This was a direct challenge to the Allied powers, Britain, France, and Italy. Hitler announced his intention of building up the army to 36 divisions (550 000 men) together with the creation of a military air force.
		• The Allies responded with the formation of the **Stresa Front**.
		• Hitler got away with it, although his actions prompted France and Soviet Russia, followed by Soviet Russia and Czechoslovakia, to sign **mutual assistance pacts**.
June 1935	Anglo-German Naval Agreement.	• The pact allowed Germany to have a fleet that was 35 per cent the size of Britain's, with submarines at 45 per cent. This pact essentially legalised German naval rearmament and was made without obtaining the prior agreement of France or Italy.
		• This gave the impression that it was quite in order for countries to pursue their national interests regardless of others.
		• Mussolini felt encouraged to apply the same selfish principle to extending Italy's colonies.

▲ **Table 3.2**

▲ **Fig. 3.4** Vote count during Saar plebiscite, January 1935

▲ **Fig. 3.5** German pocket battleships in port at Kiel, June 1935

Saar

A region of Germany important for coal production, with a population of around 800 000.

Stresa Front

A united stand made by Britain, France, and Italy against Hitler's violations of the disarmament clauses of the Treaty of Versailles announced in March 1935. The Front issued a strongly worded protest. It was soon undermined when Britain negotiated the Anglo-German Naval Agreement of June 1935.

Mutual assistance pact

This is an agreement between two or more countries whereby one country promises to help another in return for a promise of a similar kind.

How far did Hitler reveal his true intentions between 1936 and 1938?

By the beginning of 1936 Hitler had been in power for three years. Up to this point not a shot had been fired in anger against a foreign power by a German soldier. During the next three years it was still not clear to most western statesmen what Hitler intended. His methods were highly questionable but his objectives often appeared quite reasonable.

The remilitarisation of the Rhineland, March 1936

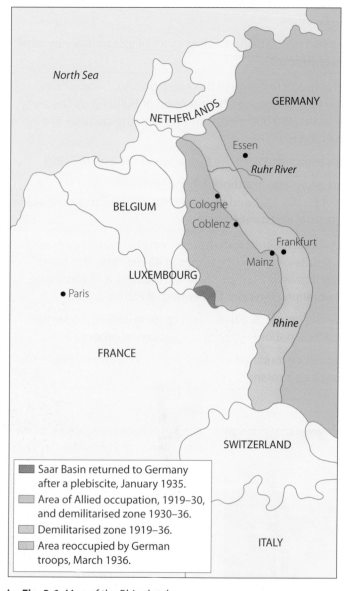

Saar Basin returned to Germany after a plebiscite, January 1935.

Area of Allied occupation, 1919–30, and demilitarised zone 1930–36.

Demilitarised zone 1919–36.

Area reoccupied by German troops, March 1936.

▲ **Fig. 3.6** Map of the Rhineland

▲ **Fig. 3.7** German troops crossing Rhine to reoccupy the Rhineland, March 1936

THE GOOSE-STEP

"GOOSEY GOOSEY GANDER,
WHITHER DOST THOU WANDER?"
"ONLY THROUGH THE RHINELAND—
PRAY EXCUSE MY BLUNDER!"

▲ **Fig. 3.8** British cartoon about the remilitarisation of the Rhineland published in March 1936

SOURCE 4

Hitler's reflections on the remilitarisation of the Rhineland several years later from *Germany* by Robert Gibson and Jon Nichol published in 1985.

The 48 hours after the march into the Rhineland were the most nerve-racking in my life. If the French had then marched into the Rhineland we would have had to withdraw with our tails between our legs, for the military resources at our disposal would have been wholly inadequate for even a moderate resistance.

SOURCE 5

Extract from the diary of William Shirer, an American journalist working in Berlin in 1936.

Hitler has got away with it! France is not marching. Instead it is appealing to the League! No wonder the faces of Hitler and Goering and Blomberg and Fritsch [Nazi leaders] were all smiles this noon. Oh, the stupidity (or is it the paralysis?) of the French! I learnt today on absolute authority that the German troops had strict orders to beat a hasty retreat if the French army opposed them in any way.

The Rhineland had been declared a demilitarised zone by the Treaty of Versailles which also authorised an army of occupation on the west bank for a period of 15 years. In fact, the Allied troops left five years ahead of schedule. From the German point of view a demilitarised Rhineland was a constant reminder of Germany's humiliation and disadvantage as, in theory, it enabled western armies to invade at will, as happened in January 1923.

With two divisions of troops against a possible opposition force of two hundred divisions, German forces marched into the Rhineland in March 1936.

As Hitler had correctly predicted, neither the French nor the British had any desire for war over this issue. The Rhineland was widely regarded as Germany's "backyard" and both French and British leaders realised that it was foolhardy to risk European peace over whether or not German troops should be allowed to occupy part of their own country. Furthermore, the French were in the middle of a financial crisis and facing elections in six weeks' time.

Hitler followed his Rhineland triumph with further promises of peaceful intentions, suggesting a 25-year non-aggression pact with the western powers.

DISCUSSION

1. What is the message of the cartoonist in Figure 3.8?

2. What do Sources 4 and 5 suggest was the main reason that Hitler was able to remilitarise the Rhineland successfully?

3. How far does Figure 3.8, together with Sources 4 and 5, support the view that Hitler outwitted his opponents in March 1936?

The Spanish Civil War, 1936–39

In July 1936 General Franco started the Spanish Civil War when he led a right-wing revolt against the democratically elected, republican government of the Popular Front—a mixture of socialists, communists, anarchists and syndicalists. Franco's right-wing, nationalist alliance included the Falange, Spain's fascist party founded in 1933.

Hitler, along with Mussolini, decided to support his fellow fascist, Franco, while Stalin, the leader of Soviet Russia, supported the Republicans. Britain and France decided not to become involved. The Spanish Civil War became a battleground for rival ideologies and thousands of volunteers flocked to Spain in order to check the spread of fascism. After more than thirty months of bitter struggle, in which three quarters of a million lives were lost, the Nationalists emerged victorious and Franco established a fascist-style government. From Hitler's point of view the war offered a series of opportunities:

▲ **Fig. 3.9** Guernica, Northern Spain, after a bombing raid, May 1937

What Hitler hoped to achieve	What Hitler actually achieved
If Franco was successful then Spain would become a German ally. This would provide a hostile presence on France's south-western border and hopefully provide Spanish naval bases for the German navy.	Following the surrender of Madrid to the Nationalists in March 1939, Spain failed to become an ally of the fellow fascist powers and instead opted for neutrality during the Second World War, allowing Franco to concentrate on Spain's domestic problems.
Germany's armed forces, especially the Luftwaffe, could be tested in what could be considered a dress rehearsal for a full-scale European war.	The Luftwaffe was able to practise and perfect dive-bombing techniques in the ruthless assault on Guernica in the Basque region of northern Spain.
Since Mussolini was joining Hitler in assisting Franco, Hitler hoped that this joint action might provide the occasion to detach the Italian leader from his association with Britain and France and draw him into an alliance with Germany.	Hitler succeeded in persuading Mussolini to abandon Britain and France. While still not a formal ally, Mussolini made it clear in a speech in November 1936, that Germany and Italy now formed an "axis", the "Rome-Berlin Axis". This represented an important staging post on the road to a formal alliance.
Hitler hoped that a long drawn-out civil war in Spain would distract western diplomats and officials from the affairs of central Europe. Spain could, therefore, act as a smokescreen for Hitler's attentions elsewhere.	To a large extent this happened, as the Spanish Civil War lasted for the best part of three years. During this time Hitler was able to take successful action over Austria and Czechoslovakia in central Europe.

▲ Table 3.3

The Anti-Comintern Pact, November 1936

This was a pact signed by Germany and Japan in 1936, with Italy joining in November 1937. The agreement was nominally directed against the Comintern, the Soviet agency for promoting communist revolution abroad. The real purpose of the treaty was to ensure that neither Germany nor Japan would assist Soviet Russia if the latter attacked either country.

The Anschluss, March 1938

One of Hitler's foreign policy aims was to include all German-speaking peoples in the Reich so as to form a Greater Germany. The largest concentration of German speakers outside Germany was in Austria which had a population of approximately seven million. Union between Germany and Austria was forbidden by the Treaty of Versailles but much of that treaty now lay in tatters.

The main problem lay with Italy. Italy had so far regarded Austria as within its sphere of influence and had authorised military movements in 1934 to prevent such a union happening then. But Hitler's relationship with Mussolini had improved since 1934 and Hitler was in a stronger military and diplomatic position.

In February 1938 a meeting took place between Hitler and the Austrian Chancellor Schuschnigg to discuss the persecution of Austrian Nazis by Austrian government forces. During this meeting Schuschnigg was bullied by Hitler into appointing Seyss-Inquart, a leading Austrian Nazi, as Minister of the Interior. Suspecting that Hitler wanted to destroy Austrian independence, Schuschnigg decided to hold a plebiscite on this issue on 13 March. When Hitler found out he demanded Schuschnigg's resignation and

QUICK QUESTION 4

Why would Britain and France have been alarmed by the signing of the Anti-Comintern Pact?

CONSULTING THE ORACLE.
(As recorded by Mr. Punch's magic microphone.)

HERR HITLER. "WHAT IS YOUR MESSAGE FOR GERMANY?"
SIGNOR MUSSOLINI. "TELL HER SHE MUST BE CAREFUL TO KEEP ON THE RIGHT SIDE OF ITALY."
HERR HITLER. "AND HOW CAN SHE MAKE SURE OF DOING THAT?"
SIGNOR MUSSOLINI. "BY KEEPING ON THE OTHER SIDE OF AUSTRIA."

▲ **Fig. 3.10** British cartoon about Mussolini's attitude towards a union between Germany and Austria published in June 1934

his replacement by Seyss-Inquart. Schuschnigg reluctantly agreed and Seyss-Inquart became Chancellor. He immediately requested the assistance of Germany in restoring order.

Having first secured Mussolini's support, Hitler ordered the German army into Austria on 12 March 1938 proclaiming the Anschluss to have taken place. Plebiscites held in early April confirmed these events in both Austria and Germany, with an overwhelming number of votes in favour of the union.

The Anschluss was Hitler's most daring action to date. For the first time the German army had been deployed across German frontiers. It would be hard to imagine a greater challenge to Britain and France, yet they did nothing apart from issue protests to Germany. In fact, there was little they could do without the support of Italy and any action would have appeared to be contrary to the wishes of the Austrian people. Hitler had increased German territory, population, and resources, adding to Germany's military capacity. He had also increased his confidence and contempt for the opposition of Britain and France.

GOOD HUNTING

Mussolini. "All right, Adolf—I never heard a shot"

▲ **Fig. 3.11** British cartoon about Mussolini's attitude towards a union between Germany and Austria published in February 1938

13·MÄRZ 1938
EIN VOLK EIN REICH
EIN FÜHRER

▲ **Fig. 3.12** Nazi poster celebrating the Anschluss, 13 March 1938; the caption says: "One People, One Empire, One Führer"

DISCUSSION

Why are the messages of the cartoons in Figure 3.10 and Figure 3.11 so different?

Das ganze Volk sagt am 10. April ja!

▲ **Fig. 3.13** Nazi poster for the Anschluss plebiscite of 10 April 1938; the caption says: "The whole people say Yes!"

The Sudetenland

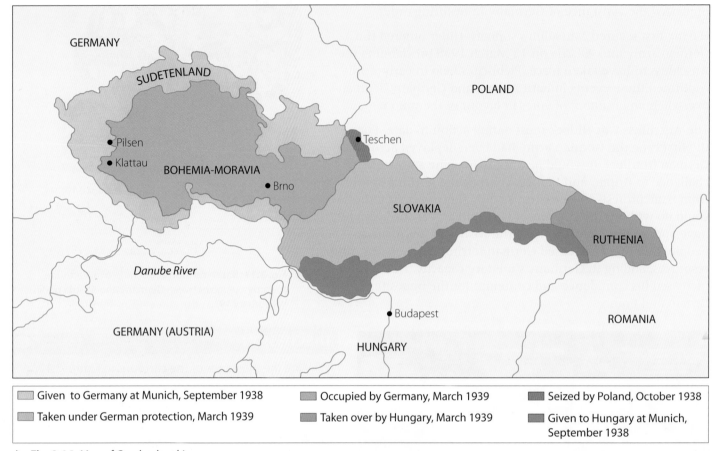

GERMANY

SUDETENLAND

POLAND

● Pilsen

● Teschen

● Klattau

BOHEMIA-MORAVIA

● Brno

SLOVAKIA

RUTHENIA

Danube River

GERMANY (AUSTRIA)

● Budapest

ROMANIA

HUNGARY

Given to Germany at Munich, September 1938	Occupied by Germany, March 1939	Seized by Poland, October 1938
Taken under German protection, March 1939	Taken over by Hungary, March 1939	Given to Hungary at Munich, September 1938

▲ **Fig. 3.14** Map of Czechoslovakia

The Sudetenland was populated by three and a half million Germans, former subjects of the Austro-Hungarian Empire. It was conveniently located within Czechoslovakia but on the border with Germany. Hitler disliked the very existence of Czechoslovakia for several reasons.

- It was a creation of the Treaty of Saint Germain, part of the Versailles Settlement.

- It had an alliance with Soviet Russia and France.

- It had a democratically elected government.

The Sudeten Germans, under their leader Henlein, were complaining of discrimination by the Czech-dominated government.

At first Hitler encouraged protests and demonstrations by the Sudeten Germans. He thought about seizing the Sudetenland in May 1938 but was dissuaded by the prospect of war with Czechoslovakia, Soviet Russia, and France backed by Britain. This was no more than a delay, however, and by September western statesmen feared that Hitler would use force to resolve the issue unless they could come up with a plan.

The Munich Agreement

Two summit meetings took place between the British Prime Minister Neville Chamberlain and Hitler.

Date	Location	Matters decided/discussed
15 September 1938	Berchtesgaden, Bavaria	• Areas of the Sudetenland, where the majority of the population was German, should be handed over to Germany. • This was subject to approval by the British, French, and Czech governments.
22 September 1938	Bad Godesberg, Rhineland	• Chamberlain reported the approval given by the British, French, and Czech governments to the matter discussed above. • Hitler now claimed that he must have the Sudeten territories immediately. • Hitler demanded that the Czechs withdraw from the Sudeten areas by 1 October to avoid the certainty of conflict.

▲ **Table 3.4**

Chamberlain was appalled by Hitler's change of heart at Bad Godesberg and returned to London to prepare for war. Instructions were issued for the mobilisation of the French army and the British navy. When Hitler realised that he was on the brink of a European war he agreed to Chamberlain's suggestion, supported by Mussolini, of an international conference to settle the dispute. The Munich Conference met on 29 September 1938.

The Munich Conference	
Participants	**Matters decided**
Neville Chamberlain (Britain) Adolf Hitler (Germany) Benito Mussolini (Italy) Edouard Deladier (France)	• The Sudetenland would be transferred to Germany over a 10-day period. • Plebiscites would be held in any areas where there was doubt over the dominant nationality. • The four powers would guarantee the remainder of Czechoslovakia once Polish and Hungarian claims had been met.

▲ **Table 3.5**

When given the terms of the Munich Agreement, Czech government ministers had little option but to agree to the break-up of their country as the alternative was for Czechoslovakia to face the full force of the German army on its own.

A few hours after the signing of the main agreement Chamberlain made a personal visit to Hitler armed with a document that he invited Hitler to sign. This document pledged Hitler and Chamberlain to do everything to promote the peace of Europe and to use the "method of consultation" to resolve any mutual differences. Hitler had no objection to adding his signature to a collection of vague promises while Chamberlain was able to return to London claiming that he had brought "peace for our time".

▲ **Fig. 3.15** Mussolini, Hitler, Chamberlain, and Deladier meet in Munich, September 1938

The Munich Agreement	
For	**Against**
• Neville Chamberlain did not think that Britain was sufficiently prepared or united to fight a war in 1938. • Britain's air defences were incomplete. Britain was vulnerable to a knock-out blow from the Luftwaffe. • The **British Dominions** were not united behind the prospect of war in 1938. This had changed by September 1939. • A war in 1938 would have been seen as a war against the principle of self-determination. In 1939 it was seen as a war to prevent German domination of Europe.	• Britain and France had abandoned Czechoslovakia to her fate. • Munich came to be seen as the supreme example of the policy of appeasement. • If war had broken out in October 1938, Britain and France would have had the support of the 36 divisions of the Czech army fighting behind their well-prepared defences. • In the event of war, Britain and France might have had the assistance or neutrality of Soviet Russia.

▲ **Table 3.6** Arguments for and against the Munich Agreement

▲ **Fig. 3.16** Evacuation of Czech citizens from the Sudetenland, October 1938

British Dominions

Self-governing territories within the British Empire such as Canada, Australia, New Zealand, and South Africa.

SOURCE 6

Neville Chamberlain speaking about the Munich Agreement in a radio broadcast on 1 October 1938.

I believe that it is peace for our time … peace with honour.

SOURCE 7

The *Daily Express* comments on the Munich Agreement, 30 September 1938.

People of Britain, your children are safe. Your husbands and your sons will not march to war. Peace is a victory for all mankind.

SOURCE 8

Winston Churchill speaking in the House of Commons during the debate on the Munich Agreement, October 1938.

We have suffered a total and unmitigated defeat … you will find that in a period of time … Czechoslovakia will be engulfed in the Nazi regime.

SOURCE 9

Hitler speaking in private about the Munich Agreement, October 1938.

That senile old rascal Chamberlain has ruined my entry into Prague.

SOURCE 10

Advice from a senior general to the British Cabinet, 20 September 1938.

… from the military point of view, time is in our favour, and that, if war with Germany has to come, it would be better to fight her in say 6–12 months' time, than to accept the present challenge.

DISCUSSION

1. How do you explain the different impressions given by Sources 6 and 8?

2. Does the information contained in Source 10 mean that Churchill's judgment in Source 8 was wrong?

3. To what extent do Sources 6 to 10 support the view that the Munich Agreement was a political success for Neville Chamberlain?

4. How might each of the following have reacted to the Munich Agreement? Explain your answer.

   a. A German living in the Sudetenland

   b. A member of the Czechoslovakian government

   c. An English citizen living in London

   d. A member of the Soviet government

⟶ Was the policy of appeasement justified?

It is easy to criticise the policy of appeasement. It is claimed that this policy was morally wrong and led directly to the sacrifice of Czechoslovakia. It certainly boosted the self-confidence of Hitler, encouraging him to make further demands and providing him with additional territory and resources. While Britain and France may have gained time to improve their defences, Germany also used this time to strengthen its army, navy, and air force.

In the years following the Second World War appeasement was regarded as a policy of concession, weakness, and cowardice that made war more rather than less likely to occur. Yet the appeasers were all people of intelligence with a sense of realism. They had good reason to try to come to terms with the dictators and accommodate their wishes. Given the advantage of hindsight, appeasement may not have been the right policy, but it certainly made sense at the time.

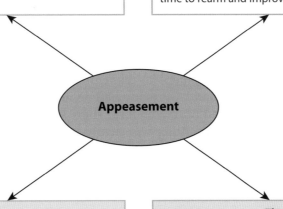

Correcting the injustices of Versailles

By the 1930s many thought that Versailles had been too harsh on Germany. While no-one liked Hitler's bullying methods there was some sympathy for his main demands. Few thought it unreasonable that Germany should be allowed the means to defend itself, secure its frontiers or make common cause with the substantial pockets of Germans living under foreign rule.

Until March 1939 there was good reason to accept Hitler's demands while deploring his diplomatic behaviour. A strong-arm approach would have run the risk of upsetting public opinion, offending the British Dominions, who supported the notion of self-determination, and intensifying the German sense of injustice.

Increasing militarism of Japan and Italy

During the late 1930s Germany was not the only threat to world peace. Both Japan and Italy became increasingly aggressive and militaristic following the successes of Manchuria and Abyssinia respectively. Whereas Italy actively supported General Franco during the Spanish Civil War and, in April 1939, invaded and overran Albania, Japan invaded the rest of China in 1937. There was a real possibility that Britain could find itself at war with Germany, Italy and Japan simultaneously with only France as a major ally. The chiefs of the British armed services did not think that Britain could win such a war.

Appeasement reflected Britain's military weakness in the face of these dangers. It seemed unwise to issue threats which could not be backed by adequate force. Meanwhile Britain gained valuable time to rearm and improve its air defences.

A popular policy

The appeasers were all leaders of democratic countries where governments were decided by free elections. All politicians working in a democracy have to take account of public opinion if they are to survive.

Public opinion in Britain and France was overwhelmingly for peace during the 1930s. Deeply affected by the experiences of the First World War there was little support for rearmament or a stronger stand against Germany, Italy and Japan.

Threat of communism

Aggressive German expansion was not the only problem faced by western Europe during the 1930s. There was the simultaneous threat of Soviet Russia and world communism.

Some western politicians feared communism more than Nazism. One way to reduce the potential threat of Soviet Russia was to ensure that there was a strong, anti-communist state in central Europe committed to its destruction. Germany fitted the bill perfectly. Anti-communists found it convenient to support appeasement.

▲ **Fig. 3.17** Reasons for appeasement

Select one of the following statements and explain why you agree or disagree with it.

1. Appeasement was a mistaken policy because it made war more rather than less likely.

2. The main problem with appeasement was that Hitler confused it with weakness on the part of Britain and France.

3. Appeasement was a useful, time-buying exercise for the western powers. It enabled them to rearm and build up their defences.

4. Hitler should have been stopped at the time of the reoccupation of the Rhineland.

Why did Britain and France adopt a policy of trying to deter Germany after March 1939?

In March 1939 Britain and France largely abandoned their policy of trying to appease Hitler in favour of a policy of deterrence. The reason for this major change in direction lay with what happened to Czechoslovakia.

The invasion of Czechoslovakia

Czechoslovakia was a multinational state inhabited by Czechs, Magyars, Slovaks, and Ruthenes as well as other nationalities. Once the Sudetenland was transferred to Germany the rest of the state began to break up. Nevertheless, Czechoslovakia remained a country rich in agriculture and industry, resources that Hitler very much wanted to obtain for the benefit of Germany. He finally made his strike in March 1939. President Hacha of Czechoslovakia was bullied into placing the fortunes of his country in the hands of the German Reich and the German army occupied Prague on 15 March 1939.

These events are complicated but important for what they reveal about Hitler's true intentions. Up until and including the Munich Agreement, every territorial change sought by Hitler could be justified on the grounds of self-determination—allowing land mainly populated by Germans to transfer to the German Reich.

The events of March 1939 were different. Here Hitler was taking new territory simply in order to increase the power of Germany. Germany had no more right to Czechoslovakia than it did to Belgium or Luxembourg. There were no Germans living in the newly acquired territories. Hitler was clearly straying well beyond the acceptable principles of achieving his Greater Germany. He was now making a bid to dominate Europe by force.

Date	Event
June 1935	Anglo-German Naval Agreement
December 1935	Hoare-Laval Pact (Abyssinia)
March 1936	Largely passive reaction of British and French following the German reoccupation of the Rhineland
March 1938	Largely passive reaction of British and French following the Anschluss
September 1938	Munich Agreement regarding the Sudetenland

▲ **Table 3.7** Examples of appeasement

Date	Event
September 1931	Japan invades Manchuria.
October 1935	Italy invades Abyssinia.
July 1937	Japan invades rest of China.
April 1939	Italy invades Albania.

▲ **Table 3.8** Japanese and Italian aggression 1931–9

Date	Event
July 1934	Italy opposes German plans to unite with Austria.
April 1935	Italy joins the Stresa Front directed against German rearmament.
October 1935	Germany continues to trade with Italy during the Abyssinian crisis.
July 1936	Italy joins Germany in assisting Franco in the Spanish Civil War.
November 1936	Mussolini refers to a Rome-Berlin Axis.
September 1937	Mussolini visits Hitler in Berlin.
November 1937	Italy joins Germany and Japan by signing the Anti-Comintern Pact.
March 1938	Mussolini agrees to the Anschluss.

September 1938	Mussolini persuades Hitler to agree to the Munich Conference.
May 1939	Italy signs a formal alliance with Germany, the Pact of Steel.
September 1939	Italy remains neutral when Britain and France declare war on Germany after Mussolini informs Hitler that he is not yet ready for war.

▲ **Table 3.9** German/Italian relations 1934–9

	Territory (km²)	Population (m)
Germany in 1935	452 000	64
Austria	84 000	6.7
Germany in March 1938 after Anschluss with Austria	536 000	70.7
Sudetenland	29 000	3.6
Germany in October 1938 after taking over the Sudetenland	565 000	74.3
Bohemia-Moravia	49 000	7.5
Germany in March 1939 after expansion into Bohemia-Moravia	614 000	81.8
Overall percentage increase between 1935 and March 1939	36%	28%

▲ **Table 3.10** The expansion of German territory and population 1935–9

The British-French guarantee to Poland

There was little the British or French could do to save Czechoslovakia in March 1939 but there was no longer any doubt about Hitler's ambitions. Poland was almost certainly going to be his next target for the following reasons.

- Poland was a recreation by the Versailles Settlement.
- Poland included territory that had been part of Germany prior to 1919 such as West Prussia.
- The Polish Corridor separated East Prussia from the main bulk of German territory.
- Danzig, located in the Polish Corridor, was populated mainly by Germans.

Hitler began by demanding the return of Danzig together with the establishment of German-controlled transport links across the Polish Corridor. Although Hitler's demands over Poland appeared just as reasonable as they had over the Sudetenland, the events of March 1939 led to the policy of appeasement being replaced by one of deterrence.

On 31 March a British-French guarantee was given to Poland that promised that Poland would receive British and French support and assistance if attacked. Britain and France also began to think in terms of constructing a grand eastern alliance against Germany to present her with the prospect of a major war on two fronts should Germany decide to attack Poland.

For this eastern alliance to be effective Soviet Russia had to be persuaded to become a member. Unsuccessful attempts were made by the British and the French to achieve this during the spring and summer of 1939. A major problem was that Stalin feared he was being drawn into a war with Germany. When the project failed, Poland was left with two western allies, Britain and France, neither of whom was in a position to provide immediate assistance in the event of a German invasion.

How important was the Nazi–Soviet Pact?

One of the most astonishing and surprising events resulting from Hitler's foreign policy was the announcement in late August 1939 of the Nazi–Soviet Pact, otherwise known as the Molotov–Ribbentrop Pact. Publicly, this amounted to a 10-year non-aggression pact. Privately, it contained clauses relating to the future partition of Poland.

At first sight this agreement appeared an extremely unlikely event. Here were two states representing ideological opposites, fascism and communism, making a deal with one another. Hitler had never made any secret of his hatred for communism and in *Mein Kampf* had argued in favour of the destruction of Soviet Russia. Stalin was well aware of German intentions and expected an invasion of his country at some point.

Yet on another level this pact made perfect sense. Hitler wanted to ensure that, having defeated Poland, he was not attacked by Soviet Russia while he dealt with Britain and France. Stalin hoped that an Anglo-French/German war would last many years and wanted to buy time to strengthen his defences and build up his military machine. Stalin also feared a war on two fronts given the current hostility of Japan.

So it suited the short-term ambitions of both Germany and Soviet Russia to do a deal with one another. The immediate result, of course, was to seal the fate of Poland. If Hitler invaded, as he now made immediate plans to do, there was absolutely nothing that Britain or France could do to assist their ally other than wage a general war against Germany. Hitler had no reason to suppose that Anglo-French opposition would be any more serious than it had been over Czechoslovakia. Also Hitler's diplomatic hand had strengthened since the Munich Agreement as Italy had become a formal ally in the Pact of Steel of May 1939.

▲ **Fig. 3.18** British cartoon about the Nazi–Soviet Pact published in September 1939

DISCUSSION

1. What does the cartoon in Figure 3.18 tell you about the Nazi–Soviet Pact?

2. How far do Sources 11 and 13 suggest that Hitler overreacted regarding the benefits of the Nazi–Soviet Pact in Source 12?

3. To what extent do Sources 11 to 15 support the view that it was Hitler who gained most from the Nazi–Soviet Pact in Source 12?

Why did Britain and France declare war on Germany in September 1939?

Britain and France declared war on Germany following the German invasion of Poland on 1 September. The immediate reason for this action was that Germany had ignored an ultimatum demanding that its army be withdrawn from the invaded areas. But the real reason behind the declaration of war went beyond what was happening in Poland. It had become clear that Germany was making a bid for European domination. Not to have declared war would have been an acceptance of this domination.

Why did Britain and France regard this action as a sign of Germany's intention to dominate Europe?

Hitler had already shown that his ambitions went beyond achieving a Greater Germany with his actions over Czechoslovakia in March 1939. Until then it had been just possible to interpret Germany's territorial expansion in Austria and the Sudetenland as in line with the principle of self-determination for German-speaking peoples. The events in Czechoslovakia showed that Hitler's real agenda was the domination of Europe by force.

The invasion of Poland was regarded by Britain and France as a continuation of this process even though Germany had legitimate grievances over Danzig and access across the Polish Corridor.

Why was Hitler not deterred by the British-French guarantees to Poland?

When Britain and France declared war on Germany in September 1939 Hitler was taken by surprise. He did not think they would take this action despite their guarantee to Poland.

This was partly because once the Nazi–Soviet Pact had been signed Hitler could not see how Britain and France could give effective help to Poland. In his mind this made a declaration of war quite pointless. It was also because Hitler was aware of how Britain and France had reacted to his previous violations of the peace settlement. He had decided that it would be out of character for them to go to war over a territory over which Germany had such strong claims.

Britain and France were possibly to blame, having behaved in such a way that allowed Hitler to draw this conclusion. They had done little more than protest over issues such as German rearmament, the remilitarization of the Rhineland, and the Anschluss. When Hitler had demanded the Sudetenland Britain and France found a way for it to be transferred to Germany. None of this looked like the behaviour of countries that would eventually make a firm stand.

So, in one sense, war broke out because of a miscalculation on Hitler's part. Yet there seems to be little doubt that European war would have broken out sooner or later. All Hitler's rearmament plans were geared towards a war in the near future and he was set upon demonstrating Germany's new-found strength.

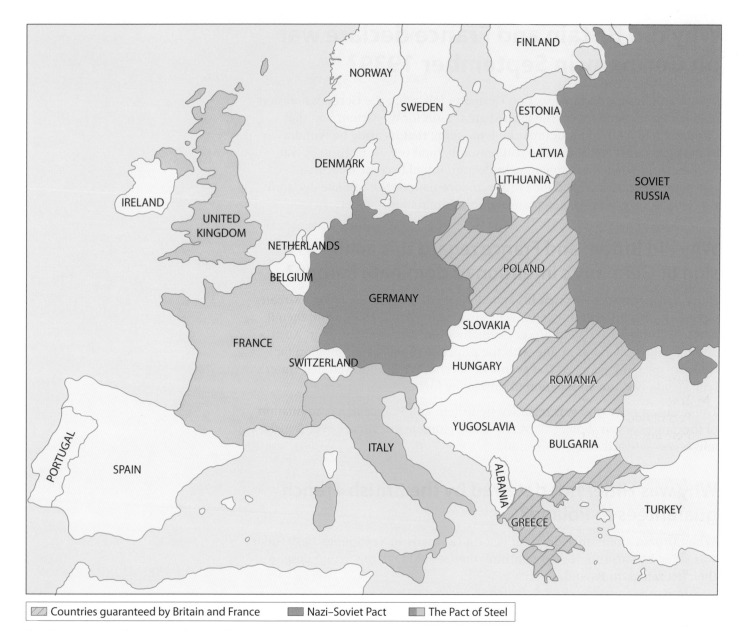

Countries guaranteed by Britain and France	Nazi–Soviet Pact	The Pact of Steel

▲ **Fig. 3.19** Map of Europe on the eve of war, August 1939

In addition, the patience and tolerance of Britain and France had run out in early 1939 and after the events of March there was a general acceptance that war was just around the corner.

DISCUSSION

Which of the following do you think was most responsible for the outbreak of the Second World War? Explain your answer.

1. Appeasement
2. The Treaty of Versailles
3. The failure of the League of Nations
4. Hitler's foreign policy aims

▶ The Paris Peace Settlement provided a series of long-term causes of the Second World War by creating a number of dissatisfied powers, failing to disable Germany, and giving Hitler a foreign policy agenda.

▶ The League of Nations was unable to make a success of collective security as it failed to restrain Japan and Italy, failed to bring about world disarmament, and left Britain and France without the means to check the ambitions of Hitler.

▶ Hitler's foreign policy significantly increased the power and prestige of Germany between 1933 and 1939 with the annexation of Austria and parts of Czechoslovakia. As Britain and France gave in to his demands he developed contempt for the democracies.

▶ The policy of appeasement came to its climax in September 1938 when the Munich Settlement effectively gave the Sudetenland of Czechoslovakia to Germany.

▶ After the German occupation of Prague in March 1939 Britain and France decided to try to deter Hitler by giving a guarantee of support to Poland. Attempts were also made to draw Soviet Russia into an eastern alliance against Germany.

▶ These attempts came to nothing with the announcement of the Nazi–Soviet Pact of August 1939. Hitler now thought there was nothing to prevent him from invading Poland.

Revision tips

● Make sure you understand why Japan, Italy, and Germany were dissatisfied with the Paris Peace Settlement.

● You need to be familiar with the failures of the League of Nations over Manchuria and Abyssinia, and understand why the collapse of collective security left Britain and France dangerously exposed to the ambitions of Japan, Italy, and Germany.

● You need to grasp the essentials of Hitler's foreign policy between 1933 and 1939, especially regarding the reoccupation of the Rhineland, the Anschluss, and the Czechoslovakian crisis.

● You must understand why Britain and France adopted a policy of appeasement towards Germany and Italy and be able to give examples of this policy.

● You must also appreciate the impact of the events of March 1939 which led to a major change in British and French foreign policy towards Germany. What was so different about the German occupation of Prague?

● The circumstances surrounding the signing of the Nazi–Soviet Pact must be understood. Why did Stalin prefer to make a deal with Germany rather than Britain or France? How did this pact lead directly to war?

Review questions

1. In what ways did Hitler revise the Treaty of Versailles between 1933 and 1936?

2. How far did the Treaty of Versailles cause the outbreak of war in 1939?

3. Why was the remilitarisation of the Rhineland important for Hitler?

4. Why was the Anschluss between Germany and Austria such a major achievement for Hitler in 1938?

5. To what extent was Hitler's desire for lebensraum responsible for causing war in Europe?

6. Describe the policy of appeasement.

7. "The Nazi–Soviet Pact made Germany's invasion of Poland in September 1939 a near certainty." How far would you agree with this view? Explain your answer.

4

Who was to blame for the Cold War?

Introduction

This chapter explains why the most powerful of wartime allies, the United States and Soviet Union, became enemies in a "cold war" which lasted for over 40 years.

In 1941, the last great empire of the last century joined forces with the emerging empires of the new century. However, this alliance between Britain, the United States, and the Soviet Union was not to last much beyond the defeat of Germany in May 1945.

By the end of 1949, Europe was divided into two **blocs**: those countries that were under Soviet control and those who enjoyed close relations with the United States. Many of the countries that were friendly with the United States were also members of the North Atlantic Treaty Organisation (NATO), an armed alliance of states.

The division of Europe was symbolised by the fate of Germany after the Second World War. Initially carved into four zones of occupation, with Berlin in the Soviet zone but similarly divided up, the failure of Stalin's plan to unite Berlin led to the unification of the three western zones and the formal creation of West and East Germany.

Both sides blamed each other for the breakdown in relations. The United States believed that the Soviet Union, under the dictatorial rule of Stalin, was intent in spreading its communist ideology as far as it could across Europe, and probably beyond. Stalin insisted the Soviet Union was acting to guarantee her own security after a conflict which had inflicted enormous damage on his populaiton and landscape.

Instead, he pointed to the United States' desire to build a global economic empire, with the United States at the centre, as the major cause of tension after the war, and was therefore forced to take extraordinary measures to protect the interests of the Soviet Union.

Bloc

A group of countries, tied together by military alliance and/or different ideologies.

▲ **Fig. 4.1** The "Big Three" pictured during the Yalta Conference, February 1945; Winston Churchill, Prime Minister of Britain 1940–5; Franklin Delano Roosevelt, President of the United States 1932–45; Stalin, leader of the Soviet Union 1924–53

The aims of this chapter are to examine the origins of the Cold War, including:

- the 1945 summit conferences and the breakdown of the US–Soviet alliance in 1945–6
- Soviet expansion into eastern Europe to 1948 and American reactions to it
- the occupation of Germany and the Berlin Blockade
- the creation of NATO and the Warsaw Pact.

Why did the US–Soviet alliance begin to break down in 1945?

Ideological differences

At the root of the tension between the United States and Soviet Union was a clear difference in how they believed society should be organised. For many historians, this meant that a breakdown in relations after the Second World War was inevitable.

America was a **democracy**, with free, multi-party elections. The US economy was **capitalist** and people were largely free to hold any religious or political belief. Freedom of speech was an important feature of American life. The rights of ordinary Americans were laid out and protected by a written **constitution**.

The Soviet political system was based on **communism**, with one-party rule and no political opposition allowed. Although a constitution was produced in 1936, Soviet citizens had few political rights. Millions of innocent people were persecuted during the 1930s and religious beliefs were not tolerated. Most of the economy was controlled by the state and was subject to long-term central planning.

After the Communists came to power in Russia in October 1917, several western powers including the United States and Britain intervened in the Russian Civil War against the Communists. This contributed to Soviet fears about future attacks from capitalist countries. During the 1930s, Stalin believed that Britain and France were happy for Hitler to expand in the east, and this contributed to his decision to seek a defensive alliance with Germany in August 1939 called **the Nazi–Soviet Pact**.

For their part, western political leaders were suspicious of the Soviet Union for two reasons. Firstly, they feared that the Communists shared the ambitions of the Russian Tsars who had preceded them and wanted to expand into central Europe and the eastern Mediterranean. Secondly, senior Communists had talked about the need for a worldwide revolution, increasing the likelihood of a conflict between communism and capitalism at some point in the future.

These tensions contributed to an uneasy relationship during the Second World War.

Wartime disagreements

After the Soviet Union was invaded by Germany in June 1941, the public was presented with a very positive image of relations between the United States, Britain, and the Soviet Union. These emphasised the common goal of defeating Nazism, and the terrible conditions which the Russian people endured on the Eastern Front.

The allies cooperated extensively during the war. British merchant ships braved the horrors of the Baltic to supply the Soviet Union with much needed materials, while the United States agreed to extend the **Lend-Lease** programme to the Soviet Union.

President Roosevelt, Stalin, and Winston Churchill met for the first time at Tehran in November 1943, where they agreed on a date for the invasion of France, while military officials and politicians regularly met to discuss details of organising the war.

Democracy

A form of political system based on popular consent.

Capitalist

A form of economic system where most of the economy is privately owned.

Constitution

A set of rules which outline the powers of a country's political institutions and the rights of its citizens.

Communism

An ideology which aims to create an equal society, where the economy is controlled by the people and private ownership does not exist.

Nazi–Soviet Pact

An agreement signed by Ribbentrop (German Foreign Minister) and Molotov (Soviet Foreign Minister) which led both countries to invade Poland.

Lend-Lease

From 1941, the United States lent, leased, and sold military equipment to countries fighting Germany, Italy or Japan.

However, beneath the surface, tensions between the western and eastern allies were ever-present. Stalin's obsessive secrecy prevented him from sharing his battle plans with either Britain or the United States, while Churchill would not share his knowledge of the **Enigma** codes with the Soviet Union. British and American pilots who flew supplies and aircraft to the Soviet Union often complained that the Soviets did not seem to trust them. The sailors who brought supplies to the Soviet Union were usually given a small amount of money to spend, but they were not allowed to move freely around Soviet ports.

At a political level, suspicions about the conduct of their allies were voiced in Whitehall, Washington, and Moscow.

Enigma

A machine used to send encrypted signals intelligence to German armed forces during the Second World War. The Germans however did not know that, British code-breakers at Bletchley Park were able to break the code.

QUICK QUESTION 1

As the war went on, who do you think had more reason to be suspicious of their fellow allies, the United States or the Soviet Union?

SOURCE 1

A telegram from the British Foreign Secretary Anthony Eden to the British Embassy in Moscow, 17 February 1943.

In conversation recently with a member of this department, Soviet Ambassador referred to suspicions harboured by his countrymen that this country was not pulling its weight and devoting its full energies to the war against Germany.

SOURCE 2

Extract from a Foreign Office report on attitudes in the United States towards the Soviet Union commenting on a campaign launched by the *Chicago Tribune* newspaper against the Soviet Union, 6 April 1943.

1. *The USSR is represented as being an aggressive and almost entirely amoral power. It is pointed out that she only entered the war because of Hitler's attack, and was not in any way opposed to Germany or Fascism on moral grounds.*

2. *3rd March I had a long private conversation, lasting some three hours, with Mr Leon Stolz, Editorial Editor of the Tribune. He at once raised the question of Russia's future intentions. I asked him why he was so interested in that problem now. He replied that the end of the war in Europe was obviously near and people had to be awakened to the menace of Bolshevism.*

SOURCE 3

Extracts from the minutes of meetings of the British Cabinet on the question of the future of Poland, 17 January 1944.

THE FOREIGN SECRETARY reported that he had now received a further communication from the Polish Government. This was under examination, and [the Foreign Secretary] sought clarification or guarantees on a number of important and difficult points.

The following points were made in the course of the discussion which followed:

a. *Did the Russians really want an independent Poland? Or had they in view a puppet Government under Russian control and a Soviet Republic? The Foreign Secretary said there were increasing signs which pointed in the latter direction (in other words, he thought they wanted to make Poland a Soviet Republic under their influence).*

Attitude towards Germany and the post-war world

By the end of 1944, two things had become obvious: the Allies were going to win the war and the Soviet Union was going to play a much greater role in world affairs than she had done before the war. In October 1944, Churchill met Stalin to discuss post-war "**spheres of influence**", where the two leaders agreed to assign their respective influences in south-eastern Europe.

The "Big Three", Stalin, Churchill, and Roosevelt, leaders of the Soviet Union, Britain, and the United States respectively, met twice in 1945 to discuss the nature of the post-war world. The first meeting was at Yalta in the Soviet Union in February 1945. By then it was clear that the war was coming to an end, even though there was still a lot of hard fighting to come. All three leaders wanted to discuss the war, but they were all more focused on the future.

Spheres of influence

A territory where one country has political or economic control.

ISSUE	AGREEMENT
1. What to do with Germany after it was defeated	<ul><li>Only unconditional surrender would be acceptable.</li><li>There was to be no separate peace.</li><li>Germany (and its capital Berlin) would be temporarily divided into four occupation zones.</li><li>Germany's eastern border would be moved westwards.</li><li>Reparations would be payments in kind, a total of $20 billion to be paid, half of this going to the Soviet Union.</li></ul>
2. Establishment of the United Nations	<ul><li>Initially it was to consist of all the states at war with Germany.</li><li>The Security Council would consist of five permanent members, each with a power of veto.</li><li>Arrangements were made to convene the United Nations held in San Francisco, June 1945.</li></ul>
3. Getting the Soviet Union to enter the war against Japan	<ul><li>Stalin agreed to intervene in the war against Japan after Germany was defeated.</li><li>In return, the Soviet Union was given territory lost to Japan during the 1904–5 Russo–Japanese War, and Outer Mongolia and Manchuria would become Soviet "spheres of influence".</li></ul>
4. The future of Poland	<ul><li>A provisional government would be established incorporating members of the pro-Soviet "Lublin" government, and the exiled "London" Poles, who fled from the German and Soviet armies in 1939.</li><li>Free and fair multi-party elections would be held as soon as possible.</li></ul>

▲ **Table 4.1** Agreements made at the Yalta Conference

Historians disagree in their views of the Yalta Conference. Some, like the one in Source 4 below, believe that it was a good example of wartime cooperation. Other historians believe Yalta marked the beginning of the end of the wartime alliance.

SOURCE 4

P. M. H. Bell, *The World Since 1945: an international history*, published in 2001.

Yalta did not partition the world. It did not divide Europe, though it did place Poland firmly in the Soviet sphere of influence. It did not see the beginning of the Cold War, but plotted a feasible course towards bringing the Second World War to a conclusion and setting up a framework for the post-war world. The Grand Alliance was still in being.

SOURCE 5

Robert Service, *Stalin*, published in 2004.

Clever though he was, Stalin was no diplomatic genius. Yet the Big 3 had conflicting interests and he took advantage. Stalin had been given his inch and he took a mile. Already the idea had formed in his head that the USSR should conquer territory in the eastern half of Europe so as to have a buffer zone between itself and any Western aggressor.

The leaders of Britain, United States, and the Soviet Union met again in **Potsdam** near Berlin in July 1945, two months after Germany's unconditional surrender. Developments in eastern Europe and changes in personnel ensured that the meeting at Potsdam had a very different feel to the meeting in Yalta.

DISCUSSION

What were the main achievements of the Yalta Conference?

QUICK QUESTION 2

Why do you think the Allies did not insist on signing a written peace treaty with Germany after the Second World War?

Potsdam

A city 15 miles south of Berlin, where Churchill, Stalin, and President Harry Truman met to discuss the post-war world.

What changed between the Yalta Conference and the Potsdam Conference?

A number of changes took place between these two important meetings that affected the outcome of the Potsdam Conference.

Roosevelt had died in April, after suffering a massive brain haemorrhage. His successor, Vice-President Harry S. Truman, was inexperienced in dealing with international affairs and believed that Stalin should keep to the agreements made at Yalta.

Winston Churchill began the conference as British Prime Minister but there was an election in Britain in the middle of the conference. Churchill's party, the Conservatives, were heavily defeated and he was replaced by Labour leader Clement Attlee.

The Soviet Union had liberated eastern Europe and was starting to install sympathetic governments, while targeting political opponents. No free elections had so far been held in any of these countries.

On the eve of the conference, Truman informed Stalin that the United States had successfully tested an atomic weapon. The United States and Britain had kept their plans to develop an atomic weapon secret during the war; little did they know that Soviet agents had infiltrated both the **Manhattan Project** and British Intelligence, and had already provided the Soviet leader with valuable intelligence about the atomic bomb.

There was no change in the Soviet Union: Stalin was still its leader. He was still determined to look after the interests of the Soviet Union. His top priorities were getting reparations out of Germany and making sure that his country would never again be invaded by Germany or any other western power.

On the face of it, Potsdam marked a significant deterioration in relations between the Allies.

- The Allies didn't agree over the future government of Poland and the **Soviet-controlled government at Lublin** continued to run the country.
- They disagreed over the future of Germany. Stalin wanted to dismember Germany, and prevent it developing its own industry.
- The Soviet Union wanted access to Germany's industrial heartland in the Ruhr. This was rejected.
- Stalin wanted to gain a foothold in Japan, a demand that Truman rejected.

In spite of these quite major disagreements, the great powers were able to agree on several significant areas.

- The Polish/German border was to be settled at the Oder-Neisse Line.
- Germany would be **denazified** and war crimes trials were to be held in Germany and Japan.
- Germany would be governed by an Allied Control Council in Berlin, where each decision required a unanimous verdict and the country would be treated as a single economic unit. It was agreed that none of the occupying powers could make decisions on Germany's future without agreement from the other powers.

President Harry Truman

Born in 1884, Truman spent his early life as a farmer in Independence, Missouri. He entered Congress in 1934, and was plucked from the Senate by President Roosevelt to be his vice-presidential candidate in 1944. He had only spent a few months as Vice President before Roosevelt died, making Truman the 33rd President of the United States.

DISCUSSION

1. How did the conferences at Yalta and Potsdam each contribute to the breakdown in relations between the Soviet Union and its wartime allies?

2. Why was it harder for the allies to reach agreement at Potsdam than it was at Yalta?

Manhattan Project

The US research project tasked to develop an atomic bomb.

Soviet-controlled government at Lublin

Set up during the liberation of Poland in 1944, it was dominated by socialists and refused to acknowledge the authority of the exiled Polish government based in London.

Denazified

An Allied initiative to purge German society and politics of any Nazi influence.

- Each country was allowed to take reparations from its own zone of occupation. The Soviet Union could also take some equipment from the industrialised western zones.
- The Council of Foreign Ministers (CFM) would be established to deal with the defeated European countries.

The conference clearly illustrated the differing views of the Soviet Union and the western powers over the future of Germany and Poland. It also put off making some very important decisions by passing them on to the Council of Foreign Ministers and the Allied Control Council.

With Germany defeated, occupied, and in ruins, attention now turned to the process of reconstruction. The conference at Potsdam had mostly dealt with general principles; as each of the four powers began to turn these principles into action, competing visions of Germany's future began to emerge.

In the eastern zone, the Soviets prioritised collection of reparations in kind as a contribution to its immense domestic rebuilding programme. However, Britain and the United States believed that production from the factories in their zones should be traded for agricultural produce in the Soviet zone. Since the Soviets disagreed, the Americans had to pay for food imports themselves, while Britain introduced bread rationing at home in 1946 so it could export wheat to Germany.

In May 1946, the commander of the American zone, General Clay, stopped the delivery of reparations to the Soviets, and two months later merged the American and British zones into a single economic unit called "Bizonia".

Divisions emerged in how the four occupying powers approached the political structure of their respective zones. While the Soviets merged the Social Democratic and Communist parties into the Socialist Unity Party, in the western zones a multi-party system emerged which represented the respective political traditions of the United States, France, and Britain.

QUICK QUESTION 3

Considering the number of points that were agreed upon at the Potsdam Conference: do you consider the Conference to be a failure or a success?

TASKS

1. Summarise the main ideological differences between the United States and Soviet Union using the table below.

	United States	Soviet Union
Political system		
Economic system		

2. Using the information provided above, explain how the experience of the Second World War contributed to the breakdown in relations after 1945. Use the following headings to structure your work:
   - Soviet concerns about British and American behaviour
   - American concerns about the Soviet Union
   - British concerns about the Soviet Union.

How had the Soviet Union gained control of eastern Europe by 1948?

Stalin had intended to create "spheres of influence" in eastern and central Europe for some time. Indeed, his dealings with Roosevelt and Churchill had convinced him that this would be acceptable to the western powers. By the end of 1948, the extent of Soviet control in eastern Europe stretched, in the famous words of Winston Churchill, from "Stettin in the Baltic to Trieste in the Adriatic". According to western observers, Stalin also had ambitions to extend his influence into the Mediterranean and beyond.

However, Soviet control over eastern Europe was not achieved immediately and, as the table below illustrates, Stalin used a variety of methods to assert his influence in each of the different countries.

Country	Background	Status in the Second World War	Methods used	Date when Soviet control established
Poland	Peasant-based economy Traditional hatred of Soviet Union Two governments: in London and Lublin	Divided between Germany and Soviet Union, then wholly occupied by Germany	Soviet troops remained after liberation New government formed in June 1945 dominated by "Lublin" Poles Opposition leaders arrested and murdered Rigged elections in 1947 gave communists 80% of the vote	1947
Romania	Monarchy Little support for communism	German ally	Soviet troops remained after liberation Soviets accepted a coalition government in 1945, accepting key positions for communists Gradually took over the police and security forces Rigged elections in 1946 gave the communists and their allies 90% of the vote "Show trial" of main opposition leader in October 1947 King Michael forced to abdicate in December	1947
Bulgaria	Monarchy Historically close to Russia	German ally	Soviet troops remained after liberation Initially joined a coalition with other parties, the Fatherland Front Purged rival groups from the Fatherland Front Monarchy abolished in 1946 New constitution in 1947 effectively destroyed parliamentary democracy and opposition parties were disbanded	1947

Country	Background	Status in the Second World War	Methods used	Date when Soviet control established
Hungary	Agriculture-based economy Little support for the communists	German ally	Soviet troops remained after liberation Communists won 17% of the vote in November 1945 elections but were given control of the Ministry of the Interior Used secret police to discredit and persecute rival politicians and parties Rigged elections in 1947 gave communists control of a coalition government Social Democratic Party and Communist Party merged in 1948	1948
Czechoslovakia	Established democracy before 1939 Strong support for communists President Beneš prepared to cooperate with Stalin	Invaded by Germany in March 1939	Soviet troops left after the war Post-war elections gave communists leadership of a balanced, coalition government Politicians gradually assumed control of key government ministries allowing them to arrest political opponents Foreign Minister Jans Masaryk, a popular and non-communist politician, murdered in May 1947 All non-communist members of the government resigned in February 1948, with communists filling vacant positions	1948

▲ **Table 4.2** Stalin's takeover of eastern Europe

▲ **Fig. 4.2** Map of eastern Europe c. 1945

" WHO'S NEXT TO BE LIBERATED FROM FREEDOM, COMRADE?"

▲ **Fig. 4.3** A cartoon by David Low printed in the *Evening Standard*, 2 March 1948

QUICK QUESTION 4

Study Figure 4.3. Are you surprised the British viewed Stalin in this way?

Elsewhere, Stalin was prepared to grant neighbouring or nearby countries more freedom. Although the Soviet Union retained control of Finland's foreign policy, it gave up control over domestic policy to the Finnish government. In Yugoslavia, where the partisans had liberated the country without Soviet assistance, **Tito** established a communist state with close ties to the Soviet Union, but which wasn't controlled by it.

Stalin didn't get everything he wanted during this period, however. Between June 1945 and August 1946, he put continued pressure on the Turkish government to give the Soviet Union a naval base on the Dardanelles, a narrow strait linking the Mediterranean and the Black Sea. This had been a long-standing goal of the Russian Tsars since the end of the Crimean War in 1856. When Stalin saw that Truman was prepared to support the Turkish government's opposition to his proposal he backed down.

Tito

A veteran of the Russian Revolution and Spanish Civil War, Josip Broz known as "Tito" (1892–1980) led the partisan resistance movement against the German occupation of Yugoslavia. At the end of the war, he became Premier of Yugoslavia, establishing a communist state which, from 1948, was not part of the Soviet Bloc.

DISCUSSION

1. According to Stalin's critics in the west, what motives did he have for expanding Soviet territory in eastern Europe?

2. Look at Figure 4.3. What is David Low's message? Explain your answer using the source and your own knowledge.

3. Look at the map in Figure 4.2. In what ways could you use this source to defend Stalin's actions after the Second World War?

4. Can you identify any common features in methods Stalin used to takeover each country in eastern Europe 1944–8?

How did the United States react to Soviet expansionism?

Although the United States had no real interest in the area taken over by the Soviet Union, the Americans soon started to compare Stalin's actions to Nazi aggression in the 1930s and 1940s.

Early uncertainty

Truman's initial response to the changed situation in Europe was confused and uncertain. On the one hand he dismissed his Commerce Secretary Henry Wallace for arguing that the United States must build bridges with the Soviet Union. However, he also locked away a secret report recommending a tougher stance towards the Soviets (see Source 6).

However, two important contributions to the debate over future American policy towards Europe and the Soviet Union had a significant impact on the President and provided him with a clearer sense of direction.

The first contribution came from the "long telegram" written by George Kennan, an American diplomat based in Moscow and an expert on Soviet policy. Kennan provided Truman with an invaluable insight into Soviet attitudes after the Second World War and provided guidance on how to manage the problem.

George Kennan's "long telegram", February 1946

What did it say?

- The Soviet Union *was* hostile to the United States, but the reasons for hostility arose out of the Soviet government's long-term feeling of domestic insecurity, which went back for hundreds of years and included a fear of its own people and what might happen if they found out about alternative systems of government.

- Communist ideology did not create this insecurity, but it fitted in with it very well, as Marxism suggests that conflicts in society cannot be solved peacefully. This helped the Russian government to justify the kind of relentless hostility to the outside world which it had always felt anyway.

- The effect of this insecurity was that no Soviet government would try to make a peaceful settlement with the United States. Therefore, attempts made under Roosevelt and afterwards to bring the Soviet Union into a long-term partnership were futile.

- The way to defeat the Soviet Union was by "a policy of firm **containment**", because although the Soviets would try to fill any space they could, they wouldn't push if they found immovable resistance. In other words, the bad news was that the Soviets would never stop trying to take over the world; the good news was that they weren't in any hurry, and could be stopped at any *one* point of pressure.

- However, contrary to what the Soviet leaders believed (Kennan said), their rule would collapse one day with an internal struggle for control, which would transform the Soviet Union "overnight from one of the strongest to one of the weakest and most pitiable of national societies". Therefore the United States only had to contain the Soviet Union when and where it was aggressive, and then wait for the inevitable collapse of the Soviet Union as it struggled to maintain a policy of foreign expansion, while struggling to provide basic goods for its own population.

George Kennan

US diplomat and expert on Soviet Affairs. Based in Riga, Latvia before the Second World War, his "Long Telegram" and 1947 article for the journal *Foreign Affairs*, written anonymously as "Mr. X", had a huge impact on Truman's doctrine of containment.

QUICK QUESTION 5

How important did Kennan believe ideology was in driving the Soviet Union's expansionist policies after 1945?

Containment

Truman developed this strategy 1945–7, which was intended to prevent the Soviet Union expanding any further. Its main components were the Truman Doctrine and Marshall Aid.

The following month, Truman listened to former British Prime Minister Winston Churchill deliver a powerful case for greater American intervention in Europe's affairs. Churchill's "Iron Curtain" speech at Fulton, Missouri highlighted not only the extent of Russian control in eastern Europe but the threat to the rest of the Europe if firm action wasn't taken.

SOURCE 7

Extract from a speech given by Winston Churchill in Fulton, Missouri in March 1946.

A shadow has fallen upon the scenes so lately lighted by the Allied victory. Nobody knows what Soviet Russia and its Communist international organization intends to do in the immediate future.

From Stettin in the Baltic to Trieste in the Adriatic, an iron curtain has descended across the continent. Behind that line lie all the capitals of the ancient states of Central and Eastern Europe. Warsaw, Berlin, Prague, Vienna, Budapest, Belgrade, Bucharest and Sofia, all these famous cities and the populations around them lie in what I must call the Soviet sphere, and all are subject in one form or another, not only to Soviet influence but to a very high and, in some cases, increasing measure of control from Moscow.

The Communist parties, which were very small in all these Eastern States of Europe, have been raised to pre-eminence and power far beyond their numbers and are seeking everywhere to obtain totalitarian control. Police governments are prevailing in nearly every case, and so far, except in Czechoslovakia, there is no true democracy.

DISCUSSION

Do you think Churchill gave his speech in Fulton, Missouri (Source 7) for the same reasons Clifford and Elsey wrote their report for President Truman (Source 6)?

Development of the "containment" doctrine

Matters were brought to a head for Truman by events in the Mediterranean. In March 1947 Britain announced that it could no longer afford to sustain its support for the Greek government in the civil war that had been going on between royalist and Yugoslav-backed communists since the liberation of Greece in 1944. If the United States wanted to prevent Greece, and possibly Turkey, falling into communist hands, it would have to act decisively and quickly.

There were further fears that the communist parties in France and Italy, both sponsored by Moscow, would come to power. Both countries were experiencing terrible economic hardship after the war, made worse by a poor harvest in 1946–7, and the failure of the coalition governments in both countries to deal with the situation made the possibility of a communist takeover more likely.

In response, Truman introduced a policy of containment which consisted of two main elements: a commitment to help any country threatened by totalitarian aggression known as "the Truman Doctrine" and the creation of the European Recovery Programme or "Marshall Aid".

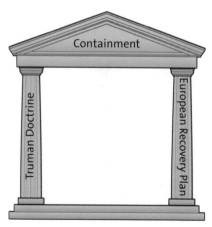

▲ **Fig. 4.4** Truman's policy of containment

The Truman Doctrine (March 1947)

Truman persuaded **Congress** to provide $400 million in economic and military aid for Greece. He described the world as divided between the free and the oppressors and provided an open-ended commitment to defend free countries threatened by aggressive neighbours throughout the world.

The European Recovery Programme (Marshall Aid)

This was announced at Harvard University by Secretary of State George Marshall in June 1947. The aims of the plan were to stabilise the economies of Europe and prevent the growth of communism in European democracies. Sixteen countries accepted "Marshall Aid" and it would also be applied to the western zones in Germany (in breach of the Potsdam agreement).

Congress

The main law-making institution in the United States.

It lasted for four years and provided $13.3 billion for European recovery. By providing loans to other countries, Marshall was hoping to create stronger markets for US exports. Stalin refused to allow Soviet bloc states to participate.

Although Congress placed a strict timescale on the duration of Marshall Aid, the doctrine of containment remained in place throughout the Cold War and influenced the policies of successive American presidents until the collapse of communism in 1991.

Stalin's response

Stalin didn't appear too concerned by the launch of the Truman Doctrine, but regarded Marshall Aid as a serious threat to Soviet interests. He recognised that the programme would require recipients to bring their economic policies into line with American interests. This would undoubtedly undermine his control over eastern Europe. More importantly, however, he regarded it as an act of ideological warfare, through the creation of a US-dominated capitalist alliance directed against the Soviet Union.

In response, Stalin convened a conference of Communist Party leaders in September 1947, where the assembled leaders were left in no doubt about how threatening the implementation of Marshall Aid could be for the future of communism in Europe. The conference also established **COMINFORM** (Communist Information Bureau), whose purpose was to maintain the unity of the assembled nations under Moscow's control. Stalin also used this as an opportunity to tighten his control over Czechoslovakia, the only country which still retained some political independence from the Soviet Union.

COMINFORM

Set up by the Soviet Union to ensure all the communist parties of eastern and western Europe followed the Soviet model of communism.

SOURCE 8

Extract from an article in the Soviet newspaper *Pravda* commenting on the Marshall Plan, 29 June 1947.

It is clear that the restoration and further development of the national economy of European countries would be facilitated if the United States of America, whose productive capacities have not only diminished during the war but have considerably increased, could give that economic help which these countries require. At the same time it is known that the USA herself is also interested in utilising her credit possibilities for the expansion of her external markets …

TASKS

3. Copy the following table and use it to explain how Stalin was able to carry out his takeover of eastern Europe by 1948.

Common factors between eastern European countries that helped him take control	Individual factors of eastern European countries that helped him take control

4. Why did Truman introduce the policy of containment? You should refer to the following points, and any others you can think of, in your answer.

- Stalin's failure to keep to his promises from Yalta and Potsdam
- George Kennan's analysis
- Churchill's speech at Fulton, Missouri
- The growth of the Soviet empire in eastern Europe
- Threats to Greece and Turkey
- Economic crisis in western Europe 1946–7

DISCUSSION

What point is the Soviet Newspaper trying to make in Source 8?

What were the consequences of the Berlin Blockade?

Of all the issues that the former allies faced, perhaps none was as difficult to resolve as the future of Germany. Even so, there was broad agreement on the major issues.

- In the short term it was agreed that the country would be divided into four zones and the country's permanent fate would be dealt with in a future peace conference.

- The city of Berlin, located in the middle of the Soviet zone, would also be temporarily divided into four zones.

- The Soviet Union was allowed to take reparations payments from Germany.

- The Polish border would be pushed westwards and established on the Oder-Neisse Line (see map below).

- The wartime powers also agreed to denazify, demilitarise, and democratise Germany.

- A Control Council consisting of representatives from all four occupying powers would decide matters affecting the whole of Germany.

However, between the end of the Potsdam Conference and the end of 1947, divisions over the future of Germany started to push the former allies further apart.

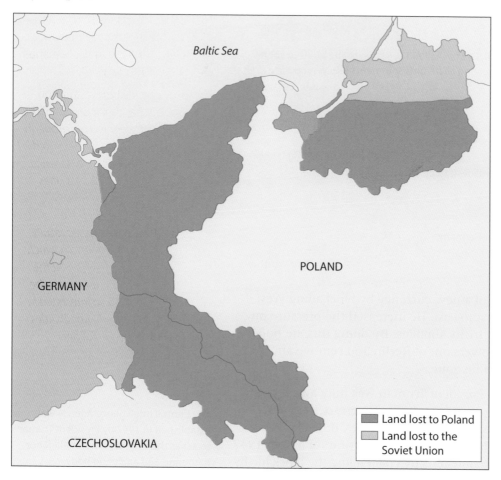

◀ **Fig. 4.5** Land lost to Poland and the Soviet Union

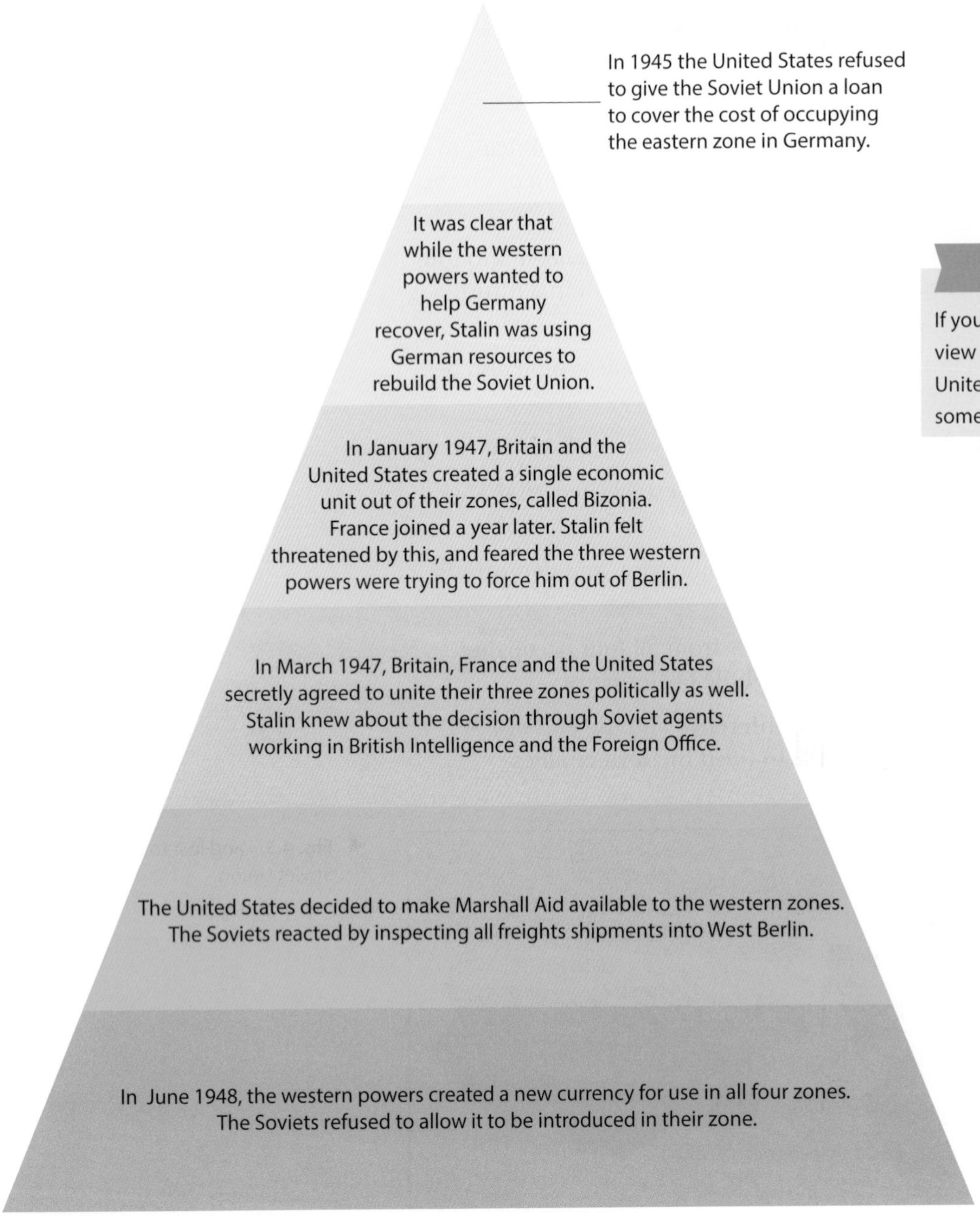

In 1945 the United States refused to give the Soviet Union a loan to cover the cost of occupying the eastern zone in Germany.

It was clear that while the western powers wanted to help Germany recover, Stalin was using German resources to rebuild the Soviet Union.

In January 1947, Britain and the United States created a single economic unit out of their zones, called Bizonia. France joined a year later. Stalin felt threatened by this, and feared the three western powers were trying to force him out of Berlin.

In March 1947, Britain, France and the United States secretly agreed to unite their three zones politically as well. Stalin knew about the decision through Soviet agents working in British Intelligence and the Foreign Office.

The United States decided to make Marshall Aid available to the western zones. The Soviets reacted by inspecting all freights shipments into West Berlin.

In June 1948, the western powers created a new currency for use in all four zones. The Soviets refused to allow it to be introduced in their zone.

▲ **Fig. 4.6** The Allies move further apart over Germany

QUICK QUESTION 6

If you were Stalin, why might you view the policies of Britain and the United States towards Germany with some suspicion?

The blockade

Stalin responded to the introduction of a new currency by blockading West Berlin, blocking all traffic moving west to east. He increased the pressure on the city by turning off all gas and electricity supplies. By doing this, he hoped that he could force the other three powers out of Berlin and remove an awkward symbol of western life from his zone.

Declassified **CIA** reports indicate that President Truman was fully aware of the Soviet plans to remove the western powers from Berlin. Even so, the question of how to respond to this threat was a difficult one to answer. If he allowed the blockade to succeed, he would have demonstrated his "doctrine" of March 1947 to be an empty threat, but at the same time directly challenging the blockade by driving armed convoys through the Soviet zone would be highly provocative.

CIA

The Central Intelligence Agency was established in 1947 by President Truman to act as the United States' intelligence gathering and analysing body.

Britain, the United States, and France quickly decided not to back down over West Berlin and pledged to supply the city's inhabitants via a huge airlift.

Operation Vittles, as the airlift was known, lasted for 11 months, involved nearly 300 000 flights and brought over two million tons of cargo to the beleaguered city. Coal, food, petrol, and other resources were transported by air from three bases in the western sectors of Germany. By mid-1949, planes were landing in West Berlin at a rate of one every two minutes.

Although the Soviets did not fire directly on the incoming aircraft, they deployed a range of obstruction tactics which included jamming radios and shining searchlights to temporarily blind pilots.

Stalin lifted the blockade in May 1949, having failed in his goal of uniting the city under Soviet control. The efforts of the British and American air forces, coupled with the remarkable determination of the two million Germans in West Berlin, ensured that the three western powers maintained control of the city. However, the airlift had not been achieved without significant cost. Sixty-five German, British, and American lives were lost during the operation to keep the city alive.

▲ **Fig. 4.7** Berlin airlift planes at Berlin's Templehof Airport, August 1949

SOURCE 9

Extracts from the final report of the British Air Ministry on the Berlin Blockade published in 1950.

The blockade of Berlin was the result of a situation which developed mainly as a consequence of decisions made during the war. It was the climax of one phase of a planned and deliberate attempt by the Russians to force the Western allies out of Berlin.

The Potsdam Agreement consisted of a comparatively short statement of principle and was not a statute book for the government of Germany. Consequently, co-operation and good faith on the part of the Allies was required if co-ordinated and effective government of Berlin was to be obtained. Unfortunately, the Russian attitude prevented this.

Owing to this lack of collaboration, the four-power control of Berlin was bound to fail and gradually the administration of the Eastern and Western sectors of the city grew farther apart until the sectors became virtually two separate cities with separate city governments and separate police forces. The split between the two sectors was made complete by the Allied currency reform which was introduced in June 1948. This was caused by the Soviets refusal to co-operate and resulted in each sector having a different currency.

The consequences of the blockade

In many ways, the crisis completed the breakdown in relations between the superpowers and established a political, economic, military, and territorial division of Europe which would last for 40 years.

In April 1949, the United States pledged to join the **North Atlantic Treaty Organisation (NATO)**, the first time in the country's history that it had committed itself in peacetime a military alliance, and one which would not require an attack on the United States to involve it in possible military action. Eleven other states joined NATO in 1949: United Kingdom, Canada, France, Denmark, Iceland, Italy, Norway, Portugal, Belgium, Netherlands, and Luxembourg.

The western powers had encouraged political activity in their zones since elections were held to elect a mayor for Berlin in June 1947. That election had been won by a former communist Ernest Reuter, who was a strong critic of the Soviet Union. Meanwhile the creation of a new constitution for the country started the following year.

In May 1949, the formal political unification of the western zones took place with the creation of the Federal Republic of Germany (West Germany), with the Basic Law providing the basis of the new country's constitution. The first national elections took place in August 1949 and Konrad Adenauer, leader of the right-wing Christian Democrats, became the first Chancellor of West Germany. Although Adenauer had control over domestic policy, the occupying powers still controlled West Germany's foreign policy until 1951, when the West German Foreign Office was created.

West Berlin was not part of West Germany, and British, French, and American forces remained there to defend the city from a future attack from the east.

The Soviets reacted swiftly to the changing situation in Germany. In October, they created the German Democratic Republic (East Germany), based on the People's Council formed in 1948 in the Soviet zone. All positions in the new state were in the hands of the communist Socialist Unity Party (SED) created in 1946 by the forced merger of the Social Democratic Party and German Communist Party in the Soviet zone.

East Berlin was part of East Germany, and became the country's capital.

Although the Soviet Union did not immediately create a military alliance to mirror NATO, it did tighten its control over its satellite states. COMINFORM had been created in 1947 to coordinate the activities of European communist parties, and in January 1949 the Council for Mutual Economic Assistance (COMECON) was created with the object of directing the national economies of the Soviet bloc.

After the successful testing of an atomic weapon by the Soviet Union in August 1949, the superpower cooperation which had successfully defeated the Axis powers, and developed a model for the post-war world, had turned into Cold War.

Although the Berlin Blockade had highlighted the west's vulnerability to Soviet aggression in East Berlin, the conclusion of the crisis arguably stabilised

NATO

The western military alliance against the Soviet Union.

SOURCE 10

Article 5 of the North Atlantic Treaty

The parties agree that an armed attack against one or more of them in Europe or North America shall be considered an attack against them all.

Konrad Adenauer

Mayor of Cologne before being replaced by the Nazis in 1933, he was restored to this position by the Americans after the Second World War. He helped found the Christian Democratic Union (CDU) and became West Germany's first Chancellor in 1949.

DISCUSSION

1. Why was it so difficult to reach agreement over the future of Germany after the Second World War?

2. Was Stalin right to feel threatened by the actions of the western powers over Berlin in 1947–8?

3. Outline the main features of the Berlin airlift.

4. In your opinion, how serious was the threat posed by the Berlin Blockade? Did it bring Europe close to war?

5. "The Berlin Blockade marked the start of the Cold War." How far do you agree with this statement?

the situation regarding Germany's position in Europe, as West German politicians were now under no illusions about the commitment of the three western powers to its security and development.

However, the issue of possible West German rearmament threatened to undermine this stability.

Before 1950, the priority of the United States was to develop better relations between western European states, and therefore supported the development of the **European Coal and Steel Community (ECSC)**. Wary of French opposition to German rearmament, US Secretary of State, Dean Acheson believed that dispute over German reunification could scupper the ECSC.

In May 1955, West Germany joined NATO, but only on the condition that it possessed no biological, chemical or atomic weapons, while Britain and the United States pledged to maintain forces in West Germany. Shortly after this the United States, France and Britain formally ended their post-war military occupation of Germany.

The Warsaw Pact

The response to these developments from the Soviet Bloc was swift. On 14 May 1955, eight communist countries agreed in Poland to unify their armed forces under a central command. The Warsaw Pact consisted of the following states: Albania, Bulgaria, Czechoslovakia, East Germany, Hungary, Poland, Romania, Soviet Union.

SOURCE 11

ARTICLE 4 OF THE WARSAW TREATY of Friendship, Co-operation, and Mutual Assistance, which established the Warsaw Pact.

In the event of an armed attack in Europe on one or several states that are signatories of the Treaty by any State or group of States, each State that is a Party to this Treaty shall in the exercise of the right to individual or collective self-defence in accordance with Article 51 of the Charter of the United Nations Organization, render the State or States so attacked immediate assistance…by all the means it may consider necessary, including the use of force.

The formation of the Warsaw Pact was a direct response to the rearmament of West Germany, and its incorporation into NATO. Soviet Premier Marshal Bulganin said West Germany's rearmament turned Germany into "the principal hotbed of the danger of war in Europe". However, this also provided an opportunity for the Soviet Union to place its satellite states' military forces on a more organised footing.

Although a joint command structure for the Warsaw Pact was established for the armed forces, the Soviet Union completely dominated the organisation.

- The Commander-in-Chief was always a Soviet army officer, with its HQ in Moscow. The first Commander-in-Chief was Marshal Ivan Stepanovich Koniev.

- The Deputy Commander-in-Chief and Chief of the Joint Staff were also Soviet officers.

- So too were the Commander-in-Chief for the three separate branches of the armed forces.

While the creation of the Warsaw Pact allowed the Soviet Union to strengthen its forces across eastern Europe, it also provided a further mechanism to keep the eastern bloc countries in line.

European Coal and Steel Community (ECSC)

Created by the 1951 Treaty of Paris, the European Coal and Steel Community created a common market for coal and steel for the six countries who signed the treaty. These were: France, Italy, Belgium, Netherlands, Luxembourg, and West Germany.

Who was the more to blame for starting the Cold War: the United States or the Soviet Union?

Arguments over who was responsible for the start of the Cold War have divided historians since the late 1940s. While most historians originally placed the blame on Stalin, the emergence of a new group of historians in the 1960s prompted a rethink over America's own role in starting the conflict. However, the collapse of communism and with it the release of previously classified documents allowed access to the debates taking place within the Soviet empire and led to a further shift in historical opinion.

In what ways was Stalin to blame?

The Soviet Union's, and therefore Stalin's, guilt for starting the Cold War can be demonstrated in several ways. Firstly, a number of historians argue that communist ideology was expansionist and universal. By this, they mean that the Soviet Union could not co-exist with capitalism and therefore intended to impose its own system of government throughout the world.

There is a considerable amount of evidence to support this view.

- Stalin did not abide by the agreements he had made at Yalta. Between Yalta and Potsdam, he had installed communist governments in Poland and Romania and went on to impose Soviet systems throughout eastern Europe in the years following the war. Political opposition was banned and opponents were frequently jailed or murdered.

- The creation of COMECON ensured that each country followed the Soviet model of economic policy.

- He frequently used ideological language when condemning the west and justifying his own actions.

- The establishment of COMINFORM was a clear sign that he intended to undermine capitalist society through national communist parties.

Other historians have argued that personalities were the most significant factor in the origins of the Cold War. In particular, John Lewis Gaddis suggests that without Stalin, it is unlikely the Cold War would ever have taken place.

Stalin, after all, was the one constant from the pre-war era through the wartime peace conferences right up to the division of Europe in 1949. He also maintained a firm grip on Soviet foreign policy, dictating a more confrontational approach to relations with the west than that advised by several Soviet diplomats.

THE BIRD WATCHER

▲ **Fig. 4.8** The Bird Watcher, published in *Punch* in July 1948

> **" ** *This war is not as in the past; whoever occupies a territory also imposes on it his own social system.* **"**
>
> Stalin speaking to a Yugoslav communist leader in 1945

Maxim Litvinov, Soviet Deputy Foreign Minister, in conversation with American journalist Edgar Snow in June 1945.

Why did you Americans wait till right now to begin opposing us in the Balkans and Eastern Europe? You should have done this three years ago. Now it is too late.

> **❝** *Stalin's postwar goals were security for himself, his regime, his country, and his ideology, in precisely that order.* **❞**
>
> John Lewis Gaddis

How can Stalin's role in the Cold War be defended?

There are some historians who defend Stalin's actions during the Cold War. They argue that Soviet security concerns at the end of the war were the biggest influence on its policy towards eastern Europe and its former wartime allies, and that Stalin's actions after the Second World War were purely defensive in nature.

These security concerns stemmed from historical fears about invasion from the west after the Russian Civil War, and Stalin's belief that Britain and France had deliberately allowed Nazi Germany to expand eastwards (i.e. towards the Soviet Union) during the late 1930s. Stalin's suspicions about the motives of the western powers increased as a result of certain British and American actions during the Second World War.

- Britain refused to share details of the German secret Enigma codes.

- From Stalin's perspective, the western Allies deliberately delayed opening a second front in the west until 1944 in order to weaken the Soviet Union (which had been engaged in brutal conflict with Germany since June 1941).

- The United States kept details of the Manhattan Project secret from the Soviet Union.

Stalin also detected a significant shift in American policy after the death of President Roosevelt. Before April 1945, relations between the superpowers had been reasonably good. However, Roosevelt's successor President Truman adopted a more hard line policy over issues such as Poland, the future of Germany, and the ending of Lend-Lease loans to the Soviet Union.

> **DISCUSSION**
>
> Was Truman as much, if not more, to blame as Stalin for the start of the Cold War?

Furthermore, a comparison of the respective losses of the Soviet Union and its wartime allies suggests that Stalin's desire to impose his own system on eastern Europe was largely driven by the need to aid Soviet post-war recovery. Soviet losses, including civilian deaths, have been estimated to be almost 20 million, whereas total American losses were less than half a million. In addition, while mainland America did not experience any wartime action, much of the land occupied by the German army in the Soviet Union was completely destroyed. Cities such as Leningrad and Stalingrad experienced horrific sieges, and approximately 25 million Soviet citizens were left homeless after the war.

This goes some way to explaining Stalin's deep concern over the future of Germany and, to a lesser extent, Poland. Above all, he feared the emergence of a united, industrialised, and remilitarised Germany which could focus on expanding towards the east in the future. The introduction of a new currency in the western zones of Germany and leaked intelligence regarding the proposal for political unification of the three zones provoked him into taking drastic action over Berlin.

▲ **Fig. 4.9** Enigma machine

In what ways was the United States to blame?

Revisionist historians thus place the bulk of the blame for starting the Cold War on the United States. Two major lines of argument have emerged among historians who blame the United States for the breakdown in superpower relations.

Argument 1: US policy was influenced by the need to create global free markets for US goods

- The United States ended its Lend-Lease arrangements with the Soviet Union in 1945.
- Marshall Aid was not designed to prevent European economies from collapsing; its true purpose was to provide a market for US goods and to ensure the preservation of a capitalist, free market system.
- The creation of Bizonia and later introduction of a new currency into the western zones was a clear breach of the Potsdam agreement, and was an attempt to impose a capitalist system across the whole of Germany.

Argument 2: US policy was influenced by important personalities such as President Truman

- Truman had been very aggressive in his dealings with Molotov, the Soviet Foreign Minister, during meetings in April 1945.
- Truman believed the US atomic monopoly would allow it to dictate terms at the Potsdam Conference.
- The Truman Doctrine and Marshall Aid were regarded by the Soviet Union as highly provocative and designed to isolate the Soviet Union.

◀ **Fig. 4.10** Arguments blaming the US for the breakdown in superpower relations

QUICK QUESTION 7

When do you think the Cold War began? What would this suggest about the main cause, or culprit, behind the start of the Cold War?

SOURCE 14

Malenkov, a senior Soviet politician, presents his view of the US containment policies, September 1947.

The ruling clique of American imperialists has taken the path of outright expansion, of enslaving the weakened capitalist states of Europe. It has taken the path of hatching new war plans against the Soviet Union and the new democracies. The clearest and most specific expression of the policy is provided by the Truman-Marshall plans.

SOURCE 13

Extract from the Novikov telegram, an interpretation of US foreign policy written by the Soviet Ambassador to the US, Nikolai Novikov, 27 September 1946.

The foreign policy of the United States, which reflects the imperialist tendencies of American monopolistic capital, is characterized in the post-war period by a striving for world supremacy. This is the real meaning of the many statements by President Truman and other representatives of American ruling circles; that the United States has the right to lead the world. All the forces of American diplomacy—the army, the air force, the navy, industry, and science—are enlisted in the service of this foreign policy. For this purpose broad plans for expansion have been developed and are being implemented through diplomacy and the establishment of a system of naval and air bases stretching far beyond the boundaries of the United States, through the arms race, and through the creation of ever newer types of weapons.

DISCUSSION

How useful is Malenkov's view as evidence of the US being blamed for the origins of the Cold War?

How can the role of the United States be defended?

Despite these arguments condemning the behaviour of the United States, there are still some arguments that support the actions taken by American leaders at this time.

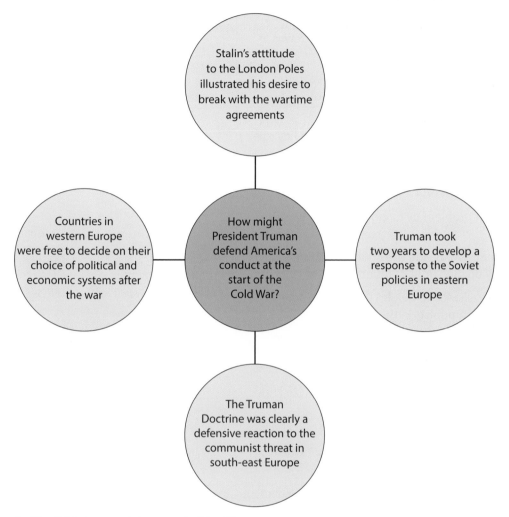

▲ **Fig. 4.11** Arguments in support of the US

The circles contain:

- Stalin's atttitude to the London Poles illustrated his desire to break with the wartime agreements
- Countries in western Europe were free to decide on their choice of political and economic systems after the war
- How might President Truman defend America's conduct at the start of the Cold War?
- Truman took two years to develop a response to the Soviet policies in eastern Europe
- The Truman Doctrine was clearly a defensive reaction to the communist threat in south-east Europe

DISCUSSION

1. Why would Truman believe that the Soviet Union threatened peace in Europe after the Second World War?

2. Explain why the Soviet Union was more badly affected by the experiences of the Second World War than the United States.

3. Study sources 1–7 in this chapter. How far do they suggest that Stalin was mostly to blame for the start of the Cold War between 1945 and 1949?

QUICK QUESTION 8

Why was Figure 4.12 published in 1947? Use the source and your own knowledge to answer this question.

◄ **Fig. 4.12** A cartoon by Daniel Fitzpatrick of the *St. Louis Post-Dispatch* commenting on the purpose of the Marshall Aid programme, 20 July 1947

KEY POINTS

◆ The United States and Soviet Union ended the Second World War as allies.

▶ The two wartime peace conferences at Yalta and Potsdam managed to establish a framework for the post-war world.

▶ Historians disagree about when the Cold War started. Some believe it was as early as 1917, when the communists came to power in Russia.

▶ Most historians suggest that the creation of the Soviet empire in eastern Europe by 1948, or division of Germany in 1949 marked the start of the conflict.

◆ Powerful personalities, such as President Truman and Stalin, played a key role in the breakdown in relations between the United States and Soviet Union.

▶ The future of Germany proved to be the most sensitive of the issues dividing the two superpowers between 1945 and 1949.

▶ Stalin attempted to solve the German problem by forcing the three western powers out of West Berlin in 1948.

▶ The creation of West and East Germany, following the Berlin Blockade and Airlift, ensured Germany would stay divided until its reunification in 1990.

▶ The western powers set up a military alliance to defend themselves against the possibility of an attack from the communists in the east: NATO.

▶ The Soviet Union established its own military alliance, the Warsaw Pact, in response to the incorporation of West Germany in 1955.

Revision tips

● Understand the different ideologies of the United States and Soviet Union: capitalism and communism.

● Remember the main sources of disagreement between the allies at Potsdam.

● Link the development of Truman's doctrine of containment to the actions of the Soviet Union in eastern Europe.

● Consider why Germany was the most sensitive issue between the superpowers after the war.

● Compile a list of reasons why you think each of the superpowers, the Soviet Union and the United States, might have been to blame for the start of the Cold War.

● Compare the different reasons behind the creation of the two military alliances by the superpowers after 1949.

Review questions

1. What was the Yalta Conference?

2. Why did differences in ideology lead to the start of the Cold War?

3. How significant was Churchill's "Iron Curtain" speech in influencing Truman's decision to contain communism?

4. Following the Potsdam Conference, what caused an increase in tension between the Soviet Union and the west?

5. What methods did Stalin use to take over eastern Europe 1945–58?

6. Explain what the Truman Doctrine was.

7. Describe the Marshall Plan.

8. "Stalin blockaded West Berlin because he was afraid the western powers wanted to push him out of Germany." How far do you agree with this statement? Explain your answer.

9. Explain why NATO and the Warsaw Pact were formed.

10. "Blame for the start of the Cold War has to lie with Truman rather than Stalin." How far do you agree with this view?

5

How effectively did the United States contain the spread of Communism?

Introduction

After the end of the Second World War the greatest threat the United States saw was the danger of communism. The Russian Revolution in 1917 followed by the communists taking power in China led to the United States becoming concerned about its spread across the world. Russia's plans to dominate Europe and the world with a group of countries tied by their communist beliefs posed a real challenge to American economic, political, and ideological interests. The horror stories of imprisonments, labour camps, and a crackdown on personal freedoms went against the American way of life. The spread of communism was also starting to threaten American interests; Cuba had always been a satellite of American interest, providing an economic market as well as power and influence for American politicians. Castro's communists threatened this. More worryingly for President Kennedy the opportunities presented to Russia by Cuba in terms of a possible military strike at the United States were particularly frightening.

The conflict in Vietnam also presented a challenge to American influence. The fall of Korea to communism in 1948 and China in 1949 had led to a real concern that Asia would be engulfed. The United States wanted to stop this growth of a world communist power base and was willing to go to war to prevent it.

▲ **Fig. 5.1** American cartoon from 1948 on the Russian attempt to drive the western powers from Berlin

The aims of this chapter are to:

- Examine the events of the Cold War by looking at American reactions to the Cuban revolution, including the missile crisis and its aftermath.

- Consider American involvement in the Vietnam War, including reasons for involvement, tactics and strategy as well as reasons for withdrawal.

- Study America's reactions to the invasion of South Korea by North Korea, including the involvement of the United Nations, and the course of the war to 1953.

The United States and events in Korea, 1950–3

SOURCE 1

Extract from Article 42 of the UN Charter.

Security Council ... may take such action by air, sea or land forces as may be necessary to maintain or restore international peace and security. Such actions may include demonstrations, blockade, and other operations by air, sea, or land forces of Members of the United Nations.

In the event that moral, economic, or diplomatic pressure fails to deter an aggressor, the UN Charter allows for the use of armed force to restore international peace and security. Since 1945 there has been just one occasion when these extreme measures have been used: Korea.

Background

- Between 1910 and 1945 Korea was controlled by Japan.

- In 1945, Japanese troops based in Korea surrendered to the Soviet Russians in the north of the country and to the Americans in the south.

- The dividing line between the Soviet and American zones was set at the **38th Parallel**.

- In 1947, the **UNO** called for free, nationwide elections to elect a democratic government for the whole of Korea.

- In 1948, elections were held in the south under UN supervision. The Republic of Korea was set up under the presidency of Syngman Rhee, with its capital and centre of government in Seoul.

- In the same year, the Soviets established the Democratic People's Republic of Korea under the leadership of Kim Il-Sung, with its capital and centre of government at Pyongyang.

- Both the communist North Korean and anti-communist South Korean governments claimed to be the legitimate government of the whole of Korea.

Why did North Korea invade South Korea in June 1950?

Kim Il-Sung wanted to unite Korea under communist rule. By June 1950 he had good reason to presume that an invasion of South Korea would be successful and enable him to achieve his ambition.

- Kim had the support of both the Soviet and Chinese leaders, Stalin and Mao Zedong.

- North Korea's armed forces, supplied with tanks, heavy artillery, and planes by Soviet Russia, were much stronger than those of South Korea.

- Kim thought that an American response was unlikely now that China was communist and Soviet Russia had the atom bomb (since August 1949).

- Leading American politicians had made public statements that seemed to suggest that Korea was not a major American defence priority.

38th Parallel

This is the popular name given to the circle of latitude in the northern hemisphere that separates North Korea from South Korea. The parallel was chosen as the army frontier between the American and Soviet sectors of Korea in 1945 and was originally intended to be a temporary dividing line. The parallel marks the approximate start and finishing positions of the two sides during the Korean War.

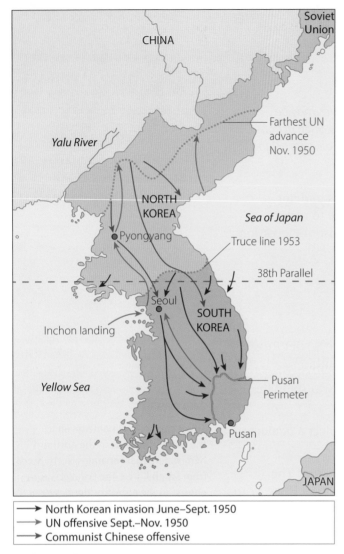

▲ **Fig. 5.2** The Korean War, 1950–3

How did the UN become involved?

The UN had been closely associated with the establishment of the new anti-communist government of South Korea, though it had been excluded from events leading up to the formation of the Democratic People's Republic of Korea. When North Korean troops crossed the border into South Korea on 25 June 1950, the Security Council met the same day.

SOURCE 2

Extract from Security Council Resolution 82, 25 June 1950.

The Security Council ... Noting *with grave concern the armed attack on the Republic of Korea by forces from North Korea,* Determines *that this action constitutes a breach of the peace, and* Calls for *the immediate cessation of hostilities;* Calls upon *the authorities in North Korea to withdraw forthwith their armed forces to the 38th parallel.*

The resolution passed on 25 June was made possible by the absence of the Soviet representative on the Security Council. Otherwise the resolution would have been vetoed. The Soviet absence was a protest against the refusal of the United States to allow communist China into the UN.

QUICK QUESTION 1

Why would Soviet Russia have vetoed the Security Council Resolution of 25 June 1950 if its delegates had been present?

When it became clear that North Korea had no intention of withdrawing its troops from South Korea, the Security Council met again and passed a second resolution.

SOURCE 3

Extract from Security Council Resolution 83, 27 June 1950.

The Security Council ... Recommends *that the Members of the United Nations furnish such assistance to the Republic of Korea as may be necessary to repel the armed attack and to restore international peace and security in the area.*

A further resolution passed 10 days later made clear how the military forces were to be organised and led.

SOURCE 4

Extract from Security Council Resolution 84, 7 July 1950.

The Security Council ... Recommends *that all Members providing military forces and other assistance pursuant to the aforesaid Security Council resolutions make such forces and other assistance available to a unified command under the United States of America.*

Troops from America and 15 other countries (Australia, Belgium, Britain, Canada, Columbia, France, Greece, Nationalist China, Netherlands, New Zealand, Panama, Philippines, Thailand, Turkey and the Union of South Africa) were sent to assist South Korea.

How did America react to North Korea's invasion of South Korea?

- The United States had been closely associated with the establishment of the Republic of Korea.

- The United States was determined to halt any further communist expansion under its policy of containment.

- The Americans regarded world communism as a single force directed from Moscow. The North Korean action was, therefore, assumed to be part of a Soviet plan.

- The United States thought that a successful conquest of South Korea would encourage a Chinese attack on **Formosa**. If South Korea and Formosa fell to the communists then the position of Japan could also be threatened. **Japan** was America's key interest in the Far East.

- In the American view, the fall of South Korea, Formosa, and Japan to the communists would represent a major shift in the power balance between the communist and capitalist world.

- It was argued that the most effective way to prevent such a shift from happening was to make a firm response to the first sign of communist aggression; this meant opposing the North Korean invasion of South Korea.

- If the UN had failed to act over this issue then there is no doubt that the Americans would have acted on their own.

- As it was, the UN action was overwhelmingly American in character: the UN forces were commanded by the American General MacArthur; half of the ground forces were American; more than 90 per cent of the air forces were American and 85 per cent of the naval forces were American.

SOURCE 5

From a British history book published in 1987.

Even in 1950 it was only the accident of the Soviet boycott that made the UN vote to intervene in Korea possible. The relatively small number of countries which then belonged to the UN, most of them sympathetic to the US, accepted American leadership in going to war for Korea. But only sixteen members provided military support. The way in which the war was fought made the presence of the UN flag seem to many to be a mockery ... Other nations were less likely to rally to the UN flag again, because of the widespread view that this was used in Korea in the interests of the United States.

Formosa

Following the victory of the Communists in the Chinese Civil War (1946–9), the offshore island of Taiwan, formerly known as Formosa, became the base for the nationalist Chiang Kai-Shek's non-communist Republic of China. These circumstances made Taiwan a key American interest in the Far East during the Cold War.

Japan

When Japan surrendered in August 1945 it was occupied by the United States and other Allied countries. With the growth in communist influence after 1945, America became committed to ensuring the economic recovery of Japan. During this process Japan became a major trading partner of the United States and America's principal ally in the Far East.

▲ **Fig. 5.3** President Truman meets General MacArthur on Wake Island during the Korean War, October 1950

B. Jefimov r. 1950

▲ **Fig. 5.4** Propaganda poster issued during the Korean War

SOURCE 6

From a Soviet history book published in 1984.

The American military intervention in Korea in the summer of 1950 made the already tense international situation even worse. The United States, having landed troops in Southern Korea after Japan's surrender in 1945, was seeking to gain control of the whole country.

By unleashing a civil war in June 1950 the South Koreans, backed by the United States, turned Korea into a place of fierce international conflict but in the end failed to achieve the aims of their Washington masters. Soviet and Chinese assistance to the People's Democratic Republic of Korea frustrated the plan to take over North Korea.

SOURCE 7

Announcement to the American people by President Truman, 27 June 1950.

In South Korea the government forces were attacked by invading forces from North Korea. The UN Security Council called on the invading troops to cease hostilities and to withdraw to the 38th parallel. This they have not done, on the contrary they have continued the attack. The Security Council called on all members of the United Nations to give assistance. I have ordered US air and sea forces to give Korean government troops cover and support.

The attack upon Korea makes it plain that communism will now use armed invasion and war. A return to the rule of force in international affairs would have far-reaching effects. The United States will continue to uphold the rule of law.

QUICK QUESTION 2

Which side produced the propaganda poster in Figure 5.4?

QUICK QUESTION 3

Why is it highly likely that the United States would have fought on its own if it had failed to get UN backing for the military operation in Korea?

DISCUSSION

1. How useful is Source 6 as evidence of American action in Korea during 1950? Explain your answer using details of the source and your own knowledge.

2. Why do Sources 6 and 7 disagree? Explain your answer using the sources and your own knowledge.

Phase 1: success for North Korea **June–September 1950**	North Korean forces successfully overran most of South Korea capturing the capital Seoul. South Korean and UN troops were confined to territory around Pusan in the south-east of the peninsula, the Pusan perimeter.
Phase 2: success for the UN **September–October 1950**	The UN and American marines now launched a two-pronged counter-attack: UN forces broke through the perimeter and headed northwards; and MacArthur led a daring seaborne attack on the west coast at Inchon, some 200 miles behind the communist lines. Seoul was relieved and North Korean troops were driven back across the 38th Parallel. At this point the original UN mission had been accomplished.
Phase 3: the UN attempt **to reunite Korea** **October–November 1950**	UN forces continued pressing northwards across the 38th Parallel, in pursuit of the long-standing UN objective of achieving "a unified, independent and democratic government" for the whole of Korea. With minimal North Korean resistance, progress was swift. Pyongyang, the North Korean capital, was captured on 19 October and just over a month later some American units reached the Yalu river on the border with China.
Phase 4: the Chinese attack **November 1950–January 1951**	Fearing an invasion of their territory, Chinese forces launched a massive counteroffensive in late November. UN forces were driven southwards and across the 38th Parallel. Seoul was again captured by the communists in early 1951. UN lines were eventually stabilised along the 37th Parallel in mid-January.
Phase 5: the UN **counter-attack** **January–July 1951**	UN counter-attacks forced the Chinese and North Koreans back to the 38th Parallel. Seoul changed hands for the last time when retaken by UN forces in March. General MacArthur argued the case for the use of nuclear weapons against China and, after disobeying orders, was dismissed by President Truman and replaced by General Ridgway.
Phase 6: stalemate leading **to an armistice** **July 1951–July 1953**	Negotiations began at Panmunjom and lasted for two years. Meanwhile fighting continued across a fortified frontier. Little territory of strategic or tactical value changed hands though many of the engagements fought over ridges or hill tops were extremely costly in terms of lives and suffering (the Battle of Bloody Ridge, the Battle of Heartbreak Ridge, the Battle of Pork Chop Hill).

▲ **Table 5.1** Events of the Korean War

What were the results of the Korean War for the UN?

- UN action over Korea showed that it was more purposeful than the League of Nations had ever been. Military sanctions had been used to reverse an act of aggression supported by two major powers (Soviet Russia and communist China).

BUT

- The UN failed to achieve its objective of a "unified, independent and democratic government" for Korea.

- The UN operation was scarred by both major misjudgments (as when MacArthur assured President Truman that the Chinese would not intervene in the war just before UN forces crossed the 38th Parallel in October 1950) and substantial damage both to property and life. Approximately four million Koreans died as a result of the war, and countless others were made homeless and destitute.

- UN action had only been possible as a result of America's refusal to admit communist China to the UN and the Soviet's protest against this decision between January and August 1950.

- Military action was made possible by the presence of large numbers of American troops that had been stationed in Japan since 1945.

- It could be argued that the United States used the UN to reinforce its foreign policy over the Korean issue. The United States was determined to end the aggression of North Korea in June 1950. The Security Council resolutions and the UN flag gave the enterprise the appearance of an international coalition against aggression. The Soviets claimed that the UN had been used as a capitalist tool against communism.

SOURCE 8

President Truman speaking at a press conference in June 1950. He was replying to a reporter who asked him whether it was correct to call events in Korea merely a policing action under the UN.

We are not at war. The Republic of Korea was unlawfully attacked by a bunch of bandits from North Korea. The United Nations held a meeting and asked the members to go to the relief of the Korean Republic, and the members of the United Nations are going to the relief of the Korean Republic, to suppress a bandit raid on the Republic of Korea. That is all there is to it.

SOURCE 9

President Truman's memoirs, 1956.

In the final analysis I did this for the United Nations. I believed in the League of Nations. It failed. Lots of people thought it failed because we were not in it to support it. OK, now we started the UN. It was our idea, and in its first big test we just couldn't let it down.

SOURCE 10

Dean Acheson's memoirs, 1969. Acheson was in charge of American foreign policy during the Korean War.

Clearly the invasion of South Korea was an open, undisguised challenge to America's internationally accepted position as the protector of South Korea, an area of great importance to the security of American-occupied Japan. To back away from this challenge, in view of the power of the USA, would be highly destructive of our strength and reputation.

▲ **Fig. 5.5** United Nations troops search North Korean soldiers, September 1950

DISCUSSION

1. How far do Sources 9 and 10 help you to decide if Truman was telling the truth in Source 8? Explain your answer using details of the sources and your own knowledge.

2. Do Sources 5 to 10 provide convincing evidence that in Korea the UN was simply a tool of the United States? Use the sources to explain your answer.

The United States and events in Cuba, 1959–62

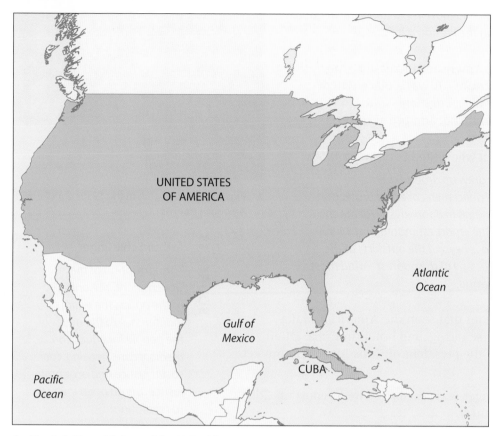

▲ **Fig. 5.6** Map of Cuba and the United States

In the **Treaty of Paris** in 1898 Cuba gained its independence from Spain. Under Cuba's new constitution, the United States had the right to intervene in Cuban affairs and to supervise its finances and foreign relations.

Cuba served an economic purpose for America as it forced the Cubans to sell raw materials for low prices. The United States also made sure that Cuba bought American manufactured goods, and by 1914 three-quarters of Cuban imports came from the United States. The United States also invested heavily in the Cuban economy. The United States controlled the railway industry, the telephone system and tobacco plantations, as well as two thirds of all arable land. The United States also took control of **Guantanamo Bay** and made it an important base for the US navy.

Cuba in the 1950s

After 50 years of independence but under a heavy American influence, discontent was spreading in Cuba. Unhappiness at American involvement in Cuba was evident among the people. The United States had a huge influence over Cuban politics. No Cuban government would be elected unless it was willing to implement policies favourable to the United States. In return for their cooperation, government ministers in Cuba received payments from American businessmen.

Treaty of Paris

A treaty ending the conflict between the United States and Spain over Spanish influence in the Americas. The Americans' victory meant that they gained influence and some measure of control over Cuba.

Guantanamo Bay

A bay on the south-east corner of Cuba which has a large harbour and is protected on one side by steep hills.

Earl Smith was the American Ambassador in Cuba between 1957 and 1959.

The United States ... was so overwhelmingly influential in Cuba that ... the American Ambassador was the second most important man in Cuba; sometimes even more important than the President [of Cuba].

The attractiveness of Cuba to visiting Americans increased. Cuba became a holiday island for rich Americans. It was a place where they could enjoy pleasures that were illegal in many states in North America. These included drinking, gambling, and prostitution.

David Detzer, an American journalist who visited Cuba in the 1950s.

Brothels flourished. A major industry grew up around them: Government officials received bribes, policemen collected protection money. Prostitutes could be seen standing in doorways, strolling the streets, or leaning from windows ... One report estimated that 11 500 of them worked their trade in Havana ... Beyond the outskirts of the capital, beyond the slot machines, was one of the poorest—and most beautiful—countries in the western world.

The relaxed government controls meant that soon the American Mafia controlled much of the gambling, horse racing, and hotels in Cuba. Often the Mafia even had agreements with the president of Cuba himself to protect its interests.

In 1955 the historian Arthur Schlesinger was asked to write a report on Cuba. He warned about the state of the country.

How did tensions develop between Cuba and the United States?

In 1959 Cuba underwent a revolution. The unpopular regime of President Batista was overthrown by the revolutionary Fidel Castro. Castro promised to restore power in Cuba to its people and to end the American corruption in the country.

Fidel Castro

Pre-political career

Born to a wealthy Cuban family with American links. Graduated as a lawyer.

Political career

Campaigned against Batista's regime in Cuba and managed to overthrow it with a guerrilla force. Gained support by promising to give the land back to the people and to defend the rights of the poor.

Character and outlook

A devisive figure, Castro gained support and fame by being someone who managed to stand up to America.

▲ **Fig. 5.7** A Cuban club in the 1950s popular with American tourists

Arthur Schlesinger

The corruption of the Government, the brutality of the police, the regime's indifference to the needs of the people for education, medical care, housing, for social justice and economic justice ... is an open invitation to revolution.

QUICK QUESTION 4

Why were Americans attracted to Cuba?

DISCUSSION

1. What problems arose as a result of the importance and power of American influence over Cuba?

2. Compare Sources 11 to 13 and Figure 5.7. How far do Sources 11 and 12 and Figure 5.7 support what Source 13 says?

3. Consider the reliability of Source 11. Why could it be called into question?

Area	Batista's Cuba	Castro's Cuba
Industry		Key industry such as the telephone company was nationalised and made cheaper to use.
Land	Seventy-five per cent of Cuba's best farming land was owned by foreign individuals or foreign companies.	Rents were cut by up to 50 per cent for low wage earners. Land was redistributed among the peasants.
Equality	Cuba followed America's lead in having segregation for blacks and whites.	Separate facilities such as swimming pools, beaches, and hotels for blacks and whites were abolished.
Education	More than 20 per cent of the Cuban population were illiterate. In rural areas over half the population could not read or write and 61 per cent of children did not go to school.	Cuba adopted the slogan: "If you don't know, learn. If you know, teach." Castro asked young students to travel to the countryside and teach the people to read and write. Free education was made available to all.
Health care	Cuba had 6 000 doctors. Of these, 64 per cent worked in Havana where most of the rich people lived.	Castro ordered that doctors had to be redistributed throughout the country; over half decided to leave Cuba. To replace them Cuba built three new training schools for doctors. Free healthcare was introduced for all. By 1970 there were more doctors per head in Cuba than in the United States.
Society		Many of the casinos and hotels used by American visitors were closed down. The Mafia were forced to leave the country.
Politics		Ninety per cent of the population supported Castro. However, Castro did not keep his promise of holding free elections.
Repression	Batista's regime had murdered over 20 000 Cubans.	Those who publicly disagreed with Castro faced the possibility of being arrested. Writers who expressed dissenting views and people he considered deviants such as homosexuals were also imprisoned.
Links with other countries	The United States dominated Cuban industry and politics.	Castro negotiated trade agreements with Russia and other communist countries to export sugar and import weapons and technology.

▲ **Table 5.2** Changes introduced under Castro

TASKS

1. Looking at the table what would go in the boxes for "industry", "society", and "politics" in the column for Batista using the information on the previous page.

2. Make a list of the reasons why Americans would not like Castro's Cuba.

How did the United States react to the Cuban revolution?

As we have already seen, the changes made by Castro reduced American influence in Cuba. America resented its loss of control over the country, but was also concerned about the spread of communist ideas so close to America. American companies and individuals had lost out as Castro's redistribution of land saw land owned by American companies being given to ordinary Cubans. Castro also nationalised a lot of industries, taking power away from American companies who had previously dominated much of Cuba's economy.

In order to try and prevent this President Eisenhower began economic sanctions. The United States stopped trading with Cuba and refused to buy Cuban raw materials and sugar. This was intended to undermine the Castro regime, or at least force a change in economic policies.

On 17 March 1960, President Eisenhower approved a plan at the meeting of the US National Security Council. America had decided to remove Castro. A budget of $13 million was agreed and plans were drawn up.

The Bay of Pigs Invasion

The **CIA** set up training camps in Guatemala and by November the operation had trained a small army for an assault landing and **guerrilla** warfare. A leading exiled politician, José Miró Cardona, was lined up to become the new president of Cuba if the plan succeeded.

Two air strikes would attack Cuban airbases to protect the landing troops. The planes were to be painted to look like Cuban air force planes. One thousand four hundred troops, including a large number of Cuban exiles living in the United States, would land at night on a remote beach in an area known as "The Bay of Pigs." At the same time paratroopers would be dropped to disrupt transportation and occupy any Cuban forces. A smaller force would land on the east coast of Cuba to create confusion in a second attack. The 1,400 troops would march on Havana, with the Cuban exiles gaining support from the Cuban population before overthrowing Castro and his government.

Failure of the plan

The Bay of Pigs Invasion was a disaster. The United States failed in both objectives: Castro was not removed and the United States had to admit responsibility for the attacks.

Why did it fail?

1. Poor secrecy: despite government efforts to keep the invasion plans covert, it became common knowledge among Cuban exiles in Miami. Through Cuban intelligence, Castro learned of the guerrilla training camps in Guatemala and was therefore prepared for an attack.

2. Failure to control the air: the plan started to unravel from the very first action. The air strikes missed many of their targets. As news broke of the attack, photographs of the repainted American planes became public and revealed American support for the invasion. Crucially the Cuban air force was left intact.

SOURCE 14

"A Program of Covert Action against the Castro Regime", an official plan for the removal of Castro by the American Government, prepared in 1960."

1. *Objective: The purpose of the program outlined herein is to bring about the replacement of the Castro regime with one more devoted to the true interests of the Cuban people and more acceptable to the U.S. in such a manner to avoid any appearance of U.S. intervention.*

CIA

The Central Intelligence Agency of America is the branch of government responsible for monitoring potential threats to the United States. Its actions are highly secretive but it is responsible for spying as well as secret operations within other countries.

Guerrilla

A type of warfare fought by an irregular armed force who often use methods such as sabotage and secret attacks.

President Eisenhower

Pre-political career

Eisenhower gained fame by being the 5-star general who had led Allied forces to victory in the Second World War.

Political career

He entered the presidential race on a policy of intervention against the spread of communism and served for two terms as president.

Character and outlook

Fair and honest, Eisenhower favoured freedoms for all and was the first president to intervene in civil rights. His fear of communism though led to an aggressive, anti-Soviet foreign policy.

3. Failure to gain support: when the invasion forces landed on the beaches along the Bay of Pigs they immediately came under heavy fire. Some escaped into the sea, others were killed or captured. Very few, if any, of the Cuban population joined the invaders.

4. Response: Castro ordered roughly 20 000 troops to advance toward the beach and the Cuban air force continued to control the skies. Without American air support and with such small troop numbers the invasion failed.

The aftermath

The captured troops were paraded by Castro and used as propaganda. His popularity increased as he repelled an American invasion. Eventually after 20 months in prison, the United States negotiated a deal to exchange the prisoners for goods scarce in Cuba, with Castro receiving baby food and medicine worth $53 million.

President Kennedy

Pre-political career

From a wealthy and powerful family, Kennedy entered politics after serving in the military in the Second World War.

Political career

Kennedy became America's second youngest president in 1961, aged only 43. His brief time in office was characterised by combating the spread of communism and the civil rights movement. He was assassinated in 1963.

Character and outlook

Kennedy was charismatic, charming, and glamorous. He was America's first TV president and drew fame and admirers for the life he lived.

QUICK QUESTION 5

Why do you think the Americans used a secret force, rather than sending its own army to overthrow Castro?

SOURCE 15

A note sent by Che Guevara to President Kennedy in August 1961.

Thanks ... Before the invasion, the revolution was weak. Now it's stronger than ever.

SOURCE 16

President Kennedy's words as reported in the *New York Times* in 1966.

[I want to] splinter the CIA into a thousand pieces and scatter it into the winds.

▲ **Fig. 5.8** This cartoon by Gib Crockett that was originally published in the Washington Star shows a very large chicken labeled "Bay of Pigs" roosting on top of the White House with the caption "Home to roost?"

Details of some of the 1,197 prisoners involved in the Bay of Pigs Invasion published by the Cuban government in 1961.

Occupations: 100 plantation owners; 67 landlords of apartment houses; 35 factory owners; 112 businessmen; 179 lived off unearned income; and 194 ex-soldiers of Batista.

Total property owned in Cuba: 923 000 acres of land; 9,666 houses and apartment buildings; 70 factories; 12 night clubs; 10 sugar mills; 24 large property owners; 5 mines and 3 banks.

An extract from a speech made by Fidel Castro in Havana in 1962.

What is hidden behind the Yankee hatred of the Cuban Revolution ... a small country of only seven million people, economically underdeveloped, without financial or military means to threaten the security or economy of any other country? What explains it is fear. Not fear of the Cuban Revolution but fear of the Latin American Revolution.

Che Guevara

Pre-political career
Born in Argentina and trained as a doctor.

Political career
Joined Castro's guerrilla force and helped seize power in Cuba. Left Cuba later in an attempt to spread the communist revolution into Bolivia where he was killed by political opponents.

Character and outlook
An intellectual and prolific writer, Guevara wanted to see all of South America united under communism.

DISCUSSION

1. What do you think Che Guevara meant in Source 15 when he thanked Kennedy for the attempted invasion?

2. What point were the Cuban government trying to make with the evidence in Source 17?

3. Why can you doubt the reliability of Rusk's account?

4. Is Castro correct in Source 18 in his views on the cause of American fear of Cuba?

▲ **Fig. 5.9** Banknote

How effectively did the United States contain the spread of Communism?

The Cuban Missile Crisis

The attempted American invasion in Cuba showed how vulnerable Castro's new regime was to American interference. The United States had made it clear that it wanted to remove Castro and install a more American-friendly ruler. Castro's country was not capable of a long-term defence against American aggression, however with support from another communist country it would be more likely to survive.

Secret U2 spy planes take photographs of the missile launchers in Cuba. President Kennedy is notified.	**15 October 1962**	
	September 1962	First nuclear missiles arrive secretly in Cuba. Reports start appearing in the United States of the missiles.
America begins military training exercises in the Caribbean, seen by some as preparation for another attempted invasion.	**July 1962**	
	July 1962	Soviet advisors tell Castro that America is planning another attempted invasion of Cuba. They advise keeping nuclear weapons on the island to prevent an attack.
America placed nuclear weapons in Turkey.	**April 1962**	
	7 February 1962	The United States impose an embargo against Cuba. Concerned that Castro's Cuba was making money from exporting goods to the American market, Kennedy banned all trade with Cuba.

▲ **Fig. 5.10** Timeline of events in the build-up to the crisis

Why were there nuclear missiles in Cuba?

There are several reasons why Russia deployed weapons in Cuba.

▶ **Political reasons**

Some within the Soviet Union felt Khrushchev was not aggressive enough towards America. They felt he was weak and in the past had appeased the Americans. A message needed to be sent out that he was strong. Cuba was an ally of the Soviet Union. Missiles there would act as a deterrent against another attack like the one in the previous year.

▶ **Military reasons**

The Soviet Union did not have a close enough base from which to strike at America. As Cuba was only 90 miles away missiles placed on the island would be able to reach the United States. The United States had recently placed missiles in Turkey which bordered the Soviet Union. Placing missiles in Cuba would give the United States less of an advantage.

▲ **Fig. 5.11** Aerial view of Mariel harbour in Cuba on 5 November 1962 during the Cuban Missile Crisis, showing the position of the missile transporters as taken by American spy planes

What options did Kennedy have?

Once nuclear weapons were confirmed in Cuba, Kennedy faced pressure to take action. He had a range of options to choose from, as set out below.

Defensive

1. No action. *The failed Bay of Pigs Invasion had shown any military action towards Cuba to be difficult.*

2. Use diplomatic measures to make the Soviet Union and Cuba remove the missiles. *Negotiation rather than aggression may help find a solution.*

3. Threaten Castro. *Give a warning to the Cuban leader about what would happen if the missiles weren't removed.*

4. Naval blockade. *Use American ships to stop any more missiles arriving on the island and also prevent supplies reaching Cuba therefore forcing Cuba to negotiate.*

5. Air strikes. *Attempting to destroy the military base from the air.*

6. Full ground invasion. *Committing American troops to the invasion of Cuba to destroy the missiles. Could possibly lead to the removal of Castro as well.*

Aggressive

▲ **Fig. 5.12** Kennedy's options

TASKS

When discussing these strategies, Kennedy and his advisors had to take into consideration how the Soviet Union and Cuba would react to decisions made by the United States. Copy the chart below. For each of the strategies given above, work out the possible impact of each action. The first one has been done for you.

Strategy	Reaction of the Soviet Union/ Cuba	Other possible consequences.
No action	Both countries see that they can do as they please.	President might lose the next election?

Other countries feel the need to "test" America? |

▲ **Fig. 5.13**

"We failed once with an invasion. Why would it work again? If we attack it makes us look too aggressive."

"We have to attack Cuba now. Only with a show of force will we keep America secure and also show these communists who is boss."

▲ **Fig. 5.14**

How effectively did the United States contain the spread of Communism?

How close was nuclear war?

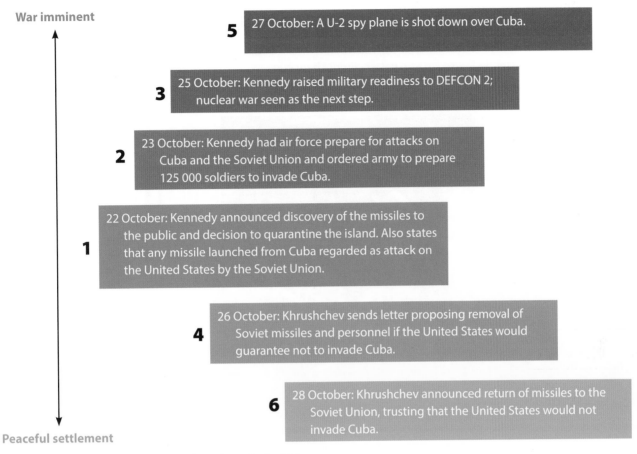

▲ **Fig. 5.15** Severity of the events of the Cuban Missile Crisis

War was averted by a deal in which the Soviets agreed to dismantle the weapon sites in exchange for a pledge from the United States not to invade Cuba. In a separate deal which remained secret for more than 25 years, the United States also agreed to remove its nuclear missiles from Turkey.

What were the long-term effects of the Cuban Missile Crisis?

SOURCE 19

Editorial from the *New York Tribune*, November 1962.

For the first time in twenty years Americans can carry their head high because the President of the United States had stood up to the premier of Russia and made him back down.

SOURCE 20

T. Howarth in *The World since 1900*, published in 1979.

Before the crisis Castro had declared himself to be a Marxist but Cuba was not a communist state. After the crisis, Cuba was as dependent on Russian aid and protection as any of the Eastern European satellites.

SOURCE 21

General William Smith, Assistant US Chief of Staff at the end of the crisis in 1962.

The [US] military were not satisfied with results, they'd only got the removal of the missiles. The US military thought that Kennedy had given away too much, had let them off too easy.

Oleg Troyanovsky, Special Advisor to Khrushchev speaking on a television programme about the crisis in 2002.

Khrushchev failed in that the missiles were withdrawn and in a way which was humiliating, but he did not fail in that America agreed not to attack Cuba, which still stands and inadvertently, it also led to a better climate between Russia and America.

"LET'S GET A LOCK FOR THIS THING"

NUCLEAR WAR

▲ **Fig. 5.18** A cartoon from an American publication shortly after the Cuban Missile Crisis ended in 1962. The two people shown are Kennedy and Nikita Khrushchev

▲ **Fig. 5.16** Castro and Khrushchev reviewing the May Day Parade in Red Square, Moscow, 1 May 1963

Bluff

The exciting NEW PARTY GAME

...OUT-GUESS AND OUT-BLUFF YOUR OPPONENTS

12 DICE
4 BEVELED
DICE CUPS WITH
VIEWING WINDOWS

▲ **Fig. 5.17** Image from the cover of a dice game called 'Bluff', marketed by Saalfield Publishing in 1963. It makes a comment on the behaviour of Kennedy and Khrushchev in the Cuban missile crisis

DISCUSSION

1. Study Sources 20 to 22. What were the consequences of the crisis?

2. Look at the cartoon in Figure 5.18. What is the cartoonist saying about relations between the Soviet Union and the United States following the crisis?

3. Are you surprised by the view in Source 21?

4. Which of the following benefited the most from the crisis?

   • Kennedy and the United States

   • Khrushchev and the Soviet Union

   • Castro and Cuba

   Explain your choice.

American involvement in Vietnam

▲ **Fig. 5.19** French prisoners being marched by the Vietminh out of Dien Bien Phu, 7 May 1954

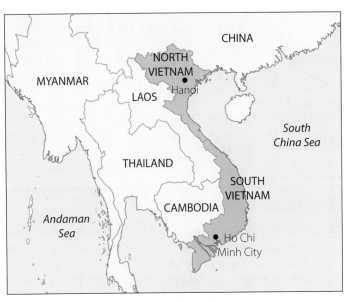

▲ **Fig. 5.20** Map showing North and South Vietnam

In 1945 Vietnam was a country with a long history of being ruled by others. The Chinese, French, and the Japanese had all attempted to control the state in South East Asia. After the defeat of the Japanese in 1945, Vietnam was once more subjected to attempts at colonisation. The French, previously rulers over what they called "French Indo-China" hoped to regain control of Vietnam but their attempts were opposed by a Vietnamese army called the **Vietminh**.

Led by Ho Chi Minh and intent on ruling their own country, the Vietminh successfully defeated the French, with the Battle of Dien Bien Phu marking the end of French involvement in Vietnam. The heavy defeat suffered led to surrender by the remaining French troops. At the Geneva Conference the French negotiated a ceasefire agreement with the Vietminh and independence was granted to Cambodia, Laos, and Vietnam.

In July 1954, France and the Vietminh agreed the Geneva Peace Accord. As part of the post-war settlement announced on 21 July 1954, Vietnam was temporarily partitioned into two parts, the north and the south. This was only meant to be temporary, before internationally supervised free elections could be held in 1956. These elections never took place. The Vietminh became the government of North Vietnam while anti-communist Vietnamese, especially Catholics, "regrouped" in the south under the leadership of Bao Dai, a former emperor of Vietnam who had abdicated in 1945.

When France left Vietnam in 1955 after its defeat in the Indo-China War, it looked like Vietnam would be allowed to rule itself. However, America saw Vietnam as a key battleground in the fight against communism.

The domino theory was first suggested by US President Eisenhower in 1954. As one country fell to communism it would be more likely that surrounding ones would be affected. Just like dominoes toppling into each other.

Vietminh

The Vietminh were founded in 1941 by the Communist Party.

> *You have a row of dominoes set up; you knock over the first one and what will happen to the last one is that it will go over very quickly.*
>
> President Eisenhower

▲ **Fig. 5.21** The domino effect, as described by President Eisenhower on page 105

After the fall of China to communism in 1949 and Korea shortly after, America thought Vietnam was next.

SOURCE 23

Former US President Dwight Eisenhower in his book *Mandate for Change* published in 1963.

It was generally conceded that had an election been held, Ho Chi Minh would have been elected Premier ... I have never talked or corresponded with a person knowledgeable in Indochinese affairs who did not agree that had elections been held as of the time of the fighting, possibly 80 per cent of the population would have voted for the Communist Ho Chi Minh as their leader.

> **DISCUSSION**
>
> Read Source 23 and consider the following question. Does the fact the United States wanted to block the election of the most popular party in Vietnam explain why it struggled in future conflict?

The United States backed the anti-communist government in South Vietnam, fearing that if it didn't, the whole of Vietnam would become communist. Soon after the peace conference the South began fighting against the **Vietcong**, a communist party based in South Vietnam which was allied with North Vietnam. In 1959, North Vietnam dramatically increased its military assistance to the Vietcong, which then began attacking South Vietnamese military units. This widened the conflict and brought full-scale war closer.

> " *If Indochina [Vietnam] falls, Thailand is put in an almost impossible position. The same is true of Malaya with its rubber and tin. The same is true of Indonesia. If this whole part of South East Asia goes under Communist domination or Communist influence, Japan, who trades and must trade with this area in order to exist must inevitably be oriented towards the Communist regime.* "
>
> Future US President and leading politician Richard Nixon, 1953.

> **QUICK QUESTION 6**
>
> Read the quote by Nixon. What factor did he see as defining whether countries turned to communism?

Vietcong

A political and military group formed to fight the South Vietnamese and then later the United States.

Why did American involvement in Vietnam increase?

Under Eisenhower

Eisenhower saw Vietnam as a crucial part of his domino theory. In 1953 Eisenhower was warned by his Chief of Staff against intervening in the war between Vietnam and France. Instead he sent American air force pilots to support the French during their military operations. When the French war effort failed he turned his attention to supporting the south and began offering military and economic aid to the new nation of South Vietnam. He also increased the number of American military advisors in South Vietnam to 900 men. This was due to North Vietnam's support of "uprisings" in the south and concern the nation would fall.

▲ **Fig. 5.22** President Eisenhower meeting President Diem of South Vietnam in Washington during a state visit in 1957

His "Eisenhower Doctrine" recommended the use of American forces to protect states in the Middle East against aggression from nations "controlled by international communism". He also encouraged economic aid to those countries with anti-communist governments. While this was directed at the safety of the Middle East, the policy can be seen in use in South East Asia as well.

Under President Kennedy

Kennedy had been advised by Eisenhower that a greater military presence in Vietnam was needed to prevent the spread of communism. Kennedy also wanted to appear strong after the failed Bay of Pigs Invasion and the Cuban Missile Crisis.

In 1961 Kennedy arranged for the South Vietnamese to receive the money necessary to increase the size of their army from 150 000 to 170 000 and sent another 100 military advisors to Vietnam to help train the South Vietnamese army.

In 1962, the Strategic Hamlet Program was introduced. The United States wanted to limit the influence of the Vietcong on peasants in the south. Peasants were moved to new villages built in areas controlled by the South Vietnamese army. This was meant to ensure that peasants could not be influenced by the Vietcong, and to keep control of the southern peasant population.

Why didn't this work?

1. The peasants did not want to move therefore the South Vietnamese army often had to force them.

2. The peasants were angry at having to travel longer distances to reach their rice fields and simply moved back.

3. Some were upset for religious reasons as they believed that it was important to live where their ancestors were buried.

4. The membership of the **National Liberation Front** had grown to over 17 000. This represented a 300 per cent increase in two years. It was estimated that the National Liberation Front controlled 20 per cent of villages in the south.

National Liberation Front

Another name for the Vietcong.

Kennedy increased the number of military advisors to 12 000 in Vietnam by the end of 1962. He also supplied South Vietnam with 300 helicopters, however, the American pilots were told not to become "engaged in combat".

On 11 June 1963, Thich Quang Duc, a 66-year-old monk, set himself on fire in protest at the South Vietnamese government. While he burned to death, the monks and nuns gave out leaflets calling for Diem's government to show "charity and compassion" to all religions. The government's response to this suicide was to arrest thousands of Buddhist monks. By August another five monks had committed suicide by setting fire to themselves. One member of the South Vietnamese government responded to these suicides by telling a reporter: "Let them burn, and we shall clap our hands."

At the beginning of November 1963, President Diem was overthrown by a military coup. After the generals had promised Diem that he would be allowed to leave the country, they changed their mind and killed him.

▲ **Fig. 5.23** Thich Quang Duc after he had set himself on fire

DISCUSSION

The death of Thich Quang Duc was widely reported in the American media. Do you think this would help the American war effort in Vietnam? Explain your answer.

Under President Johnson

After Kennedy's assassination Vice-President Lyndon Johnson took over. Johnson was a bigger supporter of the war than Kennedy, and once in office immediately asked his military chiefs to make plans should a full-scale war break out.

In August 1964 a confrontation known as "The Gulf of Tonkin Incident" resulted in the start of real warfare between America and North Vietnam. Two American warships were attacked by North Vietnamese gunboats while they were in international waters. In response the American Senate gave Johnson the power to give armed support to South Vietnam. The bombing of North Vietnam started in February 1965 and in March 1965 the first American ground troops landed in South Vietnam. By December 1965 there were 150 000 stationed in the country.

Under Johnson the American commitment was at its strongest. The number of men conscripted into the army was increased through "the draft", a lottery-style system where young men physically capable of fighting were called up to the army as needed.

What was the draft? ⓘ

The draft had been used by the United States to conscript men to its army since the nineteenth century and continued into the twentieth century. In the Vietnam War all young men who were eligible for service had to register and troops were called on as needed, usually through a "lottery" system where dates of birth were drawn. Once drawn troops had to serve for at least a year. Over two million men were "drafted" into Vietnam.

▲ **Fig. 5.24** American president Lyndon B. Johnson and General William Westmoreland, commander of American forces in Vietnam, discussing the war in Vietnam in 1964

 I do not want to be the first President to lose a war. "

Lyndon B. Johnson

Support for the war

In January 1968 there was a surprise attack by the North Vietnamese known as "the Tet offensive". North Vietnamese troops attacked nearly 30 American targets and dozens of cities in South Vietnam. Although none of the attacks succeeded in capturing territory the battle was disastrous for the American war effort. American media coverage characterised the conflict as a defeat, and public support for the war plummeted.

Another event that had a huge effect on public support for the war was the My Lai Massacre. In response to the Tet offensive, a small handful of rogue American soldiers killed hundreds of unarmed Vietnamese civilians in a small village called My Lai.

QUICK QUESTION 7

Why do you think the Tet offensive was so disastrous for Johnson?

Statement	% before TET offensive	% after TET offensive
Approves Johnson's handling of job as president	48%	36%
Approves Johnson's handling of Vietnam	39%	26%
Regards war in Vietnam as a mistake	45%	29%
Proportion classifying themselves as "hawks", that is, those in favour of military solutions to the war	60%	41%

▲ **Table 5.3** Public opinion in America

In 1968, after the horrors of My Lai and the divisions in the Democratic party over Vietnam, Johnson decided not to run again for president.

QUICK QUESTION 8

Why do you think numbers peak in 1968?

DISCUSSION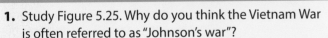

1. Study Figure 5.25. Why do you think the Vietnam War is often referred to as "Johnson's war"?

2. Considering his actions, is this a fair statement?

3. Looking at the opinion polls before and after the Tet offensive, how big a turning point was it? Explain your answer.

4. According to the Quagmire Theory, one of the ways of explaining the war in Vietnam, the United States got sucked into the conflict almost without realising it was happening. How far would you agree with this explanation of Kennedy and Johnson's increasing involvement in Vietnam between 1961 and 1965?

5. Find evidence of the following tactics used by the Americans in an attempt to control Vietnam.

   - Political interference
   - Economic aid
   - Military support

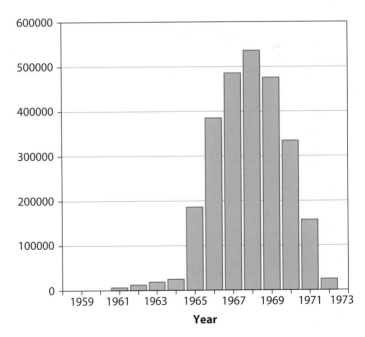

▲ **Fig. 5.25** US troops in Vietnam

The end of the war

▲ **Fig. 5.26** Nixon with advisors consulting on Vietnam

The election of President Richard Nixon in 1969 was meant to mark the beginning of the process of withdrawing US troops from Vietnam. He set about negotiating a peaceful end to the conflict having made an election promise of ending the conflict. Nixon had claimed he wanted to find "peace with honour" and set about removing America from the war. He pursued a policy called "Vietnamisation" whereby the South Vietnamese would be supported with materials and money by the Americans but the fighting would be done by the South Vietnamese army. This meant withdrawing American troops from the country. In December 1970, there were 350 000 American troops in South Vietnam. By September 1972, there were just 40 000.

However, although Nixon consistently attempted to negotiate peace, it was not only peaceful methods that he used in his efforts to end the war. In 1970, after negotiations with North Vietnam broke down, Nixon tried to force the end of the war by bombing Vietnam troop bases in Cambodia. These raids were carried out in secret to avoid international attention. The bombing failed though and in April 1970 Nixon decided to send troops in to complete the mission. This escalation of the war was badly received at home and led to demonstrations. In one of these, four students were killed when National Guardsmen opened fire at Kent State University.

▲ **Fig. 5.27** Protestors at Kent State University after an anti-war protest had led to the deaths of four students in May 1970

In the end a peace treaty was signed in 1973 in Paris. Once American support ended, there was a brief truce before fighting broke out again, this time without American involvement. North Vietnam conquered South Vietnam in 1975.

Why did the United States withdraw from the war?

Public opinion

As the mood changed in the United States, largely influenced by the media, the support for the war declined.

SOURCE 24

Gary Wieland, a soldier who served as a radio operator in the field until 1968 reflecting on the conflict in 2011.

I think the number of deaths and injuries were the primary reason Americans turned against the war. As TV coverage became more complete and graphic, Americans could see the horrors of this conflict in their own living rooms. Plus many had personally lost friends and family members. I guess we all just started to say is this worth all these lives and costs.

SOURCE 25

Walter Cronkite, highly regarded news presenter, after the Tet offensive in 1968.

To say that we are closer to victory today is to believe, in the face of the evidence, the optimists who have been wrong in the past. It is increasingly clear to this reporter that the only rational way out then will be to negotiate, not as victors, but as an honorable people who lived up to their pledge to defend democracy, and did the best they could.

SOURCE 26

President Johnson to his staff after watching Cronkite's news report live in the White House.

If I've lost Cronkite, I've lost America.

DISCUSSION

1. What do you think President Johnson meant when he said "I've lost America"?

2. Does Source 25 support what the soldier in Source 24 is saying?

The United States failed because the North Vietnamese had better tactics

The United States went into the conflict better armed, better trained, and with more sophisticated weaponry than its opponents. Yet it failed to gain control of the war. The guerrilla-style warfare of the North Vietnamese meant that the war

▲ **Fig. 5.28** An American soldier searches in a village near the town of Ben Cat for Vietcong

was not fought with large set-piece battles where American military strength would triumph, but with surprise attacks at irregular times. Therefore there was never any real evidence of progress for America.

Gary Wieland, a soldier who served as a radio operator in the field until 1968 reflecting on the conflict in 2011.

We could go for weeks walking in the country and never see an enemy troop. In fact we would go out on "search and destroy" missions after we heard rumours that some Vietcong were in the area and never see any enemy.

But then when you least expected it you would be shot at from the trees in a wooded area. Or someone would step on a pre-set trap or mortars would be shot into your camp area. Then we would return fire usually without seeing who we were shooting at. Often firing at the wooded area where the shots came from. Then you would go weeks again in the same area and not have any contact with the enemy.

The other problem was you never really knew who the enemy was. The friendly Vietnamese looked just like the enemy Vietnamese so you were never sure who was your friend and who might shoot you in the back. One example of this was when I was in the base camp and we were attacked by mortars and rifle fire at night. We return fire for an hour or so then all was quiet. The next morning we went out to do our "body count" and one of the dead enemy soldiers turned out to be the barber who came everyday to our base to give haircuts to the soldiers. I had received a haircut from this very same guy the day before.

As well as better tactics, the North Vietnamese were also better at winning the hearts and minds of the Vietnamese people. This loyalty to the people meant that the North Vietnamese retained the support of the ordinary people in Vietnam who resisted the influence of the Americans.

Vietminh directives from their conflict with France in 1948. These rules continued into the conflict with America.

1. *Not to do what is likely to damage the land and crops or spoil the houses and belongings of the people.*

2. *Not to insist on buying or borrowing what the people are not willing to sell or lend.*

3. *Never to break our word.*

4. *Not to do or speak what is likely to make people believe that we hold them in contempt.*

5. *To help them in their daily work (harvesting, fetching firewood, carrying water, sewing, etc.).*

6. *In spare time, to tell amusing, simple, and short stories useful to the Resistance, but not to betray secrets.*

7. *Whenever possible to buy commodities for those who live far from the market.*

8. *To teach the population the national script and elementary hygiene.*

A British journalist speaking on a television programme, 27 June 1993.

The American story was that this was an example of the success of their bombing and shelling campaign. They told me that it showed that the Viet Cong were so demoralised that they were having to take refuge underground. Well I must confess that I believed that version of the story. It was only later when it was discovered how enormous the tunnel complex was and how skilfully the Viet Cong used it and how the tunnels actually extended under the American base camps, that I started to think for myself and I realised that this was not a sign of how demoralised the Viet Cong had become but how determined they were.

DISCUSSION

1. Study Sources 27 and 28. Is one of these sources more useful than the other to a historian studying the Vietnam War? Explain your answer using the sources and your own knowledge.

A list of Vietcong "heroes" drawn up by an American journalist. In 1974 he researched the life of one small South Vietnamese village during the war. The villagers told him that they remembered the Vietcong in the area calling meetings of villagers in which they were told about these "heroes".

Two young women who tempted some United States soldiers to lay down their weapons, and then killed them.

An old woman who assisted guerrillas in setting up an ambush against American soldiers.

A young boy who befriended some United States soldiers and then led them into a Viet Cong ambush.

A government soldier who deserted to the Viet Cong, bringing several weapons and stolen documents with him.

A schoolboy who secretly spread the teachings of Ho Chi Minh among his classmates.

DISCUSSION

1. How far does Source 29 support the soldier's view of the difficulties of fighting in Vietnam?

2. Study the list of Vietminh directives in Source 29. What reasons can you see here for why the United States struggled to win support in Vietnam?

3. Study Sources 24 to 30. How far do these sources support the view that the Americans lost the Vietnam War because of what was happening in the United States? Use the sources to explain your answer.

KEY POINTS

▶ Why the United States became involved in Cuba

▶ American and Cuban relations

▶ The Cuban Missile Crisis

▶ Why the United States entered the war in Vietnam

▶ The development of the war

▶ The end of US involvement in Vietnam

▶ The Korean War

Revision tips

- The Bay of Pigs plan was already in place when Kennedy came to office, but he continued with it even though he was unsure of it. Be able to explain why he blamed others such as the CIA for its failure.

- Make sure you are able to fully explain the Cuban Missile Crisis and why Kennedy chose the action he did.

- Be able to explain how successive US presidents escalated the war in Vietnam. Be aware though it is not until Johnson that a large-scale ground force is committed to the war and this is only after the US navy had apparently been attacked.

- There are lots of different groups—Vietcong, Vietminh, etc.—and it can be confusing in terms of South and North Vietnam. Ensure you're fully confident about who was fighting who!

Review questions

1. How did the United States use Cuba during the 1950s and 1960s?

2. What were the main achievements of Castro's rule in Cuba?

3. Describe why the Bay of Pigs failed.

4. What were Khrushchev's reasons for placing nuclear weapons on Cuba?

5. What concession did the United States make to Russia in return for Russia's withdrawal from Cuba?

6. Why did the United States support the South Vietnamese government?

7. Why do you think Eisenhower and Kennedy were both reluctant to commit troops to Vietnam?

8. Why was the Tet offensive a turning point in the war?

9. How did American and Vietnamese tactics differ during the conflict?

10. Why did the United States withdraw from Vietnam?

How effectively did the United States contain the spread of Communism?

How secure was the Soviet Union's control over eastern Europe, 1948–c. 1989?

Introduction

The Soviet Union had been on the winning side in the Second World War. As victors, the Soviets had three main aims for Europe:

1. to create a buffer zone to the west of Russia, protecting them from any attack in the future
2. to spread communism
3. to use the resources of others to help rebuild their war-damaged country.

Communist rule was gradually established across eastern Europe as Soviet forces established control there. Through heavily supervised elections a Communist ruling party was established in each country with orders coming straight from Moscow. This "**Iron Curtain**", as it came to be known, separated Europe into two sides.

The Soviet-controlled countries in the east were tied by two binding agreements. An economic agreement was put in place in 1949 with the creation of COMECON, the Council for Mutual Economic Assistance. The Warsaw Pact set up in 1955 was a mutual defense treaty between the eight communist states of eastern Europe, with each country agreeing to support any of the others if attacked.

Iron Curtain

A line dividing Europe into the Soviet-controlled east and the capitalist west.

▲ **Fig. 6.1** Warsaw Pact members

The aims of this chapter are to:

- Examine Soviet power in eastern Europe including resistance to Soviet power in Hungary in 1956 and in Czechoslovakia in 1968, the Berlin Wall, and "Solidarity" in Poland.
- Look at Gorbachev and the collapse of the Soviet Empire.

Why was there opposition to Soviet control in Hungary in 1956 and Czechoslovakia in 1968, and how did the Soviet Union react to this opposition?

SOURCE 1

Sir Winston Churchill in a speech at Westminster College in Fulton, Missouri, 5 March 1946.

From Stettin in the Baltic to Trieste in the Adriatic, an iron curtain has descended across the continent. Behind that line lie all the capitals of the ancient states of Central and Eastern Europe. Warsaw, Berlin, Prague, Vienna, Budapest, Belgrade, Bucharest and Sofia, all these famous cities and the populations around them lie in what I must call the Soviet sphere, and all are subject in one form or another, not only to Soviet influence but to a very high and, in many cases, increasing measure of control from Moscow.

QUICK QUESTION 1

What do you think Churchill meant by the phrase "an Iron Curtain"?

Hungary

SOURCE 2

A telex message sent by the Hungarian rebels fighting the Communists, quoted in George Mikes' book *The Hungarian Revolution*, published in 1957.

We have almost no weapons, no heavy guns of any kind. People are running up to the tanks, throwing in hand grenades and closing the drivers' windows. The Hungarian people are not afraid of death. It is only a pity that we cannot last longer. Now the firing is starting again. The tanks are coming nearer and nearer. You can't let people attack tanks with their bare hands. What is the United Nations doing?

Source 2 was one of the last messages sent by the people of Hungary who rose up against Soviet rule in 1956 and demanded freedom in their country. In the uprising, some 3 000 Hungarians were killed, 12 000 were arrested, and 450 were executed. Nearly a quarter of a million people managed to take advantage of the chaos and escaped to the west.

Background

At the end of the Second World War Hungary was on the losing side. It had originally joined the war alongside the **Axis powers**, fighting with Nazi Germany and against the Soviet Union. In 1941 when Germany launched its invasion of Russia, Hungarian troops had formed part of the attack. However, by the end of the war Hungary was under Soviet control and formed part of the eastern bloc. Hungary became a satellite state of the Soviet Union, with the political ruling elite receiving orders from Moscow and communist rule was established. In 1955 Hungary was one of the countries that signed the Warsaw Pact, a military treaty linking the eastern European communist countries to the Soviet Union.

Axis powers

Germany, Italy, Japan, and their allies during the Second World War.

What caused the rebellion of 1956?

There was long-term anger about the influence of Soviet rule and the deeply unpopular communist policies.

Politics: elections had been held after the end of the Second World War. The Smallholders Party, a group working for the rights of ordinary Hungarians, won 57 per cent of the vote. The Russians, however, refused to allow the party to form a government, and instead allowed the Hungarian Communist Party to form a government with only 17 per cent of the vote. From this point on it was the party to run Hungary, despite the people's wishes.

Repression: Russian control of Hungarian society included censorship, a secret police (the AVH), and control over what schools taught. An estimated 2 000 people were executed and over 100 000 were imprisoned as the Russians took strict control over Hungary.

Religion: the Hungarians were religious but under the Communist Party religion was banned and dismissed as "dangerous propaganda". Cardinal Joseph Mindszenty, a leading Hungarian Catholic, was arrested, tortured, and put in prison.

Economics: after the war Hungary was very poor and, like a lot of Europe, needed rebuilding after years of bombing and damage. Yet much of the food produced as well as industrial goods were sent instead to Russia. This meant that standards of living dropped for ordinary people.

All these factors meant that there was a great deal of resentment of Soviet rule among Hungarians. In 1956 things reached a critical point; the Hungarian people thought change might be possible for the following reasons.

- Hungarians thought that the **United Nations** or the new American president, Eisenhower, would help them after he made supportive comments in speeches.

- Stalin had died in 1953. With his death, Russia had tried to move away from some of his policies, including the more brutal aspects. The new leader, Nikita Khrushchev, refused to allow the arrest of 400 political opponents in Hungary.

- In June 1956 workers in Poland had risen against Soviet rule and demanded change. After a tense few weeks, Russia had given in to some of their demands. This gave people hope in Hungary that the same could happen there.

The uprising begins

23 October: students in Budapest demanded an end to Soviet occupation and the implementation of "true socialism". The police made arrests. When the students attempted to aid those who had been arrested, the police opened fire on the crowd. In a symbolic gesture, a 30-foot statue of Stalin was toppled by protestors.

24 October: overnight Russian troops had been sent in to stop the protests. Soviet tanks were stationed outside the Parliament building and Soviet soldiers guarded key bridges and crossroads.

Despite this, Hungarian soldiers and workers joined the students on the streets of Budapest. The Hungarian Communist Party appointed a new Prime Minister, Imre Nagy. He asked Khrushchev to remove Russian troops from Hungary and promised the people free elections.

United Nations

The international organisation founded in 1945 to promote peace, security, and economic development.

DISCUSSION

Read Source 3. What reason does it suggest for why the Hungarians disliked Communist control?

▲ **Fig. 6.2** The head of the Stalin statue toppled by protestors

25 October: a large number of protesters gathered in front of the Parliament building. Those politicians loyal to Russia were forced to flee as the protestors took control of the running of the country. Nagy continued as Prime Minister, still promising reform.

28 October: keen to avoid bloodshed, Khrushchev agreed to the demands of Nagy to remove troops and the Russian army pulled out of Budapest.

29 October–3 November: the new Hungarian government introduced democracy, freedom of speech, and freedom of religion. Cardinal Joseph Mindszenty and other political prisoners were released from prison. Nagy also announced that Hungary was going to leave the Warsaw Pact. On 1 November he appealed to the UN for help in resolving the conflict.

4 November: one thousand Russian tanks moved into Budapest. They almost immediately captured Hungary's airfields, highway junctions, and bridges. Fierce fighting took place but Russian force was too strong for the Hungarian army and protestors.

The new leader of Hungary, Janos Kadar promised Nagy and his followers that they would be allowed to leave the country safely. Three weeks later they were kidnapped, tried, and eventually executed for treason.

DISCUSSION

Why do you think it is often students who join protests first?

▲ **Fig. 6.3** Soviet tanks take control of Budapest

SOURCE 4

Tass, Soviet news agency, 24 October 1956.

Late in the evening of October 23 underground reactionary organizations attempted to start a counter-revolutionary revolt against the people's regime in Budapest. This enemy adventure had obviously been in preparation for some time. The forces of foreign reaction have been systematically inciting anti-democratic elements for action against the lawful authority.

The Hungarian Government asked the USSR Government for help. In accordance with this request, Soviet military units, which are in Hungary under the terms of the Warsaw treaty, helped troops of the Hungarian Republic to restore order in Budapest. In many industrial enterprises workers offered armed resistance to the bandits who tried to damage and destroy equipment and to mount armed guards.

SOURCE 5

Soviet General Malashenko, an eyewitness to the event, wrote this in 1956.

The Soviet troop march into Hungary was necessary to defend the existing order and was intended to prevent Hungary from breaking away from the socialist camp, withdrawing from the Warsaw Pact and making peace with the West ...

SOURCE 6

William Tompson, a modern historian, in his book entitled *Khrushchev: A Political Life* written in 1995.

A change in the status of Hungary would have undermined the post-war status quo in Europe, and the potential ripple effects on other East European countries were extremely serious. If the Polish example had ignited Hungary, who could say what a successful Hungarian revolution would set off elsewhere in the bloc?

DISCUSSION

1. Having read Source 5 are you surprised by Source 4?

2. Why can you doubt the reliability of Source 4?

3. Read Sources 5 and 6. How useful are these two sources?

Czechoslovakia

In 1968 the "**Prague Spring**" began with the government of Czechoslovakia attempting to make reforms, improve the country, and lessen the ties to Soviet Russia. It ended with a Russia invasion, a new enforced leader and a halt to all reforms.

Much like Hungary, Czechoslovakia had fallen under Soviet rule after the end of the Second World War. Tight controls had been established on the way the country was run, how the economy was structured, and the rights people had.

▲ **Fig. 6.4** Czechs celebrate the reforms in Prague, 1968

What caused the demand for reform?

Throughout the 1960s the Czechoslovakian economy struggled. After suffering a recession during which Czech industry struggled to produce goods to sell and the standard of living for ordinary people dropped, several changes were made. The most important of these was a loosening of government controls on businesses, meaning that companies could now have more control over setting prices and wages. This was very different to communist rule.

There were also political changes. The leader of the ruling Communist Party, Antonin Novotný, was replaced after protests by students against his rule. His replacement, Alexander Dubcek, made a list of complaints against Novotný and promised change.

Proposed reforms included the following.

- The abolition of censorship, the press could now print what it wanted and started to report revelations about corruption in high places.

- Freedom of speech, citizens had the right to criticise the government.

- Members of the party were not to be unconditionally loyal to the party, but instead be honest about how the country was run. The reforms stated that each member "has not only the right, but the duty to act according to his conscience".

- The creation of workers' councils in industry.

- Increased rights for trade unions.

- Rights for farmers to form independent farms away from state control.

- A recognition of Slovak national identity and customs.

- Freedom of movement for all people.

Dubcek knew that these reforms would be seen as potentially dangerous by Moscow, and fearing a situation like that in Hungary where troops had entered the country, publicly declared that Czechoslovakia had no intention of changing its foreign policy, leaving the Warsaw Pact or ending its alliance with the Soviet Union. This was meant to reassure the Soviet Union and avoid the need for intervention from Moscow.

Prague Spring

A period of reform with the government making changes to many aspects of life in Czechoslovakia.

DISCUSSION

Which of these proposed reforms do you think the Russians would have feared the most?

Soviet response

In July 1968 the Soviet leadership announced that it had evidence that West Germany was planning an invasion of the Sudetenland and asked permission to send in the Red Army to protect Czechoslovakia. Dubcek refused. However, a month later troops from countries across the Warsaw Pact, led by the Soviets, invaded Czechoslovakia. Knowing that it stood no chance, the Czech government ordered its armed forces not to resist the invasion. The culture of reform known as the "Prague Spring" was crushed. Alexander Dubcek was taken to Moscow and soon afterwards announced that Czechoslovakia would be abandoning its reform programme.

SOURCE 7

Statement issued by Alexander Dubcek's government, 21 August 1968.

Yesterday, August 20, 1968, around 11:00 p.m., the armies of the Soviet Union, of the Polish People's Republic, of the German Democratic Republic, the Hungarian Peoples Republic, and the Bulgarian Peoples Republic crossed the borders of the Czechoslovak Socialist Republic. It happened without the knowledge of the President of the Republic. The Presidium believes that this act contradicts not only all principles of relations between socialist countries but also the basic norms of international law.

SOURCE 8

A Soviet news agency report, 21 August 1968.

The party and government leaders of the Czechoslovak Socialist Republic have asked the Soviet Union and other allies to give the Czechoslovak people urgent assistance, including assistance with armed forces. This request was brought about … by the threat from counter revolutionary forces … working with foreign forces hostile to socialism.

The leader of the Soviet Union, Leonid Brezhnev, was worried that the new ideas coming out of Czechoslovakia would spread. Other leaders in eastern Europe feared that their own people would demand the same freedom that Dubcek had allowed in Czechoslovakia. Incidentally, in 1968 Albania resigned from the Warsaw Pact because it thought that the Soviet Union itself had become too liberal since Stalin had died.

In order to stop similar events, the **Brezhnev Doctrine** was introduced. This Soviet foreign policy stated that communist countries should be mindful of how their actions impacted on other communist states. Communist countries therefore would be governed by two principles:

- a one-party system in each country
- all countries were to remain members of the Warsaw Pact.

If these conditions were not met, under the terms of the doctrine, the Soviet Union could use military force to re-establish control.

In April 1969 Alexander Dubcek was replaced as party secretary, expelled from the party, and spent the next two decades working as a clerk in a lumber yard in Slovakia. The invasion ushered in a 20-year period of so-called "normalisation". During this time, whatever happened in Czechoslovakia was coordinated with Moscow and closely monitored by Soviet army generals, **KGB** officers, and Czechoslovak collaborators loyal to the Soviet regime.

KGB

The Russian secret police.

DISCUSSION

1. During the reforms Dubcek placed great emphasis on the fact that Czechoslovakia didn't want to break from Soviet control. Why do you think he was so keen to do this?

2. Having read Source 7 are you surprised by Source 8?

3. "Both Sources 7 and 8 have little value as evidence of events in Czechoslovakia in 1968." How far do you agree with this statement?

▲ **Fig. 6.5** A street cartoon seen in Prague in 1968

QUICK QUESTION 2

Study the cartoon in Figure 6.5. What point is it making?

SOURCE 9

Mikhail Gorbachev, *Memoirs* published in 1995.

The scope and dynamic development of the reform process in Czechoslovakia had frightened our leaders into scrapping their own timid attempts at economic reform and tightening the political and ideological screws.

SOURCE 10

Lyndon B. Johnson, statement calling on the Warsaw Pact allies to withdraw from Czechoslovakia in 1968.

The Soviet Union and its allies have invaded a defenseless country to stamp out a resurgence of ordinary human freedom. It is a sad commentary on the Communist mind that a sign of liberty in Czechoslovakia is deemed a fundamental threat to the security of the Soviet system.

DISCUSSION

1. Why were the Soviets frightened of the proposed reforms in Czechoslovakia?

2. Study Figure 6.6 and Source 10. How did unrest in Hungary and Czechoslovakia during the Cold War period benefit the United States? Explain your answer.

▲ **Fig. 6.6** The funeral of Jan Palach, a Czech student who committed suicide by setting himself on fire in Wenceslas Square on 16 January 1969

How similar were events in Hungary in 1956 and in Czechoslovakia in 1968?

	How were events similar?	How were they different?
Causes	Both countries had a long-term resentment of Soviet rule.	Hungary was affected by issues in other countries: the rebellion in Poland inspired Hungary to act. Czechoslovakia was affected by issues at home: economic depression and a desire for political change.
Aims of the rebels	Both wanted to give their people more rights and lessen the control of the communist state	In Hungary these changes included withdrawing from the Warsaw Pact and Soviet influence. Czechoslovakia did not want to go that far.
Actions of the people	Both involved groups of people protesting.	In Czechoslovakia, the people's actions were largely started by the role of their leader. It was his changes that encouraged them to protest. In Hungary, it was the people who acted first.
Why the Soviet Union intervened	The Soviet Union was very suspicious and fearful that any form of rebellion/change would spread and lead to a split in its control in other countries.	The political nature of Czechoslovakia was particularly dangerous for the Soviets; they had faced people-led rebellions before like that in Hungary, but the "Prague Spring" was started by people who were meant to be under Soviet control.
How each state responded to Soviet intervention	Both leaders were removed from office. Both resulted in mass emigration.	In Hungary the people armed themselves and fought when the Soviets attacked. In Czechoslovakia, following orders from the government, the people did not fight back. In Czechoslovakia there were several protests after the Russian invasion including suicides.
Reaction of the wider world	Reactions to both were wholly negative to Soviet use of force. The situation in Hungary was discussed at the United Nations; with Czechoslovakia the Soviet actions were condemned by different countries including the United States.	With the Czechoslovakian invasion some members of the communist Warsaw Pact expressed shock at Soviet actions. The Romanian leader complained about Russian intervention.

▲ Table 6.1

DISCUSSION

Look at Table 6.1 and answer the following questions.

1. Which act of resistance achieved the most?

2. Which would have been viewed as more dangerous at the time?

3. Which would you view as more dangerous now, knowing all the information?

Why was the Berlin Wall built in 1961?

On 13 August 1961 the people of Berlin woke to find that their city had changed. Berlin, the centre of the Cold War since the division of Germany in 1945, was now a city of two halves, divided by a wall 87 miles long that separated east from west.

The wall was a surprise to most people as the leader of East Germany, Walter, had stated only two months before: "Niemand hat die Absicht, eine Mauer zu errichten!" (No one has the intention of erecting a wall!) Despite this claim, less than two months later East Germany, under instruction from Soviet Russia, built the wall.

The erection of the wall by East Germany was to prevent the mass movement of people from east to west. Nearly 2.6 million East Germans had left for West Berlin or West Germany between 1949 and 1961, some 15 per cent of the population.

QUICK QUESTION 3

Why do you think the Russians were so keen to stop people leaving East Berlin?

Why were people leaving?

The quality of life in the west was much better than that in the east after 1948. While West Germany had received financial help through the Marshall Plan from the United States to rebuild after the devastation of the Second World War, East Germany had suffered under a communist system after the control of the Soviet Union had been established.

The impact of this mass movement on East Germany was huge.

- Socially: those leaving tended to be young and well-educated. The Communist Party in East Germany feared a "brain drain" as the more intelligent left East Germany.

- Economically: East Germany lost too many skilled workers. By 1960 only 61 per cent of its population was of working age, compared to 70 per cent before the war. Engineers, technicians, physicians, teachers, lawyers, and skilled workers were all leaving in high numbers.

- Politically: the mass numbers leaving made the communist regime look unpopular. In the context of the Cold War, this was negative propaganda as the communist regime competed with the capitalist west.

As the effects of this emigration continued, the East German government saw no other way to prevent people from escaping to the west via Berlin than to close the border between East and West Berlin. At first barbed wire was used but on 13 August 1961 the first wall was built.

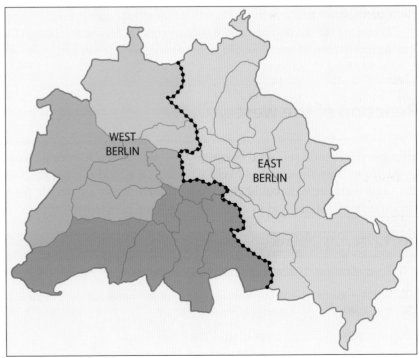

▲ **Fig. 6.7** Map of the Berlin Wall

Views of the wall in East Germany

SOURCE 11

An East German propaganda booklet dramatically described the serious nature of "the flight from the republic", published in 1955.

Those who let themselves be recruited serve West German Reaction and militarism, whether they know it or not. Is it not despicable when for the sake of a few alluring job offers or other false promises about a "guaranteed future" one leaves a country in which the seed for a new and more beautiful life is sprouting, and is already showing the first fruits, for the place that favors a new war and destruction?

SOURCE 12

From a 48-page pamphlet issued soon after the construction of the Berlin Wall by the SED (the East German ruling Marxist-Leninist party) in 1961.

On 13 August 1961, peace-loving Berliners won a battle for peace. The battle groups of Berlin's working class, along with comrades in the National People's Army and comrades of the German police of the capital of the GDR, put an end to subversive activity against the GDR by spies, slave-traders, and Revanchist organizations based in West Berlin.

SOURCE 13

From *What You Should Know About the Wall*, a brochure from the GDR defending the Berlin Wall. It was published in English for foreign distribution in 1962.

What did the wall prevent?

We no longer wanted to stand by passively and see how doctors, engineers, and skilled workers were induced by refined methods unworthy of the dignity of man to give up their secure existence in the GDR and work in West Germany or West Berlin. These and other manipulations cost the GDR annual losses amounting to 3.5 thousand million marks.

But we prevented something much more important with the wall—West Berlin's becoming the starting point for a military conflict. For the first time in German history the match which was to set fire to another war was extinguished before it had fulfilled its purpose.

▲ **Fig. 6.8** Nikita Khrushchev visiting the Berlin Wall

Reaction of the west

The reaction of the western allies was muted. Their own interests were not affected; they could still send troops to West Berlin and the wall made an attempt by invasion from the east less likely. Crucially, it was also great propaganda for the Cold War; the west could claim to be the side allowing people freedom while the communist states had to erect a wall to keep people in!

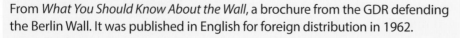

DISCUSSION

1. Study Sources 11 and 12. Which source can you trust more?

2. What reasons do the communist governments give for the construction of the wall?

3. Why was Source 13 published at the time?

4. "There is no value in using such sources to study an event as they are so obviously biased." How far do you agree with such a statement regarding Sources 11 to 13?

What was the significance of "Solidarity" in Poland for the decline of Soviet influence in eastern Europe?

In July 1980, the Polish government was facing an economic crisis. Short of money, it was forced to raise the price of goods while at the same time imposing a limit on any rises in wages. Ordinary people faced extreme poverty. This was too much for many of Poland's workers and strikes spread almost at once across the country. From these strikes developed a movement of workers which is seen by some as being part of the downfall of the control of the Soviet Union.

What happened?

On 14 August 1980, workers at the Lenin Shipyard in Gdansk went on strike, angry at the recently announced price rises and the dismissal of several workers who had complained about poor conditions. The strikers were led by Lech Walesa, an electrician. They demanded the right to form a trade union. The strike lasted a week before Communist Party negotiators arrived to begin talks with the strike committee. Despite the best attempts of the Communist government to isolate the strikers by cutting the telephone lines and censoring news reports, the workers received support from across the country. By the time the negotiations began the workers had a list of 21 demands.

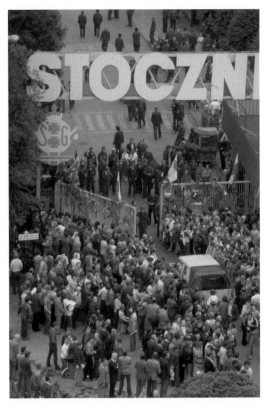

▲ **Fig. 6.9** Strike in the Lenin Shipyard in Gdansk, 1980

Some of the demands made by the strikers   ⓘ

1. Acceptance of free trade unions independent of the Communist Party and of enterprises.

2. A guarantee of the right to strike and of the security of strikers and those aiding them.

5. Availability to the mass media of information about the formation of the Inter-factory Strike Committee and publication of its demands.

8. An increase in the base pay of each worker by 2,000 zlotys a month as compensation for the recent rise in prices.

10. A full supply of food products for the domestic market, with exports limited to surpluses.

12. The selection of management personnel on the basis of qualifications, not party membership. Privileges of the secret police are to be eliminated.

19. A decrease in the waiting period for apartments.

21. A day of rest on Saturday.

On 31 August an agreement was signed meeting some of the demands. Crucially it gave workers the right to form unions independent from government control. Two weeks later a nationwide independent trade union called "Solidarity" was established. On 13 December 1981 the government declared a "state of war" and suspended Solidarity.

SOURCE 14

Radek Sikorski, a former deputy foreign and defense minister of post-communist Poland, was a high school student at the time of the strikes. He recalled the events in 2005.

"[There was] tremendous hope and a kind of electricity between people. You know, it's said that we Poles become a nation once a generation, millions of people felt that they wanted the same thing, which was free trade unions to represent them against the [Communist] Party."

QUICK QUESTION 4

Read Source 14. What reason does this give for Solidarity's success?

How did Solidarity succeed where others had failed?

Why did the Polish government agree to the demands of its workers while protests in other Soviet-controlled countries had failed?

- Organisation: the movement had a committee, spokespeople, and even a newspaper, the *Solidarnosc*. Printed on the shipyard printing press, it enabled the trade union to spread its message.

- Demands: Solidarity's 21 demands were national issues, not just local ones. By doing this the trade union secured the support from a range of the population and affected the most important industries in the country.

- Methods: the movement was careful never to use violence for fear of encouraging harsh punishments from the government.

- Support: between 1980 and 1981, 10 million people from all aspects of Polish life—students, workers, intellectuals—joined the trade union. Some 80 per cent of Poland's workforce were members.

The government, having allowed the reforms to exist, now sensed that public mood had calmed and took action to reassert control. The newly elected Prime Minister of Poland, Wojciech Jaruzelski, invited Walesa to meet to discuss his role in the new government. These discussions were a cover up though, as Jaruzelski had no intention of working with Walesa. Instead on 13 December, claiming to have recordings of Solidarity leaders planning a coup, Jaruzelski proclaimed martial law and Solidarity was outlawed. The military arrested most of Solidarity's leaders, including Walesa. It appeared that the move towards reform in Poland was over.

▲ **Fig. 6.10** A cartoon from a British newspaper dated 5 December 1980; the caption reads "Excuse me sir, is this lady bothering you?"

QUICK QUESTION 5

What do you think the message of the cartoon in Figure 6.10 is?

The return of Solidarity

In 1985 Mikhail Gorbachev became the leader of the Soviet Union. Faced with an outdated empire, he introduced a series of reforms aimed at changing the worsening economic situation across the eastern bloc. These reforms included the release of hundreds of political prisoners connected with Solidarity.

However, Gorbachev's reforms did not improve Poland's economic situation. By 1988, Poland's economy was worse than ever. Just as in 1980, strikes swept the country after food costs were increased by 40 per cent. As before, the government negotiated with Solidarity and met with Walesa to find a way to end the strikes.

On 17 April 1989, Solidarity was again legalised and the union was allowed to field candidates in upcoming elections. The union won every seat it contested in the parliament. The Communist candidate for Prime Minister failed to gather enough support to form a government, so Tadeusz Mazowiecki, a member of Solidarity, was elected as Prime Minister of Poland. Mazowiecki became the first non-Communist Prime Minister in Poland since 1945, and the first anywhere in eastern Europe for 40 years. Under Mazowiecki a Solidarity-led government was formed, and only Jaruzelski remained of the old regime.

▲ **Fig. 6.11** A Solidarity election poster from 1989, using red and white to symbolise the national colours of Poland

SOURCE 15

From a Polish website promoting Polish tourism and culture published in 2012.

The Solidarity movement received international attention, spreading anti-communist ideas and inspiring political action throughout the rest of the Communist Bloc, and its influence in the eventual fall of communism in Central and Eastern Europe cannot be understated or dismissed.

DISCUSSION

1. Read Source 15. "This source will clearly be biased towards promoting Poland, and is therefore no use to a historian studying the Solidarity movement." How true is this statement?

2. Study Figure 6.11. What is the purpose of this poster?

Mikhail Gorbachev

Pre-political career

Born into a peasant family and worked on a collective farm in his youth. Trained as a lawyer before joining the Communist Party.

Political career

Became general secretary of the Communist Party after a rapid rise through the ranks. Was seen by the West as a more moderate, younger leader.

Character and outlook

A realist, he knew that the problems facing Russia internally meant that keeping control of eastern Europe against its wishes would be too difficult.

How far was Gorbachev personally responsible for the collapse of Soviet control over eastern Europe?

Changes in eastern Europe	Date	Changes in Russia
	1985	Mikhail Gorbachev becomes leader of the Soviet Union.
	1986	President Reagan and Gorbachev resolve to remove all nuclear missiles from Europe.
	1989	
	January	Soviet troops withdraw from Afghanistan.
Poland becomes independent.	**June**	
Hungary becomes independent.	**September**	
Berlin Wall is removed and East Germany allows free movement.	**November**	
Communist governments fall in Czechoslovakia, Bulgaria, and Romania.	**December**	
	1990	
Lithuania becomes independent.	**March**	
	May	Boris Yeltsin elected as President of Russia.
Germany reunited.	**October**	
	1991	
	May	End of the Soviet Union.

▲ Table 6.2

When Lithuania became independent in 1990 the Soviet Union's control over eastern Europe was nearly over. Forty-five years of communism ended as for the first time countries elected their own democratic governments. Why did this collapse take place?

The role of Gorbachev

When Mikhail Gorbachev was elected ruler of the Soviet Union, he set about reforming the country. Realising the need for change, he set about driving the Soviet Union forwards. His major changes included attempting to modernise the Soviet Union's economy as well as attempting to tackle corruption and alcoholism.

There were two key policies: glasnost and perestroika.

Glasnost

This was the name given to the social and political reforms that Gorbachev introduced. These included more freedom for the media, allowing news to be transmitted of government corruption and criticism of government officials.

The aim of glasnost was to introduce an "openness" to society in the Soviet Union, allowing more people to be involved in the political process through freedom of expression. Gorbachev tried to encourage this by revealing parts of Russia's past that had previously been hidden, such as details about the more brutal parts of Stalin's rule.

QUICK QUESTION 6

To what extent are the policies of Perestroika and Glasnost communist?

Perestroika

The other policy was known as perestroika, meaning "restructuring". This led to a series of economic, political, and cultural reforms that aimed to make the Soviet economy a more modern and efficient system. This included:

- encouraging the private ownership of Soviet industry and agriculture
- reducing state control over imports and exports
- allowing trade with non-eastern bloc countries
- allowing foreign investments in Russian businesses
- an increase in the production and trade in consumer goods.

Actions in eastern Europe

Gorbachev's policies of promoting "openness" through glasnost applied not only within Russia; he realised that eastern Europe must be allowed to choose its own destiny. Gorbachev made it clear he would not stand in the way of attempts at democracy in Warsaw Pact countries, and that, unlike in the past, troops would not be used to keep countries tied to the Soviet Union.

There were three key reasons for this change.

- Gorbachev was a reformer. He believed the Soviet Union was out of date in controlling others and that people should be allowed a say in who ruled them.
- Economically, the union was crumbling. Food shortages were so common that by the end of the 1980s the wartime system of food cards had been reintroduced.
- Gorbachev saw his main priority as reforming Russia. To do this he couldn't be focused on maintaining control of eastern Europe. The Soviet Union could no longer afford to maintain the military presence needed to control its European satellite states.

The role of other countries

The independence movement in some eastern European countries was growing. Gradually people pressure forced the changes through.

- Poland: the Solidarity movement had shown that a unified and largely peaceful movement which wanted reform could succeed.
- Hungary: parliament adopted a "democracy package", which included trade union rights, personal freedoms, a less restricted press, more voting rights, and an acknowledgment that the uprising of 1956 was a popular movement, not a foreign insurgency.

- East Germany: mass emigration through newly opened borders raised the hope of change. When the government there moved to repress a popular movement, a visit by Gorbachev inspired the movement as he urged the Communist Party there to reform. One night by accident, an official declared an end to the restrictions on travel. With this crowds gathered and the Berlin Wall was torn down. Germany unified a year later.

- Romania: leader Nicolae Ceauşescu had stated he intended to see off any anti-communist protestors, but while he was out of the country his people began to protest. Ceauşescu ordered the protestors to be fired upon. The military refused and Ceauşescu was forced to flee. Free democratic elections were held in 1990.

▲ **Fig. 6.12** The day after freedom of movement was allowed in Germany, border guards on the wall at the Brandenburg Gate watch people move freely from east to west, 10 November 1989

Between the spring of 1989 and the spring of 1991 every communist or former communist eastern European country held democratic parliamentary elections for the first time in years. Soviet Union control was over.

External factors

It wasn't just the actions of Gorbachev though that lead to the collapse of Soviet control; there were also wider issues.

The war in Afghanistan

In what was originally an attempt to take control of the country, the Afghan militia, the Mujahideen, managed to engage the Soviets in what became a guerrilla-style war in 1979. The war badly overstretched the Soviets' economy and demoralised their military. The war led to widespread condemnation by other countries and pressure to withdraw.

▲ **Fig. 6.13** Ronald Reagan and Mikhail Gorbachev signing a peace agreement in Geneva, Switzerland in 1985

The role of the United States

The new ruler in Russia was not the only person who wanted change. President Ronald Reagan also sought to encourage an end to the Cold War. Together, Reagan and Gorbachev signed treaties to limit nuclear weapons and also encouraged people-led movements in eastern Europe. Reagan had another impact as well: by increasing military spending by a third in the United States the Soviet Union felt they could not respond in the "arms race". This meant the Soviets needed to find another way of securing peace, this time through diplomacy.

DISCUSSION

How far do you agree with the statement "it was people power that led to the fall of the Soviet Union"?

Ronald Reagan

Pre-political career

After university Reagan had been a famous actor in films and television.

Political career

He was elected president in 1980 and his time in office was marked by foreign policy in connection with the Soviet Union, Iran, and Libya.

Character and outlook

Reagan saw the Soviet Union as the "evil Empire" and wanted to see its demise. Away from politics Reagan was known to be humorous and is fondly remembered.

Who was responsible for the collapse of Soviet power?

To see Gorbachev as solely responsible is perhaps too simplistic. What Gorbachev did do was to create a climate in which people could make changes for themselves. He allowed the freedoms and the rights in Russia first, then elsewhere. The rest was done by popular movements, who for the first time were unshackled to allow them to seize power.

KEY POINTS

▶ The attempted uprising in Hungary in 1956.

▶ The attempted uprising in Czecholoslovakia in 1968.

▶ Why the Berlin Wall was built in 1961.

▶ The significance of the "Solidarity" movement in Poland.

▶ The role of Gorbachev and the collapse of Soviet control over eastern Europe.

Revision tips

- Be able to explain the causes of the uprisings in Hungary and Czechoslovakia. Remember though that after the war the Soviet Union was using these countries' resources to rebuild the Soviet Union.

- Remember the Berlin Wall still allowed for access to West Berlin from West Germany, but did not allow free movement for people from the east or into East Berlin.

- Be aware that the Solidarity movement fails initially — it is not until Gorbachev comes to power and changes are made that it finally establishes power.

- Despite Gorbachev's reforms and realistic approach, he was still a Communist. He did though allow eastern Europe to decide its own position in the Warsaw Pact. Make sure you can give clear examples of which countries leave Soviet Union control.

Review questions

1. How had the Soviet Union gained control of eastern Europe?

2. What was the Warsaw Pact?

3. Why didn't the United Nations or any western country intervene to support Hungary?

4. Why were the Russians so against the idea of reforms in Hungary?

5. What was the Prague Spring?

6. What caused the demand for change in Czechoslovakia?

7. Why were people leaving East Berlin up to 1961?

8. Why did the west do nothing about the Berlin Wall?

9. Why did the Solidarity movement succeed where the uprisings in Hungary and Czechoslovakia failed?

10. Explain Gorbachev's attitude to eastern Europe.

11. Where was the Soviet Union fighting a war during the 1980s? Why was this important to its loss of power in eastern Europe?

7 Why did events in the Gulf matter, c. 1970–2000?

Introduction

The states located around the Persian Gulf—Iran, Iraq, Kuwait, Saudi Arabia, Bahrain, Qatar, United Arab Emirates and Oman—collectively housed approximately one half of the world's known oil reserves during the last third of the twentieth century. These countries effectively controlled the economic well-being of the industrialised nations for whom oil was such a vital commodity for industry, transport and domestic use. It was therefore very much in the interests of the developed countries to pursue diplomatic and foreign policies that promoted peace and stability in this part of the Middle East. That meant conditions favourable to trade and prosperity. In turn, this guaranteed the standard of living for the populations of America and western Europe, Japan, South Africa and elsewhere. The events of the Gulf were therefore of prime concern to the rest of the world because the rest of the world depended upon steady supplies of oil at stable prices. Yet throughout this period the Gulf region was one of instability and volatility with frequent regime changes, revolts, and wars. When such events affected the production or distribution of oil there was economic and usually political crisis in the oil-consuming countries.

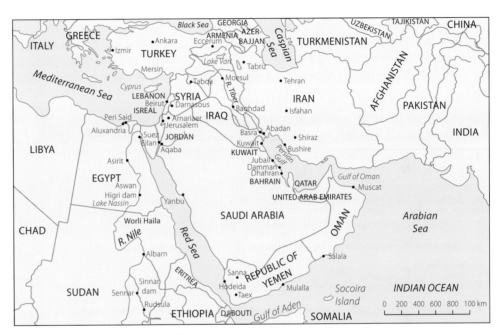

▲ **Fig. 7.1** Iraq, Iran and the Middle East

The aims of this chapter are to:

- Examine Saddam Hussein's rise to power in Iraq.

- Identify the key features of Saddam Hussein's dictatorship up to 2000 together with the consequences of his rule for different groups in Iraq.

- Look at the reasons for the revolution in Iran in 1979 including the nature of the Shah's rule.

- Consider the causes and consequences of the Iran–Iraq war, 1980–8, and examine the reasons for western involvement in the war.

- Look at the causes, course and consequences of the First Gulf War, 1990–1.

Why was Saddam Hussein able to come to power in Iraq?

Childhood and early years

At first sight it would appear that Saddam Hussein enjoyed few advantages of birth or upbringing. He was born on 28 April 1937 in Al-Ouja, a small village 13 kilometres south of Tikrit, on the western banks of the Tigris River, in north-central Iraq. His father was a poor, landless peasant who probably died before he was born while his mother, Sabha, made a living as a fortune teller. Sabha married again to Hassan al-Ibrahim who worked as a caretaker at a school in Tikrit. Saddam's stepfather was a violent bully who repeatedly humiliated his stepson and prevented him from attending school, sending him instead on petty criminal errands. One result of this was that Saddam did not begin to learn to read and write until he was 10 years old. He also spent his early years as a social outcast and used to carry an iron bar with which to protect himself against attacks.

How was Iraq governed during the twentieth century?

- Before the First World War Iraq was part of the Ottoman Empire.
- From 1919–32 Iraq was administered by Britain as a League of Nations mandate.
- From 1921 the British imposed the Hashemite monarchy on Iraq.
- In 1932 Iraq became an independent kingdom.
- The Hashemite monarchy was overthrown by General Abdul Karim Qassem in July 1958.
- Qassem was deposed by the Baath Party and military officers in February 1963.
- In November 1963 the Baath Party was ousted from power after fighting between factions within the party.
- In July 1968 President Arif was overthrown by the Baath Party and certain members of the previous regime. Ahmad Hassan al-Bakr became President.
- Saddam Hussein became President in July 1979.

SOURCE 1

From an interview given by Saddam Hussein to ABC TV about his childhood in June 1990.

Life was very difficult in Iraq. Very few people wore shoes and in many cases they only wore them on special occasions. Some peasants would not put their shoes on until they had reached their destination so that they would look smart.

TASKS

1. How useful is Source 1 as evidence of the conditions in which Saddam Hussein grew up? Explain your answer using details of the source and your own knowledge.

The influence of Khairallah Tulfah

Had it not been for Sabha's brother, Khairallah Tulfah, Saddam may have spent his life as an unknown Iraqi peasant. Khairallah, who was effectively to become Saddam's foster father, was originally an army officer in Tikrit who had been imprisoned in 1941 for joining an attempt to drive the British out of Iraq. When he was released from jail in 1947 Saddam went to live in his household. Khairallah instilled in the young Saddam an appreciation of **Arab nationalism** and a consequent hatred of the Hashemite monarchy that ruled Iraq under the watchful eye of the British. Khairallah also ensured that Saddam acquired some primary education at a local school. In 1955, at the age of 18, Saddam moved with his uncle to Baghdad where he enrolled at Karkh High School with the aim of entering the Baghdad Military Academy. It was a crushing blow to Saddam when he failed the entrance exam in 1957.

Arab nationalism

Arab nationalists opposed western interference in Arab affairs and were also in favour of a politically united Arab world. They believed that since all Arabs were linked by ties of language, religion, culture, and history there should be a single Arab nation.

From an anecdote about Saddam Hussein's conduct at school provided by one of his contemporaries.

My headmaster told me that he wanted to expel Saddam from school. When Saddam heard about this decision, he came to his headmaster's room and threatened him with death. He said: "I will kill you if you do not withdraw your threat against me to expel me from the school."

An opinion on Saddam Hussein expressed by Said Aburish, a Palestinian writer.

Saddam was an exceptionally intelligent child, a fast learner who was calculating and methodical from the start.

From a biography of Saddam Hussein written by a British author and published in 2007.

By his late teens Saddam had grown into an impressive physical specimen. At six foot two inches tall, he was unusually tall for an Arab, and had a muscular build to go with it. He spoke with a thick, peasant accent and his speech was littered with Tikrit colloquialisms, much to the amusement of the more sophisticated Baghdadis with whom he was beginning to associate.

TASKS

2. Does Source 3 make you surprised by what is said in Source 2? Explain your answer using the details of the sources and your own knowledge.

3. How far do Sources 1 to 4 provide convincing evidence that Saddam Hussein was able to rise above the disadvantages of his poverty-stricken childhood? Use the sources to explain your answer.

Early political activity

In 1957, inspired by the political views of his uncle, Saddam joined the Baath Party. This soon involved him in a variety of violent anti-government activities such as organising thugs to beat up political opponents on the streets of Baghdad. In October 1958 Saddam demonstrated his loyalty to Khairallah by carrying out an assassination of a local government official in Tikrit who had informed against him. Saddam had already established credentials as a ruthless operator and man of action. It was for these reasons that he was selected by the Baath Party to participate in an attempt to assassinate Iraq's ruler, General Abdul Karim Qassem. The attempt in October 1959 failed and Saddam was wounded but the event marked his emergence into the limelight as one of Iraq's most wanted men.

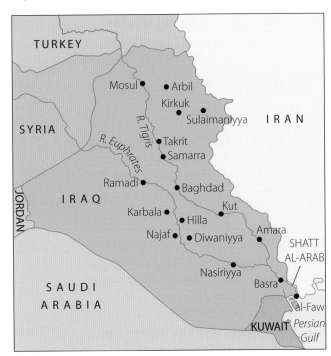

▲ **Fig. 7.2** Main towns in Iraq

Saddam was now obliged to go into exile. After three months in Damascus he left for Cairo where he spent the next three years. Much of the time was spent extending his education. In 1961, at the age of 24, he graduated from

What did the Baath Party stand for?

- The Baath Party was established in Syria during the early 1940s but soon had branches in the other Arab states.

- Its motto was "Unity, Liberation and Socialism". "Unity" implied consolidation of the Arab states into one Arab nation. "Liberation" meant freedom from non-Arab control and interference. "Socialism" required attention to the living conditions of the Arab people.

- The Baath Party was against intervention in the Middle East by the colonial powers. It was strongly against the existence of the state of Israel.

- There was often friction between the Baath Party in Syria and Iraq as to which country should lead the Arab world.

high school in Cairo and the following year enrolled for a law degree at the city's university. Legal studies were cut short, however, by the opportunity to return to Iraq following the overthrow and death of Qassem in February 1963. Qassem was replaced by a government consisting of army officers and the Baath Party. Saddam was given a minor position at the Central Farmer's Office with the task of finding ways to improve the position of the peasantry.

Building up a power base

From this unpromising position Saddam began making political alliances and friendships that would transform his position within the Baath Party. The new Prime Minister, Ahmad Hasan al-Bakr, was both from Tikrit and a kinsman, the cousin of Khairallah Tulfah. Saddam lost no time in joining his faction and proving he was indispensable. Yet the Baathists were soon ousted from power as President Abdul Salam Arif lost patience with the infighting that had broken out in the party. Paradoxically these events played into Saddam's hands, as the extremist wings of the Baath Party had become discredited whereas Bakr's position as leader of the moderates had strengthened. As Bakr's star rose within the Baath Party so did that of Saddam who won the former's trust and confidence. In February 1964 Saddam was rewarded for his loyalty by becoming a member of the **Regional Command**.

Saddam appreciated that in the violent world of Iraqi politics the key to acquiring power and staying there was armed force. As a prominent Baath Party politician Saddam now aimed to acquire responsibility for security affairs and he was soon put in charge of the Party's military organisation. He immediately began plotting a coup against President Arif scheduled for September 1964. Unfortunately for Saddam the conspiracy plans were uncovered and he spent two years in jail before escaping in July 1966.

The July Revolution 1968

After his escape Saddam concentrated on restructuring the party's organisation in Iraq, completing the formation of the security apparatus, establishing a new military force and expanding the network of branches throughout the country. But Saddam knew that these agencies were not powerful enough to bring down the Arif regime on their own. Consequently the party made contact with a group of senior army officers who held key positions within the government but were sympathetic to the Baath cause. Saddam was particularly persuasive at an emergency meeting of the Regional Command in promoting this temporary arrangement. He argued that the officers could be liquidated either during or after the revolution. The coup was bloodless, President Arif was flown to London and Bakr became President. Saddam now applied his organisational and operational skills to ensure that two of the colonels were sent abroad never to return. His reward for this work was to be made Deputy Chairman of the **Revolutionary Command Council** (RCC). After President Bakr, Saddam Hussein was now the most important person in government circles.

The road to the Presidency

It took Saddam 11 years to convert his position as President Bakr's right-hand man into the presidency itself. As early as 1972 Saddam was probably

▲ **Fig. 7.3** The death of President Qassem

QUICK QUESTION 1

What does Figure 7.3 tell you about the nature of Iraqi politics in the early 1960s?

Regional Command

The Regional Command was the supreme decision-making body of the Baath Party within Iraq.

Revolutionary Command Council

The RCC was set up immediately after the 1968 revolution to become the most important decision-making body in Iraq.

the most influential man in the government, as the President and deputy acted more as equals. Saddam moved with caution and calculation, anxious to avoid being singled out as a man with presidential ambitions. That way he was able to consolidate his political relationship with Bakr. The key to Saddam's success lay partly with the way he outwitted, outmanoeuvred and often eliminated his rivals or men who might pose a threat to his position. Having control of the party's security apparatus he was in an ideal position to uncover or invent plots and conspiracies. Saddam's targets included both civilian politicians and high-ranking military personnel. Saddam also used his influence to ensure that persons friendly to himself were appointed to the Revolutionary Command Council. During this process Saddam showed that he was the master of political cunning, always keeping a low profile and always making sure that the President's dignity remained intact.

By the early 1970s Saddam had shown that he was an extremely adept politician, both with regard to foreign and domestic issues. He was the prime mover in a series of diplomatic initiatives that led to a Treaty of Friendship and Cooperation with the Soviet Union, signed in April 1972, so ensuring that Iraq had a superpower ally. He strongly supported the nationalisation of Iraq's oil industry and directed a significant portion of the resulting new wealth towards projects that improved the lives of ordinary Iraqis such as schools, hospitals and improved transport facilities.

As President Bakr grew older and suffered from increasing health problems Saddam became the ruler of Iraq in all but name. In 1979, amid circumstances that that almost certainly involved threats and bullying, Bakr was encouraged to resign in favour of Saddam who achieved the presidency in a final bloodless move. At the age of 42 Saddam Hussein had become the unquestioned leader of Iraq.

▲ **Fig. 7.4** Saddam Hussein with President Bakr, November 1978

DISCUSSION

Which of the following reasons was the most important for Saddam Hussein coming to power?

a. Family connections

b. Saddam's political skills

c. The violent and unstable politics of Iraq

d. Saddam's ruthlessness

QUICK QUESTION 2

What does Figure 7.4 reveal about the relationship of Saddam Hussein and President Bakr?

What was the nature of Saddam Hussein's rule in Iraq?

Saddam Hussein ruled as a dictator after coming to power in 1979. Not only was he President of Iraq but his positions included those of Chairman of the Revolutionary Command Council (RCC), Prime Minister and Commander-in-Chief of the Armed Forces. He consciously modelled his regime on that of his political hero Joseph Stalin, who governed Soviet Russia between 1928 and 1953. Saddam was a keen reader of Stalin biographies and carefully studied his techniques of government. There are striking similarities between many aspects of the two men.

▲ **Fig. 7.5** Poster of Saddam Hussein

Purges and terror

Once Saddam had displaced Bakr from the Presidency, he immediately set out to deal with those who questioned the transition of power.

An obvious target was Mashhadi, the RCC's Secretary-General, who had demanded a vote on the validity of the process. Mashhadi was relieved of his duties and accused of being part of a plot to overthrow the Baathist regime. On 22 July 1979 Saddam met with a conference of senior Baath Party members. Mashhadi was brought to this meeting where he delivered a detailed but fabricated confession of his crimes against the state; this was followed by the naming of 66 alleged co-conspirators who were then led out of the hall one by one. The accused included Adnan Hussein al-Hamdani, a former close friend of Saddam's, who had only just been appointed Deputy Prime Minister and Head of the President's Office. A special court was set up to try the 66 accused of whom 55 were found guilty. Twenty-two were sentenced to death and 33 received prison sentences.

The purges and terror continued beyond this high-profile event as Saddam sought to establish his unquestioned mastery over the Baath Party and army. Hundreds of party members and military officers were purged, many of whom were executed. False accusations, arrests, torture and summary trials followed by lengthy prison sentences or executions became a regular feature of Saddam's rule by terror.

Waging war on his own people

One of Saddam's aims after becoming president was to unify the state of Iraq. This was a major challenge since the Kurds (20 per cent of the population) in the oil-rich north of the country wanted independence while the Shiites (60 per cent of the population) in the central and southern parts of the country were generally hostile to the Sunni-dominated regime. Previous governments had dealt with this problem using a mixture of diplomacy and force. These were Saddam's tactics too, except he was also prepared to use methods of exceptional brutality and ruthlessness.

His campaigns against the Kurds were at their most ferocious between 1987 and 1988 and again in 1991. During these merciless engagements Saddam destroyed half of Kurdistan's villages and towns, killed thousands of Kurds using mustard gas and cyanide, and displaced more than a million people. Many fled to Iran or Turkey while others were housed in concentration camps located in the Iraqi desert. One of the most appalling attacks took place against the town of Halabja in March 1988. Iraqi planes spread poison gas over the area killing 5,000 men, women and children while inflicting injuries on another 10 000.

Saddam took action against the Shiites in 1991 with similar levels of brutality. After the outbreak of revolts which started in Basra and then spread to the holy cities of Najaf and Karbala, the Republican Guard stormed into the rebel strongholds carrying out arrests and summary executions. Civilians were roped to the front of tanks to act as human shields while women and children were shot on sight. In the same year the Marsh Arabs of south-east Iraq came under attack. Saddam was determined to construct a new waterway in the region which involved destroying the marshes and displacing a group of Arabs whose culture stretched back centuries. Some of the Marsh Arabs moved voluntarily, some were the victims of chemical weapon attacks while others starved to death once their food source had been destroyed. The population of Marsh Arabs dropped from 250 000 to approximately 30 000.

Personality cult

Saddam realised that his dictatorship was unlikely to survive in the long term if it was based upon fear, terror, and military campaigns. He needed to cultivate popularity and make the Iraqi people love and adore him. With this in mind he set about projecting an image of himself as an all-powerful, father-style leader of the nation.

A permanent exhibition about Saddam was established in Baghdad, his life story regularly featured in newspapers and magazines, and an autobiographical film about his early life, "The Long Days," was produced by the Iraqi Ministry of Information. The press, radio and television made constant attempts to glorify Saddam's achievements while picture portraits of the Iraqi leader adorned street corners and decorated party and government offices. By the early 1980s some 200 songs had been written in praise of Saddam Hussein and the evening television news would begin with a "Saddam song".

One of Saddam's favourite routines was to visit ordinary Iraqi homes and villages in disguise in order to discover what people were thinking of him and his policies. His hosts would pretend not to recognise their famous visitor and expressed delight and surprise when the President finally revealed his true identity. In order to appear to attend as many functions and official engagements as possible Saddam resorted to the practice of using doubles or lookalikes; these men were given months of training during which they studied videos of Saddam's public appearances.

Images of Saddam sprang up everywhere and streets and squares were named after him. Statues, murals and paintings were commissioned to ensure that no Iraqis could remain in ignorance for long as to who was their leader.

▲ **Fig. 7.6** Mural of Saddam with shovel and wheelbarrow

QUICK QUESTION 3

What impression of Saddam Hussein is created by the images in Figures 7.6 and 7.7?

▲ **Fig. 7.7** Saddam with flying doves

Modernisation

With the nationalisation of the Iraqi oil industry in 1972 oil revenues dramatically increased from $476 million in 1968 to $26 billion in 1980. This led to a massive improvement in national finances, providing the resources to carry out an extensive modernisation programme of both the economy and social facilities and institutions. The new-found wealth was also used to fund wage rises, tax cuts, and subsidies for basic foodstuffs. Modernisation was a key way by which Saddam built up his support base among the Iraqi people.

Unfortunately, after the early 1980s social spending had to take second place to the demands of the military as Iraq became embroiled in war.

Extension of electrification	Electrification was extended throughout the country ensuring that even remote villages became connected to the grid. Poor families sometimes received gifts of televisions and refrigerators.
Heavy industry	Often using foreign technicians and experts, Saddam developed the country's heavy industry involving steel, petrochemicals, and coal. Massive new industrial complexes were constructed at al-Zubair and Basra.
Railroads and oil pipelines	Railroads were built as was a countrywide network of oil pipelines with terminals in Syria and Turkey.
Media	A new radio and television network was established which enabled government propaganda to reach an even wider audience.
Social improvements	There were major building programmes of schools, houses, and hospitals. School and university enrolment increased significantly and a major campaign was launched to end adult illiteracy. Hospital treatment was made free.

▲ **Fig. 7.8** Modernisation in Iraq

Military expansion

The same oil revenues that enabled Saddam to introduce a programme of modernisation also enabled him to convert Iraq into a major military power. The major supplier of conventional arms to Iraq was Soviet Russia followed by France, but arms imports also arrived from most of the major European states together with Yugoslavia and Brazil. With these contacts Saddam was able to purchase tanks, bombers, helicopters, transport aircraft, surface-to-air missiles, artillery, and electronic equipment. The army increased from 10 to 12 divisions.

Saddam also wished to build up an arsenal of non-conventional weapons—chemical, biological, and nuclear. By July 1979 he had constructed his first chemical warfare plant near Akashat. During the 1980s, with the help of various foreign companies, he was producing significant quantities of Distilled Mustard, a blister agent, together with Tabun and VX, both of which attack the human nervous system. The biological weapons industry increased in capacity and began producing agents such as anthrax, typhoid and cholera.

Saddam's nuclear weapons programme was less successful. As a preliminary step he purchased the Osiraq research reactor from France in 1976 but the Israelis destroyed it in a bombing raid in June 1981. Further attempts to develop a nuclear capacity were frustrated by Allied bombing raids during the Gulf War in 1990.

DISCUSSION

- Why would Saddam Hussein have wanted to convert Iraq into a major military power?

- Why would Israel have wanted to destroy Iraq's nuclear programme?

- Why would Saddam Hussein have wanted to build up a stockpile of chemical and biological weapons?

- Why do you think so many countries were willing to assist Iraq's military expansion programme?

Family member	Relationship to Saddam Hussein	Positions held
Khairallah Tulfah	Uncle and father-in-law	Mayor of Baghdad
Adnan Khairallah	First cousin	Member of RCC, Defence Minister
Hussein Kamil Majid	Second cousin and son-in-law	Minister of Industry and Military Industry
Hisham Hassan Majid	First cousin	Governor of Babil Province
Ali Hassan Majid	First cousin	Minister of Local Government, Defence Minister, Interior Minister, Head of Party Intelligence (Makhabarat)
Barzan Ibrahim	Half-brother	Head of Makhabarat, Ambassador to the United Nations
Wathban Ibrahim	Half-brother	Governor of Salah al-Din, Head of State Internal Security
Sibawi Ibrahim	Half-brother	Deputy Chief of Police, Head of Makhabarat
Izzal Ibrahim	His daughter was married to Saddam's son	Vice Chairman of the RCC
Uday Hussein	Eldest son	Head of Iraqi Olympic Committee, Head of Iraqi Soccer Federation

▲ **Fig. 7.9** Saddam Hussein's use of family relatives in the structure of Iraqi government

Totalitarianism

Saddam aspired to and ultimately achieved absolute power in Iraq. Ruling with a small group of trusted Baath Party associates and family relatives, he controlled virtually every aspect of life—social, economic, political and military.

- Young schoolchildren were introduced to Baath ideas and taught to worship their glorious leader. Similar brainwashing took place throughout the various Baath Party youth organisations.

- Censorship and a tightly controlled media meant that Iraqis were unlikely to hear or read any views critical of the Saddam regime. It was a capital offence to criticise government policy or join an opposition party.

- Special courts run by the President's office delivered verdicts of which Saddam would have approved.

- While the economy was a mixture of state owned and privately run enterprises, all production was geared to the needs of the state.

- Membership of the Baath Party was essential for a public career in the army and civil service or for admission to higher education.

SOURCE 5

From a biography of Saddam Hussein written by a British author and published in 2007.

Much was made in the Iraqi press of Saddam's devotion to his family, and his everyday involvement with his children. Iraqis learned about his hobbies, such as fishing and gardening. In everything he said and did Saddam presented himself as the role model for all Iraqi families.

SOURCE 6

From an article about Saddam Hussein published in the *Daily Telegraph* in January 2007.

Opponents were exterminated (one wavering minister was shot dead during a cabinet meeting). Those spared a firing squad were subjected to videos showing the execution of their friends. Among the forms of torture common in Baghdad's military prisons were the amputation of sexual organs, the hammering of nails into the body and the dissolving of limbs in vats of acid. Even his closest relations were not safe. In 1996 Saddam had two of his sons-in-law killed for defecting to Jordan, having lured them back to Iraq with a false pardon.

From a biography of Saddam Hussein written by an Israeli-born expert on the Middle East and published in 2002.

With one in seven Iraqis a Party member of one rank or another, the common definition of Iraq as a state of informers can hardly be considered an exaggeration …

Eavesdropping, spies and informers are a constant threat. A joke or derogatory comment about the President, the RCC, the Baath Party or the National Assembly can cost people their lives according to a state decree of November 1986 which prescribes the death penalty for the deliberate and public insult of these institutions.

DISCUSSION

For each discussion question, explain your answers using details of the sources and your knowledge.

1. Does Source 5 make you surprised by what is said in Source 6?
2. How far do Sources 6 and 7 provide a similar view of Saddam's rule by fear?
3. How does the view of Saddam in Sources 5 to 7 compare to the quick impression you decided upon based on Figures 7.6 and 7.7 (page 140)?

Why was there a revolution in Iran in 1979?

On 16 January 1979 Shah Muhammad Reza Pahlavi, more commonly known as the Shah of Iran, left his country never to return. The 53-year-old Pahlavi dynasty and the 2500-year-old monarchy had been swept away by a popular protest movement that led directly to the establishment of an Islamic republic under the leadership of Ayatollah Khomeini. The Shah had offended almost every sector of society and the last year of his rule was punctuated by marches, demonstrations, violent clashes between the protestors and the authorities, shootings, deaths and widespread strikes. A mass rally held in Tehran on 11 December 1978 involving a crowd of more than two million people demanded "The Shah Must Go". Although the fate of the Iranian monarchy was decided between 1977 and 1979, the pressures that led to the final events had been building up during the last quarter of a century.

Date	Details of event
9 January	Protest in holy city of Qom against an official newspaper editorial denouncing Khomeini. Five fatalities.
18 February	Violent clashes between protestors and authorities in Tabriz involving government use of tanks and helicopter gunships to regain control. Thirteen fatalities.
19 August	The Cinema Rex in Abadan was burnt down killing more than 400 women and children. Both SAVAK and militant Islamists were suspected of the arson.
8 September	Protest against the Shah's rule in Jaleh Square in Tehran, despite the introduction of marital law. When the crowd refused to disperse troops opened fire killing 84 people. This event became known as Black Friday.
11 December	More than two million people went to Shahyad Square in Tehran. Their demands included the establishment of an Islamic Republic, the return of Khomeini and the overthrow of the Shah. The scale of the protest exposed the inability of the government to enforce law and order.

▲ **Fig. 7.10** Events of 1978

Opposition to foreign influence

The Shah's reign had begun in 1941 following the abdication of his father Reza Khan. While he controlled the army, for the first 10 years of his reign Muhammad Reza ruled as a constitutional monarch but then a crisis arose in 1951.

The Prime Minister, Mohammad Mussadeq, nationalised Iran's oil industry thereby upsetting the British who controlled Iran's oil through the Anglo-Iranian Oil Company. Mussadeq was popular with the Iranian people because he insisted upon Iranian independence from foreign domination. The Shah regarded him as a threat because he argued in favour of more limited powers for the monarchy. With the help of the CIA and MI6, the Shah overthrew Mussadeq in a military coup during August 1953.

This coup, which had no popular support, meant that after 1953 the rule of the Shah would be associated with the British and the Americans whose prime interest in assisting the Shah had been to safeguard oil supplies to the west—Iran possessed the third largest oil reserves in the world. The resentment of the Iranian people over this event was to fester and grow during the next two decades.

The influence of the United States became more apparent when the Shah began importing large quantities of American foodstuffs, including cattle and poultry, which undercut the efforts of local farmers. The Shah also damaged the interests of the bazaar merchants when he tried to introduce American-style shopping malls.

Dissatisfaction with the Shah's modernisation programme

Modernisation of Iran's transport network, industry, and education system had begun during the 1920s under Reza Khan. Shah Muhammad Reza continued these plans and launched what became known as a "White Revolution" after 1963. The main features of this programme were land reform, industrial expansion and health and educational reforms. Yet many of the reforms were soon regarded as inadequate or simply backfired. Land reform, for example, was designed to modernise Iran's rural areas by redistributing land among the peasantry. In fact, most peasants ended up with holdings only just sufficient to support their families and so were no better off than landless labourers. Most villages still lacked piped water, electricity, roads and other basic services.

The health reforms increased the number of doctors, nurses, and hospital beds, but in the mid-1970s Iran still had the one of the worst infant mortality rates and doctor–patient ratios in the Middle East. Similarly the expansion of education did not significantly reduce the high levels of adult illiteracy or alter the low proportion of people in higher education.

By the late 1970s the distribution of income in Iran was more unequal than it had been 20 years earlier, with the richest 10 per cent accounting for 37.9 per cent of expenditure compared to 1.3 percent for the poorest 10 per cent. This inequality was particularly obvious in Tehran where the rich lived in luxurious palaces while the poor were housed in shanty town hovels. A member of the royal family was rumoured to have asked why, if people did not like being stuck in traffic jams, they didn't buy helicopters. The insensitivity of the ruling regime was also underlined by instances of conspicuous consumption such as the Shah's multimillion-dollar coronation in October 1967 and the Shahyad Monument built to remind everyone of the achievements of modern Iran under the Pahlavi dynasty.

DISCUSSION

In what ways might the unequal distribution of wealth have affected:

- Iran's economy
- Iran's political stability?

Those opposed to the Shah's rule compared the scale of urban poverty and unemployment with the vast sums spent on military expansion. By 1975 Iran had the largest navy in the Persian Gulf, the largest air force in western Asia and the fifth largest army in the world. This was funded by oil revenues that had increased from $34 million in 1954–5 to $20 billion in 1975–6. Iran was unquestionably a wealthy country but the majority of the people saw very modest, if any, improvements to their standards of living.

Resentment at autocratic and repressive government

After 1953, the Shah made sure that the cabinet and parliament were packed with individuals agreeable to himself. Prime ministers were usually hand-picked personal favourites and ministers were mostly young, western educated, and prepared to accept the Shah's leadership. Under such a system the main political parties—Melliyun, Iran Novin and Mardom—became a sham and were sometimes referred to as the "yes" and "yes, sir" or "yes, of course" parties. Nevertheless, in March 1975, the Shah decided to establish a one-party state declaring the existence of a new Resurgence Party. It immediately began making new enemies for the Shah's regime by waging an anti-profiteering campaign in the bazaars and attacking the clerical establishment. One of the more insensitive acts of the new party was to introduce a new imperial calendar which supplanted the Muslim calendar. Iran changed overnight from the Muslim year 1355 to the imperial year 2535.

Opposition to the Shah's rule was rooted out by SAVAK: a new intelligence service or secret police. Established in 1957 with the help of the FBI and the Israeli Mossad, it expanded into an organisation of 5,000 agents and an unknown number of informers. Its task was to act as the Shah's eyes and ears, to impose censorship, and to screen government and university appointments. SAVAK became known for its brutal tactics, including torture, forced confessions, and summary execution.

Despite the ever-widening hatred for his regime, the Shah authorised a relaxation of police controls in 1977. This was largely a response to increasing international condemnation of human rights violations in Iran. He also agreed to release a number of political prisoners, allow the Red Cross into prisons, and introduce measures to ensure a fair trial in the courts. These concessions gave a massive boost to opposition groups who immediately became more evident and vocal, issuing newsletters, publishing manifestoes, and organising new protest. The Shah had obviously hoped that a tactical retreat would save the monarchy. Instead it unleashed an unstoppable wave of mass protest.

The leadership of Ayatollah Khomeini

By the mid-1970s there was widespread political and popular opposition to the Shah. Socialists and nationalists, Islamic and Marxist groups had very different agendas and ideologies but shared one common objective: the overthrow of the Pahlavian monarchy. The Shah had lost the support of clerics, merchants, unemployed migrants from rural areas, school-leavers who could not gain places at university, and university graduates who could not find employment. This opposition needed an inspirational leader to provide a rallying cry that would unite the disparate groups. Ayatollah Khomeini fulfilled this role.

Although a leading Muslim cleric and scholar, Khomeini was also a keen political activist who had been forced into exile in 1964 for undermining

▲ **Fig. 7.11** Demonstrators attending a rally around Shahyad Square during the Iranian Revolution

DISCUSSION

Does the Shah bring about his own downfall by relaxing the restrictions on his people?

the Shah with his preaching and writing. He had been particularly critical of the Shah's readiness to submit to foreign influences. Most of Khomeini's exile was spent in the Iraqi city of Najaf. He sent tapes of his political message across the border into Iran. Ordinary Iranians were able to listen to Khomeini's simple, clear articulation of their grievances and hopes for the future. Khomeini avoided any mention of his desire to establish an Islamic government. He concentrated on issues that would gain most support from his audience. He fiercely denounced the Shah for such offences as supporting Israel against the Muslim world, wasting resources on military expansion, neglecting problems in rural villages, and failing to combat crime and alcoholism. He also coined catch-phrases and sound bites that could be used as slogans.

Khomeini spent the final months of his exile in France, directing the final stages of the revolt against the Shah. He made it clear that he would not return to Iran until the Shah had left. On 1 February, two weeks after the Shah departed, Khomeini landed in Tehran in an Air France jet from Paris. The welcoming crowds numbered more than three million. Over the next 10 days the end of the Pahlavian dynasty was confirmed as the army declared its neutrality, street fighting removed any remaining defenders of the old regime, and thousands of civilians celebrated.

Some of Khomeini's slogans
"Islam represents the slum dwellers not the palace dwellers."
"The poor die for the revolution, the rich plot against the revolution."
"Islam will eliminate class differences."
"In Islam there will be no landless peasants."

▲ **Fig. 7.12**

DISCUSSION

Which of the following factors was the most decisive in ending the regime of Shah Muhammad Reza Pahlavi?

a. The appeal of Ayatollah Khomeini

b. Heavy-handed government control

c. The overthrow of Prime Minister Mussadeq in 1953

d. Military expansion

▲ **Fig. 7.13** Ayatollah Khomeini returns to Iran from exile, 1 February 1979

What were the causes and consequences of the Iran–Iraq War, 1980–8?

Iraq's land and air invasion of western Iran in September 1980 started an eight-year war bringing destabilisation to the region and devastation to the participants. Few modern conflicts have been so long, bloody, and pointless. The causes are both long-standing disputes and more immediate considerations. Some claim that Saddam was the undoubted aggressor, but it could also be argued that invading Iran was a pre-emptive strike—he wanted to destroy Khomeini before Khomeini destroyed him.

Territorial disputes

Iran and Iraq shared a border of more than 1,400 kilometres and much of the friction between the two countries involved territorial issues. Two areas of particular dispute were the Shatt al-Arab waterway and the Iranian province of Khuzestan.

The Shatt al-Arab waterway

The Shatt al-Arab is formed by the confluence of the Tigris and Euphrates rivers. It connects the Iraqi city of Basra and the Iranian cities of Abadan and Khorramshahr to the Persian Gulf. The waterway was important to Iran and Iraq for their oil exports, but especially important to Iraq as its only outlet to the sea. Arguments over navigation rights and the precise location of the Iraq–Iran border along the southern 105-kilometre stretch of the river had been ongoing since the sixteenth century. In 1937 the two countries signed a treaty favourable to Iraq: the boundary was to be marked by the low-water mark on the river's eastern bank. This was the case until 1969 when the Shah of Iran rejected the 1937 treaty and refused to pay the Iraqis any more shipping tolls.

Khuzestan

The south-western Iranian province of Khuzestan was oil rich. The majority of residents were non-Persian and most were Arabs who had cultural connections with their Iraqi neighbours to the west. Saddam claimed a historical right to control the province and encouraged the Arab residents to revolt against the Shah's rule. In retaliation Iran encouraged the Kurds in the north of Iraq to take up arms against Saddam's regime, providing them with military training and equipment.

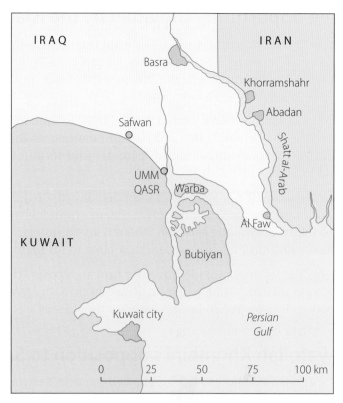

▲ **Fig. 7.14** Kuwait, Basra and the Shatt al-Arab

Algiers Agreement

Saddam was astute enough to realise that a full-scale war with Iran during the early 1970s would lead to an Iraqi defeat as Iran then had the fifth most powerful army in the world. Having ended up losing several skirmishes and minor battles, he decided to make a tactical retreat by signing the Algiers Agreement of 1975. In return for Iran ending its support for the Kurdish separatists within Iraq, Iraq dropped its claims to Khuzestan and conceded that the border between Iran and Iraq along the Shatt al-Arab should follow the deep waterline. Although the Algiers Agreement normalised relations between Iraq and Iran it was regarded as a setback by Saddam and he was determined to regain the lost ground. Shortly before invading Iran in September 1980 Saddam renounced the Algiers Agreement.

Domination of the Gulf

The Iran–Iraq War can be regarded as part of the age-old contest for power and dominance in the Middle East between the Persians and the Arabs. This contest began in the ancient civilisations of Persia and Mesopotamia. By the 1970s Iran (Persia) and Iraq (Mesopotamia) were still the only serious contenders to lead the region as they alone had the necessary financial and military resources. Saddam Hussein hoped that with the annexation of Khuzestan and renewed control of the Shatt al-Arab, Iraq's oil reserves could be significantly expanded at the expense of its main rival. This would shift the balance of power from Iran to Iraq. He also hoped to make Iraq the leader of the Arab world following Egypt's expulsion from the **Arab League** in 1979 as a result of its peace accords with Israel.

Arab League

The Arab League was established in 1945 to promote the political, economic and cultural interests of the Arab countries. Founder members included Egypt, Iraq, Saudi Arabia, and Syria.

The opportunity provided by the Islamic Revolution

In 1975 Iran was clearly more powerful than Iraq as demonstrated by the Algiers Agreement. The Islamic Revolution of 1979, however, seemed to provide a temporary change in the power balance and this was an opportunity that Saddam was keen to exploit.

In particular, the overthrow of the Shah led to an ending of the alliance between the United States and Iran and that meant that the Iranian army was deprived of American-supplied spare parts for its tanks, armoured vehicles and artillery.

Furthermore, the Islamic Revolution led directly to a major purge of the senior ranks in the Iranian army. Saddam's thinking was that Iran's political instability, diplomatic isolation, and military disintegration provided a unique chance for him to deliver a knockout blow to his main foreign enemy.

Delay would only provide Iran with time to recover. In fact, this line of thought turned out to be a miscalculation on Saddam's part: Iran was not as weak as it appeared to be and early Iraqi successes were soon reversed.

QUICK QUESTION 4

Why did Saddam Hussein think that the Islamic Revolution provided Iraq with a good opportunity to attack Iran?

Ayatollah Khomeini's opposition to Saddam Hussein

The Islamic Revolution led to renewed tensions between Iran and Iraq. This was partly over religious issues. Iran was a Shiite Muslim state governed by leading Muslim clerics according to Muslim law. By contrast Iraq was a secular state and most of its leading politicians were Sunni Muslims, even though Sunni Muslims made up less than 20 per cent of the Iraqi population. Ayatollah Khomeini regarded Saddam's regime with contempt, partly because of its religious composition, partly because he still felt bitter about his expulsion from Iraq in 1977. From June 1979 Khomeini began appealing to Iraqi Shiites to overthrow the Baath regime and establish another Islamic republic. In 1979–80 anti-Baath riots broke out in Shiite areas of Iraq and Shiite militants began a programme of assassination against leading Baath officials and politicians. Saddam regarded these developments with concern and became convinced that Khomeini was deliberately trying to undermine his government. In his view the best form of defence was attack.

Western involvement in the war

The main interest of the western powers during the war was to preserve the balance of power in the Middle East and to ensure the uninterrupted flow of oil supplies from the region. The United States did not have much enthusiasm for either Saddam Hussein or Khomeini but of the two the Americans preferred the former. The worst case scenario for the west would have been the victory of Iran followed by the installation of an Islamic revolutionary government in Baghdad. Kuwait, Saudi Arabia, and the other Gulf states would then have faced the Islamic threat. This would have introduced a high degree of instability and volatility into the region and left the west without friends in an area of major economic importance. Hence American policy was directed at ensuring that, at the very least, Iraq did not lose the war. Accordingly, the United States supplied Iraq with arms, intelligence, and finance. Britain, France, and West Germany supplied military equipment to Iraq.

American involvement became more direct during a phase of the fighting known as the "War of the Tankers". From May 1984 both sides attacked each other's oil tankers and merchant ships hoping to damage the opponent's trade. The United States sent warships to the Gulf to guarantee oil supplies and engaged in attacks on Iranian oil installations and Iranian gunboats.

Partly as a result of western assistance to Iraq, by the end of the war Iraq possessed a clear advantage over Iran in terms of tanks, fighter aircraft, helicopters and artillery. It was partly this Iraqi superiority in military equipment that persuaded Khomeini to agree to a ceasefire in August 1988.

Consequences of the war

With the Iran–Iraq War producing no winner, the nature of the peace reflected the stalemate that had dominated the hostilities during the previous six years. Neither side achieved its war aims with both Saddam and Khomeini remaining in power. There was no change in the Iran–Iraq border and the pre-war status quo was restored. Neither was there any long-term diplomatic change as the western powers were soon aligned against Saddam in the First Gulf War.

▲ **Fig. 7.15** Iranian woman visiting cemetery for victims of the Iran–Iraq War

The war had inflicted substantial carnage and devastation on both sides. The death toll for Iran was approximately one million out of a total population of 50 million. Iraq, with a much smaller population of 17 million, lost between one quarter of a million and half a million lives. The fatalities on both sides, therefore, represented around 2 per cent of each population. If the number of people seriously wounded or psychologically damaged had been included then these figures would have been much higher.

Economic damage was also considerable. In just eight years Iraq had been transformed from one of the richest countries in the world to a bankrupt state. It owed $80 billion in foreign debt and annual oil revenues had more than halved to $11 billion. Investment in social projects such as housing, schools, and hospitals had to make way for austerity. While Iran incurred a smaller foreign debt, it also faced bankruptcy and the value of its oil revenues had approximately halved to $10 billion. One immediate impact on the people of Iran was that their living standards plummeted.

Yet despite the obvious futility of the war, Saddam Hussein claimed that it had been a glorious victory for Iraq. He had halted the spread of the Islamic revolution and prevented Khomeini from toppling his regime. By surviving he had triumphed. An imposing monument to this achievement soon appeared in Baghdad consisting of two pairs of giant crossed swords clasped by huge bronze fists. Yet Saddam privately recognised that the Iraqi people would not be bought off for long with extravagant symbols. He needed to find a new way of increasing the wealth of his country.

▲ **Fig. 7.16** The Swords of Qudisiyah, Baghdad

SOURCE 8

From the website of the Iran Chamber Society—a non-partisan organisation seeking to promote Iranian culture and history.

At the end, virtually none of the issues which are usually blamed for the war had been resolved. When it was over, the conditions which existed at the beginning of the war remained virtually unchanged. The UN-arranged cease-fire merely put an end to the fighting, leaving two isolated states to pursue an arms race with each other, and with the other countries in the region.

SOURCE 9

From a history of Iran published in 2008.

One final bloodletting came in 1988, immediately after Khomeini ended the war by accepting a UN-mediated ceasefire. He announced that he had no choice but to "drink the poisoned chalice." In four short weeks, special courts set up in the main prisons hanged more than 2,800 prisoners – Amnesty International described them as "prisoners of conscience."

DISCUSSION

1. Does Source 8 make you surprised by what is said in Source 10? Explain your answer using the details of the sources and your knowledge.

2. How does Source 11 help you to understand Khomeini's attitude towards the ceasefire as described in Source 10? Explain your answer using the details of the sources and your knowledge.

3. How far do Sources 8 to 11 support the view that the ceasefire of August 1988 represented a victory for Saddam Hussein?
   Use the sources to explain your answer.

FP ▶ Why did the First Gulf War take place?

On 2 August 1990 Saddam Hussein ordered the invasion of Kuwait. Within 24 hours an Iraqi force of 100 000 troops and 300 tanks had crushed the 16 000-strong Kuwaiti army and gained control of the principality. The ruler of Kuwait, Sheikh Jaber Al-Sabah, together with most of his family, escaped to Saudi Arabia. Iraq was immediately condemned in the Arab League and at the United Nations which imposed economic sanctions. Furthermore, Saudi Arabia, fearing that it would become the next victim of Iraqi aggression,

SOURCE 10

From a history of Iraq published in 2000.

When the cease-fire was accepted by Iran in July 1988 Saddam Hussein trumpeted the victory of Iraq. In terms of his redefinition of the country's war aims, Iraq had indeed been victorious since it had thwarted Iran's attempt to overthrow his regime. It had survived the strains of eight years of war with its principal figures still in place.

appealed for American military assistance. Saddam's unprovoked aggression had united almost the entire international community against him yet, in his own mind, there had been compelling reasons for his action.

The historical claim

Until the end of the First World War Kuwait had officially been part of the Turkish Empire's province of Basra but the ruling Al-Sabah family had enjoyed a large measure of independence. The British had accepted responsibility for Kuwait's defence and foreign affairs in 1899 and in 1922 had helped establish Kuwait's boundaries with Iraq and Saudi Arabia. The association between Kuwait and Basra led a number of Iraqi rulers to insist that Kuwait was rightfully part of Iraq. Both King Ghazi in the late 1930s and President Qassem in 1961 had demanded the incorporation of Kuwait into Iraq. The involvement of the British led to Iraqi claims that the very existence of an independent Kuwait, which made Iraq a virtually landlocked state, was only due to imperialist meddling in Arab affairs.

Saddam Hussein's domestic position

Despite Saddam's attempt to represent the Iran–Iraq War as an Iraqi victory, he realised that the Iraqi people would soon see through the propaganda—in reality their country had endured a costly and bloody conflict that had essentially ended where it started. Iraq displayed many of the characteristics of a defeated power as inflation was followed by price controls, Iraqi prisoners remained in Iranian hands, and demobilised troops joined the ranks of the unemployed. Reconstruction projects remained on hold. Since July 1988 there had been at least four assassination attempts on Saddam's life involving army officers, some of whom served in the Republican Guard, his elite bodyguards. Saddam desperately needed to secure his rule and Kuwait seemed the answer to his problem. He could pose as the liberator of a territory which many Iraqis regarded as rightfully theirs, improve Iraq's access to the Gulf, and acquire a much stronger position with regard to the world's oil markets.

Financial and economic factors

During the Iran–Iraq War Saddam received loans of approximately $40 billion from Saudi Arabia and Kuwait. Given Iraq's post-war shortage of money and crippling debt he asked both countries to write off their loans to Iraq on the grounds that he had halted the spread of the Islamic Revolution and thereby directly benefited both countries. He also demanded new loans amounting to $30 billion to finance reconstruction. Both Saudi Arabia and Kuwait refused. Saddam was also annoyed that both countries had increased their oil production so bringing down the international price of oil and reducing Iraq's oil revenues to the tune of $89 billion between 1981 and 1990. Saddam asked both countries to bring their oil production into line with the quotas fixed by OPEC. Yet again Saudi Arabia and Kuwait refused. Saddam also claimed that Kuwait was illegally extracting Iraqi oil from the Rumaila oil field close to the Kuwait–Iraq border by engaging in slant drilling. The value of the oil so "stolen" amounted to $2.4 billion. Saddam now accused both Gulf states of effectively waging economic war against his country and threatened dire consequences if the matter could not be resolved.

SOURCE 11

From the Military Analysis Network, Iran–Iraq War (2002)

Casualty figures are highly uncertain, though estimates suggest more than one and a half million war and war-related casualties – perhaps as many as a million people died, many more were wounded, and millions were made refugees. Iraq's victory was not without cost. The Iraqis suffered an estimated 375 000 casualties, the equivalent of 5.6 million for a population the size of the United States. Another 60 000 were taken prisoner by the Iranians.

QUICK QUESTION 5

Why did Saddam Hussein think that Saudi Arabia and Kuwait should cancel their loans to Iraq after the Iran–Iraq war?

Establish regional leadership

The Iran–Iraq War had, in part, been an attempt by Iraq to establish regional dominance over the Gulf. Although Iran had been seriously weakened the attempt had failed since Iraq secured no new territory or other advantages. The invasion of Kuwait was a renewed attempt to alter the power balance in the Gulf. If successful Iraq would not only acquire massive new amounts of oil wealth but also 120 miles of Gulf coastline that included a large natural harbour. Iraq would also be in an excellent position to dominate Saudi Arabia and achieve in a southerly and western direction what it had failed to achieve in an easterly direction against Iran. Saddam Hussein hoped to become the most powerful Arab leader in the Middle East.

Expected American reaction

If Saddam Hussein had known in advance that his invasion and occupation of Kuwait would create such a storm of both Arab and international protest then he might have concentrated on diplomatic means to achieve his objectives. Prior to August 1990 Saddam's main concern had been to ensure that the United States remained neutral in any move he made against Kuwait. Washington had been sending conflicting signals as to its reaction to the nature of Saddam's regime, with Congress arguing for sanctions but President Bush and his chief advisors stating they were against such measures. In order to find out the likely attitude of the American administration to his intended invasion of Kuwait, Saddam summoned the American ambassador April Glaspie to Baghdad for a meeting on 25 July 1990. Glaspie apparently gave Saddam the clear impression that the matter was not one of key concern to the United States. Saddam's very real threats were mistakenly interpreted as bluster and posturing and were not met with firm responses. As a result Saddam drew the conclusion that his adventure would be unopposed.

Operation Desert Shield 7 August 1990–17 January 1991	After the invasion and occupation of Kuwait by Iraq in August 1990 there was no further fighting for over five months. During this interim period there was a build-up of American, French and British troops in Saudi Arabia. Meanwhile a series of United Nations resolutions first demanded an Iraqi withdrawal from Kuwait, then imposed economic sanctions on Iraq, and finally set a deadline for Iraqi withdrawal pending military action.
Operation Desert Storm 17 January–28 February 1991	Air war (17 January–23 February 1991): Coalition planes and helicopters attacked Iraqi military targets in Kuwait and Iraq itself. Iraq retaliated by launching SCUD missiles on Israel (unsuccessfully trying to provoke an Israeli attack on Iraq), by blowing up Kuwaiti oil wells, and by pouring millions of gallons of crude oil into the Persian Gulf. Iraq also briefly invaded Khafji in Saudi Arabia before being driven out by Coalition forces.
	Ground war (24–28 February 1991): Coalition forces invaded Iraq and Kuwait forcing Saddam Hussein to order an Iraqi withdrawal from Kuwait. Approximately 10 000 retreating Iraqi troops were killed by Coalition bombing along the "Highway of Death", a six-lane motorway connecting Kuwait City with Basra. The US Army destroyed 186 Iraqi tanks and 127 armoured vehicles at the Battle of Medina Ridge south-west of Basra. On 28 February President Bush announced a ceasefire and declared that Kuwait had been freed from Iraqi occupation.

▲ **Fig. 7.17** The main events of the First Gulf War

What were the consequences of the First Gulf War?

There could be no disguising the fact that Saddam Hussein had suffered a massive and humiliating military defeat. His forces had been ejected from Kuwait within 100 hours of the beginning of the ground war and much of his country's economic infrastructure had been destroyed by Coalition air attacks. Coalition targets had included power stations, oil refineries, road, bridges, and water purification plants. Yet Saddam survived the devastation and took immediate action to strengthen his regime. He brutally crushed revolts that broke out in the south and north of the country when the Shiites and the Kurds tried to exploit the post-war trauma of his government.

The main casualties of the war were the Iraqi people who had sustained significant losses with civilian fatalities of up to 100 000 and combat fatalities of over 20 000. They now had to suffer shortages of food and medical supplies, inadequate supplies of clean drinking water, and much reduced access to welfare services. The continuation of sanctions meant that Iraq was unable to sell its oil abroad with the financially disastrous results for the country as a whole.

America retained a military presence in Saudi Arabia, using it as a base to enforce the "no-fly zones" that were established to prevent Saddam from carrying out further atrocities against his own people in the southern and northern sectors of the country. America's objective at this point was not to topple Saddam but rather to contain his excesses. Saddam may have been a thoroughly distasteful dictator but at least he was a strong leader whose rule was preferable to Washington than a spread of the Islamic Revolution.

Nevertheless, the stage had been set for possible future international intervention in Iraq unless Saddam Hussein fully complied with UN Security Council Resolution 687 which called on him to dismantle his nonconventional weapons, biological, chemical and nuclear. Saddam had largely lost the trust of most of the international community through his actions against Kuwait. During the 1990s those countries with a major stake in the stability of the Gulf region began wondering whether their interests were best served by Saddam Hussein's continuing presence or his removal from power.

DISCUSSION

How could the oil production of Saudi Arabia and Kuwait affect the oil revenues of Iraq?

KEY POINTS

▶ Saddam Hussein's rise to power including the influence of Khairallah Tulfah and Ahmad Hasan al-Bakr.

▶ The nature of Saddam Hussein's rule in Iraq between 1979 and 2000.

▶ The nature of the Shah's rule in Iran and the reasons for the Iranian Revolution of 1979.

▶ The causes and consequences of the Iran–Iraq War 1980–8, and the reasons for western involvement in the war.

▶ The causes, course and consequences of the First Gulf War of 1990–1.

- You will need to have a good understanding of how Saddam Hussein became President of Iraq despite having few advantages of education and upbringing. The influence and support of family relatives is central to this understanding. You must also appreciate Saddam Hussein's individual qualities such as his physical strength, utter ruthlessness, and organisational skills. Once a prominent politician, his cunning, outmanoeuvring of rivals, and ingratiation with superiors became the essential means of achieving the presidency.

- For the nature of Saddam Hussein's rule up to 2000 you must become familiar with the key features of his rule such as terror and repression, war against his own people, and ways of boosting popular support through social reforms and propaganda.

- Understanding the reasons for the Iranian Revolution of 1979 involves looking at the nature of the Shah's rule together with the counter attractions of the various opposition groups led by the charismatic Ayatollah Khomeini. You need to be able to identify the mistakes made by the Shah after 1951 and how these mistakes impacted upon the population of Iran.

- You must become familiar with the main causes of the Iran–Iraq War, especially the territorial disputes and religious differences. You must also appreciate that, despite the rhetoric of Saddam Hussein, the war did little but impoverish the two participants.

- Similarly you require a clear understanding of the reasons for Saddam Hussein's invasion of Kuwait in August 1990—financial, strategic, and domestic. Why did he think that he would get away with it? Why was the war over so quickly and how did the defeat affect the future of Saddam Hussein's regime?

Review questions

1. Explain the role of Khairallah Tulfah in Saddam Hussein's rise to power.

2. Why did Saddam Hussein spend 11 years as President Bakr's deputy?

3. How did Saddam Hussein use his family members to assist his rule after 1979?

4. What were the main features of Saddam Hussein's personality cult?

5. Why did the Shah of Iran set up SAVAK in 1957?

6. Explain the term "White Revolution" in connection with the rule of the Shah of Iran.

7. How far was the Shah of Iran personally responsible for the overthrow of his regime in 1979?

8. Explain the importance of the Shatt al-Arab waterway to Iraq.

9. What were the main terms of the Algiers Agreement of 1975?

10. Why was Ayatollah Khomeini so opposed to Saddam Hussein's government in 1979–80?

11. How far was Saddam Hussein's invasion of Kuwait in 1990 a direct consequence of the Iran–Iraq War of 1980–8?

8

The First World War, 1914–18

Introduction

The First World War marked, for some historians, a watershed in modern history. Some regarded it as an event closing the door on the long nineteenth century, with the end of secret treaties and grand old empires (and Emperors) which characterised that period. For other historians, the war signalled the start of a new 'thirty years war' which did not truly end until Germany's defeat in 1945.

A war which started with a complex German plan for victory on two fronts, but quickly resulted in Germany fighting a defensive war in the west while being sucked further and further into the Russian Empire. Meanwhile, her allies proved to be more of a drain on resources than an asset, while her enemies acquired a powerful new ally (the United States), whose entry forced Germany to gamble in March 1918: a gamble which ultimately brought about its defeat on the Western Front in November 1918.

This chapter outlines the major campaigns of the conflict, but also considers the impact of the war on the home front, and its expansion onto other continents, the air and sea. Throughout the chapter a keen focus is maintained on why Britain, France and the United States were able to force Germany and her allies to agree to an armistice, and ultimately weighs up the relative importance of the various factors that contributed to the defeat of the Central Powers, consisting of Germany, Austria-Hungary, the Ottoman Empire, and later Bulgaria.

The aims of this chapter are to:

- Look at the Schlieffen Plan in operation.
- Consider the Battles of Mons, the Marne and Ypres, the reaction to the "stalemate", and the nature and problems of trench warfare.
- Consider the main battles of the war including the Somme and Verdun, the leadership and tactics of Haig at the Battle of the Somme, and the use and impact of new methods of warfare.
- Discuss the war at sea, the Battle of Jutland and its consequences, the use of convoys and submarines and the U-boat campaign.
- Look at the reasons for, and results of, the Gallipoli campaign.
- Consider the impact of war on civilian populations.
- Study events on the Eastern Front and the defeat of Russia.
- Consider the impact and importance of America's entry into the war.
- Understand why the German offensive of 1918 was unsuccessful.
- Look at conditions in Germany towards the end of the war, including the Kiel Mutiny and German Revolution, and the abdication of the Kaiser.
- Discuss the armistice.

Why was the war not over by December 1914?

The outbreak of war in 1914 posed a huge problem for Germany. The layout of Europe meant it was in the middle of two of its enemies: France and Russia. If both attacked at the same time, Germany would have no choice but to fight on both sides of the country. This would mean splitting its forces and dramatically reducing the potential strength of the German army.

Germany had suspected for several years that a European war was coming in which it would have to fight both France and Russia. It therefore had begun planning a strategy to avoid having to fight both at the same time. In 1905, Alfred von Schlieffen, German Army Chief of Staff, created an approach to any European war which involved fighting both countries.

How was the Schlieffen Plan intended to work?

It would take Russia six weeks to fully mobilise and organise its army for an attack upon Germany, therefore Germany had these six weeks to defeat France. Schlieffen thought that if this happened, Britain would not yet have joined the conflict and without France, both Britain and Russia would not continue to fight.

The plan involved using 90 per cent of Germany's armed forces to attack France. Schlieffen thought the Germans should attack through Holland and Belgium. The remaining 10 per cent of the German army would be sent to the east to stop the expected Russian advance.

Why didn't the plan work?

Schlieffen retired in 1906. Some in the German high command had thought his plan was too daring. His successor Helmuth von Moltke changed the plan, reducing the commitment of troops left to contain Russia in the east. Moltke also changed the route of the proposed attack, avoiding Holland and taking instead a more direct route through Belgium.

How important was Belgium's reaction to the Schlieffen Plan?

The plan depended upon speed of attack through Belgium so that France could be defeated quickly. However, the Germans encountered fierce resistance from the Belgians.

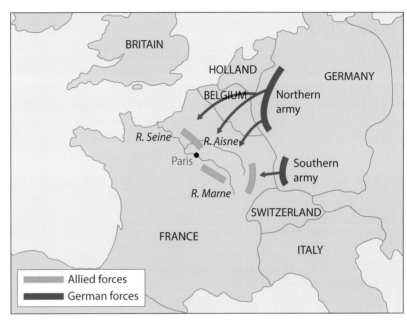

▲ **Fig. 8.1** Diagram of Schlieffen Plan

BRAVO, BELGIUM!

▲ **Fig. 8.2** This cartoon from 1914 shows a man (wearing a hat labelled "Germany") threatening a boy (with hat labelled "Belgium") while the latter defends a gate marked "No Thoroughfare"

What role did Britain and France play?

While the Germans were initially successful, they faced stubborn resistance from Allied troops along the Seine river in France. The battle of the Marne as it became known saw the German forces split into two and eventually retreat due to the combined forces of the BEF and the French 5th army.

FP How successful was the British Expeditionary Force (BEF)?

The British response to the German aggression of the Schlieffen Plan was to despatch the BEF to France. The BEF was Britain's standing army, designed to be able to respond quickly to threats abroad. It was only relatively small, and at the time of the outbreak of war, stood at around 120 000 men. The Kaiser of Germany was alleged to have given the order to "exterminate...the treacherous English and walk over General French's contemptible little army", giving the BEF the nickname of The Old Contemptibles!

The BEF was sent to stop the German advance. It first engaged the Germans at the Battle of Mons in Belgium, where just the number of German soldiers forced the British to retreat. It was, however, far more successful fighting in tandem with the French at the battle of Marne, in which Paris was protected.

FP Why did both sides introduce trenches?

Following the German retreat after the battle of the Marne both sides tried to outflank each other to gain control of the war. Three months of mobile conflict followed as the two sides fought but neither seized the advantage. This became known as the "race to the sea" as the Germans attempted to gain control of the channel ports thereby cutting off supplies coming from Britain. There were several battles, most notably at Ypres, but neither side could maintain control. In the end two lines emerged, with troops dug in along a long line of trench systems that stretched from the North Sea to the Swiss frontier with France. This line remained essentially unchanged for most of the war, and marked the end of a mobile conflict and the beginning of trench warfare.

Why was there stalemate on the Western Front?

By December 1914 the race to the sea was over. Neither side had managed to seize the advantage and outflank the other, therefore both sides had dug in. What had started as a war of rapid movement was now a war of attrition. Trench warfare developed, as both the German and Allied forces dug trenches as shelter from enemy fire. The trenches were used as positions from which to attack the other side.

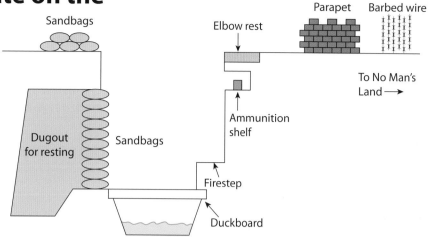

▲ **Fig. 8.3** A cross-section of a trench

What was living and fighting in the trenches like?

Soldiers did not spend all their time fighting in the trenches. A general pattern for trench routine was "4-4-4": four days on the front line, then four days in the reserve trench, and finally four days resting, usually slightly further back from the front line in a local village where the army was billeted. This pattern was theoretical though, and depended upon attacks, the availability of reserves and whereabouts on the Western Front troops were located.

The trenches themselves also varied in conditions. The First World War was fought across many different countries. The trenches in northern France and Belgium were built in chalky ground and crumbled easily. In Ypres where lots of fighting took place the ground was more boggy. Trenches were used as far as Palestine where they were built into the rock. The big dangers of life in the trenches, aside from military attacks, were the following.

- Rats and lice: they thrived in the poor conditions of mud, discarded food and other waste.

- Disease: the lifestyle of living in a trench, not washing for days or weeks, with limited toilet facilities and little chance of fresh water meant that disease was rife.

- The weather: harsh winters brought freezing temperatures; heavy rain brought flooding. In Flanders flooded trenches were waist high in water. The big danger that wet weather brought though was trench foot, a condition that crippled soldiers as the flesh on their feet wasted due to being continuously wet.

- Pyschological problems: the First World War saw many soldiers suffer from mental conditions, as well as physical ones. "Shellshock" became a term later used for those who suffered mental breakdowns due to the constant shelling and other psychological effects of this draining form of warfare.

- Boredom: there was often a long wait between major battles. During these waits, trench life was usually very tedious and hard work. Rebuilding trenches, fortifying defences and battling the elements were ways to keep boredom at bay.

▲ **Fig. 8.4** An aerial view of the trench system

QUICK QUESTION 2

Study the diagram in Figure 8.3. Does trench warfare favour the attacking or the defending side?

SOURCE 2

Robert Graves, an officer in the First World War, a poet and an author, writing in his book *Goodbye to All That* published in 1929.

Rats came up from the canal, fed on the plentiful corpses, and multiplied exceedingly. While I stayed here with the Royal Welch Fusiliers, a new officer joined the company and, in token of welcome, was given a dug-out containing a spring-bed. When he turned in that night he heard a scuffling, shone his torch on the bed, and found two rats on his blanket tussling for the possession of a severed hand.

SOURCE 3

In 1916 Lieutenant Charles Carrington kept a record of his time on the front line.

Place	Days
Frontline	65
Support	36
Reserve	120
Rest	73
Leave	17
Hospital	10

DISCUSSION

1. Read Graves' account of life in a trench in Source 2. What effect do you think events like this had on men in the trenches?

2. Study Source 3. Does Carrington's pattern of time served in 1916 match the 4-4-4 rule?

◀ **Fig. 8.5** British soldiers climbing over the parapet of their trench during the Battle of Morval in 1916

DISCUSSION

Study the photograph in Figure 8.6.

1. How does it compare with the diagram in Figure 8.3?

2. The diagram shows how trenches were meant to be built while this source shows an actual trench. What might explain the difference?

◀ **Fig. 8.6** Welsh Guards rest in a reserve trench during the Battle of Guillemont, 3–6 September 1916

Why did the war become bogged down in the trenches?

The first reason is that trench warfare was defensive rather than offensive. This can be illustrated by two case studies: the battle of Ypres and the battle of Verdun.

Case study one. The battle of Ypres, 1914

Why was it important?

The city of Ypres in Belgium saw no less than five battles during the war, but it was the first one that proved most significant in helping explain why the war became bogged down in the trenches. Ypres was important due to its location along the roads leading to the Channel ports. With the German failure at the Battle of the Marne both sides wanted to establish control of the sea.

The Allies arrived in Ypres first and manned a 35-mile long front line. The aim of the Allies was to push the Germans back, retaking the cities of Lille in France and Brussels in Belgium. The Germans were hoping for the opposite, to push through the Allies at Ypres and take the ports of Dunkirk, Calais and Boulogne.

What happened?

Fierce fighting took place for over a month. Both sides had the advantage at different points, but weaponry such as cavalry and machine guns were unable to break the stalemate. Horrific losses were suffered on both sides; an estimated half of the 140 000 British troops were killed or wounded in the battle.

Why was it significant?

Ypres marked the end of two things for the war. Firstly, it was end of the BEF. The heavy losses suffered meant that the old army was largely gone, and the British would now have to rely on volunteer recruits.

More significantly for the war it marked the end of a mobile war. Neither side had shown itself to be stronger than the other, and so two evenly matched armies had resorted to defensive formations. Across the front troops now dug in to trenches.

Case study two. The battle of Verdun, 1916

Why was it important?

The longest battle of the war was fought at Verdun. Germany believed that if it was to win the war, it had to force France to surrender, hoping that if the French did so, the British would also withdraw.

SOURCE 4

German Chief of Staff, Erich von Falkenhayn, to the Kaiser, Wilhelm II, on Christmas Day 1915.

The string in France has reached breaking point. A mass break-through – which in any case is beyond our means – is unnecessary. Within our reach there are objectives for the retention of which the French General Staff would be compelled to throw in every man they have. If they do so the forces of France will bleed to death.

To make this breakthrough, the Germans attacked the town of Verdun. Verdun was important to the French because of its history: it was a heavily fortified town built to withstand Prussian attacks in the 1880s. Verdun was a symbol of French military pride. The Germans hoped a victory here would deal a devastating blow to French morale.

DISCUSSION

Study Source 4. How does Von Falkenhayn show a negative attitude to outright German victory? Does this suggest a long war was likely?

What happened?

The Germans subjected Verdun to an intense bombardment. As the French sent extra forces to defend the town the Germans attacked. Their aim was to break through and open up the French line for a devastating assault. The French were unprepared for such a large assault, and at one point an army of 200 000 French faced up to over a million German soldiers. Despite these numbers though, the Germans were unable to make a significant breakthrough. They got close several times, but the dogged determination of the French, despite huge casualties, kept the Germans at bay.

Why significant?

The battle was the longest fought in the entire war and crucially led to the battle of the Somme as the French persuaded the British to move to an offensive elsewhere to ensure that the Germans would need to withdraw some of their troops from Verdun.

The other significance of Verdun was that it showed how hard a breakthrough was to achieve. Despite vast numbers of men, as long as the defending side were willing to suffer large casualties there seemed little chance of a breakthrough with trench warfare. Other methods of warfare were needed.

FP How important were new developments such as tanks, machine guns, aircraft and gas?

The second reason that the war became bogged down in the trenches was that new technologies did not lead to a breakthrough in the stalemate.

The tank

Tanks were first used by the Allies at Flers, on the Somme, on 15 September 1916. There were initial fears among the British leadership that tanks were not up to the harsh conditions, but after the failure to achieve a breakthrough at the Somme, they were put into use.

The first deployments were not a complete success. Of the 59 tanks in France, only 49 were considered to be in good working order. Of these, 17 broke down before they had even had a chance to engage the enemy. However, their impact was, at first, successful. The sight of the tanks created panic and had a profound effect on the morale of the German forces.

The head of the Tank Corps Colonel John Fuller was convinced that the tank was vital to winning the war. He persuaded Sir Douglas Haig to ask the government to supply him with another 1,000 tanks. He offered clear guidance on how they should be used in order for success. At times this worked, such as at Amiens in August 1918 where General Henry Rawlinson used over 400 tanks supported by soldiers and aircraft to break through the German front line.

SOURCE 5

An account by British soldier Arnold Ridley after the war in *The Train and Other Ghosts* published circa 1970.

We in the ranks had never heard of tanks. We were told that there was some sort of secret weapon and then we saw this thing go up the right hand corner of Delville Wood. I saw this strange and cumbersome machine emerge from the shattered shrubbery and proceed slowly down the slope towards Flers.

DISCUSSION

1. Read Sources 5 and 6. How do they compare in their view of the first experience of the tank?

2. Did tanks live up to this expectation?

Philip Gibbs was a journalist who reported the war on the Western Front.

It is impossible to revive the extraordinary thrill and amazement, the hilarious exultation with which these things were first seen on the fields of the Somme. It had been a secret, marvellously hidden. We war correspondents, who came to hear of most things in one way or another, had not heard a whisper about it until a few days before these strange things went into action.

▲ **Fig. 8.7** British machine gunners using a machine gun and wearing their gas masks near Ovillers during the Battle of the Somme

The machine gun

Both sides used the machine gun as an effective weapon. Capable of firing 400–600 rounds of small-calibre ammunition per minute, each one had the firepower of about 100 rifles. Larger machine guns required a crew of three to six men and were positioned on a tripod. For added protection, German machine guns were often housed inside concrete blockhouses. Smaller machine guns were manned by one or two soldiers and were deployed effectively along the Western Front, particularly by the Germans.

Gas

The use of chemical weapons and in particular poison gas was limited. Despite the horrors that it caused, it only accounted for 4 per cent of war deaths. Nevertheless, it was a terrifying weapon that caused panic and fear among troops. The two most common chemical weapons used were mustard gas and chlorine gas. Mustard gas was the most lethal of all the poisonous chemicals used during the war. Small amounts were added to high explosive shells and then released. Once in the soil, mustard gas remained active for several weeks.

British gas casualties: 1914–18	Deaths	Non-fatal
Chlorine	1,976	164,457
Mustard gas	4,086	16,526

▲ **Fig. 8.9**

▲ **Fig. 8.8** A cartoon from 1916 called "The Gas Fiend"

DISCUSSION

Study the cartoon in Figure 8.8. Why do you think gas in the picture is shown as a snake? What message do you think the cartoon is trying to make?

An extract from a poem by British soldier Wilfred Owen entitled "Dulce et Decorum est" (1917). The title means "it is sweet and right", referring to the phrase "Dulce et decorum est pro patria mori", a phrase used by supporters of the war that it was a noble sacrifice to die for your country.

Gas! Gas! Quick, boys! An ecstasy of fumbling,

Fitting the clumsy helmets just in time,

But someone still was yelling out and stumbling

And floundering like a man in fire or lime.

Dim through the misty panes and thick green light,

As under a green sea, I saw him drowning.

In all my dreams, before my helpless sight,

He plunges at me, guttering, choking, drowning.

If in some smothering dreams, you too could pace

Behind the wagon that we flung him in.

And watch the white eyes writhing in his face,

His hanging face, like a devil's sick of sin;

If you could hear, at every jolt, the blood

Come gargling from the froth-corrupted lungs,

Obscene as cancer, bitter as the cud

Of vile, incurable sores on innocent tongues,

My friend, you would not tell with such high zest

To children ardent for some desperate glory,

The old Lie: Dulce et decorum est

Pro patria mori

DISCUSSION

Read the poem in Source 7.

1. What impact would poems like this have on people in England with regards to their feelings about the use of gas in war?

2. What similarity is there between the psychological effect of gas and the psychological effect of tanks? Look back at Sources 5 and 6.

Aircraft

The First World War also saw the introduction of the use of aircraft in conflicts. Aircraft did not yet play a decisive role as in later conflicts, but did serve a purpose. The main role of aircraft at the time was observation and reconnaissance, allowing battlefield positions and troop movements to be observed from the air. The usefulness of aircraft, however, was limited by the ability to communicate. With no radios to communicate between land and air, it took valuable time for messages to be passed on to ground troops. As well as observing, there were some attempts at bombing raids, however, these were also limited.

Country	Aircraft	Airships
Germany	246	11
Austria-Hungary	35	1
Britain	110	6
France	160	4
Russia	300	11
Belgium	25	–

▲ **Fig. 8.10**

TASKS

1. Read the two statements below. Which of the new methods of warfare does each apply to? Find evidence for both.

   a. It was a more defensive, than offensive method.

   b. It was a new method that had yet to reach its potential.

2. Which of the two explanations above do you think is the more important in explaining why there stalemate on the Western Front?

What was the significance of the battles of Verdun and the Somme?

By 1916 the First World War had been raging for nearly two years. Since the winter of 1914 the fighting had been a stalemate. On 1 July 1916 the British tried to break through the enemy lines with an all out attack on the German trenches at the battle of the Somme. The battle was designed to relieve pressure on the French at Verdun, as well as securing an all important breakthrough of the German line.

Why was the attack launched?

The German attack at Verdun had stretched the French; an attack by the British would mean that the Germans had to withdraw some of their troops from Verdun. There was a widespread belief that a major victory on the Western Front could result in a decisive breakthrough in the war

A major victory would have three effects on the Germans: it would weaken their army, reduce their morale, and force their army to be stretched further.

The Commander-in-chief of the British army Field Marshal Sir Douglas Haig believed in the "Big Push". He was convinced that the enemy could be overwhelmed by sheer weight of numbers.

The plan

Step one
Heavy shelling for 7 days in the run up to 1 July. Shelling designed to remove German defences, inflict heavy casualties and clear barbed wire. Additionally 5 large mines were planted beneath the German trenches to cause maximum damage.

Step two
Coordinated infantry advance at 7.30 am on 1 July. Soldiers told to walk slowly rather than charge at speed in order to clear remaining Germans from front line trenches.

Step three
Second wave of attack including cavalry would sweep through the seized trenches and onwards, attacking the fleeing Germans.

▲ Fig. 8.11

On the day

The Battle of the Somme was one of the biggest battles of the war so far, and initial newspaper reports showed it to be a success.

The reality of the Somme, however, was very different to those initial reports. 1 July 1916 was the worst day in the history of the British army. German soldiers survived the shelling before the attack as they were dug into an elaborate trench system deep underground with all the food and supplies

SOURCE 8

Taken from *The Times* newspaper, 3 July 1916.

"The Day Goes Well." At about half-past 7 o'clock this morning a vigorous attack was launched by the British Army. The front extends over about 20 miles north of the Somme. The assault was preceded by a terrific bombardment lasting about an hour and a half. It is too early as yet to give anything but the barest particulars, as the fighting is developing in intensity, but the British troops have already occupied the German front line. Many prisoners have already fallen into our hands, and as far as can be ascertained our casualties have not been heavy.

they needed and were therefore largely undamaged by the bombardment. Once the shelling stopped, the Germans knew an attack was coming. Twenty thousand British troops were killed and 40 000 were wounded on the first day of the attack. The British shelling before the attack had been largely ineffective. It had failed to clear the barbed wire or damage the German machine guns. Very little ground was gained; few German trenches were taken and held.

The battle of the Somme continued from July until November 1916. Far from being a rapid breakthrough for the British forces, it turned into a battle of attrition that by the end of the fighting had claimed a million casualties on all sides.

Why did the attack fail?

SOURCE 9

George Coppard was a machine-gunner at the Battle of the Somme. In his book *With A Machine Gun to Cambrai* he described what he saw on 2 July 1916.

It eventually became clear that the German line followed points of eminence, always giving a commanding view of No Man's Land. Immediately in front, and spreading left and right until hidden from view, was clear evidence that the attack had been brutally repulsed. Hundreds of dead, many of the 37th Brigade, were strung out like wreckage washed up to a high-water mark. Quite as many died on the enemy wire as on the ground, like fish caught in the net. They hung there in grotesque postures. Some looked as though they were praying; they had died on their knees and the wire had prevented their fall. From the way the dead were equally spread out, whether on the wire or lying in front of it, it was clear that there were no gaps in the wire at the time of the attack.

Concentrated machine gun fire from sufficient guns to command every inch of the wire, had done its terrible work. The Germans must have been reinforcing the wire for months. It was so dense that daylight could barely be seen through it. Through the glasses it looked a black mass. The German faith in massed wire had paid off.

How did our planners imagine that Tommies, having survived all other hazards – and there were plenty in crossing No Man's Land – would get through the German wire? Had they studied the black density of it through their powerful binoculars? Who told them that artillery fire would pound such wire to pieces, making it possible to get through? Any Tommy could have told them that shell fire lifts wire up and drops it down, often in a worse tangle than before.

The battle of the Somme was a horrific loss of life, for very little land gained. When the battle ended in November 1916, the British had made gains of just over 7 miles.

It was also significant for several other reasons.

- The Allies first realized just how long this war could be.

- The soldiers were heavily demoralised.

- New technology, designed to be decisive, had been limited by the poor conditions. Tanks struggled in the mud and over half of the tanks deployed on the Somme broke down before they even reached the front line.

DISCUSSION

1. Read the newspaper report in Source 8. Does the fact the report is inaccurate mean it is of no use to a historian studying the battle of the Somme?

2. Why is the report as incorrect as it is?

DISCUSSION

Read Source 9. What evidence can you find that the outcome of the first day was due to:

a. German strengths

b. poor Allied preparation and planning?

The First World War, 1914–18

Does General Haig deserve to be remembered as the "Butcher of the Somme"?

Some of the criticism after the Somme was directed at the leader of British forces Field Marshall Sir Douglas Haig. Historians since have portrayed the soldiers as being sacrificed in an unwinnable battle, and have instead looked at them as "Lions, led by Donkeys", meaning those in positions of power were responsible for the loss of life.

Haig famously claimed that the heavy bombardment before the battle meant that "not even a rat would be alive" and so instructed the army, mainly made up of new recruits, to approach the German trenches at walking pace to help avoid confusion. Is the criticism of Haig fair though? Or was he doing the best he could with limited resources?

Some see Haig as directly responsible.

SOURCE 10

Fred Pearson, a private on the Western Front, commenting on Haig in a local newspaper in 1966.

The biggest murderer of the lot was Haig. I'm very bitter; always have been and always will be and everybody else that knew him. He lived almost 50 kilometres behind the line and that's about as near as he got. I don't think he knew what a trench was like. And they made him an Earl and gave him £100,000. I know what I'd have given him.

SOURCE 11

John Laffin, a military historian, writing in his history book *British Butchers and Bunglers of World War One* (2003). Laffin earned his living taking people on battlefield tours and researched the war from the soldiers' viewpoint.

Haig and other British generals must be blamed for wilful blunders and wicked butchery. However stupid they might have been, however much they were the product of a system which obstructed enterprise, they knew what they were doing. There can never be forgiveness for their sheer incompetence.

SOURCE 12

David Lloyd George, British Prime Minister during the First World War, writing in a book about his war-time experiences *War Memoirs* (1935).

Haig was a second-rate Commander in unparalleled and unforeseen circumstances. He was not endowed with any of the elements of imagination and vision. He certainly had none of that personal magnetism which has enabled great leaders of men to inspire multitudes with courage, faith and a spirit of sacrifice. He was incapable of planning vast campaigns on the scale demanded on so immense a battlefield.

However, it can be argued that this view of Hague is misleading.

SOURCE 13

Part of a report sent by Douglas Haig to the British cabinet following the Battle of the Somme (December 1916).

A considerable portion of the German soldiers are now practically beaten men, ready to surrender if they could, thoroughly tired of the war and expecting nothing but defeat. It is true that the amount of ground we have gained is not great. That's nothing. But we have proved our ability to force the enemy out of strong defensive positions and to defeat him. The German casualties have been greater than ours.

DISCUSSION

Study Sources 10, 11 and 12.

1. Read Source 11. Why can the reliability of this source be questioned?

2. Ready Source 12. Can you see any reason why the Prime Minister would look to distance himself from associating with Haig?

3. "The writer of Source 11 is obviously biased towards ordinary soldiers and therefore the source is of no use". How far would you agree with this statement?

A former soldier writing as a historian, Gordon Corrigan from the book *Mud, Blood and Poppycock*, page 198.

Generals, and indeed officers of any rank, may seem uncaring to the civilian mind. A commander cannot allow the death of one, or a hundred or a thousand of the men placed under him to affect his performance. If he does, that commander cannot properly discharge his responsibilities to the others who are still alive. Life has to go on, and while any commander will miss a fallen comrade, and regret his passing, he must move on: there is little time to mourn. Any general will make plans with the possibility of casualties well to the forefront of his thinking, but war is a nasty business, and killing is part of it. British generals were not uncaring but they accepted, as they had to, that the very nature of the war, would lead to many deaths however hard they tried to avoid them.

Alfred Duff Cooper, a soldier in the Grenadier Guards during the war, writing in his biography of Sir Douglas Haig. He was a friend to the Haig family and was officially invited to write Haig's biography by his family after Haig's death. He later became a Conservative MP and Secretary of War from 1935–37.

Great War and the mists created by prejudice, propaganda and false witness begin to scatter, the figure of Haig looms ever larger as that of the general who foresaw more accurately than most, who endured longer than most and who inspired most confidence amongst his soldiers. Haig believed from the first that the German line could be broken and it was. In moral stature, Haig was a giant. It may be easy in history to find a more brilliant man, but it would be hard to find a better one.

DISCUSSION

1. Study Source 13. Haig's statement that "The German casualties have been greater than ours" was correct. Does that mean his tactics were justified?

2. How far does Source 14 explain the negative views expressed in Sources 10 and 11?

3. Does who the author is make Source 15 unreliable? Explain.

4. To what extent is it impossible to come to a judgment as to whether General Haig deserves to be remembered as the "Butcher of the Somme"?

How important were other fronts?

FP Who won the war at sea?

In the years leading up to 1914, each of the major powers had devoted a huge amount of resources to developing large and powerful navies. In the case of Germany, its decision to launch a major naval construction programme led to an **arms race** with Britain which significantly added to the tension between the two alliances. Surprisingly, however, there were relatively few major naval engagements during the First World War, and those that did take place failed to provide a decisive outcome. Even so, the ability of Britain to gain and maintain control of the English Channel and North Sea played a significant part in her eventual victory in the war.

The main aims of British and German naval policy differed at the outbreak of war. From the British perspective, the priority had to be on preserving the supply lines between Britain and her major trading partners, and between Britain and northern France. A further aim was to choke German into submission through the implementation of a **blockade** of Germany's narrow coastline.

Germany's main aim, by contrast, was more limited. There is considerable evidence to suggest that the rapid development of its navy was intended to perform more of a deterrent role than an actual combatant function and, as a result, its primary role during the war was intended to sustain this function, while carrying out small attacks to reduce the size of the Royal Navy, in the hope it would be a useful negotiating tool in future peace negotiations. However, the enormous cost of constructing the navy resulted in a large pressure to use it in actual combat. As a result, the German navy carried out

Arms race

Germany launched a naval race with Britain at the end of the nineteenth century. Britain responded by introducing a new class of battleship, the Dreadnought, in 1905.

Blockade

A form of economic warfare where one country attempts to prevent goods or equipment being imported to its rival.

small, close attacks on British forces, laid minefields in the North Sea and deployed its developing submarine force to achieve these goals.

The earliest uses of the navy were, with two notable exceptions, mostly intended to gain control of the North Sea, an objective vital to the fulfillment of both sides' naval aims during the war.

Early naval operations, 1914/1915

28 August 1914 Battle of Heligoland Bight. A large British force targeted German shipping at its naval base in Heligoland, resulting in the deaths of 712 German sailors and 6 ships for the loss of 35 British sailors and no ships sunk.

⬇

1 November 1914 Battle of Coronel. A small German fleet of modern cruisers commanded by Admiral von Spee sank two British cruisers with the loss of 1600 British lives off the coast of Chile. This was the first British naval defeat since 1812.

⬇

8 December 1914 Battle of the Falkland Islands. A new British fleet, assembled to hunt down von Spee's forces, gained revenge for the Battle of Coronel, sinking four German ships and inflicting 1871 fatalities for the loss of 10 men and no ships on the British side.

⬇

16 December 1914. The German High Seas Fleet attacked 3 towns on the east Yorkshire coast (Scarborough, Whitby and Hartlepool), which resulted in 137 fatalities.

⬇

24 January 1915 Battle of Dogger Bank. After intercepting German radio messages, the British knew German High Seas Fleet was heading for Dogger Bank, where it cut off the German forces and managed to sink 1 armoured cruiser and inflict 954 fatalities.

▲ **Fig. 8.12**

SOURCE 16

Taken from Hew Strachan's *The First World War* published in 2003 by Simon and Schuster.

Once the war was declared, the Royal Navy had no strategic interest in fighting a major action against the German navy. As the world's greatest sea power, Britain enjoyed maritime supremacy. Its task was to defend what it had.

QUICK QUESTION 3

Who do you think had achieved most from the early naval encounters 1914/15?

DISCUSSION

Why was control of the sea vital to both Britain and Germany during the First World War?

Battle of Jutland

Within the Royal Navy, and the public at large, there remained a desire to achieve the type of decisive major naval victory which would rank with previous naval victories such as this experience occurred on 31 May 1916 at Jutland.

The aims of the commanders of both sides reflected the broader aims of Germany and Britain in the war at sea. Scheer's plan was to lure the British Grand Fleet from its base at Rosyth by way of decoy attacks on merchant shipping in the North Sea, and then use the remainder of his fleet to destroy parts of Jellicoe's forces. In doing so, he hoped to reduce the size of the British fleet, bringing it closer to the size of the German fleet. Unfortunately for Scheer, Jellicoe was aware of his plan and had sailed out of port much earlier than Scheer expected, and was instead lying in wait to achieve his objective: inflicting as much damage as possible on the High Seas Fleet.

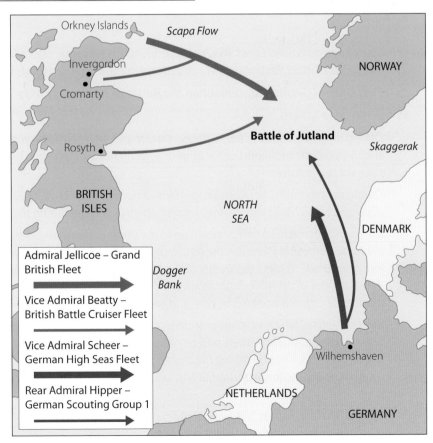

▲ **Fig. 8.13** The planned routes of German and British forces at the Battle of Jutland

While Jellicoe's fleet outnumbered that of Scheer, the decision to provide greater speeds and better guns at the expense of stronger armour would prove costly during the battle. Within the first hour of the battle starting, German gunfire had sunk HMS Indefatigable, and HMS Queen Mary costing 2,868 lives. However, Jellicoe had planned to lure Scheer into a trap, hoping that he would pursue the remnants of Admiral Beatty's ships. This resulted in main fleets facing each other by early evening in a fog of heavy smoke and with poor communications within each fleet. The ensuing battle only lasted a few minutes, but the damage caused by the huge British guns and the realisation that he was sailing into a trap forced Scheer to sail for home. Using his submarines for cover, he was able to prevent Jellicoe mounting an effective pursuit and managed to reach port the following morning.

Jutland was the biggest battle in naval history, featuring 250 ships and 100 000 men over the course of three days. Both sides claimed the battle as a victory.

Who won the Battle of Jutland?	
Was it Germany?	**Was it Britain?**
Lost 11 ships, including 1 battle cruiser	Lost 14 ships, including 3 battle cruisers
Lost 3,058 dead and wounded	Lost 6,784 dead, wounded and captured
Able to deploy 10 large ships immediately after the battle	Able to deploy 24 large ships immediately after the battle
Never risked a major sea battle again	Maintained its control of the North Sea
	Able to sustain its blockade of the north German coast.

▲ **Fig. 8.14**

Admiral Reinhard Scheer
(1863–1928)

Commander of the High Seas Fleet from January 1916, he had joined the German navy in 1879 and taken command of his first ship in 1907.

Sir John Jellicoe
(1859–1935)

Jellicoe was appointed commander of the Grand Fleet at the start of the war. He was cautious in his use of the fleet, aware of the damage which a major naval defeat could do to Britain's prospects in the wars as a whole.

SOURCE 17

Source Records of the Great War, Vol. IV, ed. Charles F. Horne, National Alumni 1923. From http://firstworldwar.com/source/jutland_1stgermanreport.htm.

First Official German Statement on the Battle of Jutland, 31 May-1 June 1916

Berlin, June 1, 1916

During an enterprise directed to the northward our high sea fleet on May 31st encountered the main part of the English fighting fleet, which was considerably superior to our forces.

During the afternoon, between Skagerrak and Horn Reef, a heavy engagement developed, which was successful to us, and which continued during the whole night.

In this engagement, so far as known up to the present, there were destroyed by us the large battleship Warspite, the battle-cruisers Queen Mary and Indefatigable, two armoured cruisers, apparently of the Achilles type; one small cruiser, the new flagships of destroyer squadrons, the Turbulent, Nestor, and Alcaster, a large number of torpedo-boat destroyers, and one submarine.

By observation, which was free and clear of clouds, it was stated that a large number of English battleships suffered damage from our ships and the attacks of our torpedo-boat flotilla during the day engagement and throughout the night. Among others, the large battleship Marlborough was hit by a torpedo. This was confirmed by prisoners.

Several of our ships rescued parts of the crews of the sunken English ships, among them being two and the only survivors of the Indefatigable.

On our side the small cruiser Wiesbaden, by hostile gunfire during the day engagement, and his Majesty's ship Pommern, during the night, as the result of a torpedo, were sunk.

The fate of his Majesty's ship Frauenlob, which is missing, and of some torpedo boats, which have not returned yet, is unknown.

The High Sea Fleet returned to-day [Thursday] into our port.

Source Records of the Great War, Vol. IV, ed. Charles F. Horne, National Alumni 1923. From http://firstworldwar.com/source/jutland_1stbritishreport.htm.

SOURCE 18

First Official British Statement on the Battle of Jutland, 31 May-2 June 1916

London, June 2, 1916

On the afternoon of Wednesday, the 31st of May, a naval engagement took place off the coast of Jutland.

The British ships on which the brunt of the fighting fell were the battle-cruiser fleet and some cruisers and light cruisers, supported by four fast battleships. Among these the losses were heavy.

The German battle fleet, aided by low visibility, avoided a prolonged action with our main forces. As soon as these appeared on the scene the enemy returned to port, though not before receiving severe damage from our battleships.

The battle-cruisers Queen Mary, Indefatigable, and Invincible, and the cruisers Defence and Black Prince were sunk.

The Warrior was disabled, and after being towed for some time had to be abandoned by her crew.

It is also known that the destroyers Tipperary, Turbulent, Fortune, Sparrowhawk, and Ardent were lost, and six others are not yet accounted for.

No British battleships or light cruisers were sunk.

The enemy's losses were serious. At least one battle cruiser was destroyed and one was severely damaged. One battleship is reported to have been sunk by our destroyers.

During the night attack two light cruisers were disabled and probably sunk.

The exact number of enemy destroyers disposed of during the action cannot be ascertained with any certainty, but must have been large.

Further Statement

Since the foregoing communication was issued a further report has been received from the Commander-in-Chief of the Grand Fleet stating that it has now been ascertained that our total losses in destroyers amount to eight boats in all.

The Commander-in-Chief also reports that it is now possible to form a closer estimate of the losses and the damage sustained by the enemy fleet.

One dreadnought battleship of the Kaiser class was blown up in an attack by British destroyers and another dreadnought battleship of the Kaiser class is believed to have been sunk by gunfire.

Of three German battle-cruisers, two of which are believed were the Derfflinger and the Luetzow, one was blown up, another was heavily engaged by our battle fleet and was seen to be disabled and stopping, and the third was observed to be seriously damaged.

DISCUSSION

How far was the battle of Jutland a British victory?

TASK

How far do Sources 17 and 18 agree on the results of the battle?

One German light cruiser and six German destroyers were stunk, and at least two more German light cruisers were seen to be disabled. Further repeated hits were observed on three other German battleships that were engaged.

Finally, a German submarine was rammed and sunk.

Tactics at sea

Blockades

If Jellicoe had not provided the hoped for major military victory at Jutland, his decision to mount a blockade of Germany's ports proved to have a much greater impact on the outcome of the war. Britain had used commercial blockades as a method of warfare since the eighteenth century, and the Royal Navy was given the task upon the outbreak of hostilities in August 1914. Soon after, the North Sea was declared to be a British military area, and all neutral merchant ships were intercepted and searched for any materials which could be used to help the German war effort.

The impact of the blockade on Germany was substantial. Both Germany's ability to feed her population and service her armaments industry were badly affected. Imports fell by 60 per cent during the war, creating a slow but ever-tightening stranglehold on the German economy. In February 1917, daily rations dropped from a daily average of 2,240 calories per person to 1,000 calories per person, forcing many people to rely heavily on ersatz goods and causing food riots across Germany and Austria-Hungary. Furthermore, the shortage of potatoes in 1917 created the turnip winter, a period when turnips, a vegetable hitherto seen fit to feed only animals, replaced the potato as a staple in the German diet.

SOURCE 19

Taken from http://www.nationalarchives.gov.uk/pathways/firstworldwar/transcripts/spotlights/cabinet_memo_blockade.htm.

MEMORANDUM IN REGARD TO THE PRESENT POSITION OF THE BLOCKADE, JANUARY 1st, 1917.

All the evidence available tends to show that, with some minor exceptions, practically no goods coming from overseas are getting through to Germany. For this purpose, fish caught by any of the northern neutrals and landed in a northern country is regarded rather in the light of home produce than in that of goods from overseas. The chief minor exceptions are certain colonial goods, such as tobacco, coffee, and cinchona from the Dutch colonies, and wines and spirits, as to which we have had a good deal of difficulty with the French. It is possible that, in addition to these, there may be some slight leakage by way of Sweden, because we are much hampered by the Swedish laws in getting information as to the export trade from Sweden to Germany. With regard to the other three northern neutrals, we have fairly complete returns, partly official and partly those furnished to us by our own agents, and these all go to show that practically none of the export trade from the northern neutrals to Germany consists of overseas goods.

▲ **Fig. 8.15** Berlin inhabitants cutting up a horse for meat during fighting in the city, undated

Submarine warfare

Britain, of course, was also vulnerable to the threat of blockade with 60 per cent of all food consumed in Britain in 1914 having to be imported. Germany launched a campaign of **unrestricted submarine warfare** in 1915 designed to target military and merchant ships leaving or heading towards Britain. International outrage at this tactic peaked when a German U-boat sank the passenger liner Lusitania on 7 May 1915, with the loss of 1,198 lives. Pressure from the United States increased when a US liner, the Arabic, was sunk in August that year bringing about the possibility of US intervention in the war. This led Germany to temporarily abandon the policy.

However, by the start of 1917, a combination of factors forced a rethink in Berlin. Germany's failure to achieve victory on the Western Front, with the likely impact of American soldiers in Europe, and the dangers of combatting the Royal Navy on the surface, persuaded Chancellor Bethmann-Hollweg to resume the policy of unrestricted submarine warfare.

The effects of the campaign were devastating on Britain. Germany believed that losses of 600 000 per month would be enough to bring about a British collapse, and by April 1917 that number had been comfortably exceeded. During the spring and summer Britain and her allies lost 1,505 merchant sailors and 2,775,406 tons of shipping, forcing Britain to introduce food **rationing**.

To counter the threat posed by the U-boats, Britain deployed a range of strategies and by the end of 1917 the worst of the danger was over. Germany's unrestricted use of submarines had succeeded merely in drawing America into the conflict and had failed to force Britain out of the war.

Q ships

Heavily armed ships, disguised as merchant vessels, were deployed to lure submarines to the surface where they could be attacked. Guns were hidden under fake lifeboats and funnels. Their record, however, was mixed. The total of 6 U-boats sunk by these vessels in 1917 must be set against the 23 Q ships which were themselves sunk by U-boats that year.

Mines

Thousands of mines were laid across the North Sea, with the 180-mile stretch between Norway and the Orkneys and Heligoland Bight providing especially dangerous for German submarines.

▲ **Fig. 8.16**

Convoy system

From summer 1916, merchant ships crossed the Atlantic in large numbers, escorted by battleships, and in some cases by aircraft as well. This made it harder for U-boats to pick off isolated ships and made it dangerous for them to attack in daylight. In addition, the battleships and planes could drop depth charges where they believed submarines to be present. This strategy was very effective in reducing the number of ships sunk, and between May 1917 and the end of the war only 168 (out of a total of 16 539) were sunk by U-boats across the Atlantic.

Unrestricted submarine warfare

A strategy deployed by Germany at times during the war. German U-boats would target any ship which appeared to be en route to Britain and Ireland.

Rationing

A measure to designed to ensure the regular supply of food and materials to a population. People would be issued with a ration card and only allowed to purchase a set amount of the rationed goods.

QUICK QUESTION 4

How do you think neutral countries would react to the policy of unrestricted submarine warfare?

DISCUSSION

1. Describe the main ways each side attempted to gain control of the sea during the period 1914–17.

2. What do Source 19 and Figure 8.15 tell us about the impact of the British blockade of Germany?

3. What were the main features of unrestricted submarine warfare?

4. Why was the convoy system more effective than other method of tackling the U-boat threat?

Why did the Gallipoli campaign of 1915 fail?

On 25 April 1915, British, French, Australian and New Zealand troops launched an invasion of Turkey designed to provide the outright victory which was lacking on the Western Front, and to provide assistance to their ally Russia by knocking Turkey out of the war.

Previous attempts to knock out the guns on the Gallipoli shoreline had been frustrated by a combination of bad weather, mines in the Dardanelles Straits and the organisation of the Turkish defenders by the German general Liman von Sanders.

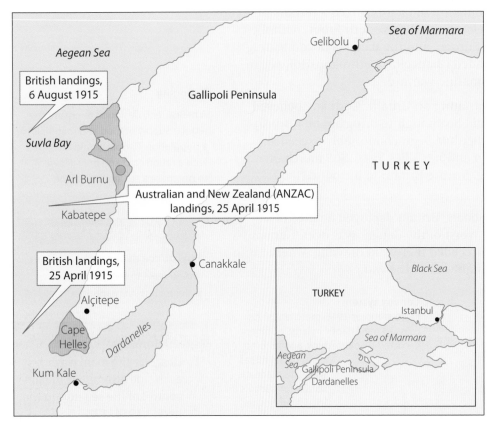

▲ **Fig. 8.17** Map of the Gallipoli campaign, April–December 1915

The combined allied forces at Gallipoli came under the command of General Sir Ian Hamilton. Hamilton had been advised by Greek military leaders that he would need 150 000 men to take Gallipoli, but Lord Kitchener, who opposed the plan, only approved the deployment of half that number. To make matters worse for Hamilton all element of surprise had been lost after the March naval raids leading to the arrival of 70 000 new Turkish troops to defend the peninsula.

QUICK QUESTION 5

Why did Britain decide to launch an offensive against the Turks?

Sir Ian Hamilton (1853–1947)

Placed in command of the ill-fated Gallipoli expedition due to his role as Commander-in-Chief of British forces in the Mediterranean, Hamilton had previously seen action in the Boer Wars and Russo–Japanese War. He was replaced by General Munro in October 1915, thereby effectively ending his military career.

From *Gallipoli* by Michael Hickey published in 1995.

There was a lack of up to date knowledge about Turkish troop positions… Hamilton's only intelligence consisted of a 1912 manual on the Turkish army, some old (and inaccurate) maps, a tourist guide book and what little could be found out from the Turkish desk at the Foreign Office.

The landing on 25 April aimed to establish two bridgeheads, one at Helles in the south and the other at Kabatepe. The British invasion at Helles resulted in heavy casualties, with 20 000 of the invading force of 70 000 killed or wounded. Many of the casualties were suffered on Beach V where an old trawler, the River Clyde was used to land the troops. Unfortunately, the Turkish machine gunners had a direct line of fire on the troops inflicting heavy casualties on the invaders. With Hamilton commanding the invasion miles offshore on the *Queen Elizabeth,* he was unable either to grasp the enormity of the crisis unfolding or make the necessary changes to the landing. Further north, at ANZAC Cove, as Kabatepe became known, the landings did not proceed any better. The troops were dropped off 1,500 metres from the designated drop off point, and were then confronted by steep cliffs preventing the ANZAC forces making any progress inland. Over 2,000 Australians were casualties on the first day of the landing.

Conditions were tough for all at Gallipoli, and the intense summer heat made matters worse. Shortage of fresh water, fly-ridden food, and difficulties burying corpses meant that sickness and disease spread quickly among the malnourished men. The onset of winter failed to bring any relief as torrential floods threw men out to sea, and snow brought with the dangers of frostbite.

Taken from Fred Waite's *The New Zealanders at Gallipoli* published in 1919.

Countless hordes of flies settled on everything edible. The soldiers waved them off. The black cloud rose and descended among the filth on the other side of the parapet. Presently they were back again on the food,—and so on, from the jam to the corpse, and back again to the jam, flitted the insect swarm, ensuring that the germs of most things undesirable were conveyed to the soldier's system through his mouth.

▲ **Fig. 8.18** Stores and dug outs at W beach, Gallipoli front

Unable to move troops off the beach in either the north or south of the peninsula, Hamilton decided to launch a second invasion in August at Suvla Bay. While ANZAC forces mounted a diversionary attack at ANZAC Cove, 20 000 British troops under the command of General Stopford came ashore at Suvla Bay facing very little opposition. However, Stopford's reluctance to push inland and the arrival of more Turkish defenders mean that this invasion resulted in the same stalemate which had afflicted the landings elsewhere.

British Commander-in-Chief Sir Ian Hamilton describes the battle of Sari Bair, which followed the landings at Suvla Bay in August 1915. Located at http://firstworldwar.com/source/saribair_hamilton.htm.

The first step in the real push – the step which above all others was to count – was the night attack on the summits of the Sari Bair ridge.

The crest line of this lofty mountain range runs parallel to the sea, dominating the under features contained within the Anzac position, although these fortunately defilade the actual landing-place. From the main ridge a series of spurs run down towards the level beach, and are separated from one another by deep, jagged gullies choked up with dense jungle.

…The New Army troops attacked with a fine audacity, but they were flung back from the height and then pressed still further down the slope, until General Baldwin had to withdraw his command to the vicinity of the Farm, whilst the enemy, much encouraged, turned their attention to the New Zealand troops and the two New Army battalions of No. 1 Column still holding the southwest half of the main knoll of Chunuk Bair.

Constant attacks, urged with fanatical peristence, were met here with a sterner resolution, and although, at the end of the day, our troops were greatly exhausted, they still kept their footing on the summit. And if that summit meant much to us, it meant even more to the Turks.

At daybreak on Tuesday, August 10th, the Turks delivered a grand attack from the line Chunuk Bair Hill Q against these two battalions, already weakened in numbers, though not in spirit, by previous fighting.

First our men were shelled by every enemy gun, and then, at 5.30 a.m., were assaulted by a huge column, consisting of no less than a full division plus a regiment of three battalions. The North Lancashire men were simply overwhelmed in their shallow trenches by sheer weight of numbers, whilst the Wilts, who were caught out in the open, were literally almost annihilated.

▲ **Fig. 8.19** Troops landing on the beach at Gallipoli

Hamilton was replaced in October by General Sir Charles Munro. Faced with little prospect of success at Gallipoli, and after enduring appalling weather conditions, he took the decision to withdraw the Allied troops in November 1915. Helles was the last beach to be evacuated in January 1916. In total, over one million men were involved on both sides in the Gallipoli campaign; over one third became casualties. The invaders lost over 44 000 men in one of the biggest military blunders of the war, meaning that the search for an alternative to the war of attrition in Belgium and northern France was over. The expedition's failure also resulted in two prominent political casualties. In November Winston Churchill resigned from the government, followed in December by the replacement of Asquith as Prime Minister by David Lloyd-George.

SOURCE 23

Extract from *Gallipoli* by John Masefield (1916) who was present at Gallipoli.

No such gathering of fine ships has ever been seen upon this earth, and the beauty and the exultation of the youth upon them made them seem like sacred things as they moved away. All that they felt was a gladness of exultation that their young courage was to be used. They went like Kings in a pageant to their imminent death.

The campaign came, more than once, very near to triumph, achieve the impossible many times, and failed, in the end from something which had nothing to do with arms nor with the men who bore them.

TASKS

1. Source 10 comes from a piece of British government propaganda. Does this mean it is of little use to an historian studying the Gallipoli campaign? Explain your answer using details of the source and your knowledge.

2. Use the sources, images and the text to explain the role of the following factors in the failure of the Gallipoli campaign:

   a. poor leadership

   b. Turkish defences

   c. the conditions facing the men at Gallipoli.

Why did Russia leave the war in 1918?

Russia entered the war in August 1914 with the largest land army of any the combatants, and the speed of her mobilisation in the early weeks of the war caught her enemies by surprise. However, by the summer of 1917 Russia was all but finished as a major partner in the entente war effort and was forced to sign a humiliating peace treaty with Germany in March 1918.

The war had started well for Russia, as the bulk of the Russian population rallied behind the Tsar's call to arms and the army enjoyed early successes against Austria-Hungary in the south and Germany in the north. At the battles of Tannenberg and Masurian Lakes, however, the two Russian armies suffered a heavy defeat at the hands of Hindenburg's German force and suffered losses of approximately a quarter of a million men. Samsanov, the commander of the Russian 2nd Army, was so traumatised by the defeat at Tannenberg that he shot himself rather than face the Tsar after the battle. This pattern of defeats continued in the north, until the Russians were able to hold off the German advance into their Polish territories by the end of the year.

While the Russian army was able to prevent a significant loss of land on the Austrian Front, 1915 brought further retreats in the face of the German advance. Warsaw fell on 4 August and only the huge reservoir of men at their disposal and the extremities of the winter weather prevented total capitulation. Commanders complained of shell shortages, while the new Minister of War, Polivanov, became exasperated at the lack of coordination between generals along the front line, and between the General Headquarters and the Ministry of War.

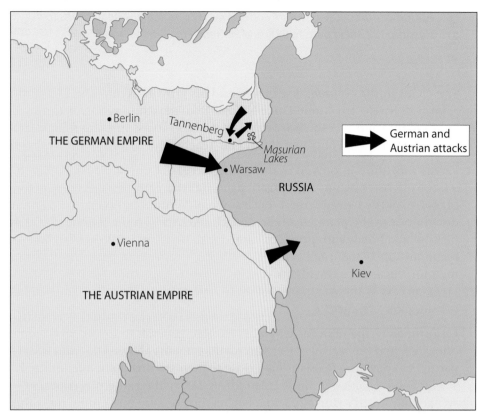

▲ **Fig. 8.20** Map of the Eastern Front

German and Austrian attacks

SOURCE 24

Taken from *The Eastern Front, 1914–17* by Norman Stone published in 1975.

Certainly shell was exaggerated as a feature of Russian military defeats in the spring and summer of 1915. The Germans' artillery superiority on the eastern front was no greater, and indeed was usually smaller than the western powers' artillery superiority in France, which got them nowhere.

▲ **Fig. 8.21** Tsar Nicholas II visiting the Russian front, May 1915. Grand Duke Nikolai Nikolaevich, Commander-in-Chief of the Russian Army is standing furthest to the right on the picture.

Taken from *The First World War* by Hew Strachan published in 2003.

At Gorlice-Tarnow (1915) the Central Powers collected 334 heavy guns to 4 Russian, 1272 field guns to 675, and 96 trench mortars to none.

The chaos in the command structure and his growing sympathy for political reform in Russia led Grand Duke Nikolai Nikolaevich to resign as Commander-in-Chief in August 1915. Tsar Nicholas' decision to assume the role proved to be one of the most controversial and far-reaching decisions of the entire war.

Russia's fortunes improved in the spring of 1916. General Brusilov planned a large offensive against the Austrians in Galicia, with the aim of relieving pressure on the beleaguered French town of Verdun and tying the Germans down prior to the planned Anglo-French offensive on the Somme at the start of July. In a break with previous campaigns, Brusilov implemented large-scale reconnaissance and intelligence gathering in order to prepare his officers and men for the attack. The offensive, which began on 4 June, was, initially, a great success as the Austrians lost up to half its army, and were pushed back a considerable distance.

Unfortunately, the reluctance of other Russian generals to follow up the initial offensives and the arrival of German reinforcements allowed the Alliance partners to push the Russians back close to their starting point and inflicted 1.5 million casualties on the Russian forces. While the battle was critical in weakening Austria-Hungary and relieving the pressure on Verdun, most Russians were dismayed at the failure of the army to once again deliver a clear victory.

General Brusilov (1853–1926)

One of the most talented of all the Russian officers serving on the Eastern Front, Brusilov's plan to smash through the Austrian lines in Galicia nearly succeeded in knocking Austria out of the war.

How did the war affect Russia?

Military
A series of defeats against Germany outweighed the successes Russia had against the Austrians. By the end of 1916, German forces had invaded Russia, and approximately 1.5 million men had lost their lives during the war. Furthermore the loss of land created a huge refugee problem as families were forced to escape the invading German forces.

Economic
Two inter-related issues created the biggest problems. A shortage of food in urban areas coupled with the government's decision to print money to pay for the war resulted in chronic inflation. The shortages were a result of peasant hoarding of grain and the inability of the transport network to withstand the pressures imposed on it by the demands of modern warfare. The impact on prices was dramatic: prices in Moscow more than doubled in the first year of the war, and trebled again by the start of 1917.

Political
Although most political parties supported the war in August 1914, the majority of Duma deputies joined a new opposition group, the Progressive Bloc in August 1915. The Bloc promised to help the war effort but wanted liberal political reforms introduced once the war was over. Nicholas rejected the offer and sacked ministers who supported it. Nicholas became more isolated during 1916 as his decision to become Commander-in-Chief left Alexandra and Rasputin in charge in Petrograd. Leaders gradually removed ministers who were not 100 per cent loyal to the Tsar, and replaced them with incompetent supporters such as Boris Stürmer. Ultimately, it was the regime's inability to tackle the food shortages which led to its downfall in 1917.

▲ **Fig. 8.22**

In February 1917, Nicholas II was forced to abdicate and a **Provisional Government** was established to rule Russia until a new Constituent Assembly could be formed. The Provisional Government was limited from the start by its lack of legitimacy and the fact it had to share power with a council of workers and soldiers called the **Petrograd Soviet**. Its decision to remain in the war arguably added to its unpopularity, particularly after an unsuccessful attempt to make a breakthrough on the Austrian front in June 1917.

▲ **Fig. 8.23** Russian deserters forced back, 1917

While a revolt against the government was crushed in July, as well as an attempted military coup in August, the future of the Provisional Government remained uncertain. A well-organised communist revolution led by the Bolsheviks in October 1917 overthrew the Provisional Government and introduced a series of radical reforms.

SOURCE 26

Extract from The Decree on Peace, 27 October 1917.

The Workers' and Peasants' Government, created by the revolution of October 24–25, and drawing its strength from the Soviets of Workers', Soldiers', and Peasants' Deputies, proposes to all warring peoples and their governments to begin at once negotiations leading to a just democratic peace. A just and democratic peace for which the great majority of wearied, tormented and war-exhausted toilers and labouring classes of all belligerent countries are thirsting, a peace which the Russian workers and peasants have so loudly and insistently demanded since the overthrow of the Tsar's monarchy, such a peace the government considers to be an immediate peace without annexations (i.e., without the seizure of foreign territory and the forcible annexation of foreign nationalities) and without indemnities.

Among its early decrees was a decision to end the war with Germany. The Decree on Peace invited all combatant nations to begin negotiations, to give up their claims to any territory gained during the war, and called for territorial settlements to be based on the principle of self-determination. An armistice with the Central Powers was agreed by the middle of December, and peace negotiations commenced one week later.

The Bolshevik delegation was led by Commissar for Foreign Affairs Leon Trotsky, whose apparently contradictory negotiating strategy of "**no war, no peace**" seemed to reflect the conflict within the Bolshevik leadership over the peace negotiations.

Provisional Government

After the abdication of Nicholas II in February 1917, a temporary government was established by members of the Duma. It only intended to remain in power until elections to a new Constituent Assembly had been held.

Petrograd Soviet

The main council of workers and soldiers created during the February Revolution. It maintained control of the army and jointly ruled Russia with the Provisional Government under an arrangement known as Dual Authority.

QUICK QUESTION 6

Why do you think Britain and France insisted Russia would have to pay back her war loans immediately if she pulled out of the war after the Tsar's abdication?

No war, no peace

Trotsky, Commissar for Foreign Affairs in the Bolshevik government, deployed this delaying strategy while negotiating a peace treaty with Germany. He did not intend to carry on the war, but would not agree to peace under the terms offered by the Germans.

While Lenin was anxious to begin building a socialist state in Russia and therefore pushed for a swift resolution to the talks, the majority of the party's Central Committee wanted to drag the talks on as long as possible, believing that similar socialist revolutions were imminent in Germany and Austria-Hungary.

Trotsky's recollections of the peace negotiations from his autobiography *My Life*.

It was obvious that going on with the war was impossible. On this point there was not even a shadow of disagreement between Lenin and me. But there was another question. How had the February revolution, and, later on, the October revolution, affected the German army? How soon would any effect show itself? To these questions no answer could as yet be given. We had to try and find it in the course of the negotiations as long as we could. It was necessary to give the European workers time to absorb properly the very fact of the Soviet revolution.

Frustrated by Trotsky's willingness to reach an agreement, the Germans ended the armistice in February 1918. Both sides agreed to sign the Treaty of Brest-Litovsk on 3 March 1917; a treaty which would exact a high price from the Russians for exiting the war, and would lead to the start of a further three years of civil war.

DISCUSSION

Look carefully at the photograph and source on page 179 and the source on this page. Using the information in the sources and your own knowledge, explain why the Bolsheviks were keen to negotiate a peace deal with Germany.

◀ **Fig. 8.24** Map of the Treaty of Brest-Litovsk

The main terms of the Treat of Brest-Litovsk

Russia lost:

- more than 290 000 square miles of land, including Finland, Latvia, Lithuania, Estonia, Belarus, and the Ukraine
- a quarter of its population
- a quarter of the its industry
- 90 per cent of its coal mines.
- all Turkish lands gained in the Russo–Turkish War of 1877–78, which were to be returned to the Ottoman Empire.

1. Produce a graph charting Russia's military performance 1914–18. An example for how this could be laid out is provided below.

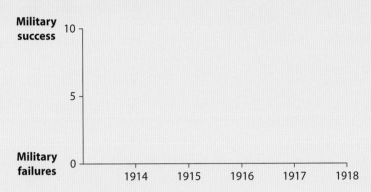

2. Write a speech defending Nicholas' decision to become commander-in-chief in August 1915, and one which criticises it.

3. Which was the most damaging feature of the Treaty of Brest-Litovsk for Russia?

What was the impact of war on civilian populations?

The outbreak of war brought many new restrictions on people's way of life. In August 1914, the British government introduced the Defence of the Realm Act (DORA) which gave the government wide-ranging powers to secure "public safety". These sweeping powers included the introduction of press censorship, imprisonment without trial, reduced licensing hours and the introduction of British Summer Time.

While it was late to join the war, the United States quickly passed major pieces of legislation to restrict any action which might threaten the war effort. The 1917 Espionage Act made it illegal to interfere with the recruitment of troops or to pass on classified information. Conscious objection was also an offence under this Act. A year later, the Sedition Act made it an offence to use abusive language about the US Constitution, the armed forces or the government. As a result of the Act, mail could be denied anyone thought to be in breach of its terms.

Perhaps the greatest impact on the civilian populations was the need to recruit sufficient manpower to fight the war. Although each of the major combatants, with the exception of Britain, had a large army in 1914, each country introduced conscription. Britain relied on a volunteer army for the first two years of the conflict, managing to recruit over 3 million men between 1914 and 1916. However, the cumulative effects of campaigns such as Mons, Ypres and Gallipoli meant that conscription was introduced for all single men aged 18–41 in January 1916. The measure was extended to all men within that age range in May 1916.

Approximately 16 000 men refused to be conscripted, and these were know as **conscientious objectors**. While approximately half of these accepted a non-combatant role in the armed forces, a significant minority did not and were either imprisoned or forced to join a military unit in France.

Most of the combatant nations experienced a shortage of food as a result of the war. While there were some common reasons for these shortages, such as the

Conscientious objectors

After the introduction of the 1916 Military Service Act, which introduced conscription, thousands of men applied to be exempted from military service on the grounds of their conscience.

conscription of farm workers into the army, other causes such as blockades or inadequate railway networks also made a large contribution in individual cases.

Britain was especially vulnerable to blockade as it imported large amounts of food and other raw materials from other countries. As is described earlier in the chapter, the German campaign of unrestricted submarine warfare and the British naval blockade had a devastating effect on its enemy's economy.

QUICK QUESTION 7

What factors might influence someone to become a conscientious objector during the First World War?

How did Britain and Germany attempt to tackle the problem of food shortages?	
Britain	**Germany**
Increased area of farmland in order to produce more food.	Developed *ersatz* (substitute) goods such as acorns and beechnuts as a coffee substitute.
Increased imports from the United States.	Clocks were moved forward an hour to give workers the opportunity to work in their gardens after work.
Introduced rationing in January 1918, starting with sugar and meat, but later extended to other goods during the year.	Millions of pigs were slaughtered in order to save grain.
	After the disastrous potato harvest in 1916, turnips were issued as a replacement.
	Limited rationing was introduced in 1914.

▲ **Fig. 8.25**

DEFENCE OF THE REALM.
E.P. 6.
MINISTRY OF FOOD.
BREACHES OF THE RATIONING ORDER
The undermentioned convictions have been recently obtained:—

Court	Date	Nature of Offence	Result
HENDON	29th Aug., 1918	Unlawfully obtaining and using ration books	3 Months' Imprisonment
WEST HAM	29th Aug., 1918	Being a retailer & failing to detach proper number of coupons	Fined £20
SMETHWICK	22nd July, 1918	Obtaining meat in excess quantities	Fined £50 & £5 5s. costs
OLD STREET	4th Sept., 1918	Being a retailer selling to unregistered customer	Fined £72 & £5 5s. costs
OLD STREET	4th Sept., 1918	Not detaching sufficient coupons for meat sold	Fined £25 & £2 2s. costs
CHESTER-LE-STREET	4th Sept., 1918	Being a retailer returning number of registered customers in excess of counterfoils deposited	Fined £50 & £3 3s. costs
HIGH WYCOMBE	7th Sept., 1918	Making false statement on application for and using Ration Books unlawfully	Fined £40 & £6 4s. costs

Enforcement Branch, Local Authorities Division,
MINISTRY OF FOOD.
September, 1918.

▲ **Fig. 8.26** Breaches of the Rationing Order

Food shortages in Russia were largely attributable to two main causes: the poor quality of the country's railway network and the the lack of incentive for peasants to produce more food as the war dragged on. As well as decreasing amounts of food in the cities, the main consequence was a sharp increase in inflation. Between 1914 and 1916, the cost of meat rose by 232 per cent, and the average price of food by nearly 90 per cent.

However, not every country experienced food shortages: the United States was able to feed its own population while providing essential supplies for her allies. Meanwhile France was still able to feed its population due to the amount of agricultural land unaffected by the war.

The First World War proved to be a watershed in providing employment opportunities for women which had hitherto been denied them across Europe. In Russia, women made up 43 per cent of the industrial workforce, and even recruited a female battalion in 1917. Women in Britain also made up a significant proportion of the workforce by 1918; the number increasing from 24 per cent in 1914 to 37 per cent in 1918. In France, approximately one third of the labour force working in arms production was women.

However, these statistics are slightly misleading as the total number of women working in all sectors across Europe increased by only 1 million. What appears to have happened is that women in low-paid, usually domestic, jobs took the opportunity to move into better paid jobs in munitions factories and public transport.

The need to increase food production provided further opportunities for women to work in different sectors. Across Europe, many women worked on the land from the earliest stages of the war, and in 1915 created the Women's Land Army offered a skilled female farming workforce.

Conditions for women during the war differed across the continent. Women in France benefited from the general increased in farm incomes and from allowances paid by the government to soldiers' wives. However, this contrasted sharply with the experience of women in Germany where the effects of food shortages and the effects of influenza lead to sharp increase in the death rates for women in 1917 and 1918.

Once the war was over, considerable public pressure forced most women out of their new jobs and back into their pre-war occupations. Even so, women in most of the combatant nations were rewarded for their efforts during the war by the being given the vote. Britain, Canada and Austria granted it in 1918, Germany in 1919 and the United States in 1920.

▲ **Fig. 8.27** Certificate issued to members of the Women's Land Army, 1915

QUICK QUESTION 8

Why did the British government issue the certificate in Figure 8.27?

SOURCE 28

Notice stuck to a wall of a French munitions factory at the end of the war.

Now you may best serve your country by returning to your former pursuits, busying yourselves with peacetime activities.

As well as the estimated 10 million fatalities on the battlefield, deaths on the home front were significant in number too. Approximately 940 000 civilians lost their lives due to military action, with a further 5.9 million dying from disease, malnutrition and accidents. The arrival of Spanish flu during the last stages of the war inflicted further fatalities in addition to these figures.

TASKS

1. What do you understand by the term "total war"? In what ways could the First World War be said to be an example of a "total war"?

2. Britain relied on imports to a much greater extent than did Germany during the war. Why do you think the impact of food shortages was so much greater in Germany than in Britain?

3. How far did the war have a positive effect on civilian populations?

Why did Germany ask for an armistice in 1918?

FP What was the importance of America's entry into the war?

The United States had maintained a policy of **isolation** throughout the nineteenth century, but effectively broke its policy of neutrality in 1914 when it agreed to a British request to stop selling arms to Germany. However, it did not agree to formally join the war against Germany and her allies until April 1917. The decision to declare war was a result of several factors.

With the development of mass communications and sea transport, the United States developed closer links with Europe and therefore had no wish to see a single dominant power emerge victorious from the war, particularly if this dominant power represented political views at odds with the US belief in democracy. Furthermore, the policies of Germany during the war pushed the United States closer to the Entente powers. The use of unrestricted submarine warfare appeared to highlight the aggressive nature of the Central Powers, and President Wilson reacted furiously to US fatalities caused by U-boat attacks, culminating in 100 American deaths on the Lusitania in May 1915.

President Wilson spent much of 1915 and 1916 attempting to broker a peace between the two sides, but met with no success. After Germany resumed her campaign of unrestricted submarine warfare in February 1917, US public opinion became more convinced of the need to go to war, opinion which was hardened by the publication of a telegram intercepted by the British sent by the German Foreign Minister Arthur Zimmermann to the German ambassador to Mexico offering United States territory to Mexico in return for joining the German cause. On 6 April Wilson declared war on Germany.

While the size of US forces in 1917 was not large enough to cause any great alarm to the Central Powers, the US army consisted of approximately 130 000 soldiers, over the course of the following 21 months its contribution to the Allied war effort would be hugely significant.

Initially, US assistance was limited to bolstering the anti-submarine capabilities of her allies, sending destroyers and merchant ships, and assisting with mining operations in the North Sea. While US land forces only arrived in small numbers, 300 000 were in France by March 1918, their presence helped to plug the gaps created by Ludendorff's offensive launched on 21 March. The arrival of a further 800 000 soldiers between May and July 1918 allowed the Allies to transfer their more experienced soldiers away from quieter parts of the Western Front to combat the follow-up German offensives in June and July.

US forces never gained the key victory its commander General Pershing desired but their arrival provided a huge psychological boost to the Entente powers, coming as it did after a disastrous 1917 when the submarine campaign, the effects of Passchendaele and the Bolshevik revolution threatened to push victory still further out of sight. This effect was compounded by the effects on the balance of forces on the Western Front: as the German army was losing 1.75 million men between 21 March and 11 November, their opponents were being boosted by the arrival of an ally who had managed to recruit nearly 5 million men by the end of the war.

Isolation

US foreign policy since the late eighteenth century had avoided any involvement in European affairs.

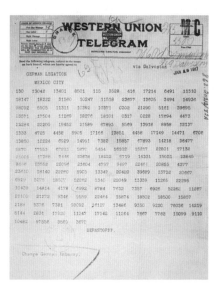

▲ **Fig. 8.28** The Zimmermann telegram

QUICK QUESTION 9

President Wilson failed to broker a peace deal between Germany and her enemies in 1915 and 1916. Why do you think this was?

Why was the German offensive of 1918 unsuccessful?

In January 1918, German prospects in the war were not good. The Germans were still committed to a war on the Eastern Front, but they had recruited all remaining reserves and the submarine campaign had failed to deliver a knock-out blow against Britain. Furthermore, the United States was expected to deliver large numbers of men to bolster its opponents in the west. General Ludendorff conceived of a plan to draw Allied forces away from Flanders, where he hoped to launch a decisive campaign designed to push the BEF into the sea. The decision to go ahead with "Operation Michael", Germany's last chance of victory, was made on 10 March 1918.

Erich Ludendorff (1865–1937)

Due to his successes early in the war, capturing Liege in the west and defeating the Russian forces in the east, Ludendorff was promoted to Quartermaster-General under Hindenburg and the two officers ran Germany as a "**silent dictatorship**" from 1916. He was chiefly responsible for persuading Wilhelm II to accept an armistice in November 1918 and then spent much of his life after the war perpetuating the "stab in the back" myth. He was an accomplice of Adolf Hitler in the failed 1923 Beer Hall Putsch.

The offensive started at 4am on 21 March. The German army amassed its troops south of Arras in the St Quentin sector. The offensive was, initially, a huge success with German forces advancing 35 miles in the first 3 weeks. Subsequent attacks in June and July pushed the Allies within five miles of Paris before being stopped by a Franco-American counter-offensive. The British had lost 178 000 including 70 000 men who were taken prisoner; the French lost an estimated 77 000 casualties. German casualties were even higher, suffering over 1 million casualties during the offensives of 1918.

The reasons for the failure of Ludendorff's plan stem largely from its initial success. By breaking out of the heavily fortified **Hindenburg Line**, the Germans transformed a war of attrition into a war of movement, a move which played into the hands of an enemy with more men, tanks and aircraft. In addition, the ground captured in the first weeks of the campaign now had to be occupied and defended, something Hindenburg realised he was unable to do after the 1916 Somme Offensive, hence his retreat and the shortening of his defensive lines.

The successful French counter-attack at the Marne in July was critical in forcing Ludendorff back onto the defensive: he called off his offensive in Flanders and was forced to fight a desperate rearguard action until the end of the war. The French success demonstrated the shift in Allied tactics, with surprise attacks and creeping barrages supporting infantry advances, reinforced by an overwhelming superiority of shells and tanks.

Allied superiority in material was reflected in numerical superiority. A serious influenza epidemic resulted in half a million cases in the Germany army, adding to the impact of the losses incurred since March. At the start of August, it was reported that only 2 of its 13 divisions were fit for action and a further 5 only good for defence.

Silent dictatorship

As chiefs of the German High Command, Hindenburg and Ludendorff were able to create a position by September 1916 where they had the dominant influence over civilian and military matters in Germany, and both the Kaiser and Reichstag were relegated in importance.

Hindenburg Line

German forces on the Western Front retreated to a shortened defensive position after the battle of the Somme. Featuring concrete bunkers, fortified villages, underground tunnels and protected by rows of barbed wire, it was meant to provide an impregnable position from which to prevent further Allied advance.

▲ **Fig. 8.29** German soldiers training before Operation Michael

These factors had an impact on German morale with alcohol abuse, shirking and desertion becoming a feature of what was previously a highly disciplined armed force.

The turning point on the Western Front was the defeat at Amiens in August. On 8 August, a combined Allied infantry, artillery, tank and air offensive, coupled with precise intelligence of the location of enemy artillery resulted in an advance of 8 miles, described by Ludendorff as the "black day of the German army". The tactical innovations displayed by the French at the Marne and the British at Amiens were significant in making the type of breakthrough which had eluded the Allies in 1916 and 1917. While casualties were still heavy between August and the end of the war, with the breaking of the Hindenburg Line at the end of September, it became a question of when, rather than if, Germany would surrender in 1918.

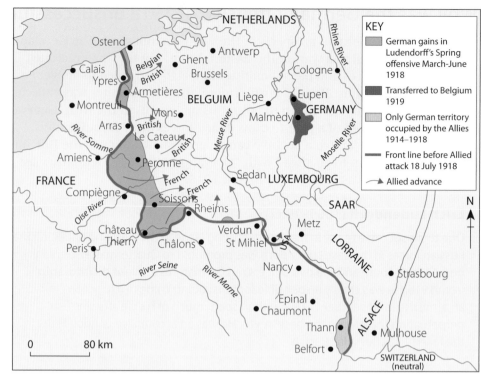

▲ **Fig. 8.30** The 1918 German Offensive

SOURCE 29

Taken from *The Myriad Faces of War* by Trevor Wilson published in 1986.

The Germans had purchased a tactical success at the price of a strategic calamity. They had sustained irreplaceable casualties to the tune of 250,000 men. And they had overrun territory that, a year before, they had gone to great trouble to abandon.

Why did revolution break out in Germany in October 1918?

During the last two years of the war, the German political system seemed to move in two divergent directions. On the one hand, Generals Hindenburg and Ludendorff interfered in domestic affairs under the auspices of directing the country's war effort, to the extent that some historians refer to the period 1916–18 as the "silent dictatorship". However, at the same time, the Reichstag started to take a more active role in questioning the direction of the war effort and the composition of the government. By November 1918, these two trends had converged to overthrow the Empire and create a new republic.

The main long-term cause of the German revolution was war weariness. In July 1917, the Reichstag demanded a peace without major annexations and reparations, although it was not until the end of September 1918 that Ludendorff was willing to consider a "revolution from above" in order to prevent widespread mutiny and a possible revolution.

The German revolution seemed to happen in two separate stages. The first stage took place between 3–26 October. On 3 October, Prince Max von Baden, a liberal monarchist was appointed chancellor, and formed a new government consisting of liberal and socialist Reichstag members. He quickly asked President Wilson for an armistice, but Wilson insisted that any peace negotiations take place with true representatives of the German people, that is, not the generals or the Kaiser. On 26 November, the Kaiser created a series of measures called the October Reforms which radically transferred power from the elite to the Reichstag: the old system of government, established by Bismarck in 1871, had been overthrown and a parliamentary monarchy put in its place.

The trigger for the second stage of the German revolution was a mutiny of sailors at the main naval bases of Kiel and Wilhelmshaven. The mutiny was a reaction to a plan devised by Naval Supreme Commander Admiral Reinhardt Scheer to end the war with a large naval assault on Britain's High Seas Fleet. Tired, hungry, and aware that armistice talks were ongoing, most of the sailors either refused to return from leave or refused to set sail on 30 October. Soldiers' Councils were set up, which soon included industrial workers from Kiel among its number.

Within a week, riots had broken out across Germany, with Kurt Eisner establishing a Bavarian Democratic and Social Republic in Munich on 8 November, while the capital Berlin became the centre of political intrigue which resulted in the abdication of the Kaiser. The issue of the Kaiser's position appeared to be the only obstacle to ending the war; President Wilson had stated that Wilhelm would not be allowed to participate in any peace talks. Fearing imminent civil war, a delay to the end of the war, and a more radical socialist revolution, Prince Max announced Wilhelm's abdication on 9 November, and appointed SPD leader Friedrich Ebert as the new chancellor. Wilhelm fled to the Netherlands shortly afterwards.

Why was the armistice signed?

On 28 September, Ludendorff and Hindenburg agreed that Germany had no choice but to surrender. Failure to do so would likely result in the complete destruction of the German army and the invasion of Germany. By the start of November, German forces were in a state of permanent retreat, and morale had all but collapsed. The timing of the decision was influenced by events both on the Western front and other fronts. The impact of the Allied breakthrough was compounded by the Bulgarian defeat at Monastir-Doiron, prompting a call for an armistice at the end of September, followed by Turkey agreeing to a peace deal on 30 October and Austria four days later.

The defeat of the Central Powers was largely due to events on the Western Front.

TASKS

1. What do you understand by the term "revolution from above"?

2. In what ways do the events of October and November 1918 represent a "revolution from above"?

3. Is it possible to argue that it was pressure from below that led to the Kaiser's abdication, rather than the actions of politicians in Berlin?

QUICK QUESTION 10

Was Germany's defeat in the First World War inevitable?

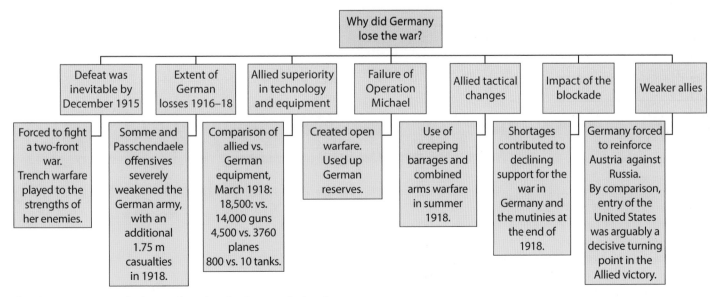

▲ **Fig. 8.31** Factors which contributed to the Germans losing the war

- ▶ The Schlieffen Plan
- ▶ Life in the trenches
- ▶ Different methods of warfare
- ▶ While the war at sea was inconclusive, the impact of the Allied blockade and Britain's ability to see off the U-boat threat played a significant part in Germany's eventual defeat.
- ▶ The attempt to achieve victory by opening up new fronts proved disastrous as the Gallipoli expedition illustrated.
- ▶ The overthrow of Nicholas II and the eventual Russian withdrawal from the war removed the threat of a two front war, but the entry of America into the war provided a greater threat to the Germans.
- ▶ The failure of the Ludendorff Offensive, combined with the collapse of the home front not only led to Germany's defeat on the battlefield and the abdication of the Kaiser in November 1918.

Revision tips

- Trench warfare didn't begin at the start of the war. Fighting in Trenches developed as a result of neither side being able to seize the advantage in those early exchanges. Both sides attempted to take control, but after the battle of the Marne it became apparent that they were too evenly matched.

- The battle of the Somme was launched as a direct consequence of the battle of Verdun. The British hadn't intended to launch an offensive at the Somme, and this can explain why so many were killed.

- Consider how far Germany's defeat was inevitable after the failure of the Schlieffen Plan

- Think about the differing contributions of the following features to the defeat of Germany in 1918: Allied naval blockade, new technology, the entry of the United States into the war, and the failure of the Ludendorff Offensive.

- Look at the ways in which Britain was able to cope better with the threat posed by Germany to its food supplies than Germany was with the threat posed by the Royal Navy to its supplies.

Review questions

1. Why was Britain able to withstand the U-boat war in 1917–18?

2. How far do you agree with the view that Britain won the war at sea?

3. How far do these sources in this chapter provide convincing evidence that failure of the Gallipoli campaign was mostly due to poor military leadership? Use the sources to explain your answer.

4. Study Figure 8.26. What can you learn from this about the impact of the war on Britain? Support your answer with reference to the source.

5. How far was the failure of the Ludendorff responsible for the defeat of Germany in 1918?

9 Germany, 1918–45

Introduction

Shortly before the signing of the armistice on 11 November 1918, Wilhelm II, Kaiser of Germany, abdicated. His autocratic system of government was replaced with a democracy soon to become known as the Weimar Republic. This experiment with democracy was to last for 14 years before it was destroyed by the establishment of Hitler's dictatorship. The **Third Reich**, intended to last for 1,000 years, collapsed in 1945 following the suicide of its creator, Adolf Hitler, and the military defeat of Germany.

Third Reich

The term used to describe the Nazi regime in Germany from 1933 to 1945.

The aims of this chapter are to:

- Examine the Revolution of 1918, the establishment of the Republic, and the Versailles Settlement and German reactions to it.

- Look at the Weimar constitution, the main political divisions, and the role of the army as well as the political disorder of 1919 to 1923 including economic crises and hyperinflation, and the occupation of the Ruhr.

- Consider the Streseman era as well as the cultural achievements of the Weimar period.

- Examine the early years of the Nazi Party, including Nazi ideas and methods, the Munich Putsch, and the roles of Hitler and other Nazi Leaders.

- Study the impact of the Depression on Germany, the political, economic, and social crisis of 1930 to 1933, the reasons for the Nazis' rise to power, Hitler taking power, the Reichstag fire, and election of 1933.

- Examine Nazi rule in Germany including the Enabling Act, the Night of the Long Knives, the death of Hindenburg, the removal of opposition, methods of control and repression, and the use of culture and mass media.

- Consider Nazi economic policy including rearmament.

- Look at different experiences of Nazi rule including women and young people, the rise of anti-Semitism, persecution of minorities and opposition to Nazi rule.

- Consider the impact of the Second World War on Germany including the conversion to a war economy and the Final Solution.

Was the Weimar Republic doomed from the start?

How did Germany emerge from defeat at the end of the First World War?

The events of October to November 1918 are sometimes referred to as "the German Revolution". Following a naval mutiny at Kiel and soldiers' and workers' rebellions spreading to other German ports and cities, the German Kaiser was persuaded to abdicate. He fled to exile in Holland. Political power was immediately assumed by Friedrich Ebert, the leader of the Social Democratic Party, the largest party in the Reichstag. Amid conditions of considerable social unrest, violence on the streets and political chaos, a German Republic was declared with Friedrich Ebert as Chancellor. His first tasks were to restore law and order and hold democratic elections as soon as possible.

Restoring law and order was not going to be easy as there was one extremist political group committed to the overthrow of the new government. This Bolshevik-inspired party was the Spartacist League. At the end of December 1918, the party changed its name to the German Communist Party and made immediate plans to seize power. The attempted revolution of January 1919 is referred to as the Spartacist Uprising.

▲ **Fig. 9.1** Spartacist poster

Leaders	• Karl Liebknecht and Rosa Luxemburg
Objective	• The overthrow of Ebert's moderate government based on parliamentary democracy • The establishment of a communist-style government based on soldiers' and workers' councils, or soviets, across the towns and cities of Germany. There would be no national parliament.
Methods	• Formation of a Revolutionary Committee • Seizure of some newspaper offices in Berlin • Organisation of a general strike • Armed street fighting against opponents and the erection of barricades.
Government response	• Force by the army and Freikorps who seized the Spartacist headquarters and crushed the uprising • Liebknecht and Luxemburg were murdered.
Reasons for failure	• Spartacists were divided as to which tactic should be used—delay or immediate violent seizure of power • Death of leaders • Loyalty of the army and ruthless methods of the Freikorps.
Significance	• Showed the weakness of the new government as it had to rely upon the services of an independent group, the Freikorps, over which it had little control • Led to a number of further communist rebellions (including Bavaria, April 1919 and the Ruhr, March 1920) which were similarly crushed by the Freikorps • Communism remained a significant influence in German politics throughout the 1920s and early 1930s.

▲ **Table 9.1** The Spartacist Uprising, January 1919

QUICK QUESTION 1

How far does Source 1 agree with the message of the poster in Figure 9.1?

SOURCE 1

Extract from an article written by the Spartacist leader, Rosa Luxemburg, December 1918.

All this resistance must be broken step by step, with an iron fist and ruthless energy. The violence of the bourgeois [middle-class] counter-revolution must be confronted with the revolutionary violence of the proletariat [urban working class]. Against the attacks, insinuations, and rumours of the bourgeoisie must stand the inflexible clarity of purpose, vigilance, and ever ready activity of the proletarian mass.

Party	Support-base	Political position	Votes (millions)	% of vote	Seats
Social Democrat	Urban working class and lower middle class	Moderate, democratic socialist	11.5	37.9	165
Centre Party	Roman Catholic	Democratic conservative	6.0	19.7	91
Democratic Party	Middle class	Left-wing liberal democrat	5.6	18.6	75
Nationalist People's Party	Landowners and wealthy industrialists	Anti-Weimar Republic	3.1	10.3	44
Other			4.3	13.5	48
Total			30.5	100	423

▲ **Table 9.2** German political parties and the January 1919 general election

Ebert's Social Democratic Party emerged as the largest party after the general election of January 1919 (see Table 9.2). It was now the task of the newly-elected assembly to devise a constitution for the new republic. As Berlin was still affected by lawlessness and street fighting, the National Assembly met in the small town of Weimar which gave its name to the new constitution and republic which was finally approved at the end of July 1919 (see Figure 9.2).

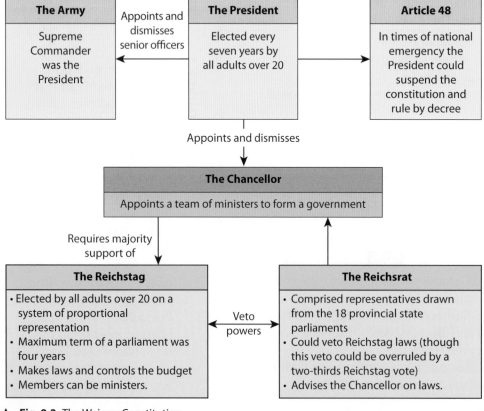

▲ **Fig. 9.2** The Weimar Constitution

Proportional representation	• This system of election meant that the proportion of votes received by a political party would be approximately equal to the proportion of seats allocated in the Reichstag. • One advantage of this system over many others was that it was considered to be fair. There were also disadvantages. • By allowing a party that won a small proportion of the vote some seats, small extremist parties were able to gain a foothold in the Reichstag and receive publicity for their cause. • Proportional representation encourages voting for a broad range of parties as there are no wasted votes. This means that it is extremely difficult for any one party to gain 50 per cent or more of the vote; this never happened during the years of the Weimar Republic. • All governments were, therefore, **coalition** governments. These often proved to be short-lived creating political uncertainty and instability. There were nine general elections during the years of the Weimar Republic—on average, approximately one every eighteen months.
Article 48	• Arguably, this gave the President too much power as it allowed him to discard the democratic system of government. • Between 1929 and 1933, Presidential Decrees were used with increasing regularity. This helped to undermine respect and confidence in the new parliamentary democracy.
Forward-looking features	• The granting of equal voting rights to all Germans; men and women were treated equally under the voting system. • The granting of human and civil rights such as the rights to free speech, free worship, and the holding of public meetings. • In some respects the Weimar Constitution was the most democratic and progressive in the world.

▲ **Table 9.3** The Weimar Constitution included a number of interesting and controversial features

Coalition

A coalition government is made up of representatives from a number of different political parties in order to command a majority.

What was the impact of the Treaty of Versailles on the Republic?

The army

The Treaty of Versailles was unpopular with most Germans, but it was the right wing that was strongest in its opposition. In particular, the army resented the disarmament clauses that limited the number of troops to 100 000. Many discharged soldiers joined the Freikorps as a way of continuing their military life. But this development concerned the Allies who regarded the numbers enrolled in the Freikorps as part of the 100 000 limitation. When the Weimar Government attempted to implement an Allied request that the Freikorps be disbanded there was a revolt, the Kapp Putsch.

Who were the Freikorps?

• A group of ex-soldiers who shared strong anti-communist views and a taste for violence.

• They were a volunteer force initially formed by Ebert on the eve of the Spartacist Uprising.

• They were armed, well equipped, and numbered about 4,000 in January 1919.

The economy

The Treaty of Versailles stripped Germany of European territory, resources, colonies, and its merchant navy. It also imposed reparations, assessed in 1921 at £6.6 billion. The Weimar government argued that this amount placed an impossible strain on an economy already burdened with war debts and deprived of the means to create wealth. In 1922 the government failed to pay its second instalment of reparations. The French thought that the Germans were bluffing and simply trying to avoid their treaty obligations. Together with the Belgians, they decided to occupy the **Ruhr** in January 1923. The intention was to seize coal to the value of the money owed. But the action misfired and led to a serious economic and financial crisis.

- The German government authorised passive resistance to the French. This meant that the German population of the Ruhr refused to work in the mines or accept orders from the occupiers.

- Amid violence and shootings, the French responded by expelling some 100 000 Germans from the Ruhr.

- Since the Ruhr was one of the main wealth-producing areas in Germany, the revenue of the government fell at the very time that it needed to find more money to support the Germans still living there. The expelled Germans also had to be rehoused.

- In order to bridge the gap between income and expenditure the government decided to print money. This action led quickly to hyperinflation during the second half of 1923. In effect, the currency collapsed and many Germans resorted to bartering—exchanging goods for other goods or services.

Leader	• Dr Wolfgang Kapp
Objective	• The overthrow of the Weimar government and its replacement by a Nationalist government
Methods	• Freikorps units marched on Berlin
Government response	• Unable to rely on army support, the government fled to Dresden
	• Appealed for assistance from the Berlin workers
Reasons for failure	• A general strike in Berlin brought the capital to a halt—transport, public utilities, civil service, etc.
Significance	• The government survived but it had not been able to restore order using its own law-enforcing agencies
	• While the army did not actively support the putsch, neither did it assist the government.

▲ **Table 9.4** The Kapp Putsch, March 1920

Ruhr

A wealthy, industrial region in the Rhineland area of western Germany.

▲ **Fig. 9.3** German poster protesting at the French occupation of the Ruhr

▲ **Fig. 9.4** German woman feeding banknotes to her cooking range

QUICK QUESTION 2

Why was the poster in Figure 9.3 published in 1923?

QUICK QUESTION 3

What does the photograph in Figure 9.4 tell you about the German hyperinflation of 1923?

Definition	• A very rapid rise in prices, wages, and salaries.
Winners	• Owners of goods and property that held its value—landowners, owners of industrial premises, plants, and machinery • Those who owed money—debtors.
Losers	• Pensioners and those on fixed incomes • Savers with substantial cash balances • Those who were owed money—creditors • Those who were paid at long intervals i.e. monthly salaries.

▲ **Table 9.5** Hyperinflation, July–November 1923

Month	German marks
Jan	372 477
Sept	269 439 000 (269 million marks)
Oct	1 347 070 000 000
Nov	87 000 000 000 000 (87 trillion marks)

▲ **Table 9.6** Number of German marks needed to buy one ounce of gold in 1923

SOURCE 2

Memories of a German historian from *Germany 1918–49* by A. White and E. Hadley published in 1990.

*In early 1923, when I was a student in Freiberg some 30 miles from the Swiss border, there was a regular arrival of Swiss visitors from nearby Basel. They were quite ordinary people who came for a day's shopping and enjoyment. They filled the best cafes and restaurants and bought luxury goods. Most of us had little money and could never afford to see the inside of all those glamorous places into which the foreigners crowded. Of course we were envious. Contempt for such visitors combined with envy produced in most of us a great deal of **nationalist** and anti-foreigner feeling.*

Nationalist

Someone who strongly identifies with the fortunes of his or her country. A nationalist would be an enthusiastic supporter of foreign policy or international sporting success.

QUICK QUESTION 4

How far does Source 2 show that people were harmed by hyperinflation?

The Weimar government response

There was a clear danger in the summer of 1923 that the economy and political system of the Weimar Republic would collapse. Germany was saved from this outcome by the actions of Gustav Stresemann, who became Chancellor and Foreign Minister in August 1923. The key features of Stresemann's rescue plan were as follows.

• Passive resistance in the Ruhr was ended.

• The currency was stabilised with the introduction of the provisional Rentenmark.

• Reparation payments to the Allies were resumed.

These initiatives, though highly unpopular at the time, laid the foundations for a period of economic and political recovery between 1924 and 1929.

To what extent did the Republic recover after 1923?

If the period 1919 to 1923 was defined by economic crisis and attempts to overthrow the Weimar Republic, the next six years were characterised by economic recovery and political stability. After steering Germany away from disaster during the last five months of 1923, Stresemann continued to use his influence to bring about a full return to normality (at least it appeared that way at the time).

Dawes Plan

In April 1924, an important step forward was taken with the Dawes Plan. This linked reparations payments to economic performance and provided an American loan of 800 million gold marks to help kick-start the economy. Further loans followed. From now on Germany needed only to pay what it could afford in reparations. A permanent currency, the Reichmark, replaced the Rentenmark. These initiatives brought about a marked economic revival: inflation fell, industry expanded, and exports increased. By 1928, industrial production exceeded pre-war levels for the first time.

Renewed economic crisis

Despite these encouraging advances, there were also some worrying problems: unemployment remained stubbornly high, the farming sector never recovered, and, most importantly, much of the economic revival was based on American loans. Shortly after the Wall Street Crash of October 1929, the American economy went into recession triggering a worldwide economic downturn. American business failure put pressure on the banking system and many of the loans offered to Germany in the period since 1924 were recalled. This meant that the German economy suffered a double blow. Not only did it have to cope with the onset of world depression and the consequent reduction of orders for export items, but it had to repay substantial amounts of money to the United States. Investment projects were cancelled and unemployment began to rise to alarming levels. At its worst, in 1932, German unemployment stood at six million, or one third of the workforce. This was about 10 per cent higher than the unemployment levels found in other capitalist countries such as France, Britain, and Japan.

Return to political instability

With the onset of economic depression in Germany, many of the achievements of the period 1924–9 began to unravel. Whereas combined support for the two extreme parties of the left and right, the Communists and Nazis, stood at 13 per cent in the 1928 general election, this figure rose to 31 per cent in 1930 and 52 per cent in 1932. At the same time, support for the moderate parties that had made up the coalitions of the Weimar governments began to contract. It would appear that the Weimar Republic could only prosper under favourable conditions.

FP What were the achievements of the Weimar period?

Political

Stresemann's main achievement was to improve Germany's profile within the international community. When he became Foreign Minister in August 1923, Germany was still regarded with distrust and suspicion. By the time of his death in 1929, Germany was engaging on equal terms with the major powers of the world.

As a result of Stresemann's emergency measures introduced in the late summer and autumn of 1923, France was reassured and agreed to leave the Ruhr by July 1925. The Locarno Treaties of 1925 placed Germany on an equal level with

---

Why did the Weimar government fail to deal with the economic depression? ⓘ

- After the hyperinflation of 1923, printing money and increasing public expenditure was not considered to be a responsible option.

- The coalition parties could not agree among themselves the best way to solve the crisis.

- The adopted policies of tax increases and wage and welfare cuts were unpopular, reduced demand in the economy, and led to the Social Democrats resigning from the government.

the other signatories in providing guarantees for the frontiers of Germany, France, and Belgium. Rehabilitation continued in 1926 with Germany's admission to the League of Nations. Further recognition of Germany's new position came with the Young Plan of 1929 which reduced reparations from £6.6 billion to £2 billion. At this point Germany was regarded as a responsible member of the international community.

Cultural

The 1920s was a decade of cultural revival in Germany, especially in Berlin. The dawn of a new democratic republic with its commitment to civil liberties, including the lifting of censorship, encouraged the activities of artists, writers, film and theatre directors, and designers. Expressionism, the rejection of traditional forms, and critical interpretations of the new political and social order became key features of the new art. At a more popular level there was an expansion in the number of night clubs, dance halls, cafés, and restaurants, with increased opportunities for cabaret artists, singers, and dance bands. Many of these creative developments were regarded with shock and disgust by those on the right wing of German politics. They regarded the artistic experiments as a sign of decadence, corruption, and moral decay. Hence, under the Nazi regime, many of the artists, writers, and thinkers were forced to take refuge abroad, especially if they had Jewish or left-wing connections.

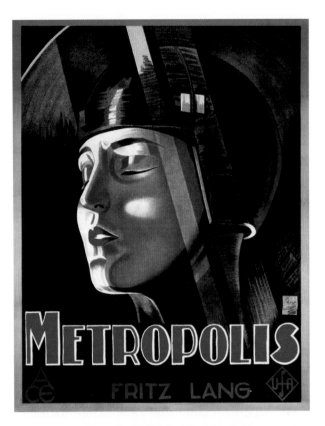

▲ **Fig. 9.5** Poster advertising the film *Metropolis*

DISCUSSION

Why do you think traditional elements of society disliked the cultural changes occurring in Germany at the time?

Literature	Bertolt Brecht and Kurt Weill, *The Threepenny Opera* (1928)
	Thomas Mann, *The Magic Mountain* (1924)
	Herman Hesse, *Steppenwolf* (1927)
	Erich Remarque, *All Quiet on the Western Front* (1924)
Art	George Grosz, *Grey Day* (1921)
	Otto Dix, *Big City* (1928)
Film	*Metropolis*, directed by Fritz Lang (1927)
	The Blue Angel, directed by Josef von Sternberg (1930)
Architecture	The Bauhaus style founded by Walter Gropius

▲ **Table 9.7** Some examples of Germany's cultural revival, 1919–33

DISCUSSION

How far would you agree with the view that Gustav Stresemann saved the Weimar Republic from disaster?

Why was Hitler able to dominate Germany by 1934?

FP What did the Nazi Party stand for in the 1920s?

January 1919	Establishment of German Workers' Party by Anton Drexler, a Berlin locksmith.
September 1919	Adolf Hitler joined the party and was soon taking on responsibility for publicity, propaganda, organisation of meetings, and public speaking.
February 1920	The Party published its 25-Point Programme and renamed itself the National Socialist German Workers Party (Nazis for short). By the summer it had adopted the swastika as its emblem.
July 1921	Hitler replaced Drexler as leader.
August 1921	Hitler founded the SA or Storm Troopers.
November 1923	Unsuccessful attempt to seize power in the Beer Hall or Munich Putsch.

▲ **Table 9.8** Early history of the Nazi Party

When the German Workers Party, the forerunner of the Nazi Party, was first founded in 1919 there was no doubt that it was strongly nationalist and anti-Semitic (anti-Jewish). These characteristics remained key features of the Nazi Party throughout the 1920s. The early objectives of the Nazi Party were announced in February 1920. The 25-Point Programme included the following policy aims.

The union of all Germans in a Greater Germany—this involved expanding Germany's frontiers to include Germans living in Austria, Poland, and Czechoslovakia
The destruction of the Treaties of Versailles and Saint Germain
Additional territory for food supplies and settlement of surplus population
German citizenship to be reserved for those of German blood, thereby excluding Jews
No more immigration of non-Germans and recent immigrants to be expelled from Germany
All citizens to have equal rights and obligations
Nationalisation of public industries
Profit-sharing in heavy industries (coal, iron and steel, shipbuilding, etc.)
Improved welfare provision for the elderly
Special state provision for the education of gifted children
Encouragement of physical fitness, sport, and gymnastics for the young
The formation of a strong central government

Nationalisation

Involves the state taking over a privately-run firm or industry so that the profits can be directed into the national treasury.

Profit-sharing

Normally the profits of a firm or company go to the owners or shareholders. With profit-sharing, any surplus is often divided among the entire workforce.

The Munich Putsch, November 1923

To begin with, the Nazis hoped to win power through a violent overthrow of the Weimar Republic. After all, Mussolini had come to power in Italy in 1922 through a demonstration of force. It was while the hyperinflation was still raging that Hitler planned his Munich or Beer Hall Putsch.

Leader	• Adolf Hitler
Objective	• The violent overthrow of the Weimar government and its replacement with a Nazi government.
Reasons why Hitler thought he would be successful	• The Weimar government was particularly unpopular in the late autumn of 1923: the ending of passive resistance in September looked like the government was giving in to the French; hyperinflation was at its height; it looked as if the government was tolerating left-wing state governments in Saxony and Thuringia; and Germany resumed reparations payments. • Hitler thought that his collaborator, General Ludendorff, would be able to use his influence to persuade the army to support his putsch. • Hitler also thought that leading members of the Bavarian state government could be persuaded to join him.
Events	• On 8 November, Hitler and 600 Storm Troopers forced their way into a meeting between the Bavarian Prime Minister, Gustav Kahr, and some local businessmen. • At gunpoint, Kahr was persuaded to announce that he supported the revolution. • The next day Kahr went back on his promise to support Hitler. • Hitler staged a march through the streets of Munich in order to gain public support. • Armed police brought the march to an end; 16 Nazis were killed and Hitler dislocated his shoulder; Hitler and Ludendorff were arrested.
Reasons for failure	• Crucially the army remained loyal to the Weimar government. • Prior to the putsch, the government had taken decisive action to depose the left-wing state governments in Saxony and Thuringia. • This action helped determine the loyalty of leading Bavarian politicians. • Hitler's Nazi Party was only small with approximately 3,000 members.

▲ **Table 9.9** The Munich or Beer Hall Putsch, November 1923

Although the Munich Putsch was a humiliating failure, leading to Hitler's trial and imprisonment and the banning of the Nazi Party, the event gave Hitler considerable publicity; his trial was given national coverage in the newspapers. Perhaps most importantly, the putsch convinced Hitler that his tactics had been wrong. He now decided to achieve power by constitutional means. That meant developing and expanding the organisation of the Nazi Party, contesting seats at general elections, and building up a power base in the Reichstag.

SOURCE 3

Extract from a letter written by Hitler in 1924 from *Hitler* by J. C. Fest published in 1974.

Instead of working to achieve power by an armed coup we shall have to hold our noses and enter the Reichstag against the Catholic and Marxist deputies. If outvoting them takes longer than outshooting them, at least the results will be guaranteed by their own Constitution! Any lawful process is slow. But sooner or later we shall have a majority – and after that Germany.

Mein Kampf

Although sentenced to five years imprisonment, Hitler served less than nine months in Landsberg Castle. He made use of his time by writing a book, *Mein Kampf* (My Struggle), which was a mixture of autobiography and political beliefs. It emphasised the superiority of the German or Aryan race, the dangers of communism, and Germany's destiny as the dominant state in Europe. The book became a bestseller and the royalties provided Hitler with a much needed income.

Nazi tactics, 1924–9

Nazi policies underwent a number of changes during the middle years of the Weimar Republic. While the two keystone principles of nationalism and anti-Semitism remained, the Nazis were prepared to revise virtually any of their other policies to achieve maximum popularity. Propaganda, in the form of posters, pamphlets, and slogans, was used to promote issues that were important to audiences. It was very much a case of finding out what potential supporters wanted and then devising policies that suited. When the Nazis discovered that they were picking up support among farmers, for example, they began to devise policies that addressed their fears and needs. Hitler's principal concern was achieving power and he was prepared to use any means to achieve it.

Emphasis was placed on expanding party membership, which increased from 3000 to over 100 000, and improving the professionalism of the party machine. Party activists were given coaching and training in public speaking, and propaganda methods were refined and improved. By 1929 the Nazi Party was well prepared to take advantage of any change in circumstances that might favour its cause. The Wall Street Crash and the advent of world depression provided just such an opportunity.

FP Why did the Nazis have little success before 1930?

While the Nazi Party made considerable progress in terms of its organisation, membership, and finances during the 1920s, it made little impact in elections. It was too small to contest the 1919 or 1920 elections, and had to wait until May 1924 before it could test its national popularity. It achieved a respectable first showing with 6.5 per cent of the popular vote. This initial success may have been due to the publicity enjoyed by Hitler during his trial in March 1924. It must have been a bitter disappointment, therefore, when it proved impossible to build on this support in the election of December 1924. It appeared as if the Nazis had already peaked, for their vote was cut by more than half and continued to decline for the May 1928 election. At this point, with support of 2.6 per cent, the Nazi Party looked very much on the edges of German politics.

The reasons for this lack of electoral success can be found in the improvement that was taking place at the same time in the Weimar Republic—economic, political, and international. As has been seen, Stresemann steered the Republic away from the economic crisis of 1923 and pointed Germany along the way to recovery. The moderate parties that made up the Weimar coalitions were the main winners from this process, with the Social Democratic Party improving its share of the vote in each of the elections held during this period.

Date	% Vote	Reichstag seats
May 1924	6.5	32
Dec 1924	3.0	14
May 1928	2.6	12

▲ **Table 9.10** Nazi Party general election results, 1924–8

SOURCE 4

William Shirer's verdict on the May 1928 general election from *The Rise and Fall of the Third Reich* published in 1959. Shirer was an American journalist living in Berlin.

Nazism appears to be a dying cause. It got support because of the country's problems such as hyper-inflation and the French invasion of the Ruhr. Now that the country's outlook is bright it is dying away. One scarcely hears of Hitler except as the butt of jokes.

QUICK QUESTION 5

Are you surprised by Shirer's assessment of the fortunes of the Nazi Party in Source 4?

Times were improving, or at least appearing to improve, and German voters could see little reason to switch their support to an untested, extreme right-wing party whose leader had recently been convicted of high treason.

Why was Hitler able to become Chancellor by 1933?

The Nazis and world economic depression

The world depression transformed the prospects of the Nazi Party. In Germany there were wage cuts, short-time working, unemployment, homelessness, and poverty on a scale never seen before. The established parties that made up the Weimar coalitions, such as the Social Democrats, took the blame. In desperation, voters changed support to the parties that had been the most critical of the Weimar coalitions, the Communists and the Nazis. The breakthrough point for the Nazis came in the general election of September 1930. Unemployment stood at more than two million and the Nazis polled over six million votes, making them the second largest party in the Reichstag next to the Social Democrats. The Communists, with more than 4.5 million votes were the third largest party.

	1930 September		1932 July		1932 November	
	Seats	% Vote	Seats	% Vote	Seats	% Vote
Nazis	107	18.3	230	37.3	196	33.1
Communists	77	13.1	89	14.3	100	16.9

▲ **Table 9.11** General election results, 1930–2: the Nazi and Communist vote

Over the next 18 months, the economy continued to deteriorate and the Nazis used every opportunity to attack the coalition government and criticise its inability to provide effective solutions. The Nazi propaganda machine, led by Josef Goebbels, was now working at full capacity as the Party message was spread by thousands of posters, pamphlets, and broadsheets, while those already faithful to the Party were invited to attend torch-lit parades and mass rallies. The Nazis were the masters of spectacle and pageantry and seemed to offer hopes of a brighter future. They were also masters of modern technology. During the 1932 presidential election, when Hitler stood against Hindenburg, the Nazi leader was flown by aeroplane from one speaking venue to the next so that he was able to visit up to five cities on the same day.

The economic depression also boosted the fortunes of the Communist Party, who argued that the root of the problem was the capitalist system. This played into the hands of the Nazis who posed as the strong defenders of the existing order. Communists were portrayed as scheming revolutionaries in league with the Jewish community and their meetings were regularly disrupted by bands of violent SA men. Wealthy industrialists began contributing to the Nazi Party in order to prevent the Communists from taking power.

▲ **Fig. 9.6** Nazi election poster, "Our Last Hope: Hitler", 1932

DISCUSSION

What is the message of the Nazi election poster in Figure 9.6?

Political manoeuvrings, 1932–3

In the general election of July 1932, with unemployment heading towards six million, the Nazis became the largest party in the Reichstag polling more than 13 million votes. Normally, the leader of the largest party could be expected to become Chancellor, but Hindenburg had no intention of appointing a man he had privately described as "the vulgar little corporal". Instead, Franz von Papen, a member of the Centre Party, was invited to form a government. Without Nazi cooperation, however, von Papen was unable to devise a stable coalition that would be supported in the Reichstag. A second general election was therefore held in November.

Although the Nazis lost two million votes and 34 seats in this election, they remained the largest party in the Reichstag. Von Papen found that it was still impossible to form a stable coalition and von Schleicher, a former army general, became Chancellor in early December. But without Nazi cooperation von Schleicher experienced similar problems to von Papen, and it soon became clear that he too would be unable to command a Reichstag majority. At this point von Papen, who had become a rival of von Schleicher, began to play the part of power broker in order to displace von Schleicher and return to a position of political influence.

Towards the end of January 1933, von Papen managed to persuade Hindenburg to agree to a political deal whereby Hitler would become Chancellor with von Papen as Vice-Chancellor. Hitler was to be offered just three Cabinet positions in a total of 12 ministers. The calculation was that, without a majority in either the Reichstag or the government, any extreme Nazi policies could be resisted.

How did Hitler consolidate his power in 1933–4?

When Hitler became Chancellor of Germany on 30 January 1933, his influence was limited on account of the agreement made with Hindenburg and von Papen. He was simply the head of yet another Weimar coalition government. It took approximately 18 months to convert his position into one of absolute power. The first stage in this process was to call for a general election to be held on 5 March. This was meant to be a free and peaceful election, but there was much police and SA violence conducted against the Communists and other opposition groups. The most infamous event of the campaign occurred one week before polling day.

The Reichstag Fire

On the evening of 27 February the Reichstag building burnt down. A Dutch Communist, van der Lubbe, was arrested in the Reichstag grounds and charged with starting the fire. Hitler immediately claimed that this was proof of a Communist plot against the state, and persuaded President Hindenburg to issue an emergency decree which suspended personal freedoms and increased police powers. He also used the opportunity to whip up public fear against the supposed Communist threat.

THE TEMPORARY TRIANGLE.

Von Hindenburg and Von Papen (*together*)—
"FOR HE'S A JOLLY GOOD FELLOW,
FOR HE'S A JOLLY GOOD FELLOW,
FOR HE'S A JOLLY GOOD FE-EL-LOW,
(*Aside:* "Confound him!")
AND SO SAY BOTH OF US!"

▲ **Fig. 9.7** British cartoon, "The Temporary Triangle", *Punch Magazine*, 8 February 1933

The general election of 5 March 1933

With control of the police and extensive influence over the newspapers and radio stations, Hitler was obviously hoping to achieve a vote of 50 per cent or more in the March election. That would enable him to lead a Nazi government

SOURCE 5

In 1945, General Franz Halder recalled how Hermann Goering, a leading Nazi, had claimed responsibility for the Reichstag Fire. Goering later denied making any such statement during his evidence to the Nuremberg Trials. This extract has been taken from *Germany 1918–1945* by G. Lacey and K. Shephard published in 1997.

At a luncheon on the birthday of the Führer in 1942 the conversation turned to the topic of the Reichstag building. I heard with my own ears when Goering interrupted the conversation and shouted: "The only one who really knows about the Reichstag is I, because I set it on fire!"

QUICK QUESTION 6

How useful is Source 5 as evidence of Nazi involvement in the Reichstag Fire?

QUICK QUESTION 7

What is the message of the cartoon in Figure 9.7?

without coalition partners. But, in the event, the Nazis received 43.9 per cent of the vote. This was a much higher level of support than any other party had achieved during the years of the Weimar Republic but it meant that Hitler still needed the support of the Nationalists.

The Enabling Act, 23 March 1933

In order to increase his powers and be able to govern without the Reichstag, Hitler next introduced an Act which would establish his dictatorship. It achieved the necessary two-thirds support of the Reichstag by a mixture of threats and promises. SA and SS troops stood both inside and outside the Kroll Opera House where the vote was held, brandishing their weapons and chanting menacing slogans. Only the Social Democrats dared oppose the measure which was passed by 441 votes to 94.

A legal dictatorship

Hitler was now a legal dictator. In theory he now had the powers to act as he pleased. In practice, however, there were a variety of organisations and institutions that could have frustrated his will or even overthrown him.

- The unions could have organised a general strike as they did to destroy the ambitions of Wolfgang Kapp in 1920.
- The opposition parties could have regrouped and challenged the legality of Hitler's recent actions.
- The Civil Service could have stalled procedures and made it difficult to introduce Nazi laws.
- The state governments could have pursued non-Nazi policies.
- The army could have organised a coup authorised by their Supreme Commander, President Hindenburg.

Hitler had to resolve all of these potential problems before he could be in total control.

The consolidation of power, March 1933–August 1934

Trade unions	• In May 1933, the trade unions were abolished, their leaders arrested, their premises and equipment seized and their funds confiscated.
	• A Nazi-led German Labour Front was set up in its place to which all workers had to belong. Strike action became illegal.
Political parties	• By July 1933, all political parties apart from the Nazi Party had been banned and Germany became a one-party state.
Civil Service	• The Civil Service was purged of all Jews and "enemies of the state" in order to make it loyal and reliable.
The 18 state governments	• In April 1933, Nazi state governors were appointed with powers to make state laws. State parliaments were abolished in early 1934.

▲ **Table 9.12** Hitler's measures to remove any opposition

By the spring of 1934 Hitler's power was nearly complete, but there remained the problem of the army. Hitler was also worried about the growing independence of Ernst Röhm, leader of the SA. He decided to strike at the end of June.

Reasons	• If Hitler did not send a clear signal to those in the army that they were to remain a special, highly-trained, professional body, central to his plans, then there was the danger that they would launch a coup against him.
	• Senior army generals had heard that Röhm was in favour of merging the army with the SA under his leadership. These generals were upset by such rumours and unsure as to how Hitler regarded the idea.
	• Hitler was beginning to see Röhm as a threat because he was expressing disappointment with Nazi achievements and arguing in favour of a "second revolution". This would have involved introducing radical policies such as nationalisation which would have upset business leaders.
	• Hitler needed to reassure the army and show the SA leadership who was in control.
Events	• On the night of 30 June 1934, Röhm and other SA leaders were arrested and shot. During the next two weeks several hundred senior SA men and other rivals and potential enemies, including von Schleicher, were also murdered by the SS.
Effects	• The army could no longer be in any doubt that Hitler favoured it in preference to the SA.
	• The SA was brought firmly under the control of Hitler's leadership.
	• When President Hindenburg died on 2 August 1934, Hitler proclaimed himself Chancellor and Reich Führer. As such he was Head of State and Commander-in-Chief of the Army. Every soldier was required to swear an oath of personal loyalty to Adolf Hitler. Hitler's dictatorship was now a matter of fact as well as a matter of law.

▲ **Table 9.13** The Night of the Long Knives, 30 June 1934

▲ **Fig. 9.8** SA parade through Berlin, March 1933

What was the difference between the SA and the SS?

- Established in 1921, **the SA** (also known as the Storm Troopers or Brownshirts) were the private army of the Nazi Party.

- By 1934 it had become a vast organisation with more than two million members.

- Although often crude and thuggish in its methods, it had helped the Nazis in their rise to power by terrorising their opponents, especially the Communists.

- **The SS** was formed in 1925 as a personal bodyguard for Hitler.

- It was an elitist, highly disciplined, and utterly ruthless force.

- Under Himmler's leadership, membership increased from a few hundred to over 50 000 between 1929 and 1933.

- Members wore black uniforms with a skeleton head on their caps.

The Nazi regime

How effectively did the Nazis control Germany, 1933–45?

FP **How much opposition was there to the Nazi regime?**

In the last general election held under the Weimar Republic in March 1933, the Nazis gained support from nearly 44 per cent of the German population. More than half of the country preferred a non-Nazi option at this point. There were further elections and referendums held during the Third Reich revealing a surge in support for the Nazi regime—with approval rates of over 90 per cent—but these polls do not accurately show support for the Nazis. This was partly because opposition parties were banned and partly because the votes were counted and published by the Nazis themselves.

Gauging opposition to the Nazis is always going to be difficult as few active opponents survived the regime to tell their story and the Gestapo or secret police tried to suppress information about opposition activities. It would appear that the Nazis enjoyed considerable support between 1933 and 1942 and there was no large-scale organised opposition during these years. Once the war began to go badly for Germany, then opposition became more widespread and serious. The main sources of opposition to the Nazis are summarised in Figure 9.9.

Trade unions

Officially banned in May 1933 but some activists, with links to left-wing groups, continued their work in secret organising illegal strikes, demonstrations, and works-to-rule.

Left-wing groups

Communists and Social Democrats both maintained underground networks after 1933. Anti-Nazi actions included the distribution of pamphlets, the deployment of posters and slogans, and the printing of illegal newspapers. Strikes among industrial workers were encouraged.

Right-wing groups

The most important Conservative opposition group was the Kreisau Circle (named after Kreisau in Silesia) which organised secret discussion meetings on how Germany would be governed after Hitler's removal. Membership included army officers, aristocrats, and professional persons.

Opposition to Nazis

Youth

The Edelweiss Pirates and Navajos provided a refuge for anti-Nazi teenagers. They picked fights with members of the Hitler Youth, distributed pamphlets and broadsheets, and scrawled graffiti on walls.
Similar action was carried out by The White Rose, a group of Munich University students.

The churches

A number of churchmen from both the Roman Catholic and Protestant churches spoke out against the Nazi regime.
In 1941, the Catholic Bishop Galen of Münster spoke out strongly against euthanasia, forced sterilisation, and concentration camps. As a result of this the programme of euthanasia was stopped.
The Protestant Pastor Niemöller was another outspoken critic of the Nazis who formed a rival church to the Nazi Reich Church. He spent eight years in a concentration camp.

The army

General Beck's plans to overthrow Hitler during the late 1930s were impeded by the successful and bloodless takeover of Czechoslovakia.
When Germany's military fortunes changed after the disastrous defeat at Stalingrad, senior army officers planned to assassinate Hitler. The bomb plot of 20 July 1944 failed and led to 5,000 executions.

▲ **Fig. 9.9** Opposition to the Nazi regime

How effectively did the Nazis deal with their political opponents?

The fact that there were no significant revolts or rebellions against Nazi rule suggests that the methods of law enforcement and control must have been extremely effective. There was certainly no repeat of the putsches and uprisings that plagued the early years of the Weimar Republic. There were occasional conspiracies and plots, but only Reinhard Heydrich among the senior Nazis was assassinated and this act took place outside Germany. To ensure absolute obedience to Nazi rule the favoured methods were persuasion and indoctrination, but there were always those who remained unresponsive. For such persistent opponents the Nazis relied upon force and terror. Figure 9.10 outlines the main features of the Nazi police state which enforced the laws of the Nazi regime and dispensed Nazi justice.

Informers

Local Nazi officials reported on the reliability of local residents, while everyone was encouraged to be vigilant and report anti-Nazi talk and activities. In some cases husbands reported on wives, children on their parents, and ordinary people on their neighbours. This system created enormous fear as well as enabling private scores to be settled.

The SS

Led by Heinrich Himmler, in pursuit of enemies of the state SS troops had extensive powers to arrest, detain without charge, interrogate, and search and confiscate property.
The SS was responsible for running the concentration camps and implementing Nazi racial policies including the Final Solution.

The Gestapo

This was the secret state police brought under the general control of Himmler and the SS in 1936. It was probably the most feared arm of the law by ordinary citizens. It had sweeping powers to spy on Germans by tapping telephones, intercepting mail, and using information from a network of informers. Arrests could result in being sent to a concentration camp without trial.

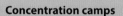

Concentration camps

These were large-scale prisons for critics and opponents of the Nazi regime, though other groups were sent there such as gypsies, beggars, tramps, and the work-shy. Conditions were basic and the discipline harsh with many deaths from beatings, torture, or other forms of ill-treatment. Prisoners were used as slave labour working in quarries, agriculture, and forestry. During the Final Solution, these camps were used for the extermination of the Jewish population.

Nazi courts and judges

The Nazis took over control of the existing court system, requiring magistrates and judges to take an oath of loyalty to Hitler. Jewish judges and lawyers were sacked. Special courts were set up for dealing with political crimes.
Capital offences were increased from 3 to 43 between 1933 and 1943, and the minimum age for the death penalty was reduced to 16. Telling anti-Nazi jokes and listening to a foreign radio station both carried the death sentence.

▲ **Fig. 9.10** The Nazi police state

How did the Nazis use culture and the mass media to control the people?

In 1933, Josef Goebbels was appointed Minister for Propaganda and Enlightenment. It was his job to persuade the German people of the benefits of Nazi rule. This was achieved by trying to ensure that everything that was seen or heard was consistent with Nazi policy and ideals. It would make the task of the Nazi leaders much easier if they were ruling over a nation that shared their thoughts and beliefs. Goebbels aimed to make every aspect of German culture and every form of communication dedicated to the task of producing loyal Nazis and followers of Adolf Hitler.

Art and architecture	• Goebbels disapproved of much of the artistic output of the Weimar Republic which was considered "degenerate". • Art galleries were forced to remove expressionist paintings and sculptures and replace them with exhibits which illustrated the heroic qualities of the Aryan race. • Favoured public architecture was classical in style, stone-built, and emphasised the authority of the state.
Music	• The classical music of Beethoven, Bruckner, and Wagner was particularly favoured. Jewish composers such as Mendelssohn and Mahler were blacklisted. • Military-style music was very acceptable. • Some popular music, especially folk song, was encouraged, but jazz music was banned as it originated in the black community.
Literature	• Books were censored and libraries and bookshops had to remove the output of Jewish and Communist authors from their stock. • In May 1933, Goebbels supported a public book burning event when students in Berlin threw some 20 000 books, considered un-German or Jewish, on to a huge bonfire. • Books about war heroes, the achievements of Adolf Hitler, or the importance of the family were encouraged.
Film and theatre	• Goebbels realised that the German public wanted to be entertained at affordable prices. • Films and plays were sometimes based on historical themes so audiences could draw parallels with the Third Reich such as *The Great King* (1942), starring Otto Gebühr, which depicted the life of Frederick the Great. More often the films were based on love stories or adventurous exploits. • Propaganda films vilified the Jews (*Jew Süss*, 1940), attacked the British as brutal imperialists (*My Life for Ireland*, 1941), or celebrated the wonders of the Nazi Regime (*The Triumph of the Will*, 1935). Admission to cinemas was only possible at the beginning of the programme so audiences were unable to miss the official newsreels that broadcast the Nazi message.
Newspapers	• All newspapers and magazines were brought under Nazi control. Jewish and anti-Nazi publications were closed down. • Editors had to attend a daily press briefing where they were told what to print.
Radio	• All radio stations were brought under Nazi control. • Cheap radios, called "The People's Receiver", were made available—70 per cent of German households had a radio by 1939. These sets were unable to receive foreign broadcasts. • Radios were installed in cafés, bars, and factories, while loudspeakers were positioned in the streets and other public places so that important announcements and Hitler's speeches could be heard by everyone.

Mass rallies	• The Nazi calendar was filled with special anniversaries—Hitler's birthday, the Founding of the Nazi Party Day, War Heroes Day, etc.—which provided opportunities for celebration accompanied by marches, parades, torch-lit processions, speeches, and pageantry.
	• The most spectacular of these occasions was the annual mass rally at Nuremberg held over the course of a week in September. Hundreds of thousands of people were accommodated in four vast arenas where they were entertained by military bands, marches, flying displays, and speeches by the leading Nazis. The purpose of these occasions was to reinforce the personality cult of Hitler and to encourage loyalty and support for the Nazi regime.
	• At a more local level, campaigns were regularly organised by the SA or Hitler Youth in order to raise funds for the Nazi Party. On "one-pot Sundays", families were expected to cook the midday meal in a single pot and hand over the money saved to Party collectors.
Posters	• Goebbels literally bombarded the German people with posters that carried the Nazi message: promoting the personal image of Hitler, encouraging Germans to buy radios, emphasising the virtues of traditional family values, appealing for new recruits to the Hitler Youth, or warning against the influence of the Jews.
Sport	• The 1936 Berlin Olympics presented Goebbels with a perfect propaganda opportunity to advertise the achievements of the Nazi state.
	• The technical facilities were superb: a new 100 000 capacity stadium equipped with television cameras, a photo-electronic timing device, and a giant, mounted stopwatch that all the spectators could see.
	• The performance of the German athletes was also impressive and Germany topped the medal table. In defiance of Hitler's race theories, however, the black American Jesse Owens was the star athlete of the games winning four gold medals and breaking 11 Olympic records.

▲ **Table 9.14** Controlling the German people through culture and media

Goebbels was keenly aware that the spoken word was perhaps the most effective means of communication and persuasion, and here the Nazis held a trump card: the extraordinary speaking abilities of Adolf Hitler.

SOURCE 6

Josef Goebbels on Hitler's effectiveness as a speaker, 1936.

He speaks his heart, and therefore reaches the hearts of those who hear him. He has the amazing gift of sensing what is in the air. He has the ability to express things so clearly, logically and directly that listeners are convinced that that is what they have always thought themselves. That is the true secret of the effectiveness of Adolf Hitler's speeches.

SOURCE 7

Otto Strasser on Hitler's effectiveness as a speaker, 1940, taken from *Germany* by R. Gibson and J. Nichol published in 1985. Strasser was expelled from the Nazi Party in 1930. He spent the years of the Third Reich in exile.

Adolf Hitler ... sniffs the air. For a minute he gropes, feels his way, senses the atmosphere. Suddenly he bursts forth. His words go like an arrow to their target. He touches each private wound on the raw, liberating the mass unconsciousness, expressing its innermost aspirations, telling it what it most wants to hear.

SOURCE 8

Hermann Rauschning, *Hitler Speaks*, 1939. Rauschning briefly joined the Nazi Party in the early 1930s but cancelled his membership in 1934. He then fled to the United States where he became a fierce critic of Hitler and the Nazis.

Hitler stamped his feet, and banged his fist on tables and walls. He foamed at the mouth, panting and stammering in uncontrolled fury.

QUICK QUESTION 8

How far do Sources 6 and 7 agree about Hitler's speaking abilities?

DISCUSSION

Do Sources 6 and 7 make you surprised by what Hermann Rauschning wrote in Source 8?

Why did the Nazis persecute many groups in German society?

During the years of the Third Reich, the Nazis persecuted a wide range of people including Jews, Gypsies, homosexuals, prostitutes, drunkards, beggars, the aged, and the mentally handicapped. All these groups were considered incompatible with either Nazi ideas about a master race or ideas about the efficient operation of the Nazi state.

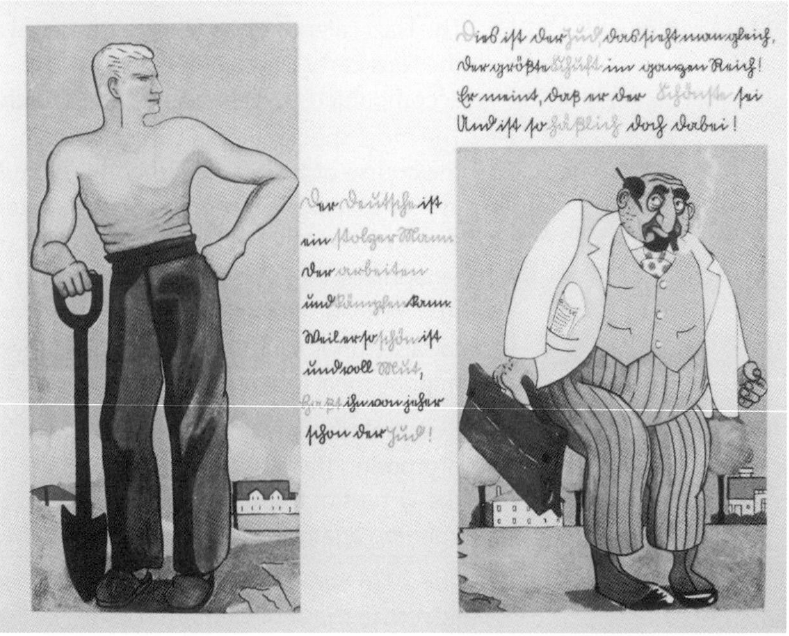

The Master Race theory

In Hitler's view the German people constituted a race, the Aryan race. He also believed that Aryans were naturally superior in terms of intelligence, physique, and work ethic. This would ensure, so Hitler thought, that eventually Germany would rule the world. To take account of setbacks such as Germany's defeat in the First World War or the economic crises of 1923 and 1930–3, Hitler argued that potential Aryan supremacy had been undermined by Jews intent on undermining the German state.

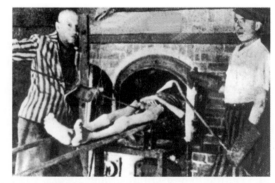

▲ **Fig. 9.11** Comparison of an Aryan with a Jewish man taken from a Nazi school textbook. While the Aryan can "work and fight" the Jewish man is "the greatest scoundrel in the whole Reich".

To preserve the purity of the Aryan race, it was essential to maintain its separateness from other races and discourage contact between Germans and non-Germans.

The efficiency requirement

Hitler also believed that Germany was overburdened with undesirables— people who refused to pull their weight, were work-shy, or preferred a life of anti-social behaviour such as alcohol or drug addiction. In addition, progress in medical science meant that many now survived disabling conditions and diseases. Hitler regarded all such people as a drain on the resources of the state. They contributed little yet cost vast amounts of money in terms of care and welfare. These resources could be better deployed supporting the fit and healthy.

How did the Nazis separate the Jews from the Aryans?

- To underline the need to draw a line between Aryans and the Jewish community, a boycott of Jewish shops and businesses was ordered in April 1933.

- This was followed by anti-Jewish articles in the press together with "Jews not wanted" signs that were displayed in cafés and public places.

- Jews were also purged from government employment.

- In 1935, the Nuremberg Laws denied German citizenship to Jews and prohibited sexual contact between Jews and non-Jews.

▲ **Fig. 9.12** Concentration Camp in Dachau, Germany

- In November 1938, on Kristallnacht (Night of Broken Glass), Jews suffered attacks on their synagogues, shops, and private houses carried out by SA men posing as ordinary German citizens.

- After Kristallnacht, Jews were forbidden to own shops or engage in trade, forbidden to attend German schools, and banned from all public and private recreational venues such as theatres and concert halls.

- In response to these measures, by the outbreak of war, 40 per cent of the 550 000 German Jews had left the country.

How were the Gypsies treated?

- In some ways the Gypsies were regarded as more offensive than the Jews as they violated both the racial and efficiency requirements.

- Like the Jews they were subject to discrimination over citizenship and marriage.

- Many were arrested without cause and sent to concentration camps.

- In 1938, all Gypsies were required to register with the authorities.

▲ **Fig. 9.13** Pile of prosthetic devices belonging to people with disabilities murdered at Auschwitz Concentration Camp, Poland

What happened to the "Undesirables"?

- Popular resentment against such people—juvenile delinquents, tramps, the disabled, etc.—was increased by a propaganda campaign.

- This was followed by a Sterilisation Law in July 1933 which authorised the sterilisation of people with certain, rather unspecific, illnesses. This measure was so loosely interpreted that nearly 700 000 persons were sterilised before the fall of the Nazi regime.

- Many others were sent to concentration camps.

- In 1939, the Nazis began killing the mentally ill in a secret euthanasia campaign. The victims included handicapped infants, children, and teenagers. Methods ranged from starvation to gas chambers. Following protests, especially from the Catholic Church, the campaign was brought to an end in 1941, but not before more than 70 000 people had lost their lives.

Was Nazi Germany a totalitarian state?

A totalitarian state can be defined as a type of rule where the government controls all aspects of public and private life with the aid of propaganda and terror. All aspects of public and private life would include the political system, the economy, and social, cultural, and religious activities. Certainly Nazi Germany is often referred to as a totalitarian state alongside Stalin's Russia, Mao's China, and the current regime in North Korea. There can also be little doubt that the Nazi regime aimed to be a totalitarian state. But it is also true that there has never been a perfectly totalitarian state as various groups have always managed to escape the control of the state. How true was this in Nazi Germany?

The political system	• Nazi Germany was a one-party state with a charismatic leader at its helm. • There were small underground cells of Communists, Social Democrats, and other outlawed political opponents, but the Gestapo ensured that they were never able to seriously threaten Nazi rule. • Hence the Nazi government successfully controlled virtually all aspects of political life in Germany.
The economy	• The economy of Nazi Germany was largely in the hands of private enterprise; most industries and financial services enjoyed a measure of independence. • There was government regulation and intervention especially in industries connected to war production; the Nazi-controlled German Labour Front also took over responsibility for directing the workforce. • Overall, Nazi control over the economy was far from complete.
Society	• As will be seen, the Nazi government exercised considerable control over German women and children. • A significant minority of teenagers rebelled against being forced to conform. • The leisure time for many adults was organised through the *Strength through Joy* organisation. • Nazi control over German society was extensive but not complete.
Mass media and culture	• Nazi control over the newspapers, radio, film, theatre, books, etc. was more or less complete.
Religion	• The Nazis never managed to control the Catholic Church which retained its independence, though many individual priests were sent to concentration camps for speaking out against the regime. • Attempts to form a Protestant Reich Church under a Nazi bishop were frustrated by the creation of the breakaway Confessional Church, founded by Martin Niemöller.

▲ **Table 9.15** The extent to which Germany was a totalitarian state

In many ways, therefore, Nazi Germany can be considered to be a totalitarian state with the economy and religion being the main exceptions. Yet the totalitarian nature of the Nazi regime would have been more convincing if the government machine had worked more effectively. As it was, Hitler applied the methods of divide and rule in order to protect his own position. Rivalries between leading Nazis and their departments were deliberately encouraged by Hitler to prevent alliances being formed against him. Furthermore, Hitler became increasingly bored by administrative detail and often delayed making decisions. Nazi government was defined by power struggles, inefficiency, inconsistency, and improvisation. If it was a totalitarian system it could have been managed more successfully.

What was the Strength through Joy organisation? ⓘ

• This was an offshoot of the German Labour Front.

• It organised leisure and recreational activities for German workers: subsidised theatre, cinema and opera tickets, affordable cruises, hikes, and other holidays together with a range of sporting activities.

What was it like to live in Nazi Germany?

FP ## How did young people react to the Nazi regime?

The Nazis affected the lives of young people through two main channels: the education system and the youth movement. The Nazis were aware that if the Third Reich was going to last a thousand years then it was necessary to produce future generations of loyal Nazis. The combined impact of school and youth movement would ensure that young Germans emerged as adults fully familiar with and accepting of Nazi ideas.

Nazi schools

Before 1933, German schools were run by the local state governments. As soon as the Nazis came to power, however, all schools were placed under the control of the Ministry of Education in Berlin. This ensured uniformity across the country and allowed a number of further changes.

To make sure that teachers could be relied upon to support the Nazi message, they were required to take a loyalty oath to Hitler and join the Nazi Teachers' League. Jewish teachers were sacked.

The curriculum was changed to take account of Nazi ideas. Biology and history lessons were particularly affected as textbooks had to be rewritten to reflect Nazi race theories and Germany's progress towards its destiny as the world's most powerful nation. Religious education was scrapped and much greater emphasis was placed on sport and physical education.

The Hitler Youth

After school young people were encouraged to join the Hitler Youth. This organisation was established during the 1920s alongside a variety of other German youth groups, many of which were linked to political parties or the churches. Most of these other groups, including the boy scouts, were banned by the Nazis in the eighteen months following Hitler's appointment as Chancellor. Under the leadership of Baldur von Schirach, the Reich Youth Leader, the Hitler Youth was organised into separate sections for boys and girls and for different age groups. From 1936 membership became virtually compulsory, though as late as 1940 nearly a million young people had still not joined the Hitler Youth.

For boys the experience of the Hitler Youth was designed to make them into good soldiers. They were taught basic military training and discipline which included drill, camp craft, map reading, cleaning and firing a rifle together with a host of activities to enhance fitness such as athletics, cross country running, camping, hiking and trekking. There was also political indoctrination with members having to learn about the evils of Jewry, the injustices of the peace settlement or the biography of Hitler's life. Girls, who at fourteen joined the League of German Maidens, were prepared for motherhood. Together with an emphasis on fitness, this involved the teaching of domestic skills such as cooking, sewing and managing a household budget.

▲ **Fig. 9.14** Hitler Youth recruitment poster, 1930s

QUICK QUESTION 9

How useful is the poster in Figure 9.14 as evidence of the nature of the Hitler Youth?

Age	Girls	Boys
10–14	League of Young Girls	German Young People
14–18	League of German Maidens	Hitler Youth

▲ **Table 9.16** The Hitler Youth

Teenage rebels

While many young Germans enjoyed the sporting and other leisure opportunities offered by the Hitler Youth, it was not to everyone's taste. One group of largely middle and upper middle class teenagers, members of the "Swing" movement, liked long hair, jazz music and dancing the jitterbug. The most important centres of the movement were in the cafés, clubs and dance bars of Hamburg and Berlin. While not overtly political, members of the Swing movement still offended the authorities by their appearance and clothes. The boys wore homburg hats, long English-style sports jackets, colourful scarves, Union Jack pins and carried umbrellas while the girls wore short skirts, make-up and nail varnish. Their loose morals, preference for English and American culture and tolerant attitude towards the Jews were further reasons why the Swing movement was objectionable to the Nazi regime. In 1941 over 300 members of the movement were arrested: identified leaders were sent to concentration camps while others were forced to have their hair cut or were sent back to school under close supervision.

The Edelweiss Pirates were a group of working class adolescents aged between 14 and 17—the gap years between leaving school and military conscription. Rather than an organised movement they were a collection of teenage groups associated with various German towns and cities, such as "The Roving Dudes" from Essen or the "Navajos" from Cologne. What they all shared in common was a strong distaste for the strict regimentation and sexual segregation of the Hitler Youth.

The Edelweiss Pirates believed in freedom of expression and collected in gangs at street corners, sang anti-Nazi songs, taunted members of the Hitler Youth and painted graffiti on walls and public buildings. They also organised hiking and camping trips. During the war their activities became more threatening to the Nazi government and included acts of sabotage, the sheltering of army deserters and the distribution of Allied war leaflets. After assassinating a Gestapo chief in Cologne in 1944, 12 of their ring leaders were publicly hanged. Other arrested members had their heads shaved or were sent to concentration camps.

SOURCE 9

Post-Second World War memories of a former Hitler Youth leader.

If other people rave about their time in the Hitler Youth, I cannot share their enthusiasm. My memories are that it was very oppressive. In our troop, activities consisted almost entirely of military drill. Even at sport or shooting practice we had to do drill first. Every day was the same monotonous routine. Then there was the endless marching. It was more punishment than fun. The slightest sign of weakness meant more drill! But, there was method in this madness: from childhood onwards we were drilled in toughness and obedience.

SOURCE 10

Post-Second World War memories of a former member of the Hitler Youth.

I was full of enthusiasm when I joined the Hitler Youth at the age of 10. What boy isn't fired up with the ideals of comradeship, honour and loyalty? Then the trips! Is there anything nicer than enjoying the splendour of the homeland in the company of one's comrades? There was always something different to do. We often went on marches on a Sunday. What joy we felt to be able to go on these trips. Playing handball or football on the meadows or bathing in a lake far away from the noisy city was a means of relaxation as well as building us up physically.

DISCUSSION

1. Having read Source 10, are you surprised by Source 9?

2. In view of the fact that membership of the Hitler Youth became virtually compulsory from 1936, are you surprised by the statistics in Source 11?

3. How far do Sources 9 to 12 support the view that the Hitler Youth movement ensured that all young Germans became loyal Nazis?

	Hitler Youth membership	Population of 10–18 year olds	Hitler Youth membership as % of 10–18 year olds
1935	3 943 303	8 172 000	48
1936	5 437 601	8 656 000	63
1937	5 879 955	9 060 000	65
1938	7 031 226	9 109 000	77
1939	7 287 470	8 870 000	82

▲ **Table 9.17** Membership figures for the Hitler Youth, 1935–9

Edelweiss Pirate Song

We march by banks of Ruhr and Rhine
And smash the Hitler Youth in twain.
Our song is freedom, love and life,
We're the Pirates of the Edelweiss

How successful were Nazi policies towards women and the family?

The Nazis believed in traditional family values: marriage, the raising of children within marriage, and the central role of women as wives and mothers. The Nazis believed in the family partly because it gave stability to society, but most importantly because it provided the best prospect of raising the birth rate. Since 1900, the German birth rate had been falling as many women concentrated on pursuing jobs and careers. During the years of the Weimar Republic women acquired new freedoms including the right to vote and stand for Reichstag elections, the right to enter the professions such as law and medicine, and equal pay with men. This was a process the Nazis were determined to put into reverse.

The Nazis were determined to boost the birth rate because if Germany went to war, then more and more German men would be required to replace losses at the battlefront and work in the war-supporting industries. There had to be enough members of the master race to occupy defeated territories and populate new colonies and conquests. Hence the majority of policies that the Nazis adopted towards the family were designed to encourage marriage and childbearing.

Measures designed to reverse the progress made by women during the 1920s	• Women were deprived of the vote and prevented from sitting in the Reichstag. • Women were either forced out of the professions or had their numbers substantially reduced. • Women were requested to stick to the "three Ks"—Kinder, Kirche und Küche (Children, Church and Kitchen).

Measures designed to encourage marriage and child bearing	• Marriage loans, worth about six months wages, were offered to newly-wed couples; the loan was then gradually reduced as children were born.
	• Fertility medals were awarded to women: bronze for five children, silver for six children, and gold for eight children or more.
	• Family allowances were introduced whereby families received a weekly welfare payment for each child; maternity benefits were also increased.
	• Classes in home-craft and parenting skills etc. were provided by the Nazi organisation for women, the German Women's Enterprise.
Child bearing outside marriage	• Under the Lebensborn programme, selected unmarried women were encouraged to get themselves impregnated by racially pure SS men and donate the child to the Führer to be reared in a state institution.

▲ **Table 9.18** Nazi policies towards women and the family

These policies did increase the birth rate which went up from 15 per thousand in 1933 to 20 per thousand in 1939. The number of marriages also increased from half a million in 1932 to three-quarters of a million in 1934. But family size remained much the same with most couples opting for a maximum of two children.

After 1937 the Nazi regime had to perform a u-turn in its policy towards women. This was because the increasing labour demands of German industry, especially those firms involved in rearmament, could no longer be met from the pool of unemployed men which was now becoming exhausted. Women were needed back in work and many were soon having to cope with the competing demands of husbands, children and employers. The marriage loan system was cancelled and women were required to perform a compulsory "duty year" which usually meant working on a farm or in a family home in return for board and lodging. The labour shortage was not resolved through female employment, however. In 1939 there were fewer women employed in Germany than had been the case ten years before. This was partly because of resistance from women themselves, who were not attracted by low wages and poor working conditions, but also from employers who often preferred foreign labour and resented having to provide facilities for female employees. After 1939 the Nazi regime became increasingly confused in its attitude towards women as it tried to pursue two contradictory objectives: the increase in the birth-rate which required women's presence in the home, and the wellbeing of the war economy which required women's presence on the factory floor. Perhaps the best example of the contradictory nature of Nazi attitudes towards women came when German women were even given employment in the German armed forces where they performed administrative, communications, nursing and other non-combative work. By 1945 there were approaching half a million female auxiliaries in the German armed forces.

▲ **Fig. 9.15** The Perfect Aryan Family, 1930s

QUICK QUESTION 10

How useful is the picture in Figure 9.15 as evidence of Nazi attitudes towards the family?

Did most people in Germany benefit from Nazi rule?

Those who suffered from Nazi rule were a minority in German society: Jews, Gypsies, committed Communists and Socialists, non-conformists of all descriptions, devout Christians, members of most religious sects—in fact anyone who was not an Aryan and who possessed strong and independent views that challenged Nazi ideology. The majority of Germans were Aryans, according to the Nazi definition, and were probably much more concerned with issues such as family life, standard of living, employment, etc. than political matters. It would appear that, until war broke out in 1939, the majority of Germans accepted the Nazi regime because their lives had improved since the days of the Great Depression.

SOURCE 13

Extract from *Mastering Modern World History* by N. Lowe published in 1982.

It would be wrong though to give the impression that Hitler hung on to power by terrorising the entire nation. In fact this was not the case at all as far as the great majority of Germans were concerned. Provided you did not mind losing freedom of speech and thought, and did not happen to be a Jew, you could usually exist quite happily under the Nazi system.

Working class	• The main improvements came with the reduction of unemployment from six million to a few hundred thousand.
	• This was achieved partly through public works schemes such as the autobahn-building project, partly through enlisting all 18–25 year olds in National Labour Service for six months, and partly through rearmament. The Nazi plans for self-sufficiency or autarky may also have been a factor.
	• Rearmament reduced unemployment when men were conscripted into the army, and also when the various supply industries such as armaments, engineering, and chemicals had to be expanded.
	• Support of the working class was retained in many cases through the benefits provided by the Strength through Joy organisation (Kraft durch Freude).
Farmers	• While farmers resented the increase in government intervention and regulation, they benefited from a number of Nazi policies: price guarantees for their produce, reduction or elimination of debts, and protection against their estates being broken up to pay death duties.
Businessmen and industrialists	• Small operators gained from Nazi laws to restrict the number and growth of department stores and the removal of Jewish businesses.
	• Large firms gained contracts from the rearmament programme and also benefited from the absence of trade unions and the elimination of the Communist threat. Substantial profits were made by big business during the years of Nazi rule.

▲ **Table 9.19** Benefits under Nazi rule

LAUFE SKI
mit »Kraft durch Freude«

▲ **Fig. 9.16** Strength through Joy poster, "Go Skiing", 1930s

What was autarky?

- Hitler wanted to make Germany as self-sufficient as possible during the 1930s to reduce imports of raw materials and food.

- This would both save money and reduce the effectiveness of an Allied wartime blockade.

- Production of steel, rubber, and oil was increased and schemes were devised whereby certain products could be produced from substitutes: coffee from acorns, petrol from coal, and textiles from pulped wood.

- Autarky had limited success and in 1939 Germany still depended upon imports for a number of essential materials.

Quite apart from any material improvements enjoyed by the population, Hitler created a "feel-good-to-be-German factor". This was a psychological benefit and resulted from the way he destroyed the hated Treaty of Versailles. By 1939, Germany had regained her position in the international community and this was something in which many Germans could take pride.

How did the coming of war change life in Nazi Germany?

When war broke out in September 1939, Germans were immediately affected by shortages of labour, food, and clothing. Yet, for the first two years of the conflict, any inconveniences suffered were offset by Germany's military victories as first Poland, then Norway, Denmark, the Low Countries, France, and finally western Russia, fell victim to the might of the German armies. New luxury items such as furs and perfumes were imported from the conquered territories, though few of them found their way into the households of ordinary Germans; they became the possessions of the rich or of high-ranking Nazi officials.

The turning point in the war occurred during the winter of 1941–2 when the German army suffered its first serious reverses against the Russians. From this point onwards there was an intensification of the problems that had afflicted Germany from the start of the war, but without the compensating comforts of military success (although Goebbels' propaganda machine did its best to hide the truth from the German population). Disillusionment with Hitler and the Nazis became more widespread, encouraging the activities of opposition groups.

Shortages	• Food rationing was introduced in September 1939 followed by clothes rationing in November.
	• Other items in short supply included soap, toilet paper, and tobacco.
	• By 1945, food shortages had become so acute that Germans had to scavenge for food from rubbish tips and even ate the meat from dead horses.
	• For those with money there was a flourishing black market.
	• Labour shortages became increasingly serious as more and more men were called up to the war front. They were replaced by women, prisoners of war, and people from conquered territories.
Bombing	• This had a dramatic impact on the lives of the German population as 3.6 million homes were destroyed with a similar number of civilian fatalities. Many more were made homeless and 2.5 million children were evacuated to rural areas.
	• Cities particularly badly damaged by Allied bombing raids included Berlin, Cologne, Hamburg, and Dresden where as many as 150 000 people lost their lives during two days of intensive bombing in February 1945.
Total War	• A series of emergency measures were introduced by Goebbels in mid-1944 in order to direct all the resources of Germany towards the war effort. These included the reduction of rail and postal services, the closing of all places of popular entertainment (except cinemas which were necessary for propaganda purposes), and the raising of the age limit for compulsory female labour to 50.
The Final Solution	• The killing of Jews began in 1941. The executioners were a branch of the SS, the Einsatzgruppen, who followed the German armies as they marched eastwards during the invasion of Soviet Russia. Approximately 800 000 Jews were killed, mainly by shooting, at this stage in the war.
	• At the Wannsee Conference in January 1942, the decision was taken to eliminate all European Jews. This was to be achieved by evacuating all Jews by rail to a number of remotely-located extermination camps in Poland such as Chelmo, Treblinka, and Auschwitz.
	• The death camps were equipped with gas chambers and crematoria.
	• In total the Nazis killed about 6 million Jews through gassing, shooting, working to death, or starvation. The work was kept secret and the Nazis tried to cover up their murderous activities during the final stages of the war by ripping up the railway tracks leading to the death camps.

▲ **Table 9.20** Effects of war in Germany

▲ **Fig. 9.17** German woman searching for food, 1945

▲ **Fig. 9.18** Berlin after Allied bombing raid, 1943

KEY POINTS

► The first, troubled phase of the Weimar Republic, 1919–23, characterised by economic crisis and political instability.

► The second phase of the Weimar Republic, 1923–9, characterised by economic recovery, political stability, and cultural revival.

► The final phase of the Weimar Republic, 1929–33, characterised by economic collapse and a resort to political extremism.

► The growth of the Nazi Party and the rise of Hitler, 1919–33.

► How and why Hitler became Chancellor in January 1933.

► Hitler's consolidation of power, 1933–4.

► The main features of the Nazi state.

QUICK QUESTION 11

How useful is the photograph in Figure 9.18 as evidence of the impact of Allied bombing on Germany during the Second World War?

Revision tips

• You need to know the main features of the Weimar constitution such as Article 48, the voting system of proportional representation, and the powers of the President and Chancellor.

• You must be familiar with the main events of the period 1919–23 such as the Spartacist Uprising, the Kapp Putsch, and the French occupation of the Ruhr leading to the hyperinflation of 1923.

• You must also understand how Stresemann defused the 1923 crisis and set Germany on course for recovery.

• The impact of the Great Depression on Germany is crucial for an understanding of the rise in political extremism—Communism and Nazism.

• An outline of the history of the Nazi Party and the rise of Hitler has to be mastered and you should be familiar with key aspects of the 25-Point Programme of 1920 and the circumstances surrounding the Munich Putsch.

• The change in Nazi tactics after 1923 is also important in understanding how the Nazis successfully exploited the deepening economic problems after 1929.

• The events leading up to Hitler's appointment as Chancellor are complicated but concentrate on the position of the Nazis in the Reichstag and the rivalry between von Papen and von Schleicher.

• Hitler's consolidation of power involves understanding how he dealt with the trade unions, political parties, the SA, and the army. Don't fall into the common trap of thinking that the SA was destroyed during the "Night of the Long Knives".

• The main features of the Nazi state are relatively straightforward to understand. Make sure that you can illustrate every general point you make with a short but precise and accurate example.

Review questions

1. Describe the main features of the Weimar Constitution.
2. What was the Kapp Putsch of 1920?
3. What problems did the Weimar Republic face in 1923?
4. Why did the Munich Putsch fail?
5. How did the Nazi Party gain support before 1933?
6. What was autarky?
7. Why did the role of women change under the Nazis?
8. How far did Nazi policy towards young people create loyal Nazis?
9. How effective was the Nazi use of propaganda and the media?
10. Describe the activities of the SS and Gestapo.

10 Russia, 1905–41

Introduction

The Russian **Empire** in 1900 was one of the most vast and diverse countries in the world. More than 19 different nationalities lived in the country with only 40 per cent of the population speaking Russian as their first language. A train journey from Moscow in the east to Vladivostok in the west would have visited two continents and covered over 6,000 kilometres. The whole journey would have taken no less than a week!

As well as the size of the country itself, the challenges facing Russia in 1900 were also huge. Russia's sprawling state was in dire need of modernisation in every way to meet the challenges posed by the new century. While the likes of France, Germany, and Britain grew to be industrial superpowers Russia was some way behind.

Empire

Where one country rules over other territories for economic and political control.

The aims of this chapter are to:

- Examine the main features of Tsarist rule and Russian society before the First World War including the 1905 revolution and its aftermath and attempts at reform.

- Consider the First World War and its impact on the Russian people.

- Study the March revolution of 1917 and the establishment of the Provisional Government and the Soviets, including the growing power of revolutionary groups.

- Examine the reasons for the failure of the Provisional Government.

- Look at the Bolshevik seizure of power, including the role of Lenin.

- Examine the main features of Bolshevik rule, the Civil War and War Communism, and reasons for the Bolshevik victory.

- Study the Kronstadt Rising and the establishment of the New Economic Policy.

- Look at Lenin's death, the struggle for power and the reasons for Stalin's emergence as leader by 1928.

- Examine Stalin's dictatorship, including the use of terror, the Purges, propaganda, and official culture.

- Consider Stalin's economic policies and their impact, including the modernisation of Soviet industry, the Five-Year Plans, and collectivisation in agriculture.

- Examine life in the Soviet Union, including the differing experiences of social groups, ethnic minorities, and women.

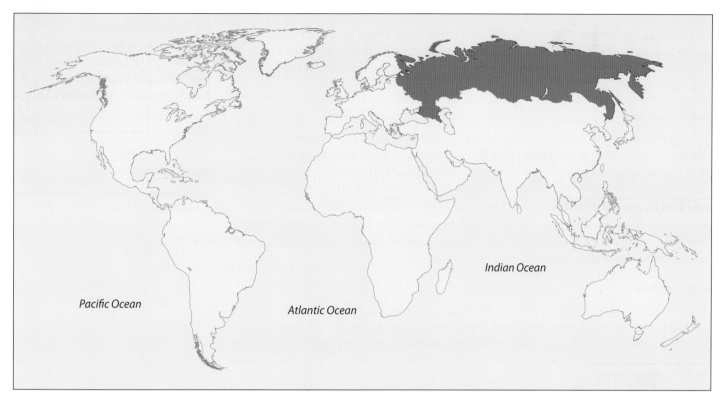

▲ **Fig. 10.1** Map of Russia in 1900

Why did the Tsarist regime collapse in 1917?

How well did the Tsarist regime deal with the difficulties of ruling Russia up to 1914?

The Russian people were unhappy for a number of reasons.

The peasants

According to the 1897 census, 77 per cent of Russians were classified as peasants. The peasants had been "freed" from virtual slavery in 1861—previously they were known as **serfs** and had been tied to the land which they worked. This end to slavery was a good thing for their freedom, but meant a large proportion of the peasantry were left to fend for themselves, working hard to support their families. Agriculture was hideously outdated with no knowledge of modern methods. When conditions were right, the peasantry had enough to live off. When harvests were bad though or disease spread, thousands often died of illness and starvation.

Serfs

Unfree peasants under feudalism; the enforced labour of serfs on the fields of landowners was a key part of nineteenth century Russia.

The Tsar

Russia was ruled by one of the oldest royal families in the world, the Romanovs. Nicholas II, the current Tsar, had inherited the throne from his father in 1894. Nicholas II believed he had a god-given duty to rule over Russia, and was not someone who wanted to bring democracy to the country.

Nicholas was aware of the need to bring Russia in line with other superpowers emerging in Europe but he didn't want to do this at the expense of his own power. He had to find a way to bring progress and modernisation to Russia, and harness the great potential available in a country so diverse. He also had to manage his people, a growing middle class who wanted representation in government and a huge peasant class that suffered occasional famines and widespread poverty. All was not lost though; the people were loyal to the Romanovs and the Tsar was worshipped by his people.

Nationalities

Russia at the time was made up of an estimated 200 different nationalities. The majority of the population were Slavs, but there were many minorities and much religious diversity. A policy of "**Russification**" had been introduced to try and unite those living in the Empire, but it had brought about widespread dissatisfaction. Areas such as Finland were being forced to accept the Russian language in areas such as schools and in local government. Several of these nationalities wanted regional control away from the influence of the Tsar. This led to tensions.

Languages

With so many nationalities, a range of languages were spoken across the country. The government's policy of Russification forbid the use of local languages but this had been widely ignored, particularly in rural areas.

State of industry

Russia's industry was beginning to grow in 1900. The high proportion of peasants had meant that the focus was previously on agriculture, but attention began to shift towards industry. The development of the railway gives evidence of this, in attempting to improve communications across the vast country as well as assisting with increasing demand for raw materials and creating jobs.

The problem was that developing railways was not enough by itself to bring Russia up to the level of an industrial nation. Money needed to be invested in industry and this money needed to come from somewhere, either from the peasantry or from expensive foreign loans. This growing industrial state also needed workers, meaning some of Russia's large peasant population would need to move to the cities.

Political opposition

Russia's largely rural population of peasants had been ruled over by the Tsars as an **autocracy**. The population was relatively easy to control as any disturbances were relatively localised. Furthermore the illiterate nature of the peasantry had made organised revolt less likely.

An updated and modernised Russia would lead to more people coming into contact with each other. This would increase the chance of organised opposition as a better educated workforce became more aware of their rights. Furthermore prosperous industry would create a middle class in Russia whose demand for political change and representation in government would be very difficult to ignore.

> *I shall maintain the principle of autocracy just as firmly and unflinchingly as it was preserved by my unforgettable dead father.*
>
> Nicholas II

Russification

People were forced to speak Russian and adopt Russian customs.

Autocracy

A government by an individual with unrestricted authority.

TASKS

1. Make a list of priorities for the Tsar in 1900. Which order would you put them in? Why?

2. Who posed the greatest threat to Nicholas's future—the peasants or the working class? Explain.

How did the Tsar survive the 1905 revolution?

▲ **Fig. 10.2** A painting of "Bloody Sunday" by Ilya Efimovich Repin

In 1905 Russia experienced an attempt at revolution. A peaceful protest by women and children quickly turned into a bloody massacre that had wide-ranging effects across the country. These events became known as the revolution of 1905.

What caused the uprising?

The causes of the events of 1905 can be seen as a combination of short- and long-term factors.

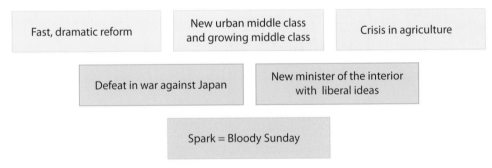

▲ **Fig. 10.3** Factors in the uprising

Long-term factors included the following.

1. **Reform** had been fast and dramatic. Improvements had been made with a 6 per cent annual economic growth compared to 2 per cent in Britain and France. The downside of this was experienced by the average worker. A Russian industrial employee worked on average an 11-hour day, with a 10-hour day on Saturday. Conditions in the factories were extremely harsh and little concern was shown for the workers' health and safety. Attempts by workers to form trade unions were resisted by the factory owners.

Reform

Make changes in an area of society, typically in order to improve it.

2. This new urban working class, along with a growing middle class created for the first time in Russia, wanted political representation to have some way of getting across their views.

3. The crisis in agriculture of poor farming techniques combined with a rapid growth in population meant that those in the countryside were also feeling rebellious.

Short-term factors included the following.

1. In 1904 Russia had gone to war against Japan. Russian hopes for a quick and morale-boosting victory had quickly faded and defeat seemed almost inevitable. The Russian fleet had sailed halfway around the world to be defeated by a far smaller nation.

2. The appointment of a new minister of the interior, Svyatopolk-Mirsky, had led to a growth in **liberal** ideas. The new minister had publicly stated he favoured a liberal approach to rule and had indirectly encouraged those pressing for concessions.

Liberal

A political ideology that seeks to maximise personal freedoms.

The spark was Bloody Sunday.

The events of Bloody Sunday

The revolution was sparked by an event that became known as "Bloody Sunday". On 22 January 1905 a priest called Father Gapon led a peaceful demonstration of 200 000 men, women and children to the Winter Palace in St Petersburg calling for reform and an end to the war. They aimed to deliver a petition to Tsar Nicholas II. The Tsar was not there, but the police and troops guarding the palace opened fire to disperse the protestors. Ninety-six were killed according to official estimates, while the opposition claimed the figure may have been as high as 4,000.

QUICK QUESTION 1

Compare Figure 10.2 with Figure 10.4. Is one of these sources more reliable than the other as evidence of the events of Bloody Sunday?

▲ **Fig. 10.4** A still from a film about the Russian Revolution of 1905. The film was not made until the 1920s, after the Tsar had been overthrown

Effects of the uprising

The shooting in Palace Square in St Petersburg had a huge effect on the people of Russia as it destroyed their confidence in the Tsar. Although he hadn't been actually in the palace when the protestors arrived and so hadn't personally ordered the troops to fire, the killings destroyed the centuries' old belief among common people that the Tsar was the "Little Father" who had their interests at heart. This never recovered, and after 1905 the Tsar's position changed.

The events of Bloody Sunday soon spread across Russia and its empire.

- Peasants attacked the houses of nobles throughout the country.

- Strikes took place all over the country. By the end of January over 400 000 people were on strike.

- Major universities closed down when the whole student body complained about the lack of civil liberties by staging a walkout.

- Workers from key industries including lawyers, doctors, engineers, and other middle-class workers established the Union of Unions and demanded a constituent assembly.

- In October, 1905, the railway workers went on strike which paralysed the whole Russian railway network.

- Vladimir Lenin, Leon Trotsky, and other **Mensheviks** established the St Petersburg **Soviet** in October 1905. Over the next few weeks over 50 of these soviets were formed all over Russia. They demanded better representation for workers.

- Perhaps most crucially, in June 1905 sailors on the **Potemkin** battleship protested against the serving of rotten meat. The captain ordered that the ringleaders be shot. The firing squad refused to carry out the order and joined with the rest of the crew in throwing the officers overboard. The Potemkin mutiny spread to other units in the army and navy. This dramatic event raised the prospect of the Tsar losing control of the army at a time of impending loss in the war with Japan.

▲ **Fig. 10.5** Picture of the Potemkin

Lenin

Pre-political career

Born to wealthy parents, he turned against the Romanovs after the execution of his brother for his part in a plot to kill Nicholas II's father.

Political career

As leader of the Bolsheviks Lenin was responsible for the seizure of power in 1917, victory in the Civil War, and the consolidation of Communist rule.

Character and outlook

An intellectual, Lenin was well travelled and well read; he was also a realistic though and knew that the problems in Russia needed to be dealt with before communism was developed.

Mensheviks

A faction of the Russian revolutionary movement that emerged in 1904 after a dispute between two sides of the party. The party divided into the "Mensheviks" and the "Bolsheviks".

Soviet

A council made up of workers.

Potemkin

The Potemkin was a battleship of the Imperial Russian Navy. The ship was made famous by the Battleship Potemkin Uprising, a rebellion of the crew against their oppressive officers in June 1905.

QUICK QUESTION 2

Figure 10.5 is from a film. Does that mean it is of no value to a historian studying the 1905 revolution?

Why was the Tsar able to survive the 1905 revolution?

In the end the Tsar managed to survive the revolution, but only just. In an attempt to calm the situation, he crucially granted reforms for those who demanded political change. The **October Manifesto** was a huge step towards democracy for Russia. After centuries of autocratic rule Russia was now for the first time offering its people freedoms and rights.

Manifesto of 17 October 1905
On the improvement of order in the state

The disturbances and unrest in St Petersburg, Moscow and in many other parts of our Empire have filled Our heart with great and profound sorrow. The welfare of the Russian Sovereign and His people is inseparable and national sorrow is His too. The present disturbances could give rise to national instability and present a threat to the unity of Our State. The oath which We took as Tsar compels Us to use all Our strength, intelligence and power to put a speedy end to this unrest which is so dangerous for the State. The relevant authorities have been ordered to take measures to deal with direct outbreaks of disorder and violence and to protect people who only want to go about their daily business in peace. However, in view of the need to speedily implement earlier measures to pacify the country, we have decided that the work of the government must be unified. We have therefore ordered the government to take the following measures in fulfillment of our unbending will:

1. Fundamental civil freedoms will be granted to the population, including real personal inviolability, freedom of conscience, speech, assembly and association.

2. Participation in the Duma will be granted to those classes of the population which are at present deprived of voting powers, insofar as is possible in the short period before the convocation of the Duma, and this will lead to the development of a universal franchise. There will be no delay to the Duma elect already been organized.

3. It is established as an unshakeable rule that no law can come into force without its approval by the State Duma and representatives of the people will be given the opportunity to take real part in the supervision of the legality of government bodies.

We call on all true sons of Russia to remember the homeland, to help put a stop to this unprecedented unrest and, together with this, to devote all their strength to the restoration of peace to their native land.

▲ **Fig. 10.6** October Manifesto

▲ **Fig. 10.7** From a British newspaper, the *Daily Mirror* published on 3 November 1905; the caption reads "Tsar's troubles not nearly over yet"

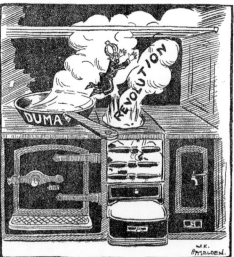

▲ **Fig. 10.8** A cartoon from a British newspaper published in 1906; the caption reads "From the frying pan to the fire"

October Manifesto

The reforms put in place after the 1905 revolution.

Nicholas II, from his diary two days after the October Manifesto.

There were only two ways open; to find an energetic soldier and crush the rebellion by sheer force. That would mean rivers of blood, and in the end we would be where we had started. The other way out would be to give to the people their civil rights, freedom of speech and press, also to have laws conformed by a State Duma—that of course would be a constitution.

Almost everybody I had an opportunity of consulting, is of the same opinion. We discussed it for two days and in the end, invoking God's help I signed. This terrible decision which nevertheless I took quite consciously. There was no other way out but to cross oneself and give what everyone was asking for.

DISCUSSION

Study Source 1.

1. Why did the Tsar give concessions to the people?

2. How far is the Tsar in favour of reform? How can you tell?

3. How far does Figure 10.7 support Source 1? Explain.

QUICK QUESTION 3

What is the cartoonist's message in Figure 10.8?

The beginnings of repression

The October Manifesto marked the end of widespread unrest started by the events of 1905. The manifesto had the effect of dividing those who opposed the Tsar; some liberal groups felt that the reforms went far enough and addressed their demands while others felt that this reform did not go far enough. The most notable of these was the St Petersburg Soviet, who publically denounced the plan (see Source 2). In December 1905, Trotsky and the rest of the executive committee of the St Petersburg Soviet were arrested. Others followed and gradually Nicholas II and his government regained control of the situation.

SOURCE 2

Leon Trotsky, speaking in 1905 after the manifesto had been published.

Citizens! Now that we have got the ruling clique with its back to the wall, they promise us freedom. They promise us electoral rights and legislative power. Who promises these things? Nicholas II. Does he promise them out of his own free will? Or with a pure heart? ... Do not be quick to celebrate victory ... look around citizens, has anything changed?

Trotsky

Pre-political career

Raised as part of a wealthy Jewish farming family, Trotsky left home to study mathematics but soon turned to revolutionary politics.

Political career

Originally a Menshevik, Trotsky's conversion to the ideas of Lenin soon saw him established as a key part of the party in both the events of 1905 and the 1917 revolution. After Lenin's death he was expected to succeed him.

Character and outlook

An intellectual who was well travelled, Trotsky often appeared aloof to others and at times arrogant.

How far was the Tsar weakened by the First World War?

The fall of Nicholas II happened in 1917. One of the key reasons put forward by historians is the role of the First World War in his downfall. But before this can be accepted as true there needs to be a careful study of Russia in the years before the outbreak of war. Was Russia calm in 1914 or were there tensions that could easily unravel?

Russia from 1906–14

The key decision at this time was the appointment of Peter Stolypin. This was an important appointment as he became the Tsar's closest advisor. Stolypin was a traditional figure who believed that Russia needed to modernise its agriculture and create a new class of peasants. He was not a **liberal** though and believed that the power should still rest with the Tsar.

There are three main areas in this period influenced by the work of Stolypin.

1. Political reform

The demand for representation was a key point for the rebels of 1905. The October Manifesto had granted a State **Duma** where laws would be passed. Immediately before the first Duma met though the Tsar issued the

Liberal

Someone who believes in giving the people more power and freedom.

Duma

The Russian parliament created in 1905 under the October Manifesto.

Fundamental Laws. This meant that the two Dumas that met before 1914 achieved very little. The Tsar often dismissed the elected ministers as he didn't agree with what they wanted. In the end the Duma was full of largely pro-Tsar representatives who didn't want change.

The October Manifesto had led to a real chance of representation in Russia in 1905. The Fundamental Laws and the "reforms" of June 1906 severely limited the impact of the manifesto and by 1914 Russia was heading back towards its undemocratic past. This doesn't mean though that the Duma was worthless—the third and fourth Dumas brought significant reforms including a doubling in the number of primary schools in this period and an increase in the expenditure on health.

2. Agricultural reform

Russia's backward peasantry had been crying out for reform for decades. Stolypin set out to harness the power that the peasants potentially possessed in order to use them to supply a modernised Russia with food.

The problem was the peasants didn't produce enough food. Their reliance on traditional methods of farming meant they largely only produced enough for themselves to eat and not enough of a surplus to feed Russia's growing industrial classes. They also depended upon the local **mir** for support.

Stolypin passed his land law in 1906 in an attempt to modernise the peasantry. His reforms were dramatic. Peasants were able to buy more land that was made available to them through the establishment of "the peasants land bank". This encouraged peasants to farm privately.

Stolypin wanted to create a new class of "sober and strong peasants". By encouraging them to leave the mir, farm for themselves, and build up their own farms, he envisioned a middle-class peasant emerging. It had some success—by 1913 nearly three million peasants had left their communes and set up on their own.

3. Repression

The revolution in 1905 had shown that there were those capable of undermining the regime through demonstrations and violence. The Tsar had ensured that concessions were offered to the majority, but the minority of those dissatisfied with the manifesto needed dealing with.

The state responded to these groups in a brutal manner. Twenty thousand were exiled from Russia and over one thousand were hanged. This became known as "Stolypin's necktie". The role of the **Okhrana** was also increased. This was the Russian secret police who imprisoned suspects and monitored opponents of the regime.

Fundamental Laws

The Fundamental Laws were a way for Nicholas to regain control over the country after giving away some power in the manifesto. It ensured the Tsar still had control over the laws passed by giving him an overall veto. He also retained for himself certain rights: that to declare war, to control the church, and to dissolve the Duma whenever he saw fit. The Tsar also had the power to appoint and dismiss ministers.

Mir

The mir was the local commune, often very conservative organisations that restricted peasants from purchasing new machinery and decided what peasants grew.

Repression

The oppression or persecution of an individual or group for political reasons.

Okhrana

The secret police force of the Russian Empire under the Tsars.

SOURCE 3

Nicholas II, telegram to the president of the Duma, 1 March 1917.

There is no sacrifice that I would not be willing to make for the welfare and salvation of Mother Russia. Therefore I am ready to abdicate in favour of my son, under the regency of my brother Mikhail Alexandrovich, with the understanding that my son is to remain with me until he becomes of age.

TASKS

Stolypin was assassinated in 1911 in mysterious circumstances. Use the information on this page to write an obituary for him. You could choose to write from the perspective of someone who favoured him, or from an opponent of the regime.

DISCUSSION

Read Source 3. Having studied the Tsar, are you surprised by this source? Explain your answer using details of the sources and your own knowledge.

Abdication of the Tsar

In 1917 the unthinkable happened. Tsar Nicholas II, Romanov ruler of Russia, head of the oldest dynasty in Europe, abdicated. He stepped down, intending his son to rule after him. This never happened and Nicholas would be the last Tsar to ever rule Russia.

Why was there a revolution in March 1917?

The downfall of the Tsar can be seen as the final event caused by a series of problems in Russia.

The build up:

Russia enters the war with the support of its people.	**1914**	Outbreak of war is greeted with initial enthusiasm as workers and peasants rally to the cause.
Battle of Tannenberg, over 30 000 Russian troops were killed or wounded and 90 000 were captured.	**1914**	Initial enthusiasm for war starts to disappear as people at home hear of defeats and losses
This linked the Tsar to the country's military failures and during 1917 there was a strong decline in support for his government.	**September 1915**	The Tsar assumed supreme command of the Russian Army fighting on the Eastern Front, leaving his unpopular wife in charge at home.
By this time Russia had lost around 1.7 million soldiers, with another 2 million held as prisoners of war, and a further million missing. The disastrous attempts to halt the Germans' Gorlice–Tarnów Offensive led to these huge losses.	**October 1916**	Not only was morale now fading, but also as the regular army fell more and more workers from the cities were forced to join the army.
This led to food shortages in the cities and high prices meant the poor struggled to afford food.	**The winter of 1916–17 was severe.**	Food shortages got worse in the countryside.
The price of goods in Petrograd (the new name for St Petersburg) had increased sixfold.	**January 1917**	The War was having a disastrous impact on the Russian economy. Food was in short supply and this led to mass discontent.
	The revolution of January 1917	In an attempt to increase their wages, industrial workers went on strike and in Petrograd people took to the street demanding food.
A large crowd marched through the streets of Petrograd breaking shop windows and shouting anti-war slogans.	**11 February 1917**	
	22 February	The owners of the Putilov Ironworks locked out its workforce after they demanded higher wages. Twenty thousand workers took to the streets. The army was ordered to disperse the protestors but soldiers refused to fire on their own people. In some cases the soldiers joined the protestors in demanding an end to the war.
Protestors demanded bread and marched to nearby factories bringing out over 50 000 workers on strike.	**23 February, International Women's Day**	
	26 February	Nicholas II ordered the Duma to close down. Members refused and they continued to meet and discuss what to do. Rodzianko, President of the Duma, sent a telegram to the Tsar suggesting that he appoint a new government. When the Tsar did not reply, the Duma nominated a Provisional Government headed by Prince George Lvov.

200 000 workers were on strike. Nicholas II, who was still away at the front, ordered the commander of the Petrograd garrison to suppress "all the disorders on the streets of the capital". The following day troops fired on demonstrators in different parts of the city. Others refused to obey the order and soldiers joined the striking workers in the streets.	**27 February**	
	28 February	Fearing that unrest at home would harm the war effort, the Russian army high command suggested that Nicholas II should abdicate in favour of a more popular member of the royal family. Grand Duke Michael Alexandrovich refused to accept the throne.
The Tsar abdicated leaving the Provisional Government in control of the country.	**1 March 1917**	

▲ **Fig. 10.9** Timeline leading up to the 1917 revolution

FP ▶ Why was the revolution of March 1917 successful?

It can be argued that Nicholas's refusal to allow political reform led to the revolution which overthrew him.

SOURCE 4

Grand Duke Alexander Mikhailovich, letter to Nicholas II, January 1917.

The unrest grows; even the monarchist principle is beginning to totter; and those who defend the idea that Russia cannot exist without a Tsar lose the ground under their feet, since the facts of disorganization and lawlessness are manifest. A situation like this cannot last long. I repeat once more - it is impossible to rule the country without paying attention to the voice of the people, without meeting their needs, without a willingness to admit that the people themselves understand their own needs.

It can be argued that Nicholas's military failings were to blame for the revolution.

SOURCE 5

Alexander Kerensky, speech in the Duma, 13 February 1917.

There are people who assert that the Ministers are at fault. Not so. The country now realizes that the Ministers are but fleeting shadows. The country can clearly see who sends them here. To prevent a catastrophe the Tsar himself must be removed, by force if there is no other way.

It can also be blamed on two other figures: Gregory Rasputin and the Tsar's wife, Tsarina Alexandra.

Rasputin

Rasputin was a hugely controversial figure. Raised as a peasant from Siberia, he had initially joined a monastery before leaving Russia to travel. While travelling he claimed he had special healing powers that allowed him to treat the sick. On his return to Russia a bishop introduced him to the Tsar and Tsarina. Their son Alexis suffered from a rare disease called haemophilia, meaning the blood does not clot if a wound occurs. When Alexis was taken seriously ill in 1908, Rasputin was called to the royal palace. He managed to stop the bleeding and from then on became a close confidant of the Tsar and his family.

DISCUSSION

1. How far does Source 4 support Source 5?

2. Is either of these sources the more reliable? Explain your answer

N. IVANOV : CARICATURE OF RASPUTIN, "RUSSIA'S RULING HOUSE"

▲ **Fig. 10.10** A Russian cartoon published in 1916 with the caption "The Russian Tsars at home"

Rasputin was a controversial figure. There were wild rumours regarding his private conduct and during the war, when the Tsar went to lead the troops, he increasingly took a prominent role in running the country. His "visions" ensured he offered advice on who should be in key positions of government and even where troops should be deployed. Many people hated Rasputin, with one politician complaining that "the Tsarina's blind faith in Rasputin led her to seek his counsel not only in personal matters but also on questions of state policy".

Rasputin was murdered in dramatic circumstances at the end of 1916 but by this stage the damage of association with such a figure had been done to the Tsar.

The Tsarina

Born in Germany, the Tsar's wife was also a controversial figure. She was deeply unpopular in Russia—not only was she German, from the country Russia was now fighting, but she made it known she disliked Russia and the thought of any form of democratic change. When the Tsar went to lead the troops at the front, the Tsarina took responsibility for domestic policy. Rasputin served as her advisor and over the next few months she dismissed ministers and their deputies in rapid succession. Rumours began to circulate that she and Rasputin were leaders of a pro-German court group and were seeking a separate peace with the Central Powers. Some politicians were deeply concerned.

The impact of the war

The cause of all the problems that emerged for the Tsar was undoubtedly the First World War. It brought all of Russia's problems under the spotlight and made many of them worse. The impact of it was in two key areas. Firstly by demoralising the people; effects of war left the people of Russia starving, demoralised by high casualties and angry at the government for forced grain requisition and shortages. The war also had another more devastating effect, by revealing the failings in the Tsar's leadership. His decision making was exposed to be poor, and his steadfast refusal to allow the politicians a say in how Russia was run, and instead relying on the dubious council of the Tsarina and Rasputin, was not popular. The War wasn't the only reason why Nicholas II fell, but it did create a situation which it was impossible for him to recover from.

How did the Bolsheviks gain power, and how did they consolidate their rule?

When the Tsar abdicated, Russia was left in a state of chaos. Without a clear ruler and embroiled in a European conflict, Russia needed leadership quickly. The unenviable job of leading the country was left to the politicians. The Duma took over and it set up a **Provisional Government**, a temporary 12-man executive led by Alexander Kerensky. The intention was for elections to be held late in 1917 and for an elected government to take Russia forwards. The elections never happened and in November 1917 there was another revolution.

QUICK QUESTION 4

Look at Figure 10.10. What does the cartoonist suggest about the influence of Rasputin?

> " General Alexseyev told me later about his profound concern on learning that a secret map of military operations had found its way into the Tsarina's hands. But like many others, he was powerless to take any action. "
>
> Alexander Kerensky

Provisional Government

The emergency or interim government set up when a political void was created by the collapse of Tsarist rule.

How effectively did the Provisional Government rule Russia in 1917?

The fall of the government can be seen to have occurred because of its failure to address several key problems facing Russia.

Problem	Details	Significance
Russia's involvement in the war	Anxious not to be associated with failure and wanting a chance for a share of the spoils of war, the Provisional Government agreed to continue with the First World War. In July, the government launched the "Kerensky offensive", an attempt to gain territory in the west and push the Germans back. The offensive failed. By the summer of 1917 an estimated two million soldiers had run away and some soldiers killed their officers rather than fight. It was a disaster.	The fall of the Tsar can be attributed to problems that stemmed from the war. By not removing Russia from the war the government in effect allowed these problems to continue. The effects continued both for the soldiers and those at home, where between February and July 568 factories closed in Petrograd with the loss of 100 000 jobs.
The role of the Petrograd Soviet	Alongside the Provisional Government existed another political body which also helped rule Russia in a system of "dual authority". The Petrograd Soviet had existed since the revolution of 1905, largely made up of workers, Mensheviks, and socialists. It had influence and control over the railways, the troops, the factories, and the power supplies.	The situation of "dual authority" meant that there were two, often contradicting, voices for people to listen to. The Petrograd Soviet was probably more powerful, but it wouldn't take power. Its leaders did not feel that Russia was ready for a workers' revolution and also felt that on a more practical level, they would not be able to run Russia, as the army leadership and the middle class didn't support them. What their presence did do though was undermine the Provisional Government.
The issue of land	After the March revolution peasants had taken to the seizing of land. Some soldiers returned and used their weapons to seize land from the nobility. Manor houses were burnt down and in some cases wealthy landowners were murdered. The Provisional Government was against this, not against the principle of land redistribution, but of the way it was carried out. It wanted to do it within the framework of the law.	The Provisional Government failed to control the peasants, or please them over the issue of land. This made the politicians appear to be failing to understand the poor or be willing to meet their needs.
Unrest among the people	Food shortages, unemployment, and high prices had brought about the downfall of the Tsar and remained an issue. Grain seizures continued in order to feed the troops fighting in the war. Although the government increased the price paid by 100 per cent this didn't persuade the peasants to sell as there was little to buy and what was available remained expensive.	The people were unhappy as they lacked the basics to live. Food shortages led to the threat of famine and the people began to demand an end to the war.

▲ Table 10.1

Did the Provisional Government achieve anything?

Although only in power eight months, the Provisional Government managed several reforms.

- The secret police (the Okhrana) was disbanded.

- An amnesty was announced for political and religious prisoners.

- Personal freedoms such as freedom of speech and religion were granted.

- The death penalty was abolished.

FP Why were the Bolsheviks able to seize power in November 1917?

The **Bolsheviks** wanted a quick revolution, where the industrial working class would seize power from the politicians. The fall of the Tsar was not enough and they wanted further change.

The role of Lenin

The Bolsheviks were led by Vladimir Lenin who returned to Russia on a sealed train provided by the Germans after the fall of the Tsar. On his return to Russia he sought to gain power for the Bolsheviks. He published his April Theses in which he attacked Bolsheviks for supporting the Provisional Government and not pushing for revolution. Lenin urged the peasants to take the land from the rich landlords and the industrial workers to seize the factories.

The July Days

The decision taken to continue the war and to launch a large offensive backfired. As the summer offensive of 1917 faltered and conditions at home didn't improve, food remained scarce and what food there was proved to be too expensive for many. Soldiers and sailors took to the streets of Petrograd in July 1917 and they were soon joined by workers in the factories. Riots occurred on 16 and 17 July. The government was forced to bring in troops to end the riots.

After the July Days the Provisional Government became more hard line in approach. Kerensky, the new leader, reintroduced the death penalty and imprisoned leading Bolsheviks. Many others, such as Lenin fled into exile in Finland.

Source 7 on page 236 was the revolutionary cry by Vladimir Lenin to the people of Russia in October 1917. These three things defined what the Bolskeviks were promising, and also what the people of Russia wanted. After the failure of the Tsar and the Provisional Government to deliver on the failings of Russia, the people turned to the promises offered by Lenin.

The Kornilov affair

The Provisional Government lacked support on all sides as its unpopularity grew. The events leading to its demise are near farcical though.

Kerensky attempted decisive action. Appointing a new Supreme Commander of the armed forces, General Kornilov, Kerensky authorised him to impose order in the capital Petrograd. Kornilov took loyal troops with him to establish control. Kerensky panicked when he saw what was happening, realising

Bolsheviks

Members of the left-wing majority group of the Russian Social Democratic Workers' Party that adopted Lenin's ideas.

DISCUSSION

How did the the Provisional Government help the Bolsheviks gain popularity?

that a popular and well-supported army leader was marching on the capital. Uncertain of the support of his army generals, Kerensky was forced to ask for help from others including the Bolsheviks. Within a few days Bolsheviks had enlisted 25 000 armed recruits to defend Petrograd. They dug trenches and fortified the city, making themselves look like the defenders of the city. Kornilov's attempt to seize power collapsed without bloodshed as his troops refused to fight against members of the **Petrograd Soviet**.

Although Kerensky survived the Kornilov affair, the event weakened the Provisional Government and paved the way for the Bolsheviks to seize power shortly after in the November Revolution. The fact that Kerensky had also armed the **Red Guards** meant that when the November Revolution came the Red Army was more powerful due to Kerensky's help than it probably would have been otherwise.

The real winners were the Bolsheviks. They were credited with saving the city and the workers who formed the Red Guards were sympathetic to the Bolsheviks. Kerensky had lost a lot of support and his power base was rapidly disappearing. On 7 November, Kerensky was informed that the Bolsheviks were about to seize power. He decided to leave Petrograd. Later that day the Red Guards stormed the Winter Palace and members of Kerensky's cabinet were arrested. The Provisional Government was now replaced by an administration headed by Vladimir Lenin.

TASKS

1. Create a list of reasons why the Provisional Government fell from power. Divide this list into two categories: "Mistakes by the Provisional Government" and "Strengths of others". Which side is the stronger argument?

2. Compare why the provisional government fell with the reasons for the fall of the Tsar. Did the Provisional Government learn anything from the Tsar's mistakes?

3. How effective at ruling Russia was the Provisional Government?

Terms used

There are many different terms used for both the rulers of the country, and the country itself. Lenin's party was formed as the Bolsheviks in 1903 and whenever this term is used it only refers to this party. In 1918 the Bolsheviks became the Russian Communist Party, and therefore the term "Communists" is also used to describe them. Gradually the name "Bolshevik" was used less and less as the party became more established.

The names for the country are equally confusing! The Russian Empire had been disbanded when Tsar Nicholas II abdicated. However, in 1922 the Soviet Union was formed at the end of the Civil War, uniting Russia with the Ukraine and Belarus. In the 1940s the Empire grew until it was disbanded in 1991.

Why did the Bolsheviks win the Civil War?

The first major decision by Lenin was to end Russia's involvement in the First World War. The Treaty of Brest-Litovsk signed in March 1918 meant that Russia's withdrawal from the conflict cost the country territory that included a quarter of the Russian Empire's population, a quarter of its industry, and nine-tenths of its coal mines. One of the reasons for this was the Civil War that had broken out once the Bolsheviks had seized power. Once in control Lenin's Bolsheviks faced opposition from all sides.

Despite the fact they were heavily outnumbered, the "Reds" managed to win the conflict. This can be seen to be because of their own strengths, as well as the failings of the "Whites".

The Reds	V	The Whites
The Bolsheviks		Supporters of the Tsar
		Military commanders who wanted to stay in the war
		Many foreign nations including Britain, the United States and France

▲ **Fig. 10.11** Who fought in the Civil War?

The role of Leon Trotsky

Trotsky was a brilliant organiser. Despite having no military training, he proved an excellent commander of the new Bolshevik army, the Red Army. Trotsky promoted men based not on their class but on how well they did in combat. He also was a great motivator; he had his own armoured train and visited the Red Army at the front to boost morale.

The Red Army

The newly formed army of the Bolsheviks were well supplied and well organised. To support the new army who lacked experience, Trotsky worked with ex-Tsarist officers as he knew that they had the military experience the Red Army lacked.

▲ **Fig. 10.12** Leon Trotsky addressing Red Army troops during the Civil War

Support

Lenin was very clever and knew that he had to win the war at all costs. Lenin had ordered that supplies of food went first to soldiers, and then what was left went to those who lived in the cities. This meant that men flocked to join the Red Army, if only to be fed.

War Communism

This was designed to provide an economy that met the needs of the war. It brought in strict methods of control through the nationalising of industry, meaning the government took over and ran the factories, enforcing strict discipline. Striking workers could be shot and rationing was introduced for workers.

The policy worked as it was meant to help win the war. However, it caused many hardships for ordinary Russians. Peasants refused to cooperate in producing food as the government took away far too much of it. Workers began moving from the cities back to the countryside, where the chances of food were greater. Between 1918 and 1920, Petrograd lost 75 per cent of its population, while Moscow lost 50 per cent. By 1921, the output levels

> **❝** *I give warning that if any unit retreats without orders, the first to be shot down will be the commissary of the unit, and next the commander. Brave and gallant soldiers will be appointed in their places. Cowards, dastards and traitors will not escape the bullet. This I solemnly promise in the presence of the entire Red Army.* **❞**
>
> Leon Trotsky, order issued to the Red Army during the Civil War

of heavy industry had fallen to 20 per cent of those in 1913. The forceful removal of grain combined with the effects of seven years of war and a severe drought, contributed to a famine that caused around eight million deaths.

If Trotsky was the heart of the military effort, Lenin ensured that the people were kept under control. The secret police, the Cheka, was responsible for hunting out possible opponents to Lenin.

The Whites weaknesses

The Whites were divided. They were a mixture of Tsarist forces who wanted the return of the Romanovs, liberal groups who wanted reforms, and foreign nations who wanted to keep Russia in the First World War. With so many groups involved, no one person could be appointed to act as their sole commander. With no unified leadership, the Whites were much weakened.

The Whites failed to secure the support of the people of Russia. Lenin had promised land to the peasants while the Whites wanted to return Russia to Tsarist days. This meant the peasants feared a return to the old order where the peasants were repressed. Bolshevik **propaganda** also reinforced this fear.

The role of foreign nations

The Allies had wanted to keep Russia fighting in the war. However as time went on, France and Britain worried about how far they were committing to a lengthy, expensive war in Russia. Reports started to emerge of atrocities by White soldiers in Russia, something that turned public support away from the war even further. At the end of the First World War on 11 November 1918, the Allies withdrew from Russia.

The cost of the war was dramatic though: 800 000 soldiers were killed and it is estimated that eight million died from starvation and disease as result of the war.

FP How far was the New Economic Policy a success?

SOURCE 10

Kronstadt Provisional Revolutionary Committee, 4 March 1921.

Comrade workers, red soldiers and sailors. We stand for the power of the Soviets and not that of the parties. We are for free representation of all who toil. Comrades, you are being misled. At Kronstadt all power is in the hands of the revolutionary sailors, of red soldiers and of workers.

In 1921 the sailors at the Kronstadt Naval Base revolted. Angry about the lack of democracy and the policy of War Communism, their revolt lasted nearly three weeks and it took the involvement of the Red Army to stop them.

The protests at Kronstadt showed Lenin that something needed to change. Although a revolutionary, Lenin seemed aware that a more realistic approach to ruling was needed. Conditions for most Russians had deteriorated; by 1918 the average wage was a quarter of that in 1913. By the middle of the Civil War it was less than 10 per cent.

To improve the situation Lenin introduced the New Economic Policy (NEP). This change regained the support of the peasantry and gained support from the workers. There was also a more pressing need to return to previous levels of production as soon as possible.

SOURCE 8

Felix Dzerzhinsky, interviewed in Novaia Zhizn, 14 July 1918.

We stand for organized terror—this should be frankly admitted. Terror is an absolute necessity during times of revolution. Our aim is to fight against the enemies of the Soviet Government and of the new order of life. We judge quickly. In most cases only a day passes between the apprehension of the criminal and his sentence.

Propaganda

A form of communication that is aimed at influencing the attitude of others towards some cause or position.

SOURCE 9

Leaflet issued by the Bolsheviks in Mourmansk in 1919.

For the first time in history the working people have got control of their country. We in Russia have succeeded. We have thrown off the rule of the Tsar, of landlords, and of capitalists. But we have still tremendous difficulties to overcome. We cannot build a new society in a day. We deserve to be left alone. We ask you, are you going to ruin us? To help give Russia back to the landlords, the capitalists and Tsar?

TASKS

"The Bolsheviks won the Civil War because of their own strengths rather than the weaknesses of the Whites." How far do you agree with this statement? Explain your answer.

What changes were made under the NEP?

The policy was very uncommunist in style. Lenin believed that Russia was not "Civilised enough for Socialism" and so designed the NEP around a more capitalist model. It meant the following changes were introduced.

Feature	What it meant
Private ownership allowed	Factories employing less than 20 people were no longer owned by the state.
Foreign trade allowed, encouraging links with other countries	Despite Russia being Communist some countries now returned to trading with Russia. This meant a boost to the economy.
State control of big industry	This remained from "War Communism". It still was an indication of the Bolsheviks' Communist beliefs.

▲ **Table 10.2**

Did it work?

There were some successes.

- By 1926 production returned to 1913 levels.
- Peasants benefited as there was better food distribution.
- "Nepmen" appeared, private traders who bought from the peasants and sold to the working classes. Some made great profits.

There were also some failures.

- Industrial workers fared no better under the scheme. They resented the success of some Nepmen.
- In a wider context, the 1920s was a time of great success across the world as Germany, the United States, and Japan flourished. In this setting the achievements of the Russian economy were not impressive.

SOURCE 11

Victor Serge, *Memoirs of a Revolutionary*, 1945.

The New Economic Policy was, in the space of a few months, already giving marvellous results. From one week to the next, the famine and the speculation were diminishing perceptibly. Restaurants were opening again and, wonder of wonders, pastries which were actually edible were on sale as a rouble apiece. The public was beginning to recover its breath, and people were apt to talk about the return of capitalism, which was synonymous with prosperity. On the other hand, the confusion among the party rank-and-file was staggering. For what did we fight, spill so much blood, agree to so many sacrifices? asked the Civil War veterans bitterly.

QUICK QUESTION 5

Study Source 11. Was Victor Serge in favour in of the NEP? How can you tell?

Stalin

Pre-political career

Born in Georgia, the young Joseph Stalin was educated at an Orthodox school before becoming radicalised by reading Lenin's work. He joined the Bolsheviks and was involved in various criminal activities.

Political career

Stalin rose to power by holding a wide variety of roles in government until Lenin's death. After a decade-long fight for power he established himself as undisputed ruler of Russia. His dictatorship would last over 20 years and was one of the most brutal in history.

Character and outlook

Autocratic and ruthless, as Stalin's rule went on he became increasingly paranoid and unpredictable.

How did Stalin gain and hold onto power?

In 1924 Lenin died. He had suffered several strokes after a failed assassination attempt in 1922. The next most prominent member of the Bolsheviks was Leon Trotsky, whose leadership of the Red Army to victory in the Civil War seemed to make him the natural replacement. However it was Joseph Stalin, a relatively minor member of the party, who became ruler of Russia.

FP Why did Stalin, and not Trotsky, emerge as Lenin's successor?

There are three key reasons why Stalin, and not Trotsky became leader of Russia.

Luck

In 1922 Lenin had written his last will and testament. Lenin's testament was highly critical of Stalin. However it was also highly critical of other members of the party, including Trotsky. It was never published in Russia, as the others mentioned feared it would harm their chances as well as Stalin's.

Policy

The battle over who would lead Russia was also a battle of policy, about where Russia would go next. It had been seven years since the revolution, and through the Civil War and the NEP some thought the Communist Party had lost its way. There were two main issues to be discussed.

a. The Permanent Revolution versus socialism in one country

The aim of communism was that it spread across the world. Only by a "world revolution" would the future of communism be secure. The idea of the Permanent Revolution was put forward by Trotsky who favoured putting all efforts into supporting the working class in other countries to stage their own revolutions.

Stalin argued for "Socialism in one country". He suggested that Russia should focus on cementing its own revolution in Russia to show what a model communist country would look like. This, he said, would allow Bolshevik control to be firmly established over Russia before attempting to spread communism elsewhere.

b. To continue or not with the NEP

The NEP had some success in boosting the Russian economy. It was however very uncommunist in style. It was creating a rich class of peasants and some were benefiting from private industry. Some favoured ending the NEP and pushing forward with mass industrialisation, while others wanted to keep the policy going. Stalin didn't make it clear what he favoured at first, but arguments between the two sides meant that Trotsky and several other contenders isolated themselves from support.

SOURCE 12

Arthur Ransome, from the British newspaper *The Guardian*, 23 January 1924.

Lenin had a sudden relapse yesterday, became unconscious, and died an hour later, just before seven in the evening. When Congress met at eleven this morning, Kalinin announced Lenin's death in a few broken sentences. Almost everybody in the great theatre burst into tears, and from all parts came the hysterical wailing of women. Tears were running down the faces of the members of Congress. Even the irreconcilable enemies of the Revolution are unable to disguise their respect for one of the greatest figures in Russian history.

SOURCE 13

Lenin's political will and testament, issued in December 1922.

Comrade Stalin, having become General Secretary, has concentrated enormous power in his hands: and I am not sure that he always knows how to use that power with sufficient caution. I therefore propose to our comrades to consider a means of removing Stalin from this post and appointing someone else who differs from Stalin in one weighty respect: being more tolerant, more loyal, more polite, more considerate of his comrades.

Trotsky

Stalin and Trotsky couldn't have been more different. Trotsky was an intellectual; he was seen as arrogant by some of the party. Furthermore he refused to criticise Stalin publicly as he assumed he would naturally be Lenin's successor. He underestimated Stalin.

Stalin on the other hand presented himself as a humble man from a peasant background. Furthermore he showed cunning in presenting himself as Lenin's natural successor. He made the most of all opportunities to show himself to be like Lenin, publishing pictures of them together and even being the leading mourner at Lenin's funeral. Trotsky wasn't there as Stalin had told him it was a different day.

TASK

"Source 12 is by a known Communist sympathiser and so is clearly of no use." How far do you agree?

▲ **Fig. 10.13** Stalin at Lenin's funeral, 21 January 1924

▲ **Fig. 10.14** Lenin and Stalin together; this photograph was taken in Lenin's last years and released by Stalin

DISCUSSION

1. What evidence is there to support the view that Stalin succeeded Lenin due to:

   a. the mistakes of others

   b. his own strengths?

2. To what extent was Lenin just another Tsar?

Why did Stalin launch the Purges?

At the end of the first of Stalin's great Five-Year Plans there was unrest emerging in Russia. Some felt that the speed of change was too rapid, and key members of the party wanted the return of Leon Trotsky, who had been exiled since Stalin had taken over. Then in 1934 a dramatic event occurred which led to a huge change.

The event was the murder of Sergei Kirov, a leading politician. Using his death as the reason, Stalin started a wave of terror known as the "**Great Purges**" which led to the death of thousands of politicians, members of the armed forces, and wider society.

Great Purges

The removal of people who are considered undesirable by those in power from a government, from another organisation or from society as a whole

SOURCE 14

By Alexander Orlov, an NKVD officer who escaped from Russia to the Untied States.

Stalin decided to arrange for the assassination of Kirov and to lay the crime at the door of the former leaders of the opposition and thus with one blow do away with Lenin's former comrades. Stalin came to the conclusion that, if he could prove that Zinoviev and Kamenev and other leaders of the opposition had shed the blood of Kirov, "the beloved son of the party", a member of the Politburo, he then would be justified in demanding blood for blood.

TASKS

1. Study Source 14. It has been widely suggested that Stalin was responsible for the death of Kirov. Why might he have done this?

2. Can you see any problems with the reliability of Orlov's account?

The purges under Stalin were dramatic. While a clearing out of the membership of the Bolsheviks had regularly happened in the past; it had never been on such a scale as it was under Stalin or as violent.

The Purges had three phases.

1. The chistka of 1932–5. Twenty per cent of party members were expelled non-violently as part of a cleaning out of undesirables. These were mostly people who had joined the party for their own advantage rather than for ideological reasons.

2. The show trials. Prominent old Bolsheviks were publicly tried and executed. The government used these during the Great Terror as political rituals, which were intended to mobilise the population against the class enemies within the Soviet Union. The proceedings were often filmed to be used as propaganda in cinemas.

3. The Yezhovshchina 1937–8. Named after Yezhov, the head of the **NKVD**, this was the period when thousands of party members and members of the armed forces were denounced, arrested, and imprisoned. Many were executed and many more died in the labour camps. Yezhov drew up a list of over 250 000 "Anti-Soviet Elements"; this included scientists, artists, writers, and musicians as well as managers and administrators.

NKVD

The public and secret police organisation of the Soviet Union that directly executed the rule of power of the Soviets, including political repression, during the era of Joseph Stalin.

How many were killed?

According to the Soviet archives the NKVD detained 1 548 366 victims, of whom 681 692 were shot. Some estimates by modern historians put this figure as two or three times higher.

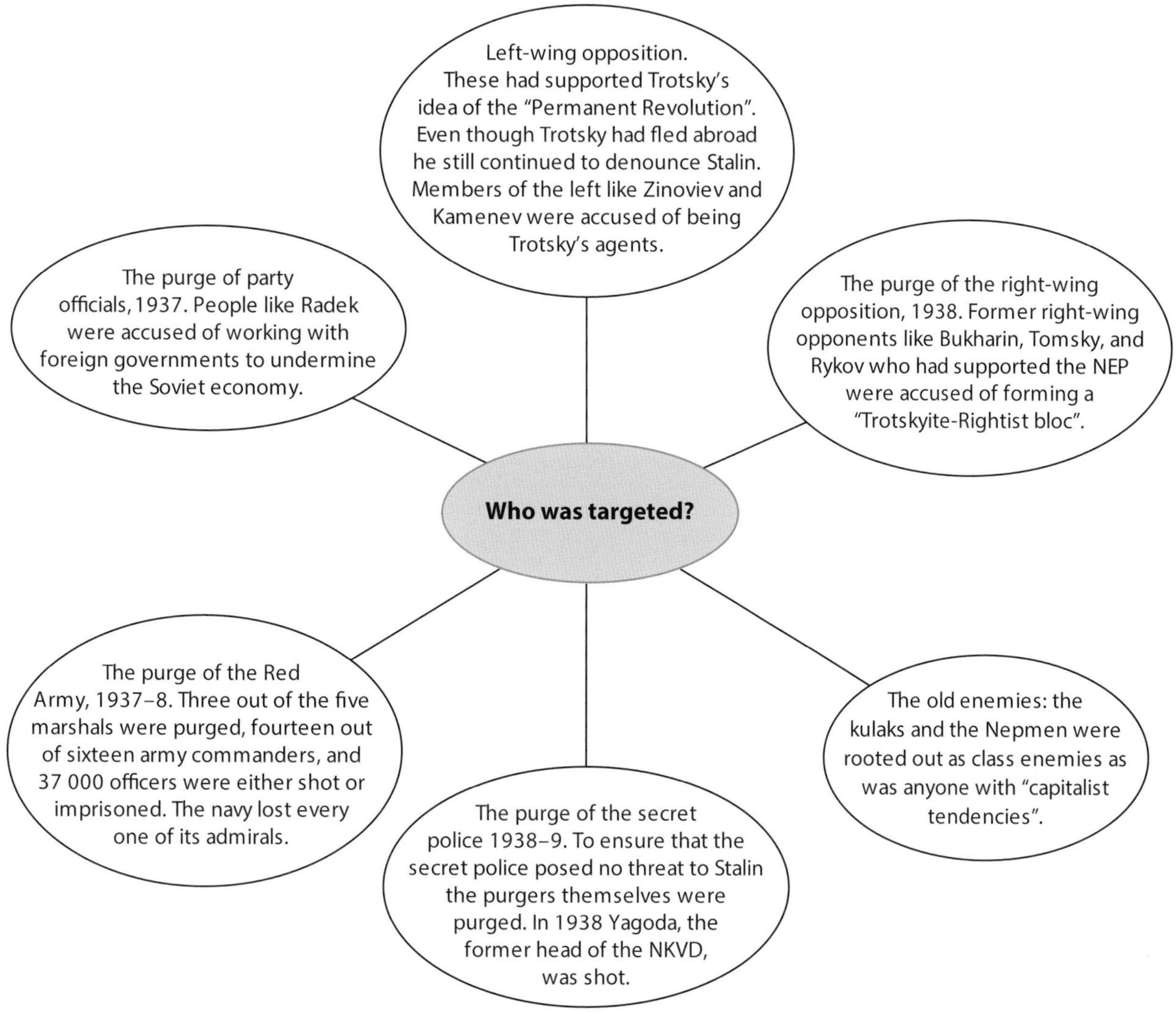
Left-wing opposition. These had supported Trotsky's idea of the "Permanent Revolution". Even though Trotsky had fled abroad he still continued to denounce Stalin. Members of the left like Zinoviev and Kamenev were accused of being Trotsky's agents.
The purge of party officials, 1937. People like Radek were accused of working with foreign governments to undermine the Soviet economy.
The purge of the right-wing opposition, 1938. Former right-wing opponents like Bukharin, Tomsky, and Rykov who had supported the NEP were accused of forming a "Trotskyite-Rightist bloc".
Who was targeted?
The purge of the Red Army, 1937–8. Three out of the five marshals were purged, fourteen out of sixteen army commanders, and 37 000 officers were either shot or imprisoned. The navy lost every one of its admirals.
The purge of the secret police 1938–9. To ensure that the secret police posed no threat to Stalin the purgers themselves were purged. In 1938 Yagoda, the former head of the NKVD, was shot.
The old enemies: the kulaks and the Nepmen were rooted out as class enemies as was anyone with "capitalist tendencies".

▲ **Fig. 10.15** Groups targeted during Stalin's purges

DISCUSSION

1. Under the Tsars 3,932 persons were killed for political crimes from 1825 to 1910. How does this compare to the brutality of Stalin?
2. Explain Stalin's motivation in terms of:
   - securing his position as ruler of Russia
   - controlling his people
   - bringing about dramatic change.
3. Study the cartoon in Figure 10.16. What is the cartoonist's view of Stalin's purges?

COMRADE STALIN, HAVING RUN OUT OF PLOTTERS, EXECUTES HIMSELF FOR TALKING IN HIS SLEEP.
OLD LOW'S ALMANACK
PROPHECIES FOR 1931

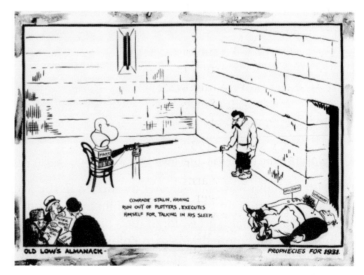

▲ **Fig. 10.16** A cartoon from a British newspaper in 1931: the caption reads "Comrade Stalin, having run out of plotters, executes himself for talking in his sleep"

What methods did Stalin use to control the Soviet Union?

Propaganda

SOURCE 15

A saying popular in the 1930s.

To oppose Stalin was to oppose the party. To oppose the party was to oppose the state. To oppose the state was to be in the pay of the Fascist organisations of the West.

One of the key parts of Stalin's rule was the cult that developed around him. Stalin was central to everything in Russia and was perceived to be the embodiment of everything good in the country. This meant the following.

- His image was everywhere. Pictures, statues, and propaganda posters all celebrated Stalin's image.

- Places were named after him. There were no fewer than 16 cities named after him in eastern European countries under Russian control.

- Mothers taught their children that Stalin was "the wisest man of the age".

- Famous photographs were changed to make him the hero of the revolution, and obliterate the names of purged people such as Trotsky.

▲ **Fig. 10.17** A propaganda poster showing Stalin and Lenin from the Spanish Bolshevik party from 1947

▲ **Fig. 10.18** A propaganda poster from 1941 which shows Stalin surrounded by children

This cult of Stalin was made greater by success in the Second World War. Increasingly statues and pictures made him appear god-like. The glamour of the propaganda also grew; for Stalin's birthday each year the celebrations became more and more dramatic to enforce the cult and show that Russia's success was dependent on Stalin.

QUICK QUESTION 6

Study Figure 10.17. Why do you think Stalin was often shown with Lenin in images?

Terror

By 1941 Stalin had established almost complete control over all aspects of Russia.

Politically

Political rivals such as Kirov and Trotsky had been murdered, purges of the party had been carried out, and anyone suspected of disloyalty had been expelled, imprisoned or put on trial in public. The result was Stalin had established himself as the only political figure with any influence. Stalin's purges had also gone wider: 81 of the 103 generals and admirals of the armed forces were executed.

Ordinary people

Some 20 million Russians had been sent to Gulags where millions died. Those who remained lived in fear of the NKVD, the secret police who enforced Stalin's rule across Russia. Stalin had introduced Russification, where only Russian customs and language were allowed and both the Christian and Muslim religions were persecuted. Those who cooperated and joined the party were entitled to some rights such as jobs, holidays, housing, and education. All lived in fear though of the seemingly random nature of the persecution.

Society

All areas of life were controlled by Stalin's rule. All forms of media, such as books, films, art, and plays were influenced and only allowed if their plots, characters and ideals matched Stalinist beliefs. Stalin believed that all of the arts should portray the working man's struggle to achieve communism and therefore tightly controlled everything.

▲ **Fig. 10.19** Cattle trucks filled with prisoners about to be transported to Siberian camps

How complete was Stalin's control over the Soviet Union by 1941?

Russia had always had prisoner camps in Siberia, the coldest and most inhospitable part of Russia. Under Stalin these camps known as gulags were used by Stalin for opponents of his regime. It is estimated that around 50 million died in Soviet gulags between 1930 and 1950.

SOURCE 16

An account of life in a gulag by V.T. Shalamov. He was imprisoned in one of Stalin's gulags for more than 20 years. From "Dry Rations," a short story from *Kolyma Tales*, published in 1976.

Each time they brought in the soup ... it made us all want to cry. We were ready to cry for fear that the soup would be thin. And when a miracle occurred and the soup was thick we couldn't believe it and ate it as slowly as possible. But even with thick soup in a warm stomach there remained a sucking pain; we'd been hungry for too long. All human emotions—love, friendship, envy, concern for one's fellow man, compassion, longing for fame, honesty—had left us with the flesh that had melted from our bodies ...

SOURCE 17

An account of living through the Terror, by Nadezhda Khazina. From *Hope Against Hope* published in 1971.

In the period of the Yezhov terror—the mass arrests came in waves of varying intensity—there must sometimes have been no more room in the jails, and to those of us still free it looked as though the highest wave had passed and the terror was abating. After each show trial, people sighed, "Well, it's all over at last." What they meant was: "Thank God, it looks as though I've escaped." But then there would be a new wave, and the same people would rush to heap abuse on the "enemies of the people."

The principles and aims of mass terror have nothing in common with ordinary police work or with security. The only purpose of terror is intimidation.

SOURCE 18

From an unnamed woman who lived through Stalin's purges, taken from Orlando Figes' *The Whisperers* published in 2007.

We were brought up to keep our mouths shut. "You'll get into trouble for your tongue"— that's what people said to us children all the time. We went through life afraid to talk. Mama used to say that every other person was an informer. We were afraid of our neighbours, and especially of the police ...

DISCUSSION

These three sources come from books written a long time after the purges. Does this lessen their value as evidence? Explain your answer.

What was the impact of Stalin's economic policies?

SOURCE 19

Stalin at the 15th Party Congress.

The Soviet Union is fifty to a hundred years behind the advanced countries, and thus must narrow this distance in ten years. … Either we do it or we shall be crushed.

Stalin's words were very dramatic. He was right though, Russia drastically needed to modernise. To do this he needed to industrialise Russia. This process had started under Nicholas II but more was needed.

Why did Stalin introduce the Five-Year Plans?

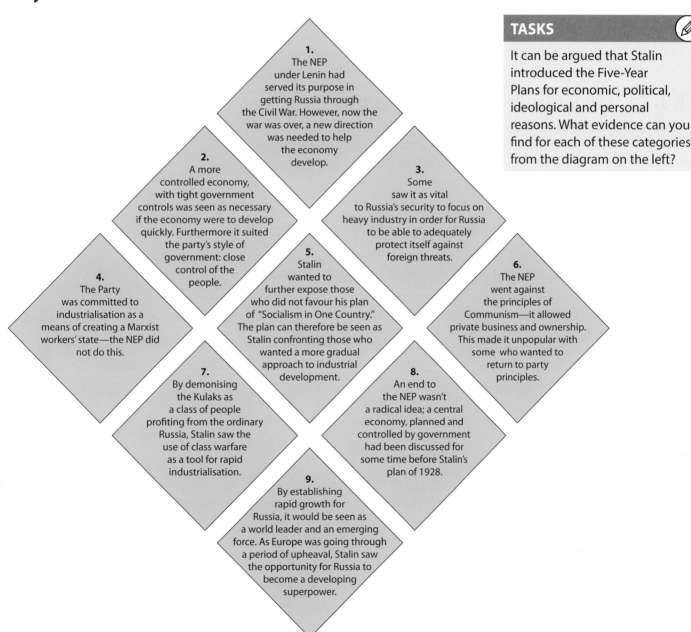

1.
The NEP under Lenin had served its purpose in getting Russia through the Civil War. However, now the war was over, a new direction was needed to help the economy develop.

2.
A more controlled economy, with tight government controls was seen as necessary if the economy were to develop quickly. Furthermore it suited the party's style of government: close control of the people.

3.
Some saw it as vital to Russia's security to focus on heavy industry in order for Russia to be able to adequately protect itself against foreign threats.

4.
The Party was committed to industrialisation as a means of creating a Marxist workers' state—the NEP did not do this.

5.
Stalin wanted to further expose those who did not favour his plan of "Socialism in One Country." The plan can therefore be seen as Stalin confronting those who wanted a more gradual approach to industrial development.

6.
The NEP went against the principles of Communism—it allowed private business and ownership. This made it unpopular with some who wanted to return to party principles.

7.
By demonising the Kulaks as a class of people profiting from the ordinary Russia, Stalin saw the use of class warfare as a tool for rapid industrialisation.

8.
An end to the NEP wasn't a radical idea; a central economy, planned and controlled by government had been discussed for some time before Stalin's plan of 1928.

9.
By establishing rapid growth for Russia, it would be seen as a world leader and an emerging force. As Europe was going through a period of upheaval, Stalin saw the opportunity for Russia to become a developing superpower.

TASKS

It can be argued that Stalin introduced the Five-Year Plans for economic, political, ideological and personal reasons. What evidence can you find for each of these categories from the diagram on the left?

How did it work?

The party set targets for heavy industry through Gosplan, the central state planning commission. These targets were passed to regional administrators, who passed them on to directors of industrial enterprises such as factory owners. The state therefore controlled what was to be produced and how much, ensuring that Russia would have enough of what was needed.

What happened?

The first Five-Year Plan trebled the production of electricity, doubled that of coal and iron, and saw huge new tractor works being built. However, there was a lack of skilled workers and a decline in consumer industries.

The second Five-Year Plan saw chemical industries grow, railways linking cities, and by 1937 Russia was self-sufficient in machine making. However, oil wasn't produced at the expected rate, consumer goods were ignored, and ice cream production was severely lacking.

Under the third Five-Year Plan heavy industry continued to grow but the focus shifted to defence and rearmaments as war approached. Steel and oil production fell and consumer industries were ignored.

FP Why did Stalin introduce collectivisation?

Russia's potential strength lay in its agricultural power. If the millions of peasants in Russia could be put to good use for the economy the country could produce far more and be more effective. Therefore the plan for agriculture was based around the idea of **collectivisation**. It had several benefits.

- The Bolsheviks could dictate production.

- It stopped the creation of the "kulak" class of peasant—rich peasants who went against communist ideology.

- It allowed for the use of big machinery instead of small private farms.

- Most importantly the government would be able to force the production of large amounts of grain which could be exported to pay for the necessary imports of technology and expertise to feed the growing population.

How did it work?

The idea that peasants could be farmers themselves was, in the view of the Bolsheviks, not working. Instead peasants were placed on state farms where under direction from a central committee they farmed the land. Each household had one acre of private land; here members of the household could grow what they wanted. Workers received no wage, but they got a percentage of the profit that the farm made at the end of the year. The problem was very few farms made a profit, therefore peasants received no money. This made what they did with their private plots of land crucial. It is estimated that these plots produced 70 per cent of meat consumed in Russia and were vital for the economy.

Collectivisation

A policy, pursued between 1928 and 1933, to consolidate individual land and labour into state farms.

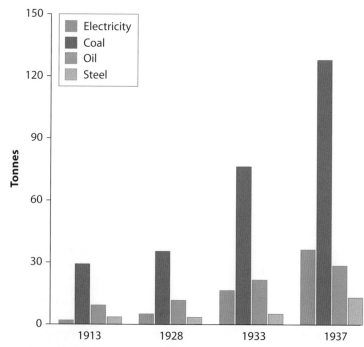

▲ **Fig. 10.20** Russia's manufacturing output

How successful were Stalin's economic changes?

Industry

At face value, the statistics look impressive—between 1928 and 1940 coal output rose from 35 million to 150 million tonnes, steel from 3 million to 18 million tonnes, and oil from 12 million to 26 million tonnes. By 1940 Russia produced 20 per cent of the world's manufacturing output.

Agriculture

In 1928 0.03 million tonnes were exported for sale abroad. By 1933 1.69 million tonnes were exported.

The advances therefore in heavy industry were impressive. It is important though to consider the wider effects of Stalin's dramatic economic changes

Key strengths

- Russia was stronger militarily—Russia entered the war in 1941 and without industrialisation, it would probably have lost. There was considerable emphasis on defence in the Plans, and the materials produced during the plans also enabled Russia to be equipped with the tools to defend itself. However there were other military effects. Part of the Plans involved building industry in safer areas deep inside the country, meaning that key production didn't fall into German hands. Some historians have also argued that the pressure on the population, which was part of fulfilling the Plans, created a siege mentality which prepared the population well for the rigours and sacrifices of the war years.

- It helped develop Russia—education programmes in the collectives, a big increase in urbanisation and some evidence of an increased standard of living in the later 1930s meant that for some, things got better.

- It transformed the way Russia worked—new chemicals for farming, new machines in factories, Russia began to resemble the industrialized nations of Europe.

Key failings

- The cost to human life—some 5 million died due to famine in 1933, caused by collectivisation. Furthermore, up to 10 million were deported and imprisoned due to perceived opposition to the Plans. Some historians estimate a total of 40 million died due to the economic hardship the new plans brought.

- Economic failings—the emphasis on quantity through improbably high targets was often at the expense of quality, as workers were desperate to meet the target regardless of how good the product was. There was also much inefficiency; productivity was often low and industry was very labour-intensive.

> **QUICK QUESTION 7**
>
> To what extent can the argument "the end justifies the means" be applied to Stalin's economic changes?

What was the impact of Stalin's reforms on ethnic minorities and women?

The role of women in Stalin's Russia was meant to be crucial. The Communist Party saw women as equals to men, and if dramatic economic change was to be carried out, women would be needed to play their part.

Policies towards women

In 1935 Stalin believed the family to be in decline. To counter this, a new family law was introduced in 1936.

- Divorce was made more difficult.

- Abortion was made illegal except for medical reasons.

- Tax breaks were introduced for families having more children.

Women in the work place

In order to promote the idea of women working, several incentives were put in place.

- Free health care

- Accident insurance in the work place

- An increased number of crèches for the children of working mothers

- Paid holidays

- Some factories even established "sitting" services for mothers so that they could work even while caring for children.

Did it work?

By 1939 women made up a significant part of the work force. They formed:

- 33 per cent of engineers

- 79 per cent of doctors

- 43 per cent of the industrial workforce.

Why did all this happen?

Under Stalin's rule, the policies towards women often brought benefits, however these measures were taken often without women's rights in mind. Stalin wanted to increase his workforce, therefore needed a higher birth rate for the future, hence the policies towards the family, and also needed workers for the immediate, explaining why he improved conditions for women.

Was it all positive for women?

Even though women benefited from many policies, they still often occupied lower positions in the workplace and still faced discrimination. Women were also expected to work in the home in addition to working in the work place, leaving little time for any other activities such as higher education. They also were restricted from holding high Party positions under Stalin, showing that the idea of equality was not yet established.

Ethnic minorities

Stalin's history in the Communist Party meant that he should have had a clear understanding of the role of minorities in Russia. Under Lenin he had acted as Commissar of Nationalities and as a Georgian was aware of the differing nationalities that made up his empire. However, his approach to minorities was to discourage, rather encourage differing national identities within his Russia.

Stalin saw the pull of different nationalities as a barrier to the development of Russia, and therefore sought to unite all who lived in Russia with a series of

DISCUSSION

"Women under Stalin weren't important, but they were necessary". What is meant by this statement?

measures designed to bring all in line. This "Russification" was not a new idea; it had been tried under the Tsars, but under Stalin it took on a harder edge. Stalin wanted people not to see themselves as Russian, or Ukranian, but as "Soviets".

In order to achieve this, several measures were put in place. Teaching the Russian language in all schools became mandatory, some 1.5 million ethnic minorities were deported back to Asia and non-Russian members of the Communist elite in positions of power were removed. At the same time, anti-semitic measures also began to be introduced.

Was he successful?

Yes	No
Natural events such as the famine in 1932 and the Second World War destroyed a lot of the non-Russian elites, meaning that new people in positions of power could be selected by Stalin.	Attempts to convince minorities to be "Soviet" rather than their own nationalities failed, and Stalin resorted to using the purges of the 1930s to target Latvians, Estonians, Finns, Poles and Hungarians within the Soviet elite.
Russia's eventual victory in the war meant that he could promote Russian nationalism and show it to be the conqueror of Nazism.	Measures were deeply unpopular, with some groups joining the sides of the Nazis during the Second World War and actually fighting against the Russians.
Millions of minorities left Russia under his rule.	Despite attempts to enforce changes in language and education, different identities remained strong, particularly in rural areas.
Power was removed from the smaller republics in the Soviet Union with Moscow retaining control over the Empire.	

FP How were the Soviet people affected by these changes?

The whole programme of "cooperatives" was presented through propaganda and socialist ideology, although the forced collectivisation of agriculture had little to do with genuine Marxist doctrine. Collectivisation caused uproar and resistance. Stalin used force, terror, and propaganda to force through his measures at high speed. Peasants resisted by eating their own animals and fighting those who enforced it.

By 1930 the party claimed that over half of the peasants had been moved to collective farms. However, the cost for the people involved was high. Peasants had resisted the change, knowing that it was a loss of independence for them. The worst of these effects though came in 1932 as famine spread across Russia. Modern historians put the numbers killed at around seven million peasants.

▲ **Fig. 10.21** With the men away serving as soldiers in the Soviet Army, these women have taken over the farming duties at their collective farm

A letter from an unnamed peasant to a newspaper in 1930 after collectivisation had begun.

Comrades, you write that all the middle peasants and poor peasants join the kolkhoz (collective farms) voluntarily, but it is not true. For example in our village of Podbuzhye all do not enter the kolkhoz willingly. When the register came round, only 25% signed it, while 75% did not. If anyone spoke out against it, he was threatened with arrest and forced labour. Collective life can be created when the entire mass of the peasants goes voluntarily, and not by force.

From a modern historian.

According to official Soviet figures some 24 million peasants disappeared from rural areas with only an extra 12.6 million moving to state jobs.

By M. M. Khatayevich, Ukrainian communist leader in 1936.

A ruthless struggle is going on between the peasantry and our regime. It's a struggle to the death. This year was a test of our strength and their endurance. It took a famine to show them who is master here. It has cost millions of lives, but the collective farm is here to stay. We've won the war.

▲ **Fig. 10.22** A woman driving a tractor on a collective farm, 1928

DISCUSSION

1. Study Figure 10.21 and Figure 10.22. Why were they published?

2. Compare Source 20 and Figure 10.21. How similar are they?

3. What do you think Source 22 means when it says "We've won the war" in the last sentence?

4. "Stalin's Five-Year Plans affected the Soviet people more than they affected the economy." How far do you agree with this statement? Explain your answer.

Religion, art and culture

Stalin's rule extended over every sphere of Russian existence. There was no area of society where the tight control of Stalin was not felt, even in wider everyday life.

The Bolsheviks saw religion as a barrier to the construction of an equal communist society. The government promoted atheism through education in schools, propaganda, discriminatory laws, and a terror campaign against religious believers. By 1939, there were fewer than 500 churches in Russia, compared to 54 000 in 1917. The Bolsheviks had churches pulled down and thousands of monks and nuns were persecuted and killed. Despite this, the Russian people still saw themselves as religious. A census in 1937 saw 60 per cent of the population describe themselves as Christian and during the Second World War the Church again became an important institution.

The arts were closely monitored under Stalin's rule. Only art sending out the right message was allowed; artists who dared criticise the regime or send out anything perceived to be the wrong message were repressed. Writers and musicians were often singled out for persecution and the secret police enforced a banned list of authors. Books were removed from libraries and destroyed. Even the famous were not except from being a target. Renowned musician Dmitri Shostakovich saw his music banned twice and Igor Stravinsky was denounced by the regime.

Art was also tightly controlled to ensure it communicated the message of Socialist realism—a style of art designed to spread the key messages of communism which often showed the poor in a favourable light. This style of art was meant to praise Stalin's policies.

▲ **Fig. 10.23** A painting entitled "Collective Farm Harvest Festival" by Sergei Gerasimov from 1937 shows hardworking peasants celebrating their first harvest on their new collective farm

▲ **Fig. 10.24** A painting entitled "Black Earth" by Alexander Gerasimov from 1930

Review questions

1. What were the main areas of weakness for the Tsar in 1905?

2. Why was the Tsar not in favour of the October manifesto?

3. Why did the First World War weaken the Tsar?

4. Why did the Tsar not survive in 1917 when he had done so in 1905?

5. Why did the Provisional Government stay in the First World War?

6. Why did the Provisional Government make the reforms it did?

7. Who fought against the Bolsheviks in the Civil War?

8. What are the differences between the policies of war communism and the NEP?

9. What were Lenin's achievements?

10. Why did Stalin become Lenin's long-term successor despite Lenin's will criticising Stalin?

11. Who was targeted during the purges? Why?

12. How true is it to say that with regards to Stalin, "the ends justify the means?" Explain.

11 The United States, 1919–41

Introduction

During the 1920s the majority of Americans were able to enjoy the highest standard of living ever seen. A startling array of consumer goods was available and recreation time was enriched by the expansion of the leisure industries such as cinema, radio, and sport. America appeared affluent and unstoppable in its search for material improvement. Yet alongside these new-found riches there was poverty, intolerance, and unprecedented levels of organised crime. America was a country of stark contrasts.

The economic bubble burst in 1929 with the Wall Street Crash which signalled the beginning of a nationwide slump that spread worldwide. Unemployment soared and the hopes of the post-war generation were dashed. Roosevelt's New Deal was a brave attempt to rescue America from this economic catastrophe, but it proved only partially successful. Full economic recovery was not achieved until the Second World War.

The aims of this chapter are to:

- Look at the expansion of the US economy during the 1920s, including mass production in the car and consumer durables industries, the fortunes of older industries, and the development of credit and hire purchase.

- Evaluate the decline of agriculture as well as looking at weaknesses in the economy by the late 1920s.

- Consider society in the 1920s by examining the "Roaring Twenties", film and other media, Prohibition and gangsterism, race relations, discrimination against black Americans, the Ku Klux Klan, and the changing roles of women.

- Examine the Wall Street Crash and its financial, economic, and social effects, as well as the reaction of President Hoover to the Crash.

- Look at the Presidential election of 1932 including Hoover's and Roosevelt's programmes.

- Study Roosevelt's inauguration, and the "Hundred Days".

- Consider the New Deal legislation, the "alphabet agencies" and their work, and the economic and social changes they caused.

- Examine the opposition to the New Deal among the Republicans, the rich, business interests, the Supreme Court, and radical critics such as Huey Long.

- Assess the strengths and weaknesses of the New Deal programme in dealing with unemployment and the Depression.

How far did the US economy boom in the 1920s?

▶ On what factors was the economic boom based?

America's economic boom of the 1920s had solid foundations extending back to the nineteenth century. By 1900 America was already one of the world's leading producers of oil, coal, iron, steel, engineering products, and textiles. These thriving basic industries provided an excellent platform for later economic growth.

The First World War presented the United States with increased opportunities for export as the warring European nations were unable to trade with their colonies and required supplies of food, raw materials, and military equipment. Whereas Germany, Britain, and France were exhausted by the war, the American economy emerged strong and reinvigorated. But there were other factors that underpinned the economic advances of the 1920s.

Bakelite

An early plastic that did not conduct electricity and was resistant to heat. As a result of these properties it was used in products such as saucepan handles and electrical plugs and switches.

Line production

Most manufactured articles are the result of a number of production tasks or processes. In line production these actions are performed in sequence by specialist workers or tools as the product passes through the factory.

Invention and innovation	• After 1917 there were a number of important breakthroughs involving new products and means of production. • The building industry benefited from new machines such as concrete mixers, pneumatic tools, and power shovels. • Communications were speeded up by automatic switchboards, dial phones, and teletype machines. • Advances in chemicals and synthetics brought rayon, **Bakelite**, and cellophane into common use.
Electrification	• The widespread availability of electricity meant that homes and industry now had a clean, cheap, and efficient power source. • Domestic appliances powered by electricity such as fridges, washing machines, and vacuum cleaners became affordable to ordinary Americans.
Mass production	• This was made possible by adapting the **line production** techniques of a Chicago slaughterhouse. • Henry Ford used assembly line production in the manufacture of cars but the same techniques were applied to the production of many other items from radios to cigarette lighters. • Mass production led to a fall in prices.
The motor industry	• The motor car was central to America's economic success. • By 1929 one American in five owned a car compared to one in forty-three in Britain. • The car industry, which employed up to half a million workers, stimulated road and hotel construction, the building of roadside filling stations, and the development of suburbs and holiday resorts. • It also boosted a range of other associated industries: plate glass, rubber, steel, leather, and upholstery.
Mass-marketing	• Mass production required ways of mass selling and advertising became a major industry during the 1920s. • Commercials were devised for the radio and the cinema while giant posters pasted onto billboards became a familiar sight along the highways. Magazines, newspapers, and mail order catalogues were also used to promote the new merchandise.

Hire purchase	• Customers who could not afford to buy a product outright were able to pay by instalments under a hire purchase agreement. • Since the cost of living was falling for many Americans, with wages rising and both food and manufactured goods becoming cheaper, this seemed a sensible way to buy.
Government policy	• The Republican governments of the 1920s followed financial policies that were considered favourable to business: low taxation, high **tariffs** and an absence of regulation or government intervention. This policy is sometimes known as laissez-faire.

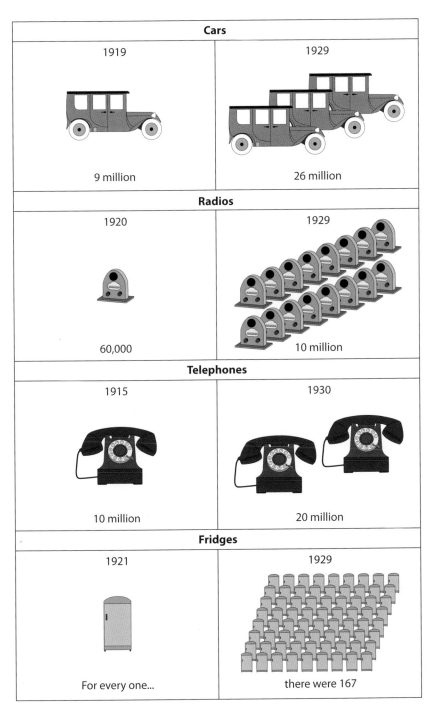

▲ **Table 11.1** Sales of consumer goods, 1915–30

Tariffs

Tariffs are taxes on imports. The effect is to raise the price of the imported item making it more expensive. Tariffs are used partly to raise money and partly to protect home industries from foreign competition.

Warren Harding	1921–3
Calvin Coolidge	1923–9
Herbert Hoover	1929–33

▲ **Table 11.2** Republican Presidents of the United States, 1921–33

Why did some industries prosper while others did not?

While the 1920s saw economic expansion in many industries, some went into decline. Overall growth never affects every part of the economy in the same way. The increase in car ownership, for example, had a negative impact on the number of people travelling by train. In general, the new industries flourished while the traditional industries declined, but this was not always the case. Steel, oil, and construction, for example, continued to expand during the 1920s even though they were all well-established industries.

Building and construction

The 1920s were the golden age of building and construction in America as new businesses required factories, offices, shops, and showrooms connected by new roads. Many skyscraper projects were designed during this time including New York's Chrysler Building and the 102-storey Empire State Building, both completed during the early 1930s. Less eye-catching was the increase in the number of homes, schools, hospitals, and other public buildings.

Cotton and woollen textiles

The general increase in the standard of living coupled with the increase in the number of shops and department stores meant that there was increased demand for clothes. But since these were often manufactured from synthetic fibres such as rayon and celanese (artificial silk) there was actually less demand for cotton and woollen textiles. The problem for the traditional textile industry was made worse by the change in fashions—shorter hemlines for women's skirts and dresses meant that less material was used. Textile operatives in the cotton and woollen industries were among the lowest paid factory workers.

▲ **Fig. 11.1** Construction workers attaching steel beams to the framework of the Manhattan Company Building, 1930s

Steel

The steel industry did not share the fate of some other older industries, partly because of the demands of the car industry which used 20 per cent of steel output. Other demand came from the building industry which required steel girders, while most new industries were equipped with machinery that made use of steel or used steel components in its products.

Coal

As with textiles the coal industry suffered from overproduction. Oil, gas, and electricity were increasingly used as alternatives both in domestic homes and in industrial premises. Existing users of coal could often burn the fuel more efficiently, so adding to the reduction in demand. The industry was plagued by wage cuts, pit closures, and strike action.

Motor cars

This was the undoubted success story of the 1920s. The industry was dominated by three firms: Chrysler, Ford, and General Motors. Henry Ford led the field, reducing the cost of his Model T from $850 in 1908 to $290 in the 1920s. This was made possible through the achievement of high volume sales—15 million Model T Fords had been manufactured by 1927. Workers at Ford's Detroit factory were paid high wages but they had to sign agreements to say that they would not join unions.

SOURCE 1

Henry Ford writing about the Model T Ford car, 1922.

I will build a car for the great multitude ... It will be constructed of the best materials, by the best men to be hired, after the simplest designs that modern engineering can devise. But it will be so low in price that no man making a good salary will be unable to own one–and enjoy with his family the blessing of hours of pleasure in God's great open spaces.

SOURCE 2

Alistair Cooke writing about the Model T Ford car, 1973. Alistair Cooke was a British/American journalist, television personality, and broadcaster. He spent much of his life reporting on aspects of American life for the BBC.

It is staggering to consider what the Model T was to lead to in both industry and folkways. It certainly wove the first network of paved highways ... Beginning in the early 1920s, people who had never taken a holiday ... could now explore the South, New England, even the West, and in time the whole horizon of the United States. Most of all, the Model T gave to the farmer and rancher, miles from anywhere, a new pair of legs.

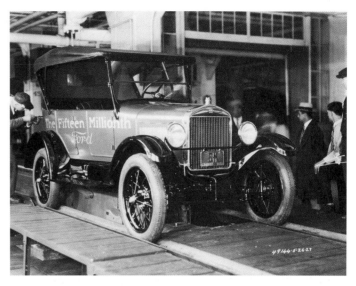

▲ **Fig. 11.2** The 15 millionth Model T Ford car coming off the production line at the Dearborn factory, May 1927

▲ **Fig. 11.3** Advertisement for a Buick car, 1928

DISCUSSION

1. How useful is Source 1 as evidence of the qualities of the Model T Ford car?

2. What impact did the Model T Ford car have on the lives of the American people according to the writer in Source 2?

Why did agriculture not share in the prosperity?

The most striking example of an industry that was unable to share in the prosperity of the 1920s was agriculture, which employed more than a quarter of the working population. During the First World War American agriculture had boomed as grain from the **midwestern** and **southern** states had been exported to Europe. With the aid of new machinery, such as combine harvesters, production increased, prices rose, and American farmers were able to make substantial profits. But the good times came to an abrupt end following the armistice.

Why was this?

There were a number of reasons that agriculture missed out on the growth experienced elsewhere.

- Demobilisation in Europe meant that former agricultural workers returned to their farms and began producing food again. American imports were no longer needed.

- American tariffs made selling to Europe even more difficult. European countries found it hard to sell in American markets thereby earning the dollars with which to purchase American produce.

- American agriculture also began facing competition from Canada and Argentina who began supplying grain to the world markets.

- American patterns of food consumption were changing. An increasingly prosperous population preferred more luxurious foods, such as fresh fruit and vegetables, to cereal products. Furthermore, the banning of alcohol under the Prohibition laws meant that the consumption of barley in making beer fell by 90 per cent.

All this meant that American agriculture was suffering from overproduction and prices fell. Profits were squeezed and many small farmers could no longer afford their rents or mortgage payments. Evictions and forced sales followed. There were one million fewer farms in 1930 than in 1920.

It was the small farmers and labourers who suffered the most. The larger operators, equipped with modern machinery, were still able to make profits. These included some of the fruit growers of California and Florida together with the cereal farmers of the Midwest.

The plight of the farming sector was bad for the whole economy. This was partly because so many Americans, approaching half the total population, lived in rural areas with their livelihoods dependent on the well-being of the farming community. As agricultural incomes dropped, so demand for manufactured goods dropped also, creating unemployment in the industrial areas.

Did all Americans benefit from the boom?

We have already seen how the economic boom failed to improve the lives of farmers and agricultural labourers and those who worked in certain traditional industries such as coal and textiles.

Unemployment was an obvious problem but low wages also prevented a significant part of the labour force from joining in the new prosperity.

Midwestern states

A portion of the central United States including states such as Illinois, Kansas, and Ohio. The region is mostly lowland and provides some of the richest farming land in the world. Chicago is the largest city followed by Indianapolis, Columbus, and Detroit.

Southern states

Also called the American South or Dixie and includes Florida, Texas, and Louisiana. Until the mid-twentieth century the region relied heavily on farming. Dallas, Houston, Atlanta, and New Orleans are among the major cities of the area.

Female cotton operatives, for example, could be paid as little as $9 a week at a time when $48 was considered to be the minimum necessary to maintain a basic standard of living. Estimates of the number of Americans living beneath the poverty line vary, but some put it as high as 60 per cent of American families in the late 1920s. In addition to the groups already mentioned were three particularly vulnerable groups in society who found it difficult to find work.

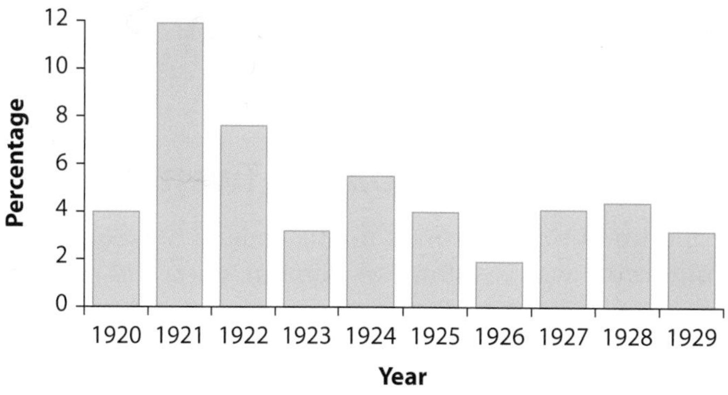

▲ **Fig. 11.4** American unemployment 1920–9

Black Americans

Until the end of the First World War the population of black Americans was concentrated in the states of the South such as Texas and Louisiana. Here they worked as labourers or **sharecroppers**. With the onset of the agricultural slump of the 1920s, approximately 750 000 of these black workers were laid off by their white landlords. Those who remained experienced poverty and extreme forms of racial discrimination.

Sharecropper

An agricultural worker who passes on a share of his crop to the landowner in return for land to farm.

Many took the decision to try to find alternative work in the northern cities. While the cities provided greater employment opportunities many of the jobs available were in the lowest paid sectors: domestic service, casual labouring, and building work. Most of the new industries which offered higher wages operated a whites-only employment policy. Blacks met with considerable discrimination, especially with regards to housing where they were segregated into slum areas such as Harlem in New York. It is fair to say that the vast majority of black Americans were excluded from the benefits of the boom.

Native Americans

During the nineteenth century, American Indians had been gradually forced off their land and by the early 1920s were living in reservations specially provided for them by the American government. The reservations were located in areas with poor soil so that growing crops was difficult. Those who remained on the reservations lived a primitive way of life compared to western standards, suffering from poverty, poor education, and ill health. Those who left and tried to mix with white society met with prejudice and discrimination, finding that the main job opportunities lay with low-paid work. As with the black Americans, the new prosperity largely passed them by.

New immigrants

With the exception of the American Indians, America is an immigrant society. The population arrived from Europe and elsewhere over three centuries. The earliest immigrants, largely from northern Europe and Scandinavia, together with their descendants, came to resent the later waves of immigration from southern and eastern Europe and Russia. The new immigrants found that only the lowest-paid jobs were available to them and as with the black Americans and American Indians they suffered from discrimination on account of their religion (many were Jews or Catholics), lack of education, and ability to drive down wages. Unemployment rates among new immigrants remained high throughout the 1920s.

How far did US society change in the 1920s?

What were the "Roaring Twenties"?

America in the 1920s was not just a land of economic prosperity. For a minority it was a country of glamour, glitz, and partying. This life of excess and frivolity was projected across the nation through the mass media so that few Americans were totally unaware of the new age and the daring new ways of the younger generation. This was the decade of short skirts and make-up, bobbed hair, cocktail drinks, nightclubs, the Charleston, the saxophone, jazz, and Hollywood. In many ways it was a time of rebellion against the starchiness of nineteenth century standards of dress, morals, and social behaviour. But millions of Americans were envious or disapproving spectators of the racy lifestyles enjoyed by the young, rich city-dwellers. The "Roaring Twenties" was more an image than a reality for the majority of the population.

▲ **Fig. 11.5** King Oliver's Creole Jazz Band with Louis Armstrong, 1920s

Movies	<ul><li>Cinema provided an opportunity for escapism for many Americans and audiences more than doubled during the 1920s reaching 95 million in 1929.</li><li>Hollywood launched stars such as Charlie Chaplin, Mary Pickford, Douglas Fairbanks, and Rudolf Valentino who became some of the world's first celebrities.</li><li>"Talkies" arrived in 1927 and millions flocked to watch and hear Al Jolson in *The Jazz Singer*.</li><li>The hairstyles, clothes, make-up, perfumes, and mannerisms of the stars were copied by impressionable Americans.</li><li>There were concerns, however, that films were corrupting public morals so the industry introduced a code of practice which, among other restrictions, limited the length of on-screen kisses and banned nudity.</li></ul>

Jazz	• Jazz music was the popular music of the 1920s giving rise to the term "Jazz Age".
	• Along with Blues music it originated in the African American community of the south. It was often performed by black musicians who had migrated to the northern cities of New York, Philadelphia, and Chicago.
	• Jazz was linked to dance music and led to the formation of many nightclubs such as the Cotton Club of Harlem, New York which launched the career of Duke Ellington.
	• Jazz appealed to young whites who found it exciting, dynamic, and modern. Older Americans found it threatening as it broke with tradition and was seen as a corrupting influence.
Radio	• By 1930, 40 per cent of American households possessed a radio.
	• The first national network, the National Broadcasting Company (NBC), was set up in 1926 following the establishment of more than 500 local commercial radio stations.
	• Radio was used to broadcast light musical entertainment to a mass audience, producing the age of the great dance bands. Orchestras led by Joe Candullo, Meyer Davis, and Jean Goldkette would play tunes such as *Swanee River Blues, Black Bottom* or *Gimme A Little Kiss, Will Ya, Huh?*
	• Radio also provided a fresh start for some of the artists such as comedians, impersonators, instrumentalists, and vocalists of the declining vaudeville or variety theatres.
Cars	• The car made possible much of the activity that characterised the "Roaring Twenties" by giving many Americans a freedom of movement they had never known before.
	• It provided an easy means of visiting clubs, cinemas, and restaurants and created opportunities for taking day trips and other holidays.

▲ Table 11.3

How widespread was intolerance in US society?

American society in the 1920s was full of contradictions and contrasts. We have seen how free expression and a rejection of old-fashioned values was fashionable among the young. More established Americans wanted to maintain traditions and were fearful of those groups who were thought to threaten the American way of life: new immigrants, communists, anarchists, trade unionists, Catholics, blacks, and Jews. It was the ambition of many to maintain the supremacy of the white, Anglo-Saxon, Protestant community (WASPs).

The Red Scare, 1919–21

Most of the immigrants to America during the first two decades of the twentieth century came from southern and eastern Europe. It was thought that many of the new immigrants had been infected with communist and anarchist ideas following the Bolshevik Revolution in Russia of 1917. A wave of strike action during 1919 seemed to confirm these fears. Further evidence of a supposed conspiracy against the state was provided in the same year by a series of bomb blasts, one of which damaged the home of the Attorney General, Mitchell Palmer.

Employers and government authorities made a firm response to these events. The strikers were faced with lockouts and heavy-handed tactics. The bombings led to the rounding up of suspected anarchists and communists in what was known as the "Palmer Raids" which led to arrests and deportations.

The Red Scare was stoked up by hysteria in the press and the readiness of local politicians to see plots and conspiracies behind every protest in favour of improved wages or working conditions. No evidence of a serious threat to the state was ever uncovered.

Religious intolerance

Fundamentalist Christians, concentrated in the rural areas of the South and Midwest, believed in a literal interpretation of the Bible. This included the belief that after making the world in five days, God created Man on the sixth. More progressive, urban Christians accepted Darwin's theory of evolution that claimed that humans had evolved from more primitive life forms over millions of years. In six states including Tennessee the Fundamentalists succeeded in outlawing the teaching of evolution.

The differences between the two sides came to a head in what became known as the Monkey Trial. A Tennessee biology teacher, John Scopes, deliberately broke state laws by teaching evolution. His trial took place in July 1925. It became a showcase for the arguments for and against evolution. Scopes was defended by a leading criminal lawyer, Clarence Darrow, while the prosecution was led by a Fundamentalist, William Jennings Bryan. While Scopes was found guilty and fined $100, the trial was widely regarded as a triumph for the evolutionists as Bryan was ridiculed when he tried to defend the Bible's version of the creation of mankind.

Immigration policy

In order to preserve the supremacy of white, northern Europeans a series of immigration laws was passed during the 1920s which restricted entry to the United States. These represented a form of government-sponsored discrimination against certain national groups.

The Emergency Quota Act passed in 1921 set a total annual limit for immigrants of 357 000. More controversially, it also set up a quota system whereby the annual number of immigrants from any one country was restricted to 3 per cent of the numbers from that same country living in the United States in 1910. This had the effect of reducing the numbers of immigrants from southern and eastern Europe by more than 75 per cent.

In the National Origins Act passed in 1924 the total limit was reduced to 150 000 while the quota was reduced to 2 per cent of 1890 figures (before the main influx of southern and eastern European immigrants began). Immigrants from Asia including China and Japan were completely barred. Following this Act about 85 per cent of immigrants came from northern Europe. The quotas remained in place until the mid-1960s.

SOURCE 3

Extract from a speech made to Congress by Democratic Senator for Alabama, James Thomas Heflin, 1921.

Thousands come here who never take the oath to support our Constitution and to become citizens of the United States. They pay allegiance to some other country while they live upon the substance of our own. They fill places that belong to the loyal wage-earning citizens of America. They preach a doctrine that is dangerous and deadly to our institutions. They are of no service whatever to our people. They constitute a menace and danger to us every day ...

SOURCE 4

Extract from the Republican Party's election manifesto, 1920.

The immigration policy of the U. S. should be such as to insure that the number of foreigners in the country at any one time shall not exceed that which can be assimilated with reasonable rapidity, and to favour immigrants whose standards are similar to ours.

The selective tests that are at present applied should be improved by requiring a higher physical standard, a more complete exclusion of mental defectives and of criminals, and a more effective inspection ...

DISCUSSION

1. What does Source 3 say are the reasons behind America's immigration policy in the 1920s?

2. How does the writer of Source 4 suggest that America's immigration procedures can be improved?

3. Is one of these sources more useful than the other as evidence about attitudes towards immigration in the 1920s?

The Ku Klux Klan

The most extreme and notorious example of intolerance and racism during the 1920s was the Ku Klux Klan, originally formed as a secret anti-negro society after the Civil War of 1864–5. During the twenties the Klan revived and expanded, claiming to have a membership of five million in 1925. Membership included a number of high-ranking politicians and government officials. It attracted those who felt that crusading action was necessary to protect American values against the dangers of blacks, Jews, Catholics, and foreigners. Many supporters came from small towns and rural areas that had been largely excluded from the new prosperity. The Klan devised secret codes and elaborate rituals, sometimes burning crucifixes. It had a uniform of white-hooded sheets. More extreme forms of persecution, mainly directed against blacks, included beatings, mutilations, and lynchings.

After 1925 the membership of the Klan declined following a number of successful prosecutions for violent activities. One of the Klan leaders was convicted of the rape and murder of a woman on a train in Indiana. The image of the Klan was permanently damaged.

▲ **Fig. 11.6** Members of the Ku Klux Klan surround a burning cross, 1925

Why was Prohibition introduced, and then later repealed?

Nationwide prohibition was introduced by the 18th Amendment of the American Constitution. From 1920 it was illegal to manufacture, transport or sell alcoholic drinks. The ban was to be enforced through the Volstead Act of 1919 which defined alcoholic drinks as those that contained more than 0.5 per cent alcohol. Prohibition was to last until 1933 when the legislation was repealed by the 21st Amendment. There are a variety of reasons for the introduction of this extraordinary experiment in social behaviour.

Pressure groups	• A number of societies, such as the Anti-Saloon League and the Women's Temperance Union, had been campaigning for the abolition of alcohol since the nineteenth century. • It was argued that alcohol was the cause of much poverty, crime, and ill health. • The "dries" (supporters of Prohibition) were particularly influential in rural areas of the South and Midwest and, by 1914, had managed to persuade some state governments to ban alcohol within their states.
First World War	• Many American brewers were of German descent. It was claimed that alcohol was linked to German aggression and that it was unpatriotic to consume alcoholic drink. • Many believed that grain made into alcohol could be better used for making bread.
Support of politicians, churchmen and industrialists	• Politicians began to realise that they could pick up votes, especially in small-town America, by supporting the campaign for Prohibition. By 1918 alcohol was already banned in 18 states. • The Protestant Church supported the cause as it believed that alcohol was associated with a decline in moral standards and family life in the big cities. • Some industrialists such as Nelson Rockefeller argued that Prohibition would be good for the economy as it would reduce absenteeism and promote hard work.

▲ Table 11.4

Why Prohibition failed

Even though Prohibition originally enjoyed considerable national support, it soon became clear that the 18th Amendment was a disastrous mistake. This was partly because although there was a majority in favour of Prohibition, it was never an overwhelming majority.

Prohibition may have worked in traditional, small-town, rural America but the story in the big cities was very different. It was not illegal to purchase or consume alcohol and drinking continued behind closed doors. "Speakeasies" or illegal drinking bars became commonplace in towns and cities, with New York supporting some 32 000 such establishments by 1929. Private deliveries of wines and spirits were made to the homes of the rich while those of lesser means produced their own "moonshine" or home-brewed alcohol in illegal stills.

▲ Fig. 11.7 Anti-Prohibition demonstration, 1920s

In order to clamp down on illegal manufacture and trading, the government appointed several thousand enforcement agents. However, there were too few, they were poorly paid, often privately opposed to Prohibition, and therefore vulnerable to the threats and bribes made by criminal gangs. Nearly 10 per cent of agents were sacked for taking bribes.

The illegal sale and distribution of alcohol provided a golden business opportunity for criminal gangs. They organised the smuggling of rum from the West Indies and whisky from Canada ensuring that the speakeasies were properly supplied with "bootleg" or illegal liquor. Gang wars broke out in cities such as New York and Chicago as criminal rivals fought for control of different city blocks. Murder and corruption became common means of removing business obstacles. Between 1926 and 1927 there were 130 gangland murders in Chicago for which the killers escaped without punishment. In the St Valentine's Day Massacre of 1929, thought to be masterminded by Al Capone, seven members of a gang were gunned down by rivals in a Chicago garage.

State officials, judges, senior police officers, and jury members were often bought off with bribes or threatened with their lives. Profitable control of the liquor trade enabled the criminal gangs to extend their activities into other areas such as protection and prostitution. It looked as if Prohibition had promoted lawbreaking on an unprecedented scale.

	1921	1925	1929
Number of illegal distilleries seized	9746	12 023	15 794
Gallons of distilled spirits seized	414 000	1 103 000	1 186 000
Number of arrests	34 175	62 747	66 878

▲ **Table 11.5** Work of the Federal Prohibition Agents

By the early 1930s it appeared increasingly difficult to justify Prohibition and the 18th Amendment became increasingly unpopular. It appeared quite illogical to spend vast amounts of money on ineffective law enforcement. It also seemed absurd to continue with a law that suppressed an industry that could have employed thousands at a time of mounting unemployment. In 1933 President Roosevelt supported the 21st Amendment which repealed the 18th Amendment and ended Prohibition.

SOURCE 5

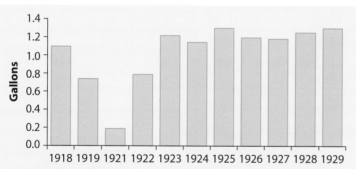

▲ **Fig. 11.8** Statistics on consumption of alcoholic beverages per head in the United States, published by a New York university in 1932

SOURCE 6

A view of Prohibition published by an American Church in 1962.

The 18th Amendment and the Volstead Act were enforced in the United States wherever they had popular support. In the rural South and West, Prohibition was effective and in some cases still is but it has been said that the only effect of Prohibition was to replace good beer with bad gin. In 1931 a Federal Commission showed that in the big cities the law was openly defied and in the smaller towns, populated by miners and industrial workers, the law was simply ignored. The federal government never had more than 2500 agents enforcing the law. In one year in New York 7000 arrests for liquor violations resulted in 17 convictions.

DISCUSSION

1. What can you tell from Source 5 about the effects of the introduction of Prohibition in 1920?

2. How far does Source 6 show that Americans opposed Prohibition?

3. Is one of these sources more useful than the other as evidence about Prohibition?

FP How far did the roles of women change during the 1920s?

Before the First World War the vast majority of adult women occupied traditional roles as wives and mothers. This was a position fully supported by the Church. Most women couldn't vote and any paid work was limited to occupations such as domestic service, secretarial work and teaching. Dress was restrictive and included corsets and full-length skirts and dresses with tight waists. There were also limitations on public behaviour which was expected to be modest, polite, and discrete. In practice this meant no drinking or smoking and, if unmarried, no male company without a chaperone. The First World War saw women performing men's work in the war industries as male labour was required in the armed services. After the war most women went back to traditional types of work.

The 1920s witnessed what appeared to be a revolution in the role of women, many of whom were referred to as "flappers".

Politics	• In 1920 women got the vote in all states. They now made up 50 per cent or more of the electorate.
Work	• The number of women in employment increased by 25 per cent to 10 million by 1929.
	• Office work and manufacturing accounted for much of the increase and in some new industries, such as electronics, women were preferred to men.
Dress	• Corsets were abandoned and women began wearing shorter, lighter skirts and dresses that were often sleeveless. The new fashions and new materials, such as rayon, permitted greater movement and self-expression.
Lifestyle	• Women began smoking, drinking, and kissing in public. Chaperones were no longer required.
	• Women also drove cars. It has been suggested that Henry Ford introduced coloured cars in 1925 as a response to the female market. Previously all Ford cars had been black.
	• Short hair and make-up became symbols of the new freedom.
	• Women were acting with more independence. The divorce rate increased from 100 000 in 1914 to 205 000 in 1929.

▲ Table 11.6

It would be misleading, however, to claim that these changes affected the majority of women. Most of the so-called "flappers" were young, wealthy, middle and upper middle class women from the large towns and cities. Women living in smaller communities and rural areas were less affected by the changes and continued their traditional roles and restricted lives: managing the home, bringing up children and earning enough money to ease the family budget. In fact many women, influenced by conservative and religious values, strongly opposed the new changes that they saw reported in the newspapers and magazines. Within this group were immigrant mothers and daughters who were used to accepting the role of the father as head of the family. Even labour-saving devices only affected the lives of a minority and in 1930, 70 per cent of households did not possess vacuum cleaners while 76 per cent lacked a washing machine. Furthermore, although all women got the vote and experienced improved employment opportunities, few achieved power in either politics or the boardroom. Women continued to be paid less than men for exactly the same type of work, which is why some employers preferred a female work force. The "flappers" were a showy and noisy minority who made a considerable impact in the media and in contemporary literature and film, but were completely unrepresentative of America as a whole. The role of the average American woman changed very little during the 1920s.

▲ **Fig. 11.9** Two flappers dancing on top of a Chicago hotel, 1926

What were the causes and consequences of the Wall Street Crash?

FP ## How far was speculation responsible for the Wall Street Crash?

What are shares?

- If a business wants to raise money then a common way of achieving this is by selling shares. A shareholder owns a part or a share of a business.

- Shares are bought and sold on a stock market. If there are more people wanting to buy than sell, then the price of the shares will rise. If there are more people wanting to sell than buy, then the price of the shares will fall.

- Each year a business will normally pay out a proportion of its profits to the shareholders. This is known as a dividend.

- A shareholder may therefore make money in two ways: by selling the shares when they rise in value and by receiving a dividend while the shares are owned.

- If the business makes a loss, or its prospects look poor, then the likelihood is that the share price will fall and there will be no dividend. In these circumstances the shareholders will lose money.

Wall Street, New York was the main American stock market where company shares were bought and sold. In October 1929 the panic selling of shares in this market led to a "crash" which marked the beginning of the Great Depression. The Wall Street Crash had a variety of causes and there is little doubt that the actions of **speculators** were partly responsible.

During the 1920s the American stock market was steadily rising. Speculators could buy shares in a growth company only to sell them a few weeks or months later in order to pocket an easy gain. From the mid-1920s many speculators bought shares "on the margin". This meant borrowing money from the banks to fund the share purchase. The loan was repaid when the shares were later sold. Banks were prepared to lend up to 90 per cent of the share price.

This practice was fine providing the share market continued to rise. If, however, it fell then speculators could end up bankrupt, as could the banks themselves. This is what happened in the months following October 1929.

Speculators

These are people who buy and sell shares simply in order to make quick profits. Anyone with a bit of money can become a speculator.

Date	Stock market	% loss
Highest point, 3 September 1929	381.17	
Black Thursday, 24 October 1929	299.47	(21.43)
Black Tuesday, 29 October 1929	230.07	(39.64)
End of first wave of selling, 13 November 1929	198.69	(47.87)
Lowest point, 8 July 1932	41.22	(89.19)

▲ **Table 11.7** Dow Jones Index 1929–32

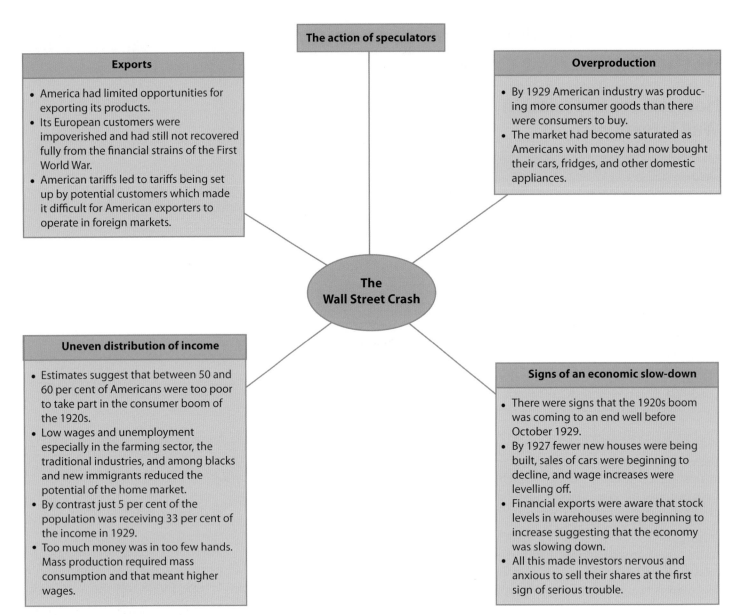

The action of speculators

Exports
- America had limited opportunities for exporting its products.
- Its European customers were impoverished and had still not recovered fully from the financial strains of the First World War.
- American tariffs led to tariffs being set up by potential customers which made it difficult for American exporters to operate in foreign markets.

Overproduction
- By 1929 American industry was producing more consumer goods than there were consumers to buy.
- The market had become saturated as Americans with money had now bought their cars, fridges, and other domestic appliances.

The Wall Street Crash

Uneven distribution of income
- Estimates suggest that between 50 and 60 per cent of Americans were too poor to take part in the consumer boom of the 1920s.
- Low wages and unemployment especially in the farming sector, the traditional industries, and among blacks and new immigrants reduced the potential of the home market.
- By contrast just 5 per cent of the population was receiving 33 per cent of the income in 1929.
- Too much money was in too few hands. Mass production required mass consumption and that meant higher wages.

Signs of an economic slow-down
- There were signs that the 1920s boom was coming to an end well before October 1929.
- By 1927 fewer new houses were being built, sales of cars were beginning to decline, and wage increases were levelling off.
- Financial exports were aware that stock levels in warehouses were beginning to increase suggesting that the economy was slowing down.
- All this made investors nervous and anxious to sell their shares at the first sign of serious trouble.

▲ **Fig. 11.10** Causes of the Wall Street Crash

FP What impact did the Crash have on the economy?

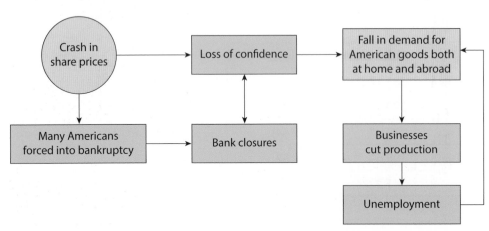

▲ **Fig. 11.11** The economic impact of the Wall Street Crash

The Wall Street Crash was not the primary cause of the Great Depression that followed although it certainly contributed. It was the structural weaknesses in the American economy—overproduction, uneven distribution of incomes, poor level of exports—that was to pitch the nation into depression.

The impact of the Crash and the onset of recession is summarised in Figure 11.11. After the first series of business and bank failures the whole economy had to adjust to a general reduction in trade and demand for American goods. Businesses had to reduce their operations by sacking workers and reducing the wages of those who remained. It became a vicious cycle as these actions took even more money out of the economy and further reduced the demand for goods. When it became clear that there would be no easy return to the good times, business confidence collapsed which meant that expansion projects were put on hold. Confidence also affected consumers who were unwilling to make expensive purchases at a time when jobs were insecure.

America was the largest capitalist economy in the world and when it went into recession the other major capitalist economies were dragged down too. This was because Americans could no longer afford to buy any foreign imports meaning that other countries lacked the dollars to buy American exports. Rising unemployment in Europe and Japan helped to increase unemployment in America.

▲ **Fig. 11.12** "Black Friday", an American cartoon of the Wall Street Crash

What were the social consequences of the Crash?

The Crash led directly to bank and business failures and the rise of unemployment. By 1933 nearly one in four of the workforce was out of a job. There were no **welfare benefits** to assist households that were suddenly without an income, but rents and mortgages still had to be paid. Some survived with the help of families, friends, and neighbours. Others were evicted from their homes and were reduced to begging on the streets, scavenging rubbish dumps for scraps of food, and sleeping on park benches.

Welfare benefits

Payments made by the government to assist the old, sick, and unemployed.

Shanty towns made up of makeshift huts and tents were constructed on the edges of towns and cities and became known as "Hoovervilles", named after the man whose presidency coincided with the Crash and its most severe consequences. During the day the desperate populations of these cardboard communities were dependent on soup kitchens and public relief schemes provided by local government. But by 1932 more than 100 of these authorities had no money left.

▲ **Fig. 11.13** A "Hooverville" in Seattle, 1934

One of the most striking images of the time was the arrival in Washington DC of around 25 000 destitute army veterans during the early summer of 1932. They had been promised a war service bonus to be paid in 1945 but, in view of the economic situation, wanted it brought forward to 1932. Following the refusal of **Congress** to pass a Bonus Bill the "Bonus Army" began a peaceful protest camped in a Hooverville opposite the White House. President Hoover, however, regarded this as a threat to the institutions of government and requested the help of the army to clear the site. The camp was destroyed with the aid of tanks, machine guns, and tear gas. Two veterans were killed and nearly a thousand were injured.

▲ **Fig. 11.14** The burning of the Bonus Army's encampment, Washington DC, 1932

Congress

The American law-making assemblies: the House of Representatives and the Senate.

Other instances of violence and protest took place in rural areas. Farmers were among the worst affected by the depression as the drop in city incomes made it even harder for them to sell their produce. Evictions and seizures of land were sometimes resisted with the erection of highway barricades and stand-offs between the sheriffs and local farmers. Yet most of the bankrupted farmers accepted their fate and took to the road in search of casual work.

SOURCE 7

Frederick Lewis Allen, American historian, *Since Yesterday* published in 1939.

Among the comparatively well-to-do ... the great majority were living on a reduced scale ... These people were discharging servants, or cutting servants' wages to a minimum ... In many pretty houses, wives ... were cooking and scrubbing. Husbands were wearing the same suit longer, resigning from the golf club, deciding, perhaps, that this year the family couldn't afford to go to the beach for the summer ...

SOURCE 8

Alec Wilder was interviewed by Studs Terkel in Hard Times, 1970.

I knew something was terribly wrong because I heard bellboys, everybody, talking about the stock market. About six weeks before the Wall Street Crash, I persuaded my mother in Rochester to let me talk to our family adviser. I wanted to sell stock which had been left me by my father. He got very sentimental: "Oh your father wouldn't have liked you to do that." He was so persuasive, I said O.K. I could have sold it for $160,000. Four years later, I sold it for $4,000.

DISCUSSION

What can you tell from Sources 7 and 8 about how previously prosperous Americans experienced the Great Depression?

Why did Roosevelt win the election of 1932?

In the November 1932 presidential elections the Democratic Party candidate, Franklin D. Roosevelt defeated Herbert Hoover's attempt to win a second term by a landslide victory. Roosevelt polled 7 million more votes than his rival who won only 6 out of 48 states. This was the Republicans' greatest defeat up to that time.

Hoover's weaknesses

Hoover was unlucky in that he had been elected president just as the 1920s boom was beginning to come to an end. His presidency was therefore associated with business and bank closures, a failing economy and rising unemployment.

With the benefit of hindsight, Hoover's early reactions to the depression were misplaced. He, along with many Americans, interpreted the early depression as a normal business downturn. Consequently his first strategy was to sit it out until prosperity returned.

When it became clear that the economy was in more serious trouble than first thought, Hoover did take action to stimulate business and employment but it was all regarded as too little and too late.

Hoover was against the federal government providing welfare support for the unemployed as he thought this would undermine the American values of self-help and rugged individualism. But given the scale of the jobless problem this made him appear unsympathetic and indifferent to the human side of the depression. Hoover's action over the Bonus Army confirmed this view.

During the 1932 campaign Hoover did not project himself as a man of vision ready to experiment with new ideas. He came across as grim-faced and thoroughly conservative in his approach.

How did President Hoover try to combat the Great Depression?

- In 1930 taxes were cut by $130 million to inject more purchasing power into the economy.

- Tariffs were increased by the Hawley-Smoot Act (1930) to protect American-produced food and goods.

- Money was provided to finance a building programme to create more jobs. The most famous project was the Hoover Dam on the Colorado River.

- Employers were encouraged to make voluntary agreements with their employees to maintain wages and production.

- The Reconstruction Finance Corporation (1932) was set up to provide loans, amounting to $1,500 million, to businesses facing hard times.

- The Federal Farm Board was set up to buy surplus produce in an attempt to stabilise prices.

Roosevelt's strengths

Roosevelt belonged to the Democratic Party which had been out of power since 1921. He therefore had no responsibility for the policies that had led up to the Great Depression.

In 1928 Roosevelt had become Governor of New York State and organized schemes to help the elderly and unemployed. This gave him a reputation for understanding the plight of the poor.

Roosevelt had an upbeat personality and appeared warm, charming, and optimistic on the campaign trail. Many Americans admired the way he had fought against personal difficulties when he contracted polio, a paralytic illness, in 1921.

While Roosevelt was often unspecific about exactly how he would rescue America from the depression, the electorate was infected by his confidence and determination to fight against the odds. The promise of a "new deal for the American people" caught the imagination of the public.

How successful was the New Deal?

What was the New Deal as introduced in 1933?

The New Deal is the term applied to the various measures introduced by Roosevelt between 1933 and 1938 to rescue America from the effects of the Great Depression. It had three main aims:

- relief or assistance for the unemployed and poverty-stricken

- recovery and rebuilding of the American economy

- reform to create a more fair and just society.

The New Deal was not a logically planned programme worked out in advance and introduced according to a scheduled timetable. It was much more a case of the President sitting down with his advisors and working out what needed to be done to solve particular problems. The first phase of the New Deal introduced between March and June 1933 is normally referred to as the First Hundred Days. A main feature of this first phase was the creation of **alphabet agencies**.

Alphabet agencies

Government agencies known for convenience by their initials.

▲ **Fig. 11.15** "The Spirit of the New Deal", American political cartoon, 1933

DISCUSSION

- Identify the different people in Figure 11.15.

- How does the cartoon in Figure 11.15 suggest that the NRA was meant to work?

The First Hundred Days	
Banks	• The banking system was close to collapse as customers were panicking and withdrawing their savings, making further bank closures more likely. • Roosevelt ordered a four-day national bank holiday while the Emergency Banking Act was passed through Congress. • Unsound banks, about 5 per cent of the total, were then closed down while the remainder were helped with government grants and advice. • Roosevelt explained what he was doing to the American people through a national radio broadcast, the first of his fireside chats. Those with savings were asked to return their money to the banks when they reopened. Public confidence was restored and the banking system survived.
Unemployed	• Unemployment stood at nearly 13 million in 1933, approximately 25 per cent of the workforce. • The Civilian Conservation Corps (CCC) was set up to provide voluntary employment for young men aged 18 to 25. • Living in government camps, they carried out conservation work, planting new forests, strengthening river banks for flood control, and clearing scrubland. • Wages were low but the scheme provided work for over two million men during the nine years of its existence. • The Public Works Administration (PWA) provided jobs by initiating major construction projects such as dams, bridges, railways, schools, hospitals, and houses. • The PWA spent $7 billion between 1933 and 1939 creating millions of jobs for skilled workers. • The Civil Works Administration (CWA) aimed to provide temporary work over the winter of 1933–4. • Four million jobs were created building roads, airports, and schools before the scheme ended in April 1934.
Farmers	• The collapse of food prices after 1929 had left the farming industry in crisis. • The Agricultural Adjustment Agency (AAA) paid farmers to take part of their land out of cultivation and reduce their livestock. • Millions of acres of sown land were ploughed up and six million piglets were slaughtered. • Prices rose and between 1933 and 1939 farmers' incomes doubled. • Farm labourers were not helped by this measure, however, and many found themselves unemployed.
Industry	• The National Industrial Recovery Act set up the National Recovery Administration (NRA) aiming to stabilise production and prices, and improve working conditions and pay. • In an attempt to achieve this, voluntary codes were drawn up for each industry that enabled employers to regulate prices, output, hours, and wages. • Businesses that signed up to their industry code were able to display the NRA badge, a Blue Eagle with the motto "We Do Our Part". The public were encouraged to buy products and services from companies displaying the badge. • The scheme definitely led to an improvement in working conditions and reduced the incidence of child labour. It also put an end to price-cutting wars. But it tended to favour the large firms who sometimes forced the smaller firms out of business. When the scheme was declared unconstitutional by the Supreme Court in 1935 Roosevelt made no attempt to revive the idea.
The Poor	• The Federal Emergency Relief Administration (FERA) had a budget of $500 million to assist those in desperate need. • The money was used to fund soup kitchens, provide clothing and bedding, and set up work schemes and nursery schools.

▲ Table 11.8

What was the Tennessee Valley Authority (TVA)?

- This was one of the most exciting and eye-catching projects of the First Hundred Days.

- The Tennessee Valley was a vast, depressed region crossing seven states. The local agriculture had been badly affected by floods and soil erosion. Over half the population of 4.5 million were on government relief schemes in 1933.

- The TVA aimed to restore the prosperity of the area: forests were planted, a series of hydroelectric dams were built, and flood prevention schemes were introduced. New industries were attracted by cheap electricity and good transport facilities.

- The TVA became a showcase for the New Deal.

SOURCE 9

Extract from F. D. Roosevelt's first speech as President, 4 March 1933.

The only thing we have to fear is fear itself. Our first and greatest task is to put people to work. This is a problem we can solve, if we face it wisely and with courage. It can be done partly by the Government itself. We must deal with unemployment as we would deal with the emergency of war.

SOURCE 10

Extract from an American history book, 1996.

The Alphabet Agencies, from 1933, hired the unemployed to construct or repair schools, hospitals, airfields and roads. The CCC, also introduced in 1933, put people to work maintaining natural treasures such as beaches, forests and parks. These were successful as they helped to reduce unemployment, gave dignity back to the unemployed and gave families the chance to survive and stay together. However, the Agencies were only relief measures, and not meant to be continued long-term.

How far did the character of the New Deal change after 1933?

While most of the best-known alphabet agencies were created during the First Hundred Days there was still much work to be done and a number of further important initiatives were introduced between 1935 and 1937. Collectively they are known as the Second New Deal. Here the emphasis was on helping the victims of the depression and creating a fairer, more just America.

The Wagner Act, 1935

This replaced part of the National Industrial Recovery Act which had been declared unconstitutional by the Supreme Court. Senator Wagner introduced an Act that supported the rights of workers to form trade unions and bargain with their employers. It outlawed a number of unfair practices used by employers to prevent union development such as the dismissal of workers who were trade union members. It also set up the National Labour Board to act as a referee between the trade unions and management.

The Social Security Act, 1935

For the first time the Federal government took responsibility for providing old age pensions, unemployment benefit, and help for such groups as the

DISCUSSION

1. What can you tell from Source 9 about unemployment by 1933?

2. How far does Source 10 show that Americans benefited from the alphabet agencies?

3. Is one of these sources more useful than the other as evidence of Roosevelt's determination to solve the problem of unemployment?

sick and disabled. Pensions and unemployment relief were based on an insurance scheme funded by taxes levied on workers and employers. If a worker became unemployed the insurance scheme provided a payment until new employment was found. This was a landmark piece of social legislation as it contradicted the belief among many Americans that individuals should provide for their own welfare.

The Works Progress Administration (WPA), 1935

This addressed the persistent problem of unemployment. It supported a broad range of projects and work programmes: the building of schools, hospitals, and highways together with a 1,600 km windbreak of trees to stop further soil erosion from the Dust Bowl. There were also schemes to provide employment for artists, actors, and writers. The National Youth Administration, a junior section of the WPA, provided part-time work and vocational training for young people.

The Resettlement Administration (RA), 1935

The RA focused on the plight of farm labourers, sharecroppers, and tenant farmers who had been made unemployed through the operation of the AAA. It aimed to move 500 000 families to areas of better land and resettle them in houses.

In 1937 the RA was replaced by the Farm Security Administration (FSA) which provided loans for land purchase by these groups. Labour camps were also set up to help migrant workers. While some farming families undoubtedly benefited from these measures, the position of many farm workers remained extremely poor.

DISCUSSION

Is Figure 11.16 in favour of Roosevelt and the New Deal? How can you tell?

Why did the New Deal encounter opposition?

There is no doubt that the New Deal involved a major increase in the amount of state intervention. It may have been a series of bold, imaginative, and radical new policies but it could have been a lot more extreme. It did not seek to apply communist or socialist solutions to the Great Depression; there was no nationalisation or major redistribution of wealth. Consequently there were some critics who thought that Roosevelt did not go far enough. Yet at the other end of the scale, conservative Americans felt that Roosevelt was too radical and too ready to move the frontiers of state action ever forward. Roosevelt found out that one problem of being a **moderate** was that he could be attacked from both left and right.

▲ **Fig. 11.16** "Ring around a Roosevelt—Pockets full of dough", American political cartoon, 1938

Moderate

A politician who favours the middle ground of policy, rejecting extreme solutions

Radical opposition to the New Deal	
The "Radio Priest" and the National Union for Social Justice	• Father Coughlin from Detroit was originally a supporter of the New Deal but he soon became disillusioned. He felt that Roosevelt was failing to tackle the problems of the poor. • He broadcast his ideas on radio every Sunday evening to an enormous national audience of some 40 million Americans. • He also founded the National Union for Social Justice which, at its height, had a membership of 7 million.
Townsend Clubs	• Dr Francis Townsend from Illinois was the author of the Townsend Plan. • All people over 60 were to receive a pension of $200 a month provided they retired and spent the money within the month. The pension was to be funded by taxation. • The plan was devised to help older people, create jobs for the young, and inject money into the economy. • Millions of old people joined Townsend Clubs which campaigned for the plan.
Huey Long's "Share our Wealth" scheme	• Senator Huey Long, a former Governor of Louisiana, planned a major redistribution of wealth to stimulate the economy. • His "Share our Wealth" scheme included confiscation of large fortunes, lump sums for American families, pensions, minimum wages, and free education. • It was claimed that Huey Long had 7.5 million supporters in 1935 and he developed presidential ambitions. In September 1935, however, he was assassinated by the son-in-law of one of his political opponents.

▲ Table 11.9

Conservative opposition to the New Deal	
Republicans	• Republicans believed in minimal government intervention, low taxation, low government expenditure, self-help, and individual responsibility. • The New Deal was seen to undermine what were regarded as core American values. • Some of Roosevelt's initiatives such as the TVA and the NIRA were compared with the Stalinist economic planning of Soviet Russia. • It was also claimed that Roosevelt had become too powerful and was acting like a dictator.
The Liberty League	• Business leaders formed the Liberty League in 1934 to unite opposition to the New Deal. • Roosevelt was accused of moving towards socialism and destroying the free enterprise spirit of America. • In particular, businessmen disliked Roosevelt's support for the trade unions, having to contribute towards the unemployment insurance scheme, and the various codes of the NIRA.
States' rights campaigners	• Some state governors, including Governor Kump of West Virginia, argued that the New Deal laws and regulations conflicted with the rights of state governments to manage their own affairs. • Campaigners for the preservation of states' rights objected to those schemes, such as the TVA, that compelled state governments to cooperate with the federal government.

The Supreme Court	<ul><li>The main task of the Supreme Court was to decide if measures passed by the President and Congress were consistent with the American Constitution.</li><li>During the 1930s most of the nine judges were old, conservative, and Republican.</li><li>They had a natural political dislike for the New Deal and declared both the NRA and the AAA unconstitutional.</li><li>After his victory in the 1936 presidential election Roosevelt decided to try and sort out the Supreme Court. He wanted to appoint an additional six judges who would agree with his policies.</li><li>This plan misfired and Roosevelt was accused of trying to "pack the court" and overthrow the Constitution.</li><li>Nevertheless, the Supreme Court began to drop its opposition to the New Deal and upheld two key measures in 1937, one of which was the pensions section of the Social Security Act.</li></ul>

▲ Table 11.10

▲ **Fig. 11.17** "Do we want a ventriloquist act in the Supreme Court?" American political cartoon, 1937

▲ **Fig. 11.18** "The Trojan Horse at our gate", American political cartoon, 1935

DISCUSSION

1. Who are the people in the cartoon in Figure 11.17?

2. What is the message of the cartoon in Figure 11.17?

3. Why does the cartoonist make use of the image of a Trojan Horse in Figure 11.18?

4. How does the cartoonist show his opposition to Roosevelt's methods in Figure 11.18?

SOURCE 11

From an interview with a farmer by a member of the Federal Writers' Project, 1938.

Hard work from sunrise to sunset, mixed with common sense to manage their money, that's what supports the people and the Government. Now this government has taken those virtues away from millions of labouring men. This Social Security thing and the Old Age pensions, they ain't right. America isn't a free country like it was when I was young because the government's telling everyone what to do now and how to do it. Most people today are looking for someone to support them without work and if they keep this idea in their heads much longer most of us will have to live in caves or old shacks.

SOURCE 12

From an American history of government, 2005.

In 1936 Roosevelt's attempt to reform the Supreme Court because of its rulings against New Deal laws was met with political opposition and the Senate voted 70 to 20 against it. The Supreme Court was shaken by the President's action and did begin approving most of the main measures of the Second New Deal. In 1938 Congress rejected the President's proposal that the increased role of the government in running the country needed to be permanent. In 1939 Roosevelt used his authority to create the Executive Office to enable the President to wield more power with Congress. The Executive Office is still part of government today.

DISCUSSION

1. What can you tell from Source 11 about the New Deal?

2. How far does Source 12 show that President Roosevelt was more powerful than the opposition?

3. Is one of these sources more useful than the other as evidence about the impact of the New Deal on the United States?

FP Why did unemployment persist despite the New Deal?

When Roosevelt became President, unemployment stood at 12.8 million or nearly 25 per cent of the workforce. By the end of 1941 when America entered the Second World War, it had fallen to 5.6 million. As Figure 11.19 shows, however, while unemployment fell between 1933 and 1937 it then rose sharply in 1938 before continuing its downward trend. Unemployment never fell below 5 million during the years of the New Deal despite Roosevelt's efforts to stimulate the economy. There are a number of possible explanations for this.

The home market

Many Americans remained on low incomes during the 1930s, reducing the amount of money that could be spent on American goods. This was especially the case in rural areas which depended upon the recovery of the farming industry. While most agricultural prices rose after 1933, wheat and cattle prices did not reach their 1929 levels until after America entered the war. Cotton prices recovered in 1941 (see Table 11.13). This meant that although the position in rural areas improved, the improvement was very slow.

The foreign market

There was a limit to how much America's exporting industries could expand and take on more workers because all its overseas customers were also suffering from depression and high levels of unemployment. Tariffs remained firmly in place and also became common practice in Europe and Japan, reducing the scope for growth in international trade.

Improved production methods

As agriculture continued to use more machinery and less labour there were reduced opportunities for employment in farming. In industry, modern methods of production involving assembly lines and automatic tools meant that fewer factory workers were required.

The business cycle

There was very little that Roosevelt could have done to get rid of the business cycle altogether, especially since it had become a global event. The world economy improved between 1933 and 1937 but then briefly fell back into recession. America's increased unemployment in 1938 was reflected in all the capitalist economies.

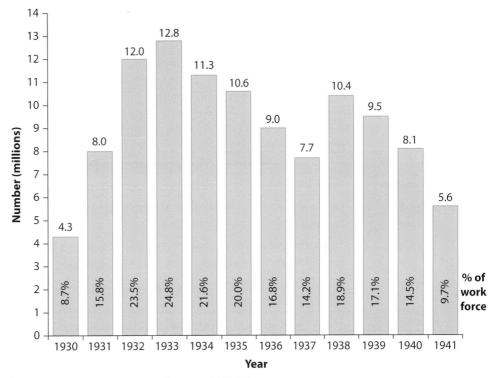

▲ **Fig. 11.19** American unemployment 1933–41

Year	Head of cattle ($)	Cotton per lb (Cents)	Wheat per bushel ($)
1929	58.47	16.78	1.04
1933	19.74	10.17	0.74
1936	34.06	12.36	1.03
1941	43.20	17.03	0.94

▲ **Table 11.11** Selected American Farm Prices 1929–41

Self-inflicted unemployment

For business to survive, especially during a recession, it has to become as efficient as possible. If there is overproduction then production capacity may have to be reduced and this will almost certainly involve the loss of jobs. This is precisely what happened in the farming industry. Roosevelt approved action which led directly to increased unemployment. The alternative would have been for him to watch the farming sector collapse.

The limitations of the New Deal

While the New Deal involved a dramatic increase in state power it was far from complete. Roosevelt did not and could not have taken over total control of the economy. Congress would never have allowed this. Instead he tried to provide solutions to the different problems associated with the depression. It was a bit like a doctor dealing with the various symptoms of an illness while hoping that the patient would recover without major surgery. The American economy did recover but at a frustratingly slow pace. It would take the demands of war to complete the transformation into economic prosperity.

Did the fact that the New Deal did not solve unemployment mean that it was a failure?

Opinions differ on the success or failure of the New Deal. Critics on the right wing of American politics claim that it began the movement towards "big government" and undermined those very qualities that had made America great. Critics on the left criticise Roosevelt for not doing enough. Others see the New Deal as steering a middle course between revolution and stagnation.

Civil rights laws

Laws to reduce or end racial discrimination.

The New Deal as a failure	
Unemployment	• Unemployment never fell below 14 per cent of the workforce between 1933 and 1939.
Trade unions	• Businessmen and industrialists strongly disliked the encouragement given to unions under the Wagner Act. • Some companies were prepared to use violence to break up strikes and sit-ins. In 1937 10 Chicago steel workers were shot dead by police while taking part in a strike march.
Small farmers	• Tenant farmers, labourers, and sharecroppers were forced off the land by government plans to reduce agricultural production.
Black Americans	• The New Deal did not end racial discrimination in American society. • Roosevelt needed the support of Democrats in the South and this prevented him from introducing **civil rights laws** which they would have opposed. • Although some blacks made gains in employment and housing they did not benefit as much as whites.
Industry	• Industrial recovery may have been held back by the increase in rules and regulations, the increases in taxation, and the encouragement given to trade unions.
Second World War	• Well before America entered the Second World War in December 1941 it had increased defence spending and begun supplying armaments and other goods to Britain and France. • These actions clearly had a stimulating impact on the American economy. Arguably it was rearmament rather than the New Deal that was primarily responsible for the economic revival of 1940 and 1941.

▲ Table 11.12

The New Deal as a success	
Unemployment	• Unemployment fell by over 30 per cent between 1933 and 1939.
Trade unions	• Trade union membership increased to over 7 million following the Wagner Act. • Many strikes were settled in the workers' favour. • Working conditions generally improved as did workers' pay.
Farmers	• Large-scale farmers benefited from the reductions in acreage and livestock, and the increase in prices.
The poor	• Millions of Americans were protected from the worst effects of the depression by the introduction of welfare payments and other emergency benefits such as food, clothing, and shelter. • America became a more compassionate society.
Industry	• Much business was saved by Roosevelt's speedy action to save the banking system. • Future industrial development and prosperity was stimulated by the construction of schools, roads, railways, bridges, and hydroelectric dams.
Morale	• Roosevelt's policies gave many Americans new hope, new confidence, and a sense of purpose. • The New Deal ensured that America survived the Great Depression without resorting to extreme solutions. Neither communism nor fascism had much support in America during the 1930s.

▲ Table 11.13

- ▶ The economic boom of the 1920s: why it happened, its main features and why it did not benefit all industries and all Americans.

- ▶ Social changes in the 1920s including intolerance, Prohibition, and the apparent revolution in the role of women.

- ▶ The causes and economic and social consequences of the Wall Street Crash.

- ▶ The 1932 Presidential election.

- ▶ The New Deal: what was it, how was it introduced, why did it give rise to fierce opposition, why did it fail to eliminate unemployment, how successful was it?

Revision tips

- The role of the automobile industry and mass production should be a main focus when revising the 1920s boom. Remember that the term "boom" is a generalisation and there were plenty of exceptions including agriculture and the older industries.

- You must be familiar with the nature of the "Roaring Twenties". But, as with changes in the role of women, you must appreciate that it affected a tiny minority in American society. Most Americans were not partying throughout the 1920s and most young American women remained unliberated.

- You must understand why America sometimes appeared an intolerant society during the 1920s. Why did the WASPS feel so threatened and how did they try to preserve their supremacy? Make sure you have covered Prohibition. You need to know why it was introduced, how it affected American society, and why it was repealed after 13 years.

- The Wall Street Crash does not need to be a difficult topic. Remember that Wall Street was simply a marketplace for company shares. Try to work out what types of American would (a) lose heavily (b) remain largely unaffected, and (c) gain from the Crash. What is the difference, if any, between the Crash and the onset of the Depression?

- If writing about why Roosevelt won the 1932 Presidential election, remember that the outcome reflected Hoover's weaknesses as well as Roosevelt's strengths.

- The New Deal is a key topic and there is a lot of detail to master. Don't let this overwhelm you. Break it up into manageable sections such as the First Hundred Days or Second New Deal and so on. Keep on going back over material you have already revised. Only rarely does information sink in thoroughly after one reading. Detail is important but so also is the "big picture". Make sure that at the end of your revision you are equipped to answer the general questions on the New Deal such as whether it was an overall success or failure.

Review questions

1. Describe the economic boom of the 1920s in the United States.

2. How did the availability of hire purchase contribute to America's economic boom?

3. How did popular entertainment change in the United States in the 1920s?

4. "Prohibition caused far more problems than it solved." How far do you agree with this statement? Explain your answer.

5. What was the effect of the Wall Street Crash on American citizens?

6. How did President Hoover respond to the Wall Street Crash and the onset of World Depression?

7. What was the New Deal?

8. Why was there so much opposition to the New Deal?

China, c. 1930–c. 1990

Introduction

By the eighteenth century the ruling Qing dynasty had established China as a growing power. However, the late nineteenth century saw a change in fortunes for China. The Boxer rebellion in 1900 was a brutal clash within China that resulted in foreign intervention and the partitioning of the country.

The Chinese Revolution of 1911 followed in which the last emperor of China was overthrown. In order to unite China, a Nationalist party was formed by Sun Yat-Sen. His party, the Kuomintang (KMT), was based upon three principles: nationalism, to rid China of foreign interference; democracy, to give the people the power to rule China; and social reform, to improve the lives of all Chinese, especially the peasants. He wanted to make China a free, prosperous, and powerful nation.

> ❛❛ *Let her sleep, for when she wakes, she will shake the world.* ❜❜
>
> Napoleon Bonaparte

Throughout the 1920s and 1930s Sun Yat-Sen's successor, Chiang Kai-shek, attempted to seize control of China but the Nationalists faced tough opposition with the emergence of the Chinese Communist Party. The Communists, led by Mao Zedong, had originally been part of the Kuomintang but had been expelled in 1925. These rival parties clashed as they tried to control China but their clashes had to be put on hold in 1936 when the Japanese invaded China.

Die Schantung-Bahn.

John Bull: So wird's gemacht! Ich betäube den Chinamann mit Opium, du plünderst ihn inzwischen aus, und nachher teilen wir!

▲ **Fig. 12.2** The slaughter of Chinese troops in the Boxer rebellion

▲ **Fig. 12.1** In this source from 1914 figures representing Britain and Japan have joined forces to exploit China for money and resources

An account of the Rape of Nanjing by Edgar Snow, an American journalist, 1941.

The Japanese entered Nanking on December 12th, as Chinese troops and civilians were still trying to withdraw to the north bank of the Yangtze River, debouching through the one remaining gate. Scenes of utmost confusion ensued. Hundreds of people were machine-gunned by Japanese planes or drowned while trying to cross the river; hundreds more were caught in the bottleneck which developed at Hsiakuan gate, where bodies piled up four feet high.

Twelve thousand stores and houses were stripped of all their stocks and furnishings, and then set ablaze. Civilians were relieved of all personal belongings, and individual Japanese soldiers and officers stole motor-cars and rickshaws and other conveyances in which to haul their loot to Shanghai. The homes of foreign diplomats were entered and their servants murdered.

The Japanese invasion of China in 1936 was dramatic in terms of the speed of its initial success. Japanese forces quickly captured the key cities of Shanghai and Nanjing, where brutal atrocities by Japanese troops in an event now referred to as the Rape of Nanjing saw the destruction of the city with an estimated quarter of a million Chinese civilians killed.

The aims of this chapter are to:

- Look at the why China becomes a Communist State in 1949, including the Communist Long March, the importance of the Communist settlement at Yenan, and the outbreak of the Civil War.

- Study the aftermath of the Second World War in China, including the reasons for the victory of the Communists in the Civil War and the establishment of the People's Republic in 1949.

- Look at Communist rule in the 1950s and 1960s, including agrarian and industrial reforms such as the Five-Year Plans and the Great Leap Forward.

- Consider the social changes and impact on the Chinese people of the new regime, including people's courts and the treatment of the landlords, and the establishment of collectives and communes.

- Examine social changes in the role of women, health, education, and propaganda and the destruction of traditional culture.

- Study Chinese foreign policy, including the changing relationship with the Soviet Union and relations with regions such as Tibet, India, Vietnam, and Taiwan.

- Look at China's closer relations with the United States from 1970, the situation in Hong Kong, and the impact on China's relations with the rest of the world of economic liberalisation since Mao's death.

- Examine the Communist Party dictatorship, including the repression of political opposition, the Hundred Flowers Campaign, treatment of minority groups, the Cultural Revolution, the role and status of Mao, the power struggle after Mao's death and the re-emergence of Deng, and the social and political consequences of economic change in the 1980s and 1990s.

Why did China become a Communist state in 1949?

The Nationalists and the Communists joined forces to fight the Japanese. However, the war effort had a very different impact on these two sides.

Why did the Communists undertake the Long March in 1934?

In 1925 the Kuomintang (KMT) elected a new leader. Chiang Kai-shek took charge, and made his main aim the removal of the Communist party in China. Chiang, along with other powerful rich landowners in China was scared that the growth of Communism in China would be a direct threat to their power. The two sides had previously worked together in government, and had been a strong alliance. This was about to change.

The Shanghai Massacre

Gradually the Communists were excluded from key roles. In 1927 this led to persecution. In the city of Shanghai, Chiang ordered that leading members of the cities communist party be arrested. Three hundred were rounded up, and Communist members of the government were expelled. As the Communist Party and local supporters took to the streets in protest, Chiang ordered the army to seize control. Violent attacks led to an estimated 1,000 arrests, 300 public executions and some 5,000 missing people. Further attacks on Communists in other cities followed, and by the end of 1928 an estimated 300 000 people had been killed in anti-communist action. In June 1928, Chiang's government secured control of Beijing, establishing control for the Kuomintang. Chiang Kai-shek was now to be the sole legal government of China.

The five extermination campaigns

The persecution of the Communists continued. Chiang, eager to eradicate the force completely, launched a full scale military campaign. As the KMT became more powerful, it looked like the end for the Communist forces. A major KMT victory at Jiangxi in 1931 forced the Communists to retreat.

The Long March

Facing annihilation, the communists escaped the KMT in a dramatic retreat. Travelling some 8,000 miles in 370 days, the Long March, as it became known passed through at times almost impassable terrain to escape the KMT. In the end, only one-tenth of the troops that left Jiangxi arrived in Yenan, on the edge of the Gobi desert in northern China.

Communist historians later claimed that the march crossed 24 rivers, 18 mountain ranges (5 covered with snow) and 11 provinces before it ended at the caves of Yenan. During the march, 235 days were occupied by day marches and 18 by night marches. The army averaged a skirmish a day and spent 15 days in major battles.

> ### Chiang Kai-shek
> Born to relatively wealthy parents in a coastal region of China. The son of a merchant, he joined the Chinese military. He returned to take part in the rebellion that established China as a republic. He joined Sun Yat-Sen's Nationalist party and was appointed to develop the new Chinese army. After Sun's death in 1925 he was appointed to lead the party.

▲ **Fig. 12.3** Chinese Communists pictured in rocky terrain during the Long March, 1934–5

Why is the Long March significant?

- **It secured Mao's position.** Mao's leadership during the retreat gained him the support of the members of the party.

- **It was great propaganda.** The harsh experiences of the Long March would come to represent a significant episode in the history of the Communist Party of China.

- **It gave the party time to rebuild.** The isolation that the rural north of China gave the Communists allowed the party time to restructure, organise, and recover from the fighting with the KMT.

- **It gained support for the party.** Travelling to rural China, the CCP lived and worked alongside the Chinese peasantry. Often overlooked by the KMT, these peasants grew to support the Communists due to their work and co-operation with them. The Communists redistributed land to the peasants and armed them with captured Kuomintang weapons.

SOURCE 2

Mao wrote in 1935:

"The Long March is a manifesto. It has proclaimed to the world that the Red Army is an army of heroes, while the imperialists and their running dogs, Chiang Kai-shek and his like, are impotent. It has proclaimed their utter failure to encircle, pursue, obstruct and intercept us. The Long March is also a propaganda force. It has announced to some 200 million people in eleven provinces that the road of the Red Army is their only road to liberation."

TASKS

Study Source 2. Why did Mao see the Long March as important?

Do you have any reason to doubt the reliability of what Mao says?

What was the importance of the Communist settlement at Yenan?

At the end of the Long March the Communists set up their headquarters at Yenan, and stayed there for the next 13 years. Here Mao set about indoctrinating his followers with Marxist-Leninist ideas tuned to Chinese conditions. Mao also made an important part of the work in Yenan focusing his followers on leading and supporting the peasantry. He wanted his CCP to be the party of the people, and therefore taught his followers to live their lives as the peasants did, and be an army designed to fight wars in defense of the people.

A growth in support

As the Communists remained in Yenan, their support started to grow. Some visitors went just to be curious, including some western visitors. Others however, flocked there to be part of the revolution that was proclaiming. Despite the huge losses during the Long March, the Communists numbers recovered. Membership reached 100 000 in 1937 and grew to 1.2 million by 1945.

Broader coverage

Mao was also able to generate interest from abroad. Visiting journalists came to Yenan to report on the settlement there, including an American Journalist, Edgar Snow whose book "Red Star over China" brought Mao's work to an international audience. It also meant that stories of KMT atrocities could be told to a wider audience.

How far did the Second World War weaken the Nationalist government?

There were several factors that weakened the Nationalist government.

Focusing on the Communists

Chiang Kai-shek saw the threat of the Communists as greater than that of the Japanese, and wanted to wipe them out before attacking the foreign invaders. This made the Nationalists unpopular with the Chinese people.

As Japanese incursions continued into China, Chiang looked weak in the face of his generals by failing to address them. These generals, in what became known as the Xian incident, forced a change of policy. Rather than focus on fighting the Communists, Chiang was forced into opening a "Second United Front" where nationalists and communists combined to resist the Japanese.

Wasting foreign funds

During the war against the Japanese the Chinese received aid from Britain, France, and the United States, where public opinion was strongly anti-Japanese. Once the Japanese attacked the United States at **Pearl Harbor** this aid increased. This support though was not well used by the Nationalists. The KMT rapidly became corrupt, with leading officials and military leaders hoarding foreign funds and weapons. The American President Truman wrote that, "the Chiangs, the Kungs, and the Soongs [were] all thieves", having taken $750 million in American aid without any visible results.

Military mistakes

Chiang Kai-shek proved reluctant to engage the Japanese in military confrontation, further frustrating foreign allies who felt the Nationalists weren't doing enough to stop the Japanese. Too often he adopted defensive positions and ignored the advice of American military advisors who urged him to attack the Japanese as they lacked troops. This annoyed both foreign supporters and the Chinese population who wanted to see their own government fight the Japanese.

How far did the Second World War strengthen the Communists?

The impact of the war was very different for the Communists. They took a different approach in their fight against the Japanese. While the Nationalists received arms and supplies from the west, the Communists were forced to rely on guerrilla-style warfare tactics against the Japanese. They organised local Chinese resistance forces in areas occupied by the Japanese in an attempt to sabotage the enemy war effort. They destroyed railways, ambushed troops, and disrupted Japanese supply lines. These sabotage operations deeply frustrated the Japanese army and led it to employ the "Three Alls Policy" (kill all, loot all, burn all), which led to Japanese war crimes being committed.

Why was there widespread support for the Communists among the peasants?

The tactics of the Japanese increased the support of the Communists among the Chinese peasants as they appeared to be the party willing to take direct action against the invaders.

Pearl Harbor

A harbor on the Hawaiian island of Oahu. An attack on this port by Japan brought the United States into the Second World War.

> *The Japanese are a disease of the skin, the Communists are a disease of the heart.*
>
> Chiang Kai-shek, 1936

TASKS

1. Imagine you are a Chinese peasant. Why are you more likely to support the Communists than the Nationalists? Explain your answer.

While the Nationalists attempted to control urban areas against the Japanese, the Communists took control of large areas of rural China. In areas under their control they introduced several key reforms to improve peasants' lives, reducing maximum rents from 37.5 per cent to 22.5 per cent of crops and increasing taxes for the rich. Furthermore, the brief cease in fighting between Nationalists and Communists after the Xian incident allowed the Communists time to expand their strength under the new united front and gain further support.

As the Japanese were driven out of the countryside, Mao's Communists were able to rely on the peasantry for support.

Why was there a civil war and why did the Communists win it?

By 1940, the war in China had become a stalemate. The Japanese lacked the large numbers of troops needed to secure the country, but the Chinese lacked the aggression and offensive push needed to remove Japanese troops from their homeland. The deciding factor came from outside of China: the Japanese attack at Pearl Harbor brought the conflict in the Far East to a global level. With America in the war Japan was forced to fight on two fronts and after the two nuclear bombs of 1945, the Japanese were defeated. The Japanese surrender caused clashes between the KMT and the Communists and Civil War broke out. So why did the Communists win?

Strengths of the Communists

Crucially the Communists continued the tactics that had served them so well in the fight against the Japanese. They continued to win support in rural areas meaning the biggest class of people in China, the peasants, largely supported Mao's troops.

Failings of the KMT

The corruption which had hindered the KMT's war effort also meant that the KMT struggled to win support during the Civil War. Ordinary people lost faith in the ability of Chiang's government to solve the economic problems the country faced and turned towards the Communists.

KMT troops also began to turn away from the party and instead joined the Communists. Not only did they desert, but they also took valuable supplies and weapons with them.

Influence of foreign countries

At first the west, and even the Soviet Union, supported Chiang's attempts to control China. However, as Chiang struggled to win and aid was needed elsewhere, America withdrew support and remained neutral. Without powerful foreign aid the KMT could not beat the Communists.

Tactics

The Communists used the guerrilla tactics that had served them so well against the Japanese. Aware that their main force was smaller and less well supplied than the KMT, they adopted a policy of not attacking the main Nationalist forces in set-piece battles and were even willing to give up land rather than face heavy defeats. Instead they focused on calculated attacks against smaller targets and causing supply problems to the KMT, while continuing to gain support among the peasants.

What is really important to consider is the contrasting ways in which each side appeared. The KMT were the party of corruption who relied upon foreign support and focused on the urbanised cities, leaving the peasant majority to its own devices. In contrast the Communists were the party of the people, visibly present in the rural areas where most lived and keen to introduce measures that the people wanted. They had successfully defended China against the foreign invaders and seemed to be the underdog. By winning hearts and minds the Communists were able to win the war.

In 1949 the Communists captured the key city of Shanghai and the KMT were forced to flee. Chiang Kai-shek left for Taiwan with what remained of his support. China was declared a People's Republic under Communist control.

SOURCE 3

Extract from a speech by Mao in August 1945.

Once in power, Chiang Kai-shek, far from being grateful to the people, knocked them down and plunged them into the bloodbath of ten years of civil war. During the present War of Resistance the Chinese people again defended him. This war is now ending in victory and Japan is on the point of surrender, but he is not at all grateful to the people. On the contrary, thumbing through the records of 1927, he wants to act in the same old way. He says there has never been any "civil war" in China, only "bandit suppression". Whatever he likes to call it, he wants to slaughter the people.

SOURCE 4

Extracts from a report made by Mao, 25 December 1947.

Our principles of operation are:

1. *Attack dispersed, isolated enemy forces first; attack concentrated, strong enemy forces later.*

2. *Take small and medium cities and extensive rural areas first; take big cities later.*

3. *Make wiping out the enemy's effective strength our main objective; do not make holding or seizing a city or place our main objective.*

4. *In every battle, concentrate an absolutely superior force (two, three, four and sometimes even five or six times the enemy's strength), encircle the enemy forces completely, strive to wipe them out thoroughly and do not let any escape from the net. Strive to avoid battles of attrition in which we lose more than we gain or only break even. In this way, although we are inferior as a whole (in terms of numbers), we are absolutely superior in every part and every specific campaign, and this ensures victory in the campaign.*

7. *Strive to wipe out the enemy through mobile warfare. At the same time, pay attention to the tactics of positional attack and capture enemy fortified points and cities.*

9. *Replenish our strength with all the arms and most of the personnel captured from the enemy. Our army's main sources of manpower and matériel are at the front.*

▲ **Fig. 12.4** General Chiang Kai-shek in discussions with foreign diplomats, including the British ambassador

DISCUSSION

1. How far does what you know so far about the war effort support what Mao says about Chiang Kai-shek in Source 3?

2. Study the photograph in Figure 12.4. Why does this support the idea that Chiang Kai-shek was unpopular due to his lifestyle and the way he behaved?

3. Study Mao's report to his troops in Source 4. Does this help to explain why Mao was victorious in comparison to Chiang?

How far had Communist rule changed China by the mid-1960s?

At the beginning of this chapter there was a quote by Napoleon about the potential of China. In 1949 once Communist rule was established, Mao wanted to awaken this potential in the country. He wanted to make China a great military power which would dominate other countries but China was poor, with over 90 per cent of its population peasant farmers. If China was to be strong, prosperous, and independent, then both Chinese industry and farming had to be reformed.

DISCUSSION

1. Evolution rather than revolution. How true is this of Mao's stated intentions?

2. Can you see a reason why Mao wanted his plans to sound like gradual change?

After nearly 20 years of fighting there were many problems facing China. The country had little industry. What had existed had been destroyed by so many years of war. Money was valueless and in the towns there was high unemployment.

The countryside was experiencing food shortages; and if the countryside was not producing food, then the cities were bound to be short of food as well. To make the situation worse China's population was increasing by 14 million a year.

What changes in agriculture did Communist rule bring?

In 1949 agriculture was dominated by wealthy landlords who controlled the lives of the peasants who worked for them. Mao and his Communist Party wanted to redistribute the land in line with communist principles, giving power and status to the peasants at the expense of the landlords.

Agrarian Reform Law

In 1950 in the first step to achieve their aims in rural areas, Communist Party officials encouraged peasants to take over in a series of land reforms. Animals, machinery, and land were given to the peasants.

At the same time, persecution of former landlords started. Peasants were encouraged to come to meetings and display their anger at the way their landlords had treated them in the past. These were called **"speak bitterness" meetings**. Often they resulted in landlords being beaten up or harassed.

To take this a stage further the Communist Party encouraged peasants to put their former landlords on trial in **"people's courts"** where their crimes could be heard. These crimes could be the mistreatment of peasants, charging excessive rents or low prices for grain. Once on trial the landlord's fate would be decided by a jury of peasants, often the people who had worked under the landlord! In the worst cases landlords were executed for their perceived crimes, others were imprisoned.

It is thought that as many as one million ex-landlords were executed between 1949 and 1953 while others were sent to special camps to be re-educated.

Mao Zedong

Mao was the son of a peasant farmer in a rural part of China. He was a keen reader but was forced to leave school by his father who needed his help on the farm. He spent his teenage years and early twenties studying the work of revolutionaries and nationalists from other parts of the world. He eventually joined the Nationalist party under Sun Yat-Sen and was appointed head of the peasant training branch of the party. He eventually left the party to join the growing Chinese Communist Party.

> *It will take many years to raise China from her low economic position. China must use elements of urban and rural capitalism which will help the national economy. Our present policy is to control not eliminate capitalism.*
>
> Mao in the 1950s

"Speak bitterness" meetings

Meetings in which the peasants were encouraged to air grievances towards their landlords. Previously the peasants had not been allowed to do so.

People's courts

Courts made up of local people who would "try" people accused of crimes. Those on trial were often landlords.

Why was land redistributed?

Land redistribution was in line with communist theory, it give the power to the people. It was also a reward to the peasants for their support of the Communists during the Civil War. The landlords were often the traditional supporters of the Nationalist party so by removing their influence, a threat had been neutralized.

Cooperative and collective farms

The Agrarian Reform Law was only the first step towards achieving a communist agricultural system. Despite the changes there were still problems with the new system of peasant ownership. Plots of land were very small, preventing the use of machinery while farming methods were often very traditional using animal and human labour, with simple ploughs.

Mao felt that farm production was not rising quickly enough to pay for his planned industrial changes. He was also worried that private ownership of peasant farms might lead to new class inequalities. Therefore cooperative farms were introduced in 1953.

▲ **Fig. 12.5** The caption reads "Receiving instruction in new farming methods, which includes the delivery of a new tractor", 1953

QUICK QUESTION 1

The Communists used propaganda to encourage peasants to join the cooperatives. Why would the poster in Figure 12.5 appeal?

Cooperative farming meant that between 30 and 50 families in one village joined their land together to make one bigger, more efficient farm. Although the families still legally owned their plots of land, the land was actually on permanent loan to the cooperative, which paid each family a rent for its use. The families then farmed the cooperative together.

In 1955 these cooperatives moved towards collective farms. In these several villages, roughly 200 families or more, joined their cooperatives into larger units called collectives. By 1956, 95 per cent of peasants were in collectives.

Private ownership, except for small gardens, ceased to exist. Families no longer owned their land; instead they received a wage for their work with the land owned by the state.

What was the impact of the Communists' social reforms?

The establishment of Communist rule meant mass social change. As well as the agricultural and industrial reforms, Mao's policies reached deeper into society in several key ways.

Some of these were positive

- Health care became free. China had a history of herbal remedies but the Communist party promoted prevention against disease instead through sensible measures. This dramatically reduced illness rates and also increased the numbers of doctors in rural areas.

- Education for all was improved. Mao was aware the peasants would need some form of basic education in order to operate machinery and play a part in industrial development. To tackle problems a nationwide literacy drive was introduced. Mao had no wish for universities or places where intellectuals would study and challenge his policies, instead he wanted all to have a basic standard of literacy. By the 1960s this had been achieved; over 90 per cent of the population could read and write.

Health care became free. China had a history of herbal remedies but the Communist Party promoted prevention against disease instead through sensible measures.

Education for all was improved. Mao was aware the peasants would need some form of basic education in order to operate machinery and play a part in industrial development. A nationwide literacy drive was introduced.

▲ **Fig. 12.6** A Communist propaganda poster from 1953 showing workers in a collective farm preparing to submit a production report to Mao

QUICK QUESTION 2

Study the poster in Figure 12.6. To what extent has Mao transformed farming with his collective farms?

How successful were the Five-Year Plans in increasing production?

At the same time as the dramatic changes in agriculture were introduced, Mao also set about revolutionising Chinese industry. Mao wanted to make China a world leader in production and use this power to develop its military. In order to do this rapid development was needed. Mao decided to follow the Russian model that had so dramatically developed the Soviet Union. In 1953 he launched the first of his Five-Year Plans.

What were the Five-Year Plans?

The principles of the plans were very straightforward.

- Private businesses and industries were taken over and placed under state control.
- All decisions about the economy were decided by the government.
- Production targets were set by the government for each factory. Each target had to be met within a five-year time span.

Communist ideology formed part of the five-year plan ethos. Targets were seen as essential for the greater good, so in failing to fulfill them you were failing your people. To encourage workers to be more productive, those who reached the targets set earned rewards such as access to more food, better accommodation, and even better schools!

Did the Five-Year Plans result in an increase in production?

Substance	Amount in 1952	Target for 1957	Amount actually achieved in 1957
Steel	1.3 million tonnes	4.1 million tonnes	5.2 million tonnes
Coal	63 million tonnes	113 million tonnes	124 million tonnes
Pig iron	1.9 million tonnes	4.7 million tonnes	5.8 million tonnes
Oil	0.4 million tonnes	2 million tonnes	1.4 million tonnes
Cement	2.6 million tonnes	6 million tonnes	4.6 million tonnes
Chemical fertiliser	0.2 million tonnes	0.6 million tonnes	0.7 million tonnes

▲ Table 12.1

The first Five-Year Plan was a huge success. The experience of Soviet advisors helped to organise the Chinese economy and the propaganda of the Communists helped motivate the workforce. The plans transformed China with rapid growth in the size of cities and the development of infrastructure such as railways.

TASKS

Using the data in Table 12.1, draw a graph showing the increase in these substances.

The Great Leap Forward

▲ **Fig. 12.7** A poster advertising the Dazhai Commune in Shanxi province

The success of the Five-Year Plans convinced Mao of the enthusiasm and work ethic of the Chinese workers. In 1958 Mao announced the "**Great Leap Forward**", a bold economic plan to quickly develop China's economy. Mao proudly proclaimed that China would overtake Britain in production of steel and other products within 15 years.

The centrepiece of the plan was the development of communes. The collective farms already established would be developed rapidly into new communes, vast collections of farms joined together taking in whole villages and sometimes even towns. The aim was not just to serve a farming purpose but also to use the peasantry to help develop industry.

Communes were also to be the lowest level of local government and served as a way to control the peasantry. Mao intended to use the communes to control the productivity of peasant labour, using them for work on large-scale projects, such as building tunnels and bridges when needed. The campaign created about 23 000 communes, with over 700 million people living in them.

SOURCE 5

Mao in an article called "Communes are Better" published in the *People's Daily* in August 1958.

It is better to set up people's communes. Their advantage lies in the fact that they combine industry, agriculture, commerce, education and military affairs. This is convenient for leadership.

> ❝ *It is possible to accomplish any task whatsoever.* ❞
>
> Mao, 1958

Great Leap Forward

Economic plan to increase China's production of materials announced in 1958.

DISCUSSION

1. Where does Mao see the impact of the communes? On the lives of the peasants or of the people?

2. Look at the name of the article from the newspaper in Source 5. What does it suggest about the public reaction to communes if there is a need to write such a piece?

Life on the communes

The population in the communes was organised into specific groups for work.

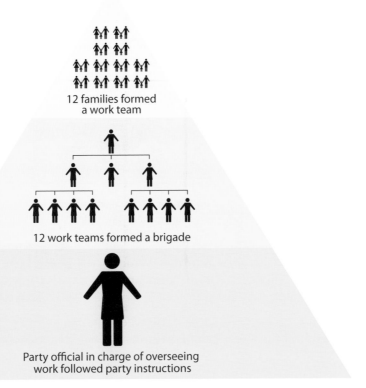

12 families formed a work team

12 work teams formed a brigade

Party official in charge of overseeing work followed party instructions

▲ **Fig. 12.8** The groups within communes

It wasn't just farming though that developed on the communes. All aspects of life were provided for for the thousands of families who moved onto them. Schools were built, entertainment provided, provision was even made for young children who were not old enough for school and for the elderly who were past working age.

The other mass development on the communes was the use of propaganda. Workers were exposed to it everywhere in order to encourage productivity. Large speakers were even erected in the fields so workers could hear motivational political speeches by Mao!

Communes also contributed to industrial production in a less obvious way. Private enterprise flourished, as communes set up "backyard" production plants. Some 600 000 furnaces produced steel for the communes producing an estimated 11 million tonnes.

At first it looked like the campaign was a huge success. Not only had large numbers joined the communes, but production also showed signs of progress. Iron production increased 45 per cent in 1958 and there were rises in steel and timber production.

However, gradually it became clear the impact was actually far from positive.

▲ **Fig. 12.9** Backyard furnaces on a collective, 1958

What were failures of the Great Leap Forward

Targets became unrealistic and if commune leaders refused to accept the targets they were labelled "bourgeois reactionaries" and sent to prison. The standards of the rapidly produced machinery were exposed as poor. Tools often fell to pieces when first used and others were unusable as they were so badly made.

The crucial backyard furnaces also had a negative effect as they took workers away from the fields meaning desperately needed food was not being harvested. Also coal was needed to fire them leading to shortages for China's rail system which depended on coal to drive its trains.

It became clear that the production figures so proudly declared by Party leaders were not true. This meant valuable food was sold abroad as officials wrongly believed enough food remained in China to feed its people.

▲ **Fig. 12.10** Child and a famished man on a street during the Great Leap Forward

There was a shortage of skilled labour in the new factories as former farmers were employed. While they were away from the fields the fertile crop land went to waste.

All these failings led to one huge problem for the Chinese: famine. Between 20 and 40 million starved to death as a result of the Great Leap Forward, making that famine the largest in world history.

> **SOURCE 6**
>
> Liu Binyan, journalist for the *People's Daily*.
>
> *The slogan was "struggle hard for three years, change the face of China. Catch up with Britain and catch up with America". It was completely unrealistic.*

By 1959, it was obvious that the policy was a failure. The Party blamed Mao and he was forced to resign from his position as head of state, remaining only as Party Chairman. His replacements abandoned the Great Leap Forward and quickly reintroduced private ownership of land and dismantled the communes.

DISCUSSION

1. The Great Leap Forward was Mao's personal idea and he was the driving force behind it. Does this explain why Mao was forced from power?

2. Study Source 6. *People's Daily* is the state newspaper. If this criticism was published by the state, what does it show about how the state later regarded the Great Leap Forward?

The Dazhai Commune

- The Dazhai Commune is a good example of the problems with the Great Leap Forward.

- It was one of the most famous communes in China.

- Reportedly built up from the ruins of a great flood by 500 peasants, it boasted record grain productions and it provided a model for other communes across China.

- It was visited by foreign leaders and dignitaries and used by China as a model of all it achieved.

- However it was revealed later that Dazhai was a sham. The record grain reports were fiction, production figures were exaggerated and the commune was heavily funded by the state.

Did the Chinese people benefit from Communist rule?

The reforms in health care and education benefited all. By the 1960s over 90 per cent of the population could read and write.

The role of women greatly improved under the Communists. Traditionally in Chinese society women were treated as second-class citizens. Marriages were arranged and it was common for men to marry more than once. If divorce did happen it was very rare, and all property went to the man.

The cruel nature of the treatment of women can be seen most dramatically with the practice of foot binding. Foot binding was an ancient tradition in China, where a girl's feet would be tightly wrapped in bandages with her toes tucked under the soles. The bandages would be tightened each day causing excruciating pain. If a woman's feet weren't bound she was considered unsuitable for marriage. In fact, it was preferred that the foot be around 3 inches in length.

Mao saw the role of women as crucial to the development of the Chinese state, and wanted to move the focus from women producing for the home to producing for the state. Key changes were introduced.

1. Husbands were not allowed to marry more than once and infidelity was made illegal.

2. In 1950, Mao introduced the Marriage Reform Law which banned forced marriages. The law was straightforward: "All marriages are to be based on the free consent of men and women."

3. Wives with unbound feet were encouraged and the practice was removed from society.

4. Divorce was made easier to obtain and women maintained their share of wealth.

5. Women were encouraged to work and become Communist officials.

6. The same educational opportunities were available to men and women.

▲ **Fig. 12.11** Chinese peasants are taught to read and write as part of Chairman Mao's Great Leap Forward

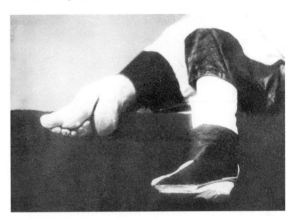

▲ **Fig. 12.12** The practice of binding feet caused damage to the structure of the foot

TASKS

1. Read Source 7. Does this show Mao's policy towards women to be a success? Explain.

2. Did the Chinese people benefit from Mao's rule?

SOURCE 7

From "A Documentary of Revolution in a Chinese Village" by William Hinton, 1966.

"*Among those who were beaten was poor peasant Man-ts'ang's wife. When she came home from a Women's Association meeting, her husband beat her as a matter of course, shouting, 'I'll teach you to stay home. I'll mend your rascal ways.' But Man-ts'ang's wife surprised her lord and master. Instead of staying home thereafter, she went the very next day to the secretary of the Women's Association and registered a complaint against her husband. After, in a discussion with the members of the executive committee, the secretary called a meeting of the women of the whole village. At least a third, perhaps even half of them, showed up. In front of this unprecedented gathering of determined women a demand was made that Man-ts'ang explain his actions. He said that he beat* his wife because she went to meetings and 'the only reason women go to meetings is to gain a free hand for flirtation and seduction'.*

This remark aroused a furious protest from the women assembled before him. They rushed at him from all sides, knocked him down, kicked him, tore his clothes, scratched his face, pulled his hair and pummeled him until he could no longer breathe.

'Stop, I'll never beat her again,' gasped the panic-stricken husband who was on the verge of fainting under their blows.

They stopped, let him up, and sent him home with a warning – let him so much as lay a finger on his wife again and he would receive more of the same 'cure'."

What was the impact of Communist rule on China's relations with other countries?

What have been China's changing relationships with neighbouring states?

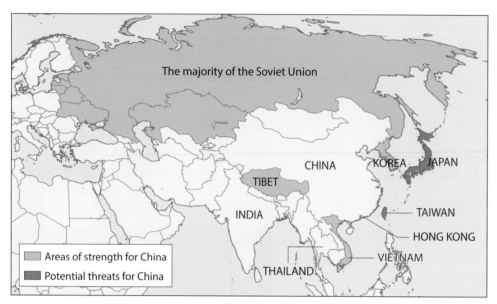

▲ **Fig. 12.13** China's relationships with its neighbours

Japan

The war had left relations between the two at an all time low. A peace treaty was not signed until 1976.

Taiwan

At the end of the Civil War the KMT had fled there under Chiang Kai-shek. They threatened to invade China, and received support in weapons and supplies from America. An attack never came though.

Tibet

The holy region of Tibet caused several problems for China. A rebellion in the 1950s had to be suppressed by troops, leading to the persecution of Tibet's religious leaders by the Chinese.

Korea

The Korean War, a struggle between the communist North and the democratic South supported by the United States, had threatened China after Chinese supplies and troops were sent to aid the North. Chinese troops became engaged in clashes with the United States which briefly threatened an invasion.

Soviet Union

Despite both being communist, relations between China and the Soviets were never easy. Both Stalin and Mao viewed the other as inferior and relations soured as Mao openly criticised the Soviet model of communism.

Vietnam

The Chinese offered support to Ho Chi Minh's communist forces in their fight against the democratic South aided by the United States. Although they never sent troops, aid and supplies were offered. The communists eventually won and united the two sides of Vietnam.

Hong Kong

Despite its close proximity to China, Hong Kong was controlled by the British. China left the territory alone, anxious not to provoke a clash with Britain.

DISCUSSION

1. Are any of China's strengths actually potential threats?
2. How isolated was China internationally? Explain.

How have relations between China and the Soviet Union developed?

Relations between the two great Communist superpowers of Russia and China have changed greatly since the Civil War.

Improving relations

The Soviet Union and China signed the Sino-Soviet Treaty of Friendship and Alliance in 1950, which comprised a $300 million low-interest loan and a 30-year military alliance between the two countries.

Tensions began to rise though as China sought to displace the Soviet Union as the ideological leader of the world communist movement. Mao stated that Asian and world communist movements should follow China's model of peasant revolution, not the Soviet model of a workers' revolution.

Relations stayed in place nevertheless as tensions over Korea meant both worked together through fear of an American attack there.

During the 1950s, the Soviet Union supported China in following the Soviet model of central planning, focusing on heavy industry.

After Stalin's death in 1953 relations again improved with an official visit by Premier Nikita Khrushchev. During this visit Russia formally handed over the Lüshun (Port Arthur) naval base to China.

The Soviets also provided technical aid in 156 industries in China's first Five-Year Plan, and 520 million roubles in loans. Experts from the Soviet Union travelled to China to assist with the Five-Year Plans and collective farms.

There was also some success in foreign policy. China and the Soviet Union persuaded the Democratic Republic of Vietnam, led by Ho Chi Minh, to temporarily accept the division of Vietnam.

Deteriorating relations

However Khrushchev's post-Stalin policies began to irritate Mao as he stated that Stalin had been wrong to rule the Soviet Union as a dictator in sole control, much like Mao was.

Khrushchev also favoured good relations between communist and capitalist nations which directly challenged Mao's own policy of only working with communist states. The final blow for Mao came as the Soviet Union pursued better relations with the United States, and ignored China's pleas for help in a dispute with India. Khrushchev withdrew all experts from China leaving some projects unfinished.

During the Cultural Revolution relations got even worse. After clashes over the rights to the border between the two countries, the red guards attacked the Soviet embassy in Beijing. Both sides began gathering troops at the border between the two countries. Conflict seemed likely.

Since 1976 relations have remained poor. During the Soviet Union's war in Afghanistan the Chinese supported the Afghan rebels. A state visit by Gorbachev in 1989 did little to improve terms.

DISCUSSION

1. Why is Stalin's death such a turning point in relations between China and the Soviet Union?

2. What evidence can you find that it is ideological differences that have led to poor relations between the two?

China, India and Tibet

The history of China and Tibet had always been linked. In 1913 a decision had been reached that Tibet would, in theory, remain under Chinese rule, but in practice Tibet was free to be an autonomous state, free to observe its own religious customs and practices which were set by its ruling leader, a religious figure known as the Dalai Lama. By 1945 areas of Tibet had fallen under Indian control while still preserving its autonomy.

Once the Civil War was over Mao looked to make Tibet a permanent part of China and remove the influence of India. Mao also wanted to remove the influence of Buddhism in the region, and therefore the power of the Dalai Lama. Direct negotiations began between India and the Communists in a friendly manner; India made it clear it had no political claim over Tibet and also had been one of the first major countries to recognise and acknowledge Mao's China. An agreement was signed by Tibet in May 1951 recognising Chinese rule over the country but guaranteeing that the existing political and social system of Tibet would continue.

Panch Shila

In April 1954, India and China signed an eight-year agreement on Tibet called Panch Shila. Meaning the Five Principles of Peaceful Coexistence, it was meant to promote understanding between China and India over Tibet and other issues. Cultural exchanges between the two countries began, an exchange of artists and writers as well as political meetings.

Growing tension

In 1954, India published new maps that included the boundaries of India with China. As Indian map makers finalized routes, clashes at the border began to develop. In January 1959, The Chinese stated in a letter to the Indian leader that their borders were incorrect and that 104 000 km² of territory shown on Indian maps was in fact Chinese land. As tensions grew between the two sides the Dalai Lama and thousands of Tibetan refugees fled to India.

Outbreak of hostilities

In 1962 these disputes resulted in a brief war. Chinese forces proved too strong though, and Indian forces were pushed into retreat before a ceasefire was declared after just a month of fighting.

Several small conflicts followed in the next decade, with India blaming these on Communist uprisings in India. In 1967, a peasant uprising in India received Mao's backing for a time.

Worsening of relations

China continued to support the Communist party in India and also provided support for other groups who were against the Indian government. Relations further worsened when China came out in support for Pakistan during the 1965 war with India. China also accused India of assisting rebels in Tibet. The contact established early in Mao's reign of political and cultural exchanges virtually ceased, and trade between the two of wool, furs and spices also stopped. It was not until the early 1990s that relations between the two began to improve.

TASKS

Why were China's relations with India poor in the period 1950–62?

China and Taiwan

In 1949, as the Communist Party won the Chinese Civil War, the KMT retreated to Taipei, in Taiwan, proclaiming the Republic of China (ROC) from there. Taiwan had been a Japanese territory up until 1945 and since that point had been closely linked with Chiang Kai-shek's China. After 1949, it became a base for members of the KMT and followers of Chiang to flee to, escaping persecution in Mao's China.

Continuation of war

War was officially still declared between the two states until 1979. Early on in 1950, the Communists attempted to seize control through an invasion of the island of Kinmen. A fierce battle was fought, but the Communists were defeated. Other attempts were also made, including some successes such as the Communist conquest of Hainan Island in April 1950, and capture of the Wanshan Islands off the Guangdong coast. In response to these attempts the Taiwanese closed its ports to all foreign ships. As road routes were largely non-existent, the only way for contact between the two was by sea. This closure meant suffering for fishermen from both sides.

Foreign intervention

The Taiwanese did receive some support from the Americans, who saw Taiwan as a vital staging point if they were ever forced to invade Communist China. Arms and supplies were sent in order for the country to defend itself; a resolution was also passed in the United States congress to support Taiwan militarily during a military clash known as the First Taiwan Strait crisis in September 1954. Although this conflict quickly ended, it did show the level of tension between the two sides.

Both governments claimed to be the legitimate government of China, and labeled the other as illegitimate. Each side used propaganda, showing the other to be suffering and living in poor conditions. Until 1971 the exiled government in Taiwan continued to be recognised by most countries as the true government of China. The Communists were recognised by fellow Communist states, as well as the United Kingdom and the Netherlands.

Improving relations

In 1979, as relations between Communist China and the United States improved, the United States stopped recognising the government in Taiwan as the legitimate rulers of China. This seemed to signify a chance for relations to improve. However, the ruler of the ROC in Taiwan, President Chiang Ching-kuo claimed a "three noes policy" of "no contact, no compromise, and no negotiation." It was not until 1987 that the ROC government began to allow visits to mainland China. As travel began again between the two states, relations improved and discussions began.

China and Vietnam

In theory relations between Vietnam and China should have been the strongest of all its neighbouring states. Both had suffered at the hands of Japanese occupation, and both had growing Communist movements.

During the Vietnam War, where the Communist north fought against the Democratic South allied with the United States, the Chinese Communist Party provided arms, military training and essential supplies to the north. However, all this support was dependent on the North Vietnamese refusing all Soviet aid.

Despite this aid there were tensions. China wanted to see Vietnam as a similar Communist movement, looking to spread its ideas abroad. The Vietnamese Communist Party wanted to focus on developing its own brand of nationalism. Alongside this distrust, there were also tensions regarding land. Both sides claimed sovereignty of the Islands in the South China Sea, as well as oil deposits in the Gulf of Tonkin.

Sino-Vietnamese War

In 1976 Vietnam invaded Cambodia, provoking tensions with China. This, and Vietnam's close ties to the Soviet Union, made China consider it a threat. Vietnam further worsened tensions by signing a treaty of friendship with the Soviet Union, a country where China had increasingly poor relations.

In February 1979, fighting broke out. The Chinese People's Liberation Army attacked northern Vietnam and for a time a full scale conflict seemed likely. Peace talks broke down in December 1979 and mass troop build ups from both sides occurred at the border. This fighting continued throughout the 1980s as China tried to force Vietnam to withdraw from Cambodia.

In September 1990 at secret peace talks both sides reached an agreement. Vietnam had withdrawn from Cambodia and relations between the two improved.

▲ **Fig. 12.14** A propaganda poster produced in the early 1970s by the Chinese for the Northern Vietnamese Army in the fight against the United States

China and Hong Kong

An island off the south coast of China, Hong Kong had been part of the British Empire since 1842. As China developed as a communist state, Hong Kong benefited in the following ways.

1. Migrants fled China because of ongoing Chinese Civil War. This increased Hong Kong's population dramatically.

2. When the People's Republic of China was proclaimed in 1949, more migrants fled to Hong Kong for fear of persecution by the Communist Party.

3. As the Communist Party took control of the economy, many businesses in major Chinese cities, for example Shanghai, moved to Hong Kong.

Improving relations

During the 1980s Hong Kong started to work with China on a series of joint projects that brought the two countries closer together. As part of China's developing relations with other countries, in 1984 Britain and China reached an agreement that Hong Kong would revert back to Chinese authority in 1997. While now a part of China, its commercial, social, and legal aspects will remain independent of China until 2047, at which time China will be able to exercise its authority.

FP▶ Why did China try to improve relations with the United States after 1970?

Positive relations between China and the United States	Negative relations between China and the United States
The United States provides arms and support for the Chinese in their fight against the Japanese.	1950–3: Korean War. China aids the communist North against the democratic South. The United States supports the South. Chinese and American forces clash.
	1960s: the United States blocks China joining the UN.
1971: American envoy Henry Kissinger visits China to negotiate trade agreement. In the same year China is allowed to join the United Nations. The American table tennis team are invited to tour China, making them some of the first Americans to be allowed into the country since the revolution.	1960s: Vietnam War. China and the United States once more clash, supporting opposing sides.
1972: Chinese–American trade agreement. Peace treaty also signed.	
1978: the Chinese Prime Minister visits the United States for official state trip.	

▲ **Fig. 12.16** A huge rally against the actions of the United States in Vietnam and other Asian countries in Tiananmen Square, Beijing in 1971

▲ **Fig. 12.15** Closer relations with the United States from 1970

As you can see from the timeline above, relations between China and America dramatically improved after 1970. This was quite remarkable given the hostility between the two previously. Mao had even stated in 1964 that "US imperialism is the most ferocious enemy of the people of the entire world".

Why did relations improve?

America's reasons	China's reasons
The wars in Korea and Vietnam had been a failure for America. Nixon wanted to find a new way of dealing with communist countries.	China wanted access to American trade and business expertise. After the failure of the "Great Leap Forward" it badly needed the help.
America saw the worsening relations between China and the Soviet Union as an opportunity to divide the two further. If it could establish links with China it would isolate its Cold War enemies.	As relations soured with the Soviet Union, China didn't want to be isolated from another world superpower.

▲ **Table 12.2** Improved relations between China and the United States

How far was China established as a superpower by the time of Mao's death?

By 1976 the Soviet Union and the United States were undoubtedly world **superpowers**, but how far could China also be put in this category?

Superpower

A powerful and influential nation, especially a nuclear power, that dominates its allies or client states in an international power bloc.

Definition of a superpower	Does this match Mao's China?
A powerful and influential nation	Powerful indeed. China's population of nearly 100 million was more than four times that of either America or the Soviet Union.
	Influence was also growing. China had been admitted to the United Nations and was an important nation in discussions with the United States and the Soviet Union.
especially a nuclear power	Yes. In 1967 the Chinese had tested their first hydrogen bomb, making them capable of nuclear weapons.
that dominates its allies or client states in an international power bloc	China had been an important ally to Korea and also aided Vietnam. It controlled Tibet and had defeated India in a brief clash over territory.
	It didn't, however, control other territories and indeed faced the threat of Taiwan close to its borders.

▲ **Table 12.3**

So was China a superpower?

Some would say yes, definitely! Looking at everything in context, from where China had come in 1945 it was definitely a growing world power. Its size meant that others had to pay attention to it and it dominated Asia.

Others would say no, not yet! It was an important power, but not yet a superpower. Industrially and militarily it lagged behind the Soviet Union and America and didn't yet have influence over other states.

How far have China's relations with other countries improved since Mao's death?

The improvements in relations with other countries that had begun in 1970 developed further after Mao's death.

▶ **The return of territories**

In 1997 it negotiated the return of Hong Kong from Britain. In 1999 Macau was returned from Portugal.

▶ **China's response to a changing world**

China was able to resist the spread of the collapse of communism that began in 1989 after the fall of the Soviet Union. It helped that Mao had distanced China from the Soviet Union.

▶ **Further developments**

The country's admission into the World Trade Organization in 2001 allowed greater economic links with other countries to be formalised and cemented China's role as a world leader. Beijing's selection to host the Olympic Games in the summer of 2008 was generally considered a great success. In 2010 the highly successful Shanghai World Expo was held, showcasing its rapidly developing economy and technological advances.

However while these events are positive, there have been some exceptions. China clashed with Vietnam, an Asian and communist ally, over its invasion of Cambodia in 1978.

The bloody suppression of the demonstrations such as the one in Tiananmen Square also led to widespread condemnation from foreign states. The United States, the European Community, and Japan imposed sanctions after the events.

▲ **Fig. 12.17** Tiananmen Square protests

Has Communism produced a cruel dictatorship in China?

FP▶ Why did Mao launch the Cultural Revolution?

Reasons for China	Reasons for Mao
Divisions in China were starting to reappear. Those less well off and poorly educated seemed to be turning against the spirit of the revolution.	Since the failure of the Great Leap Forward Mao had lost his position as Chairman of the state. He wanted to return to a powerful position.
After the enthusiasm of the 1950s had faded young people seemed less connected to the communist model.	As the Great Leap Forward had been widely discredited, Mao was worried his position in history was under threat. A new movement would help re-establish his influence.
Elements of capitalism such as private trade had made certain people richer than others.	Mao was concerned that the revolution in China was heading towards a Soviet model, where certain groups became more powerful and privileged. He wanted to stop this.
	Mao's successor, Liu Shaoqi, the State Chairman of China, didn't favour the collective farms and factories Mao had introduced. He saw Liu Shaoqi as a threat to what he had achieved.

▲ **Table 12.4** Reasons for the Cultural Revolution

The Cultural Revolution was an attempt by Mao to reimpose his authority on the Party and, therefore, the country. It began as a way of refreshing the revolution in China. Mao wanted to create a China in which peasants, workers, and educated people worked together—a classless society where all were equal. To do this he wanted to use young people to force change. Mao told them the revolution was in danger and that they must do all they could to stop the emergence of a privileged class in China where others were left to struggle. Mao argued this is what had happened to the revolution in the Soviet Union under Stalin and Khrushchev and that it would happen in China if the reforms of Liu Shaoqi continued.

▲ **Fig. 12.18** Cultural Revolution propaganda poster depicting Mao Zedong above a group of soldiers from the People's Liberation Army; the caption says "Closely follow Chairman Mao; forge ahead amid the wind and the waves"

QUICK QUESTION 3

Study the poster in Figure 12.18. What is the message? Who is China promoting a similarity to? Why?

▲ **Fig. 12.19** Workers with their copies of the Little Red Book

▲ **Fig. 12.20** A political rally at a unit of the People's Liberation Army, China during the Cultural Revolution

The Sixteen Points: Guidelines for the Great Proletarian Cultural Revolution published in 1966.

The masses of the workers, peasants, soldiers, revolutionary intellectuals, and revolutionary cadres form the main force in this Great Cultural Revolution. Large numbers of revolutionary young people, previously unknown, have become courageous and daring pathbreakers.

Why did the Cultural Revolution end?

As the violence got out of hand, members of the Party became concerned that China was heading for another civil war. A leading politician, and one of those who had encouraged all Party members to submit themselves to criticism, Zhou Enlai, urged for a return to normality.

This, together with the expulsion of Liu Shaoqi in 1968, meant Mao had forced the removal of a potential rival in the Party and therefore saw no need for the Cultural Revolution to continue.

What was the impact of the Cultural Revolution in China?

Persecution

Millions of people in China were persecuted during the Cultural Revolution. Those identified as enemies of the state were accused of the crime of being "revisionist" and of profiting from the work of others. Punishment came in many forms, with thousands suffering beatings, imprisonment, rape, and torture. It wasn't just physical abuse that they suffered as property was seized and medical attention was denied for those deemed a threat. People were also forcibly moved to the countryside to be re-educated in the ways of the revolution.

Nien Cheng, a victim of the Cultural Revolution.

A young man—a Red Guard, with an armband. He came up to me and he said: We are the Red Guards. We have come to take revolutionary action against you.

Education

The closure of schools and colleges led to a lowering of academic standards. Even the education that remained was directed towards communist ideology. This brainwashing meant that the skills needed for the workplace were not taught and subsequently workers struggled. The university entrance exams were cancelled after 1966 and were not restored until 1977.

Some regions had illiteracy rates as high as 41 per cent 20 years after the revolution. The elimination of qualified teachers meant many areas were forced to rely upon chosen students to re-educate the next generation.

Art and culture

The Chinese were encouraged to ignore traditional arts and ideas, instead praising Mao. Traditional Chinese traditions such as fortune telling, feng shui, and classical Chinese literature were discouraged and only authors and artists endorsed by the regime were encouraged.

Historical sites, artefacts, and museum pieces were also destroyed as Mao sought to remove influences of past generations. Priceless pieces were removed from private collections and destroyed. Others were smuggled abroad and sold to prevent destruction. There are no records of how much was destroyed or how much damage was done.

On society

People were encouraged to question their parents and teachers, which had been strictly forbidden in traditional Chinese culture. Slogans such as "Parents may love me, but not as much as Chairman Mao" were common.

The Chinese were also encouraged to be fearful of other countries, especially after relations soured with the Soviet Union. Red Guard attacks on foreigners were common and in 1967 the British Embassy was burned down in protests over Hong Kong.

What was it like to live in China under Mao?

Mao's rule in China lasted 23 years. Estimates vary on the final number, but some historians estimate as many as 50 million died under his rule. When studying Mao's China it is important to be aware of several parts of his rule.

Persecution

In 1953 Mao stated that "95 per cent of the people are good". The remaining five per cent were classed as "counter-revolutionaries". These included KMT sympathisers, Christians, and those who didn't conform with the Party's ideals. Those classed as threats to the state were persecuted in a variety of ways. Exclusion from society came first, with access to good jobs restricted. Physical beatings and, finally, imprisonment followed

SOURCE 10

A modern historian.

No-one was safe from criticism: writers, economists and anyone associated with the man Mao considered his main rival—Liu Shao-chi. Anyone who was deemed to have developed a superior attitude was considered an enemy of the Party and people.

SOURCE 12

An account of life on a commune by Frank Dikötter in *Mao's Great Famine: The Story of China's Most Devastating Catastrophe.*

One record shows how a man was branded with hot metal. People were forced to work naked in the middle of winter; 80 per cent of all the villagers in one region of a quarter of a million Chinese were banned from the official canteen because they were too old or ill to be effective workers, so were deliberately starved to death.

SOURCE 11

Washington Post, 17 July 1994.

During the 1970s, U.S. government officials using satellite photographs and other information, estimated that between 2 million and 6 million Chinese were in prison at one time. Based on an assumption that between 5 and 10 percent of all prisoners die while in prison, scholars conclude that perhaps 3 million to 6 million people died in Chinese prisons in the Mao era.

Propaganda

Propaganda was central to communist rule in China. Mao used mass media, most notably posters, to spread simple messages to the people. They were most commonly used to spread the message of new policies and to legitimise his actions. The success of Mao's propaganda was its simplicity; he was able to communicate effectively with China's millions of peasants who were largely illiterate.

▲ **Fig. 12.21** Chinese propaganda poster in which Chinese children parade with banners of their two heroes: Mao and Stalin, printed at a time when China was trying to maintain good relations with the Soviet Union

▲ **Fig. 12.22** Chinese propaganda poster with image of Mao appearing above marching workers

▲ **Fig. 12.23** A large statue of Chairman Mao Zedong in Zhongshan Square (once called Red Flag Square) at Shenyang, Liaoning Province, China

DISCUSSION

The propaganda of Mao was largely based on his image and relied heavily on people trusting in his word. In which other dictatorships have you seen such a "cult" develop? Why do you think dictators present themselves in such a way?

The Hundred Flowers Campaign

The complex nature of Mao's rule can be difficult to interpret. He wanted to dramatically develop China, but his actions and callous policies led to the deaths of millions. Some see him as a hero and the father of modern China. Others see him as a cruel dictator with no regard for human life. A single policy of Mao's reveals his complexity. In 1957 Mao launched his "Hundred Flowers Campaign" with the slogan "Letting a hundred flowers blossom and a hundred schools of thought contend is the policy for promoting progress in the arts and the sciences and a flourishing socialist culture in our land". Mao wanted to address the direction of the revolution. He claimed he wanted the Chinese to analyse the direction their country was heading in. Stating that criticism was good and healthy, Mao encouraged people to speak about the excesses they saw. Thousands of opinions were voiced.

Rather than addressing concerns that would move the revolution forward, the suggestions were directed at Mao, leading politicians, and the revolution itself. The campaign was suspended and the persecution of intellectuals, students, artists, and professors quickly followed.

The Hundred Flowers Campaign shows the two sides to Mao's character. Firstly, he attempted to reform China, encouraging freedom of speech. Secondly, he brutally repressed those who spoke out.

DISCUSSION

Did Mao deliberately launch the campaign to drive those who were likely to criticise the regime out into the open, knowing that repression would then quieten any in the future who may speak out? Or did Mao launch the campaign with the best of intentions, only to repress views reluctantly when he feared he was losing control?

Does Mao's motivation matter when assessing his rule if ultimately his regime led to the deaths of 50 million?

How was the power struggle after the death of Mao resolved?

▲ **Fig. 12.24** Chairman Mao Zedong's body lying in state at the Great Hall of the People, Beijing, 1976

In 1976 Mao Zedong, revolutionary leader of China, died. This, and the purge of the "**Gang of Four**", allowed China to attempt to move in a new direction.

" News of Chairman Mao's death has spread quickly through the Chinese capital. Many people are wearing black armbands. Groups have paid tribute opposite a huge portrait of Chairman Mao at the main entrance to the Forbidden City. His body will now lie in state at the Great Hall of the People. A memorial service will be held in Tiananmen Square on 18 September. Everyone except those performing essential tasks will be expected to maintain a three minute silence. "

BBC report on reaction to Mao's death in 1976.

SOURCE 13

A college professor, taken from *Intellectual opinions of the Hundred Flowers Movement* published in 1957.

The Party members, due to their occupying positions of leadership and being favorably situated, seem to enjoy in all respects excessive privileges.

Gang of Four

The four leading members of the Communist Party who, along with Mao, were the leaders of the Cultural Revolution. They were Jiang Qing, Wang Hongwen, Yao Wenyuan and Zhang Chunqiao.

Power struggle

After Mao's death two groups of politicians emerged, both anxious to lead China forward. Mao had indicated that the new Chairman of the Party should be Hua Guofeng. On 6 October 1976, shortly after the death of Mao, Hua removed the Gang of Four from power by arranging for their arrests in Beijing. He then took on the titles of Party Chairman and Chairman of the Central Military Commission. Hua insisted on largely continuing the policies of Mao, despite a feeling that these policies had alienated large elements of society.

In contrast to Hua was Deng Xiaoping. Deng had a mixed history under Mao—he had served in a variety of roles, including that of political commissar in the army during the civil war, and rising as high as First Vice-Premier, in practice running daily affairs within China. However, he hadn't always been popular and after opposing elements of the Cultural revolution he was expelled from power and sent to the work in a tractor factory in rural Jiangxi province as a regular worker.

Deng offered a different route forward from Hua, taking China in a new direction, away from the previous regime. In 1977 Deng was restored to important positions within the Party, including Vice-Chairman of the Central Committee and Chief of the General Staff of the People's Liberation Army. These roles allowed him to arrange his supporters in the party into powerful positions and through this increase his support. Once restored to authority Deng encouraged public criticism of the Cultural Revolution, strengthening his own position as someone who had previously stood against it while at the same time weakening Hua, who still stood for Mao's policies. As his support crumbled, Hua was removed from his top leadership positions by 1980. Hua was allowed to keep certain titles, but his power was removed. A new regime in China had begun, with Deng's supporters instilled as **Premier** and **General Secretary** of the Party. The Party made further changes in 1982. In response to concerns that one person might again become too powerful in the Party, the position of Chairman was removed. China was gradually distancing itself from Mao's reign.

Economic change

A new 10-year plan was put together in early 1978 to achieve rapid economic growth. This marked a new direction for the Chinese economy as it moved towards a more western-style economy. New measures were introduced such as resuming foreign trade and borrowing from foreign investors in order to create capital to speed up the country's modernisation.

Prices paid for farm products sharply increased in 1979, pumping significant additional resources into the agricultural sector. The collective farming system was gradually dismantled in favour of a return to family farming. Peasants were also allowed far greater choice in what crops to plant, and many abandoned farming altogether, establishing small-scale industries, transport companies and other services. Exceptionally good weather during the early 1980s contributed to record harvests.

A fresh start

The new regime of Deng Xiaoping tried to appease Chinese society after the excesses of Mao's rule. Thousands of political prisoners were released from

Premier

The head of the Chinese government.

General Secretary

The highest position in Chinese politics. The holder of the position generally is the leader of China.

labour camps and previous convictions for criticising the Party were removed from people's records. Criticising policy of the regime was no longer illegal, and the role of the public security (secret police) forces was cut back substantially.

How far did economic development of the 1980s produce social and political change?

These new changes and attempts at tolerance however led to problems in the late 1980s. Disaffection with the government spread and it was again students—eventually joined by many others—who took to the streets in cities from April to June to demand greater freedoms. These protestors were met with government force as they used the army to suppress this unrest in early June. This was captured in the world's press, as protestors in Tiananmen Square were attacked leading to the loss of life.

KEY POINTS

▶ The establishment of a communist state in China in 1949.

▶ The nature and development of communist rule in China by the mid-1960s.

▶ The impact of communist rule on China's relations with other countries including Russia and the United States.

▶ The Cultural Revolution, the Hundred Flowers Campaign, and other key developments of Mao's reign.

▶ A range of opinions on whether Mao's reign was a cruel dictatorship.

Revision tips

- Make sure you can explain why the failings of the Nationalists led to their defeat in the Civil War. It's crucial to look at their failings in direct contrast to the strengths of the Communists—for every area that Chiang failed in, Mao was able to show a strength.

- Life under Mao changed dramatically for all through huge economic developments and social reforms, massive changes in education and the role of propaganda. Don't forget the cruel side of Mao's rule, or that all change was ideologically motivated; all aspects of life were controlled to enforce the communist ideal.

- China's often confusing relations with other countries needs careful study. See relations between China and the two superpowers at the time, the Soviet Union and the United States, as interlinked. As relations deteriorate with one, they improve with the other.

Review questions

1. What was the "Rape of Nanking"?

2. Why did the Communists support increase because of the war?

3. Describe how foreign nations were involved in the Chinese Civil War.

4. Explain how Mao was a factor in the victory for the Communists.

5. Why did the Mao target landlords for repression?

6. Which was the more successful—the agrarian changes or the industrial ones?

7. The Great Leap Forward was motivated by ideological rather than economic reasons. How far do you agree with this view?

8. Give three examples of positive social change for Chinese people living under communism.

9. What evidence can you find that Mao moved China away from its traditional customs of the past?

10. Why, despite being both being communist, did China and Russia not have a close relationship?

11. For what reasons did relations improve between China and the United States?

13 South Africa, c. 1940–c. 1994

Introduction

The history of South Africa in the second half of the twentieth century is essentially the history of the rise and fall of apartheid. Although apartheid was not officially introduced until after the victory of the National Party in the 1948 general election, it was built upon the foundations of nearly forty years of formal segregation—the separation of whites and non-whites. Following the establishment of the Union of South Africa in 1910, segregationist customs were increasingly the subject of government legislation. Apartheid was a logical progression from this state of affairs except that existing policies were developed and applied more thoroughly and systematically and enforced with even greater levels of brutality.

Apartheid resulted from the fact that South Africa was, as it still is, a multicultural society. The main division was between the whites and non-whites. The whites were themselves divided into two groups: descendents of the original seventeenth century Dutch settlers known as the **Boers** or Afrikaners and descendents of the later British settlers. The non-white population had three main elements: black Africans, many of whom were descended from the original inhabitants, coloureds who were people of mixed race, and Asians who were originally brought in as slaves during the late seventeenth century from parts of the Dutch Empire. In addition a large group of Indians began migrating to southern Africa from the 1860s to work on the sugar plantations.

During the late nineteenth century there was a struggle for political control of southern Africa between the British and the Boers. The climax of this struggle came with the Boer or South African War of 1899 to 1902. British victory meant that the two former Boer republics, Transvaal and Orange Free State, joined with the two British colonies of the Cape and Natal to form the Union of South Africa. The new nation was set up as a dominion within the British Empire. But most unfortunately for the non-white population the British were so anxious that the two white groups should be able to live in harmony together that they approved a constitution that effectively handed over power to the Boers or Afrikaners. Determined to preserve and enforce white supremacy the Boers could now pass laws to suit themselves.

Boers

Descendants of the Dutch-speaking population who settled in southern Africa during the seventeenth century. The word "Boer" means farmer.

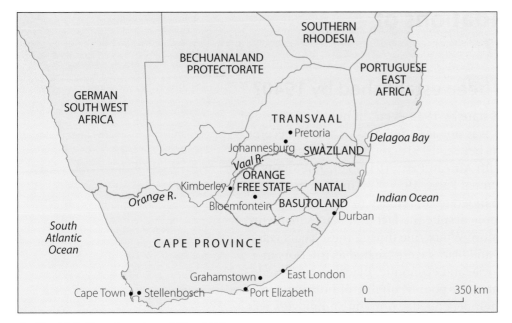

▲ **Fig. 13.1** Map of southern Africa, 1910

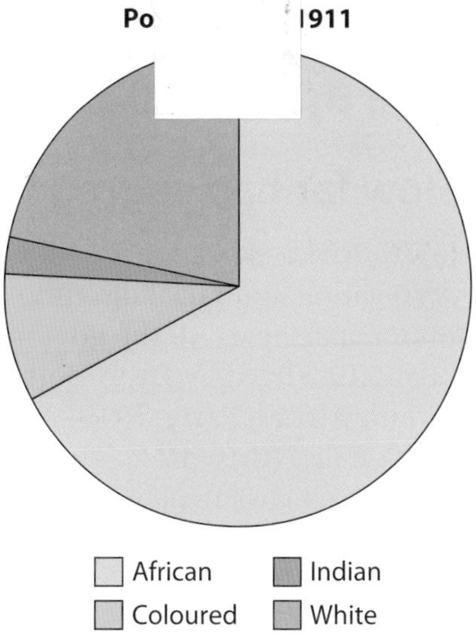

Po — 1911

- African
- Coloured
- Indian
- White

▲ **Fig. 13.2** Composition of South African population, 1911

The aims of this chapter are to:

- Consider the foundations of the apartheid state by looking at how far segregation had been established by 1940 and what the impact of government policies on the non-white population had been.

- Look at the development of the South African economy between 1910 and 1945 with special reference to gold mining, agriculture, and the manufacturing industry.

- Study the impact of the Second World War on South Africa and the reasons for the victory of the National Party in the 1948 general election.

- Review the main features of the apartheid state after 1948 and look at its impact on the white and non-white peoples of South Africa.

- Examine the growth of opposition to apartheid together with the effects of the government response to opposition by the mid-1960s.

- Consider the significance of the policies of the National Party governments between 1966 and 1980 together with the nature of black opposition during this period.

- Look at how economic factors improved lives by 1980.

- Examine the impact of external opposition to apartheid.

- Examine the policies of P. W. Botha and explain why violence increased during his presidency.

- Look at the nature of the transition to black majority rule between 1989 and 1994 and assess the contribution of individual leaders to the collapse of apartheid.

What were the foundations of the apartheid state?

FP How far had segregation been established by 1940?

South Africa was a highly segregated state by 1940 even though the process of segregation and racial discrimination was not as complete as it was to become under apartheid. All the governments between 1910 and the introduction of apartheid, led by Louis Botha (South African Party, 1910–19), Jan Smuts (South African Party, 1919–24 and United Party, 1939–48) and James Hertzog (Nationalist Party, 1924–39) believed in white supremacy to varying degrees and passed laws to achieve this outcome despite the fact that blacks made up more than 65 per cent of the population. White rule during these years was exclusively for the benefit of whites, and blacks were treated as inferiors in every department of life—political, social and economic. Blacks were forced onto the least productive land, allocated the poorest quality of housing and given only low-paid menial work. Their dependence on white employers was guaranteed by the introduction in 1925 of a poll tax on adult black males; cash to pay the tax had to be earned in the white-controlled factories, mines or farms.

Whites wanted blacks only for their cheap labour. They did not want to live or work alongside blacks, who were effectively excluded from all forms of white society. During the Depression of the early 1930s the South African government took a number of steps to assist the whites, including the provision of low-cost housing and measures to assist white farmers. The plight of blacks was ignored.

Yet, although this system seems repugnant when judged by modern standards, it was not so different from conditions in many of the European colonies in Africa. Racial discrimination was also the norm in many parts of the United States during the 1920s and 1930s.

The political system

- Following the formation of the Union of South Africa in 1910, a new constitution provided for a parliament consisting of a lower house—the House of Assembly, and an upper house—the Senate. Membership of parliament was restricted to white men. Voting for parliament was also largely restricted to white men although a small number of non-white men were allowed to vote in Cape Province and an even smaller number in Natal Province.

- The Natives Representation Act (1936) removed the existing voting rights of non-white men in Cape Province replacing them with the right to elect three whites to represent them in the House of Assembly. Africans in all four provinces were also given the right to elect indirectly a total of four white senators.

Sexual relations

- The Immorality Act (1927) made extra-marital intercourse between a white person and a black person a criminal offence carrying a sentence of up to five years for males and up to four years for females.

Land ownership

- In 1900 nearly 90 per cent of blacks lived in rural areas working as small farmers. The expanding towns and cities provided a market for their surplus produce and many of the farms were successful and prosperous businesses.

- Some blacks farmed as **share croppers** whereby a share of their output was given to the landowner as a form of rent.

- The problem with this state of affairs was that cheap labour was wanted in the mines and on the large farms run by whites.

- An "alliance of gold and maize," (mine owners and large-scale farmers) put pressure on the government to take action.

- The Natives Land Act (1913) allocated just over 7 per cent of South African land to the black population. This portion was increased to 13 per cent in 1936. Share cropping was banned.

- Blacks were not allowed to buy or rent land outside their reservations. Such land was for the use of whites only.

Share cropper

Farmers who gave a share of their output to the landowner as a form of rent.

Housing

- The Native Urban Areas Act (1923) introduced segregated housing for whites and blacks in town and city areas. It also provided for the building of new black townships.

- The thinking behind the Act was that towns ought to be regarded as white areas only, with blacks admitted only when required to attend to the needs of the white population as domestic servants or factory workers.

Travel

- The freedom of Africans to move around their country at will was severely limited by the pass system.

- Every black male over 16 was obliged to carry a pass which contained personal and work details and had to be presented to the police on demand.

- The system was used by the authorities to control and monitor the movement of black Africans. White farmers, for example, used passes to ensure that their African labourers completed their work contracts as it was illegal for them to leave the farms without a pass. Passes were also used to ensure that blacks moved out of the towns as soon as their work was complete.

- Failure to produce a pass on demand could result in a jail sentence or deportation to a black reservation.

Employment

- A colour bar had existed in the mining industry during the late nineteenth century but it had been a matter of custom rather than law. In 1911 the government introduced the Mines and Works Act which banned strikes by African mineworkers and gave white workers exclusive access to skilled jobs in the mines.

- The Native's Labour Regulation Act (1911) defined the conditions for African employment. Africans were to be recruited in rural areas, fingerprinted and given passes which allowed them to enter urban areas. The penalty for breaking their employment contract or staying in the cities beyond the term of their contract was hard labour for up to two months.

- The Industrial Conciliation Act (1924) effectively prevented black workers from joining trade unions.

- The Mines and Works Amendment Act (1926), also known as the Colour Bar Act, revised the parent Act of 1911 and reinforced the colour bar in the mining and other industries.

What was the impact of government policies on the non-white population by 1940?

The virtual exclusion of non-whites from the political system meant that there was no political incentive for white politicians to pass laws that protected or improved the position of the non-white majority. Quite the reverse happened, in fact, with non-whites paying through their taxes and food prices for subsidies to assist the white farming community. In view of this it is hardly surprising that there was a sharp deterioration in the social and economic position of non-whites.

Land

- As a result of the Natives Land Act African farming gradually collapsed. The reserves were so overpopulated with both people and livestock that the streams and waterholes dried up and much of the land suffered from soil erosion. Prosperous peasants disappeared and the quality of life plummeted with more than 20 per cent of children dying before their first birthday.

- Schooling was left to the underfunded missionary societies who were unable to offer a basic education to more than 30 per cent of African children.

- As was undoubtedly the intention of the white politicians the reserves became reservoirs of cheap, unskilled labour for white farmers and industrialists. African men were forced out to work by financial necessity, becoming victims of the migrant labour system.

What was the migrant labour system?

- Blacks were recruited from their Homelands or reserves to work in the mines and factories managed by white business people.

- They would normally sign a contract which entitled them to a wage, food and living quarters in a segregated compound. Breaking the contract was a criminal offence.

- When the contract expired the worker would return home to his Homeland.

- Wages were low and conditions in the living compounds were basic.

- Blacks were attracted by the opportunity to earn some cash in order to pay taxes and add to the family income. But men might not see their wives and children for many months during which time they were subject to harsh work discipline and long hours.

Housing

- The Native Urban Areas Act led to most South African towns having starkly contrasting residential sectors. Typically, whites would live in spacious leafy and paved suburbs with detached houses, some of opulent design, equipped with every available amenity.

- Some comfortable distance away black Africans lived in very different locations with houses often constructed of mud or corrugated iron standing on tiny plots of land with outside earth closets and occasional standpipes for water supply. Roads and paths were little more than dust tracks.

Travel

- Under the system of segregation the pass laws applied to African men only and when an attempt was made to extend the system to women in 1913, a series of demonstrations and protests forced the authorities to back down.

- An important effect of the pass system on African males was to turn large numbers of them into criminals. In 1930 for example, 42 000 Africans were convicted for offences against the pass laws in the Transvaal.

- The pass system became one of the most hated features of segregationist rule.

Employment

- One of the main results of segregation in the workplace was that wages for non-whites were set substantially below those of the white population.

- In 1938/9 the average per capita pay for white employees in manufacturing industry was £240 whereas for Africans it was £47. In mining the disparity was even greater with white gold miners earning 11.7 times the wages of African miners in 1911 with the disparity increasing after that date. White farmers paid their African workers lower wages than they could earn in manufacturing or mining.

- Furthermore, white workers often qualified for pensions and holidays with pay which Africans did not receive. Neither did Africans receive the same level of disability allowance paid to whites.

- The net effect of all this was that by 1940 the material gap between whites and blacks was both wide and rigid. White income was approaching ten times that of Africans. This meant that the gap in the standard of living between the two groups was correspondingly high with blacks unable to afford more than the bare necessities of life.

	Population (millions)	Income per head (£)
Whites	2.0	130
Asians and coloureds	1.0	21
Africans	6.6	10
Total population	**9.6**	**36**

▲ **Table 13.1** Population and income per head in South Africa 1936

How successful was the economic development of South Africa by 1945?

Despite the impact of the 1930s Great Depression the economy of South Africa was in a far stronger position in 1945 than it had been in 1910 with national income tripling during this period. By 1945 the economy was nearly self-sufficient apart from large inputs of foreign capital and technology. This expansion and improvement was mainly due to developments in gold mining, agriculture and manufacturing.

Gold mining	• Gold mining has been described as the engine of the South African economy.
	• Not only did it make a valuable contribution to jobs and output, it accounted for up to 70 per cent of exports so earning the foreign exchange that was vital for the purchase of oil and advanced technology goods.
	• Gold mining helped stimulate other sectors of the economy such as the production of machinery, electrical equipment, explosives, wire cables and miner's boots. It also boosted coal mining, electricity generation and railways.
	• Banking and financial services expanded and the immigration of doctors, lawyers, geologists and accountants took place in order to meet the needs of the gold mining industry.
	• Foreign capital, entrepreneurs and skilled labour was drawn to South Africa providing funds, technical expertise and managerial skills for use in other industries.
	• Gold mining contributed to the South African treasury through the high taxes and royalties levied on the industry. This money was used to assist other sectors especially white commercial farming.
Agriculture	• Approximately one third of the working population was dependent on agriculture which contributed around 20 per cent to the total output of the economy in 1910.
	• Farmers experienced many problems during this period. During the 1920s there were severe droughts followed by the collapse of prices and markets during the Great Depression.
	• The government realised that if the farming sector was to survive then action was needed. Farmers received loans, grants, rebates on railway rates and many other forms of help.
	• It was largely black consumers, now having to pay more for their maize, milk and sugar, who paid for the government's generosity to the white farming community.
Manufacturing	• In 1910 manufacturing contributed less than 5 per cent to the total output of the economy. By 1945 this contribution had risen to over 20 per cent.
	• Manufacturing took a major step forward during the 1920s due to two government initiatives: the introduction of tariffs to protect home industries and the establishment of two major public corporations to stimulate the economy.
	• In 1923 the Electricity Supply Commission, 1923 (ESCOM) was set up to ensure the plentiful supply of cheap and efficient electricity to railways and harbours, local authorities and industry.
	• In 1928 the Iron and Steel Industrial Corporation (ISCOR) was set up to exploit the country's rich resources of coal and iron-ore. By 1940 ISCOR was producing 320 000 tons of steel meeting about one third of the national requirements.
	• Although manufacturing made impressive progress during this period it was held back by weaknesses in the home market due to the low wages paid to black Africans.

▲ Table 13.2

▲ **Fig. 13.3** Workers in a South African gold mine, c. 1932

SOURCE 1

From South African government statistics published in the 1960s.

Employment in Gold Mining	1929	1940
Black workers	200 000	383 000
White workers	23 000	41 000
State income from taxes on gold production		
	£1 600 000	£22 000 000

SOURCE 2

From *Twentieth Century South Africa* by W. Beinart published in 1994.

The worldwide economic depression of the 1930s weakened South Africa's export markets for agricultural and industrial products. The government had begun to protect prices of both wine and tobacco in the 1920s. In the 1930s this was extended to almost all agricultural produce and in 1937 the government set up marketing co-operatives for white farmers. Industry received less support but grew rapidly in the later 1930s, particularly in textiles and engineering where the workforce trebled between 1932 and 1940.

TASKS

1. What does Source 1 tell us about the gold mining industry in the 1930s? Support your answer with reference to the source.

2. How far does Source 2 show that the South African economy faced difficulties in the 1930s? Explain your answer.

3. Is one of these sources more useful than the other as evidence about the South African economy between 1929 and 1940? Explain your answer.

Why did the National Party win the election of 1948?

After the success of Jan Smuts' United Party in the general election of 1943 it looked as if the Nationalist Party, led by Dr Daniel Malan, was doomed to permanent opposition. The Nationalist Party victory in 1948 was, therefore, unexpected and dealt a mortal blow to the United Party. The Nationalists were to remain in power until 1994.

In fact, although the Nationalists won a majority of seats in parliament, the United Party won the clear majority of the popular vote. This was because the South African constitution allowed for greater representation in the rural areas than the urban areas, a provision that favoured the Nationalist Party. But even the rural bias in the electoral system does not explain why the Nationalists performed so much better in 1948 than 1943.

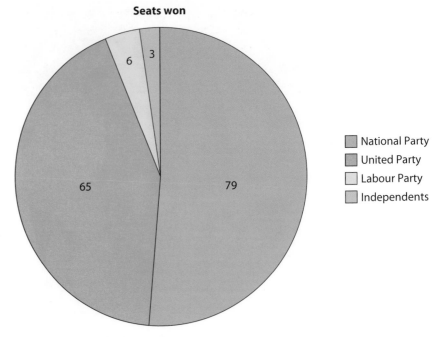

Seats won

- National Party
- United Party
- Labour Party
- Independents

▲ **Fig. 13.4** 1948 election results

The growth in Afrikaner nationalism	• 1948 coincided with a high point in the level of Afrikaner nationalism. This could be expressed politically by voting for the Nationalist Party which had been formed in 1914 to represent the Afrikaner community.
	• From the opening years of the twentieth century the Afrikaners had been developing a sense of identity and togetherness. This was encouraged by the publication of an Afrikaner newspaper, De Burger (The Citizen), from 1915. A secret society, the **Broederbond**, looked after Afrikaner interests in business and the professions.
	• Encouraged by the teachings of the Dutch Reformed Church many Afrikaners thought that they were a chosen people destined to rule over blacks and other non-whites.
The Second World War	• The Second World War led to industrial expansion in order to meet the new demand for weapons and armaments and goods which could no longer be imported.
	• Since many whites were called away to fight in the war factories responded to the labour shortage by employing more blacks—the overall number of black males working in industry increased by 70 per cent. Some blacks took over skilled and semi-skilled jobs.
	• This meant that more blacks moved to the towns where, for the first time, they began to outnumber whites. Blacks often settled in squatter camps constructed around the major urban centres.

Broederbond

A secret society that looked after Afrikaner interests in business and the professions.

	<ul><li>The government responded to these developments by relaxing some of the laws and regulations that had enforced segregation such as the Pass Laws.</li><li>With a very slight improvement in their conditions some groups of blacks decided to press for further concessions and participated in boycotts, passive resistance and strikes.</li><li>Whites were shocked and appalled by these changes which seemed to suggest that cracks were appearing in the policy of segregation. They had to decide whether Smuts or Malan had the best ideas for dealing with blacks.</li></ul>
Jan Smuts and the United Party	<ul><li>By 1948 Jan Smuts was 78 and widely regarded as out of touch. He was also regarded with suspicion for supporting the ideas of equal human rights and liberty in the Charter of the United Nations drawn up after the war.</li><li>The approach of the United Party to the racial question was that blacks were in the cities to stay and that complete segregation was completely impracticable. This was far from reassuring for most Afrikaners.</li></ul>
Daniel Malan and the Nationalist Party	<ul><li>Nationalist Party policy towards the position of the non-whites was outlined in the **Sauer Report**. It advocated total segregation or apartheid. This was what the Afrikaners wanted from their politicians.</li></ul>

▲ Table 13.3

Sauer Report

The National Party set up the Sauer Commission in 1947 to evaluate the current system of segregation. The resulting report favoured the continuation and extension of segregation across all areas of social and economic activity.

How successfully was apartheid established between 1948 and 1966?

What were the main features of the apartheid system set up by the National Party after 1948?

The policy of apartheid was introduced into South Africa by Prime Minister D.F. Malan (1948–54) and continued by his successors—J.G. Strijdom (1954–58), H.F. Verwoerd (1958–66) and John Vorster (1966–78). The essence of apartheid was the separation of whites from non-whites. But it was much more than separation. Apartheid also implied white control over the state and the greater importance of white interests over black interests. The state felt no obligation to provide equal facilities for whites and non-whites.

In many ways apartheid appears like a continuation of the segregation introduced after 1910. The main difference was that apartheid was more coherent, far-reaching and intense in its objectives.

As with segregation, apartheid was introduced by a series of laws passed by Parliament. The main apartheid laws are considered below.

Population Registration Act, 1950

- If laws were going to be introduced to separate whites from non-whites then it was obviously important to be able to identify to which race every person belonged.

- This Act attempted to define or classify every South African as white, black or coloured.

- In most cases the process of classification was straightforward but problems arose with the classification of the children of mixed marriages.

- At first, racial group was determined by considering the community into which the individual had been accepted. In the early 1960s, however, greater stress was placed on the individual's appearance.

- The law proved difficult to enforce and led to some absurd classifications whereby sibling members of the same family with the same parents were classified differently.

Prohibition of Mixed Marriages Act, 1949

In order to preserve racial purity this law made marriages between whites and members of other racial groups illegal.

Immorality Amendment Act, 1950

This amendment extended the parent Act of 1927 by banning sexual relations between whites and any non-whites.

Group Areas Act, 1950

- In order to ensure that whites, blacks and coloureds lived separately this law divided the whole of South Africa into racial areas. Only one race was allowed to live in each area.

- Implementation of the act meant that some groups living in the "wrong" area had to move. Most of those affected were non-whites. An estimated 3.5 million people were uprooted between 1960 and 1983.

- One notorious removal made under the Act was Sophiatown, four miles west of Johannesburg. This was a township where blacks had owned land for more than thirty years and had developed a distinct and lively community. In 1955 the government forcibly removed the inhabitants of Sophiatown to Meadowlands 12 miles from the city.

- The Act proved impossible to implement fully and in 1980 over 60 per cent of blacks still lived outside their designated areas.

Abolition of Passes and Coordination of Documents Act, 1952

- This Act contradicted its title by strengthening the pre-war pass laws.

- It replaced existing passes for black male Africans with a 96-page "reference book" which included an individual's photograph, fingerprints, address, marital status, employment record, details of taxes paid and place of residence.

- After 1956 the system was extended to include black women.

- Failure to produce the reference book on request was a criminal offence carrying a jail sentence.

- In a typical year there would be over 100 000 arrests under the Act.

▲ **Fig. 13.5** Black South African displaying pass book

Native Laws Amendment Act, 1952 ✓

- This law attempted to control and restrict the movement of blacks into white areas.

- Blacks were banned from remaining in urban areas for more than 72 hours without a permit stating that they were legally employed.

- There were exceptions for blacks who had been born in urban areas, had lived there continuously for 15 years or had worked for the same employer for 10 years

Separate Representation of Voters Amendment Act, 1956

- Cape coloureds were no longer allowed to vote with whites in national elections. Instead they were given separate elections to elect four white MPs to represent them in parliament.

- Only whites would now be able to choose the government.

Bantu Education Act, 1953

- All black schools were brought under the control of a government department, the Native Affairs Department.

- Government grants for missionary schools (they had previously educated 90 per cent of African pupils) were withdrawn forcing most of them to close down.

- Black children would now be taught a different curriculum from whites which prepared them for life as part of a permanent underclass. They were often taught in their native language.

- Money allocated to black education was reduced producing larger classes, poorer quality buildings and equipment and less-qualified teachers.

- A later law introduced apartheid at university level banning non-whites from previously mixed universities and setting up new colleges for Africans, coloureds and Indians.

The Reservation of Separate Amenities Act, 1953

- All races were to have separate amenities—toilets, parks, beaches, cemeteries—and they did not need to be of equal quality.

- Apartheid signs were erected throughout South Africa.

The Bantu Self-Government Act, 1959

- This law was the centrepiece of Prime Minister Verwoerd's vision for an all-white South Africa.

- The Act created eight **Bantustans** based on the original African reserves or homelands each of which was allocated to a particular ethnic group. These Bantustans were intended to be the homelands for all blacks.

Bantustan

Territory set aside as a homeland for black South Africans.

- The newly established regions were eventually intended to become self governing and in 1963 the Transkei became the first Bantustan to have its own parliament elected by blacks.

- The policy of Bantustans provided a way for the government to eject all blacks from white areas who were not employed or needed for the functioning of the economy such as women, children, the old and the unemployed.

- The Act was criticised because the total area of the Bantustans comprised only 13 per cent of the area of South Africa and much of the land was infertile. The Bantustans were often fragmented and KwaZulu, for example, was divided into 26 different bits.

- Bantustans failed to provide the final answer for apartheid as blacks continued to live outside their homelands in squatter camps outside the cities and other illegal residences. By 1980 only just over half of those who should have lived in Bantustans actually did so.

▲ **Fig. 13.6** Scene from Langa Township near Cape Town

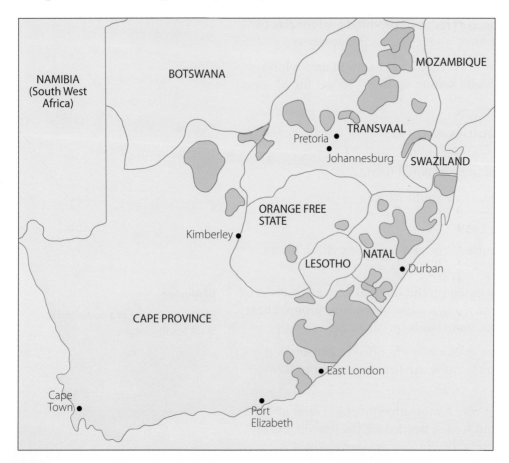

◀ **Fig. 13.7** Map of the proposed location of the Bantus or Homelands

From a South African newspaper report of a case under the Pass Laws, 1967.

Mrs Mpemba, a mother of eight children, has been told that as her husband is no longer living in Langa she has no right to live there and must leave. Because she has lived in Langa for 25 years she also does not have the right to return to her place of birth. Legally, she may now not live anywhere.

From a report in the *New York Times* by an American writer who was expelled from South Africa in 1966 reproduced in *Move Your Shadow: South African Black and White*, published in 1985.

Before they went to the police station on 21 March 1960, PAC member Philip Kgosana told the crowd of 6000 in Langa township, 'Every African must make up his mind that he will never again carry a pass. In this campaign NOW and CONTINUOUSLY we are going to observe ABSOLUTE NON-VIOLENCE.' Nine days later, he repeated these points to a crowd of 30 000 that he had led in a march to Parliament in Cape Town.

TASKS

1. What can you tell from Source 3 about the effects of the Pass Laws? Support your answer with reference to the source.

2. How far does Source 4 show that Africans opposed the Pass Laws? Explain your answer.

3. Is one of these sources more useful than the other as evidence about the Pass Laws in the 1960s? Explain your answer.

What consequences did apartheid have for the people of South Africa?

The impact on whites

Most white South Africans clearly approved of apartheid for the National Party was re-elected in 1953 and 1958 with increased majorities. In 1960 a majority of white voters supported Prime Minister Verwoerd's proposal to make South Africa a republic after which it left the Commonwealth. In the 1961 general election the National Party won 105 seats with a majority of 59 over the opposition parties.

It is not difficult to understand why apartheid was so popular among whites. The economy boomed for much of the time and firms benefited from the extremely low wages they paid to black employees. Whites became as prosperous as the professional and business classes of Europe and North America enjoying one of the highest standards of living in the world. They owned cars, lived in substantial houses and apartments, many with swimming pools, and were waited upon by black servants. The quality of living was boosted by a range of excellent public services including schools, hospitals, libraries, parks, buses and trains, roads, street lighting, water, electricity and telephones.

The group who benefitted most from apartheid was undoubtedly the Afrikaners who, until 1948, had been the poor relations within the white community. In 1946 the average Afrikaner income had been less than half that of an English-speaking South African. By 1976 it had risen to approaching three quarters and continued to rise after that. But the Afrikaners made a series of broad-ranging gains and improvements.

- Afrikaners were appointed to senior as well as junior positions in all the state institutions—civil service, army, police and industrial corporations.

- The medical and legal professions came increasingly under Afrikaner control.

- The government directed official business to Afrikaner banks and gave state contracts to Afrikaner businesses.

- Afrikaners broke the stranglehold of English speakers on mining manufacturing, trade and financial services.

- Afrikaner farmers received massive state support which enabled them to introduce mechanisation and increase their profits.

The impact on non-Whites

Non-white Africans were unable to share in the increasing prosperity. The wages of blacks remained much the same and the real value of black mine wages was less in 1971 than it had been in 1911. Black factory workers earned only 18 per cent of the wages of white workers performing the same tasks. Overall, white income was ten times greater than that of blacks. By the early 1980s it was estimated that the top 10 per cent of the population received 58 per cent of the national income while the lowest 40 per cent received 6 per cent.

What this meant in practical terms was cheap, overcrowded, leaky housing with either inadequate or nonexistent public facilities. In the Homelands, women might have to walk several miles every day to collect firewood and water. It was not uncommon to find 17 to 20 persons living in a typical four-roomed house with more than six to a bed.

Inevitably the gap between white and non-white communities had an impact on health and life expectancy. The mortality rate for black and coloured infants, aged one to four, was 13 times higher than for whites.

'OUR POLICY OF APARTHEID HAS OFTEN BEEN MISUNDERSTOOD. IT CAN BEST BE DESCRIBED AS A POLICY OF GOOD NEIGHBOURLINESS'
— DR VERWOERD

▲ **Fig. 13.8** A British cartoon about apartheid published in 1961

QUICK QUESTION 1

Examine Figure 13.8. What do you think Dr Verwoerd meant by "good neighbourliness"?

Around 1970 a male could expect to live, on average, to about 65 if he was white but to only 51 if he was black. Whereas heart disease was a major killer among whites for blacks the single most important disease was tuberculosis. Many black mine workers suffered disabling injuries or contracted lung diseases.

But while the apartheid regime clearly benefited whites at the expense of non-whites, not every member of the latter group earned extremely low wages. Among the non-white community there was a very small number of university graduates, professional workers and businessmen who were able to afford better housing and enjoy a higher standard of living than the majority of their non-white fellow countrymen.

This was especially the case in the Bantustans or Homelands. Here the black leaders together with their governing councils were paid high salaries and also enjoyed generous allowances and travelling expenses. Jobs were created for government officials and civil servants. But blacks who benefited from such opportunities were relatively few in number. Life for the majority of those who lived in the Bantustans was one of grinding poverty, disease and malnutrition.

How did opposition to apartheid develop between 1948 and 1964 and what were the effects of the government's response to opposition by 1966?

The African National Congress or ANC, which became the principal anti-apartheid protest organisation, had been founded in 1912 with the aim of bringing all black Africans together as one people to defend their rights and freedoms. To begin with the ANC membership was mainly limited to educated and middle-class blacks. The strategy of the movement until the 1940s was to use the methods of persuasion. It rejected more violent methods as likely to prove counter-productive. During the 1940s, however, the ANC became revitalised largely as a reaction to increased attacks on the rights of blacks and the growth of extreme Afrikaner nationalism. These circumstances called for a more militant stance. This was supplied, in part, by the ANC Youth League whose leaders included Nelson Mandela, Walter Sisulu and Oliver Tambo. Together they aimed to involve masses of people in the militant struggle for equal rights. By 1948, after a slow start and patchy progress, the ANC was beginning to become an effective protest organisation with a large support base. Its popularity among black Africans was boosted by the victory of the National Party in the general election of 1948.

Opposition to apartheid between 1948 and 1964 and the inevitable government response consisted of a series of attempts by both sides to outmanoeuvre the other. The government was intent on making any form of overt opposition illegal just as the ANC was constantly trying to find new ways to publicise its cause and to outwit the security forces. Every act of protest or defiance prompted a brutal response followed by even more repressive laws. By the mid-1960s it looked as if the government had achieved its aim of silencing opposition by constructing a vast array of security measures.

The Programme of Action (1949–50)

In 1949 the Youth League persuaded the main body of the ANC to adopt a Programme of Action to challenge government plans for apartheid. The programme included boycotts, civil disobedience and a national day of strike action on 26 June 1950.

The Suppression of Communism Act (1950)

The government responded with new legal restrictions in the form of the Suppression of Communism Act. The Communist Party was banned and communism was so widely defined as to include virtually any organisation or political activist who was considered a nuisance by the government. This meant that the government now had the legal powers to silence any of its critics since criticism was regarded as the same thing as communism.

The Defiance Campaign (1952)

Following the Programme of Action a number of Youth League members, including Mandela and Sisulu, were elected to the ANC Executive. Using their new-found influence Mandela and the other recently-elected leaders of the ANC planned a campaign of defiance against apartheid. Beginning in April 1952 it involved peaceful defiance by a volunteer force of more than 8,000 persons. The campaigners entered 'whites only' waiting rooms on railway stations, travelled in 'whites only' railway coaches and stood in 'whites only' lines in post offices. Curfews were ignored as were areas restricted by the pass laws. The campaign was given full coverage in both the home and foreign press prompting international condemnation of the apartheid system. The campaign ended in 1953 by which time membership of the ANC had increased from 7,000 to 100 000.

The Public Safety Act, 1953

The government reacted by ordering arrests under the Suppression of Communism Act and approximately 8500 people had been arrested by December 1952. Fines were imposed followed by jail sentences when they were not paid. The main government response was the Public Safety Act which gave it the powers to declare a state of emergency and suspend all laws when public safety was supposedly endangered. The Criminal Law Amendment Act of 1953 made it a criminal offence to accompany anyone found guilty of offences unless the accused could prove his or her innocence. It was now virtually impossible to protest against apartheid and remain within the law.

Women's resistance (1955)

The Federation of South African Women (FSAW) and the ANC women's league also attempted to push for reform. The FSAW's 'Women's Charter' demanded better rights for women and a removal of all laws and customs that denied women such equality. Together with the ANC Women's League, the Federation organised scores of demonstrations outside Government offices in towns and cities around the country. The biggest of these protests was on October 27, 1955, when 2000 women of all races marched on the Union Buildings in Pretoria to demand reform. In response to these groups, the government acted and in December 1956, 156 leaders of both organisations were rounded up and detained and charged with Treason. During these trials the FSAW organised support for the accused's families.

The Freedom Charter and the Treason Trial, 1956–61

In the mid-1950s opposition to apartheid was still largely peaceful but the ANC was increasingly making common cause with other groups wanting change in South Africa. Together with anti-apartheid organisations representing whites, Indians, coloureds and trade unionists it held a Congress of the People at Kliptown near Johannesburg in June 1955.

The Congress met to discuss the Freedom Charter which set out a new vision for the future of South Africa. It called for an end to apartheid and the introduction of democracy, human rights, land reform and equality before the law.

The government decided that the Freedom Charter was an act of treason and charged 156 persons under the Suppression of Communism Act. The trial lasted for several years and, while the defendants were found not guilty, it kept most of the leaders of the opposition groups out of action for that time.

The government also introduced censorship of books and films and amended the Riotous Assemblies Act in 1956 which outlawed any public meetings which might cause problems for the government.

Sharpeville (21 March 1960)

▲ **Fig. 13.9** Aftermath of Sharpeville Massacre

In 1959 it had become apparent that continued protests in the form of bus boycotts or petitions against the pass laws were achieving very little. A breakaway organisation was formed, the Pan African Congress (PAC), led by Robert Sobukwe. Unlike the ANC the PAC did not support the Freedom Charter believing that blacks should work on their own to achieve their rights.

In March 1960 the PAC began a national campaign against the pass laws. Africans were encouraged to leave their pass books at home and then gather outside their local police stations to invite arrest. The protests were planned as a peaceful operation.

One of these demonstrations outside the police station at Sharpeville, 35 miles from Johannesburg, ended in violence when police fired on the crowd killing 69 and wounding 186. It later appeared that most of the dead and wounded had been shot in the back.

Later the same day in the Langa township near Cape Town a similar demonstration resulted in three deaths and several injuries.

Protest and demonstrations continued throughout 1960. When 30 000 Africans marched on Parliament in Cape Town, the government declared a state of emergency, arresting 18 000 and banning the ANC and PAC.

What was the role of women in the protests against apartheid?

- Women protested alongside men in the Campaign of Defiance and other general demonstrations of opposition to apartheid, but they also engaged in all-women forms of protest.

- When the Pass Law system was extended to women in 1952, women organised demonstrations against the Pass laws in many parts of South Africa and, in August 1956, occupied government offices in Pretoria.

- Black women protesters were supported by the Black Sash, an organisation of white, mainly middle class women who were also opposed to the Pass Laws and other apartheid restrictions.

- Black women were also involved in protests against government attempts to close down their shebeens, or domestic beer-halls. Following police raids and arrests near Durban in 1959, a group of women burnt down two official beer-halls leading to violent police retaliation.

SOURCE 5

From an article by the black South African journalist, David M. Sibeko, written in 1976.

The PAC branch at Sharpeville approached almost every house and the men's hostel in the township, mobilising support for the strike against passes planned for Monday, March 21, 1960.

Not a single bus moved out of Sharpeville to take passengers to work on that Monday. PAC task force members started out before the break of dawn lining up marchers in street after street. When all the groups had been assembled, the 10 000 and more men, women and children proceeded to the local police station – chanting freedom songs and calling out campaign slogans.

SOURCE 6

From the Report of the Truth and Reconciliation Commission, 1998.

In its verbal submission to the Commission the PAC emphasised the commitment of its organisers to peaceful protest.

The police refused to arrest PAC members who presented themselves for arrest. According to the police, PAC officials refused the order to disperse. However, it appears from the testimony of victims that the PAC leadership did ask the crowd to disperse but approximately 300 remained behind.

Throughout the morning police reinforcements arrived, including Saracen armoured cars. According to witnesses, they positioned themselves facing the crowd.

At 13h 15, with nearly 300 police members facing a crowd of 5000 people a scuffle broke out. According to police witnesses, stones were thrown at them and, in response, inexperienced constables began firing their guns spontaneously. However, evidence reveals a degree of deliberation in the decision to fire at Sharpeville and indicates that the shooting was more than the result of inexperienced and frightened police officers losing their nerve.

The crowd was unarmed. The majority of those killed or wounded were shot in the back.

TASKS

1. What can you tell from Source 5 about the role of the PAC at Sharpeville? Support your answer with reference to the source.

2. How far does Source 6 indicate that the police in Sharpeville were looking for a confrontation with the protesters. Explain your answer.

3. Is one of these sources more useful than the other as evidence of what happened at Sharpeville in March 1960? Explain your answer.

The Rivonia Trial and the General Laws Amendment Act, 1963

The ANC and PAC were forced to become underground organisations by government repression and formed militant wings, Umkhonto (usually known as MK) and Poqo respectively. With the failure of peaceful protest both wings adopted a policy of violent resistance.

In 1963 the police discovered the MK base at Rivonia near Johannesburg. Evidence was found linking MK to acts of sabotage. Seventeen MK leaders, along with Nelson Mandela, were arrested and put on trial for treason, an offence which could carry the death penalty. During his defence Mandela addressed the court with a four-hour speech in which he called for greater understanding between the white and black communities in South Africa. Eight of the defendants, including Mandela, were given life sentences and were taken to Robben Island, an island prison in the south Atlantic off Cape Town.

One of the most extreme laws passed in response to the escalating violence was the General Laws Amendment Act whereby police could detain for 90 days without charge and without access to a lawyer.

By the mid-1960s it looked as if the government had successfully crushed most of the internal resistance to the apartheid state. This was certainly the verdict of the business community as the inflow of investment capital and white immigration began again following the interruption caused by Sharpeville.

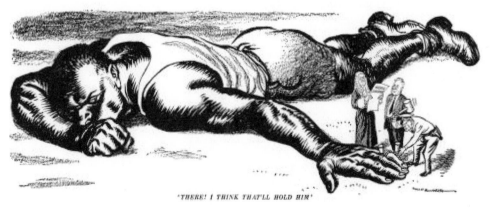

'THERE! I THINK THAT'LL HOLD HIM'

▲ **Fig. 13.10** A British cartoon about the Mandela judgment in the Rivonia Trial published in 1964

QUICK QUESTION 2

What point is the artist making in Figure 13.10 about the Mandela Judgement from the Rivonia Trial of 1963–64?

7 out of 10 shot in back
Statistics on Sharpeville

VEREENIGNIG, MAY 3
The senior district surgeon of Johannesburg, Dr Jack Friedman, told the judicial inquiry into the Sharpeville shooting to-day that his ~ropsies on 5? Af~ ~s killed there

the Langa inquiry that the police would be issued with more accurate pistols and have special training in a new kind of te~ ~as as a result of the recent

▲ **Fig. 13.11** Newspaper article headline from *The Guardian*, 4 May 1960.

QUICK QUESTION 3

Study Figure 13.11. What do you think the impact of such a headline has on the international community?

To what extent did South Africa change between 1966 and 1980?

FP How significant were the policies of the National Party governments from 1966 to 1980?

The foundations of the apartheid state were now firmly established. The period from 1966 until the end of the 1970s saw the development and intensification of existing policies as apartheid laws and regulations were tightened up and loopholes closed. There were few entirely fresh initiatives during these years rather a following through and refinement of principles that had already been accepted. Many Acts of Parliament between 1966 and 1980 had the word 'amendment' as part of their title; this indicated a change in the detail of legislation rather than the introduction of a completely new law. The theme of continuity was illustrated by the election of John Vorster as Prime Minister following the assassination of H. F. Verwoerd in September 1966. Since 1962 Vorster had been Minister of Justice in Verwoerd's cabinet a role he combined with responsibility for police and prisons. Vorster had acquired a reputation as a strict and rigid enforcer of apartheid policies. He was expected to deliver more of the same.

Security measures

- The security measures introduced after 1966 represented continuations of earlier government attempts to uncover and then stamp out resistance to apartheid rule.

- Two important new bodies were set up to co-ordinate security and intelligence matters:

- BOSS (Bureau of State Security) was established in 1969 to act as a co-ordinating link between the Security Branch of the police and the military intelligence division of the army. It reported to the PM and its activities remained secret.

- SSC (State Security Council) was established in 1972 to advise the PM on security matters and how they might affect government policy and strategy. Membership of the SSC included the PM, and the ministers of defence, justice, police and foreign affairs.

- The Terrorism Act of 1967 made terrorism a separate crime equal to treason. Apart from murder and possession of arms and explosives terrorist acts included the receiving of military training. Convicted terrorists could receive the death penalty.

- The Internal Security Amendment Act of 1976 allowed suspects to be detained without charge for a renewable period of 12 months and for potential witnesses to be detained for six months in solitary confinement. In effect this law enabled the state to detain indefinitely anyone thought to be a potential threat to law and order or to the apparatus of apartheid.

- Whereas there was a modest expansion in police numbers during the Vorster administrations there was a much more dramatic programme of military expansion. By 1978 defence accounted for over 20 per cent of the national budget and every young white man was conscripted into the army for two years. The police and security services were armed by ARMSCOR, a state corporation, which supplied guns, mortars, bombs, tear gas, napalm and other military equipment.

Propaganda and censorship

- In 1976 the SABC (South African Broadcasting Corporation) began operation with a monopoly of radio and television broadcasting. It soon became the voice of official government propaganda.

- Any attempts to report the activities of organisations such as the ANC through books, pamphlets and other sections of the communications media were checked by a rigorous system of censorship. In 1977 government censorship agencies banned 1,246 publications, 41 periodicals and 44 films.

- All this meant that many South Africans, especially Afrikaners, remained in partial ignorance about what was going on in their country.

The political system

- The Separate Representation of Voters Amendment Act of 1968 completed the abolition of non-white political representation. It achieved this by scrapping the last four parliamentary seats that had been reserved in the National Assembly for white representatives of coloured voters.

- From 1968 until the introduction of a new constitution in 1983 only whites could now vote in elections for the National Assembly.

The Bantustans or Homelands

- The Bantu Homelands Constitution Act of 1971 followed the Bantu Self-Government Act of 1959. The former Act gave the government the power to grant independence to any Homeland.

- The Transkei became independent in 1976 followed by Bophuthatwana in 1977, Venda in 1979 and Ciskei in 1981. The political leaders of these new states were African chiefs willing to collaborate with the South African government. Most of them led corrupt dictatorships. Citizens of the new states were deprived of South African citizenship.

- This policy enabled the South African government to pose as a progressive regime willing to acknowledge the self-governing wishes of black South Africans. Its real motives were more questionable. By forcing black Africans into the Homelands it was able to save considerable amounts of money for the government no longer felt obliged to provide houses, schools, hospitals and other amenities for blacks living in white areas. The Homelands became overpopulated and poverty-ridden with many blacks being forced to enter illegally the towns and cities in search of work; it was the only way to survive but carried the daily risk of arrest and imprisonment.

- Foreign powers were unimpressed and refused to recognise the territories when they became "independent" states partly because the South African government continued to control such matters as foreign policy and defence.

When Vorster was forced to resign as Prime Minister in 1978 following a scandal that involved corruption and the misallocation of public funds, the apartheid system was still fully intact. Yet there were worrying signs for the government. Despite an extensive intelligence network, substantial numbers of security personnel together with the legal powers to silence all who opposed the apartheid system, it was still unable to put an end to continuing unrest and resistance in South Africa.

To what extent did black opposition change in this period?

In the ten-year period following the Rivonia Trial and convictions, open resistance to the apartheid regime appeared to subside. This was partly the result of the draconian laws of repression together with the fact that most of the anti-apartheid leaders were either in prison (Mandela and Sisulu) or exile (Tambo). Yet black Africans were far from accepting their place as second-class citizens. Hopes of eventual freedom were fuelled by a blossoming of black culture involving both theatre and the publication of novels and poems with a strong liberationist message. Much of this literature was published abroad and then smuggled into the black townships so to avoid government censorship. Ideas of confrontation and resistance were developed among the general black population including children, students, parents and industrial workers. When a major challenge to white supremacy occurred in 1976 the government proved unable to extinguish the unrest by using the well-tested methods of repression. This was partly because the resistance was so widespread and involved tens of thousands of people.

Before the major events of 1976, however, there was an outbreak of black industrial militancy. This was caused by a series of economic factors: recession followed by inflation followed by rising unemployment. Beginning in 1973, there was an upsurge in strike action for improved wages and conditions of work. Whereas in the 1960s an annual average of 2,000 African workers had gone on strike, in 1973 nearly 100 000 black workers were involved. Workers began calling for more general improvements such as better housing, healthcare and political rights.

Soweto, 1976

What was the importance of Steve Biko and Black consciousness for the anti-apartheid movement?

- Steve Biko was a talented medical student at Natal University when he founded the exclusively black South African Students' Organisation (SASO) in 1969.

- He is also regarded as the founder of the Black Consciousness Movement of which SASO was a part.

- Black Consciousness involved pride and confidence in being black, a refusal to rely on well-meaning whites in the struggle against apartheid and a discovery of black history and culture.

- Biko was a moderate and advocated peaceful methods, but he was regarded as dangerous by the authorities, for he encouraged a greater sense of cohesiveness, solidarity and assertiveness among black people. Biko's ideas were part of the inspiration behind the Soweto protests of 1976.

- Biko was thrown out of university in 1972 on account of political activities which included the organisation of strikes on university campuses which led to 600 student arrests.

- He soon ran into trouble with the security forces and was banned, arrested, put on trial, re-arrested and ultimately bludgeoned to death in a police cell.

- Steve Biko helped to change the way that black people thought about themselves, encouraging them to continue the struggle against oppression with renewed hope and vigour.

The most important challenge to the apartheid state between 1966 and 1980 occurred in Soweto, a black township about ten miles outside Johannesburg. In 1976 over half the population was under 20 years of age and many of the young people were inspired by Steve Biko's Black Consciousness movement. On 16 June thousands of black schoolchildren demonstrated against the latest government instruction that half their subjects be taught in Afrikaans. This was widely regarded as the language of oppression and white supremacy. The protests became nationwide after the police shot and killed a thirteen-year-old African boy and then responded with tear gas and further gunfire. According to official estimates at least 575 people had been killed of whom 134 were under the age of eighteen.

▲ **Fig. 13.12** Rioting in Soweto

News of the violence swept around the world causing shock and outrage at the inhumanity and brutality of the apartheid regime. There were immediate falls in gold and diamond shares as investors began to take fright. Thousands of Africans fled across the borders and into Mozambique, Tanzania and Angola where they trained as guerrilla fighters. Resistance to the apartheid state had become both more widespread and more violent.

SOURCE 7

Entry dated 8 September 1977 from the "Occurrence Book" at Bakenstraat Police Station. This report was supplied to the inquest into the death of Steve Biko.

Maj. Snyman reports that on 7/9/77 at about 07:00 he and Siebert and Beneke [all three being police officers] ... interrogated Stephen Bantu Biko. The detainee was extremely arrogant, went berserk, took one of the chairs in the office and threw it at Snyman. With his fists he then stormed at the other members and the other members overwhelmed him. After a violent struggle, he fell with his head against the wall and with his body on the floor and in this process he received injuries on the lip and body. Warrant-Officer Beneke received an elbow injury and nonetheless did not go off duty. The district surgeon was informed and visited the detainee.

SOURCE 8

Major Snyman's evidence given to the Truth and Reconciliation Commission on 10 September 1997 regarding the instructions he received about how to account for the injuries sustained by Steve Biko during the police interrogation.

Col. Goosen [Snyman's superior] explained that the death of Biko was a great embarrassment to the security branch and the South African Government or could be a great embarrassment. It was clear that this event would have a negative impact on the image of South Africa abroad and that perhaps this could lose foreign investments for the country ... Col. Goosen explained ... that the matter had to be managed in such a way that the interests of the security branch and the South African Government could be protected. During this meeting there were instructions for everyone involved that the true facts with regard to this incident had to be adapted or simply not mentioned.

TASKS

1. What does Source 7 tell you about the circumstances in which Steve Biko received his bodily injuries during the police interrogation? Support your answer with reference to the source.

2. How far does Source 8 suggest that the South African Police had the true interests of South Africa at heart during the apartheid era?

3. Is one source more useful than the other as evidence about the activities of the South African Police with regard to the death of Steve Biko? Explain your answer.

How far did economic factors improve lives by 1980?

The South African economy was prospering for most of the period 1966 to 1980. In most years national economic growth rates averaged between 6 and 7 per cent. South African firms could earn profits of up to 25 per cent in 1980 and the value of firms operating in South Africa grew by 400 per cent during the 1970s. It did not follow from this, however, that the majority of the population benefited from the economic good times. South Africa had an exceptionally unequal distribution of wealth and income—almost certainly the most unequal in the world.

The main beneficiaries of the booming economy were the whites who enjoyed rising standards of living, high standards of health care and increasing life expectancy. In particular the white farmers, most of whom were Afrikaners, received massive state support which they used to mechanise their farms and increase output.

For black South Africans the story was very different. Indeed, the success of the South African economy was, to a large extent, built on the foundations of low labour costs. Until the early 1970s the income gap between black and white employees continued to widen: in 1970, white manufacturing and construction workers earned approximately six times what black workers could earn and white mineworkers earned 21 times as much as blacks. There were some improvements during the 1970s and the wages of blacks began to rise as a result of competition between employers for experienced workers. This meant that income gap between whites and blacks began to narrow but it still remained high. Blacks were also badly affected by a steep rise in unemployment during the 1970s such that by 1977 about 26 per cent of blacks were unemployed. The human cost of these statistics was an increase in poverty, malnutrition and disease.

The plight of many blacks can be illustrated from the state of the Homelands where more than half of the population of blacks South Africans were living by 1980. The population densities in some of these crowded territories rose to disastrous levels. The 1980 population densities per square kilometre for Transkei, Ciskei and Qwaqwa, for example, were 55, 82 and 298 respectively. The white areas in the Cape had a corresponding population density of 2. In practical terms this meant that agricultural cultivation was impossible in the Homelands and their landscapes became marked by deforestation and dust bowl conditions. The majority of the population lived below the poverty level and suffered from high levels of infant and child mortality as a result of inadequate nutrition.

Hence the impressive economic performance of South Africa up to 1980 resulted in health, happiness and the good life for much of the white population but under-nourishment, squalor and early death for many of those who made up the majority population of blacks.

What was the impact of external opposition to apartheid?

The United Nations

After 1966 the system of apartheid in South Africa came under increasing international criticism. The principal mouthpiece for this criticism was the United Nations whose General Assembly had been passing annual resolutions condemning apartheid since 1952. By 1967 the General Assembly had set up a Special Committee on Apartheid together with a Unit on Apartheid which produced publications which drew attention to the nature and effects of racism in South Africa. In 1973 the General Assembly declared apartheid to be "a crime against humanity" and four years later the Security Council passed a resolution calling for an arms embargo against South Africa.

The Organisation for African Unity

There was also mounting criticism of apartheid within Africa itself as the process of decolonisation swept across the continent. Between 1966 and 1968 three neighbours of South Africa gained their independence from Britain—Lesotho, Botswana and Swaziland. In 1975, following a coup in Lisbon, Angola and Mozambique gained their independence from Portugal. These events helped to swell the membership of the Organisation of African Unity (OAU) founded in 1963. The OAU had set up a Liberation Committee with headquarters in Tanzania which provided refugees from South Africa with education and military training.

Muldergate

Such developments could not be ignored by the South African government. It devoted considerable time, energy and resources to foreign propaganda in order to minimise the effects of the anti-apartheid criticism and gain favourable comment in the foreign press and media. It was in connection with this activity that John Vorster had to resign. The 'Muldergate' scandal was named after Dr Mulder, the Information Minister. His department had secretly used £40 million of government money to win influence abroad through bribes and the purchase of luxury flats to entertain journalists, politicians and other influential persons.

What are sanctions?

- Sanctions can take many forms. They are designed to force a government to alter course. They can be imposed by a government or an organisation.

- Economic sanctions involve refusing to trade with a country or offer it loans. If a country relies upon international trade for its economic wellbeing this can cause considerable inconvenience.

- The only successful sanctions levied against South Africa before 1980 concerned sport.

- The 1970 South African Cricket tour to England was cancelled by the MCC (Marylebone Cricket Club) and by the 1977 Gleneagles Agreement in Scotland, the Commonwealth banned sporting contacts with South Africa.

- From the mid-1980s economic sanctions against South Africa became increasingly effective as both the United States and the EEC (European Economic Community) took action. An important landmark came in 1985 when the American Chase Manhattan Bank refused to lend any further money to South Africa until apartheid was ended.

Sanctions

Yet given the very substantial international condemnation of apartheid the South African government remained absolutely steadfast in its support for the apartheid system. This was largely because the criticism consisted merely of words rather than words and deeds. If, for example, comprehensive trade sanctions had been imposed on South Africa the South African government might have been forced to alter course since South Africa had no oil reserves, depended upon foreign capital and relied upon imports both for advanced technology and for heavy plant and equipment. The reasons for inaction on the part of the international community concern trade and business, South Africa's economic and military dominance of southern Africa and international politics.

Trade and business

If effective economic sanctions had been imposed on South Africa these would have had a double-edged effect. Certainly South Africa depended on trading links with the rest of the world but then the world economy depended upon South Africa for a broad range of essential minerals as indicated in Table 13.4. In addition to these minerals South Africa was also a major producer of gem diamonds and an important producer of asbestos, coal, copper, iron, nickel and zinc.

Another reason for not imposing sanctions was the fact that South Africa was a major focus for American, Japanese and European investment. By 1978 some $26.3 billion of foreign capital was invested in South Africa. A principal reason for this was the excellent investment returns. American returns averaged 14 per cent between 1976 and 1978. Of course these profits were partly due to the low labour costs which resulted from the apartheid system.

Governments of industrialised nations felt compromised by calls for the imposition of sanctions against South Africa and reluctant to take actions which would have damaged their national interests.

Mineral	%	Applications
Gold	60	Jewellery, Investments, Electronics
Platinum Group of Metals	47	Car Exhausts, Oil Refineries
Chromium	33	Steel Production
Vanadium	42	Steel Production

▲ **Table 13.4** South Africa's share of world mineral production in 1979

South Africa's economic and military dominance of southern Africa

While all of South Africa's neighbours would have liked to take action to end apartheid they were not in a position to do so. South Africa was the dominant military power in the region and most of its neighbours depended on it for economic survival. Lesotho, for example, was entirely surrounded by South African territory and its main source of wealth came from the wages its population earned in South African mines, factories and farms. Botswana and Swaziland were also partially surrounded by South African territory and would not have been able to resist effectively an attack by South African forces. Zambia imported food from South Africa and depended upon South African railways and ports for most of its overseas trade.

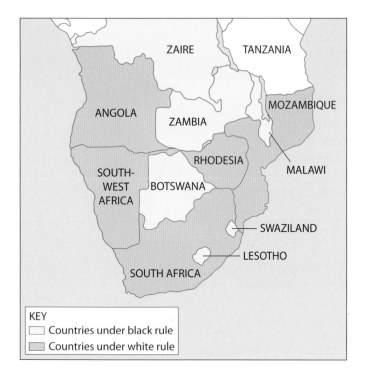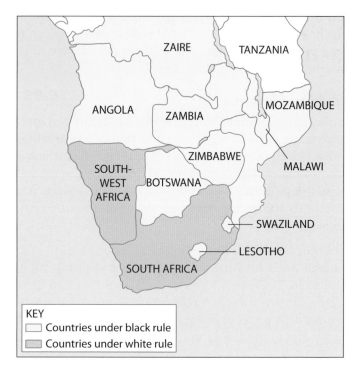

▲ **Fig. 13.13** The changing face of southern Africa

International politics

Opposition to apartheid became entangled with Cold War issues. After the Second World War most of the world divided into either the capitalist group of nations, led by the United States, or the communist bloc led by Soviet Russia. The two superpowers were engaged in a struggle for power, influence and control of resources which involved Europe, parts of Asia, the Middle East and Africa. South Africa was firmly in the capitalist camp and considerable amounts of South African government propaganda were directed at presenting attempts to end white supremacy as a communist-inspired movement. It was true that the ANC had close links with Soviet Russia which provided education and training for South African refugees and was the main supplier of arms for the MK, the military arm of the ANC. But the ANC was not a communist organisation neither were prominent members such as Tambo and Mandela communists. Nevertheless, American and other western leaders regarded support for sanctions as much the same thing as support for the communist cause. This was because sanctions were bound to weaken the position of the South African government. It was unthinkable that the Cape should fall under communist influence or that Soviet Russia should gain control over South Africa's mineral wealth. The best way of ensuring that this did not happen, as far as many western nations were concerned, was by opposing sanctions.

Why did white minority rule come to an end?

What were the effects of the policies of P. W. Botha?

P. W. Botha became Prime Minister in 1978 following the resignation of John Vorster. Botha wanted to uphold the apartheid regime but realised that the current system was not working. In particular, it was failing to deliver enough trained black workers for industry. Botha clearly felt that his country was under siege both from enemies abroad and within South Africa. He described South Africa's predicament as "Total Onslaught" for which he intended to apply the solution of "Total Strategy". At home this involved following a dual policy of rigorously enforcing the law while introducing very moderate reform in order to blunt the opposition to apartheid. Abroad this meant raiding ANC bases, carrying out political assassinations and exploiting western concerns about the threat of communism.

Trade Union reform

- This followed a period of increasing industrial militancy as illegal black unions were formed during the 1970s.

- Employers wanted a definite and recognised body with which to negotiate and were upset by the number of unofficial strikes. They also wanted an end to job reservations for whites as they were suffering from shortages of skilled labour.

- Consequently from 1979 black trade unions were recognised by law and given access to the industrial court together with the right to strike. Job reservations for white workers were abolished.

- The legislation backfired on the government as the black trade unions gave black Africans useful experience in democratic organisation and the new unions became increasingly militant: whereas in 1974, 14 167 working days had been lost this had risen to 365 337 in 1982, just over one million in 1986 and to nearly six million days in 1987.

Constitutional reform

- A new constitution came into force in 1984.

- The new South African Parliament consisted of three chambers: a House of Assembly comprising 178 white members elected by whites; a House of Representatives comprising 85 coloured members elected by coloureds; and a House of Delegates comprising 45 Asian members elected by Asians. This meant that when joint sessions were held the whites held a majority of up to 48 members.

- A State President, elected mainly by whites, selected a cabinet from members of the three chambers.

- If Botha hoped that the new constitution would look like power sharing and win the support of the 2.6 million coloureds or the 800 000 Asians he was soon to be disappointed. Approximately 40 per cent of coloureds and Asians could not be bothered to register and of those who did only 30 per cent of coloureds and 20 per cent of Asians voted in the first elections.

- Black Africans who made up 75 per cent of the population of South Africa were not included in the new arrangements although they were allowed to elect local councils. The new constitution further soured relations between blacks and the South African regime.

Reform of the Pass Laws and changes in urban living restrictions

- By the mid-1980s the government finally realised that it could not hope to prevent the movement of blacks from the Homelands to the urban areas. This was because the Homelands were incapable of sustaining their populations and Africans were forced to leave if they wanted to survive. In 1986 the government repealed the pass laws.

- It also proved impossible to enforce the Group Areas Act which banned non-whites from living in white areas. By 1986 a quarter of residents in three white Johannesburg suburbs were Asian or black. In the same year Botha extended the permit system which allowed Asians and blacks to live in certain white suburbs.

- While these reforms may have been a movement in the right direction they were unlikely to satisfy many non-whites who continued to suffer massive disadvantages in the jobs and housing markets. Whites were more likely to be employed, more likely to be fairly paid and more likely to be housed in good accommodation.

Education reform

- While Botha was not prepared to introduce a single desegregated educational system he did increase spending on schools for non-whites.

- Unfortunately most of the new money was absorbed by the expanding school population and there was little change to per capita spending. Conditions remained poor with large classes, under-qualified teachers and shortages of teaching resources and equipment. In 1986 the government was still spending seven times as much to educate a white child than a black child.

- Following the Soweto riots black school children were becoming a significant element in the anti-apartheid movement. The government had missed an opportunity to gain the support of this potentially troublesome section of the population.

Petty apartheid

- Some of the segregation laws were repealed during the 1980s including the bans on interracial sex and marriage.

- Many hotels, restaurants, trains, buses and public facilities such as cinemas were desegregated.

- Sports fixtures were allowed to take place between teams of different races.

- Examples of petty apartheid remained, however, including most swimming pools and public toilets.

- Blacks may have been admitted to hotels and restaurants but few could afford to go there in any case.

The overall impact of these reforms on the non-whites was not what Botha expected. The new constitution met with large-scale opposition from non-white groups who combined to form the United Democratic Front (UDF). Collectively the reforms raised expectations but failed to deliver what non-whites were demanding—the abolition of the entire apartheid system and the introduction of one person one vote.

For the white population of South Africa the reactions were more varied. Moderates together with many businessmen and industrialists supported Botha's reforms. Hardliners felt that Botha was undermining the apartheid state and broke away from the National Party to form the Conservative Party of South Africa in 1982. In the 1987 general election the Conservative Party polled 26 per cent of the vote. Even more extreme was the Afrikaner Resistance Movement, led by Eugene Terreblanche, which used swastika-like emblems and made it quite clear that its members were prepared to fight to preserve white supremacy.

What was the significance of individual leaders in the collapse of apartheid?

Oliver Tambo (1917–1993)

Oliver Tambo was one of the most influential post-war leaders of the ANC who helped transform the organisation into a radical national freedom movement. Following the Sharpeville massacre Tambo was sent by the ANC to travel abroad to establish ANC offices in foreign capitals and to help mobilise international opinion against the apartheid system. By 1990 there were 27 of these unofficial embassies in various African and European countries. During the 1970s Tambo addressed the United Nations and other international gatherings on the subject of apartheid helping to raise the prestige and status of the ANC to that of an alternative South African Government. Tambo was President of the ANC between 1967 and 1991. It was he who in 1985 told people in the townships to make South Africa ungovernable. Perhaps more than any other leading figure he helped to hold the ANC together during the later years of apartheid.

Joe Slovo (1926–1995)

Joe Slovo was a white defence lawyer, active communist and leading ideas-man for the ANC. In 1963 he fled South Africa to spend 27 years in exile. He helped to found the Umkhonto we Sizwe (MK), the military wing of the ANC and in the late 1970s he masterminded a large number of MK operations in South Africa from Mozambique. In 1985 Slovo became the first white member of the ANC national executive. After 1990 Slovo became a key negotiator between the various anti-apartheid groups and the National Party. He was personally responsible for a "sunset clause" which provided an element of protection for whites under the interim constitution.

Desmond Tutu (1931–)

Desmond Tutu was an articulate and tireless campaigner against apartheid which he denounced as "evil and unchristian". In particular, he campaigned in favour of equal rights for all South Africans, a common system of education, abolition of the hated pass laws and an end to forced relocation to the Homelands. As a prominent Anglican priest (his positions included Bishop of Johannesburg, Archbishop of Cape Town and Secretary-General of the South African Council of Churches) his views on such matters as economic sanctions, which he favoured strongly, and a peaceful reconciliation between all parties involved in apartheid, was guaranteed a worldwide audience. In 1984 Tutu was awarded the Nobel Prize for Peace. He played a major role in persuading whites that they would not become the victims of revenge in a new South Africa but would be treated with fairness and consideration.

F. W. de Klerk (1936–)

F. W. de Klerk was the first South African president to accept that apartheid was not working and had to be dismantled. He also accepted that a new political system, based on non-racial democratic principles, was essential to avoid South Africa tearing itself apart. While de Klerk vigorously defended the position of the white community, as he was expected to do, he also possessed sufficient flexibility and political vision to put first the interests of his country as a whole. De Klerk was desperate to avoid South Africa becoming engulfed by civil war and persevered with the peace discussions in the face of some provocation from those on the extremist wing of the ANC and a deteriorating relationship with Nelson Mandela. De Klerk's achievement was to help steer South Africa away from white supremacy, with the support of the majority of whites, towards a new phase in its history. For this task he was awarded the 1993 Nobel Peace Prize, together with Mandela, for his role in ending apartheid.

Mangosuthu Buthelezi (1928–)

Mangosuthu Buthelezi was one of the most enigmatic, controversial and divisive members of the anti-apartheid movement. Although a member of the ANC Youth League between 1948–50 he later left the ANC becoming Chief Minister of the Zulu homeland of KwaZulu. For this decision he was bitterly criticised as being a collaborator of the National Government. Yet during the 1970s Buthelezi was also party to a declaration which called for the peaceful pursuit of political change together with a Bill of Rights. After 1990 Buthelezi represented the Inkatha Freedom Party and supported the idea of a federal republic to protect the ethnic rights of the Zulus and his own personal political position. At first he refused to participate in the negotiations leading up to the 1994 election, thereby sparking off a serious outbreak of violence and killings between ANC and IFP supporters. Buthelezi changed his mind at the last moment.

Nelson Mandela (1918–2013)

Nelson Mandela was the principal negotiator, representing the ANC, in the talks leading up to the 1994 election after which he became President of South Africa. Mandela had a clear and firm strategy during these talks which was to end the apartheid system and establish a new constitution. The latter would provide for one person, one vote within a united South Africa. He also wanted reconciliation between the different ethnic groups so that whites remained within the country and continued to apply their managerial and technical skills. Mandela was not, therefore, against making minor concessions to whites providing his overall strategy remained in place. Like de Klerk, Mandela also faced provocations during the discussions, this time from white extremists who wanted to undermine the peace process. Mandela was appalled, especially when he realised that there were links between the government and the extremists, but he kept his eye on the ultimate objective of black majority rule. Mandela attracted considerable praise for refusing to allow any bitterness or desire for revenge, as a result of his long years of imprisonment, to affect his desire for a fair and just settlement for all South Africans. Mandela died in December 2013, aged 95.

QUICK QUESTION 4

Explain what the sunshine clauses were.

QUICK QUESTION 5

Which three of these six people won the Nobel Peace Prize at some point in their lives? Why?

QUICK QUESTION 6

Which of the six individuals had the biggest impact abroad in changing opinion about apartheid?

Why did violence increase between 1980 and the early 1990s?

From the time of the Soweto riots of 1976 violence and unrest was never far below the surface in many of the African townships. In September 1984, however, there was a new surge of mass protest and violence in parts of the Vaal Triangle to the south of Johannesburg as a reaction to the imposition of increased rents and electricity charges. Exploiting the new levels of community discontent the ANC called for people to "Make apartheid unworkable! Make the country ungovernable!"

There was a speedy reaction to this request and the black local government system in the townships broke down as a result of attacks on government buildings and assassinations against black councillors and police who were regarded as collaborators with the apartheid system. Many resigned their positions but the violence continued with protestors using the necklace (a burning tyre placed around the victim's neck) as a murder weapon.

School boycotts protesting against substandard teachers and resources added to the confusion such that in the words of one government minister South Africa was "at the edge of anarchy and bloody revolution" by the early summer of 1985.

▲ **Fig. 13.14** Suspected police informant saved from "necklacing"

Causes of the new violence

This upsurge in violence had causes that went considerably beyond the specific issues involved such as rents, electricity charges or shortages of school textbooks.

- The most obvious underlying cause was continued opposition to the apartheid system combined with outrage and disappointment at Botha's new constitutional reforms; these excluded blacks altogether from national politics and placed the other non-white groups in an inferior position. It was quite clear by 1984 that the government had no intention of moving towards a genuinely democratic political system.

- In such a free and democratic political system opposition could be voiced in the media, on the streets and in the ballot box. None of these options were available to blacks in South Africa at this time. Violence may have appeared to be the only way of making a difference.

- There can also be little doubt that the community violence was a response to very considerable violence, torture and murder deployed by the government security services. Police killings, many of them shootings at funerals and protest marches, increased from less than 100 in 1984 to more than 500 in 1985.

- This state-sponsored violence became even easier to commit when President Botha declared a State of Emergency in 1985 in order to try and regain control over South Africa. The government was given sweeping new powers which included new restrictions on press reporting and taking pictures of the unrest. Civil liberties were suspended so that the authorities could resort to arrests without warrants, detentions and treason trials—unofficial estimates put the number of people detained under the emergency regulations as high as 29 000, many of whom were children. There were reports of intimidation of suspects and the widespread use of torture and violence involving beatings, electric shocks and strangulation.

- After 1980 attacks by the ANC on government buildings and power installations from bases outside Africa were easier to carry out with the ending of white rule in Rhodesia now renamed Zimbabwe. In 1981 the ANC launched over 80 armed attacks. Between June 1986 and September 1988 the ANC was allegedly responsible for more than a hundred explosions causing 31 deaths and 565 injuries in various city-centre streets, restaurants, cinemas, shops and sporting venues.

- Some of the violence may have had little to do with the struggle for political freedom. Among the black population of South Africa there were tribal jealousies and rivalries particularly between the Xhosa tribe and the Zulus. The general lawlessness almost certainly provided an opportunity for the settling of tribal scores and quarrels.

By 1989 there was a state of deadlock if not civil war. The government was unable to re-establish control over the black townships yet the opposition to apartheid was unable to overthrow the government. The verdict of many businessmen and industrialists was to leave South Africa altogether. Firms that pulled out at this time included Barclays, Esso, IBM, Peugeot and Pepsi Cola.

Internal unrest and deteriorating economic prospects were not the only problems facing the South African government. As a result of the ending of the Cold War in the late 1980s South Africa was no longer useful to the west as an anti-communist ally. The isolation of the apartheid regime was almost complete and these circumstances reinforced the need for constructive negotiations as recognised by both the government and the ANC.

SOURCE 10

From an article by an Afrikaner journalist in 1990.

Pieter Botha was certainly more reasonable than any of the earlier National Party leaders. He recognised blacks as permanent residents of white cities and granted them the right to own houses and land in the townships. He permitted the rise of a real black opposition and allowed trade unions to organise openly. He got rid of some of the worst apartheid laws and offered a vote of sorts to the Coloureds and Indians. To pay for this and other reforms he taxed the whites heavily. As a result his party split.

SOURCE 9

From a speech by Reverend Allan Boesak, a leading anti-apartheid activist, at the beginning of the United Democratic Front in 1983.

*We want our rights here in a united, undivided South Africa. We do not want them in poor homelands. We want all our rights, we want them here and we want them **NOW**. We have been jailed, exiled, killed for too long. **NOW** is the time.*

TASKS

1. What can you tell from Source 9 about the United Democratic Front? Support your answer with reference to the source.

2. How far does Source 10 show that President Botha was willing to end the dominance of the white minority? Explain your answer.

3. Is one of these sources more useful than the other as evidence about the strength of opposition to apartheid in the 1980s? Explain your answer.

To what extent was there a smooth transition of power between 1989 and 1994?

In August 1989 President Botha resigned following a stroke. He was replaced by F. W. de Klerk who had served as one of the more conservative-minded members of his cabinet. From this point until May 1994 South Africa made the change from white majority to black majority rule.

Prior to the point that he became President, de Klerk was regarded as a defender of the apartheid regime. But he was also a political realist and, soon after taking office, took the view that apartheid was effectively finished in South Africa. He thought this because of the appalling violence in the townships, the deteriorating economy and the absence of friends and allies abroad.

De Klerk stood at the political crossroads in 1989. One route led to yet more repression, civil war, economic catastrophe and a declining quality of life. The other involved the ending of apartheid, negotiations and the establishment of a new political system. The former route was one of despair, the latter held out some hope for the future. De Klerk felt that he had little choice if he had the best interests of his country at heart.

De Klerk's early initiatives are summarised below:

September 1989	During General Election campaign de Klerk promised that apartheid would be reformed.
September 1989	A march for peace and the ending of apartheid, involving 30 000 demonstrators, held in Cape Town, was allowed to go ahead.
October 1989	Walter Sisulu released from jail.
February 1990	Unbanning of ANC, PAC and the Communist Party; release of political prisoners who had been jailed for non-violent offences and the suspension of capital punishment; unconditional release of Nelson Mandela after 27 years of imprisonment.

▲ Table 13.5

From May 1990 onwards there were discussions between de Klerk and Mandela concerning the future of South Africa. Ultimately these discussions led to South Africa's first democratic election held on 27 April 1994. In the meantime, however, the talks were conducted against a backcloth of continued violence and killings and attempts by both sides to undermine the peace process in order to gain political advantage. In the five year period between 1990 and 1994 there were, on average, more than 3 200 deaths per year due to political violence. This violence reflected the complexities and seemingly irreconcilable issues facing the chief negotiators.

Problems facing de Klerk

- Although de Klerk had won a parliamentary majority in the 1989 general election his National Party polled less than half the popular vote. To the right of the National Party was the Conservative Party which polled 31 per cent and wanted a return to full apartheid. Even within the National Party there were members who believed that de Klerk was betraying the whites and wanted the government to fight for a military victory over the opposition. De Klerk regained the initiative over his critics by holding a referendum, for or against the peace process, among the white electorate in March 1992. A clear majority, 68.7 per cent, supported de Klerk's policy.

- There was also the problem of de Klerk maintaining control over his own security forces that, on a number of occasions, took the law into their own hands and carried out killings, kidnappings, torture and other atrocities. An early example of this occurred in March 1990 when police gunned down eleven demonstrators at Sebokeng, thirty miles south of Johannesburg.

- Mandela became convinced that a government-backed "Third Force," consisting of men from the security services, was acting to disrupt the talks and show that blacks were unfit to rule. It was suspected, and later proved true, that this "Third Force" was deliberately stoking up trouble between the ANC and Inkatha. On 17 June 1992 armed Inkatha supporters killed 46 residents of the black township of Boipatong. It was alleged that police trucks had brought the assassins to the township; certainly the security forces had done nothing to prevent the massacre or bring those responsible to justice. De Klerk denied all knowledge of government involvement in such events but many suspected otherwise.

Problems facing Mandela

- In much the same way that de Klerk was unable to speak for all whites so Mandela was unable to speak for all blacks. There were members of the ANC who opposed the negotiations fearing that Mandela would make too many concessions to the whites. Instead they would have preferred to concentrate on the armed struggle to secure victory. Mandela was opposed to this approach since he thought that the country would be torn apart and the whites, many of whom were essential for the economic wellbeing of South Africa, would leave the country.

- Perhaps Mandela's main problem concerned Chief Buthelezi, Prime Minister of KwaZulu, one of the Homelands, and head of Inkatha. Buthelezi was a Zulu nationalist and hoped to make KwaZulu an independent state. This was at odds with Mandela's ambitions for a unified South Africa. Friction between Inkatha and the ANC sometimes escalated into violence that threatened to destroy the sometimes fragile relationship between Mandela and de Klerk. Mandela refused to be blown off course by these serious distractions, however, and ultimately persuaded Buthelezi to participate in the elections.

The Interim Constitution

- During 1993 and early 1994 the National Party, the ANC and other groups agreed on an interim constitution under which South Africa would be ruled by a Government of National Unity.

- There was a form of power sharing for five years whereby any party with over 5 per cent of the vote would be able to have a seat in the cabinet and any party with over 20 per cent of the vote would be able to appoint a Deputy President.

- No party would have the right of veto, as wanted by the whites, but any new constitution would have to have support of at least 66 per cent of the members of parliament.

- These arrangements were accompanied by a Bill of Rights and guarantees for the jobs and pensions of whites working in the civil service, judiciary, police and army.

The April 1994 elections

These were the first democratic elections to be held in South Africa with some 16 million blacks allowed to vote for the first time. The ANC won a convincing victory with 62.5 per cent of the vote. The National Party polled 20.5 per cent and Inkatha won 10.5 per cent. In May, Nelson Mandela became President and de Klerk a Deputy President. Buthelezi became a minister in Mandela's government. Shortly afterwards, in a spirit of reconciliation, Mandela declared to his supporters "This is a time to heal the old wounds and build a new South Africa".

▲ **Fig. 13.15** A British cartoon about the ending of apartheid showing de Klerk and Mandela published in 1993

SOURCE 11

From President de Klerk's televised speech to Parliament in 1990.

The prohibition of the ANC, the PAC and the Communist Party is now ended without conditions. These organisations over the years have alleged that they resorted to violence because the Government did not wish to talk to them. This justification for violence exists no longer – the Government wishes to talk to all leaders who seek peace. The time for talking has arrived and whoever still makes excuses does not really wish to talk.

SOURCE 12

From Nelson Mandela's autobiography published in 1994.

At the end of March 1994 thousands of Inkatha members armed with spears and other weapons marched through Johannesburg and an Inkatha group attacked the ANC headquarters. Fifty-three people died and it seemed South Africa was on the brink of internal war. Mr de Klerk and I were determined that Inkatha would not succeed in postponing the election and they did not. The ANC won 62 per cent of the vote in the April election. Mr de Klerk made a gracious speech ending three centuries of white minority rule. At every opportunity I said all South Africans must now join hands and say we are one country, one nation, one people, marching together into the future.

QUICK QUESTION 7

In Figure 13.15. why does the cartoonist show de Klerk and Mandela holding a park bench?

QUICK QUESTION 8

What is the main message of the cartoon in Figure 13.15?

TASKS

1. What can you tell from Source 11 about President de Klerk? Support your answer with reference to the source.

2. How far does Source 12 show that by 1994 South Africans were willing to work together to make 'one country, one nation'? Explain your answer.

3. Is one of these sources more useful than the other as evidence about the ending of white minority rule? Explain your answer.

► The segregation era, 1910–48, and the nature of white rule.

► The apartheid state, 1948–89.

► The transition to a new non-racial, democratic political system, 1989–94.

Revision tips

- For the segregation era you need to be familiar with the details of the various Acts (Natives Land Act, 1913, Native Urban Areas Act, 1923, etc.) whereby segregation was introduced. You also need to be able to explain the nature of the migrant labour system and the pass laws. Make sure you understand why black resistance to segregation achieved so little during this period. How did the Second World War alter the balance between blacks and whites?

- You need to understand why and how the National Government introduced a policy of apartheid. This will include a working knowledge of the key pieces of legislation discussed in the text. You must be familiar with the opposition to apartheid and the government response to this opposition. You should also revise the Defiance Campaign, The Freedom Charter, the Treason Trial of 1956–61 and Steve Biko's Black Consciousness Movement. Sharpeville and Soweto are also key topics.

- Make sure you understand how and why apartheid began to unravel beginning with the moderate reforms of P. W. Botha and leading on to the radical initiatives of de Klerk. The importance of external opposition and economic sanctions will be very important. You will need to be able to explain why, despite apparent improvements, violence increased during this period. You will also need to understand the motivations behind the actions of Chief Buthelezi. The roles of Mandela and de Klerk are pivotal in understanding the transition to a new political system between 1990 and 1994.

Review questions

1. What restrictions were placed on the political rights of non-whites in South Africa between 1910 and 1948?

2. Why did the political fortunes of the Nationalist Party recover so dramatically between 1943 and 1948?

3. What was the Black Sash?

4. What were Bantustans?

5. Explain the role of Steve Biko in the fight against apartheid.

6. "Apartheid was a completely successful system for the benefit of South Africa's white population between 1948 and the early 1970s". How far do you agree with this view? Explain your answer.

7. What sanctions were imposed on South Africa before 1980?

8. How did Mandela and de Klerk contribute to the ending of apartheid in South Africa?

9. Why did it become increasingly difficult to enforce the system of apartheid after the mid-1970s?

10. How important were international factors in the ending of apartheid in South Africa?

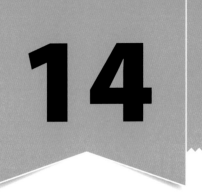

14 Israelis and Palestinians since 1945

Introduction

The land know as Palestine or Israel finds itself at the centre of a conflict based around religious claims, being regarded as a holy land for Jews, Christians and Muslims, and geopolitics. The land is at a key point, guarding access to Syria, Lebanon, the Mediterranean and Egypt. Since 1945, this conflict has resulted in three major wars, almost constant low-level terrorism, numerous political assassinations, and the failure of either superpower to bring about a sense of order to the region.

From the sixteenth century until the end of the First World War, the Middle East was governed by the Ottoman (Turkish) Empire. The Turks sided with Germany and Austro-Hungary during that conflict, and Britain and France made promises to both Arab and Jewish leaders that they would provide them with respective homelands in the Middle East in return for their support during the war.

Britain's failure to act on either guarantee undermined its credibility with both groups; something which made it very difficult to maintain a presence in Palestine after the end of the Second World War. A bitter civil war between Arabs and Jews broke out in 1947, which developed into a major conflict after the formal declaration of the state of Israel in May 1948. The legacy of this war, with Israeli expansion, huge numbers of Palestinian refugees, and resentful Arab neighbours lasts to the present day. In spite of the best efforts of numerous US presidents Israeli prime ministers and Arab leaders, no settlement is in sight, and the fate of Palestinian people looks no nearer to being resolved.

This chapter outlines the long-term origins of the conflict, before looking in detail at not only the causes and effects of military actions during the period, but many attempts to resolve the conflict through bargaining and diplomacy rather than with bullets and devastation.

The aims of this chapter are to:

- Consider the Arab and Jewish peoples of Palestine with regards to differences in culture, race, and language, as well as the aftermath of the Second World War including Jewish immigration, Jewish nationalism and the ending of the British mandate.

- Look at Israel and its Arab neighbours including the Suez War (1956), the Six-Day War (1967), and the Yom Kippur War (1973), and Israeli incursions into Lebanon.

- Examine moves towards peace, Camp David and subsequent negotiations, and the position of the Palestinians including the refugee problem, Palestinian nationalism and the formation of the PLO, activities of the PLO and international acceptance, the role of Arafat, relations between the PLO and Arab states, and relations with Israel and moves towards the creation of a Palestinian state.

- Study the state of Israel including social organisation, the experiences of men and woman in national service, and the kibbutz.

- Consider relations between Jews and Arabs within Israel and the occupied territories, problems of new Jewish settlements, and differing viewpoints among Israelis on dealing with Arab neighbours.

- Explain how differing beliefs among Palestinian groups in the 1980s and 1990s have impacted upon the peace process.

How was the Jewish state of Israel established?

FP What were the causes of conflict between Jews and Arabs in Palestine?

The conflict between Israelis and Palestinians comes from longstanding historical claims which both groups have on land in the Middle East. The Jews can trace their occupation of Palestine to approximately 1000 BCE, where they lived until being expelled by the Romans around 135 CE. The Muslims occupied the region from the seventh century as the Arab Empire spread throughout the Middle East and North Africa.

Whereas the Jews spread across Europe, the Arab Empire gradually declined and fell under the control of the Turks. However, by the end of the nineteenth century, with the Turkish Empire falling apart and the persecution of Jews in Europe increasing, both groups developed plans to create a homeland in Palestine.

Theodore Herzl's ideas gave rise to the development of **Zionism**, a movement which supported the creation of a Jewish state in Palestine. Between 1880 and 1914, approximately 60 000 Zionists left Europe and established lives in Palestine.

Zionism

A form of Jewish nationalism which supports the creation of a Jewish homeland in Palestine.

SOURCE 1

From *The Jewish State* by Theodor Herzl, 1896.

Palestine is our ever-memorable historic home. The very name of Palestine would attract our people with a force of marvellous potency. If His Majesty the Sultan were to give us Palestine, we could in return undertake to regulate the whole finances of Turkey. We should there form a portion of a rampart of Europe against Asia, an outpost of civilization as opposed to barbarism. We should as a neutral State remain in contact with all Europe, which would have to guarantee our existence.

The desire for self-determination was strong in Arab national identity and it consisted of strong anti-Turkish and anti-European colonialist elements. Rising levels of Jewish immigration and competition over land gave it a strong anti-Zionist element too. However, before the First World War, Arab nationalism struggled to present itself as a unified force due to regional and personality clashes.

It was British involvement in the First World War which gave hope to both Jews and Arabs that their aims would be fulfilled, and created further potential for conflict between them. The British offered to create an Arab homeland in return for assistance in the war against the Turks. At the same time, the British Foreign Secretary Arthur Balfour promised Lord Rothschild, a leading British

DISCUSSION

How far were other countries responsible for the emergence of Jewish and Arab nationalism before 1914?

Theodore Herzl

Hungarian journalist and author, and often referred to as the father founder of modern Zionism. He believed that anti-semitism would only be ended when the Jewish people had their own state.

Jew, that his government would support the creation of a Jewish homeland after the war.

At the end of the war, control over the region was passed to the British under the terms of a League of Nations mandate. Between 1919 and 1939, the British struggled to keep the peace with the Arabs who were resentful about the British "betrayal" at the end of the war and the large increase in Jewish settlers during the inter-war period. Zionists, meanwhile, feared that British strategy was aiming for the creation of an Arab state in Palestine and the obstruction of Jewish interests there.

Perhaps surprisingly, Arab–Jewish relations in the mandated territories were relatively smooth in the first few years after the mandate was created. However, Arab fears that Jews were attempting to seize control of Jerusalem's Wailing Wall in August 1929 caused a series of riots which left 133 Jews and 116 Arabs dead. The greatest impact of these riots was felt by the ancient Jewish community in Hebron: 67 people were murdered, forcing the British army to evacuate the remaining 484 survivors to Jerusalem for their own safety.

Unfortunately, the British government's reaction to the attacks further increased tension between the two groups, while increasing levels of Jewish immigration to Palestine further inflamed Arab opinion increasing levels of Jewish immigration further inflamed Arab opinion.

Date	Number of Jews	Jews as % of population
1918	60 000	9
1931	175 000	18
1939	429 000	28

▲ **Table 14.1** Increase in the size of the Jewish population of Palestine 1918–39

1936: the Arabs rose up against the British and started a revolt which lasted for three years.

1937: a British government report created a plan to partition the area into two states.

1939: with war in Europe looming, the British government produced a White Paper which attempted to pacify the Arabs. Its terms, which included no reference to partition, outraged Jews.

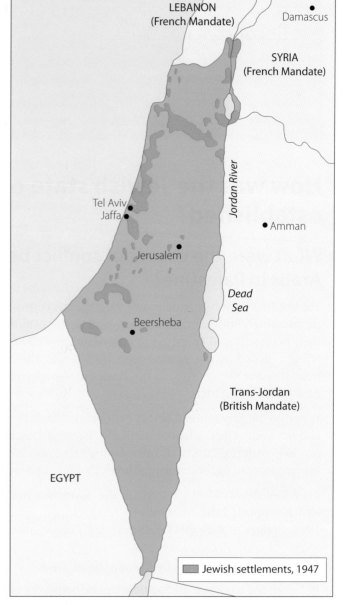

▲ **Fig. 14.1** The British mandate in Palestine

 Jewish settlements, 1947

DISCUSSION

How far was British policy to blame for the unrest in Palestine after the First World War?

TASKS

1. How did the First World War and its aftermath increase tension between Jews and Arabs in Palestine?

2. Explain what is meant by the term "League of Nations mandate".

3. In what ways did British policy in Palestine contribute to tension in the region?

4. Look at Source 1. Why was this source published in 1896? Answer this question by using details of the source and your own knowledge.

5. Why did Britain produce the White Paper in 1939?

What was the significance for Palestine of the end of the Second World War?

Palestine remained peaceful during the Second World War. This was due to several reasons.

- Most Arabs supported the terms of the White Paper. More extreme Arab nationalists, who opposed the plans, were undermined due to their links with Nazi Germany.

- Increased demand for food stimulated production and brought prosperity to the region.

- The Arabs were too divided to coordinate a further campaign against the British.

- Jewish settlers in Palestine believed that Britain had to be supported in its efforts to defeat Germany.

- The main Zionist militia, the Haganah, was keen to provide military assistance to the British so they could gain access to weapons and military training.

- After an initial increase during 1939–40, Jewish immigration fell sharply due to the German occupation of Europe.

- Haganah also assisted the British in hunting down Jewish terrorists who had assassinated Lord Moyne, the British Resident Minister for the Middle East in 1944.

- Approximately 20 000 Palestinian Jews enlisted in the British Army.

- Jewish leaders realised that US involvement in the conflict would increase their chances of creating a homeland once the war was over.

During the course of the war, both the British government and Jewish leaders made plans for the future of the Middle East after the war. The British plan, approved by the Cabinet in January 1944, included proposals for Jewish and Arab states, with Britain retaining a small area under its mandate. The Jewish plan, outlined by the World Zionist Organization at a conference in 1942, demanded the creation of a Jewish state in Palestine and unlimited Jewish immigration into the region.

SOURCE 2

Zionist leader, David Ben Gurion on the attitude of Jewish settlers at the outbreak of the Second World War.

We must assist the British in the war as if there were no White Paper and we must resist the White Paper as if there were no war.

David Ben Gurion

Polish-born Jewish leader, who became the first Prime Minister of Israel in 1948. He was prominent in establishing relations with West Germany and launching the 1956 war against Egypt.

SOURCE 3

Extract from the Biltmore Programme, adopted by the Extraordinary Zionist Conference at the Biltmore Hotel of New York City, 11 May 1942.

5. In the new values thus created, their Arab neighbours in Palestine have shared. The Jewish people in its own work of national redemption welcomes the economic, agricultural and national development of the Arab peoples and states. The Conference reaffirms the stand previously adopted at Congresses of the World Zionist Organization, expressing the readiness and the desire of the Jewish people for full cooperation with their Arab neighbours.

6. The Conference calls for the fulfillment of the original purpose of the Balfour Declaration and the Mandate which recognizing the historical connection of the Jewish people with Palestine was to afford them the opportunity, as stated by President Wilson, to found there a Jewish Commonwealth.

When the war was over, both Arabs and Jews once again felt that there were strong reasons for optimism.

Why did the Arabs believe that the creation of a homeland was likely after 1945?

- Prominent Arabs, such as King Abdullah of Transjordan and Ibn Saud of Saudi Arabia, had welcomed the 1939 White Paper and believed that its terms would be implemented after the war.

- The wartime British Foreign Secretary, Anthony Eden, was strongly opposed to partition and the creation of a Jewish state.

- The Arabs knew that Britain wanted to maintain access to oil in the region, and this would mean establishing good relations with Arab states.

- The leaders of Egypt, Lebanon, Iraq, Saudi Arabia, Syria, and Yemen formed the **Arab League** in March 1945. The aim was to coordinate the campaign to create an Arab state, and to resist both the creation of a Jewish state and increased Jewish immigration.

- By the end of the war, it was clear that Britain could no longer afford to maintain a large empire.

Why did Jews believe that the creation of a homeland was likely after 1945?

- The effects of the Holocaust had created considerable sympathy for the Jews, and increased support among political leaders for a Jewish homeland.

- The new Labour government, elected at the end of July 1945, was believed to be more sympathetic to the Zionist cause. In 1944, the Labour Party Conference stated its support for the creation of a Jewish homeland.

- The role of Haganah during the war was thought to have persuaded British politicians to support a Jewish homeland.

- Haganah's stockpiling of weapons, and the military experience gained during the war, was also thought to have placed the group in a strong position should it have to fight either Britain or Arabs to achieve its goals.

- The Democratic and Republican parties both endorsed the Biltmore programme in the 1944 US Presidential elections.

- President Truman, the new President of the United States, believed that European Jews should be able to establish a homeland in Palestine.

The ambitions of both Jews and Arabs were dented by Britain's reluctance to withdraw swiftly from the Middle East. Foreign Secretary Ernest Bevin's goal was to preserve a British trusteeship over a new Palestinian state, which would maintain British control over the eastern Mediterranean. However, three related developments conspired to obstruct his and Britain's intentions for the region.

- Britain's attempts to limit Jewish immigration provoked an international outcry. Bevin rejected David Ben Gurion's plea to allow 100 000 Holocaust survivors to enter Palestine, in defiance of President Truman's public support for Ben Gurion's request. Instead, Britain transported several illegal immigrants in Palestine back to Europe, detaining many of them in internment camps in Cyprus. In an attempt to create a political solution to the future of Palestine, Home Secretary Herbert Morrison and US Ambassador Henry Grady produced a report recommending the creation of a single Palestinian state. The state would contain separate Jewish and Arab

DISCUSSION

How far does the evidence from the period 1939–45 suggest that the supporters of a Jewish homeland believed they would only achieve their aims through violence?

Arab League

An organisation of Arab states designed to encourage collaboration between them and protect their interests in the region.

DISCUSSION

Would you agree that it was events in Europe rather than the Middle East which increased Jewish demands for a homeland?

provinces, and allow 1 000 000 Jewish immigrants to enter the new state within a year. President Truman not only refused to support the proposal, but actually outlined his own plans for a two state solution in October 1946.

- The United States' role in pushing Britain towards a swift withdrawal from Palestine was the second factor which contributed to the change in British policy. With Congressional mid-term elections approaching in November 1946, and under strong pressure from Zionist sympathisers in Congress, Truman pressurised the British to lift their limits on Jewish immigration and to accept a two state solution. The media in the United States even played its part: an American film crew recorded a British destroyer dragging the *Exodus*, a ship with 4,500 Jewish passengers who had escaped Europe but were sent back to Germany by the British on prison ships because they did not have permission to enter Palestine, into port at Haifa.

- Arguably the most important factor in Britain's decision to withdraw was the intensely violent campaign of terror waged by armed Jewish militants against British forces in Palestine. During the period 1946–8, approximately 220 British soldiers were killed by Jewish terrorists. While the three main Jewish groups differed in their tactics and attitude towards civilian casualties, they united under the banner of the Hebrew Resistance Movement in an attempt to force the British out of Palestine.

The Hebrew Resistance Movement

The Movement consisted of the following.

The Haganah The military wing of the Jewish Agency, it was initially reluctant to use violence against the British. It wanted to focus on attacking military targets and key elements of the infrastructure.

Irgun This represented a more radical from of Zionism. Led by a Polish Jew, Menachem Begin, it declared war on the mandate in 1944. Less reluctant to target civilians or Arabs, it was primarily responsible for the attack on the King David Hotel, 22 July 1946.

The Leh'i Created by Avraham Stern, who was killed by the British in 1942. It was responsible for the murder of Lord Moyne in 1944.

Examples of the movement's successes against the British:

31 October/1 November 1945 Simultaneous attack on British patrol boats, the railway network, and a goods yard.

25 February 1946 20 planes destroyed in an attack on 3 airfields.

25 April 1946 A Leh'i attack in Tel Aviv resulted in the death of seven British soldiers.

16/17 June 1946 All but one of the 11 road and rail bridges linking Palestine to its neighbours were destroyed.

22 July 1946 Attack on the King David Hotel, Jerusalem.

The most notorious act committed against the British was the attack on the King David Hotel in July 1946. The hotel served as the British administrative base in Palestine, and had been a longstanding target of Irgun and Leh'i. In response to a British crackdown on suspected Jewish terrorists, Irgun managed to bring down a whole wing of the hotel, killing 92 people in the process. Twenty-eight of the victims were British, 41 were Arab, and

SOURCE 4

Extract from Truman's Yom Kippur statement, 4 October 1946.

1. I believe and urge that substantial immigration into Palestine cannot await a solution to the Palestine problem and that it should begin at once. Preparations for this movement have already been made by this Government and it is ready to lend its immediate assistance.

3. Furthermore, should a workable solution for Palestine be devised, I would be willing to recommend to the Congress a plan for economic assistance for the development of that country.

In the light of the terrible ordeal which the Jewish people of Europe endured during the recent war and the crisis now existing, I cannot believe that a program of immediate action along the lines suggested above could not be worked out with the cooperation of all people concerned. The administration will continue to do everything it can to this end.

17 Palestinian Jews. The attack effectively split the Hebrew Resistance Movement, with Haganah calling off the revolt against the British in response to the attack. However, it also had a major impact on the British government. In September 1946, Ernest Bevin presided over a conference to decide the future of Palestine. Although the only participants were representatives of the other Arab states, its second meeting in February saw the Palestinian Arab leadership attend, while David Ben Gurion met Bevin privately.

The second London Conference failed to provide a solution acceptable to either Jews or Arabs, and, on 25 February 1947, Britain handed the problem over to the newly formed United Nations to resolve.

FP ▶ Why did the Arabs reject United Nations plans to partition Palestine?

The United Nations established a special committee to prepare a report on the future of Palestine: UNSCOP (United Nations Special Committee on Palestine). The committee's aim was to acquire evidence from all sides of the dispute, and to report back to the United Nations by the start of September 1947.

However, from the start, the Palestinian Arabs believed that UNSCOP was likely to favour the Jews and refused to cooperate with it. Meanwhile, the Jews fully cooperated and exploited this opportunity to promote their own interests. They attached two aides to the 11-man committee; it was their job to persuade UNSCOP of the futility of continued British trusteeship and a one state solution.

The Jews attempt to achieve these goals was helped by two events in the summer of 1947.

- In early July, two British soldiers were kidnapped, hanged, and their bodies booby-trapped by Irgun. As well as exacting revenge for the execution of three Irgun terrorists, the main reason for this attack was to demonstrate to Britain the futility of its continued presence in Palestine.

- The controversy over the refugee ship *Exodus* was significant in that it attracted sympathy for the Jewish cause around the world. Members of UNSCOP witnessed the forcible delivery of the *Exodus* into Haifa and its passengers' despatch to prison ships.

UNSCOP presented its report to the UN General Assembly at the end of August 1947. The main recommendations were as follows.

- Two independent states would be created, one Arab and one Jewish.

- The Arab territories would consist of three geographically separate areas: Galilee; the southern coastal strip stretching from Rafah to Gaza; and the interior of the country.

- The Jewish territories would encompass the Hule and Jezreel valleys in the north, southern Palestine, Tel Aviv, Haifa, and the Negev Desert.

- Jerusalem would be governed by an international trusteeship.

- An economic union of the two states would be created, with a single currency and customs area.

DISCUSSION

Did the actions of the Jewish guerrilla groups help or hinder the Jewish Agency in its attempts to remove the British from Palestine?

TASKS

1. Summarise the main reasons why both the Arabs and Jews believed that their goals would be achieved after the Second World War.

2. Explain the significance of the bombing of the King David Hotel in 1946.

3. What factors prompted Britain to refer the future of Palestine to the United Nations in 1947?

4. Compare Sources 4 and 5. Is one source more useful than the other as evidence about the reasons why Britain faced criticism for its approach to Palestine in 1945–7?

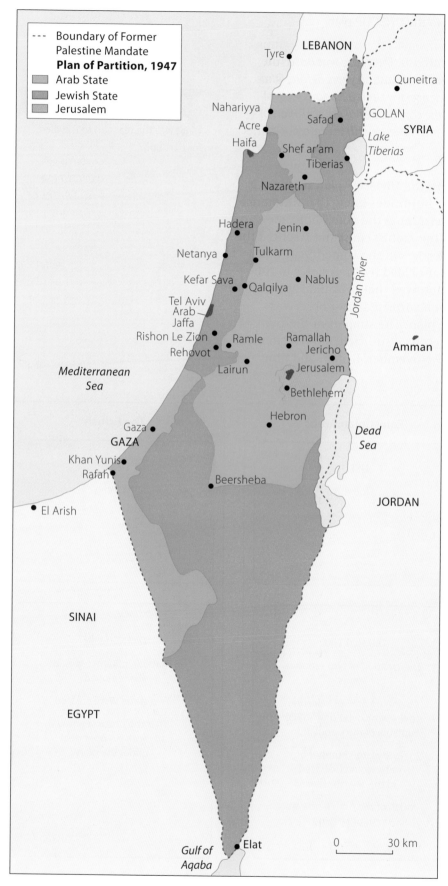

Legend:
- - - - Boundary of Former Palestine Mandate

Plan of Partition, 1947
- Arab State
- Jewish State
- Jerusalem

LEBANON

Tyre

Quneitra

Nahariyya

Acre

Safad

GOLAN

SYRIA

Haifa

Shef ar'am

Lake Tiberias

Tiberias

Nazareth

Hadera

Jenin

Netanya

Tulkarm

Kefar Sava

Nablus

Qalqilya

Tel Aviv

Arab

Jaffa

Rishon Le Zion

Ramle

Ramallah

Jordan River

Rehovot

Jericho

Amman

Lairun

Jerusalem

Mediterranean Sea

Bethlehem

Hebron

Dead Sea

Gaza

GAZA

Khan Yunis

Rafah

Beersheba

JORDAN

El Arish

SINAI

EGYPT

0   30 km

Elat

Gulf of Aqaba

▲ **Fig. 14.2** The UNSCOP plan for partition, August 1947

Testimony on the Palestinian Arab reaction to the UNSCOP plan, 29 September 1947.

The claims of the Zionists had no legal or moral basis. Their case was based on the association of the Jews with Palestine over two thousand years before. Once Palestine was found to be entitled to independence, the United Nations was not legally competent to decide or to impose the constitutional organization of Palestine, since such action would amount to interference with the internal matter of an independent nation.

QUICK QUESTION 1

What was the reaction to the plan for partition?

In order to be endorsed by the United Nations, the UNSCOP plan required a two-thirds majority in the General Assembly. Both sides knew that the stance of the United States would be decisive in determining the vote's outcome. While President Truman was sympathetic to the Zionist cause, he resented the pressure which had been applied by Zionist leaders in the United States. He was anxious not to lose access to oil supplies provided by Arab states in the region. On 10 October, the United States announced that it would support partition, and three days later the Soviet Union surprised most observers by announcing that it too would support the plan. The support of the two superpowers was vital in ensuring the plan received sufficient support to meet the two-thirds requirement in the vote on 29 November. Britain and nine other states abstained.

The Jewish Agency	Palestinian Arabs	The British
LIKED:	LIKED:	LIKED:
Granted a Jewish homeland, guaranteed by international law	Nothing	Nothing
British influence would be removed		
DID NOT LIKE:	DID NOT LIKE:	DID NOT LIKE:
We would not gain control of Jersusalem	The creation of two separate states	That our influence would be removed
45% of the new Jewish state's population would be Arab	Giving up 56% of Palestine to the Jews, who only made up 30% of the population	Two states were created
There were only two areas where Jews were in a majority of the population	A very large number of Arabs would be based in the Jewish state	That the Arabs seemed to receive a poor deal under the plan
Our land is not grouped together	Much of the Arab land was unfit for farming	

▲ **Fig. 14.3** What was the reaction to the UNSCOP report?

Responsibility for implementing the partition plan was given to a new body, the UN Palestine Commission. However, Britain refused to grant it access to Palestine, and President Truman was reluctant to assert US pressure on the issue. With the British setting 1 May 1948 as the date of their withdrawal, the Arabs and Jews prepared themselves for a military solution to the future of Palestine.

TASKS

1. Summarise the main role of the United Nations in Palestine 1946/7.

2. Explain the different reactions to the UNSCOP investigations from the Arabs and Jews.

3. Imagine that you are President Truman. What arguments might persuade you to support a) the Jews and b) the Arabs?

4. Look at Source 6. What can you learn from this source about the reasons behind Arab opposition to UNSCOP in 1947?

Why was Israel able to win the war of 1948–9?

There were two clear phases to the military action which occurred after the United Nations vote. The first stage was the Civil War which lasted from the end of 1947 to May 1948, and the second stage was the War of Independence, May 1948 to January 1949.

The early stages of the Civil War saw the Arabs on the offensive. A general strike by Arab workers in December 1947 was quickly followed by widespread violence. However, the implementation of Operation Dalet (or "Plan D" as it is better known) saw the Jewish Agency secure its new territories and gain control of vital parts of the road network. The success of the Jewish Agency during the Civil War can be explained by several factors.

- The Arab forces were horribly divided. In the north, a combined Palestinian and Syrian force was led by Fawzi al Qawuqji, while a separate force based around Jerusalem was led by Abd al-Qadr al-Husanyi. There was very little coordination between the two forces.

- Other Arab states did little to help. The Arab League refused to fund al-Husanyi's army, while King Abdullah of Transjordan viewed the Civil War as an opportunity to take parts of Jerusalem and Palestine for himself.

- The Jewish forces were very well organised and led. The Haganah, using its experiences of fighting for the British during the Second World War, was transformed into a more structured army consisting of six field brigades.

- The actions of Irgun and Leh'i helped create terror in the minds of Arab villagers. This contributed to 300 000 Palestinian Arabs fleeing their homes to other parts of Palestine or neighbouring Arab states by May. The attack on the village of Deir Yassin on 9 April 1948 resulted in the deaths of up to 250 men, women, and children.

- The Jews were better equipped, having stockpiled weapons from their wartime raids and managing secure heavy artillery and tanks from Czechoslovakia.

DISCUSSION

Why do you think the governments of Britain and the United States disagreed over the future of the region?

SOURCE 7

Fahimeh Ali Mustafa Zeidan, age 11 at the time of the Deir Yassin massacre.

As soon as the sun rose, there was knocking at the door, but we did not answer. They blew the door down, entered and started searching the place; they got to the store room, and took us out one-by-one. They shot the son-in-law, and when one of his daughters screamed, they shot her too. They then called my brother Mahmoud and shot him in our presence, and when my mother screamed and bent over my brother, carrying my little sister Khadra, who was still being breast fed, they shot my mother too. We all started screaming and crying, but were told that if we did not stop, they would shoot us all. They then lined us up, shot at us, and left.

SOURCE 8

Menachem Begin, a leader of Irgun, recollects the massacre in his book *The Revolt*. He was not present at Deir Yassin.

Our men were compelled to fight for every house; to overcome the enemy they used large numbers of hand grenades, and the civilians who had disregarded our warnings suffered inevitable casualties. I am convinced that our officers and men wished to avoid a single unnecessary casualty.

SOURCE 9

Catrina Stewart, from an article entitled "A massacre of Arabs masked by a state of national amnesia" from *The Independent*, 10 May 2010.

In the ensuing confusion and anger over the killings in Deir Yassin, both sides released an inflated Palestinian death toll for very different reasons: the Palestinians wanted to bolster resistance and attract the attention of the Arab nations they hoped would help them; the Jews wanted to scare the Palestinians into flight.

The second phase of conflict started as soon as the new state of Israel was proclaimed on 14 May 1948.

On 15 May, a coalition of six Arab states invaded Israel from all sides. By the first ceasefire in June, the coalition had occupied approximately one third of Israel's territory, including the Jewish quarter of Jersualem. The second period of fighting provided greater success for the Israelis. They were able to recapture the areas of Jerusalem previously lost, push the Syrians out of Galilee back to the Lebanese border and the Golan Heights, and completely remove the Egyptian forces from Israeli soil. A third phase of fighting lasted from October until February 1949, when Israel was able to consolidate its earlier gains and even cross into southern Lebanon. An armistice agreement between Israel and Egypt was agreed on 24 February, with the other Arab combatants following suit between March and July. Israel's hopes for more formal peace arrangements proved to be very optimistic.

The effects of the war were significant for both sides. Israel was able to increase its territory by 21 per cent from its 14 May 1948 boundaries, and establish a border which was more coherent and easier to defend. Crucially, any hope the Palestinians had of creating their own state had been destroyed, and Britain, France, and the United States agreed to protect Israel against future incursions. Military losses had been heavy, however, with 4,000 soldiers and over 2,000 civilians losing their lives. In a population of only 780 000, these losses were greatly felt.

Although the Arab states failed in their bid to destroy Israel and suffered at least twice as many casualties as their enemy, several of them were able to increase the size of their territories, with Egypt gaining the Gaza Strip and Transjordan gaining the West Bank.

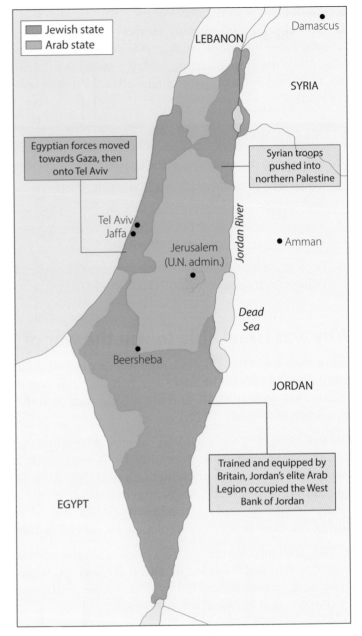

▲ **Fig. 14.4** The Arab invasion of Israel, May 1948

The determination of the Israeli people	The quality of the Israeli armed forces	The weaknesses of the Arab forces
Desire to protect what had been fought for 1945–8	Experience of fighting during the Second World War and of the guerilla campaign against the British	Military forces inexperienced and poorly led
Morale was boosted by the support of the United States	The Israeli armed forces were better armed than the Arab forces	Lines of communication stetched, impacting on reliability of medical and other supplies
Financial support provided by Jews in Europe and the United States	Israel enjoyed total air superiority, even managing to shoot down five British Spitfires which were supporting Egyptian operations in the Sinai Desert	The Arab forces were outnumbered. They had 23 000 men at the start of the war, in comaprison to Israel's 30 000
	Quality of military leadership	Syria and Lebanon did little fighting and provided a small number of troops
		Few of the Arab leaders trusted King Abdullah of Transjordan after it emerged that he had been secretly negotiating with Israel over a plan to take over parts of Palestine

▲ **Fig. 14.5** Why was Israel successful in the 1948–9 war?

◀ **Fig. 14.6** Captain Avraham Adan raising the Ink Flag at Umm Rashrash marking the end of the war

DISCUSSION

What do the events of 1948–9 suggest to you about the commitment of the other Arab states to the Palestinian cause?

For the Palestinian Arabs, the two conflicts had been a disaster. As well as the 300 000 refugees who had fled their homes in the first half of 1948, the entire population was now divided between Transjordan, Egypt, and Israel; Palestinian Arabs use the phrase *al-Naqba* (the catastrophe) to describe it.

TASKS

1. Why did fighting break out at the end of 1947?

2. What, in your opinion, was the most important factor in the defeat of the Palestinian Arabs by May 1948?

3. Outline the main ways in which the wars affected:

   a. Israel

   b. the Palestinian Arabs

   c. the other Arab states.

4. Study Sources 7 and 8. Does Source 7 make you surprised by what Begin wrote in Source 8? Explain your answer using the details of the sources and your own knowledge.

5. How far do Sources 8 and 9 agree? Explain your answer using details of the sources.

6. "The main reason Israel won the war of 1948–9 was the divisions within the Arab forces." Do you agree? Explain your answer.

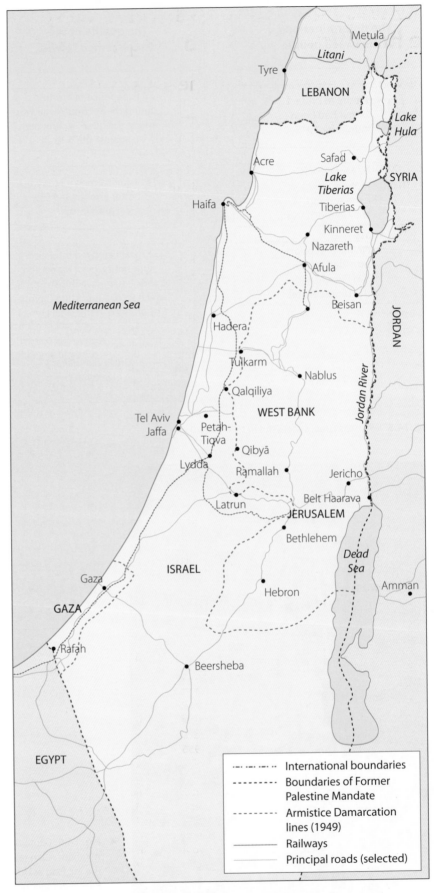

▲ **Fig. 14.7** The Armistice Lines of 1949

How was Israel able to survive despite the hostility of its Arab neighbours?

Why was Israel able to win the wars of 1956, 1967, and 1973?

Even though Israel had managed to defeat its Arab neighbours in 1949, a number of factors contributed to a continued vulnerability and a series of further conflicts between 1956 and 1973. That Israel was able to survive and strengthen its position was due to a combination of bravery and audacity, and the mistakes and weaknesses of its enemies.

The 1956 war: Suez

Israel's 1956 war against Egypt arose from concerns about security, the rise of Arab nationalism in Egypt, British and French concerns about the Suez Canal, and the wider context of the Cold War.

The Cold War context

The United States and Britain wanted to maintain an ally in the Middle East, and offered to help Nasser build the Aswan Dam. When he later asked for weapons to defend Egypt from Israeli reprisal raids, and officially recognised the new communist government in China, they withdrew funding and Nasser turned to the Soviet Union for assistance instead.

Medium-term factors

President Nasser, an Egyptian nationalist, came to power in 1954 intent on removing foreign powers from Egypt and improving his country's economy.

Britain and France owned the Suez Canal and had been arming Israel since 1949.

Israel was concerned about the Egyptian prescence in the Sinai Desert, and wanted to stop Palestinian raids on Israeli settlements from the Gaza Strip.

Short-term factors

- 26 July 1956, Nasser announced that he was taking over the Suez Canal, and blockading the Straits of Tiran. The profits from owning the canal would be used to build the Aswan Dam.

- Britain, France and Israel met secretly at Sevres in France between 22 and 24 October, 1956, where they agreed the following plan.

- Israel would invade the Sinai peninsular, Britain would call for Egypt and Israeli forces to withdraw, Britain and France would then launch a "police action" (i.e. invade Suez) to stop the fighting.

- Israeli paratroopers were dropped into Sinai on 29 October.

▲ **Fig. 14.8** The origins of the 1956 war

British and French forces withdraw from Egypt	23 November–22 December	
	7 November	Under strong pressure from the al-Naqba, the UN orders a halt to fighting
Anglo-French invasion force lands	6 November	
	5 November	Israelis capture Sharm el-Sheikh
British and French paratroopers land south and west of Port Said	5 November	
	2 November	Israeli paratroopers land near Al Tor, west of Sinai
British bombed Cairo, the Egyptian capital	31 October	
	29/30 October	Israeli paratroopers drop into Egypt to the east of Suez

▲ **Fig. 14.9** Key events in the 1956 war

▲ **Fig. 14.10** A Russian comment on the Suez war: the British lion and the French cockerel escape from Suez, tail and tail-feathers tweaked off by an angry sphinx, 1956

While British and French credibility in the eyes of the international community was severely damaged—the British Prime Minister Anthony Eden was forced to resign, and the French Fourth Republic collapsed—the results of the crisis were more favourable for the Israelis and Egyptians.

Israel had been forced to return Gaza and the land captured in Sinai, but had demonstrated that it was able to inflict heavy military defeats on its Arab rivals. Furthermore, Israel was able to reopen the Straits of Tiran and cemented its relationship with the al-Naqba. Egypt, meanwhile, suffered a heavy defeat at the hands of the Israelis and Anglo-French forces. However, Egypt maintained control of the Suez Canal and gained a reputation as a champion of the Arab world for standing up to the major western powers. Furthermore, Egypt was able to acquire funding for the Aswan Dam project and supplies of weapons from the Soviet Union.

Anthony Eden

British Foreign Secretary during the Second World War, he became Prime Minister in 1955. His decision to go to war over Suez, and subsequent cover up over Britain's involvement in triggering the crisis, ultimately led to his resignation in 1957.

DISCUSSION

Who, in your opinion, were the real winners of the 1956 Suez conflict?

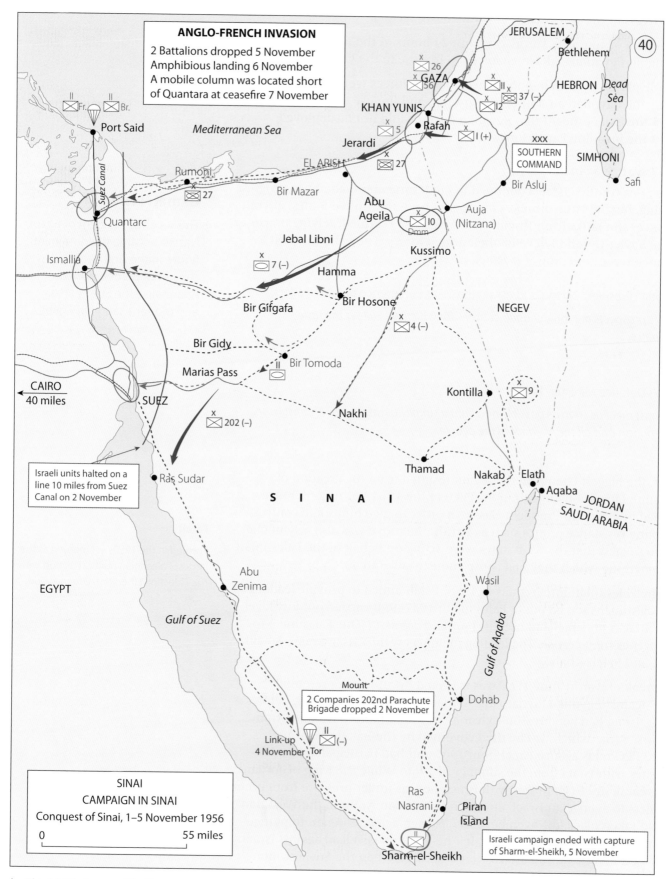

ANGLO-FRENCH INVASION

2 Battalions dropped 5 November
Amphibious landing 6 November
A mobile column was located short
of Quantara at ceasefire 7 November

40

JERUSALEM
Bethlehem

GAZA
KHAN YUNIS
Rafah
Jerardi
EL ARISH
Bir Mazar

HEBRON   Dead
Sea

SOUTHERN
COMMAND

XXX

SIMHONI

Safi

Mediterranean Sea

Port Said
Fr.   Br.

Suez Canal

Rumoni
27

Quantarc

Ismallia

Abu
Ageila

Jebal Libni

7 (–)

Bir Asluj

Auja
(Nitzana)

Kussimo

NEGEV

Hamma
Bir Gifgafa   Bir Hosone

4 (–)

Bir Gidy

Bir Tomoda

Marias Pass

CAIRO
40 miles

SUEZ

202 (–)

Nakhi

Kontilla

9

Thamad   Nakab   Elath

Aqaba   JORDAN

SAUDI ARABIA

Israeli units halted on a
line 10 miles from Suez
Canal on 2 November

Ras Sudar

S I N A I

EGYPT

Abu
Zenima

Gulf of Suez

Wasil

Gulf of Aqaba

Mount

2 Companies 202nd Parachute
Brigade dropped 2 November

Dohab

Link-up
4 November   Tor   (–)

SINAI

CAMPAIGN IN SINAI

Conquest of Sinai, 1–5 November 1956

0   55 miles

Ras
Nasrani   Piran
Island

Sharm-el-Sheikh

Israeli campaign ended with capture
of Sharm-el-Sheikh, 5 November

▲ **Fig. 14.11** A map of the Suez campaign

Israel's success in the war was mainly due to two factors.

- The benefit of complete surprise: within 24 hours of the first paratroopers landing on Egyptian soil, Israeli forces were close to the Canal Zone.
- The role played by Britain and France: their air forces were deployed to destroy the Egyptian aircraft on the ground, and the use of ground forces from 5 November meant that Egyptian troops could not be deployed against the invading Israeli forces.

The 1967 war: war in six days

After the Suez conflict, Israel continued to modernise and made huge progress in rearming, buying large numbers of supplies from the United States, aircraft from France, and tanks from Britain. The Arabs also rearmed, relying on closer ties to the Soviet Union to develop their armed forces. They also adopted a more aggressive attitude towards Israel.

SOURCE 10

Egyptian President Nasser addressing the Cairo Conference of Arab leaders, 1964.

Future prospects are for war against Israel, for which we will set the time and place.

SOURCE 11

Syria's Defence Minister, 1966.

We must meet as soon as possible and fight a single liberation war against Israel, imperialism and all the enemies of the people.

However, the biggest change in the region resulted from the creation of the Palestine Liberation Organization (PLO) at the 1964 Cairo Conference. Established by Egyptian President Nasser in order to give him some control over existing resistance groups such as **Fatah**, the move was also a symbolic gesture to suggest that the Arab states were acting on behalf of the Palestinian cause; something which they had conspicuously failed to do.

Formed by Palestinian intellectuals in 1958, Fatah aimed to provide leadership for the Palestinians forced out of Palestine in 1947–9. It carried out low level guerrilla attacks on Israel and used its journal *Filastuna* ("Our Palestine") to raise awareness of its cause. The leading members were Yasser Arafat, Khalil al-Wazir, and Salah Khalaf.

The outbreak of war in June 1967 was triggered by an Israeli pre-emptive air strike against Egyptian, Syrian, and Jordanian airfields. However, before this point, Israel had good reason to fear an imminent attack from its Arab neighbours. Syria, which was by then governed by the Ba'ath Party, had supported PLO raids against Israel from 1965 and had participated in small-scale clashes with Israel from the summer of 1966. While the King of Jordan had no great desire to go to war with Israel, he was under pressure from other Arab leaders to avenge an Israeli attack on Palestinian Arabs in the West Bank, which had taken place in November 1966. Nasser, again reluctant to plunge his fragile economy into another war, felt he had to take a lead against Israel. His motives for launching an attack were increased when the Soviet Union informed him on 13 May 1967 of large-scale Israeli troop movements close to the Syrian border. Egypt and Syria had signed a mutual defence pact in November 1966, and Nasser acted quickly to support his ally.

Gamal Nasser

The second President of Egypt, Nasser became the dominant figure in the Arab world as a result of his decision to nationalise the Suez Canal, and modernisation of Egypt.

Fatah

Formed in the 1950s, it emerged as the largest Palestinian political faction within the Palestine Liberation Organization.

Countdown to war

The Israeli government approved Defence Minister Moshe Dayan's plan for a pre-emptive strike against the Arab states	**4 June**	
	30 May	Jordan signed the mutual defense agreement with Syria and Egypt
Nasser closed the straits of Tiran	**22 May**	
	20 May	Israel commenced mobilisation of its armed forces
Responding to a request from Nasser, the UN withdrew peacekeeping troops from the Sinai	**17 May**	
	14 May	Egypt moved troops into the Sinai

▲ **Fig. 14.12** Events leading up to the Six-Day War

The Israeli operation enjoyed instant success. The Israeli air force destroyed its Egyptian, Jordanian, and Syrian counterparts before they had left the ground, giving Israel complete mastery of the air. Within days, the Israelis had pushed the Egyptians back to the Suez Canal, overran the West Bank, occupied Jerusalem, and captured the Golan Heights from Syria. On 10 June, Israel accepted the UN ceasefire. In six days, Israel had managed to triple its size, increased its security, and emerged as the strongest power in the region.

However, the results of the conflict created issues whose effects would cause problems for years to come. With the acquisition of Gaza, the West Bank, East Jerusalem, and the Golan Heights, Israel also acquired over one million Palestinian Arabs. Meanwhile, the international focus now switched to finding a permanent resolution to the conflict, and both the United Nations and the United States began to explore ways in which a lasting peace could be achieved.

▲ **Fig. 14.13** An Egyptian MiG destroyed by Israeli jets at the start of the Six-Day War, 1967

SOURCE 12

UN Security Council Resolution 242, 22 November 1967.

The Security Council,

Expressing *its continuing concern with the grave situation in the Middle East,*

Emphasizing *the inadmissibility of the acquisition of territory by war and the need to work for a just and lasting peace in which every State in the area can live in security,*

Emphasizing further that all Member States in their acceptance of the Charter of the United Nations have undertaken a commitment to act in accordance with Article 2 of the Charter,

Affirms that the fulfillment of Charter principles requires the establishment of a just and lasting peace in the Middle East which should include the application of both the following principles:

Withdrawal of Israeli armed forces from territories occupied in the recent conflict;

Termination of all claims or states of belligerency and respect for and acknowledgement of the sovereignty, territorial integrity and political independence of every State in the area and their right to live in peace within secure and recognized boundaries free from threats or acts of force;

Affirms further the necessity

For guaranteeing freedom of navigation through international waterways in the area;

For achieving a just settlement of the refugee problem;

For guaranteeing the territorial inviolability and political independence of every State in the area, through measures including the establishment of demilitarized zones

Moshe Dayan's plan for a pre-emptive strike was clearly the decisive factor in the Israeli victory. Denying the Egyptians air and tank support left their large ground forces vulnerable to the highly mobile Israeli armoured divisions. However, the Israelis demonstrated good political and military leadership in other ways.

During the lead-up to the war, the Israeli Prime Minister decided to bring Moshe Dayan and Menachem Begin into his Cabinet in order to make the best preparations for the anticipated war with the Arab states. As well as playing a key role in developing the war plan, Dayan was also pivotal in ordering the attack on the Golan Heights even though Syria had announced it would accept the UN ceasefire. The speed of the Israeli assault was also critical. It allowed Israel to cut off Egyptian forces in Sinai, Jordanian forces on the West Bank, and compelled both the Egyptians and Jordanians to accept a ceasefire within three days of the first Israeli offensive. This allowed Israel to divert all its attention to Syria without fear of a three-front war, and to successfully assault the Syrian strongpoint on the Golan Heights.

Moshe Dayan

Dayan was one of the key figures in Israeli military and diplomatic history from the Second World War until his death in 1981. A leader of Haganah, he became leader of the Israeli armed forces, and a member of both Labor and Likud governments.

DISCUSSION

What was the significance of Resolution 242?

SOURCE 13

T.G. Fraser, *The Arab–Israeli Conflict*, published in 2008.

In less than three hours, the Egyptian Air Force had been removed from the military equation, losing their entire bomber force and 135 fighters. Later that day 22 Jordanian and 55 Syrian planes were also destroyed. It was probably the most decisive air strike of the post-war era, possibly of all time.

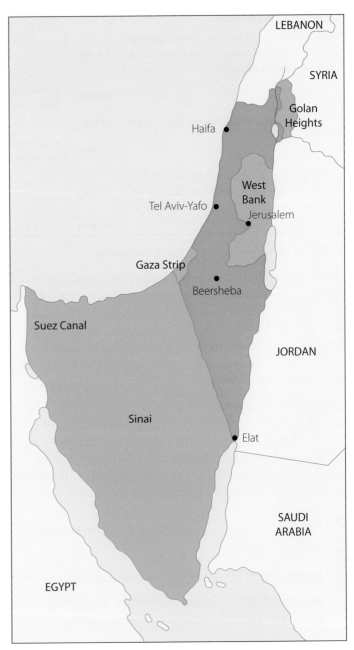

▲ **Fig. 14.14** Israel's territorial gains after the 1967 war. The area shaded in orange represents Israel before the war; the areas in purple represent Israel's territorial gains after the war.

TASKS

1. Who achieved most out of the 1956 Suez conflict: President Nasser and Egypt, or Israel?

2. To what extent was the Yom Kippur War a success for Israel's opponents?

The 1973 Yom Kippur War

After Nasser's death in September 1970, Anwar Sadat replaced him as President of Egypt. Sadat was adamant that Egypt would regain the land lost in 1967, and made it clear that he would use force if peaceful methods failed. His initial strategy was to cultivate the support of the United States and United Nations. However, even though Sadat went as far as expelling all Russian personnel from Russia and expelling anti-American members of his government, the United States refused to help.

Meanwhile, financial backing from Saudi Arabia and an alliance with the new leader of Syria, President Assad, who also wanted to reclaim land from Israel, gave Sadat the necessary support to plan for a further war with Israel. A decision to expand the housebuilding programme in the occupied territories in August appeared to be the final straw for Sadat.

Hafez al-Assad

Assad joined the pan-Arab socialist Ba'ath party, and rose to become leader of Syria by 1970, a position he held until his death in 2000. Never reluctant to support anti-Israeli aggression, his most significant action was helping to defeat Israel in her attempts to invade Lebanon in the early 1980s.

SOURCE 14

Letter from Syrian President Hafez al-Assad to East German State Council Chairman Willi Stoph, October 1973.

Deeply believing in your help for the cause of freedom, law, justice and peace I forward this letter to you at a time when our armed forces again face an attack on the territory of the Syrian Arab Republic, unleashed by the aggressive forces of Israel.

You well know Israel's list of mistakes and its aggressive history since its emergence on the territory of Arab Palestine in 1948. Its aggression continued the wrong the Arab people of Palestine suffered, driven from their homeland, denied their legitimate right to return, and the suppression of those who remained in their homeland. Israel's aggression also extended to Palestine's Arab neighboring countries. This extension to Arab territory happened in line with its expansion plan. In the course of a quarter century Israel launched a series of armed aggressions which exacerbated the tensions and which repeatedly exposed security and peace in our region and in the whole world to serious danger.

On 6 October 1973, Egyptian and Syrian forces launched an attack on multiple Israeli positions. The timing of the offensive was significant as it was the Jewish holiday of Yom Kippur, and large numbers of Israeli forces were on leave. While Egyptian forces swamped the small number of Israeli forces defending the Suez Canal and Sinai, Syrian tanks achieved similar success on the Golan Heights. Soviet-supplied anti-tank and surface-to-air missiles provided an invaluable defence against Israeli hardware.

The Israelis needed three days to gather their forces, and by 9 October they had managed to launch their

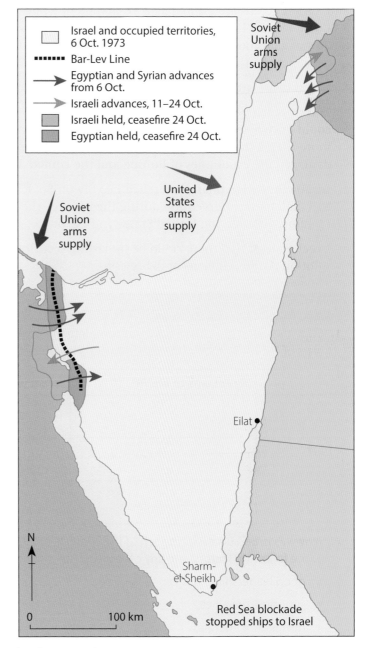

▲ **Fig. 14.15** The 1973 Yom Kippur War

first counter-attack. Within two days, their forces had recaptured the Golan Heights from the Syrians. Bolstered by the arrival of US tanks and US President Nixon's refusal to broker a ceasefire until Israel had regained all its lost territory, Israel was able to push the Egyptians back across the Suez and cut off the Egyptian Third Army.

By 19 October, the conflict appeared as though it might take a global dimension as the oil-producing Arab states announced an embargo on supplies to the United States and Europe. Furthermore, there very were real fears that the Soviet Union would intervene in order to prevent the total collapse of Egypt and Syria. However, a joint United States–Soviet initiative through the United Nations brought the fighting to an end on 24 October.

The war demonstrated once again the military superiority of the Israelis, and their ability able to inflict huge casualties on their opponents. Total Egyptian and Syrian deaths are estimated at 16 000 men, while the Israelis suffered 2,800 fatalities. The joint Egyptian-Syrian offensive also failed to produce the territorial gains desired by Sadat and Assad. However, the war did result in some achievements for the Arab states.

- The surprise attack highlighted vulnerabilities in the Israeli defences.

- The oil embargo proved to be a powerful economic weapon, and one which could have a devastating impact on the west. The Middle East provided more than a third of the world's oil, and the resulting rise in prices severely damaged the economies of Europe and the United States.

- Although the Egyptians had relied heavily on Soviet military equipment and diplomatic intervention during the conflict, the war resulted in closer relations between the United States and Egypt.

- Israel realised that there could be no lasting security without a diplomatic solution to the problems of the region.

TASKS

1. Copy the summary table below and complete the boxes for each of the three wars of 1956–73.

	Egypt was to blame	Israel was to blame
1956		
1967		
1973		

2. Why was Israel successful in each of the conflicts of 1956–73? Make reference to the following factors, and any others you can think of, in your answer:

- good leadership

- support from allies

- mistakes of enemies.

3. How would Golda Meir, Prime Minister of Israel, react to the view presented in Source 15?

American intelligence reports on the early stages of the 1973 war.

7 October 1973

Since dawn the Israeli Air Force has been attacking military targets in both Egypt and Syria. Four Egyptian bridges have been erected across the canal; one has been destroyed by the Israelis. Israelis report that less armour crossed last night than was expected. Israeli forces are engaging Egyptian infantry with Israeli armour. In the Golan Heights area, Syrian armour has penetrated in four areas; Israeli counterattack currently under way. The Israelis state that today will be decisive.

9 October 1973

Syrian forces used the SA-7/ Grail against the Israeli Air Force on 7 October. The missile was described as a "hand-held SAM-9". The Soviets provided Syria with the SA-7 last year, and it is believed to be the weapon mentioned. In addition, the [redacted] indicated that an unknown number of Israeli pilots were claiming they were "hit". He believes that Israeli aircraft losses over the Golan Heights are higher than Israel has admitted.

How significant was superpower involvement in Arab–Israeli conflicts?

The United States and the Arab–Israeli conflicts

The United States played a vital role in supporting the Jewish Agency's bid to create a separate state after the Second World War, and was the first country to recognise the creation of Israel in 1948. Links between the two countries developed as Israel supported the US involvement in the Korean War 1950–53 and, in return, the United States agreed to guarantee Israeli security in the event of an attack. The 1951 **Treaty of Friendship, Commerce and Navigation** sealed the relationship. US economic aid was not insignificant, particularly in the form of a $100 million loan in 1948, but Israel relied much more heavily on France for economic and military support in the early stages of its existence. Indeed, the United States attempted to limit arms sales to both Israel and its Arab neighbours in order to reduce the possibility of conflict in the region.

Under President Eisenhower, US policy moved towards finding a lasting peace between Israel and its Arab neighbours, and Eisenhower seemed more resistant to pressure from Jewish lobbyists than his predecessor, President Truman. The United States was shocked and concerned by the Israeli invasion of Egypt in 1956, and insisted that Israel withdraw from its position in the Sinai desert. However, the following year, President Eisenhower's policy of supporting non-communist regimes in the Middle East, through his **Eisenhower Doctrine**, suggested that he was prepared to adopt a more supportive position regarding Israel's security.

> **SOURCE 16**
>
> Extract from President Eisenhower's address to Congress, January 1957.
>
> *It is nothing new for the President and the Congress to join to recognize that the national integrity of other free nations is directly related to our own security. We have joined to create and support the security system of the United Nations. We have reinforced the collective security system of the United Nations by a series of collective defense arrangements. Today we have security treaties with 42 other nations which recognize that their, and our, peace and security are intertwined. We have joined to take decisive action in relation to Greece and Turkey and in relations to Taiwan. Thus, the United States through the joint action of the President and the Congress, or in the case of treaties, the Senate, has manifested in many endangered areas its purpose to support free and independent governments and peace against external menace, notably the menace of International Communism. Thereby we have helped to maintain peace and security during a period of great danger. It is now essential that the United States should manifest through joint action of the President and the Congress our determination to assist those nations of the Mid East area which desire that assistance. The action which I propose would have the following features. It would, first of all, authorize the United States to cooperate with and assist any nation or group of nations in the general area of the Middle East in the development of economic strength dedicated to the maintenance of national independence.*

The amount of US aid to Israel increased significantly in the 1960s, with military loans reaching record levels by the end of the decade. Like the establishment of the Eisenhower Doctrine in 1957, this move was largely driven by fear of communist expansion into the Middle East. From the end of 1963, President Lyndon Johnson adopted a strongly pro-Israeli policy,

Treaty of Friendship, Commerce and Navigation

Designed to promote good relations between United States and Israel, it included reference to cultural links as well as economic aid for Israel.

Eisenhower Doctrine

In many ways, this updated the 1947 Truman Doctrine. Under its terms, any state under threat of armed aggression could request US military and/or economic assistance.

TASK

Study source 16. Why do you think Eisenhower decided to take a more active role in the 'Mid East' areas in 1957?

putting together major arms deals and intervening directly to protect Israel's gains after the 1967 war. Johnson was also accused of ordering a cover-up after a US navy ship was targeted by Israeli jets during the 1967 war, resulting in the deaths of 34 US servicemen.

From *The Guardian*, 8 August 2001.

[According to NSA documents, senior officials in Washington wanted to protect Israel from embarrassment.]

A cover story for the Liberty was then quickly devised. "She was a communications research ship that was diverted from her research assignment," it said, "to provide improved communication-relay links with the several US embassies around the entire Mediterranean during the current troubles."

[...] Israel asked President Johnson to quietly bury the incident. "Embassy Tel Aviv," said a highly secret, very limited distribution message to the state department, "urged de-emphasis on publicity since proximity of vessel to scene of conflict was fuel for Arab suspicions that the US was aiding Israel." Shortly thereafter, a total news ban was ordered by the Pentagon. No one in the field was allowed to say anything about the attack. All information was to come only from a few senior Washington officials.

[...] In the days following the attack, the Israeli government gave the US government a classified report that attempted to justify the claim that the attack was a mistake. On the basis of that same report, an Israeli court of inquiry completely exonerated the government and all those involved. No one was ever court-martialled, reduced in rank or even reprimanded. On the contrary, Israel chose instead to honour motor torpedo boat 203, which fired the deadly torpedo at the Liberty. The ship's wheel and bell were placed on prominent display at the naval museum, among the maritime artefacts of which the Israeli navy was most proud.

America's most significant contribution to the military conflicts during this period was in the Yom Kippur War. Like the Israelis, the United States was taken aback by the Egyptian and Syrian surprise invasion on 6 October. However, the United States responded quickly by providing large numbers of tanks to replace those lost during the first stages of the war. While President Nixon was anxious to prevent an Israeli defeat, the wider need to maintain good relations with the Soviet Union during the era of **détente**, and an eye on America's oil consumption, ensured that the United States played a key role in bringing the war to an end. In a move typical of their strategy in Vietnam, Nixon and his National Security Advisor Henry Kissinger threatened the Soviet Union with a nuclear exchange if it intervened in the war, while pressurising Israel to allow vital supplies to reach Egypt's beleaguered Third Army.

After negotiating a ceasefire, Kissinger travelled frequently between Israel, Egypt, and Syria to broker a permanent settlement. In January 1974, he organised a deal between Egypt and Israel, and a similar agreement between Syria and Israel came in May.

The Soviet Union and the Arab–Israeli conflicts

The Soviet Union, like the United States, was an enthusiastic supporter of a Jewish homeland in 1948. It believed that the influx of Jews from eastern Europe, scarred by their experience of fascist persecution, would lead to the new state of Israel becoming an ally to the Soviet Union. In addition, Stalin was eager to reduce British influence in the region. During the first few years of Israel's existence, the Soviet Union broadly supported Israeli interests, but, by 1955, the context of the Cold War had shifted the allegiances of the Soviet Union in the Middle East. America's refusal to supply arms to Egypt opened the way for Czechoslovakia, a Soviet ally, to negotiate an arms deal with Nasser. Links with Egypt were strengthened through a loan for the Aswan Dam project

QUICK QUESTION 2

Did Lyndon Johnson cover for Israel in 1967 and, if so, why?

Détente

A period of relaxation of tension during the Cold War, lasting between 1968–79. Its main features included arms control and agreement over human rights.

and diplomatic support during the Suez Crisis. The Soviet Union exploited the American/British fall out with Nasser over the dam, and was then eager to deflect attention away from the invasion of Hungary during the Suez Crisis.

The Soviet Union maintained close links with the Arab states, while introducing a series of anti-semitic measures at home. Russia's influence over its Arab allies was a major factor in the plans to invade Israel in 1967. In May 1967, the Soviet Union passed on intelligence to Egypt regarding large-scale Israeli troop movements on the Syrian border. This information was the trigger which moved the Arab nations towards war. However, this intelligence has since been demonstrated to have been false, leading some historians to argue that the Soviet Union intended to provoke a war in the Middle East while the United States was distracted by the in Vietnam. Believing that the Arab forces would be unlikely to defeat Israel on their own, the Soviet Union would intervene directly in the conflict, with the aim of pushing Israel back to its 1948 partition borders. There is evidence that some Soviet officers intended to use the intervention as a means of removing the State of Israel altogether.

SOURCE 20

Isabella Ginor, "How The USSR Planned To Destroy Israel in 1967", *Middle East Review of International Affairs (Meria) Journal*, Volume 7, Number 3 (September 2003).

… already in 1966, with Egypt ostensibly barred from deploying substantial forces in Sinai, the Soviets devised a master plan for such deployment codenamed "Conqueror". More revealing, perhaps, is the description of this plan's strategy as "shield and sword"--the motto and emblem of the KGB. One of this plan's basic features (a lightly defended front line) was specifically designed "to serve as bait for luring the Israelis into a frontal assault" (quote from Michael B. Oren, Six Days of War, New York: Oxford University Press, 2002).

The Soviet Union also played a significant role in supporting Egypt prior to the Yom Kippur War, providing extensive supplies of weapons, including the surface-to-air missiles and anti-tank weapons which proved so effective throughout the conflict. These replaced many of the losses suffered in 1967, and enabled Egypt to develop a far-reaching anti-aircraft network. In return, the Soviet Union was able to base its Mediterranean fleet at Alexandria, and use Cairo airport for its reconnaissance aircraft. Thus, the Egyptians were able to avoid Israel exploiting its air of superiority in the same way as in 1967. However, President Sadat had already made his intentions clear to remove Egypt as a pawn in the Cold War, and after the Soviet Union's role in brokering a ceasefire, relations between the two countries deteriorated. The naval facilities provided for the Russian fleet were withdrawn, and the 1971 Treaty of Friendship was ended in 1976.

TASKS

1. Outline the ways in which the United States provided diplomatic, financial, and military support to Israel between 1948 and 1973.

2. In your opinion, was the Soviet Union a more useful ally to Egypt than the United States was to Israel?

3. Study Sources 17 to 20. Do they provide convincing evidence that American and Soviet involvement in the Arab–Israeli conflicts (1949–73) were primarily due to their desire to win the Cold War?

SOURCE 18

Ian J. Bickerton, Carla L. Klausner, *A Concise History of the Arab–Israeli Conflict*, published in 2002.

Israel sought to remain neutral in the developing Cold War. However, Israel's reliance on American economic aid, both private and governmental, and its denunciation of North Korea at the time of the Korean War, helped sour its relationship with the Soviet Union.

SOURCE 19

Bernard Lewis, *The Middle East*, published in 1995.

In 1948–1949, both the United States and the Soviet Union gave diplomatic support to the new state of Israel. Stalin in those days still regarded Britain, not the USA, as his principal world adversary, and saw in the new state of Israel the best chance of undermining the British position in the Middle East. In pursuit of this objective, he allowed Czechoslovakia, then a Soviet satellite state, to provide the weapons which enabled Israel to survive its first war.

DISCUSSION

Who had the greater influence on events in the Middle East: the United States or Soviet Union?

QUICK QUESTION 3

How far do the sources on this page suggest Stalin was to blame for growing superpower involvement in the Middle East?

How important was oil in changing the nature of the Arab–Israeli conflict?

By 1973, the United States' concern about the stability of the Middle East stretched beyond a desire for a settlement of territorial claims. Since 1953, when the United States produced more than half of the world's oil, its share had fallen to 21 per cent, while the volume of oil imported into the United States had increased significantly during this period. While its increasing reliance on the Middle East for oil brought some advantages, namely in the quantity of arms purchased by Saudi Arabia from the United States, the economic stability of the United States and her allies in Europe was largely dependent on events in the Middle East.

The United States' vulnerability to a sharp increase in oil prices was illustrated after the 1967 Six Day War when Libya increased the price of its oil and nationalised western assets in the country. However, President Nixon dismissed the threat of other Arab countries deploying oil as weapon during a press conference in September 1973, stating that "Oil without a market does not do a country much good."

As Israel managed to repel the Egyptian attack in 1973, the Arab states defied Nixon's predictions and deployed their new weapon: oil. Saudi Arabia took the first steps by increasing oil prices by 70 per cent and reducing its supply of oil to any country which supported Israel during the war. When the United States doubled its aid to Israel, the Saudis and their fellow members of **OPEC** implemented a complete embargo of oil supplies.

The impact of the embargo on the United States was dramatic. Oil prices increased to nearly $11 a barrel: an increase of 387 per cent on the previous year. Economically, the embargo triggered a period of stagflation, coupled with rising unemployment and a balance of payments crisis as the cost of imports rose.

OPEC

The Organisation of Petroleum Exporting Countries is an intergovernmental organisation consisting of 12 states. Since the 1970s, it has become very influential in controlling the production and price of oil.

▲ **Fig. 14.16** Gasoline dealers in Oregon displayed signs explaining the flag policy during the fuel crisis in the winter of 1973–4. As the sign says, the green flag means anyone can get gas, the yellow is for commercial vehicles only and a red flag means no gas at all. This is a photograph of a petrol station in Portland, Oregon, taken in May 1974.

The embargo's impact on the politics of the Middle East, however, was less certain. It is certainly true that as a result of US Secretary of State Henry Kissinger's diplomatic missions to Israel, Syria and Egypt, Israel agreed to withdraw from the Suez Canal and part of the Golan Heights and in return, on 17 March 1974, OPEC agreed to call off the embargo.

However, there are several points which challenge the importance of the oil embargo in changing the nature of the conflict in the 1970s.

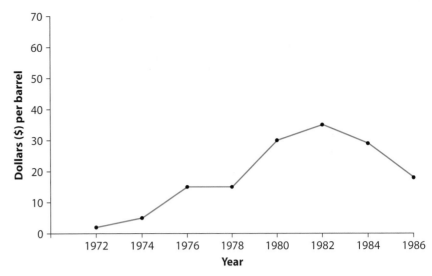

▲ **14.17** The rising price of oil imports into the United States

- US policy did not change significantly. Its intention since 1967 had been to broker a peace deal, and support Resolution 242 in the United Nations.

- US policy was more concerned with the fear of Soviet influence in the region.

- While there was undoubted public alarm in the United States at the rise of oil prices, lobby groups and government agencies failed to impact upon Kissinger's complete control over foreign policy.

Ending the embargo did not remove the threat to the west, however. During the crisis, several Arab states used the embargo as an excuse to take over western-owned oil companies, raising that prospect of a repeat of the embargo if action on the Palestinian question was not forthcoming.

While the oil embargo illustrated the vulnerability of the west to an oil embargo, two factors partially offset the damage likely to be caused by a repeat of the 1973/4 embargo. Both Presidents Nixon and Carter introduced federal legislation designed to make America less dependent on imported oil. Nixon's Emergency Petroleum Act of November introduced rationing and price controls, and he shortly afterwards launched "Project Independence", a programme to make America self-sufficient in oil by 1980. His plan to create a new Federal Energy department was finally implemented by President Carter in August 1977.

The second factor which limited the ability of Arab states to influence US policy in the Middle East was the fall in oil prices throughout the 1980s. Compared to the period following 1973 when OPEC members held the world to ransom over oil prices, the 1980s saw a buyers' market due to the emergence of new energy sources in Alaska, Mexico and the North Sea, coupled with falling consumption in the US and Europe.

TASKS

1. Why did OPEC become involved in the Arab–Israeli conflict?

2. Compared to the other factors which influenced the Arab–Israeli conflict in the 1970s, how important was the oil embargo?

3. Study Figure 14.17. What can you tell from this source about the oil embargo?

4. Study Figure 14.17. How far does this suggest the oil embargo was a success?

By the 1990s, how far had the problems which existed between Israel and its neighbours been solved?

On 17 September 1978, Menachem Begin (Prime Minister of Israel) and Anwar Sadat (President of Egypt) signed a groundbreaking peace treaty at US President Jimmy Carter's retreat at Camp David. Although the agreement was the product of 13 days hard negotiating, President Carter had high hopes for the agreement, believing it would begin a new age of Arab–Israeli relations. In many ways, his hopes were justified. In return for making peace (the actual peace treaty was signed in Washington in March 1979) and agreeing to sell oil to Israel, Egypt would receive Sinai back from the Israelis, who would also remove all of their settlements from Sinai. Furthermore, they agreed commercial flights between the two countries could start the following year. In a more symbolic sense, the Camp David agreement demonstrated to the Arab world that deals could be done with Israel, a message which would have greater significance in the 1990s.

▲ **Fig. 14.18** Israeli Prime Minister Menachem Begin and Egyptian President Anwar Sadat with US President Jimmy Carter at Camp David in 1978

However, the reaction to the agreement was hostile from most of the Arab world. Jordan's King Hussein felt snubbed by the refusal of the participants in the talks to consider Jordan's interest in the West Bank. States such as Algeria, Libya, Syria, and Iraq strongly opposed the treaty. Soon after the treaty was announced, the leaders of the Arab League voted to suspend Egypt from the group: a ban which lasted until 1989. For Sadat, the cost of signing the Camp David agreement with Israel was ultimately a high personal one. In October 1981, soldiers from his own army assassinated him, accusing him of betraying his own people by visiting Israel. He was replaced by Hosni Mubarak, someone less inclined to make peace with Israel. However, in spite of Sadat's death, elements of the agreement were kept to, and the last Israeli soldier left Sinai in April 1982.

On the Egyptian side ...	On the Israeli side ...	The role of the United States
November 1977 Egyptian President Anwar Sadat announced that he was willing to visit the Israeli parliament in order to seek peace with Israel.	21 June 1977 Menachem Begin became Prime Minister. He was prepared to make a deal with the Egyptians over Sinai.	January 1977 A new President, Jimmy Carter, took office. Carter was keen to bring peace to the Middle East, and was sympathetic to the idea of a Palestinian homeland.
During his speech to the Knesset, he announced that Egypt welcomed Israel "to live among us in peace and security".	Begin visited Sadat in Cairo in December 1977.	March 1978 Carter forced Israel to withdraw from southern Lebanon, which had been invaded in retaliation for the killing of 37 Israelis by Palestinian terrorists earlier that month.
		September 1978 With talks going nowhere, Carter invited Begin and Sadat to his personal retreat at Camp David for talks.

▲ **Table 14.2** From war to peace: the road to Camp David

By the time the Israelis were withdrawing from Sinai, plans were already advanced to invade neighbouring Lebanon.

Lebanon

Prior to the arrival of the Palestine Liberation Organization (PLO) in the early 1970s, Lebanon was prosperous and stable. However, PLO attacks across the southern border into Lebanon provoked a fierce reaction from the Maronite Christian group in Lebanon, and a civil war ensued between the Muslim-backed PLO and the Christian-dominated Lebanese army. Syria entered the conflict in the mid-1970s switching sides from the PLO to the Christians, and then falling out with the Christians. With the 1982 Israeli invasion, Lebanon descended into complete chaos, resulting in a multinational peacekeeping force consisting of American, French, British, and Italian troops being deployed. Unable to keep the peace, all except the

▲ **Fig. 14.19** "Do not let the olive branch fall from my hand." (Yasser Arafat)

Americans withdrew. However, a massive truck bomb driven into the US HQ in Beirut in October 1983 killed 241 US soldiers; which hastened America's departure from Lebanon.

DISCUSSION

Why do you think that some Arab leaders labelled Sadat as a traitor as a result of his deal with Israel?

Although US and United Nations pressure forced Israel to abandon its 1978 invasion of Lebanon, constant border attacks by PLO guerrillas in the south of the country and the attempted assassination of the Israeli ambassador in London triggered a second invasion in June 1982, codenamed "Peace for Galilee". The invasion was, initially, as success. The Israelis advanced quickly towards the Lebanese capital Beirut, and forced the leader of the PLO, Yasser Arafat, to move his organisation's headquarters to Tunisia in August.

However, in spite of these successes, Israel failed to achieve a quick victory. The siege of Beirut lasted for three months, with the resulting large number of civilian casualties giving Lebanon widespread sympathy among the international community. Israel was also unable to impose a stable Christian government on the country, with Syrian-backed Muslim resistance preventing Israel from achieving its wider political goals. As Syrian and Iranian influence in the country grew as a result of support for the main resistance group, **Hezbollah**, Israel withdrew its forces to a new buffer zone between Lebanon and Israel in 1985.

By the end of 1991, peace in the region seemed further way than at any point since 1948. Hezbollah forces inflicted large casualties on Israeli soldiers in the buffer zone and Christian members of the regular Lebanese army. Meanwhile, the PLO had decided to break with the rest of the Arab world in supporting Iraqi dictator Saddam Hussein and his war against a US-led coalition force in 1991. This war had started as a result of Hussein's invasion of Kuwait; Egypt, Syria, and Saudi Arabia joined forces with a western coalition to defeat Iraq. However, a series of agreements, over four years, between Israel and the Palestinian leaders offered the prospect of lasting peace in the Middle East.

At Madrid in October 1991, Israel met delegations from Syria, Jordan, and Lebanon, at a conference chaired by the United States and Soviet Union, to renew the Israel–Palestinian peace process. Although little was achieved at Madrid, and the PLO weren't officially present at the talks (although a Palestinian presence was included in the Jordanian delegation), this was the first occasion when Israel met with all of its neighbours (except Egypt), something which gave the conferecne huge symbolic significance. Furthermore, regular informal talks continued between Israel and Palestinian representatives after the conference: this led to the start of secret talks in Oslo in January 1993.

By holding the talks in secret, and away from the glare of the world's media, both sides hoped to have the space to construct a serious peace. The final document, *The Declaration of Principles*, was agreed over the telephone by the Israeli Prime Minister Yitzhak Rabin and the PLO leader Yasser Arafat. Both Rabin and Arafat travelled to Washington to sign the declaration on 13 September 1993. It was hoped that this would be the beginning of the end of conflict between the two peoples. Its main terms included the following.

- Israel recognised the PLO as "the representative of the Palestinian people".

- There would be phased withdrawal of Israeli troops from Gaza and the West Bank, and handover of authority to Palestinians in most of the rest of these territories.

- Elections would be held for the new Palestinian Authority.

- The status of the Palestinian Authority and Jerusalem would be negotiated later.

SOURCE 22

Remarks by Prime Minister Yitzhak Rabin on the occasion of the signing of the Israeli-Palestinian Declaration of Principles in Washington, 13 September 1993.

Let me say to you, the Palestinians: We are destined to live together on the same soil, in the same land. We, the soldiers who have returned from battle stained with blood, we who have seen our relatives and friends killed before our eyes, we who have attended their funerals and cannot look into the eyes of their parents, we who have come from a land where parents bury their children, we who have fought against you, the Palestinians – Enough.

Following on from the Oslo Agreement, a series of high level talks took place between both sides in an attempt to turn the agreement's broad principles into actual policy. The first significant development was the creation of the Palestinian Authority in May 1994, which was given control of Gaza and Jericho. This was followed in August the same year with a deal to hand over the Palestinian area

Hezbollah

Formed in 1982 by Shia Muslim clerics as a vehicle to help drive Israeli forces out of Lebanon, Hezbollah rejects the right of Israel to exist, and has frequently resorted to cross border attacks against Israeli forces.

Saddam Hussein

President of Iraq from 1973 until the US-led invasion of the country in 2003. Saddam was a controversial figure, whose war with Iran resulted in approximately one million deaths on both sides. His decision to invade Kuwait in 1991 led to a humiliating withdrawal after a broad-based coalition intervened against him. Suspicion that he still maintained weapons of mass destruction contributed to the invasion of Iraq in March 2003, and he was captured by coalition forces in December 2003. After a high profile trial, he was executed in December 2006.

of the West Bank to the Palestinian Authority. These were perceived in Israel to be triumphs of diplomacy by Foreign Minister Shimon Peres as he had succeeded in giving up much less land than the Palestinians demanded, particularly in the area surrounding Jericho. Here the Palestinians had insisted on 350 km², but Israel succeeded in providing only 24 km². Israel also managed to boost security on its eastern border by signing a treaty with King Hussein of Jordan in July 1994. Palestinians, who made up the majority of the Jordanian population, were furious with this deal as it failed to address any of their grievances with Israel.

Opposition to the agreements was not confined to Palestinians. On 25 February 1994 an Israeli officer shot dead 29 Palestinians at prayer in the Al-Ibrahami Mosque, Hebron. Another 33 Palestinians died during the rioting which followed the massacre, forcing Rabin to seal off Gaza and the West Bank. The extremist terrorist group **Hamas** retaliated by killing several Israeli officers. Hezbollah carried its war against Israel further afield, killing 96 Jews in Buenos Aires, Argentina, and bombing the Israeli Embassy in London in July 1994.

Hamas

Formed in 1987, with a short-term goal of removing Israel from the occupied territories, it aspires to create a united Palestinian homeland.

In spite of this upsurge in violence, Rabin and Arafat signalled a return to diplomacy with the traditional handshake on the lawn outside the White House on 28 September 1995. This event marked the signing of the Middle East Peace Accord, which featured the following key terms.

- Israel would withdraw from several West Bank towns and 450 villages in late 1995.

- Talks on the status of Jerusalem, West Bank, and Gaza would start in spring 1996.

- Israel would maintain control of its civilian settlements.

- The status of Hebron, a controversial Jewish settlement, was left for later negotiations.

The prospects for peace after this accord did not greatly improve. The two major Israeli political parties, Labor and Likud, adopted contrasting positions to the future of Palestine and Israel's relations with its neighbours. Likud, for example, supported the continuing expansion of Jewish settlements into the occupied territories. This tougher stance represented, to an extent, growing opposition to Rabin's concessions from extremist groups within Israel. This was most starkly illustrated by the assassination of Yitzhak Rabin by Yigal Amir, an Israeli student.

DISCUSSION

How significant was the first Gulf War in bringing the Palestinians and Israelis to the negotiating table?

Moreover, fundamental differences remained over the future of Jerusalem. A decision over the future of the city was delayed until 1999 by the Oslo Agreement, but the Palestinians demanded the return of the eastern sector of the city which was dominated by Palestinians but was captured by Israel in 1967. The Palestinians also wanted Jerusalem to be the capital of their new Palestinian state.

One curious source of tension which remained after Oslo was the future of the region's water supply. Israel retained control of the water resources found in the West Bank, and restricted the level of water usage by Palestinians. Israel's great fear was that the Palestinian Authority might gain control of the "Mountain Aquifer" in the West Bank and then be able to deny access to water to up to three million Israelis.

TASKS

1. Outline the main problems which caused tension between Israel and its Arab neighbours by the mid-1970s.

2. Why were Israel and Egypt willing to discuss peace by 1978?

3. Why did it take so long for the PLO to get involved in peace talks with Israel?

4. How far did the Oslo Agreement succeed in removing the main causes of tension between Israel and the Palestinians?

What was the impact of the Palestinian refugee issue?

FP Why were there so many Palestinian refugees?

As described earlier in this chapter, the events of 1947/1948 created a huge refugee crisis. Approximately 700 000 Arabs fled their homes and went mostly to the West Bank, Gaza Strip, Jordan, Syria, or Lebanon.

The origins of the crisis are disputed by historians and both sides in the Middle Eastern conflict. Palestinians refer to the refugee crisis as "Al-Nakba", or the **diaspora**, and claim that the Israelis pursued a deliberate policy of expulsion in an attempt to occupy as much of Palestine as possible. Evidence to support this view can be found in the existence of Haganah's Plan D and the attack at Deir Yassin. However, the Israeli position is that Arab leaders encouraged the mass exodus in order to gain support for their cause, and believe that the Arabs should shoulder most of the responsibility as they rejected the 1947 partition plan and, in so doing, started the war. However, a group of Israeli historians claim that Haganah and the Arabs should share responsibility. One of these "New Historians", Benny Morris, suggests that Haganah used psychological warfare to drive the Arabs from their villages, followed up by attacks on villages. These methods, along with Arab leaders creating mass panic among the population, resulted in large-scale escape from villages.

Diaspora

This term describes the mass exodus of Palestinians after the declaration of the state of Israel in May 1948.

SOURCE 23

Benny Morris, *The Guardian*, 14 January 2004.

No doubt, Arab fright and flight was leavened by reports of real and imagined Jewish atrocities - and there were many real ones, as the recently released documentation shows. Pillage was almost de rigueur, rape was not infrequent, the execution of prisoners of war was fairly routine during the months before May 1948.

It is clear from the new documentation that the Palestinian leadership in principle opposed the Arab flight from December 1947 to April 1948, while at the same time encouraging or ordering a great many villages to send away their women, children and old folk, to be out of harm's way. Whole villages, especially in the Jewish-dominated coastal plain, were also ordered to evacuate.

SOURCE 24

Ehud Olmert, Israeli Prime Minister, 30 March 2008.

I will not agree to accept any kind of Israeli responsibility for the refugees. Full stop.

Israel would only allow the refugees to return home if the Arab states agreed to let Israel keep the land it had won during the 1948 war. As this was unlikely to be agreed to, most of the refugees were forced to live in camps. Indeed, the Arab states had strong motives for keeping the refugee problem alive: the continued existence of the camps served as a reminder of Israeli aggression, and if the Palestinians returned "home" to their (now Israeli-controlled) villages, they would cease to be Palestinians and would be "absorbed" into the new Israeli state. In 1950, the United Nations Relief and Works Agency (UNRWA) established these camps across the Arab states and set up projects to provide education, health care, and help with farming. Even so, conditions in the camps were atrocious. In a report for the BBC, reporter Jonathan Dimbleby described the state of one camp on the Gaza Strip.

The refugee crisis worsened as a result of the 1967 war, as refugees fled from Sinai, Gaza, Jerusalem, and the West Bank. The Israeli policy of encouraging Jewish settlers meant it became impossible for Arabs to return to their homes. This policy was introduced to tie Gaza and the West Bank permanently to Israel, and was carried out by designating land in these territories as "state land". This policy meant over half of the West Bank and a third of the Gaza Strip had been secured for Israel by the late 1980s.

TASKS

1. Why has there been disagreement over the cause of the Palestinian refugee crisis?

2. In what ways could the views of Ehud Olmert in Source 23 be challenged?

3. Why did the Six-Day War contribute to the refugee crisis?

How effective was the Palestine Liberation Organization in promoting the Palestinian cause?

Faced with little hope of a return to their homes, grim conditions in the camps, and little support from Arab states for their return, some Palestinian activists organised themselves into resistance groups. In 1959, the Palestinian National Liberation Movement, or **Al-Fatah**, was formed, and began to launch guerrilla raids into Israel. In 1964, Fatah joined with other Palestinian groups to form the Palestine Liberation Organization (PLO). This organisation was dedicated to the return to the Palestinian homeland, and advocated the use of force to achieve this goal.

Al-Fatah

See definition on page 372.

Fatah attacks, 1965–7

- **January 1 1965**   Supported by Syria, Fatah carried out its first terror attack in Israel.

- **July 5 1965**   Fatah planted explosives at Mitzpe Massua, near Beit Guvrin, and on the railroad tracks to Jerusalem near Kafr Battir. In total, 39 attacks were carried out in 1965 alone.

- **1965–7**   A wave of Fatah bomb attacks targeted Israeli villages, water pipes, and railroads.

Following the defeat of the Arab states in the 1967 war, the PLO assumed a more prominent role in the conflict and used less conventional military tactics to apply pressure to Israel. Deploying a range of terrorist methods, the PLO and other Palestinian groups also demonstrated a willingness to take the struggle beyond the war against Israel, targeting western companies, and in some cases Arab leaders themselves.

Palestinian terrorism, 1970–6

- **September 1970** The Popular Front for the Liberation of Palestine (PFLP) hijacked five airliners. Three of them were landed at Dawson's Field in Jordan, the passengers were removed, and then the three planes blown up.

- **November 1971** The Jordanian Prime Minster, Wasfi Tal, was murdered by Black September terrorists in revenge for the PLO's expulsion from Jordan.

- **September 1972** The Black September group kidnapped nine Israeli athletes competing at the Olympic Games in Munich. All nine hostages were killed during a gun battle between West German police and the terrorists.

- **October 1972** Black September hijacked a Lufthansa plane and demanded the release of the terrorists jailed for their part in the Munich Olympics attack.

- **July 1976** An Air France flight was hijacked by PFLP terrorists and flown to Entebbe, Uganda. They threatened to kill the 104 Jews on the aircraft unless Palestinian prisoners were released around the world. The Israeli government responded by despatching a special-forces unit who killed the hijackers and rescued all but three of the hostages.

▲ **Fig. 14.20** A British cartoon which appeared in the *Daily Mail*, 7 September 1972

With large numbers of Palestinian refugees living in Jordan, the PLO was able to operate a virtual "state within a state" inside that country. However, King Hussein of Jordan feared a backlash from both Israel and western powers after the Dawson's Field hijacking and ordered his army to attack the PLO. Over 10 days of fierce fighting, between 3,000 and 5,000 Palestinians were killed and the PLO was forced to flee the country.

For much of the 1970s, the PLO failed to gain much ground either from Israel or the international community. Although its leader, Yasser Arafat, was invited to address the UN General Assembly in 1984, it found itself involved in a civil war in its new home Lebanon, and marginalised on the diplomatic front by the United States/Israeli/Egyptian peace talks in the latter part of the decade.

The fortunes of the organisation seemed to decline further after the Israeli invasion of Lebanon, which resulted in the PLO leadership having to flee to Tunis in 1982. While Arafat was away from the region, the PLO's links to the Palestinian people were cut, and new extremist groups stepped into the space created by the organisation's departure. With the military strategy for reclaiming Palestinian lands no longer feasible, Arafat turned to diplomacy, attempting to build better relations with the United States and Jordan. However, neither the US President nor King Hussein of Jordan were prepared to support Arafat's plan for a homeland, and several years of negotiations came to nothing.

However, an uprising in Gaza and the West Bank by Palestinian youths, called the **Intifada**, provoked a violent backlash from Israel. This in turn increased Palestinian resentment and caused outrage at Israel's tactics among the international community. More importantly, the Intifada, which lasted for three years (1987–90), made it clear that there would be no peace in the region without a solution to the Palestinian problem.

> **Yasser Arafat**
>
> Born August 4 1929.
>
> Died 11 November 2004.
>
> He became leader of the Palestinian Students' Union while studying engineering at Cairo University, and founded Fatah in 1956. He became leader of the Palestine Liberation Organization in 1969.

Intifada

An uprising against the Israeli occupation of the Palestinian territories, 1987–92

TASKS

1. Provide three reasons to explain why the Palestinians developed their own resistance groups in the 1950s.

2. Summarise the main activities of Fatah prior to the start of the 1967 Six-Day War.

3. What point is the cartoonist in Figure 14.20 trying to make?

4. How far did the activities of the PLO succeed in promoting the Palestinian cause between 1970 and 1982?

How did international perceptions of the Palestinian cause change over time?

Since its creation at the end of the 1960s, the PLO has experienced what might be thought as a surprising degree of hostility from Arab states. Jordan's problems with the PLO, described in the previous section, led to it expelling the organisation in 1970. After the PLO became involved in the Lebanese civil war, Syria attacked it in 1976. Egypt abandoned the organisation completely when making peace with Israel in 1978–9, while Syria expelled it from Syrian-controlled parts of Lebanon in 1983.

In addition, Arab states did not always back up pledges to fund the movement. In 1978, an inter-Arab agreement promised $250 million a year to the PLO and $150 million to a Jordan-PLO committee, but only Saudi Arabia paid its share.

Arab states also failed to donate much to UNRWA's relief for Palestinian refugees, with the United States contributing over 40 per cent of its budget. The PLO's financial situation deteriorated significantly after the 1991 war in Kuwait, with Gulf states cutting their funding to the organisation by approximately $10 million.

This reluctance to support the Palestinians stemmed from several causes. As Arab states saw the crisis in the Middle East as an opportunity to gain ascendancy over its Arab neighbours, so the PLO came to be used as a tool to advance the interests of particular states. The changing attitudes of Egypt and Syria during the 1960s and 1970s provided a good example of this. On the other hand, the actions of the PLO itself contributed to these attitudes. In both Jordan and Lebanon, the PLO created problems for the countries' rulers, in both cases triggering civil wars. Arafat's change of strategy in the 1980s towards a diplomatic route cost him (ironically) the support of Syria, which was backing Hezbollah and increasing its stake in Lebanon. Arafat's decision to support Saddam Hussein in the Kuwait war proved to be a disastrous mistake, placing the PLO in the position of siding with Iraq against a US-led coalition featuring Egypt, Syria, and Saudi Arabia. After 1991, the rise of more extremist groups such as Hamas, and the rise of Islamic fundamentalists, led to several Arab states carrying out their own individual negotiations with Israel. With the PLO carrying out negotiations with Israel from 1993, other Arab states could then claim that they no longer had an obligation to maintain a commitment to the creation of a Palestinian homeland.

International perceptions of the Palestinian cause have fluctuated throughout the Middle Eastern conflict. The United Nations has perhaps taken the most involved role in attempting to tackle the issue of Palestinian refugees. It responded quickly to the initial refugee crisis by establishing the United Nations Relief for Palestinian Refugees in November 1948. This provided basic amenities such as tents, food, and clothing. One month later, the United Nations passed a resolution calling for all Palestinians who wanted to, to be allowed to return to their homes. Compensation would be paid to those unable to do so. Unsurprisingly, Israel rejected this resolution, and focused on turning former Palestinian territories into land for Jewish immigrants. In December 1949, the United Nations created UNRWA in an attempt to provide work programmes for displaced Palestinians, and the UN Conciliation Committee for Palestine (UNCCP) whose main focus was the return of refugees to their own homes. However, UNCCP's attempts to resolve the issue were impeded by the contradictory demands of both the Arab states and Israel. The Arab states insisted that Israel acknowledge the right of the refugees to return home and receive compensation, while Israel would consider the issue if included in an overall peace plan for the region. By the middle of the 1950s, UNCCP was unable to find a solution acceptable to both sides, and effectively ceased operating.

UNRWA has been a longer-lasting institution and has provided relief for refugees of the conflicts after 1948, including those based in Lebanon. One important role it performs is to provide formal identification of all Palestinian refugees outside of Israel, a role which ensures that the scale and nature of the issue of the refugee crisis remains tangible. However, the United Nations has been unwilling to enforce its resolutions calling for a return to their original homes. The wider international community has been content for the United Nations to focus on humanitarian efforts, while allowing Israel to ignore the rights of Palestinian refugees since the first Arab–Israeli war. Significantly, the issue of Palestinian refugees has been absent from all major peace agreements dealing with the ongoing conflict.

DISCUSSION

What factors have made it difficult for the Palestinians to gain the support of the international community since 1948?

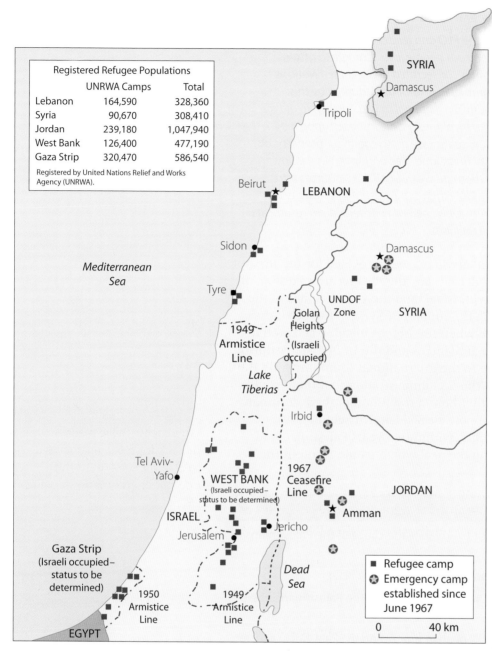

Registered Refugee Populations		
	UNRWA Camps	Total
Lebanon	164,590	328,360
Syria	90,670	308,410
Jordan	239,180	1,047,940
West Bank	126,400	477,190
Gaza Strip	320,470	586,540

Registered by United Nations Relief and Works Agency (UNRWA).

▲ **Fig. 14.21** Palestinian refugee camps, 1993

As for the international community's attitude to the Palestinian cause, it has taken a considerable period of time for attitudes of fear and hostility to change into something more sympathetic. The upsurge in Palestinian terrorism in the late 1960s and attacks on western targets at the start of the next decade led to widespread condemnation of the PLO. As head of the PLO, Arafat was personally criticised for failing to stop the growing number of attacks, and for refusing to condemn them. However, the political fortunes of the movement improved in 1974 when the PLO was recognised by the Arab League as "the sole representative of the Palestinian people". In November 1974, the PLO was granted observer status at the United Nations, and Arafat was allowed to address the UN General Assembly. Backed by support from African and Asian states, the Palestinians cause was strengthened at the United Nations, so much so that a resolution passed in November 1975 condemned Zionism as a "form of racialism".

Yasser Arafat, addressing the UN General Assembly, 13 November 1974.

In my formal capacity as Chairman of the PLO and leader of the Palestinian revolution I appeal to you to accompany our people in its struggle to attain its right to self-determination. This right is consecrated in the United Nations Charter and has been repeatedly confirmed in resolutions adopted by this august body since the drafting of the Charter. I appeal to you, further, to aid our people's return to its homeland from an involuntary exile imposed upon it by force of arms, by tyranny, by oppression, so that we may regain our property, our land, and thereafter live in our national homeland, free and sovereign, enjoying all the privileges of nationhood. Only then can we pour all our resources into the mainstream of human civilization. Only then can Palestinian creativity be concentrated on the service of humanity. Only then will our Jerusalem resume its historic role as a peaceful shrine for all religions.

Unfortunately for Arafat, little practical assistance was provided for his attempt to reclaim Palestine. Instead, the next decade saw the PLO return to a state of international isolation. Ignored by Egypt, Israel, and the United States in the 1978 and 1979 agreements, and losing the support of Syria in the Lebanese civil war, the PLO was in a poor shape when the Israelis invaded Lebanon in 1982. However, negotiations with the Jordanians and the United States during the 1980s offered some kind of return to the international community. By the end of the 1980s, it was clear even to the US administration that there could be no lasting peace in the Middle East without a resolution of the Palestinian issue. Although Arafat's misguided support for Saddam Hussein in 1991 illustrated his questionable tactical ability, within two years Palestinian and Israeli representatives were negotiating the deal which would result in the Oslo Agreement.

TASKS

1. Why were some Arab states reluctant to advance the cause of the Palestinians in the period 1948–67?

2. Why was the Israeli invasion of Lebanon important for the PLO?

3. How did the 1991 Gulf War impact on relations between the Palestinians, their neighbours, and Israel?

4. How significant has the work of the UN been in supporting the Palestinian cause?

Why has the United Nations been unable to secure a lasting peace?

United Nations attempts to resolve the Arab–Israeli conflict appear to have taken place over three different phases.

The first phase, which started during the 1948 war saw the United Nations (UN) use two tactics to achieve a lasting peace for the Middle East. The initial tactic was devised by the special UN mediator Count Bernadotte, who planned to redraw the map, and presented the original UN partition plan giving the Arabs more land in the south and Israel more land in the north. Bernadotte was assassinated by the Stern Gang shortly after presenting his plan on 17 September 1948.

The UN then played a significant role in supervising the separate armistice agreements signed between Israel and her enemies between January and July 1949. This role included the difficult task of observing a demilitarised zone between Syria and Israel, creating a buffer zone between each state. However, the UN failed to achieve its goal of a lasting peace primarily because neither side wanted it. While Egypt concentrated on domestic reforms and harassing Israel's borders, Israel settled on a new strategy for securing her future: mass immigration and creation of a modern state.

The UN's role evolved in the second phase, which covered the period between the 1956 Suez war and the 1982 Israeli invasion of Lebanon. In each of the 1956, 1967, 1973 and 1982 conflicts, the superpowers turned to the UN to act as a peace-keeper. After the announcement of a ceasefire on 6 November 1956, the UN intervened in the Suez Crisis by ordering British and French forces to leave and sending the UNEF (United Nations Emergency Force) to the canal. A year later, the UNEF was used as a pawn in President Eisenhower's negotiations with Prime Minister David Ben-Gurion over a total Israeli withdrawal. In return for this withdrawal, the UNEF would be stationed in the Sinai, providing a physical barrier between Israel and Egypt.

In 1967, UN vulnerability was illustrated in the run up to the Six Day War by Nasser's insistence that UNEF be withdrawn from Egypt, and by Israel's defiance of the **UN General Assembly**'s vote on 4 July 1967 declaring Israel's annexation of East Jerusalem to be illegal.

The most significant UN contribution to the peace process originated in attempts to restore peace after the 1967 war. Resolution 242, introduced by Britain, contained incentives for both sides to make peace. Unfortunately, the issue of Israel's newly-captured territories proved to be an insurmountable stumbling block: Israel needed the land for security, while the Arabs wouldn't negotiate until Israel withdrew. Even so, Resolution 242 remains the basis of all attempts at peace in the region.

SOURCE 27

Extract from Resolution 242

Affirms that the fulfillment of Charter principles requires the establishment of a just and lasting peace in the Middle East which should include the application of both the following principles:

(i) Withdrawal of Israel armed forces from territories occupied in the recent conflict;

(ii) Termination of all claims or states of belligerency and respect for and acknowledgment of the sovereignty, territorial integrity and political independence of every State in the area and their right to live in peace within secure and recognized boundaries free from threats or acts of force.

In 1973, the UN was once more sent to Egypt to act in a peace-keeping capacity, and in 1978 the United Nations Interim Force in Lebanon (UNIFIL) was created to oversee the Israeli withdrawal from Lebanon in 1978. After Israel's invasion of Lebanon in 1982, UNIFIL stayed behind Israeli lines attempting to offer both protection and humanitarian aid to the civilian population. However, with the intervention of the United States and a multinational force of peace-keepers into the crisis in 1982, the UN's role in the country gradually reduced.

Count Bernadotte 1895–1948

Folke Bernadotte was a Swedish noble, who gained a distinguished reputation as a negotiator during the Second World War after he managed to secure the release of several thousand prisoners of war and Jews from German concentration camps towards the end of the war. He was appointed UN Security Council mediator for the Arab–Israeli conflict in 1947.

UN General Assembly

Comprising all members of the United Nations, the UN General Assembly is the main policymaking, deliberative and representative body of the United Nations.

While the UN was actively involved in different aspects of the region's problems, the different focus of the UN General Assembly and the UN Security Council has undermined the organisation's attempts to achieve peace. Perhaps understandably, given the influx of former colonial states admitted to the UN, the General Assembly has passed many resolutions dealing with the 'Palestinian problem' or the refugee crisis. By contrast, the Security Council has displayed a reluctance to intervene on these issues, preferring to focus on conflict resolution.

This has resulted in the UN arguably presenting a divided approach to the conflict, while Israel has historically felt that the membership of the UN has resulted in a built-in anti-Israeli bias: something it could exemplify through reference to Yasser Arafat's UN address in 1974 and United Nations General Assembly Resolution 3379, adopted on November 10, 1975, which equated Zionism with racism. (This was later revoked in 1991.)

The least successful phase of UN intervention in the Arab–Israeli conflict has endured since the end of the Cold War, when the UN has failed to make any major contribution towards a peace agreement in the region. In many ways, the reasons for its failure illustrate the many problems the UN has faced in the region since 1947. Fundamentally, both sides in the conflict have only been prepared to work with the UN when they could gain something out of the arrangement. By the early 1990s, increasing American intervention in the Middle East, either through the invasion of Iraq in 1991 or the intervention of a major US statesman relying on his own lines of communication, such as Kissinger, Carter or Clinton, has eliminated the UN's peace-making role. Increasing American intervention since 1991 was directly due to the end of the Cold War, and the removal of the Soviet Union as a patron for the Arab states. As a result, states which may have traditionally looked to Moscow for aid now had to turn to Washington. This contrasted with earlier periods in the conflict when the US and Soviet influence was less pronounced, and the role of the old imperial powers Britain and France was in decline. As a result, the UN was able to provide an important role not only in resolving conflict, but additionally as an institution through which the issues underpinning the conflicts could be resolved.

In addition, the changing nature of the conflict has contributed to the reduced role of the UN in the Middle East. Since 1988, it has shifted from a conflict between nation states to one between ethnic groups. In particular, the conflict became one featuring Palestinians, featuring groups as diverse as Fatah and Hamas, and Israel instead of the Arab states and Israel. Accompanying this shift has been a radicalisation of the conflict, with extremists on both sides demonstrating a willingness to use violence where their interests are threatened either by the prospect of an unsatisfactory peace deal (eg after Oslo 1994) or perceived threats from the other side. Both developments have, in their own ways, undermined the potential for a multi-national peace-keeping organisation, such as the UN, to maintain peace and resolve the main sources of tension in the Arab–Israeli conflict.

DISCUSSION

Why do you think that the United States failed to include the UN in its peace talks with the Israelis and their enemies 1977–94?

TASKS

1. How did the role of the UN in the Middle East change between 1948–82?

2. Explain how the following factors have contributed to the UN's failure to resolve the Arab–Israeli conflict since 1948:

   a. Israeli aggression

   b. Arab aggression

   c. The changing nature of the conflict

   d. The end of the Cold War

   e. The UN's lack of credibility in the region

How have divisions within Israel affected the peace process?

Throughout Israel's history, a debate has raged just beneath the surface of political life in the country: is Israel a Jewish state or a state of the Jewish people? This is a debate that has, at its heart, a clash between Judaism and the non-religious, or secular, elements within Jewish society. The extent to which Judaism has influenced politics in Israel has varied over the years, but its broad impact on all aspects of life in the country has been hugely significant.

During the period 1948–67, an era when the Labor Party dominated Israeli politics, the focus was on building a secular, democratic state. While the central purpose of this state in the beginning was to survive, in many other ways it resembled a European-style democracy. Elections to the Knesset, the parliament, were held using proportional representation, the government was directly accountable to the Knesset, and the state was built upon the principles of the rule of law rather than religious law. In other ways, Judaism can be seen to have had a large influence on the new Israeli state. A Ministry of Religious Affairs was established in 1951, which was given responsibility for all religious services throughout the country. Rabbinical courts were established under the control of the state judicial system and have complete control over all marriage and divorce by Jews. If Jews in Israel want to have a civil marriage, they must leave the country to do so.

The election of the Likud government in 1977 gave greater prominence to religion. Menachem saw the potential to build a strong power base by using powerful aspects of Jewish symbolism, such as the Holocaust, and the importance of holy sites such as Hebron to promote a greater sense of nationalism in the country. This trend continued into the 1980s, when the Labor and Likud parties held very similar numbers of seats in the Knesset and relied on Orthodox Jewish parties to put them into government.

Among the dozen or so political parties which have seats in the Knesset, the Israeli parliament, the Likud and Labor parties have alternated in the leadership of the various coalition governments formed since the late 1940s. While both parties have maintained a hard-line stance in their negotiations with their Arab neighbours, it would be too simplistic to suggest that they have maintained a unified position in their approach to both the Arab states and the Palestinians.

Most Palestinians would argue that there are few substantive differences between the two main parties. Indeed, both parties deny the right of the Palestinians to self-determination, and reject the notion of an independent Palestinian state. For much of the period after 1948, neither party would negotiate directly with the PLO: something which only changed in 1994.

However, major differences in both aims and actual strategy did exist between Labor and Likud. The differing aims of the parties were apparent from the first days of the Israeli state: whereas Likud have consistently pursued the goal of creating a "Greater Israel", denying any claim of either the Jordanians or Palestinians over the West Bank, the Labor party believed that Israel's security would be preserved through a peaceful resolution of the Arab–Israeli conflict. As such, it was prepared to negotiate with Jordan over this area from 1947 and after the 1967 Six-Day War.

TASKS

1. List the main ways that Judaism has been politically significant in Israel since 1948. You may find it helpful to divide your response into chronological sections: 1948–67; 1968–80; 1981–95.

2. Suggest reasons why the influence of Judaism on Israel became more significant from the mid-1970s.

Likud's attitude was clearly demonstrated when negotiating the Camp David agreement, and during the multiple rounds of talks which followed the 1991 Madrid summit. In December 1977, Menachem Begin was only prepared to offer the Palestinians the right to run their own lives within the occupied territories: he refused to consider giving up Israel's sovereignty over the West Bank and Gaza. In 1991, negotiations between the Israeli and Palestinian delegations stalled over the issue of territory. The Palestinians argued that the talks should lead to the creation of an independent Palestinian state, whereas the Likud-led Israeli delegation argued that the Palestinians were a people with no national rights and certainly without a claim to independence.

The 1992 election brought Yitzhak Rabin's Labor Party to power in a landslide victory. Rabin had a reputation for a tough, uncompromising attitude towards the Palestinians, but his Labor Party campaigned on a platform of negotiating a territorial settlement with the Palestinians. He quickly outlined the main differences between Labor and Likud's approach.

- Instead of spending more money on Jewish settlements in the occupied territories, it would be directed towards improving the state of the Israeli economy.

- Priority would be given to the issue of Palestinian autonomy, with a clear goal of making peace with the Palestinians.

However, it proved difficult for Rabin to deliver on his promise to construct a historic deal with the Palestinians. Attempts by Hamas to disrupt the peace process provoked a harsh reaction from Rabin, with a mass deportation of alleged Hamas activists in December 1992: an act which was widely criticised as a breach of international law and one which could destroy the peace process.

That the peace talks did not collapse was due to a combination of factors. Shimon Peres, Rabin's foreign minister, had maintained informal links with the Palestinians during the period when Rabin appeared to be cutting back the official talks. Rabin also realised how desperate the financial state of the PLO was, and furthermore appeared close to collapse. The significance of the talks resuming was huge. For the first time, an Israeli government recognised the PLO and included its leader, Yasser Arafat, in the negotiations. Furthermore, Israel agreed on a settlement which included the potential for withdrawals from parts of the occupied territories. This, in effect, overturned previous attempts at creating a Greater Israel, and as such would have been impossible to achieve under a Likud government.

DISCUSSION

How far do you think domestic factors have influenced Israeli attitudes to the Palestinians?

SOURCE 28

Avi Shlaim, *Journal of Palestine Studies*, Winter 1994.

The very fact that Rabin reached an accord with the PLO demolishes the notion, so prevalent and persistent among Palestinians, that there is no real difference between the Labor Party and the Likud.

TASKS

1. On what issues have Labor and Likud differed in their approach to the Palestinians?

2. Why did both parties refuse to negotiate with the Palestinians for so long after the first Arab–Israeli War in 1948?

3. How far do the two main parties disagree in their approach to the Palestinians?

How have rivalries among Palestinians affected progress towards a settlement?

Since the creation of the PLO in 1964, the Palestinian resistance movement has acted as an umbrella for different groups claiming to work for Palestinian statehood. However, the dominant group remained the Fatah-inspired element of the PLO. The PLO's primary goal was to achieve a homeland for the Palestinian people, and its brand of a largely non-religious nationalism proved popular in the refugee camps of the occupied territories and Lebanon.

SOURCE 29

Extract from the Palestinian National Charter

THE PALESTINIAN NATIONAL CHARTER:

Resolutions of the Palestine National Council, July 1–17, 1968

Article 1: Palestine is the homeland of the Arab Palestinian people; it is an indivisible part of the Arab homeland, and the Palestinian people are an integral part of the Arab nation.

Article 3: The Palestinian Arab people possess the legal right to their homeland and have the right to determine their destiny after achieving the liberation of their country in accordance with their wishes and entirely of their own accord and will.

Article 5: The Palestinians are those Arab nationals who, until 1947, normally resided in Palestine regardless of whether they were evicted from it or have stayed there. Anyone born, after that date, of a Palestinian father - whether inside Palestine or outside it - is also a Palestinian.

Article 6: The Jews who had normally resided in Palestine until the beginning of the Zionist invasion will be considered Palestinians.

The dominance of the PLO started to be challenged as a result of its expulsion from Lebanon in 1982. The Israelis also secretly encouraged friction between the PLO and Islamist groups in Gaza as a way of weakening the PLO. Hamas, or Islamic Resistance Movement, was formed in 1987, and emerged as the most prominent Palestinian rival to the PLO, offering an Islamist-nationalist alternative to the secular PLO. The founder of Hamas, Sheikh Yassin, rejected peace with Israel, claiming that Israel didn't recognise the right to an independent Palestinian state, and pledged that violence and the destruction of Israel was the only way for the Palestinian people to enjoy true peace.

SOURCE 30

Extract from a CNN news report, 3 March 1996

At least 19 dead in Jerusalem bus bombing

An explosion ripped apart a commuter bus on Jaffa Street in Jerusalem early Sunday, killing at least 19 people in a grim replay of last week's deadly bombing along the same bus route and at the same time. The Israeli government responded by calling for a suspension of the Palestinian peace process.

Israel radio reported that the bus was number 18, the same number as the bus destroyed in last Sunday's suicide bombing that occurred at almost exactly the same time, 6:25 a.m. (0425 GMT). Twenty-five people were killed in that attack, for which the Islamic militant Hamas group claimed responsibility.

Israeli Prime Minister Shimon Peres was booed by the crowd gathered at the scene of the blast. The prime minister left without addressing the crowd.

A further splintering of the Arab movement occurred as a result of the PLO's exit from Lebanon. Hezbollah, 'the Party of God' was formed in 1982 to counter the Israeli invasion. It aimed to turn Lebanon into an Islamist state, although this position was softened towards the end of the decade.

In retaliation for the murder of 29 Palestinians in a mosque in Hebron by a Jewish settler, Baruch Goldstein, Hamas launched a campaign of violence against Israel, who it blamed for allowing the settlers to arm themselves. Deploying suicide bombers as its principal weapon, Hamas carried out a series of bus bombings in February and March 1996, killing nearly 60 Israelis, in retaliation for the assassination in December 1995 of Hamas bomb maker Yahya Ayyash.

The effect of these attacks was to provoke Israel into moving troops back into Gaza and the West Bank, and to close the borders between the occupied territories and Israel. This, in turn, had an adverse effect on the Palestinians who worked in Israel but were not able to cross the border to go to work.

▲ **Fig. 14.22** The official flag of Hezbollah

SOURCE 31

Extract from the Hamas charter

Article One

The Islamic Resistance Movement draws its guidelines from Islam; derives from it its thinking, interpretations and views about existence, life and humanity; refers back to it for its conduct; and is inspired by it in whatever step it takes.

Article Thirteen

[Peace] initiatives, the so-called peaceful solutions, and the international conferences to resolve the Palestinian problem, are all contrary to the beliefs of the Islamic Resistance Movement. For renouncing any part of Palestine means renouncing part of the religion; the nationalism of the Islamic Resistance Movement is part of its faith, the movement educates its members to adhere to its principles and to raise the banner of Allah over their homeland as they fight their Jihad: "Allah is the all-powerful, but most people are not aware."

In March 2002, Prime Minister Ariel Sharon launched 'Operation Defensive Shield' in response to the killing of 29 Israelis in a Hamas-organised suicide bombing. Combining helicopter gunships, fighter planes, and ground forces, the Israelis surrounded Arafat's headquarters in Ramallah, West Bank and attacked refugee camps elsewhere in the West Bank and Gaza. The construction of a security wall further into the West Bank was designed to reinforce security from attack.

However, in spite of these moves, the death of Yasser Arafat in 2004 triggered a dramatic shift in the political future of the Palestinian Authority. In elections

TASKS

1. What were the main differences between the PLO and Hamas?

2. In spite of the spate of Hamas attacks, peace talks between the PLO and Israel continued through the late 1990s. Can you think of any reason why this might have been?

held for the Palestinian parliament in 2006, Hamas won a majority of seats: a result which effectively brought the last remaining elements of the peace process to an end.

Revision tips

- Think clearly about the role that religion, settlement, and colonial powers played in causing the dispute between Jews and Arabs.

- Are there any common features of Israeli military success 1948–73?

- Has the United States or Soviet Union contributed anything meaningful to improving relations between Arab states and Israel?

- Think about the relative successes of using diplomacy and taking military action for both sides in the conflict.

- Consider the main areas of similarity and difference between the two main political parties in Israel.

- Look at the main aims and tactics of the different groups challenging Israel from 1982.

Review questions

1. Compare sources 5 and 6. Is one source more useful than the other as evidence about the reasons why Britain faced criticism for its approach to Palestine in 1945–7?

2. Describe the actions of the Jewish Resistance Movement between 1945–6.

3. Why did the Palestinians object to the 1947 partition plan?

4. Who were the Fedayeen?

5. 'The Camp David agreement solved nothing.' How far do you agree with this statement? Explain your answer.

6. Why did the Israelis establish settlements in the occupied territories?

7. What was the Intifada?

8. How far did the Labor and Likud parties agree in their approach to the Palestinians?

9. 'The Oslo Accords satisfied neither Israelis or Arabs.' How far do you agree with this statement? Explain your answer.

15

Preparing for assessment

The format of the exam

Cambridge IGCSE® History (0470 and 0977) requires you to take three components: Paper 1 and Paper 2, and *either* Component 3 *or* Paper 4.

Cambridge O Level History (2147) requires you to take two components: Paper 1 and Paper 2.

Paper 1

Compulsory

This paper requires you to answer **two** questions from Section A on the Core Content, and **one** question from Section B on the Depth Studies.

Here is the full list of Core Content topics for the 20th Century option.

1. Were the peace treaties of 1919–23 fair?

2. To what extent was the League of Nations a success?

3. Why had international peace collapsed by 1939?

4. Who was to blame for the Cold War?

5. How effectively did the United States contain the spread of Communism?

6. How secure was the USSR's control over eastern Europe, 1948–c.1989?

7. Why did events in the Gulf matter, c.1970–2000?

Here is the full list of Depth Studies.

A The First World War, 1914–18

B Germany, 1918–45

C Russia, 1905–41

D The United States, 1919–41

E China, c.1930–c.1990

F South Africa, c.1940–1994

G Israelis and Palestinians since 1945

You have **2 hours** for this paper and 60 marks are available.

In Section A, there will be four questions from the seven 20th Century History topics. You answer any **two** questions.

Section B contains two questions on each of the seven Depth Study topics. You choose **one** question to answer.

All questions are in the form of structured essays, split into three parts: (a), (b), and (c).

For IGCSE, Paper 1 makes up 40 per cent of the overall marks.

For O Level, Paper 1 makes up 55 per cent of the overall marks.

Paper 2

Compulsory

Paper 2 requires you to answer **six** questions on one specified topic drawn from the Core Content. Each option includes a range of source material relating to the prescribed topic, and the six questions are based on the source material provided.

You have **2 hours** for this paper and 50 marks are available.

Your teacher will know well in advance which option you will be taking for this paper.

For IGCSE, Paper 2 makes up 33 per cent of the overall marks.

For O Level, Paper 2 makes up 45 per cent of the overall marks.

Candidates taking **Cambridge IGCSE® History** are also required to choose one of the following:

Component 3

This is the coursework option.

The coursework is **one piece of writing of up to 2000 words** in length, based on content from any one of the Depth Studies from the syllabus, or from a Depth Study devised by the Centre. Your coursework piece will be based on a single question around the issue of significance.

Component 3 makes up 27 per cent of the overall marks.

or

Paper 4

This is the written paper option, and the alternative to the coursework option.

Paper 4 requires you to answer **one** question from a choice of two on any one of the Depth Studies that you have covered.

You have **1 hour** for this paper, and 40 marks are available.

Paper 4 makes up 27 per cent of the overall marks.

How to maximise your chances

The Cambridge IGCSE® and O Level History courses require all students to be able to demonstrate evidence of the following objectives.

Assessment Objective 1: an ability to recall, select, organise and deploy knowledge of the syllabus content.

Assessment Objective 2: an ability to construct historical explanations using an understanding of:

- cause and consequence, change and continuity, similarity and difference
- the motives, emotions, intentions and beliefs of people in the past.

Assessment Objective 3: an ability to understand, interpret, evaluate and use a range of sources as evidence, in their historical context.

You should bear these objectives in mind while undertaking your studies.

Each paper attaches different weightings to the three Assessment Objectives, so it is also important that you know what skills are assessed on each paper. They are weighted as follows:

Cambridge IGCSE® History

Assessment objective	Weighting in IGCSE %	Weighting in component %		
		Paper 1	Paper 2	Component 3/Paper 4
AO1	30	33	20	37.5
AO2	43	67	0	62.5
AO3	27	0	80	0

Cambridge O Level History

Assessment objective	Weighting in O Level %	Weighting in component %	
		Paper 1	Paper 2
AO1	28	33	20
AO2	36	67	0
AO3	36	0	80

General advice

The Cambridge IGCSE® and O Level syllabuses outline the skills a learner will have to display in order to achieve one of the top grades, which are to:

- accurately recall, select and deploy relevant historical knowledge to support a coherent and logical argument
- communicate in a clear and coherent manner using appropriate historical terminology
- demonstrate an understanding of the complexity of historical concepts
- distinguish clearly between cause and consequence, change and continuity, and similarity and difference, by selectively deploying accurate and relevant historical evidence

- show an understanding of individuals and societies in the past
- understand the importance of trying to establish motives
- interpret and evaluate a wide range of historical sources and their use as evidence
- identify precisely the limitations of particular sources
- compare and contrast a range of sources and draw clear, logical conclusions.

The following points of advice should help you in your attempts to achieve a high grade.

- **Make sure you answer the question.** Every point should relate directly to the question set. Do not attempt to fit a pre-prepared answer on a related question into your answer. It is always a good idea to use the wording of the question throughout your answer. By doing so, you will be letting the examiner know that you are attempting to do just what the question has asked.

- **Look carefully at the wording of the question.** If there is a reference to a place, event, feature, period, you should refer to those, and not to others that are not part of the question. For example, if a part b) question on the origins of the First World War asks you about *colonial* rivalry, do not write an answer about any other form of rivalry such as the arms race.

- **Look at the date range of the question.** If a date range is given do not stray beyond it as you will probably gain no credit for anything beyond the scope of the question. It is equally important to refer to events across the whole of the date range: don't restrict your answer to a small period within the date range.

- **Be specific.** Your responses will be so much more convincing if you can support a point with an example. This could be a date, statistic or a more developed explanation.

- **Think about the requirements for each type of question.** On the one hand, you should bear in mind the amount of time you should spend on each question (see the next point for more guidance on this point). However, you should also be certain that you understand the meaning of terms such as 'Describe', 'Explain', 'How far', 'Reliable', 'Useful', 'To what extent', etc. They all require different types of answer.

- **Plan your answers.** This is especially important when tackling longer responses. Students who do not plan ahead are much more likely either to drift off focus, or to produce chunks of narrative which do not relate directly to the question.

Index